An Introduction to Philosophy: Knowledge and Reality

CANADIAN EDITION

AN INTRODUCTION TO PHILOSOPHY: KNOWLEDGE AND REALITY

ROCKNEY

JACOBSEN

PEARSON

Toronto

Acquisition Editor: Matthew Christian
Program Manager: Madhu Ranadive
Marketing Manager: Christine Cozens
Developmental Editor: Johanna Schlaepfer
Project Manager: Andrea Falkenberg
Production Services: Shruti Awasthi, Cenveo® Publisher Services
Permissions Project Manager: Erica Mojzes
Text Permissions Research: Varoon Deo-Singh, EPS
Cover Designer: Alex Li
Cover Image: RYGER/Shutterstock

Credits and acknowledgments for the material borrowed from other sources and reproduced, with permission, in this textbook appear on the appropriate page within the text.

3 2019

Library and Archives Canada Cataloguing in Publication

Jacobsen, Rockney, 1951-, author
An introduction to philosophy : knowledge and reality / Rockney Jacobsen.

Includes bibliographical references and index.
ISBN 978-0-13-344447-6 (pbk.)

1. Philosophy—Textbooks. I. Title.

BD21.J33 2014 100 C2014-907219-8

PEARSON

ISBN 978-0-13-344447-6

Brief Table of Contents

Table of Contents

Preface

FOR INSTRUCTORS

An Introduction to Philosophy: Knowledge and Reality is an introductory philosophy textbook designed to give students their first taste of philosophy by exposing them to problems in metaphysics and epistemology. It can serve as the sole text for a one-semester course in those areas, or as one component of a general full-year introduction to philosophy. The text takes a problem-centred, argument-driven approach to teaching philosophy, balancing features of an introductory anthology with the advantages of a single-author text.

Objective and Approach

Neither Anthology nor Single-Author Text

Philosophy textbooks tend to follow one of two models. First, there are anthologies of primary sources, containing readings from original and influential philosophical works with which the editor judges every serious student of philosophy must become familiar. This is how almost everyone in my generation learned philosophy, usually in classes of 20–25 students, where our teachers watched our faces for expressions of confusion and desperation and came to our rescue just before we went under for the last time. With motivated students, a good instructor, and a pedagogical environment with ample tolerance for attention to individual student needs, I believe this is still the best way to learn philosophy. But anthologies have the well-known disadvantage of making students almost entirely dependent on their instructor, and the classroom environments that once made them the best tool for learning philosophy are either gone or are rapidly disappearing.

The alternative—a single-author textbook—reduces the dependency of the student on the teacher, and gives students more opportunities for learning on their own. But they also deprive students of the pleasure of hearing the great philosophers speak in their own voices, and of the opportunity to practice the full range of skills they will need to consume philosophy raw. Perhaps the worst failing of single-author texts is that, in the effort to be fair, they tend to create a false equivalency among alternative philosophical positions and to encourage students in the view that, after all the arguing is done, students are free to pick and choose among philosophical positions—and even among the supporting arguments they will use to prop up their preferred positions. Although I have seen some excellent examples of single-author textbooks that avoid these pitfalls, there are too many cases where the usual complaints are accurate.

This book occupies one of many positions intermediate between an anthology of primary sources and a single-author textbook. Roughly one-third of the text consists of selections from primary sources, so students will have ample opportunity to face the challenges of working through original philosophical texts. The remainder of the text both *discusses* and *participates in* the debates in which those primary sources are involved. To purists, this will either seem to be an anthology with too much editorial intervention, or a single-author textbook that is too liberal in its use of extended quotation. But more important than the ratio of author-to-primary-source material is the principle according to which the primary material is selected.

Problems and Arguments

While insisting on the historical depth of each problem, the text takes a *problem-centred* and *argument-driven* approach to introducing philosophy. Students are introduced to familiar and longstanding philosophical problems in metaphysics and epistemology—the so-called Big Questions about personal identity, death, certainly and doubt, God, evil, and so on. In each chapter they will read selections from a number of philosophers. The reading selections are made entirely in light of their contribution to the discussion of some particular philosophical problem. My guiding thought is that students will fare much better with the readings if they can see where each fits in a discussion that the student has already been invited to join. When students are involved in the debates to which each reading contributes, they are better able to discern, to follow, and to engage the ideas and arguments in those readings. Roughly two-thirds of the book is designed to draw students into the discussion of philosophical problems, provoking them into joining the arguments; assisting them with an understanding of context; introducing the vocabulary, logic, and conceptual tools they will need; and making them aware of options to consider and objections they are bound to face. The philosophers themselves—from Heraclitus and Plato to Derek Parfit and Helen Longino—are encountered as fellow participants.

In the chosen excerpts, a philosopher might develop a substantial proposal for addressing a problem, construct an argument for or against a proposal, or offer a rebuttal of such an argument. One example illustrates how this shaped the selections in the text. René Descartes appears in more than a dozen places throughout, where he contributes to the discussion of six different philosophical problems. Most of those contributions are relatively minor (e.g., in Chapter 5, Descartes provides one of three variations on a classic argument for the immortality of the soul), but some are more substantial (e.g., his contributions to debates about mind-body dualism in Chapter 6, his theory of justification in Chapter 9, and his theory of perception in Chapter 11). Thus, in some places Descartes makes his contribution in only a single paragraph while in others he is given several uninterrupted pages to develop his arguments. In each case, I made a selection from Descartes's writings that positions his ideas in a larger discussion about a philosophical problem. Students will hear what Descartes has to say about mind and body, his views about justification and the nature of knowledge, and so on, but nowhere will they find an extended reading designed to display "the philosophy of Descartes."

In addition to being problem-centred, the direction of the discussion is driven by philosophical *arguments*. The discussion in which the primary source texts are embedded is heavily focused on the clarification, presentation, and evaluation of philosophical arguments. The basic resources students will need—for example, explanations of the components of arguments, the notions of validity and soundness, and an introduction to a range of fallacies as well as valid argument forms—are provided in the text as the need arises. In numerous places, mini lessons in logic are separated from the main text in Logic Boxes. At every stage, concern with logic or argumentation arises naturally out of the need to address the philosophical problems under discussion. For teachers who prefer to provide students with a single, more extended lesson in informal logic early in the course, Appendix A makes suggestions for re-assembling the Logic Boxes into a resource for that purpose. The hope is to increase students' logical facility both by exposing them to a wide array of arguments and by supplying them with tools that will help them articulate responses to the arguments they encounter.

My larger hope is that the text will decrease student dependence on their teachers and increase their engagement with philosophy without diluting the challenges that are an essential part of learning to philosophize.

Chapter Organization

The Topics and their Arrangement

There may be too many topics covered in the text for a one-semester introduction to metaphysics and epistemology, so the text has some flexibility for alternative course designs built into it. In their current arrangement, many chapters build on others in ways I believe to be helpful, but only a willingness to make modest use of the glossary is needed to implement alternative arrangements of the material.

Some chapters can be skipped over without loss of continuity. For example, you might ignore the general considerations about identity and change (Chapter 2) and go directly to the problem of personal identity (Chapters 3 and 4); you might prefer to skip the topics of death and immortality (Chapter 5); or, if you think functionalism is too challenging for first-year students, you can skip Chapter 7. The problem of freedom and determinism (Chapter 8) can also be passed over. For those who prefer to do less philosophy of religion, the chapter on the epistemology of testimony (Chapter 13) or the one on the problem of evil (Chapter 14) can be left out.

You might also choose to avoid certain *sections* of an assigned chapter. Thus, the metaphysical arguments for immortality—the first major section of Chapter 5—can be read and discussed without taking up the question whether a person's death is a bad thing for her—the second major division of that chapter. Or Chapter 8, on freedom and determinism, can be read without the section that accuses causal determinism of committing a scope fallacy, or without the section that asks whether quantum indeterminacy accounts for freedom. Not every section is optional for understanding the issues in a given chapter, but every chapter has some sections that can be made optional.

Finally, you might prefer to *re-order* some of the chapters. You may wish to take up epistemology (Chapters 9 to 11) before covering the philosophy of mind (Chapters 6 to 7), or to discuss the philosophy of religion (Chapters 12 to 15) before taking on the problem of personal identity (Chapters 2 to 3). Perhaps you would like to introduce the philosophy of religion by addressing the problem of evil (Chapter 15) first, and then explore experiential (Chapter 13) and cosmological (Chapter 12) arguments. The table of contents reflects my preferred arrangement of these topics, but the text easily accommodates other configurations.

FOR STUDENTS

This is an *introductory* textbook in philosophy, so no previous background is presupposed in the topics discussed. This does not mean that the problems addressed are *easy*—philosophical problems rarely are. But it does mean that when we find the philosophical waters growing too deep, we will need to turn back to shore. It will often be necessary to break off discussion when there is still more that needs to be said. The hope, however, is that you will soon have the knowledge and skills you need to venture further on your own.

Do not let this lead you to the common misunderstanding that *no progress is ever made in philosophy*. Even without getting to the bottom of the problems we take on you will see that that this not true. Progress is made in philosophy whenever a new idea, a new argument, or a new way of seeing things pushes our thinking one step further down the road, leaves one bad idea behind, illuminates one previously dark corner, or brings one new possibility into view. By these measures, you will easily see that philosophy has made, and continues to make, genuine progress. And you will also make the same kinds of progress in the development of your own philosophical views.

There are two matters you should be warned about in advance. First, some of the selections from philosophers in the text were written long ago, in styles that will seem old-fashioned, just as your style will seem antiquated to your grandchildren. It takes patience and practice to become accustomed to the flow of words and ideas. The greatest challenges you will meet in reading philosophy—even when the style presents no special challenges—arise from the nature of philosophy itself. The writings of philosophers are best understood if you proceed slowly and thoughtfully, whenever possible looking for ways to restate the central ideas in your own vocabulary, and always being alert to the paths that carry a philosopher from one idea to another. The text can assist you with that process, but nothing can replace the effort you must make on your own. You will be surprised how rapidly your understanding improves.

Second, the spirit in which philosophical ideas are discussed is the spirit of critical engagement—no idea is treated as sacred. That means that when ideas are presented in philosophy, we are all invited to scrutinize and evaluate them. A good idea has only one way to establish its worth: by showing that it can survive careful scrutiny. If we shelter an idea from critical examination, we only make it look suspicious and contribute to doubts about its value. One result is that philosophical ideas are never presented as the final word on any topic—they should all come labelled as *open to further reflection and continued discussion*. Never forget that this goes for what I say in the text as well. For example, when I raise objections to a philosopher's ideas, you are expected to understand those objections, but not to treat them as the last word. Their purpose is to provoke and assist you in taking your own thinking a few steps further, not to bring your thinking to a close. In many places throughout the text I present arguments on behalf of ideas for which I have no sympathy, and I sometimes even let them have the final word in the discussion of a topic. I believe those ideas and arguments can contribute to your understanding of the issues, and I encourage you to take them seriously. But when I end my discussion of a topic, it is not because I have arrived at the views that are right, or even the views that I accept. It is because I have arrived at the place from which you should proceed on your own.

Features

Throughout the text, a number of resources help you learn philosophy. These are designed to make your life easier, so don't neglect to take advantage of them. Pay special attention to the following:

Learning Objectives

Each chapter begins with a list of objectives. Look these over before you read the chapter, and let them guide your thinking about what to look for. You can also use them to test your comprehension of the material.

Logic Boxes

Logic Boxes are scattered throughout the text. These are mini lessons in logic to help you acquire the vocabulary and tools to evaluate philosophical reasoning. They are essential for helping you achieve distance from your own reasoning in order to see and discuss it with more objectivity. (The Logic Boxes should be supplemented with information provided in Appendix A.)

Key Terms and Figures

A list of important vocabulary terms and key thinkers appear near the end of each chapter. Each term on the list is highlighted in the chapter and defined in the margin. When you have read the chapter, review the key terms to make sure you understand the new vocabulary and can give quick summaries of the relevant ideas of the thinkers listed.

Additional Readings

You will also find a short bibliography of additional readings at the end of each chapter. Turn to these when you want to learn more about the topics discussed in the chapter. Keep in mind that each chapter contains selections from the writings of well-known philosophers. When you want to enhance your appreciation of the issues raised, you might turn first to the works from which these selections have been made. (The source of each selection can be found in the references section at the end of the text. Many are available online.) If you want to pursue a particular idea to learn more about a branch of philosophy or a philosopher, the following online sources are recommended:

1. *Internet Encyclopedia of Philosophy*. (J. Fieser & Bradley Dowden, Eds.). Available at http://www.iep.utm.edu
2. *Stanford Encyclopedia of Philosophy*. (E. N. Zalta, Ed.). Available at http://plato.stanford.edu

These sources can sometimes be challenging, but they are very reliable. The recommended additional readings at the end of each chapter vary in degree of difficulty—some are relatively advanced, but most will be accessible after you have studied the material in the chapter.

Appendices

There are two short appendices to the text. Appendix A provides important additional information about the evaluation of inferences and premises. It also introduces a key idea in logic—the idea of logical, or argument, *form*—that will help make arguments and their evaluation more intuitive. Appendix B briefly discusses the two kinds of writing—*expository* and *critical*—that go into a typical philosophy essay. The mechanics of a beginning philosophy essay—what format to use for citations, whether to use footnotes or endnotes, whether to use the first-person pronoun—are matters on which your instructors will differ. Appendix B is silent about such things. But the *spirit* in which philosophy essays are written is very nearly universal, so the appendix tries to address those matters of the spirit.

RESOURCES

Pearson Custom Library

For enrollments of at least 25 students, you can create your own textbook by choosing the chapters that best suit your own course needs. To begin building your custom text, visit www.pearsoncustomlibrary.com. You may also work with a dedicated Pearson Custom editor to create your ideal text—publishing your own original content or mixing and matching Pearson content. Contact your local Pearson Representative to get started.

CourseSmart for Instructors

CourseSmart goes beyond traditional expectations—providing instant, online access to the textbooks and course materials you need at a lower cost for students. And even as students save money, you can save time and hassle with a digital eTextbook that allows you to search for the most relevant content at the very moment you need it. Whether it's evaluating textbooks or creating lecture notes to help students with difficult concepts, CourseSmart can make life a little easier. See how when you visit www.coursesmart.com/instructors.

ACKNOWLEDGEMENTS

I would like to express thanks to the many people who offered thoughtful suggestions and recommendations for creating this textbook. I especially thank the following instructors for providing formal reviews of the draft manuscript:

Ardis Anderson, University of Lethbridge
Jeremy Fantl, University of Calgary
Michael Fleming, Capilano University
Shereen Hassanein, Seneca College
Justine Noel, Camosun College
Christopher Stephens, University of British Columbia
Kira Tomsons, University of New Brunswick
Patrick Walsh, University of Manitoba

Gary Foster, Randall Keen, and Dwayne Moore read a much earlier draft of the whole and, in Randall's case, portions of the penultimate draft. All have made valuable suggestions, for which I am grateful. Kathy Behrendt and Jill Rusin made helpful suggestions about material to include in the text; I wish I could have incorporated even more of their recommendations. Philosophers with whom I have had ongoing discussions over many years about both philosophy and pedagogy have been more helpful than they are aware. I easily see the influence of Gerry Callaghan, David Checkland, Randall Keen (again), and the late Sue Campbell on many sections. The helpful suggestions and ongoing assistance of an entire team of highly professional editors at Pearson was essential to the successful completion of the project.

Finally, Renee Sylvain contributed more than I can capture in any brief note of gratitude. While writing I took full advantage of her love of ideas and her talent for grappling with them. In addition to being a source of endless insight and more helpful suggestions than I can itemize, she supplied the daily encouragement and support needed to undertake and complete the project. It is to her, with love, that this book is dedicated.

Chapter 1

Introducing Philosophy

Learning Objectives

- Compare and contrast *explanations* and *justifications*.
- Compare and contrast disagreements about matters of fact and disagreements about the nature of things.
- Explain why it is *never* necessary to rely on authorities when we decide what to believe.
- Explain why it is *sometimes* a fallacy to rely on the fact that a belief is widely held as a justification for the belief.
- Summarize Plato's allegory of the cave and explain how it expresses his view about the nature of philosophy.
- Outline Bertrand Russell's understanding of the value of philosophy.
- Explain how the practice of philosophy can contribute to self-knowledge.

In this chapter, we will sketch very provisional answers to two questions: *What is philosophy?* And *what is the value of philosophizing?* Our answers can only be provisional—after you have had a chance to explore philosophy, you will be in a better position to concern yourself with the many refinements they might need. Questions about the nature and value of philosophy are themselves philosophical in nature and, as you will soon see, philosophers value disagreement.

After comparing the distinctive kinds of interests that philosophers have in ideas and beliefs with the kinds of interests others have, we will look at one old-fashioned way of defining philosophy. Even if the definition is out of fashion (and for good reason), it can illuminate aspects of philosophy and point us in the direction of other ways of defining it.

We will then turn to several views about the *value* of philosophy—that is, to several reasons *why we should philosophize*. Although we consider several options, we will dwell in detail on only one: the idea that philosophizing can help free us from illusion and prejudice. This idea has a long history, and we will look at presentations of it by philosophers who were separated by 26 centuries.

WHAT IS PHILOSOPHY?

Those who are new to philosophy often come to it with certain misconceptions. This is hardly surprising. Although everyone has heard of philosophy, few have actually studied it. Misconceptions are also common because philosophers themselves cannot give straight and unequivocal answers to questions about the nature of philosophy. The question "What is philosophy?" is a topic for proper debate within the discipline, while the queries "What is biology?" or "What is physics?" are not questions of biology or physics. Indeed, the latter questions are more likely to be raised by philosophers of science than by practicing scientists. Self-reflective biologists might ask what biology is, and look for answers, but when they do so they are asking a *philosophical* question, not a *biological* one.

Understanding why philosophers cannot give a straightforward account of what they do might only reveal that philosophy does not have a "nature." Perhaps it is not a discipline that is very well defined, or perhaps philosophers are like the blind men who describe an elephant after touching different parts of the animal ("It is like a rope"; "No, it is like a tree trunk"; "No, it is a wall"). In that case, philosophers might need an outsider to explain how their stories fit together into a description of a single animal. Newcomers to philosophy are right to be baffled. Nonetheless, there are some things that we can say about philosophy that might be helpful.

However *philosophy* is to be defined, two ideas are widely agreed upon. First, the concerns, methods, and styles of philosophers have changed considerably since the inception of philosophy roughly 2600 years ago, and they continue to change. At any one time, different schools of philosophy use different methods, write in different styles, read different authors, and focus on different issues. Second, in all cases, the study of philosophy involves learning to philosophize and not merely learning about the philosophizing that has been done by others, just as learning to play a musical instrument requires practicing the instrument. For a variety of reasons, it might be useful to learn what different philosophers have thought at different times, and to be able to associate their names with their most important ideas. However, only when you *engage* those ideas yourself, so that they provoke you to further thoughts, will you have begun to philosophize.

Here we will take two approaches to describing philosophy. We will consider one way of saying how philosophy *differs* from some other disciplines, and we will consider one rather old-fashioned way of defining philosophy. Although very few philosophers would accept this definition today, contemporary philosophy can only be understood when it is seen as descended from this earlier conception. We will then be in a better position to ask how some philosophers conceive the value of philosophizing.

What Philosophy Is Not

In philosophy we talk a great deal about ideas, about what people believe, and about why they believe those things. Usually philosophers are concerned with ideas that are of deep significance to people—beliefs that shape our world views, beliefs about what matters and why. But philosophy should not for that reason be confused with religious doctrine and belief, or with the psychological or sociological study of beliefs. Although, like those areas of thought, philosophy is also concerned with beliefs, it is relatively indifferent to *what* people believe and is much more interested in the *rationales* for their beliefs.

Consider first the contrasts between a philosophical interest in beliefs and a religious concern with belief. Those who have religious beliefs usually begin to acquire them at an age when they are still unprepared to subject those beliefs to serious critical scrutiny, and such scrutiny is usually considered inappropriate. Religious doctrines are generally taught and learned in contexts in which they are not intended to be challenged or criticized. Philosophy is learned only later, when we have reached the age at which we can be expected to experience doubts and to seek rationales for our beliefs. The result is not that philosophy and religion are always interested in *different beliefs*, but only that they have *different kinds of interest* in beliefs. A single belief—for example, a belief that God exists—can be an expression of someone's religious faith, but it can also be a philosophical claim. The difference lies not in the content of the belief (not in *what* is believed), but in the spirit in which the belief is held and expressed. As a profession of religious faith, a belief in God is not put forward for investigation or scrutiny; it is not offered with the expectation that challenges and objections will be made or that evidence or argument might be required for it. To express belief in the existence of God *as a philosophical claim* is to put it forward in the spirit of openness to scrutiny, with the expectation that clarification and defense will be required, and with a willingness to provide a rationale for the belief.

Like philosophers, social scientists sometimes study beliefs or systems of belief. Sociologists might be interested in understanding the beliefs of a particular social group, and anthropologists might want to understand the beliefs held by members of a particular ethnic or cultural group. Like philosophers, both sociologists and anthropologists might want to understand *why* people have the beliefs they have. But the interests of philosophers and social scientists diverge in an important way: Where social scientists might like to *explain* why a group of people share certain beliefs, philosophers are interested in the rationales—the *justifications* (if any)—that can be found for those beliefs. An explanation of someone's belief tells us why they have the belief, but it can do that without justifying the belief. Consider an example.

Suppose I believe there is an elephant hiding in my office. An *explanation* for my belief might be this: I have taken a hallucinogenic drug, which causes wildly bizarre beliefs. When you learn this about me, you understand how I came to have my strange belief, but knowing the explanation of my belief *gives you no reason to suspect that my belief might be true*. On the other hand, a *justification* for my belief might be this: There are muddy elephant tracks leading down the hall toward my office; elephant odours and elephant sounds emanate from my office. When you learn the justification for my belief, you once again understand how I came to have the belief, but in this case, knowing the justification *also provides you with some reason to suspect that my belief might be true*. We can express one important difference between an explanation and a justification for a belief in this way: If the justification is any good at all, it is a reason for anyone who knows the justification to think that the belief is true. The same is not true for explanations. If you know the explanation of my belief, and you think the explanation is a good one, it still will not give you reason to share my belief. In summary, an **explanation** of someone's belief tells us why they have the belief, but it may have no direct bearing on whether the belief is true; there are perfectly good explanations for false beliefs as well as for true ones. A **justification** for someone's belief is relevant to whether the belief is true, and it provides reasons or evidence for *anyone* to think that the belief is true or likely to be true.

explanation: An account of why something happens or why it is the case. *Causal* explanations are probably the best known form of explanation—they provide an account of why an event occurred by stating its cause.

justification: A reason for believing that a proposition is true or is likely to be true.

One reason for the differences between how philosophers and social scientists attend to beliefs is that philosophers are concerned with the justifications for beliefs, while social scientists are concerned with their explanations. But why is there *that* difference? Because social scientists are interested in what people believe and why, but philosophers are interested in *what to believe* and why. We are interested in the justifications that others have for their beliefs because we want to know *what we should believe*. This is a significantly different kind of interest in beliefs and their justifications. An anthropological study of the belief system of the Yanomami people of the Amazon, or of the Ju/'hoansi of the Kalahari, is not undertaken *to decide whether the anthropologist should adopt those systems of belief*. But a philosophical investigation of the same belief systems is motivated by the questions, *Are they right?* and *Should I adopt those beliefs?*

THE LOVE OF WISDOM

The word *philosophy* comes from ancient Greek, where it means "love of wisdom." We might therefore define philosophy simply as *the love of wisdom*. But this is not a helpful definition unless we first know what is meant by *wisdom*, and about the kind of *love* that it is appropriate to have for wisdom. The simplest way to understand wisdom is to think of it as one kind of knowledge. But it is not the sort of knowledge we have when, for example, we know a friend's phone number, or know where to find the best cheeseburgers in town. Roughly 2400 years ago, philosophers began to describe the kind of knowledge that philosophy is concerned with as knowledge of the *natures* or *essences* of things. What sort of knowledge is that? A few simple examples can help.

Not Just the Facts

Shakespeare's Romeo and Juliet are sometimes used to illustrate the idea of romantic love. But did Romeo really *love* Juliet? There are reasons to be suspicious; after all, when he first announced his love for Juliet, Romeo had only just met her—he had caught a glimpse of her from across a room and, shortly thereafter, exchanged a few words with her. Is that sufficient acquaintance to actually *be in love* with someone, or is it necessary to know that person better? Part of the problem is that there are several other feelings in the same neighbourhood as love, and Romeo might have had one of those. He might, for example, have been feeling infatuation or lust. A person who is infatuated, or whose mind is consumed with lust, might not always be the best person to decide whether what they feel is love. How can we find out whether what Romeo felt was love?

Note that our question is not about whether Romeo was only *pretending* to be in love with Juliet—that is something he could easily have told us. We are instead asking whether the feelings that Romeo had for Juliet *qualify* as love. Even if Romeo could have bared his feelings to us, our question still remains: Is *that* love? To answer, we may first need to pose another question: What, after all, is *love*? Similar queries can be raised about a variety of topics: An honest disagreement over whether a trial was fair may rest on a disagreement about the facts of the case. People who are equally well acquainted with the facts—even with *all* the facts—can still have an honest disagreement about whether the trial was fair. Sometimes that disagreement persists because they disagree about the nature of fairness: Does fairness require that the accused have qualified legal representation? Does it require a mix of genders or races on the jury? Similarly, a disagreement about whether an object is really *art* may rest on a disagreement about relevant facts. Is the object an artifact produced by a person, or is it something that grew naturally in the forest? People who may know all the facts could still disagree about what makes something *art*. In each of these examples, the residue of disagreement that remains after we agree on the relevant facts is usually a disagreement about the nature of *something*: What is love, or fairness, or art?

In the preceding examples, we used a distinction between *disagreements about the facts* and *disagreements about the natures of things*. Notice that it is not always immediately obvious which sort of disagreement we might be having. Suppose that you and I disagree about how many chairs there are in the next room. This seems a clear example of a disagreement about the facts, since it can be settled to our mutual satisfaction using straightforward empirical methods, such as observing, counting, or measuring. But suppose we go into the next room to count the chairs together, and we find that we *still* disagree about whether there are (say) six chairs or only five chairs in the room. But now we are able to locate the source of our disagreement: We disagree about whether to count one piece of furniture in the far corner of the room. You insist that it is a wide, stuffed chair designed to seat two people, but I contend that it is a small sofa. What appeared to be a simple disagreement about the facts, one that we might easily settle by counting, concealed a disagreement about the nature of chairs. We assumed there would be no disagreement about the nature of chairs, or at least nothing comparable to disagreements about the nature of love, art, or justice. But not even chairs are too mundane to have natures. Whenever we pursue answers to questions about the nature of things—even if those things are only chairs—then we are doing philosophy. In the chapters that follow, we will find discussions about the natures of identity, change, persons, selves, minds, freedom, knowledge, certainty, justification, God, faith, evil, and much else.

As a lover you may wonder whether you really are in love with a certain person. If your uncertainty leads you to ask and explore the further question "What, after all, is love?," then you have begun to philosophize—you have begun to inquire into the *nature* of something. Some philosophers prefer to avoid this way of describing what they do, and say instead that they are investigating or analyzing the *idea* of love or the *concept* of love. Others state this view of philosophy using the idea of *meaning*: Instead of asking "What is the nature of love?," they might ask "What does 'love' mean?" There are differences between these ways of describing philosophy—differences that matter to philosophers. However, the varied descriptions all gesture in the same direction, and that is enough to get us started.

Philosophy and Self-Knowledge

Now we have a way to define philosophy. Philosophy is an investigation into the nature of things or, if you prefer, an investigation into concepts or meanings. If we understand *wisdom* as knowledge of natures (or concepts, or meanings), then we can follow the ancients in describing philosophy as the pursuit of wisdom. This view usually comes hand in hand with two other ideas: First, that philosophical knowledge is *prior to* other kinds of knowledge, and second, that the practice of philosophy is a route to greater self-knowledge. Consider what each of these means.

1. In the examples we used to illustrate philosophy, we employed a distinction between questions about matters of fact and questions about the nature of things. We also implied a certain relationship between the two—namely, that our disagreements

about matters of fact cannot be settled until we have *first* settled any disagreements about the nature of things. For example, it looks as though we cannot decide whether Romeo really loved Juliet until *after* we resolve the question of what love is. It seems that philosophical knowledge—knowledge of the nature of things—has to come prior to factual knowledge. Some philosophers have certainly accepted this idea—Plato, whom you will meet shortly, is a famous example—but it is not an inevitable consequence of our definition of philosophy.

Many philosophers today are inclined to say that questions about matters of fact and questions about the nature of things are so deeply entangled that we cannot hope to explore one without *at the same time* exploring the other. On this view, we cannot answer, for example, the factual question of *whether we are really free* without at the same time considering *what freedom is*, and we can only come to know what freedom is through the process of attempting to understand whether we are free. Neither question has priority; instead, we move back and forth between the two, revising and refining our views about the natures of things in light of continually evolving beliefs about what the facts are, and revising our understanding of the facts in light of our evolving views about the natures of things. So, philosophical knowledge does not provide a prior foundation for factual knowledge, but the two are woven into a single fabric in which each helps to shape and reinforce the other.

2. A second idea that commonly accompanies the view of philosophy as an investigation into the nature of things is that the *practice* of philosophy brings with it increasing self-knowledge. It is easy to see how the two ideas are linked. Once we have all the facts, we won't *disagree* about whether Romeo loved Juliet unless we disagree about the nature of love. Likewise, we won't *agree* that Romeo loved Juliet unless we agree about the nature of love. But whether we agree or disagree about Romeo's feelings for Juliet, the implication is that *we already hold some view or other about the nature of love.* If you believe Romeo loved Juliet, or if you think you have ever been in love, then you must believe you can recognize a case of love when you encounter one. You must already be operating with *some* understanding of the nature of love, and that understanding is shaping your views about what the facts are—about, for example, whether you are currently in love. Similarly, our various agreements and disagreements suggest that *we already have views* about the nature of art, fairness, freedom, and so on. We already hold philosophical views about these matters, whether or not we have given them any deliberate thought or attention.

   As you undertake the practice of philosophy, you will need to make more explicit the view about the nature of love (or fairness, or freedom, and so on) that is already shaping your judgment about whether Romeo loved Juliet (or whether the trial was fair, or whether you are free). This is an essential first step, since until your so-far-unexpressed views are brought into the light of day, they cannot undergo the kind of scrutiny (whether by yourself or others) that is needed to decide whether they are plausible views. The first step in this process—the step of making more explicit your own implicit views about the nature of things—is not (usually) a matter of simply finding the words to give outward expression to what you already think. More often it is a matter of discovering for yourself the ideas—the hidden assumptions and presuppositions—that influence how you think. This is the source of the idea that by practicing philosophy we get to know ourselves better. Perhaps it hasn't occurred to you that you may *already* be operating with philosophical ideas about the nature of love, fairness, art, freedom, knowledge, and so on. But if you are, won't it be important clarify what those views are, and decide whether they are any good? In the practice of philosophy, you bring ideas out of obscurity and make them clearer. Only then can you examine and evaluate them.

It would be an exaggeration to suggest that we each have a philosophical *theory* about, say, the nature of love. *Theory* is too grand a term for our vague implicit understanding. At the very least, we have a great many unarticulated assumptions, presuppositions, and—perhaps—prejudices, all of which influence our decision about whether Romeo loved Juliet. The processes by which we uncover our own assumptions and presuppositions, and then find the words to make them explicit, and finally subject them to critical examination—the very practices that constitute philosophizing—are also the processes by which we arrive at self-knowledge.

I mentioned at the outset that the idea that philosophy is an investigation into the nature of things is rather old-fashioned. There are other ways to define it, but they are often refinements and developments of the ancient definition of philosophy. We have already seen at least two ways in which contemporary philosophers have refined the ancient idea. Questions about the *nature* of things have sometimes been recast as questions about concepts or meanings. Furthermore, any imagined boundary between questions about matters of fact and questions about the nature of things has become blurry, and views about the priority of philosophical knowledge to factual knowledge have been widely abandoned. Nonetheless, you will not be misled if you take our old-fashioned definition of philosophy as a starting point, so long as you realize that it may need to be refined later. According to this ancient definition and, indeed, to most contemporary definitions of philosophy, our efforts to say something here about the nature of philosophy are themselves examples of philosophizing about philosophy.

Anti-Philosophical Thoughts

This way of understanding philosophy invites an obvious question: How do you decide whether the answer you settle on to a philosophical question is the *right* answer or a *good* answer? As you sharpen and polish your ideas about the nature of love, or art, or justice, you will eventually arrive at full-fledged philosophical theories about love, art, or justice. How do you tell a good philosophical theory from a bad one? As we proceed, you will encounter some of the standards a good philosophical theory is expected to meet. However, at least at the outset of the study of philosophy, it is important to avoid certain easy reactions to philosophical questions.

One common beginner's reaction is to treat such questions in the way a non-scientist might treat a scientific question; namely, by asking *whose expertise* is to be relied on for the best answer. But there are no experts to whom we can turn for an authoritative answer to philosophical questions. Philosophers, who ought to be experts on these matters if anyone is, will quickly be found to disagree with one another, and that disqualifies them from having genuine expertise about the nature of things. Although it is a good idea to consider carefully what people who have thought longer and harder about certain philosophical issues have to say, they cannot tell you what you will find when your own explorations are finished.

Logic Box

Illicit Appeal to Authority

It is common, often legitimate, and sometimes even essential to rely on the statements or "say-so" of experts who have knowledge we lack. However, it is a *fallacy* to rely on the say-so of:

1. persons who lack the expertise that is *relevant to the particular claim* being made; or
2. persons who speak about matters about which *no one* has expertise; or
3. persons speaking about matters that are known to be *widely disputed* (even among the experts, if there are any).

A good test for a legitimate appeal to authority is whether other, independent experts agree with the claim and—this part is crucial—whether *it is in principle possible for you to acquire the expertise to check the claim yourself.* When genuine experts make a claim, they will have good reason—for example, strong evidence—for the claim. That is precisely why the experts have reached agreement. Therefore, you can always bypass the experts and go straight to the evidence itself. An expert who cannot, in principle, be replaced by the evidence itself is no real expert at all. Whenever you are tempted to think that the truth of something depends only on *who* says it, you are almost certainly making an **illicit appeal to authority**.

Example: "Since Albert Einstein advocated nuclear disarmament, disarming would probably be the right thing to do."

illicit appeal to authority: Appeals to authority rely on the fact the some expert holds a belief as grounds for thinking that the belief is probably true. An appeal to authority is *illicit*, and the reasoning is fallacious, when no one has expertise in the topic of the statement, when the experts disagree about the statement, or when the person to whom one appeals for support is not a genuine expert in the topic of the statement.

At this point, it is tempting to say that if there are no authorities to whom we can turn on philosophical matters, then *people should believe whatever they want*. Or perhaps then *we are all entitled to our own opinion*. But these reactions are unjustified. If they are reactions to the absence of authorities or experts, they assume that unless there is *someone else* to whom we can turn for answers, then no answer will be better than any other. Apart from demonstrating an extraordinary subservience to authority, this erroneously assumes that the value of an idea depends on *the person* from whom it comes. If an idea has any value at all, it will have that value no matter who is responsible for it. For this reason you should always try to replace the question "According to whom?" with "*Why* should we believe that?" The first query asks for the idea's pedigree, but the second—and better question—asks for its justification.

Consider, very briefly, our two expressions of the anti-philosophical idea that if there are no experts or authorities, then any answer is as good as any other. The first is that people should believe whatever they want. *Why*? Perhaps because *it makes no difference what we believe* (about, for example, the nature of love). But it takes only a moment's reflection to remind ourselves that such ideas *do* make a difference. Because Romeo believed that what he felt for Juliet was love, he proposed marriage and—shortly thereafter—committed suicide. Romeo's beliefs about the nature of love made a significant difference to how his life went. Your belief about whether you are in love can also matter to how your life goes. Perhaps, however, the reason for thinking we should believe whatever we want is the suspicion that when there are no experts, it is because *there are no right answers*. But unless we have conducted a thorough examination of possible answers, we are not justified in thinking there are no right answers. More important, if it is true that there are no right answers, that would be a very bad reason to believe whatever we want. After all, if there are *no* right answers, then whatever we end up believing—even if it is what we *want* to believe—will be *wrong*.

Consider the second anti-philosophical claim made above—namely, that on philosophical matters, we are all entitled to our own opinions. This says more than that we all *have* our own opinions. It may be true that most of us have opinions on these matters, but *having* an opinion is not the same as *being entitled* to have it. If I steal someone's wallet, then I *have* his wallet, but I am not thereby *entitled* to it. To be entitled to something, whether it is a wallet or an opinion, means that my possession of it can be *justified*. Merely having an opinion doesn't entitle me to it. Perhaps, however, this is unfair, and the person who says we are all entitled to our own opinions is only making the perfectly correct observation that we are *legally* entitled to believe whatever we want. The law does not forbid me from believing anything I want to believe—although, of course, it can forbid me from acting on or even expressing some of those beliefs. If this is what is intended by claiming we are all entitled to our own opinions, it is a very poor recommendation for those opinions. The law permits me to believe as many *false* or *foolish* things as I want. It is not against the law to be a fool, so I am (legally) entitled to be one if I want—but that is no defense of foolishness.

After only a little scrutiny, the belief that we are all entitled to our own opinions does not seem to be an opinion to which we are entitled, and the idea that we should believe whatever we want is not an opinion we should want to hold. The belief that we can simply turn our backs on views that are *merely philosophical* is itself a philosophical view. When we try to walk away from philosophy, we always find ourselves in the middle of it. But if we are inevitably going to philosophize anyway, then—like most other things—we might as well learn to do it well.

WHY PHILOSOPHIZE?

Why bother to philosophize? Most people don't need a motive for philosophizing—their natural desire to have a better understanding of themselves and their world suffices to lead them into philosophy. There are some commonly recited answers to our question, however, and we should briefly consider a few of them.

1. There is a rather obvious side effect of philosophizing: *Philosophizing is good mental exercise*. Philosophizing frequently requires stretching ourselves in new directions. First, it requires us *to formulate new questions* that hadn't occurred to us before. Second, as we search for answers to those questions, it requires *imagining new alternatives*. So much emphasis is usually placed on the importance of reasoning in philosophy that it is easy to overlook the many ways that philosophy requires us to stretch our imaginations. Third, philosophizing requires *making reasoned choices* among the alternatives. A mental ability, like any ability, can atrophy with disuse, or it can become more highly developed with exercise. Philosophy is one arena in which we can give our minds a good workout. This is a beneficial side effect of philosophy, but not its purpose, and rarely is it anyone's real motive for philosophizing.
2. Following our discussion of the nature of philosophy, you should already suspect what one benefit will be. An obvious motive for philosophizing is simply *the desire for greater clarity* about something. Anyone who has been troubled by confusion and obscurity will understand how satisfying it can be to acquire even a bit of clarity. One way to understand an investigation into the nature of things is simply to see it as a quest for greater clarity—a quest for the clarification of concepts or meanings. When our own incomplete and implicit understanding of, for example, love is gradually transformed into a theory about the nature of love, we have achieved greater clarity.

Philosophy, if it is done with care, empowers us to better say what we mean and to mean what we say.

Clarity is not easy to achieve. Two obstacles to it deserve special mention. To be in possession of darkly obscure thoughts can give one an aura of mystery, or it can give others the impression of wisdom or profundity that surpasses their own. This explains the temptation to indulge in obscurity, but it does not justify giving in to that temptation. In such cases, to insist on greater clarity is to threaten a source of power. It is occasionally useful to remind ourselves that, for most purposes, it is better to be clear than to seem profound.

We are exposed constantly to clichés and platitudes—the little slogans we are surrounded by that we learn to recite without thinking, without realizing we are doing so, and without giving much thought to what they might mean. There are vast institutions and industries whose primary function is to supply slogans that replace thought and to encourage communication by cliché. We already saw an example of a platitude that is intended to serve that purpose: "We are all entitled to our own opinions." When we pause to reflect on what those words might mean, our platitude quickly unravels. Nonetheless, the slogan still serves a purpose: It is something we say in order to put an end to further thought or discussion. There are occasions on which it is necessary to do that, but it is a mistake to think that the cliché reveals something *true* about our opinions or about their value. We have similar slogans ready for many occasions, and they are often the first things that come to mind when it isn't obvious what to say. These are only *comfort words*: slogans, clichés, and platitudes designed to relieve us of the burden of thinking, or even to block to road to further thought. The kind of clarity we seek in philosophy requires continuing to think things through, so we need to be on constant guard against comfort words.

3. The ancient philosopher Diogenes (c. 400–325 BC) once said that "for the conduct of life we need right reason or a halter."[1] This hints at another motive for philosophizing. Since Diogenes identified philosophy with reason, we can usefully understand him as saying that either we must philosophize, or we will be led around in a halter. His suggestion, then, is that philosophy helps make us free: It allows us to escape from a life in the halter. Many other philosophers have made a similar point, but it is easily misunderstood. We tend to think of *being free* as being rid of the coercive power that *others* have over us. Freedom from coercion or enslavement by others is certainly important, but it is difficult to see how philosophy can help us gain such freedoms. We must ask what sort of freedom philosophizing might help us to attain. We will begin by examining what two philosophers, widely separated in time, had to say.

Plato: Athenian philosopher, student of Socrates, and teacher of Aristotle. Widely regarded as one of the greatest philosophers of all time, Plato wrote on almost every area of philosophy. His writings take the form of dialogues in which his philosophical mentor, Socrates, discusses philosophy with other characters.

Socrates: Highly influential Athenian philosopher best known for having stimulated Plato's thinking. His relentless demands for greater clarity and better rationales for ideas, policies, and practices led to a new style of philosophizing and eventually to his execution by the state of Athens. He left behind no writings.

One of the earliest—and certainly the most famous—appearances of the idea that philosophy helps make us free is found in *The Republic*, written by **Plato** (427–347 BC). *The Republic* is a dialogue between Plato's famous teacher, **Socrates** (469–399 BC), and a small group of philosophers and friends. In the brief excerpt below, Socrates relates a famous allegory about the nature of, and motives for, philosophy.

[1] From Laertius, Diogenes. *Lives of Eminent Philosophers*. In R. D. Hicks (Ed.) (1925)., Book VI, Chapter 2 (24). Retrieved June 29, 2014, from http://www.perseus.tufts.edu/hopper/text?doc=D.%20L.%206&lang=original.

The Allegory of the Cave[2]

And now, I said, let me show in a figure how far our nature is enlightened or unenlightened:—Behold! human beings living in an underground den, which has a mouth open towards the light and reaching all along the den; here they have been from their childhood, and have their legs and necks chained so that they cannot move, and can only see before them, being prevented by the chains from turning round their heads. Above and behind them a fire is blazing at a distance, and between the fire and the prisoners there is a raised way; and you will see, if you look, a low wall built along the way, like the screen which marionette players have in front of them, over which they show the puppets.

I see.

And do you see, I said, men passing along the wall carrying all sorts of vessels, and statues and figures of animals made of wood and stone and various materials, which appear over the wall? Some of them are talking, others silent.

You have shown me a strange image, and they are strange prisoners.

Like ourselves, I replied; and they see only their own shadows, or the shadows of one another, which the fire throws on the opposite wall of the cave?

True, he said; how could they see anything but the shadows if they were never allowed to move their heads?

And of the objects which are being carried in like manner they would only see the shadows?

Yes, he said.

And if they were able to converse with one another, would they not suppose that they were naming what was actually before them?

Very true.

And suppose further that the prison had an echo which came from the other side, would they not be sure to fancy when one of the passers-by spoke that the voice which they heard came from the passing shadow?

No question, he replied.

To them, I said, the truth would be literally nothing but the shadows of the images.

That is certain.

And now look again, and see what will naturally follow if the prisoners are released and disabused of their error. At first, when any of them is liberated and compelled suddenly to stand up and turn his neck round and walk and look towards the light, he will suffer sharp pains; the glare will distress him, and he will be unable to see the realities of which in his former state he had seen the shadows; and then conceive some one saying to him, that what he saw before was an illusion, but that now, when he is approaching nearer to being and his eye is turned towards more real existence, he has a clearer vision, what will be his reply? And you may further imagine that his instructor is pointing to the objects as they pass and requiring him to name them,—will he not be perplexed? Will he not fancy that the shadows which he formerly saw are truer than the objects which are now shown to him?

Far truer.

And if he is compelled to look straight at the light, will he not have a pain in his eyes which will make him turn away to take refuge in the objects of vision which he

[2] From Plato (380–60 BC). *Republic.* 514a–517d. (Benjamin Jowett, Trans.). Retrieved June 29, 2014, from http://www.gutenberg.org/cache/epub/150/pg150.txt. References to Plato's writings are usually given by line numbers, which can be found in the margins of most editions and translations of Plato's works.

can see, and which he will conceive to be in reality clearer than the things which are now being shown to him?

True, he said.

And suppose once more, that he is reluctantly dragged up a steep and rugged ascent, and held fast until he's forced into the presence of the sun himself, is he not likely to be pained and irritated? When he approaches the light his eyes will be dazzled, and he will not be able to see anything at all of what are now called realities.

Not all in a moment, he said.

He will require to grow accustomed to the sight of the upper world. And first he will see the shadows best, next the reflections of men and other objects in the water, and then the objects themselves; then he will gaze upon the light of the moon and the stars and the spangled heaven; and he will see the sky and the stars by night better than the sun or the light of the sun by day?

Certainly.

Last of all he will be able to see the sun, and not mere reflections of him in the water, but he will see him in his own proper place, and not in another; and he will contemplate him as he is.

Certainly.

He will then proceed to argue that this is he who gives the season and the years, and is the guardian of all that is in the visible world, and in a certain way the cause of all things which he and his fellows have been accustomed to behold?

Clearly, he said, he would first see the sun and then reason about him.

And when he remembered his old habitation, and the wisdom of the den and his fellow-prisoners, do you not suppose that he would felicitate himself on the change, and pity them?

Certainly, he would.

And if they were in the habit of conferring honours among themselves on those who were quickest to observe the passing shadows and to remark which of them went before, and which followed after, and which were together; and who were therefore best able to draw conclusions as to the future, do you think that he would care for such honours and glories, or envy the possessors of them? Would he not say with Homer,

"Better to be the poor servant of a poor master,"

and to endure anything, rather than think as they do and live after their manner?

Yes, he said, I think that he would rather suffer anything than entertain these false notions and live in this miserable manner.

Imagine once more, I said, such a one coming suddenly out of the sun to be replaced in his old situation; would he not be certain to have his eyes full of darkness?

To be sure, he said.

And if there were a contest, and he had to compete in measuring the shadows with the prisoners who had never moved out of the den, while his sight was still weak, and before his eyes had become steady (and the time which would be needed to acquire this new habit of sight might be very considerable), would he not be ridiculous? Men would say of him that up he went and down he came without his eyes; and that it was better not even to think of ascending; and if anyone tried to loose another and lead him up to the light, let them only catch the offender, and they would put him to death.

No question, he said.

This entire allegory, I said, you may now append, dear Glaucon, to the previous argument; the prison-house is the world of sight, the light of the fire is the sun, and you will not misapprehend me if you interpret the journey upwards to be the ascent of

> the soul into the intellectual world according to my poor belief, which, at your desire, I have expressed whether rightly or wrongly, God knows. But, whether true or false, my opinion is that in the world of knowledge the idea of good appears last of all, and is seen only with an effort; and, when seen, is also inferred to be the universal author of all things beautiful and right, parent of light and of the lord of light in this visible world, and the immediate source of reason and truth in the intellectual; and that this is the power upon which he who would act rationally, either in public or private life must have his eye fixed.
>
> I agree, he said, as far as I am able to understand you.
>
> Moreover, I said, you must not wonder that those who attain to this beatific vision are unwilling to descend to human affairs; for their souls are ever hastening into the upper world where they desire to dwell; which desire of theirs is very natural, if our allegory may be trusted.

Plato's grim portrait of the human predicament has us in chains, imprisoned in a dimly lit cave in which we mistake passing shadows for reality. The world outside the cave is bathed in bright sunlight, and we will only ascend toward it if we are compelled to do so. Gradually, we will overcome the pain of the harsh sunlight, and after we see the reality outside the cave, we will never again be content to live among shadows.

The Metaphysics and Epistemology of the Cave

Plato's allegory presents our predicament in two ways: one *metaphysical*, the other *epistemological*. First, the allegory gives some broad hints about Plato's theory of reality—his metaphysics. **Metaphysics** is the branch of philosophy concerned with questions about the nature of reality, questions about what kinds of things are real and what are not. Plato describes *two realms of being*, a world of appearances and a world of realities. There is the dark underground where we are imprisoned, and where everything is only illusion, but there is also the bright sunlit realm outside the cave, filled with realities about which the prisoners know nothing. There are two metaphysical realms: the shadowy world of appearances and the sunlit realities. Inside the cave we dwell among appearances, the shadows of things and the echoes of sounds. Plato believes we are like the prisoners in his allegory because we also live in a world of appearances and mistake it for reality. There is also another, higher realm of being, however, and we can aspire to knowledge of it.

metaphysics: Theory of reality. A branch of philosophy concerned with questions about what is real and about the kinds of things that exist. Longstanding debates in metaphysics include the nature of properties and substances, the nature of causation, determinism, the nature of minds and their relationship to bodies, whether God (or gods) exist, and so on.

The story of the cave is only offered as allegory, but it is rich enough to be read in a number of illuminating ways. Perhaps we can get a feel for Plato's two worlds by reminding ourselves of the contrast between the world of our daily experience and the world that our best scientific theories tell us we actually live in. The solid and stable world in which we appear to live our daily lives is nothing like the reality revealed by contemporary science. As it is described in our scientific theories, physical reality is mostly empty space, populated by whirling clouds of strangely misbehaving subatomic particles, and the earth on which we so securely plant our feet spins at 1000 miles per hour while being swept around the centre of our galaxy at nearly 500 000 miles per hour. And we aren't the least bit dizzy! We can use Plato's allegory to remind us that the way things seem is probably not how they really are, and that, like Plato's prisoners, we too are content to live among appearances.

epistemology: Theory of knowledge. A branch of philosophy concerned with the nature of knowledge, certainty, justification, and related concepts. Longstanding debates in epistemology concern what can be known and how, whether it is possible to acquire certainty, whether perception is a source of knowledge, and so on.

Plato's division of the world into two realms is mirrored by a distinction between *two ways of trying to comprehend reality*. His **epistemology**—his theory of knowledge—runs parallel to his theory of reality, but Plato's allegory only gestures toward his theory of knowledge. The "prison house," he says, "is *the world of sight*," but the world to which we ascend if we leave the cave is the "intellectual world." Plato's idea, developed in detail in other writings, is that the world we experience through our senses (the world of sight) is an illusion, and that only intellect can get beyond appearances to know reality. We *grasp* each realm of being in a different way: Our senses reveal the appearances, by which we are held captive, but our intellects are capable of climbing upward past the appearances to get occasional glimpses of reality. Alternatively put: Our senses give us only *opinions*, most of which are false; but our intellects are able to move past the appearances and can provide *knowledge*. In Plato's picture, the philosopher leaves behind the world of appearances and tries to grasp reality with her intellect. Why does she bother?

The Unconditional Love of Truth

Plato believes that after we glimpse reality, the world of appearances becomes unbearable—we "would rather suffer anything than entertain these false notions and live in this miserable manner." If we try to teach what we have learned, or—even worse—tell others that they are being seduced by illusions, they will find us ridiculous and may even put us to death (as happened to Socrates). It is better to look foolish to those who prefer to stay in chains than to accept shadows and echoes for reality. Despite his bleak picture of the *human predicament*, Plato was an optimist about *human nature*. After only a glimpse of reality, our "souls are ever hastening into the upper world where [we] desire to dwell," and, he adds, this "desire of [ours] is very natural." It is in our nature to prefer realities to appearances, or truths to falsehoods.

Perhaps Plato makes it a little *too easy* to prefer reality to illusion. The contrast between appearance and reality in his allegory is a contrast between being chained in a dark cave and roaming freely over a sunlit surface. Given *that* choice, who wouldn't prefer reality? But what would happen if reality turned out to be a cruel or unpleasant place? Would we then crawl back into a world of illusions if one were offered? Plato believes we would not, and that we would prefer realities even if they weren't more beautiful than illusions. The lovers of wisdom in us are drawn to reality as moths to a flame. Plato's philosopher is under pressure from the ridicule of peers, and even from the threat of death, to be content with appearances, but no matter how unpleasant others make her efforts to know reality, she prefers it over appearances. Plato thus sees knowledge of reality as intrinsically desirable, and our love of the truth as unconditional. He believes we would all prefer to know an unpleasant truth than to believe a beautiful falsehood, and we need no further motive to philosophize than that.

On Plato's view, our metaphysical predicament is that we live in the midst of illusion, cut off from reality. Our desire to know the reality from which we are estranged is part of human nature. The freedom that philosophy offers us is the freedom that all lovers of wisdom will naturally desire once they discover that they are chained to appearances.

The Value of Philosophy (Bertrand Russell, 1912)[3]

The ancient idea that philosophy can make us free was also defended by the twentieth century British philosopher **Bertrand Russell** (1872–1970). For Russell, the prison from which philosophy promises to free us is not a metaphysical predicament; it consists of customs and prejudices from which we must struggle to free ourselves by practicing philosophy. If you examine his words carefully, you will notice that he does not say that philosophy will free us from oppression, enslavement, or imprisonment. Rather, he says that philosophy promises freedom from *something inside us*. It promises freedom from the narrowness of our own minds, from the stubbornness, prejudice, and bigotry that so easily takes root in each of us.

Bertrand Russell: Influential British philosopher and logician who played a central role in laying the foundations for twentieth century philosophy. Russell was one of the first philosophers to make use of "the new logic" that appeared at the end of the nineteenth century to develop striking new views on metaphysics, epistemology, and the philosophy of language.

> [I]t will be well to consider . . . what is the value of philosophy and why it ought to be studied. It is the more necessary to consider this question, in view of the fact that many men, under the influence of science or of practical affairs, are inclined to doubt whether philosophy is anything better than innocent but useless trifling, hair-splitting distinctions, and controversies on matters concerning which knowledge is impossible.
>
> This view of philosophy appears to result, partly from a wrong conception of the ends of life, partly from a wrong conception of the kind of goods which philosophy strives to achieve. Physical science, through the medium of inventions, is useful to innumerable people who are wholly ignorant of it; thus the study of physical science is to be recommended, not only, or primarily, because of the effect on the student, but rather because of the effect on mankind in general. Thus utility does not belong to philosophy. If the study of philosophy has any value at all for others than students of philosophy, it must be only indirectly, through its effects upon the lives of those who study it. It is in these effects, therefore, if anywhere, that the value of philosophy must be primarily sought.
>
> But further, if we are not to fail in our endeavour to determine the value of philosophy, we must first free our minds from the prejudices of what are wrongly called 'practical' men. The 'practical' man, as this word is often used, is one who recognizes only material needs, who realizes that men must have food for the body, but is oblivious of the necessity of providing food for the mind. If all men were well off, if poverty and disease had been reduced to their lowest possible point, there would still remain much to be done to produce a valuable society; and even in the existing world the goods of the mind are at least as important as the goods of the body. It is exclusively among the goods of the mind that the value of philosophy is to be found; and only those who are not indifferent to these goods can be persuaded that the study of philosophy is not a waste of time.
>
> Philosophy, like all other studies, aims primarily at knowledge. The knowledge it aims at is the kind of knowledge which gives unity and system to the body of the sciences, and the kind which results from a critical examination of the grounds of our convictions, prejudices, and beliefs. But it cannot be maintained that philosophy has had any very great measure of success in its attempts to provide definite answers to its questions. If you ask a mathematician, a mineralogist, a historian, or any other man of learning, what definite body of truths has been ascertained by his science, his answer will last as long as you are willing to listen. But if you put the

[3] Russell, Bertrand (1912). Chapter XV. *The Problems of Philosophy*. Retrieved June 29, 2014, from http://www.gutenberg.org/cache/epub/5827/pg5827.txt.

same question to a philosopher, he will, if he is candid, have to confess that his study has not achieved positive results such as have been achieved by other sciences. It is true that this is partly accounted for by the fact that, as soon as definite knowledge concerning any subject becomes possible, this subject ceases to be called philosophy, and becomes a separate science. The whole study of the heavens, which now belongs to astronomy, was once included in philosophy; Newton's great work was called 'the mathematical principles of natural philosophy'. Similarly, the study of the human mind, which was a part of philosophy, has now been separated from philosophy and has become the science of psychology. Thus, to a great extent, the uncertainty of philosophy is more apparent than real: those questions which are already capable of definite answers are placed in the sciences, while those only to which, at present, no definite answer can be given, remain to form the residue which is called philosophy.

This is, however, only a part of the truth concerning the uncertainty of philosophy. There are many questions—and among them those that are of the profoundest interest to our spiritual life—which, so far as we can see, must remain insoluble to the human intellect unless its powers become of quite a different order from what they are now. Has the universe any unity of plan or purpose, or is it a fortuitous concourse of atoms? Is consciousness a permanent part of the universe, giving hope of indefinite growth in wisdom, or is it a transitory accident on a small planet on which life must ultimately become impossible? Are good and evil of importance to the universe or only to man? Such questions are asked by philosophy, and variously answered by various philosophers. But it would seem that, whether answers be otherwise discoverable or not, the answers suggested by philosophy are none of them demonstrably true. Yet, however slight may be the hope of discovering an answer, it is part of the business of philosophy to continue the consideration of such questions, to make us aware of their importance, to examine all the approaches to them, and to keep alive that speculative interest in the universe which is apt to be killed by confining ourselves to definitely ascertainable knowledge.

Many philosophers, it is true, have held that philosophy could establish the truth of certain answers to such fundamental questions. They have supposed that what is of most importance in religious beliefs could be proved by strict demonstration to be true. In order to judge of such attempts, it is necessary to take a survey of human knowledge, and to form an opinion as to its methods and its limitations. On such a subject it would be unwise to pronounce dogmatically; . . . we shall be compelled to renounce the hope of finding philosophical proofs of religious beliefs. We cannot, therefore, include as part of the value of philosophy any definite set of answers to such questions. Hence, once more, the value of philosophy must not depend upon any supposed body of definitely ascertainable knowledge to be acquired by those who study it.

The value of philosophy is, in fact, to be sought largely in its very uncertainty. The man who has no tincture of philosophy goes through life imprisoned in the prejudices derived from common sense, from the habitual beliefs of his age or his nation, and from convictions which have grown up in his mind without the co-operation or consent of his deliberate reason. To such a man the world tends to become definite, finite, obvious; common objects rouse no questions, and unfamiliar possibilities are contemptuously rejected. As soon as we begin to philosophize, on the contrary, we find . . . that even the most everyday things lead to problems to which only very incomplete answers can be given. Philosophy, though unable to tell us with certainty what is the true answer to the doubts which it raises, is able to suggest many possibilities which enlarge our thoughts and free them from the tyranny of custom. Thus, while diminishing our feeling of certainty as to what things are, it greatly increases our knowledge as to what they may be; it removes the somewhat arrogant dogmatism of those who have never travelled into the region of liberating doubt, and it keeps alive our sense of wonder by showing familiar things in an unfamiliar aspect. . . .

Thus, to sum up our discussion of the value of philosophy; Philosophy is to be studied, not for the sake of any definite answers to its questions, since no definite answers can, as a rule, be known to be true, but rather for the sake of the questions themselves; because these questions enlarge our conception of what is possible, enrich our intellectual imagination, and diminish the dogmatic assurance which closes the mind against speculation; but above all because, through the greatness of the universe which philosophy contemplates, the mind also is rendered great, and becomes capable of that union with the universe which constitutes its highest good.

Russell provides one version of the idea that the practice of philosophy can make us free. He believes it frees each person from "the tyranny of custom," from "the habitual beliefs of [our] age or nation," and from the "convictions which have grown up in his mind without the co-operation or consent of his deliberate reason." What needs to be emphasized is that Russell did not contend that philosophy can free us from oppression by others. The prejudices, habitual beliefs, and convictions from which we need to be freed are *our own*; they are not the habitual beliefs and convictions that only belong to others, but ones we have absorbed into our own thinking. Sometimes we need to turn inward to find the chains that bind us.

Russell characterizes the beliefs by which each person is imprisoned as the "convictions which have grown up in his mind without the co-operation or consent of his deliberate reason." These are the convictions and prejudices that have settled into our ways of thinking, even though we have not consented to their occupation of our minds. In opposition to this suggestion, we like to see ourselves as wholly independent thinkers, so if Russell's suggestion doesn't fit your view of yourself, consider the following line of reasoning.

On Having a Colonized Mind

Persons who are born into and raised in certain communities tend very strongly to have beliefs and attitudes that conform closely to the beliefs and attitudes of others in their communities. That agreement extends beyond opinions on topics where they might have *independently* arrived at the same views, as they might have independently discovered that snow is cold. Groups of people who regularly interact with one another share a great many opinions about religion, morality, and politics. There is nothing remarkable about this, and there is probably more than one explanation: group cohesion is an important evolutionary survival tool, people who regularly interact are more likely to influence one another's thinking, and we tend to associate more with people whose view of the world we already share. It is easy to find explanations for the significant amount of agreement we have with our peers but we must be careful not to think that our agreement with others *justifies* our opinions—to think so is to be guilty of a **fallacy**, a flawed form of reasoning.

fallacy: Broadly, it refers to argument in which the conclusion does not follow from the premises. More commonly the term designates a special class of relatively common arguments that make illegitimate appeals to emotion or involve logical slight-of-hand.

Logic Box

Argument from Popularity

The fact that a belief is very widely held can sometimes be a reason for thinking the belief is likely to be true, but *only* when the people who share the belief acquired it independently—not from each other, and not from the same source. In all other cases, it is a fallacy to use the fact that a belief is widely held as a reason for thinking that the belief is true. To prevent yourself from falling prey to the fallacy of the **argument from popularity**, remember that if a belief is widely held by numerous people who acquired it independently, then it cannot be difficult to check their opinion yourself. In that case, it is unnecessary to depend on the fact that others hold the belief as your sole reason for accepting it.

Example: "There is good reason to believe that there is a God; after all, people of all cultures have, at all times, believed in a God."

argument from popularity: A fallacy that concludes that a belief is true, or probably true, from the premise that the belief is widespread. The inference is fallacious since it is valid only in the special case when all those who share a belief have acquired it independently that the popularity of the belief is any evidence in its favour.

The idea that we unreflectively inherit some opinions—including important ones, about religion, politics, or morality—from our communities implies that if we were born and raised in very different families and communities, we would probably have very different beliefs and attitudes than we now have. Finally, it is obvious that we do not *choose* the families or communities into which we are born and raised. We do not *consent* to being bought up in one way of thinking or another. Thus it seems that some of the ways we think and some of the ways we feel have, in Russell's phrase, "grown up in our minds without our consent."

This conclusion, if we grant it to Russell, requires us to confront a series of questions that are not easy to answer. To begin, we need to know what, if anything, is *wrong* with having beliefs that have been shaped by others. After all, we depend on others a great deal—for schools, food, or transportation—and there seems no obvious reason we should not also depend on them for at least some of our opinions. Perhaps many of the ideas we inherited, however unthinkingly, are perfectly sound, and are much better than the ones we might have come up with on our own. Russell need not disagree with this point. His proposal is not that we toss our intellectual inheritance overboard, but that we examine and test each part of it. The convictions that survive critical examination will, after scrutiny, no longer be mere assumptions or prejudices. They will have acquired "the consent of our deliberate reason."

Russell believes that philosophy is worth doing because it can free us "from the tyranny of custom." Customs exercise a kind of tyranny over us not because there is anything wrong with them, but because they operate unnoticed and therefore go unexamined. They do their work in shaping our thinking, and our lives, without ever being recognized or acknowledged. They thus evade the kind of critical scrutiny that might determine their worth. On this view, the business of philosophy is to locate the factors that surreptitiously shape our thinking, to bring them out into the open, and to put them to the test. The result is not that we will have escaped from customs, but that the customs under which we live will operate only with our consent.

It is not impossible for people to be brought up, as a matter of local custom, to challenge authority, to scrutinize their own beliefs, and to seek justifications for their own opinions. That would be the custom of doing philosophy.

CONCLUSION

Philosophers were traditionally characterized as conducting investigations into the nature of things, but few philosophers today would accept that as a description of philosophy. The actual practice of philosophy, however, often proceeds very much *as if that is what they are doing*. In the practice of philosophy we are always seeking greater clarity about ideas and their expressions, we try to subject all ideas to careful scrutiny, and we try to let go of those ideas that do not withstand scrutiny. Plato saw these processes as attempts to free ourselves of our attachment to appearances and to get a glimpse of the realities beyond appearances; Russell saw the same practices as attempts to free ourselves from the assumptions and prejudices that have colonized our minds without our consent.

Perhaps the best way to get clear about the nature of philosophy is to try some. The chapters that follow will provide many opportunities to do just that. As you puzzle your way through the philosophical issues raised, ask yourself what assumptions or presuppositions you have uncovered in your own thinking, and always explore whether those assumptions, once they have been brought to the surface, can survive further examination.

Key Terms and Figures

explanation p. 3

justification p. 3

illicit appeal to authority p. 8

Plato p. 10

Socrates p. 10

metaphysics p. 13

epistemology p. 14

Bertrand Russell p. 15

fallacy p. 17

argument from popularity p. 18

Additional readings on the nature and value of philosophy

Joll, N. Contemporary Metaphilosophy. In J. Fieser & B. Dowden (Eds.), *Internet Encyclopedia of Philosophy*. Retrieved June 29, 2014, from http://www.iep.utm.edu.

Nagel, T. *What Does it All Mean?* New York: Oxford University Press, 1987.

Plato. *Apology*. (Benjamin Jowett, Trans., 1892). Retrieved June 29, 2014, from http://www.gutenberg.org/cache/epub/1656/pg1656.txt.

Russell, B. (1912). Chapter 15. *The Problems of Philosophy*. Retrieved June 29, 2014, from http://www.gutenberg.org/cache/epub/5827/pg5827.txt.

Chapter 2
Constancy and Flux

Learning Objectives

- Outline the central features of ancient materialism, and use the ideas of Heraclitus to illustrate each of those features.
- Explain why some ancient thinkers believed that where there appears to be change, there is really only destruction and creation.
- Outline the central features of ancient idealism, and use the ideas of Parmenides to illustrate each of those features.
- Summarize ancient atomism and explain how it can be seen as an attempt to reconcile change and sameness.
- Summarize Plato's doctrine of the Forms, and explain how it can be seen as an attempt to reconcile change and sameness.
- Explain the role of substances and qualities in Aristotle's theory of change.

We begin our introduction to metaphysics with some ideas that are historically remote, but that contain the roots of the discipline as it was practiced outside Asia—so-called "Western philosophy."[1] Several diverse schools of philosophy emerged, starting about 600 years before the Christian era: first in Ionia (along the western shores of present-day Turkey), and shortly thereafter on the island of Sicily, along the southern shores of what is now Italy, and in parts of the Greek peninsula. Collectively, these thinkers are known as the **Presocratic philosophers**, to mark the idea that the teachings of Socrates (who died in 399 BC) and his followers were an important watershed for Western thought. In this chapter, we will set up a contrast between two Presocratic schools of thought—the materialist philosophy that appeared in Ionia, and the idealist school that emerged in Sicily—and will encounter attempts to achieve reconciliation between these two schools. Nonetheless, our aim in this chapter is not primarily historical. We will use these ancient thinkers to introduce problems about the nature of change and identity, and to illustrate how our way of responding to these problems can lead to divergent theories about the nature of reality.

Presocratic philosophers: Ancient philosophers, especially in the geographical locale of present day Greece, Italy, and Turkey, who lived and worked prior to Socrates (who died in 399 BC).

[1] The label *Western* should be used with caution. There was no such thing as the West at this time, and no such place as Europe. Furthermore, many of the most important ideas developed by these thinkers originated in Babylon, India, and North Africa.

Philosophical theories can seem strange and aloof from our concerns—even more so when they are historically distant from us. To understand them, we first need to achieve a perspective from which their strangeness is minimized. One way is to remind ourselves that philosophical theories and doctrines arise as attempted solutions to problems. Understanding a theory or doctrine thus requires understanding the problem—or problems—that the theory is intended to solve. Furthermore, to evaluate such theories, we should consider their success or failure in addressing the problems that give rise to them. When we have a better perspective on these problems, then the theories intended to solve them will seem less aloof from real concerns. In this chapter, we will focus on one very deep divide between the materialist and idealist schools: their disagreement about the nature of change and identity. To understand why these schools had reason to disagree, and why their disagreement took the form it did, we will need to *feel for ourselves* the intellectual dissatisfaction that their divergent theories were meant to address.

THESEUS'S SHIP: AN ANCIENT METAPHYSICAL PUZZLE[2]

One problem that our earliest philosophical ancestors were wrestling with, and to which they had several divergent reactions, was to understand how two apparently opposite aspects of the world manage to co-exist. The world and the things in it appear to persist or last for a time, and yet during that time they regularly undergo change. On the one hand, then, we find a significant amount of constancy or stability among the things of this world: Things come into being, and then persist or endure for a time before they die or are destroyed. The chair on which I now sit will last (hopefully) for at least as long as I continue to sit at my desk; if it does, then I will stand up from the same chair I sat down on an hour ago. I drive the same car I was driving three years ago; it has endured at least that long. I look out my window and see the same maple tree I saw last year and the year before. In each of these cases, there is a connection between something *lasting*—its persisting or enduring—and its being *the same over time*. The connection between these ideas is simple: If something *persists* through time, then the *same* thing must be around at different times. We might even take this as a definition of **persistence**. When we say that an object persists for a time, we mean that it exists at one time, and it—the same object—still exists at a later time, and it exists at every time between those two times.

persistence: Something is said to *persist* from one time to a later time when the *same* thing exists at both times and at every time in between.

On the other hand, it seems obvious that the world and the things in it are constantly undergoing change. The chair I am sitting on has recently been scratched, and it has changed position many times over the past hour. My car has acquired a few minor dents and four new tires. The maple tree outside my window has grown, and it has shed and replenished its leaves many times over the years. Somehow, we hold both thoughts together: the chair, the car, or the tree is the same, and yet each has changed. Perhaps you don't recognize any "tension" between these thoughts, but our philosophical ancestors

[2] The original source for this puzzle is Plutarch, a Greek philosopher and essayist who lived approximately 46–119 AD.

thought they did. To help you to feel that tension more sharply, we'll look at an ancient puzzle about change.

Consider the following events, which occurred over a long series of days:

Theseus's ship: An ancient metaphysical puzzle used to illustrate the challenges of reconciling our ideas about change and identity.

On Day 1: **Theseus's ship** left port, carrying a cargo of lumber, which he was hired to transport to its owner at a remote destination.

On Day 2: After one day at sea, Theseus replaced a very small part of the ship (make it as small as you like—for example, toothpick size, or a single cell or molecule) with wood from the cargo hold.

On Day 3: One day later, he replaced another small part of the ship (make it the *same size* as the previous piece) with wood from the cargo hold.

On Day 4 through Day (N): Each day at sea, Theseus repeated the slow process by replacing one very small portion of the ship with one very small portion of the cargo lumber.

On Day (N): Theseus arrived at his destination, by which time he had replaced all the wood that constituted his original ship with wood from the now-empty cargo hold.

Now, is the ship in which Theseus arrived at his destination on Day (N) the *same* ship he departed in on Day 1? This deceptively simple yes or no question becomes a metaphysical puzzle when we see that there are very strong reasons for answering it both ways. In examining those reasons, we will be compelled to reflect more deeply on the nature of sameness and its relationship to change. Let us first consider rationales that might be given for either answer to our question.

The Affirmative Answer

Yes. Theseus arrived at his destination on the *same* ship on which he originally departed. The rationale for the affirmative answer takes the form of a simple but extended line of reasoning, which we will break into distinct steps:

1. Some changes in an object are so slight and insignificant that they do not prevent it from being the same object after undergoing such a change. Suppose we make the change from Day 1 to Day 2 that small and insignificant.
2. Having undergone only an insignificant change, the ship at Day 1 and the ship at Day 2 are the same ship.
3. The change made to the ship from Day 2 to Day 3 is the same size as the change from Day 1 to Day 2, and so the ship at Day 2 and the ship at Day 3 are also the same ship. Applying this reasoning consistently, we must say that the ships on *any two consecutive days* are the same ship, for all the days of the voyage.

transitivity of identity: The idea that if A = B, and B = C, then A = C. In other words, if one thing is identical to a second thing, and the second thing is identical to a third thing, then the first thing must also be identical to the third thing.

4. Identity is **transitive**; that is, if a = b and b = c, then a = c. For example, if the ship on Day 1 = the ship on Day 2, and the ship on Day 2 = the ship on Day 3, then the ship on Day 1 = the ship on Day 3.
5. Thus, the ship on Day 3 = the ship on Day 1. By making continued applications of the idea that identity is transitive, we see that the ship on Day 4 = the ship on Day 1, the ship on Day 5 = the ship on Day 1, and so on, until we reach the conclusion that the ship on Day (N) = the ship on Day 1.

Because the change made each day of the voyage was so insignificant that it does not result in a different ship, the ships *on any two consecutive days* will be the same ship. This point, combined with the transitivity of identity, requires us to conclude that the ship on which Theseus arrived at his destination and the ship on which he originally departed are the same ship, despite the fact that they are made of none of the same material. Before we allow ourselves to be persuaded by this reasoning, however, we should consider the rationale for the opposite conclusion.

argument: An argument is a series of statements, some of which (*premises*) offer support for others (*conclusions*). Arguments are used to persuade their audience of a conclusion by using the premises to *justify* the conclusion.

premise: Statement in an argument that offers support for conclusions.

conclusion: Statement in an argument that is inferred from, or supported by, premises.

deductive argument: An argument in which the premises purport to give conclusive reasons for accepting the conclusion. In a deductive argument, the premises are said to *entail* the conclusion, or the conclusion is said to *follow from* the premises.

inductive argument: In an inductive argument, premises are offered to make a conclusion probable; that is, they are meant to make the conclusion more likely to be true than to be false, but they do not purport to give conclusive support for the conclusion. Inductive arguments are referred to as *strong* or *weak* depending on *how probable* the premises make the conclusion.

The Negative Answer

No. The ship on which Theseus arrived at his destination is *not the same* ship on which he departed. Two brief rationales for the negative answer follow:

First, we might reflect that the ship on which he arrived at his destination is made of *none of the same matter* as the ship on which he departed. But a ship is only a material object; it is nothing beyond the matter it is made of. So by replacing all the matter from which it is made, we have replaced the original ship with another one.

Second, we should notice that the ship changes each day, even if only a little. But nothing can *change* (even a little) without *becoming different* in some way, and if something *becomes different* in any way, then it doesn't remain the same. So, strictly speaking, Theseus didn't arrive at his destination on the same ship on which he originally left home; indeed, it ceased to be the same ship after he made the first tiny change on Day 2 of his voyage.

We have now seen rationales or *arguments* for both the affirmative and negative answers to the question of whether Theseus arrived at his destination on the same ship on which he departed. I have expressed the argument for the affirmative answer in a form that clearly distinguishes its *premises* and *conclusions*, which we will discuss next. Although we will not do so here, it might be good exercise to rewrite both arguments for the negative answer in a form that clearly distinguishes their premises and conclusions.

The Crux of the Matter: Identity as Continuity

How do we decide which of the two responses—the affirmative or the negative—to the puzzle posed by Theseus's ship is better? Our first step is to locate the essential point of

Logic Box

The Components of Arguments

An **argument** is a series of statements in which some of the statements (**premises**) offer support for others (**conclusions**) in the series. Arguments are intended to persuade or convince their audience of a conclusion by using the premises to *justify* the conclusion. That is, the premises of an argument are presented as reasons why the audience ought to believe the conclusion of the argument. In a **deductive argument**, the premises purport to give *conclusive* reasons for the conclusion. In an **inductive argument**, the premises give reasons intended to make the conclusion probable (i.e., more likely to be true than false), but they do not purport to be conclusive.

disagreement between the two sides. In this case, we can find the crux of the disagreement by asking how someone might criticize the line of reasoning used to support the affirmative conclusion. That reasoning employed only two ideas; it simply re-applied these same two ideas over and over again. First, it used a general principle about change—in premise (1)—which said some changes in an object are so insignificant that they don't prevent it from remaining the same object. Second, it used the idea—in premise (4)—that identity is transitive. We can't very easily give up the idea that identity is transitive, since this idea is needed for even the most basic arithmetic. For example, if I know that $2 + 3 = 4 + 1$, and also that $4 + 1 = 5$, then I can rely on the transitivity of identity to determine that $2 + 3 = 5$. On the other hand, if the general principle about change stated in premise (1) is accepted, then steps (2) and (3) should also be accepted, since they are merely applications of that same principle.

So it seems that the best prospect for rejecting the line of reasoning for the affirmative answer is to challenge the general principle in (1). That is, in order to conclude that Theseus did not arrive on the same ship that he departed on, it is necessary to say that *any change*, however small, results in a *different* object. This can seem a fairly natural way to challenge the rationale here. After all, the challenge just says that nothing can change in *any way* and still be the *same* thing. If we accept that, then we must suppose that any change a thing undergoes, however small or insignificant, prevents it from being the same thing it was before the change.

We can now identify a single thesis about change and sameness that divides those who give one answer to our metaphysical puzzle from those who give the other. It is the very thesis employed in step (1) of the affirmative answer, but that is denied by the second rationale for the negative answer:

> **(C-T) Compatibility-Thesis:** Some changes in an object are so insignificant that they do not prevent it from being the same object after it undergoes such changes.

This thesis states something you probably already take for granted; it is perhaps only a common sense view about change. After all, you probably already think that if you plucked one hair from your head, the person before and after plucking the hair is one and the same person—they are both you, despite a small and insignificant change in the number of hairs on your head. According to this thesis, change and sameness are compatible.

We can summarize the important features of Theseus's story, and clarify the role of (C-T) in it, in the following way. The material composing the ship on any day we choose *overlaps* significantly with the material composing the ship on adjacent days—it is almost entirely the same material. But the material composing ships that are separated by a long stretch of days have less overlap, and there will be no overlap at all in the material composing ships that are separated by a sufficiently long stretch of time. Nonetheless, any two ships in the story that are separated by a very long stretch of days will still be connected by a long series of intermediate ships, each of which overlaps significantly with the ships on neighbouring days. There is, then, a smooth, continuous series of virtually indistinguishable ships, like links in an unbroken chain, connecting the ship on which Theseus originally left port and the ship at the conclusion of his voyage. To describe this sort of relation, wherever we find it, let us say that the ships at two remote times are *continuous* with one another—the **continuity** between them is provided by the nearly complete overlap in the material composing the ship(s) on adjacent days. Whether we agree that this is enough to make them the *same* ship, we can agree that there is substantial continuity (in this case, continuity in the material) between the two ships.

continuity: Two things are said to be *continuous* with one another when they are spatio-temporally contiguous (adjacent), and there is only insignificant change from one to the other. *Continuity* between two things requires substantial overlap in the material or characteristics of the things at different times.

We can now express the affirmative answer in this way: The ship in which Theseus arrived at his destination is *continuous* with the ship on which he began his voyage, and such continuity is enough to ensure that they are the same ship. In general, what makes a thing at one time the *same* as something at an earlier time, despite changes it may have undergone, is the continuity between them. So an object persists from one time to a later time only if there is continuity between its later and earlier stages.

We can better appreciate the idea of continuity if we consider a simple variation on the story. Suppose that on Day 1, as the cargo lumber was about to be loaded onto the ship, Theseus's ship caught fire and burned to ashes. Theseus and his crew, in order to escape liability for the disaster, worked hastily to build, from the cargo lumber still waiting on the docks, a perfect duplicate of the now destroyed ship, and then set sail on Day 2. Over a long stretch of days, they arrived at their destination on Day (N) with no lumber in the cargo hold (exactly as in the previous story). You can see that our two stories have identical endings. Indeed, if you compared the ships at the endings of the two stories, you would find that they were made of exactly the same material—even the same atoms, placed in exactly the same arrangement. But there is a very important difference between them. In the first story, there is continuity between the final ship on Day (N) and the original ship on Day 1; in the second, there is no continuity between the ship on Day (N) and the ship on Day 1. In the second story, the final ship was not a gradual development from the original ship, but a replacement for it. So if we think of identity over time as based on continuity, then one ship remained identical with the original ship and the other did not.

Opposing (C-T) is a second thesis, and one that can seem just as obvious:

> **(I-T) Incompatibility-Thesis:** Change and sameness are opposites, so nothing can both change and remain the same.

In other words, if objects change in any way, however insignificantly, then they become different in some way, and if they become different in any way, then, *strictly speaking*, they are not the same. The point can also be put the other way around: If something truly remains the same, then it doesn't change *in any way*. So defenders of (I-T) can agree that there is significant continuity between the ship on which Theseus began his voyage and the ship on which he ended it, but they do not agree that continuity is enough for sameness.

Notice that anyone who would argue on this basis that the ship on Day 2 cannot be the same as the one on Day 1 is not challenging the *reasoning* that led us from (C-T) to the affirmative conclusion. That reasoning might well be **valid**, but they are challenging the *premise* with which we began our reasoning. That premise expresses a view about the nature of identity that is, they insist, mistaken. And if our starting point is a false premise, then there is no guarantee that our conclusion will be true, even when our reasoning is impeccable.

valid argument: An argument is *valid* when its premises and conclusion are related in such a way that it is impossible for the conclusion to be false if all its premises are true. The premises of a valid argument do not have to be true, but if they are true, they guarantee the truth of the conclusion.

Both positions can seem initially plausible, but if we use (C-T) in our thinking, we are led to the conclusion that Theseus arrived at his destination on the same ship on which he

Logic Box

Valid vs. Sound

We use "true" or "false" to evaluate *statements* (premises or conclusions) in an argument, but we use "valid" or "invalid" to evaluate the *reasoning* that takes us from the premises to the conclusions. An argument is valid when *it is impossible for the conclusion of the argument to be false if all of its premises are true.* The premises of a valid argument need not be true; nor need its conclusion be true. But in a valid argument, *if* its premises were true, its conclusion would also have to be true. The validity of our reasoning from premises to conclusions is not determined by the truth or falsity of the premises.

When (i) an argument is logically valid and (ii) all of its premises are also true, then the conclusion is guaranteed to be true. It is then called a **sound argument**. Not all valid arguments are sound, since an argument can be valid and still have one or more false premises. So in deciding whether an argument is valid, you should not concern yourself with whether the premises are actually true; you only need to ask: *If* the premises *were* true, then *would* the conclusion *have to be* true? Alternatively: Would the truth of the premises *guarantee* the truth of the conclusion? If the answer is yes, then the argument is valid; otherwise it is invalid.

sound argument: A sound argument is one that is logically *valid* and that also has all true premises. We are assured that the conclusion of a sound argument is true.

left home; on the other hand, if we use (I-T) when we think about the puzzle, then we will be led to the conclusion that he was on a different ship each day of his voyage. We seem to be in a mental bind: Both propositions are plausible, and yet they lead us to opposite conclusions when we use them to reason about the world. If you can now feel the bind, you are in a good position to appreciate the theories that our philosophical ancestors were led to devise as they sought a better understanding of the nature of change and identity.

Many ancient philosophers, when grappling with this and similar puzzles, felt compelled to adopt the second thesis. They reasoned, as we have done, that since sameness and change are opposites, they are mutually exclusive, and nothing can both change (become different) and still be the same thing. Clearly, the world *appears* to somehow reconcile both change and sameness—that's why (C-T) seems so natural to us. But if change and sameness really are mutually exclusive, then we cannot trust the appearances. If persistence or sameness cannot be reconciled with change, then one of the two pervasive features of our world—either the apparent persistence of objects, or the manifest variety of changes that objects undergo—must be only appearance and not reality. A question our philosophical ancestors faced was then: Which is real—constancy or flux?

The two schools of thought we will examine—early materialism and early idealism—both accepted the idea that change and sameness are opposites and so are mutually exclusive. In other words, they both accepted (I-T), which says that if something undergoes any change at all, it ceases to be the same object. Later in this chapter, we will encounter thinkers who tried, in different ways, to accommodate both change and sameness.

EARLY MATERIALISTS: THALES AND HERACLITUS

materialism: The metaphysical doctrine that everything that exists is composed of matter; there are no non-material substances or entities.

The early materialist philosophers defended the view that everything that exists consists of matter—**materialism**. However, their understanding of the nature of matter was quite different than ours. Matter, it was widely thought, consisted of four elements: earth, air, water, and fire. If this seems strange, it might help to think of these four elements as comparable to the four most common states of matter—solid, gas, liquid, and plasma.

Thales (625–545 BC) is widely considered the first *philosopher* and also the first *scientist* (no distinction between the two emerged for a very long time). He took water to be the principle or most fundamental of the elements, in part because the characteristics of water can be used to explain so much else. Water can freeze (solidify) to become earth (solid), and it can "thin out" or evaporate to become air (gas). Air can also condense to become water again, and earth (solid) can melt to return to the form of water (liquid). He also thought that if air became still more rarified, then it would become fire.

Thales: Widely considered the first philosopher and scientist, Thales was a materialist who held that water was the first principle and the most fundamental of the elements.

Although we are uncertain about how to understand Thales's idea that water is the principle or the most fundamental element, there are two obvious interpretations. Perhaps Thales meant that earth, air, and fire are all just *different forms of water* as it solidifies or becomes more rarefied. So air is really just water in its gaseous state, and earth is water in its solid state. Alternatively, he might have meant that water was the first or *original element*, from which the other elements gradually evolved. On the first interpretation, my desk is (or is composed of) water, since everything is water; on the second interpretation, the solid matter of my desk has descended from water, but no longer is water.

Under either interpretation, Thales's view can seem bizarre, but his views include some original insights that explain why he is often considered the first philosopher and scientist. Thales's account of the world includes these ideas:

1. A wide variety of phenomena are *unified* by reducing everything to a single phenomenon.
2. The explanation of the variety of phenomena is a *natural* explanation; that is, it uses only the elements of nature itself, and does not appeal to anything mythological or supernatural (from outside the natural order).
3. The explanation of phenomena is something that can be grasped by the human intellect. This is connected with the preceding point: If explanations are not mythological, they do not invoke the caprice or whimsy of unruly and unpredictable gods.

Because he attempts to provide a natural explanation that can be grasped by the human intellect, and because he aims at such enormous generality, Thales's theory introduces a new way of thinking about the world. Others followed in his wake, and they modified or refined his approach in various directions; for example, some thought that air, or perhaps fire, but not water, was the fundamental element. Still others believed that no single element was more fundamental than others, and that different kinds of material things consisted of different mixtures of the four irreducible elements.

Heraclitus (535–475 BC), our chief representative of the materialist school of thought, considered fire to be the fundamental element. Fire can be condensed or contracted to become air, which can be further condensed to become water, which in turn can be contracted (solidified) to become earth. Fire drives the transformation of earth into water (it melts solids), and it transforms water into air (by causing water to evaporate, producing steam). Fire also directly transforms earth (solids, such as wood) into air (such as smoke). Thus Heraclitus believed that earth, air, and water were different

Heraclitus: An ancient materialist philosopher who considered fire to be the fundamental element and the driving principle behind all change.

transformations of fire, and he understood the processes of transformation to be caused by fire. Fire was the most basic element because it had the power to drive the many transformations found in nature. The fundamental constituent of all things is itself in constant motion: Fire never stands still; it is continually transforming itself and everything it touches. Heraclitus is thus the philosopher of change. His ideas have been preserved only in fragments[3]:

> (*Frag. 19*) Wisdom is one thing. It is to know the thought by which all things are steered through all things.
>
> (*Frag. 20*) This world, which is the same for all, no one of gods or men has made; but it was ever, is now, and ever shall be an ever-living Fire, with measures of it kindling, and measures going out.
>
> (*Frag. 22*) All things are an exchange for Fire, and Fire for all things, even as wares for gold and gold for wares.
>
> (*Frag. 25*) Fire lives the death of air, and air lives the death of fire; water lives the death of earth, earth that of water.
>
> (*Frag. 28*) It is the thunderbolt that steers the course of all things.
>
> (*Frag. 29*) The sun will not overstep his measures; if he does, the Erinyes, the handmaids of Justice, will find him out.
>
> (*Frag. 32*) The sun is new every day.
>
> (*Frag. 41*) You cannot step twice into the same rivers.
>
> (*Frag. 42*) For fresh waters are ever flowing in upon you.
>
> (*Frag. 81*) We step and do not step into the same rivers; we are and are not.

Consider one of the more obvious manifestations of fire, the sun. In Fragment 32, Heraclitus says that it is a new sun every day. We can be confident that he would have said the same of Theseus's ship: It was a new ship every day. The famous remark in Fragment 41 claims that we cannot step into the same river twice, and in Fragment 42 Heraclitus offers a justification for this claim: We cannot step into the same river twice because when we return to the river again, new waters are flowing between its banks, so it is no longer the *same* river. Heraclitus pushes this idea even further in Fragment 81: What prevents someone from stepping into the same river twice is both that the river is different when she returns to it again ("fresh waters are ever flowing"), but also that the person who returns to the river at a later time is a different person ("we are and are not"). Everything is in flux, and the flux runs through us, as well.

For Heraclitus, only the flux is real—everything is shot through with it. But there is still an order or pattern to this change, and this order is something that we can get to know. The suggestion in Fragment 28 is that things don't drift randomly or aimlessly from one form to another: They are *steered* by the thunderbolt (which, like the sun, is an overt manifestation of fire). Fragment 19 implies that things are steered through their many

[3] From Burnet, J. (1908). *Early Greek Philosophy* (pp. 148–150, 153). Adam and Charles Black: London.

transformations according to some order or pattern, but also that it is a pattern that we are capable of grasping. Elsewhere, Heraclitus calls the pattern ***logos*** (that is, *reason*, *law*, *rational account*), and he believes that all the ceaseless transformations happen in accord with this *logos*.

logos: A Greek term meaning *reason, law,* or *rational account*; it was used by Heraclitus to refer to an order or pattern that the human intellect is capable of discerning within the flux.

Furthermore, the key idea presented in Fragments 20, 22, and 29 seems to be that the transformations of the elements are understood on the model of *exchanges* (22), in which one thing is "exchanged" for another (air for water, water for earth, and so on). The amounts to be exchanged are *measured* (20), and so the exchange is kept balanced or just, since fire (the sun) does "not overstep his measures" (29). So, for Heraclitus, nothing is the same from one moment to the next, but there is nonetheless a kind of regularity—an order or pattern—that we can discern within the flux.

Creation and Destruction

We are accustomed to thinking that if a person pulls one hair from her head, then that person existed before she pulled out the hair, and she still exists after she pulls out the hair. Despite a change in the number of hairs on her head, something remains the same: She—the *same person*—exists both before and after the change. She persists through the changes she undergoes. Thus far, this appears to be only a common sense view of change.

We can put this point in more general terms: If an object undergoes a change, then *it* has one characteristic before the change, and *it* has a different characteristic after the change. But, if an object has different characteristics at two different times, then *it* (i.e., the *same* object) must be present at both times. On this view, an object does not undergo a change unless the *same* object exists before and after the change—unless *it* persists though the change. In a famous Sicilian novel, a character lamenting the passing of a way of life says, "If we want things to stay as they are, things will have to change."[4] We are now saying the opposite: As we usually conceive of change, if we want things to change, then things will have to stay the same—they will have to persist through the changes that they undergo. Although this might be a common sense view of change, it is does not appear to be how Heraclitus understands change, and it does not appear to be consistent with our Incompatibility-Thesis.

In Fragment 25, Heraclitus describes transformations from one element into another as the "death" of the first of those elements. We can see why he might have conceived of the transformation of earth into fire (consider the burning of a piece of wood) as the "death" of earth: The solid wood is consumed and destroyed by its transformation into flames. If the "death" of a piece of wood is its destruction, and what remains is no longer wood at all, then the original wood has ceased to exist. Heraclitus appears to view all the elemental transformations in this way: The transformation of an object of one element into another element is the destruction of the first element. What remains after a transformation is a new object or element. When he says that the sun is new each day, Heraclitus appears to mean that yesterday's sun has ceased to exist (we can imagine him thinking that it is extinguished when it sets into the sea at the end of the day), and a new sun is created (born) at the beginning of the next day. There is a daily succession of different suns, each closely resembling the others. If that is the right interpretation of

[4] From di Lampedusa, G. T. (1958). *The Leopard* (p. 21). (A. Colquhoun, Trans.) The Harvill Press: London.

his words, then the world of the Heraclitean flux would be a world in which things are continually destroyed and renewed; where similar things are created in their place—nothing persists or remains the same. On this view, if I pull one hair from my head, I—the same person—cannot remain behind to tell the tale. The resulting person is not the same person, but a new person—perhaps a very close duplicate of me, but someone who has one less hair than I have.

If this seems crazy, notice what might lead someone to believe that there is only destruction and creation: They would only need to accept the Incompatibility-Thesis, which says that no change, however small, can leave us with the same object. But, if that is true, then the flux that surrounds and runs through us is not merely "change"—at least as we ordinarily think of it—but is a continual process of destruction and creation. Persistent objects have been banished from this view of reality, and we have only *successions* of near duplicates—one object succeeding another.

flux: Change or transformation.

Thales and Heraclitus were just two of many early materialists. Despite the differences among them, most early materialists agreed that the elements of which everything is composed are continually transforming from one into another. This is the idea of the **flux**: Everything is constantly altering or changing. A few early materialists also believed that one element is more fundamental than the others, so that all the diversity in the world results from the many transformations of one principle form of matter. Finally, some thought that there exists a rational order (regularity or pattern) to the transformations of the elements (Heraclitus's *logos*) and, because of this, human beings are capable of understanding the order of things by relying on reason and experience. It is not difficult to discern in this cluster of ideas a vision of the world that is both very remote and surprisingly familiar.

EARLY IDEALISTS: PYTHAGORAS AND PARMENIDES

idealism: Used to refer to two unrelated schools of thought. In its modern use, the term refers very broadly to any school of thought that maintains that everything that exists is mental or spiritual. It also refers more narrowly to the ancient Presocratic school of thought, according to which reality is an "idealized" version of what we encounter every day.

Pythagoras: Reputed to have held the earliest and most radical version of the *idealist* world view. He thinks that numbers, and their relations to one another, are all that is real, and that all change is an illusion.

An opposing anti-materialist school of thought began by focusing on the *order*, or *pattern*, that matter follows in its transformations. Followers of this school paid close attention to what persists unchanged in an always changing world; namely, the ratios and proportions that matter appears to follow in its transformations from one state to another—what Heraclitus called their "measure." They linked these ratios to what was then known about mathematics, and attempted to understand the constancy or stability they saw in the world in terms of the constancy or stability that exists in arithmetic and geometry. Reflections that began this way quickly led the anti-materialists to early **idealism**, the view that reality is an idealized version of what we encounter in our everyday experience.

Pythagoras (580–496 BC) is reputed to have held the earliest and most radical version of the idealist world view. He believes that numbers, and their relations to one another, are all that is real. However, numbers and the mathematical relationships among them are permanent and unchanging, so all change is merely an illusion. Pythagoras makes what seems to us a wild intellectual leap. First, he identifies reality itself with the permanent unchanging order or pattern in the transformations of matter: The matter isn't what is real; nor are the transformations of it. Only the stable regularities that are revealed in the behaviour of matter are real. Then, making the leap, he identifies the permanent, unchanging reality with numbers and the relationships among them (the ratios or proportions in which things are measured and exchanged).

Two ideas might help to bring Pythagoras's curious view of reality into focus. First, ask yourself how you know that the relationships among numbers are unchanging. How do we know, for example, that 2+2 is always and everywhere equal to 4? Obviously, we haven't *checked to see* if this is so—we haven't added every pair of objects to every other pair of objects and *counted the result* to confirm that the sum is four objects. Even though we know that 2+2 is always 4, we don't appear to know this on the basis of experience. Numbers, and the relationships among them, are known by reason, not by sense experience. For Pythagoras, for whom reality consists only of numbers and the relationships among them, reality is not known by experience, but only by reason. This is part of why his view is considered a form of idealism.

Second, consider an illustration of the sort of thinking that leads to idealism. The three interior angles of a triangle add up to *exactly* 180 degrees, not more or less. But if we measure very carefully any triangle drawn on paper, we will find that it doesn't have exactly 180 degrees in its interior angles. Triangles drawn on paper and seen with our eyes are *not quite triangles*; they always fall short of being *real triangles*. The many triangular figures we can actually see, figures that are made of matter, have slightly more or less than 180 degrees in their interior angles and so are at best *approximations* of real triangles. Only an idealization of what we encounter in the imperfect world of matter—only a perfect version with exactly 180 degrees in its interior angles—is a real triangle. Generalizing this idea, Pythagoras suggests that whatever we encounter in our experience only *roughly approximates* reality—it is only a crude likeness of reality. Reality itself, the "real" reality, is a constant and unchanging ideal, knowable only by the use of reason. The flux, which our sense experience shows us, and the matter that participates in the flux are less than fully real.

Parmenides (540–470 BC), who was the most important representative of the idealist school of thought, took up the Pythagorean idea that change (the flux) is illusory, and that what is real is always constant and unchanging. Since real change is, he believes, impossible, the appearance of change around us must be only an illusion. Parmenides begins by contrasting two paths, or ways, along which we can conduct inquiries into the nature of things: the Path of Truth and the Path of Error (or appearance). Parmenides's account of the Way of Truth includes the following[5]:

Parmenides: An important representative of the ancient idealist school of thought, who took up and defended Pythagoras's theory that change is illusory. Parmenides held that we can only think about what exists, and that we cannot think about what does not exist—nothingness is unthinkable.

> Come now, I will tell thee—and do thou hearken to my saying and carry it away—the only two ways of search that can be thought of. The first, namely, that *It is*, and that it is impossible for it not to be, is the way of belief, for truth is its companion. The other, namely, that *It is not*, and that it must needs not be,—that, I tell thee, is a path that none can learn of at all. For thou canst not know what is not—that is impossible—nor utter it; for it is the same thing that can be thought and that can be.
>
> (6)
>
> It needs must be that what can be spoken and thought is; for it is possible for it to be, and it is not possible for what is nothing to be. This is what I bid thee ponder. . . .
>
> (7)
>
> For this shall never be proved, that the things that are not are; and do thou restrain thy thought from this way of inquiry.

[5] From Burnet, J. (1908). *Early Greek Philosophy* (pp. 197–200). Adam and Charles Black: London.

(8)

> One path only is left for us to speak of, namely, that *It is*. In this path are very many tokens that what is is uncreated and indestructible; for it is complete, immovable, and without end. Nor was it ever, nor will it be; for now *it is*, all at once, a continuous one . . . . I shall not let thee say nor think that it came from what is not; for it can neither be thought nor uttered that anything is not . . . . Wherefore, Justice doth not loose her fetters and let anything come into being or pass away, but holds it fast. Our judgment thereon depends on this: "*Is it* or *is it not?*" Surely it is adjudged, as it needs must be, that we are to set aside the one way as unthinkable and nameless (for it is no true way), and that the other path is real and true. How, then, can what *is* be going to be in the future? Or how could it come into being? If it came into being, it is not; nor is it if it is going to be in the future. Thus is becoming extinguished and passing away not to be heard of.
>
> . . . The thing that can be thought and that for the sake of which the thought exists is the same; for you cannot find thought without something that is, as to which it is uttered. And there is not, and never shall be, anything besides what is, since fate has chained it so as to be whole and immovable. Wherefore all these things are but names which mortals have given, believing them to be true—coming into being and passing away, being and not being, change of place and alteration of bright colour.

Central to Parmenides's thinking is the idea that, if we speak or think at all, then what we speak or think about must exist: "It needs must be that what can be spoken and thought *is*." However, a corollary of this idea is that we cannot think about what does not exist: Whatever is not is, he says, "unthinkable and nameless." We might put Parmenides's reasoning like this[6]:

1. If you are (allegedly) thinking about what does not exist, what you are thinking about is nothing; and
2. If you are thinking about nothing, then you are not thinking about anything; and
3. If you are not thinking about anything, then you are not thinking.
4. So, if you are (allegedly) thinking about what does not exist, then you are not thinking.

His idea seems to suggest that thinking or speaking is always thinking or speaking about something, and in the (alleged) case of thinking about (as he says) "what is not," there is nothing being thought. This strange idea is more easily grasped if we compare thoughts to desires. A desire is always a desire *for something*, so that when we say *we desire nothing*, that's just another way of saying *we don't have any desires*. Parmenides makes a similar claim about thoughts: To be thinking about nothing is not to be thinking at all. This idea becomes important to Parmenides and his followers because, as we will now see, if speech or thought about nothing is unintelligible, so is the idea that things can change: "becoming extinguished and passing away [are] not to be heard of."

If we cannot intelligibly speak or think about what is not, then Parmenides and his followers can easily argue that there is no change, no creation, and no destruction. Put bluntly: All such change requires that "what is not" come to be; but "what is not" cannot

[6] In this discussion I follow Plato's interpretation of Parmenides, as found in Plato's *Sophist* 237C-E.

exist, so nothing can become what it is not. Indeed, he can show that we cannot even *conceive* of such things. The needed reasoning can be represented as follows[7]:

1. Change requires that something become what it is not. (For example, it requires that a thing that is green become a thing that is not green.)
2. No thing can be what it is not. (A green thing cannot be a thing that is not green.)
3. Therefore, nothing can change. (A thing that is not green cannot become green.)

Things are even worse for change than this conclusion suggests. Parmenides's point is not merely that change is unreal; in addition, he holds that we cannot even successfully think (or talk) about change, for to think about change we must think about something becoming something it is not, and that requires us to think about something that does not exist. Not only is change an illusion, but so is the idea that we can even think there is any change. What appears to be change is an illusion; what appears to be thought or speech about change is unintelligible and incoherent.

Zeno and Motion

Zeno: A student of Parmenides who is most famous for his paradoxes of motion, arguments designed to show that real motion is impossible and the appearance of motion is always an illusion.

Zeno (489–430 BC), a student of Parmenides, laboured to support the ideas of his teacher by attempting to prove in detail that one of the most conspicuous sorts of change—motion or change of location—is impossible, and the appearance of motion is an illusion. He employed the mathematical wisdom of the Pythagoreans in the construction of his proofs. Here is a variation on one of Zeno's famous paradoxes, by which he attempts to prove the impossibility of motion:

1. On the line between any starting point and any destination point (or any point en route to the destination point), there are an infinite number of line segments (however short) that must be traversed.
2. An infinite number of line segments (however short) will be infinite in length when laid end to end.
3. Therefore, motion from any starting point to any destination point must traverse an infinite distance.
4. Nothing can traverse an infinite distance.
5. Therefore, motion from one place to another is impossible.

Like his teacher Parmenides, Zeno concludes that motion must be an illusion. What is wrong with Zeno's argument? It is not easy to say, but here is a first idea to explore. Perhaps the argument employs a false premise; namely, premise (2), which says that an infinite number of lines (however short) will, when laid end to end, form a line that is *infinite* in length. To see that this is not obvious, consider that:

a. A one-metre line (which is clearly not infinite in length) is composed of *2 half-metre lines* (placed end to end), and is the same length as
b. A one-metre line composed of *4 quarter-metre lines* (placed end to end), which is the same length as

[7] This argument is adapted from Melissus, a fifth century BC defender of Parmenides.

c. A one-metre line composed of *100 one-centimetre lines* (placed end to end), which is the same length as

d. A one-metre line composed of *1000 one-millimetre lines* (placed end to end), which is the same length as . . . and so on.

Here, we can see that the length of the one-metre line does not increase as the number of line segments composing it increases, since *as the number of line segments composing it gets larger, the length of each line segment shrinks in proportion to their total number*. However great the number (N) of line segments composing the one-metre line, their length will be 1/N, and the sum of their lengths will still be only one metre. In other words, increasing the number of line segments that compose a given line does not increase the length of the original line so long as the line segments decrease in length in proportion to their increase in number.

Whether this successfully answers the argument depends on what you think happens when N becomes infinite, and the length of each line becomes 1/infinity. It is not clear what, if anything, *that* is supposed to mean. You might also observe that this response does not answer the paradox as it is set up in premise (2) —that an infinite number of line segments, however short, will *add up* to an infinite length *when laid end to end*. In effect, the paradox begins with a very small line segment, and then *adds* another very small line segment of the same size to it, and then repeats this process of addition over and over, an infinite number of times. Our proposed criticism of the reasoning produces an infinite number of line segments *by dividing* a line over and over again. Are we really so sure that the process of *dividing* a line segment to get an infinite number of parts is equivalent to *adding* an infinite number of line segments? We will need to dig deeper if we want to dismiss the argument against motion.

RECONCILATIONS

The contrast between Heraclitus and Parmenides is stark. According to Heraclitus, nothing really persists or endures, and the appearance that some things do persist through change is merely an illusion. According to Parmenides, nothing really changes, and the appearance of ongoing flux and transformation is only an illusion.

Despite the vast gulf between these two opposing ways of seeing the world, it is important to note that the gulf becomes as wide as it does because of a common assumption—the assumption that emerged as the Incompatibility-Thesis (I-T) in our earlier discussion of Theseus's ship. One of Parmenides's followers, Melissus, expressed the central idea well when he said, "Now, if changed by so much as a single hair in ten thousand years, it will all perish in the whole of time."[8] This is a vivid illustration of the idea that if something changes in any way, however small, then the *same* thing cannot remain after the change. If what remains after a very small change is no longer the same thing that existed before the change, then the original thing no longer exists. Undergoing change is the same as being destroyed. Both Heraclitus and Parmenides accept the simple idea that *nothing can both undergo change and remain the same*. This assumption forces us to choose between change and sameness, and it doesn't allow us to have both. The next generation

[8] From Burnet, J. (1908). *Early Greek Philosophy* (p. 371). Adam and Charles Black: London.

of philosophers looked for a way to accommodate both sameness and change, and sought a reconciliation between the two.

Although we will not examine it in any detail, it is useful here to briefly consider the most famous reconciliation attempted from within the materialist camp; we will then examine in somewhat more detail one idealist effort at reconciliation—Plato's—that became what is probably the most influential theory in Western philosophy. Then we very briefly examine the reconciliation of sameness and change provided by Plato's most famous student, Aristotle, who attempted to recover at least part of the common sense view about change discussed earlier.

Democritus and Atomism

Democritus (460–370 BC) is perhaps the best known of the second wave of materialists, who were called atomists. He proposed a view of the world that was still conspicuously materialist (that is, only matter exists), but that allowed for both flux and constancy to co-exist. According to the atomists,

Democritus: The best known representative of the ancient materialist school known as *atomism.*

1. All matter consists of simple, indestructible parts called atoms (from the Greek *atomos*, meaning "can't be cut"), which themselves have no parts.
2. All change—the flux—consists of rearrangements or re-combinations of atoms. Atoms are continually reshuffled, entering into new arrangements with each other.

If all change consists of rearranging parts, and atoms have no parts, then the atoms cannot change; they persist and are indestructible. But change, when it is viewed as a reshuffling of parts, requires that the parts move, which requires space in which the parts can move. For this reason Democritus insisted that there must be regions of nothing—the **void** must also be real. He asserted, against Parmenides, that both beings (atoms) and non-being (the void) exist. In a way, his disagreement with Parmenides was also a partial concession, since Democritus agreed with Parmenides that change can only be real if non-being is also real. To accommodate change, he then assigned reality to non-being, in the form of "the void."

void: Regions of non-being or nothingness. The existence of the void was disputed by ancient philosophers, with the atomists arguing that it is needed for atoms to have a place in which to move, and their critics arguing that nothing—that is, what is not—cannot be.

For our purposes, **atomism** is best seen as one way of reconciling flux and constancy: The atoms themselves never change, but their combinations and arrangements do change. One sort of entity (the atom) is always the same and unchanging, while another sort of entity (composites or arrangements of atoms) is always changing. There is nothing that both changes and persists. Nonetheless, the unchanging atoms and the complexes made of atoms are still only matter, so the reconciliation between change and constancy is a reconciliation within a materialist perspective.

atomism: An ancient school of materialism, according to which all matter consists of indivisible and indestructible parts called atoms (from *atomos,* meaning "can't be cut"). Following the atomist view, all change consists in the rearrangement and recombination of atoms in the *void* (regions of non-being or nothingness). Because atoms have no parts, they cannot change.

Atomism did not earn a wide following for more than 2000 years. Many were deeply troubled by aspects of atomist theory. First, it appeared to conflict with official religious doctrines, by reducing persons to swarms of inert components. Second, atomism appeared to threaten the idea that we have free will by taking responsibility for actions out of our control. Our bodies, like any other physical objects, are only arrangements of lifeless parts that drift through the void and rearrange themselves in ways that are not of our choosing. Until satisfying answers could be found to questions like these, atomism remained a marginal metaphysical theory.

The most famous attempt to reconcile constancy and flux came from the great Athenian philosopher Plato (427–347 BC). We can best understand Plato's views as emerging in response to a new kind of question or demand, placed on philosophers by his teacher, Socrates (469–399 BC). Recall from Chapter 1 that philosophy was defined very early as the attempt to know the natures or essences of things. What is it that we want to know when we want to know the *essence* of something like love, beauty, or justice? Socrates insisted on greater clarity about this matter.

Socrates, Plato, and the Forms

To illustrate what Socrates wanted, consider the following extract from Plato's dialogue between Socrates and an arrogant young prophet named Euthyphro, whom Socrates encounters on the steps of the courthouse. Socrates is on his way to court to be officially charged with impiety (the charges that would eventually lead to his trial and execution), while Euthyphro is about to lay charges against his own father for negligence in the death of a labourer. Socrates claims not to understand why his own actions are impious, while Euthyphro's prosecution of his father is pious, so he seeks from the young prophet a better understanding of the nature of piety. Euthyphro gives several examples, including his own action of laying charges against his father, to illustrate what piety is. Socrates responds as follows:

> Socrates: … [J]ust at present I would rather hear from you a more precise answer, which you have not as yet given, my friend, to the question, What is 'piety'? When asked, you only replied, Doing as you do, charging your father with murder.
>
> Euthyphro: And what I said was true, Socrates.
>
> Socrates: No doubt, Euthyphro; but you would admit that there are many other pious acts?
>
> Euthyphro: There are.
>
> Socrates: Remember that I did not ask you to give me two or three examples of piety, but to explain the general idea which makes all pious things to be pious. Do you not recollect that there was one idea which made the impious impious, and the pious pious?
>
> Euthyphro: I remember.
>
> Socrates: Tell me what is the nature of this idea, and then I shall have a standard to which I may look, and by which I may measure actions, whether yours or those of any one else, and then I shall be able to say that such and such an action is pious, such another impious.[9]

essences: What all things of the same kind (e.g., all cats, all beautiful things) have in common that qualifies them to be things of that kind.

In this passage, Socrates asks for instruction on the nature or essence of piety. As he describes them, **essences** are found by determining what the many examples of things of the same kind have in common that makes them the same kind of thing. For example, Mars, Jupiter, and Saturn are things of the same kind; they are all planets. So they must share something that explains why they are all planets—they must all have the essence of planet (or planethood). Similarly, for all their differences, Fido and Rover are both

[9] From Plato. *Euthyphro* (6c–e). (Benjamin Jowett, Trans., 1889.) Retrieved June 29, 2014, from http://www.gutenberg.org/cache/epub/1642/pg1642.txt.

dogs, so they share (with all other dogs) the essence of dog (or dogginess). Essences have three characteristics. The essence will be some *one* thing that all the *many* things have in common (e.g., the essence of piety is some one thing that the many pious actions have in common, and the essence of love is some one thing that the many examples of love have in common). But things of the same kind might have many traits in common, not all of which have anything to do with the kind of thing they are. It might be true, for example, that all dogs live within 7000 kilometres of the centre of the earth, but this has nothing to do with their being dogs. The second component of Socrates's definition says that an essence is what, among the various characteristics that things of the same kind might have in common, *makes* the many different things to be things of the same kind (for example, the essence of piety is what makes the many pious actions pious). The final characteristic of essences tells us their use: An essence can be used *as a standard* by which to judge whether any particular thing is of that kind. For example, we can use the essence of piety, if we know it, to tell if some action really is pious.

At least for unclear or disputed cases, Socrates takes the view that knowledge of the nature or essence of things is needed *prior* to having knowledge of particular cases. That is, a dispute about whether an action is really pious can only be settled by first acquiring more complete knowledge of the essence of piety. The point is meant to be completely general. To know whether the animal before you is an oryx, you must first know what an oryx is, and to know that is to know the essence of oryx. Plato believes that the distinctive task of philosophy is to seek knowledge of essences, and that this knowledge will empower us to rationally settle even our most intractable of disagreements.

The Problem of the One and the Many

Plato began his investigations of change by accepting Heraclitus's doctrine that **sensible things**—things we know through sense experience—are always in flux, always undergoing change, coming into and going out of being. Plato also accepts Socrates's demand that more precise definitions must be known if we are to resolve disputes, and those definitions must tell the essences of things. Plato then provides a metaphysical theory about the nature of essences and about our knowledge of them, which closely resembles the idealism that started with Pythagoras and simultaneously provides a way of reconciling constancy and flux.

sensible things: A term used by Plato to refer to things with which we are acquainted through sense experience.

What do the many *particulars* (particular things to which the same name applies) have in common that justifies our applying the same name to them? What, for example, do beautiful things have in common that makes it appropriate to apply the word *beautiful* to all of them? Here, Socrates serves as the mouthpiece for Plato's answer:

> There is nothing new, he said, in what I am about to tell you; but only what I have been always and everywhere repeating in the previous discussion and on other occasions: . . . first of all assume that there is an absolute beauty and goodness and greatness, and the like; grant me this, . . . for I cannot help thinking, if there be anything beautiful other than absolute beauty . . . that can be beautiful only in as far as it partakes of absolute beauty—and I should say the same of everything. . . . I know nothing and can understand nothing of any other of those wise causes which are alleged; and if a person says to me that the bloom of colour, or form, or any such thing is a source of beauty, I leave all that, which is only confusing to me, and simply and singly, and

perhaps foolishly, hold and am assured in my own mind that nothing makes a thing beautiful but the presence and participation of beauty in whatever way or manner obtained; for as to the manner I am uncertain, but I stoutly contend that by beauty all beautiful things become beautiful. That appears to me to be the safest answer which I can give, either to myself or to another, and to this I cling, in the persuasion that this principle will never be overthrown, and that, to myself or to any one who asks the question, I may safely reply, That by beauty beautiful things become beautiful.[10]

Plato's answer is this: What all beautiful things have in common is *beauty*; all beautiful things partake of beauty, and that is what makes them beautiful. Similarly, all good things partake of *goodness*, and that is what makes them good. Plato develops this view by exploring two questions: What is *the nature* of this one thing that the many beautiful things share; that is, what kind of thing is beauty itself? And what is *the relationship* between the many examples of beautiful things and the one essence that all those beautiful things share?

To answer these questions, Plato draws on the Pythagorean reasoning we examined earlier in the chapter. There, as we saw, the many particular triangles that we perceive with our senses are not real triangles, but are only imperfect images of real triangles. Plato applies the idea not only to geometric figures, but to all things: Each of the many particular things we encounter in experience is but an imperfect image of a reality. Triangular things, when they are made of matter, fall short of being perfect triangles, but they qualify as triangular because they approximate ideal triangles; similarly, all beautiful things qualify as beautiful because they approximate ideal beauty. Plato refers to this ideal beauty as the **Form** of beauty. The many beautiful things thus have a common relationship to the Form of beauty; they all approximate or resemble that Form in varying degrees, which explains why they are rightly called "beautiful."

Form: Plato's term for the perfect or ideal version of each kind of thing. On Plato's view, actual instances of any kind of thing only approximate the ideal, or *Form*, for things of that kind. Forms are *intelligible things* known only to reason or intellect.

Well, but there is another thing, Simmias: Is there or is there not an absolute justice?

Assuredly there is.

And an absolute beauty and absolute good?

Of course.

But did you ever behold any of them with your eyes?

Certainly not.

Or did you ever reach them with any other bodily sense?—and I speak not of these alone, but of absolute greatness, and health, and strength, and of the essence or true nature of everything. Has the reality of them ever been perceived by you through the bodily organs? or rather, is not the nearest approach to the knowledge of their several natures made by him who so orders his intellectual vision as to have the most exact conception of the essence of each thing that he considers?

Certainly.

And he attains to the purest knowledge of them who goes to each of them with the mind alone, not introducing or intruding in the act of thought sight or any other sense together with reason, but with the very light of the mind in her own clearness searches

[10] From Plato. (n.d.). *Phaedo* (100b–e). (Benjamin Jowett, Trans.). Retrieved June 29, 2014, from http://www.gutenberg.org/cache/epub/1658/pg1658.txt.

> into the very truth of each; he who has got rid, as far as he who can, of eyes and ears and, so to speak, of the whole body, these being in his opinion distracting elements which when they infect the soul hinder her from acquiring truth and knowledge—who, if not he, is likely to attain the knowledge of true being?
>
> What you say has a wonderful truth in it, Socrates, replied Simmias.[11]

What undergoes change are the many particular things we call "beautiful," which might lose their beauty; what remains constant is the single ideal of beauty. Similarly, triangular things can lose their shape, or be destroyed, but the true triangle cannot. In effect, Plato regards the always changing things we encounter in experience (sensible objects) as mere approximations of an ideal, and those ideals (the Forms) constitute an unchanging reality knowable only by reason.

Since we are acquainted with the changing particulars only through our senses, they are sensible things, but the unchanging Forms—absolute beauty, or absolute justice, for example—are knowable only through the exercise of reason or intellect, so they are called **intelligible things**. Knowledge of reality must, then, come from reason, not from sense experience.

intelligible things: Term used by Plato to refer to things (such as *Forms*) that are knowable only through the exercise of reason or intellect; intelligible things cannot be known through sense experience.

Plato remains on the side of the early idealists, and offers a way of reconciling constancy and flux that remains friendly to idealist doctrines. He believes there are two realms of being, or two "worlds." One world, the ideal, is permanent and unchanging, consisting of ideal objects or Forms; the other is a world in perpetual flux, a realm of imperfect copies or approximations of ideal objects. Change is limited to the realm of imperfections. In contrast to the materialist (atomist) reconciliation of constancy and flux, which locates both constancy and stability *within* the material world, Plato sees the only stability or constancy as lying *outside* the material world—the unity, regularity, and stability comes from outside or above, not from within.

The Reality of the Forms

We might easily accept that there are many beautiful things, but Plato wants us to go further. In addition to the beautiful things we are acquainted with, absolute beauty also exists. Indeed, it is *more real* than the many beautiful things. A number of considerations led Plato to take seriously the idea that the perfect Form of each kind of thing exists in a separate realm. Here is the sort of reasoning for this view that impressed him[12]:

1. If one thing is more beautiful than another thing, then it more closely approximates perfect beauty.
2. One thing cannot more closely approximate perfect beauty unless there is such a thing as perfect beauty for it to more closely approximate.
3. So if one thing is more beautiful than another (however imperfect their beauty), then there must be such a thing as perfect beauty for it to more closely approximate.

---

[11] From Plato. (n.d.). *Phaedo* (65d–66b). Retrieved June 29, 2014, from http://www.gutenberg.org/cache/epub/1658/pg1658.txt.

[12] This argument is modelled after an argument in Plato's *Phaedo*, 74–76.

Logic Box

A Strategy for Evaluating Reasoning

The distinction between validity and soundness means that a deductive argument can be evaluated in two very different ways: (1) On the one hand, it can be evaluated by scrutinizing its premises: We are not required to accept the conclusion of a deductive argument if one or more of the premises used in its support is unacceptable. (2) On the other hand, a deductive argument can be evaluated by scrutinizing the reasoning that leads from the premises to the conclusion. Even if the premises are all acceptable, we are not required to accept the conclusion of a deductive argument if the reasoning it employs is not valid—that is, if the conclusion does not follow from the premises. These are tasks that should be undertaken separately in the attempt to evaluate any line of reasoning. Naturally, some bad arguments will be unsound for both reasons.

Just as you cannot be closer to the door than I am unless there really is a door, you cannot be closer to perfect beauty than I am unless there really is such a thing as perfect beauty. Although we won't attempt to do so here, it might be useful to try to say what (if anything) is wrong with this reasoning.

Plato attempted to retain the insights of both Heraclitus and Parmenides. He believed that Heraclitus was right about the material world—it is a world of flux and inconstancy, where nothing persists for long. But he also thought Parmenides was right—there is a world of ideal or perfect objects for which change is inconceivable. Plato combined these views by relegating flux and constancy to two different realms of being. His way of combining the opposing tendencies of change and constancy favoured the idealist view of reality, since the many changing particulars compose only a realm of *appearances*, and only the unchanging Forms are really real.

On Plato's view, we dwell among illusions. The flickering images, the sensible objects of our world are moving shadows cast by a constant and unchanging reality that the world of our experience can only approximate. When philosophy is conceived of as an investigation into the essences of things, philosophers must struggle against the distractions of the images around us and must seek to acquire knowledge of reality itself. Philosophers must turn away from the many fleeting but beautiful things and strive to know true beauty itself. (Good luck in the attempt.)

Aristotle: Substance and Quality

Aristotle: Ancient Greek philosopher, student of Plato, and teacher of Alexander the Great. One of the greatest philosophers of all time, Aristotle wrote on everything from logic and metaphysics to poetry and politics. His work in logic dominated philosophical thinking until the late nineteenth century, and his important contributions to the sciences, especially biology, physics, and astronomy, were not superseded until the scientific revolution in the seventeenth and eighteenth centuries.

Despite spending 20 years studying under Plato in Athens, **Aristotle** (384–322 BC) remained a highly original thinker who diverged from his teacher on many issues. For example, although Plato insists that the unchanging Forms exist separate from the changing material or sensible things, Aristotle argues that Forms are to be found *within* the sensible things. If you and I are both beautiful, it is not because we both approximate a detached but perfect beauty, but because the essential qualities of beauty are present within both of us. While Plato believes the order and regularity of nature is imposed on otherwise chaotic matter from without, Aristotle thinks regularities arise from within nature itself.

Like Plato, Aristotle believes a reconciliation of sameness and change is possible, and that the right metaphysical account of the reality will find a place for both. Consider the following brief discussion of change, taken from Aristotle's *Categories*[13]:

> The most distinctive mark of substance appears to be that, while remaining numerically one and the same, it is capable of admitting contrary qualities. From among things other than substance, we should find ourselves unable to bring forward any which possessed this mark. Thus, one and the same colour cannot be white and black. Nor can the same one action be good and bad: this law holds good with everything that is not substance. But one and the selfsame substance, while retaining its identity, is yet capable of admitting contrary qualities. The same individual person is at one time white, at another black, at one time warm, at another cold, at one time good, at another bad. This capacity is found nowhere else [than substances] . . . . It is by themselves changing that substances admit contrary qualities. It is thus that that which was hot becomes cold, for it has entered into a different state. Similarly that which was white becomes black, and that which was bad good, by a process of change; and in the same way in all other cases it is by changing that substances are capable of admitting contrary qualities . . . . Thus, in respect of the manner in which the thing takes place, it is the peculiar mark of substance that it should be capable of admitting contrary qualities; for it is by itself changing that it does so. . . .
>
> But it is by reason of the modification which takes place within the substance itself that a substance is said to be capable of admitting contrary qualities; for a substance admits within itself either disease or health, whiteness or blackness. It is in this sense that it is said to be capable of admitting contrary qualities.
>
> To sum up, it is a distinctive mark of substance, that, while remaining numerically one and the same, it is capable of admitting contrary qualities, the modification taking place through a change in the substance itself.

Aristotle's view about change can be understood by using a grammatical or linguistic distinction. When we use a sentence to make a statement, our sentence always has two parts: a *subject* and a *predicate*. A very general way of distinguishing the two is that the subject of a sentence is the part that tells us what the sentence is about (what the topic is), and the predicate is the part that says something about (comments on) that topic. For example, in the statement, "The woman is musical," the subject ("the woman") tells us what the topic of the statement is, and the predicate ("is musical") tells us something about her. Within our grammatical distinction between subjects and predicates, Aristotle sees the sign of a fundamental metaphysical distinction between *substances* and their *qualities*. A substance is a thing (like the woman) or it is stuff (like water) about which we can say a variety of different things. That is, we can make a variety of comments, or give a variety of descriptions, of one and the same substance. In discussing water, we can say, "It is liquid," "It is cold," and "It is dirty," each time referring to the same substance (with the subject "it"). But the many different predicates ("is liquid", "is cold," "is dirty") we use to describe the substance do not themselves refer to any substances—each refers to a different *quality* that the water is capable of having.

---

[13] From Aristotle. (n.d.). *The Categories* (Section 1, Part 5). (E. M. Edghill, Trans.). Retrieved June 29, 2014, from http://www.gutenberg.org/cache/epub/2412/pg2412.txt.

Aristotle's reality contains at least two radically different kinds of beings—substances and qualities. Both are found within the sensible world. Sameness and change can now be reconciled as follows: When a substance undergoes change, it remains one and the same substance both before and after the change. Because the same substance is capable of having different qualities, the same substance can have one quality at one time, and the opposite quality at a later time. That is exactly *what change is*. When water in a kettle goes from being cold to being hot, it is the same substance in the kettle, but it loses the quality of being cold and it acquires the new quality of being not-cold or of being hot.

In our example, there is a clear sense in which the quality itself does not undergo any change; that is, *the quality of being cold* does not become hot. In the same sense, the substance itself (*what it is* that is in the kettle) does not change to *a different substance*; that is, the water does not become non-water. However, in a second sense, the qualities of the water have changed—one quality has been replaced by another. The substance has also changed – it has exchanged one quality for another. Recall that Parmenides thought that such change would require 'the cold' to become 'the hot'. But, he reasoned, since it is impossible for cold to ever be hot, the change is impossible. Aristotle can now reply that Parmenides is right if he means to say that the *quality of coldness* can never become the quality of hot (that is, "not-cold"). But that does not prevent a *substance that has the quality* of being cold (at one time) from being the same substance that (later) has the quality of being hot. Sameness and change are reconciled by saying that whenever a substance undergoes change, it remains one and the same substance, but one quality is replaced with another.

A key ingredient of Aristotle's metaphysical picture of the world is evident in his account of change: Reality must contain both qualities and the underlying things or substrata that have those qualities. This duality in the world makes it possible to have both sameness and change.

CONCLUSION

Reflection on problems of the sort that arose in the puzzle of Theseus's ship led our philosophical ancestors to promote a variety of extremely general theories about the nature of reality. The metaphysical views we sampled here—early forms of materialism and idealism, atomism, Platonism, and Aristotelianism—were not the results of any special insight or intuition about the nature of reality. They were devised to address problems, and they rested on reasoning that can, with a little effort, be made explicit and evaluated. Although we encountered a number of arguments in this chapter, and I tried to make their motivations and components obvious, we did not attempt to evaluate them. In later chapters, after you have been exposed to even more arguments, we will devote ample time to their evaluation. As long as the theories of reality we encounter rest on argument, and not inspiration or insight, we can critically scrutinize them and, at the end of the day, accept or reject them on the merits of the arguments offered in their support.

Plato's ideas were important and influential, but they did not stand unchallenged in the ancient world. Even his own student Aristotle offered a powerful alternative. Nonetheless, Plato's views remained vital; indeed, some aspects of his thought continue to influence us today. A good way to see the extent of Plato's influence is to consider what later happens to the distinction between the two realms of being when it is applied to persons. Where do *we* stand in the worlds of flux and constancy? This question will be the topic of the next three chapters.

Key Terms and Figures

Presocratic philosophers p. 20
persistence p. 21
Theseus's ship p. 22
transitivity of identity p. 22
argument p. 23
premise p. 23
conclusion p. 23
deductive argument p. 23
inductive argument p. 23
continuity p. 25
valid argument p. 25
sound argument p. 26
materialism p. 26
Thales p. 27
Heraclitus p. 27
***logos* p. 29**
flux p. 30
idealism p. 30
Pythagoras p. 30
Parmenides p. 31
Zeno p. 33
Democritus p. 35
void p. 35
atomism p. 35
essences p. 36
sensible things p. 37
Form p. 38
intelligible things p. 39
Aristotle p. 40

Additional readings on sameness, change, and related aspects of ancient philosophy

Aristotle. (XXXX) *Physics* (Book I, Part 7). In R. McKeon (Ed.), *The Basic Works of Aristotle*. Random House: Modern Library.

Curd, P. & McKirahan, R. D. (1995). *A Presocratics Reader; Selected Fragments and Testimonia*. Cambridge: Hackett Publishing Company, Inc.

Mortensen, C. (2012). Change and Inconsistency. In E. N. Zalta (Ed.), *The Stanford Encyclopedia of Philosophy*, Winter 2012. Available at http://plato.stanford.edu/archives/win2012/entries/change.

Plato. (n.d.). *Euthyphro*. (B. Jowett, Trans.) Available at http://www.gutenberg.org/cache/epub/1642/pg1642.txt.

Plato. (n.d.). *Phaedo* (B. Jowett, Trans.). Available at http://www.gutenberg.org/cache/epub/1658/pg1658.txt.

Learning Objectives

- Explain the difference between numerical and qualitative identity, and use that distinction to define and clarify the problem of personal identity.
- Explain what it means to say that identity is relative to, or dependent on, the kinds of categories we are talking about.
- State Locke's contrast between "man" and "persons," and say how it matters for his proposed solution to the problem of personal identity.
- Summarize the memory criterion for personal identity, and outline Thomas Reid's most important objection to it.
- Explain the forensic conception of persons.
- Outline Reid's view about the self, and explain why he requires it to be indivisible.

In this chapter and the next we will continue to explore the ideas of identity and change, but will shift our focus to the ways in which our understanding of these ideas becomes entangled with our views about the nature of persons. The philosophical problem of *personal identity* concerns whether—and how—we can remain the same persons despite the many changes we undergo over the span of a human life. A central aim of this chapter is to clarify the problem of personal identity and to help you understand why it is of continuing interest to philosophers. This will require a deeper look into the ideas of change and identity. We will also introduce problems about the nature of persons that will surface again in later chapters.

We will discover how the problem of personal identity was first introduced by Plato, and move on to examine the ideas of John Locke and Thomas Reid, philosophers from the seventeenth and the eighteenth centuries, respectively, whose contrasting views set the stage for more recent work on personal identity. We will then be prepared to explore—in following chapters—views about personal identity that encourage us to reconsider traditional ways of thinking about the nature of persons and selves.

THE PROBLEM OF PERSONAL IDENTITY

The issues addressed in this chapter were first discussed as long ago as the fourth century BC, in writings by Plato. They begin with the recognition that we all undergo significant changes in our lifetime: a great many physical changes from child to adult, and continued changes into old age. Some of these changes are sudden and dramatic, as when a person loses a limb in an accident, for example, but most are so insignificant that they easily go unnoticed. But the shock of an old family photo, or an encounter with a friend you haven't seen for many years, shows how much difference the gradual accumulation of small changes can make over time. We also undergo significant psychological changes between infancy and adulthood. Experiences accumulate; our interests, desires, and beliefs change over time; and gradual psychological changes make our older and younger selves barely recognizable to one another. From one day to the next, you likely don't detect any change in yourself or your friends, but with a longer view it becomes appropriate to wonder, "In what sense is that small child in old family photos, with whom I have so little in common, *me*? What makes us the *same* person?"

Although philosophers have moved far from Plato's own views on these issues, he provides a good platform from which to see the problem and a range of possible answers. He enables us to see that the problem of personal identity is really a tangle of several problems about the nature of identity, persons, and survival.

Plato's Formulation: Procreation or Reincarnation

Plato famously distinguished between two "worlds," or realms of being. The first was an imperfect world of matter in endless flux, in which we live our lives in deep ignorance; the second was a world of stability, of unchanging eternal entities, each a perfect exemplar of its own kind. Plato believes that we naturally strive to approximate the eternal world more closely, and each step we take in the direction of better understanding is a step in the direction of the eternal. As the cosmos is divided into two kinds of being, so, too, are we: Plato conceives of persons as consisting of changing and perishable bodies and unchanging and immortal souls. So his division between two realms of being cuts directly through each of us.

Plato distinguishes *soul* and *body* with respect to their very different susceptibilities to change:

> . . . [T]hat the soul is in the very likeness of the divine, and immortal, and intellectual, and uniform, and indissoluble, and unchangeable; and that the body is in the very likeness of the human, and mortal, and unintellectual, and multiform, and dissoluble, and changeable.[1]

Diotima, a character in one of Plato's dialogues, expresses the opposing view. Socrates, Plato's mentor, asks Diotima to teach him about the nature of love, and in their discussion she explains the intensity of sexual desire by identifying it with the desire to procreate. The intense desire to procreate also needed an explanation, however, so Diotima suggests that, since we are mortal creatures, procreation is the closest we can come to achieving immortality. As mortal creatures we will perish, but through our descendants we can approximate the immortality that only the gods can truly have. Having descendants might seem a very poor approximation of immortality for those who seek the real thing, but, surprisingly, Diotima suggests that the relationships we have to

Diotima: A character in Plato's dialogue *Symposium*, she taught Socrates about the nature of love. Diotima discussed the problem of personal identity, where she took the position that persons do not survive change, that our future selves are related to us as our offspring, and that procreation is the closest we can come to immortality. Some scholars believe Diotima was an historical person.

[1] From Plato. (n.d.). *Phaedo*. (Benjamin Jowett, Trans.) Retrieved July 11, 2014, from http://www.gutenberg.org/cache/epub/1658/pg1658.txt.

our ancestors and descendants might be the very same relationships we have to earlier and later stages of ourselves.

> . . .[M]ortal nature is seeking as far as is possible to be everlasting and immortal: and this is only to be attained by generation, because generation always leaves behind a new existence in the place of the old. Nay even in the life of the same individual there is succession and not absolute unity: a man is called the same, and yet in the short interval which elapses between youth and age, and in which every animal is said to have life and identity, he is undergoing a perpetual process of loss and reparation—hair, flesh, bones, blood, and the whole body are always changing. Which is true not only of the body, but also of the soul, whose habits, tempers, opinions, desires, pleasures, pains, fears, never remain the same in any one of us, but are always coming and going; and equally true of knowledge, and what is still more surprising to us mortals, not only do the sciences in general spring up and decay, so that in respect of them we are never the same; but each of them individually experiences a like change. For what is implied in the word "recollection," but the departure of knowledge, which is ever being forgotten, and is renewed and preserved by recollection, and appears to be the same although in reality new, according to that law of succession by which all mortal things are preserved, not absolutely the same, but by substitution, the old worn-out mortality leaving another new and similar existence behind—unlike the divine, which is always the same and not another? And in this way, Socrates, the mortal body, or mortal anything, partakes of immortality; but the immortal in another way. Marvel not then at the love which all men have of their offspring; for that universal love and interest is for the sake of immortality.[2]

Diotima's description of the flux that runs through persons—both body and soul—sets the stage. Although, she says, *we call ourselves the same person* in old age as in youth, this might only be "succession and not absolute unity." That is, whom we *call* "the same person" might actually be a succession of closely related persons, and not one person who persists through a lifetime of changes.

Consider that your friend Mary is now 21 years old. Unless the Mary who is with you now existed more than 20 years ago, you cannot truthfully say that she is now 21. Obviously, if she came into existence only yesterday, then she is only one day old. If you think about it carefully, you might not find anything about Mary that has lasted 21 years. The cells composing her body regularly die and are replaced by new cells, at a rate that leaves her composed of all new matter roughly every seven years. Like Theseus's ship, Mary on one day may be virtually indistinguishable from Mary on the next day, but after seven years her body will be composed entirely of new matter. Furthermore, her thoughts, feelings, and desires undergo constant change, with the result that her psychological life when she is 21 might share nothing with the psychological life of her infant self. Such changes continue over time, and Mary at 80 years of age might have nothing in common with 21-year-old Mary. In what sense, then, are 80-year-old Mary, 21-year-old Mary, and infant Mary different stages of the *same person*?

---

[2] From Plato. (n.d.). *Symposium* 207d–208b. (Benjamin Jowett, Trans.) Retrieved July 11, 2014, from http://www.gutenberg.org/cache/epub/1600/pg1600.txt.

Both physically and psychologically there is normally significant overlap between persons from one day to the next—that is just what creates the appearance that we are "absolutely the same." But, like the philosophers we met in the previous chapter, Diotima does not believe that continuity is enough for identity, which is why we have only a "succession" of similar individuals, one after the other. We continue to exist, she says, "not absolutely the same, but by substitution." Diotima thus adopts the perspective of Heraclitus, for whom the sun was a new sun each day, and concludes that every day you become a new person, and your old self ceases to exist. Infant Mary, 21-year-old Mary, and 80-year-old Mary are three *distinct but related* individuals. The relationships among them are not significantly different from the relationships among Mary, her children, and her grandchildren.

Socrates, speaking for Plato, disagrees. Although he accepts that our bodies undergo constant change, and that we do not have the same bodies from one day to the next, he nonetheless insists that each of us remains the *same person* from infancy to old age. Indeed, because Plato also believes in reincarnation, he believes we remain the same person throughout many lives. Since persons persist through change, persons must be "indissoluble, and unchangeable." We must, Plato believes, be souls who have the same kind of permanence enjoyed by the gods (or the Forms).

Plato and Diotima agree that if *we* undergo change then *we* do not survive—not even for the duration of a single lifetime stretching from infancy to old age. Diotima claims that we change daily, and she accepts the consequence that even our younger and older selves, however closely related, are not the same person. Plato, however, believes that our younger and older selves are the same person, and therefore he draws the very different conclusion that we do not, despite appearances, change. Persons, then, must be unchanging (and, hence, immortal) souls. In effect, Diotima believes that each day we die and leave behind descendants to take our place; we are not the same person even over the span of a single life. Plato thinks we are unchanging souls who can acquire and discard many different bodies, both within a lifetime and over many lives. We are, in effect, reincarnated many times even within the span of a single mortal life.

The differences between Diotima's and Plato's views allow us to see three broad positions on the question whether we remain the same person for the span of a human life. First, following Plato, we might begin with the assumption that we remain the same person for a lifetime (or more), and conclude that persons are something distinct from the many changing things. Persons themselves must be incapable of change. On this view, sameness or identity is taken to be incompatible with change; persons are entities aloof from the physical and psychological flux. Second, we might follow Diotima and say that persons themselves do undergo change. We are caught up in the flux and do not persist from one day to the next. There may be continuity between our earlier and later selves, but that is not enough to make them the same person. On this second view, sameness is again incompatible with change, so each person is really a succession of brief ephemeral beings. Third, there is a possible middle ground between the two extremes. If change and sameness are somehow compatible, then if the right relationships exist between our younger and older selves, they might be the same person despite the changes we undergo. Persons will then be part of the world of change, rather than apart from it.

The disagreement between Plato and Diotima illustrates the complex interactions between three different philosophical concerns that will occupy us here and in the next two chapters: What is identity, and how, if at all, is it related to continuity? What sorts of things are persons? What are our prospects for immortality? Exploring any of these questions will inevitably entangle us in the others.

Sharpening the Problem

problem of personal identity: The philosophical problem of explaining what makes a person *numerically the same* person through the many physical and psychological changes undergone in a lifetime. Alternatively expressed, it is the problem of saying what makes our younger and older selves stages of *the same person.*

qualitative identity: Two things are qualitatively the same, or qualitatively identical, when they have the same characteristics. Two things can be qualitatively identical in one respect (in colour, for example) while being qualitatively different other respects (in shape).

numerical identity: For A to be numerically identical to B, A and B must be one and the same object. Although *two* objects can be qualitatively the same, two things cannot be *one* and the same, so they cannot be numerically identical.

The **problem of personal identity** poses the question: Given the many changes you undergo during your life, what makes you *numerically the same person* from one time to the next? Alternatively expressed, in light of the many changes you undergo in the span of a single life, what makes your younger and older selves stages of *the same person*? The debates surrounding the problem of personal identity concern identity *over time*—that is, identity from one time to another.

To understand this problem correctly, we need to be clear about the idea of *numerical sameness*, which is best understood by contrast with *qualitative sameness*.

(a) **Qualitative Identity**: Two things are qualitatively the same, or qualitatively identical, when and only when they have the same characteristics. I am not the same age or the same weight, and my hair is not the same colour, as the person who bore my name 30 years ago. Because some of my characteristics or *qualities* have changed, I am not qualitatively identical with my earlier self. Identical twins can be qualitatively identical and still be two persons, but they cannot be numerically identical and still be two.

(b) **Numerical Identity**: Despite the many qualitative changes I have undergone, we normally suppose that I am somehow *the same person*. The person who bore my name 30 years ago was *me*—his birth was my birth, his tenth birthday was my tenth birthday, his parents were my parents, and so on. That means roughly this: When we talk about him, and when we talk about me, we are only talking about *one* person—one person at two different stages of his life. A person can remain numerically the same—that is, can be just one person—over time, even if that person does not remain qualitatively the same.

The philosophical problem of personal identity is, then, the problem of explaining how it is possible for our younger and older selves, despite their many qualitative differences, to be different stages in the life of *one and the same person*.

We should consider not only the gradual and cumulative changes that all persons undergo over the duration of their lives, but also the sudden and dramatic changes that some persons experience. The great Czech writer Franz Kafka began *The Metamorphosis* as follows:

> As Gregor Samsa awoke one morning from uneasy dreams he found himself transformed in his bed into a gigantic insect. He was lying on his hard, as it were armor-plated, back and when he lifted his head a little he could see his domelike brown belly divided into stiff arched segments on top of which the bed quilt could hardly keep in position and was about to slide off completely. His numerous legs, which were pitifully thin compared to the rest of his bulk, waved helplessly before his eyes.
>
> What has happened to me? he thought. It was no dream.[3]

[3] From Glazer, N. (Ed.). (1972). *Franz Kafka: The Complete Stories*. New York: Shocken Books, 89.

Gregor Samsa's metamorphosis was sudden and dramatic. He went to bed a man, and awoke an insect. Naturally, this is fiction, but it invites the question: Do we even *understand* the idea that the gigantic insect that awoke in Gregor's bed was, in some sense, still Gregor? What could constitute the gigantic insect as *Gregor*?

Although this is a question about Gregor, it is also a question about how we conceive of persons: What view of *persons* must we have in order to think that the very same *person* who went to bed with the body of a man might later exist in the body of an insect? Questions just like this troubled the seventeenth century philosopher **John Locke** (1632–1704), who developed one of the first modern responses to the problem of personal identity.

John Locke: English philosopher who wrote on a wide range of topics. Best known as the founder of modern empiricism, and as the defender of views about natural rights and the social contract that inspired the French and American revolutions. He also developed one of the first modern responses to the problem of personal identity, and an important critique of fideism.

JOHN LOCKE ON PERSONAL IDENTITY

John Locke articulates an intuitively attractive position on personal identity. Although his powerful good sense results in a view that has gathered much criticism, Locke introduces a set of distinctions that remain helpful in contemporary discussions of the problem. The following passages from his writings confront each of our three entangled questions about the nature of identity, the nature of persons, and our prospects for immortality.

Of Identity and Diversity (John Locke, 1689)[4]

1. Wherein Identity consists.

Another occasion the mind often takes of comparing, is the very being of things, when, considering *anything as existing at any determined time and place*, we compare it with *itself existing at another time*, and thereon form the ideas of *identity* and *diversity*. When we see anything to be in any place in any instant of time, we are sure (be it what it will) that it is that very thing, and not another which at that same time exists in another place, how like and undistinguishable soever it may be in all other respects: and in this consists *identity* . . . That, therefore, that had one beginning, is the same thing; and that which had a different beginning in time and place from that, is not the same, but diverse. . . .

4. *Principium Individuationis*.

. . . In the state of living creatures, their identity depends not on a mass of the same particles, but on something else. For in them the variation of great parcels of matter alters not the identity: an oak growing from a plant to a great tree, and then lopped, is still the same oak; and a colt grown up to a horse, sometimes fat, sometimes lean, is all the while the same horse: though, in both these cases, there may be a manifest change of the parts; so that truly they are not either of them the same masses of matter, though they be truly one of them the same oak, and the other the same horse. The reason whereof is, that, in these two cases—a *mass of matter* and a *living body*—identity is not applied to the same thing.

[4] From Locke, J. (1689). *An Essay Concerning Human Understanding*. Vol. 1, Book II, Chap. XXVII. Retrieved July 11, 2014, from http://www.gutenberg.org/cache/epub/10615/pg10615.txt.

5. Identity of Vegetables.

We must therefore consider wherein an oak differs from a mass of matter, and that seems to me to be in this, that the one is only the cohesion of particles of matter any how united, the other such a disposition of them as constitutes the parts of an oak; and such an organization of those parts as is fit to receive and distribute nourishment, so as to continue and frame the wood, bark, and leaves, &c., of an oak, in which consists the vegetable life. That being then one plant which has such an organization of parts in one coherent body, partaking of one common life, it continues to be the same plant as long as it partakes of the same life, though that life be communicated to new particles of matter vitally united to the living plant, in a like continued organization conformable to that sort of plants. . . .

6. Identity of Animals.

The case is not so much different in *brutes* but that any one may hence see what makes an animal and continues it the same. Something we have like this in machines, and may serve to illustrate it. For example, what is a watch? It is plain it is nothing but a fit organization or construction of parts to a certain end, which, when a sufficient force is added to it, it is capable to attain. If we would suppose this machine one continued body, all whose organized parts were repaired, increased, or diminished by a constant addition or separation of insensible parts, with one common life, we should have something very much like the body of an animal . . .

7. The Identity of Man.

This also shows wherein the identity of the same *man* consists; viz. in nothing but a participation of the same continued life, by constantly fleeting particles of matter, in succession vitally united to the same organized body. . . . For if the identity of *soul alone* makes the same *man*; and there be nothing in the nature of matter why the same individual spirit may not be united to different bodies, it will be possible that those men, living in distant ages, and of different tempers, may have been the same man: which way of speaking must be from a very strange use of the word man, applied to an idea out of which body and shape are excluded. And that way of speaking would agree yet worse with the notions of those philosophers who allow of transmigration, and are of opinion that the souls of men may, for their miscarriages, be detruded into the bodies of beasts . . . But yet I think nobody, could he be sure that the *soul* of Heliogabalus were in one of his hogs, would yet say that hog were a *man* or Heliogabalus.

8. Idea of Identity suited to the Idea it is applied to.

It is not therefore unity of substance that comprehends all sorts of identity, or will determine it in every case; but to conceive and judge of it aright, we must consider what idea the word it is applied to stands for: it being one thing to be the same *substance*, another the same *man*, and a third the same *person*, if person, man, and substance, are three names standing for three different ideas;—for such as is the idea belonging to that name, such must be the identity . . .

9. Same man.

An animal is a living organized body; and consequently the same animal, as we have observed, is the same continued *life* communicated to different particles of matter, as they happen successively to be united to that organized living body. And whatever is talked of other definitions, ingenious observation puts it past doubt, that the idea in our minds, of which the sound man in our mouths is the sign, is nothing else but of an animal of such a certain form. Since I think I may be confident, that, whoever should see a creature of his own shape or make, though it had no more reason all its life than a cat or a parrot, would call him still a *man*; or whoever should hear a cat or a parrot discourse, reason, and philosophize, would call or think it nothing but a *cat* or a *parrot*; and say, the one was a dull irrational man, and the other a very intelligent rational parrot.

10. Same man.

For I presume it is not the idea of a thinking or rational being alone that makes the *idea of a man* in most people's sense: but of a body, so and so shaped, joined to it; and if that be the idea of a man, the same successive body not shifted all at once, must, as well as the same immaterial spirit, go to the making of the same man.

11. Personal Identity.

This being premised, to find wherein personal identity consists, we must consider what *person* stands for;—which, I think, is a thinking intelligent being, that has reason and reflection, and can consider itself as itself, the same thinking thing, in different times and places; which it does only by that consciousness which is inseparable from thinking, and, as it seems to me, essential to it: it being impossible for anyone to perceive without *perceiving* that he does perceive. When we see, hear, smell, taste, feel, meditate, or will anything, we know that we do so. Thus it is always as to our present sensations and perceptions: and by this every one is to himself that which he calls *self*:—it not being considered, in this case, whether the same self be continued in the same or divers substances. For, since consciousness always accompanies thinking, and it is that which makes every one to be what he calls self, and thereby distinguishes himself from all other thinking things, in this alone consists personal identity, i.e. the sameness of a rational being: and as far as this consciousness can be extended backwards to any past action or thought, so far reaches the identity of that person; it is the same self now it was then; and it is by the same self with this present one that now reflects on it, that that action was done.

12. Consciousness makes personal identity.

But it is further inquired, whether it be the same identical substance. . . . we losing the sight of our past selves, doubts are raised whether we are the same thinking thing, i.e. the same substance or no. Which, however reasonable or unreasonable, concerns not personal identity at all. The question being what makes the same person; and not whether it be the same identical substance, which always thinks in the same person, which, in this case, matters not at all . . . For, it being the same consciousness that makes a man be himself to himself, personal identity depends on that only, whether it be annexed solely to one individual substance, or can be continued in a succession of several substances. For as far as any intelligent being *can* repeat the idea of any past action with the same consciousness it had of it at first, and with the same consciousness it has of any present action; so far it is the same personal self. . . .

13. Personal Identity in Change of Substance.

That this is so, we have some kind of evidence in our very bodies, all whose particles, whilst vitally united to this same thinking conscious self, so that *we feel* when they are touched, and are affected by, and conscious of good or harm that happens to them, as a part of ourselves; i.e. of our thinking conscious self. Thus, the limbs of his body are to everyone a part of himself; he sympathizes and is concerned for them. Cut off a hand, and thereby separate it from that consciousness he had of its heat, cold, and other affections, and it is then no longer a part of that which is himself, any more than the remotest part of matter. Thus, we see the *substance* whereof personal self consisted at one time may be varied at another, without the change of personal identity; there being no question about the same person, though the limbs which but now were a part of it, be cut off.

16. Whether, the same immaterial Substance remaining, there can be two Persons.

As to the second part of the question, Whether the same immaterial substance remaining, there may be two distinct persons; which question seems to me to be built on this,—Whether the same immaterial being, being conscious of the action of its past duration, may be wholly stripped of all the consciousness of its past existence, and lose it beyond the power of ever retrieving it again: and so as it were beginning a new account from a new period, have a consciousness that *cannot* reach beyond this new state. All those who hold pre-existence are evidently of this mind; since they allow the soul to have no remaining consciousness of what it did in that pre-existent state, either wholly separate from body, or informing any other body; and if they should not, it is plain experience would be against them. So that personal identity, reaching no further than consciousness reaches, a pre-existent spirit not having continued so many ages in a state of silence, must needs make different persons. . . .

17. The body, as well as the soul, goes to the making of a Man.

And thus may we be able, without any difficulty, to conceive the same person at the resurrection, though in a body not exactly in make or parts the same which he had here,—the same consciousness going along with the soul that inhabits it. But yet the soul alone, in the change of bodies, would scarce to anyone but to him that makes the soul the man, be enough to make the same man. For should the soul of a prince, carrying with it the consciousness of the prince's past life, enter and inform the body of a cobbler, as soon as deserted by his own soul, every one sees he would be the same *person* with the prince, accountable only for the prince's actions: but who would say it was the same *man*? The body too goes to the making the man, and would, I guess, to everybody determine the man in this case, wherein the soul, with all its princely thoughts about it, would not make another man: but he would be the same cobbler to every one besides himself. . . .

18. Consciousness alone unites actions into the same Person.

But though the same immaterial substance or soul does not alone, wherever it be, and in whatsoever state, make the same *man*; yet it is plain, consciousness, as far as ever it can be extended—should it be to ages past—unites existences and actions very remote in time into the same *person*, as well as it does the existences and actions of the immediately preceding moment: so that whatever has the consciousness of present and past actions, is the same person to whom they both belong. Had I the same consciousness that I saw the ark and Noah's flood, as that I saw an overflowing of the Thames last winter, or as that I write now, I could no more doubt that I who write this now, that saw the Thames overflowed last winter, and that viewed the flood at the general deluge, was the same *self* . . .

19. Self depends on Consciousness, not on Substance.

Self is that conscious thinking thing,—whatever substance made up of, (whether spiritual or material, simple or compounded, it matters not)—which is sensible or conscious of pleasure and pain, capable of happiness or misery, and so is concerned for itself, as far as that consciousness extends. . . . That with which the consciousness of this present thinking thing *can* join itself, makes the same person, and is one self with it, and with nothing else; and so attributes to itself, and owns all the actions of that thing, as its own, as far as that consciousness reaches, and no further; as every one who reflects will perceive. . . .

21. Which shows wherein Personal identity consists.

This may show us wherein personal identity consists: not in the identity of substance, but, as I have said, in the identity of consciousness, wherein if Socrates and the present mayor of Queenborough agree, they are the same person: if the same Socrates waking and sleeping do not partake of the same consciousness, Socrates waking and sleeping is not the same person. And to punish Socrates waking for what sleeping Socrates thought, and waking Socrates was never conscious of, would be no more of right, than to punish one twin for what his brother-twin did, whereof he knew nothing, because their outsides were so like, that they could not be distinguished; for such twins have been seen.

22. Absolute oblivion separates what is thus forgotten from the person, but not from the man.

But yet possibly it will still be objected,—Suppose I wholly lose the memory of some parts of my life, beyond a possibility of retrieving them, so that perhaps I shall never be conscious of them again; yet am I not the same person that did those actions, had those thoughts that I once was conscious of, though I have now forgot them? To which I answer, that we must here take notice what the word *I* is applied to; which, in this case, is the *man* only. And the same man being presumed to be the same person, I is easily here supposed to stand also for the same person. But if it be possible for the same man to have distinct incommunicable consciousness at different times, it is past doubt the same man would at different times make different persons . . .

27. Consciousness unites substances, material or spiritual, with the same personality.

. . . But let men, according to their diverse hypotheses, resolve of that as they please. This every intelligent being, sensible of happiness or misery, must grant—that there is something that is *himself*, that he is concerned for, and would have happy; that this self has existed in a continued duration more than one instant, and therefore it is possible may exist, as it has done, months and years to come, without any certain bounds to be set to its duration; and may be the same self, by the same consciousness continued on for the future. And thus, by this consciousness he finds himself to be the same self which did such and such an action some years since, by which he comes to be happy or miserable now. . . .

28. Person a forensic Term.

Person, as I take it, is the name for this self. Wherever a man finds what he calls himself, there, I think, another may say is the same person. It is a forensic term, appropriating actions and their merit; and so belongs only to intelligent agents, capable of a law, and happiness, and misery. This personality extends itself beyond present existence to what is past, only by consciousness,—whereby it becomes concerned and accountable; owns and imputes to itself past actions, just upon the same ground and for the same reason as it does the present. . . .

We will draw out several important themes from Locke's views about identity and personal identity, and we will clarify some of his more challenging vocabulary along the way. Later, we will examine some objections to Locke's account of personal identity.

Themes from Locke

Several important ideas emerge from Locke's views about personal identity, ideas that have influenced all subsequent discussions of the problem. One prominent Lockean thesis that has arguably helped clarify issues more than any other is his idea that (as we might express it) *identity is relative* to the sort of thing to which it is applied. Locke also tries to clarify how the term *person* is related to the terms *man*, *consciousness*, and *self*. Finally, he provides a psychological criterion for personal identity by using memory to bind the different stages of a life into a single person.

Relative Identity Locke maintains that before answering the question of whether some object is identical or the same, we must first be clear what general concept or idea the object is to be placed under. The criteria for deciding whether one thing is identical to another will depend on (will be relative to) *the category* of thing we are asking about. Recall the case of Gregor Samsa: The insect that awoke in Gregor's bed was not *the same human being* who went to sleep there, since it was not a human being at all. But it might still have been *the same person*—it might still have been Gregor in a different (nonhuman) body. The terms *person* and *human being* describe different categories of things, and the requirements for being the *same person* might differ from the requirements for being the *same human being*.

relativity of identity: The idea, first expressed by John Locke, that the question, "Is A the same as B?" is incomplete, and cannot be answered without *specifying the kind of thing* we are asking about. A and B might be the same wood, but not the same ship, or they might be the same person but not the same man.

We might put Locke's core idea about the **relativity of identity** like this: We can't begin to answer the question about whether A is the same thing as B without first saying what sort of things we are asking about. If we simply ask whether A is the same as B, we do not have enough information to answer, and we must clarify our question. Do we want to know, for example, whether A and B are *the same person*, or do we want to know whether they are *the same man*, or *the same collection of molecules?* By itself, the question "Is A the same as B?" simply has no answer. Locke's idea that identity is relative means we can't settle questions about personal identity without first clarifying what we are asking about. The category of *person*, as Locke uses it, has several facets.

Man, Persons, and Selves Locke is careful to distinguish between what he calls *man* and *person*. He uses *man* to refer to "an animal of a certain form" (section 9). In this view, to be a 'man' is to be a member of our species—a biological organism of a certain kind. Contemporary equivalents to Locke's term *man* might be *human being* or *Homo sapien*. He restricts the term *person* to any "thinking, intelligent being which has reason and can consider itself as itself" (section 11). Although it may be that only biologically human beings then qualify as persons, it need not be so. An intelligent, rational nonhuman alien from another galaxy would probably not be a member of the species *Homo sapiens*, but it would nonetheless qualify as a person. If we could take an unbiased look at them, perhaps we would even find that orangutans or dolphins qualify as persons.

According to Locke's definition, all persons think and perceive, and they are, in addition, *conscious*. *Consciousness* is Locke's word for our awareness of our own thoughts and perceptions. It is one thing to think about a tree, or to be aware of one, but having *consciousness* requires being aware that we are aware of the tree. Persons all have consciousness of this sort. As Locke says, "When we see, hear, smell, taste, feel, meditate, or will anything, we know that we do so" (section 11). By virtue of acquiring consciousness, we become something more than "an animal of a certain form." Locke says that "it is by this [consciousness] every one is to himself that which he calls self," and that "consciousness . . . is that which makes every one to be what he calls self" (section 11). Perhaps Locke's thought is this: If I am only aware of a tree, then I am nothing to myself. If I am conscious, then I am also aware that *I* am aware, and so *I (myself)* am also part of what I am aware of. In other words, part of being conscious is having self-awareness, or awareness of one's self. We might think of a *self* as simply what each person calls herself.

Locke adds another dimension to the concept of person when he suggests that it is a forensic term. The **forensic conception of persons** says that to be a person is to have legal and moral status; persons are the bearers of rights and responsibilities. This is important, since it means that questions about whether A is the same person as B are directly tied to questions about whether A is responsible for B's actions. If your current self is the *same person* as the occupant of some earlier stage of your life, you are morally or legally responsible for the deeds of that earlier person. Responsibility is tied to our status as persons, and our status as persons is dependent on our consciousness or self-awareness. So, according to Locke's view, if I (now) am the same person as some earlier person, then I (now) am aware of, and responsible for, that earlier person's thoughts and actions. This idea explains why the metaphysical problem of personal identity is important. It is also the key to Locke's theory of personal identity.

forensic conception of persons: The idea that to be person is to be a bearer of moral and legal rights and responsibilities—*person* designates the status of having moral and legal obligations. The forensic conception contrasts with metaphysical conceptions of persons, which contend that being a person means having some distinctive component, ingredient, or capacity (e.g., soul, self-awareness, or rationality).

The Memory Criterion Locke claims that at the resurrection we will not have the same bodies, but we can still be the same persons, providing that we have "the same consciousness going along with the soul that inhabits [the new body]" (section 17). Similarly, he says, if the soul of a prince goes into the body of a cobbler while "carrying along with it the consciousness of the prince's past life," then the result will be the same person as the prince. But it will not be the same human organism or animal—that is, it will not be the same *man* as the prince. Locke's criterion for being the same person is, then, a **psychological criterion**. In other words, we will be the same person at earlier and later times so long as the right sort of *psychological connection* is preserved between our later and earlier selves. The bodily changes we undergo are irrelevant. In taking this position, Locke gives expression to an intuition shared by many: the intuition that the person we are has more to do with our psychological life than it does with our bodily appearance. Exactly what sort of psychological connection between our later and earlier selves is needed for them to be the same person?

psychological criterion: A criterion that counts a person at one time as numerically identical with that person at a later time in virtue of psychological relationships connecting the two. Locke's *memory criterion* is a well-known example of a psychological criterion for personal identity.

Locke believes that the essential psychological connection between earlier and later selves needed to make them stages of the same person is provided by *memory*. When a person who is now conscious of her current thoughts, feelings, and perceptions is also conscious (*via* memory) of the thoughts and feelings of some (any) person in the past, then those current and past persons are stages of the very same person. If a current consciousness includes awareness of having some earlier person's thoughts and feelings, or of performing some earlier person's actions, then the current person *is* that earlier person. The gigantic insect that awoke in Gregor's bed was still Gregor, simply because the insect had Gregor's memories—it remembered itself doing what Gregor did on preceding days.

Your memories thus unify or bind together your many past, present, and future selves, making them all stages of a single person. If you lose that crucial link to your past, then you will cease to be numerically identical with those past persons who bore your name, even if you retain the same body. For example, if I suffer permanent amnesia and *irretrievably* lose the ability to recall my past, then I am no longer the person who existed prior to the accident. I may well be the very same man, but I will not be the same person. Conversely, if I *do* remember the past thoughts and deeds of some earlier person, then I am that very person, even if I am not the same human being—even if, like Gregor, I am not a human being at all, or if, like the prince in the cobbler's body, I am a different human being altogether.

THOMAS REID ON PERSONAL IDENTITY

Thomas Reid: Scottish philosopher best known as a critic of the skeptical tendencies in empiricist philosophy and as a defender of common sense and direct realism. Reid developed important criticisms of Locke's memory criterion for personal identity and defended a metaphysical realist theory of the self.

A century after Locke wrote about personal identity, Scottish philosopher **Thomas Reid** (1710–1796) offered several objections to Locke's view and suggested an alternative theory. Both Reid's objections to Locke and his own theory of personal identity are found in the following selection. In the first part, Reid attempts to clarify the notion of *person*, and he defends the curious thesis that "a person is something indivisible." In reading those passages, try to understand what this means, and to understand his defense of it. Reid next discusses the notion of identity. You should carefully note what he says about the "imperfect identity" of always changing physical bodies—that is, things that are *continuous* with one another but for which we nonetheless use the term *identity*. Does Reid think of *perfect* and *imperfect identity* (continuity) as two different kinds of identity, one for persons (selves) and the other for bodies? Or does he believe that continuity is *not really identity* at all?

Of Identity (Thomas Reid, 1785)[5]

> The conviction which every man has of his identity, as far back as his memory reaches, needs no aid of philosophy to strengthen it, and no philosophy can weaken it, without first producing some degree of insanity.
>
> . . . I see evidently that identity supposes an uninterrupted continuance of existence. That which has ceased to exist, cannot be the same with that which afterward begins to exist; for this would be to suppose a being to exist after it ceased to exist, and to have had existence before it was produced, which are manifest contradictions. Continued uninterrupted existence is therefore necessarily implied in identity.
>
> . . . It is perhaps more difficult to ascertain with precision the meaning of personality; but it is not necessary in the present subject: it is sufficient for our purpose to observe, that all mankind place their personality in something that cannot be divided, or consist of parts. A part of a person is a manifest absurdity.
>
> When a man loses his estate, his health, his strength, he is still the same person, and has lost nothing of his personality. If he has a leg or an arm cut off, he is the same person he was before. The amputated member is no part of his person, otherwise it would have a right to a part of his estate, and be liable for a part of his engagements. It would be entitled to a share of his merit and demerit, which is manifestly absurd. A person is something indivisible, and is what Leibniz calls a *monad*.

[5] Reid, Thomas, Essays on the Intellectual Powers of Man. The MIT Press, Cambridge Mass., 1969. Used by permission.

My personal identity, therefore, implies the continued existence of that indivisible thing which I call *myself*. Whatever this self may be, it is something which thinks, and deliberates, and resolves, and acts, and suffers. I am not thought, I am not action, I am not feeling; I am something that thinks, and acts, and suffers. . . . My thoughts, and actions, and feelings, change every moment; they have no continued, but a successive existence; but that *self*, or *I*, to which they belong, is permanent, and has the same relation to all the succeeding thoughts, actions and feelings, which I call mine.

. . . Although memory gives the most irresistible evidence of my being the identical person that did such a thing, at such a time, I may have other good evidence of things which befell me, and which I do not remember: I know who bare me, and suckled me, but I do not remember these events.

It may here be observed, though the observation would have been unnecessary, if some great philosophers had not contradicted it, that it is not my remembering any action of mine that makes me to be the person who did it. This remembrance makes me to know assuredly that I did it; but I might have done it, though I did not remember it. . . .

The identity of a person is a perfect identity; wherever it is real, it admits of no degrees; and it is impossible that a person should be in part the same, and in part different; because a person is a *monad*, and is not divisible into parts. . . .

We probably at first derive our notion of identity from that natural conviction which every man has from the dawn of reason of his own identity and continued existence. The operations of our minds are all successive, and have no continued existence. But the thinking being has a continued existence, and we have an invincible belief, that it remains the same when all its thoughts and operations change.

Our judgments of the identity of objects of sense, seem to be formed much upon the same grounds as our judgments of the identity of other persons besides ourselves.

Wherever we observe a great similarity, we are apt to presume identity, if no reason appears to the contrary. Two objects ever so like, when they are perceived at the same time, cannot be the same: but if they are presented to our senses at different times, we are apt to think them the same, merely from their similarity.

Whether this be a natural prejudice, or from whatever cause it proceeds, it certainly appears in children from infancy; and, when we grow up, it is confirmed in most instances by experience: for we rarely find two individuals of the same species that are not distinguishable by obvious differences.

. . . It may likewise be observed that the identity of objects of sense is never perfect. All bodies, as they consist of innumerable parts that may be disjoined from them by a great variety of causes, are subject to continual changes of their substance, increasing, diminishing, changing insensibly. When such alterations are gradual, because language could not afford a different name for every different state of such a changeable being, it retains the same name, and is considered as the same thing. Thus we say of an old regiment, that it did such a thing a century ago, though there now is not a man alive who then belonged to it. We say a tree is the same in the seed bed and in the forest. A ship of war, which has successively changed her anchors, her tackle, her sails, her masts, her planks, and her timbers, while she keeps the same name, is the same.

The identity therefore which we ascribe to bodies, whether natural or artificial, is not perfect identity; it is rather something which, for the conveniency of speech, we call identity. It admits of a great change of the subject, providing the change be gradual, sometimes even of a total change. And the changes which in common language are made consistent with identity, differ from those that are thought to destroy it, not in kind, but in number and degree. It has no fixed nature when applied to bodies; and questions about the identity of a body are very often questions about words. But identity, when applied to persons, has no ambiguity, and admits not of degrees, or of more and less: it is the foundation of all rights and obligations, and of all accountableness; and the notion of it is fixed and precise. . . .

Of Mr. Locke's Account of Personal Identity

. . . This doctrine has some strange consequences, which the author was aware of. Such as, that if the same consciousness can be transferred from one intelligent being to another, which he thinks we cannot show to be impossible, then two or twenty intelligent beings may be the same person. And if the intelligent being may lose the consciousness of the actions done by him, which surely is possible, then he is not the person that did those actions; so that one intelligent being may be two or twenty different persons, if he shall so often lose the consciousness of this former actions.

There is another consequence of this doctrine, which follows no less necessarily, though Mr. Locke probably did not see it. It is, that a man may be, and at the same time not be, the person that did a particular action.

Suppose a brave officer to have been flogged when a boy at school, for robbing an orchard, to have taken a standard from the enemy in his first campaign, and to have been made a general in advanced life. Suppose also, which must be admitted to be possible, that when he took the standard, he was conscious of his having been flogged at school; and that when made a general, he was conscious of his taking the standard, but had absolutely lost the consciousness of his flogging.

These things being supposed, it follows, from Mr. Locke's doctrine, that he who was flogged at school is the same person who took the standard; and that he who took the standard is the same person who was made a general. Whence it follows, if there be any truth in logic, that the general is the same person with him who was flogged at school. But the general's consciousness does not reach so far back as his flogging, therefore, according to Mr. Locke's doctrine, he is not the person who was flogged. Therefore the general is, and at the same time is not, the same person with him who was flogged at school.

. . . It may be observed, that in this doctrine, . . . personal identity is confounded with the evidence which we have of our personal identity.

It is very true, that my remembrance that I did such a thing is the evidence I have that I am the identical person who did it. And this, I am apt to think, Mr. Locke meant: but to say that my remembrance that I did such a thing, or my consciousness, makes me the person who did it, is, in my apprehension, an absurdity too gross to be entertained by any man who attends to the meaning of it: for it is to attribute to memory or consciousness, a strange magical power of producing its object, though that object must have existed before the memory or consciousness which produced it.

Consciousness is the testimony of one faculty; memory is the testimony of another faculty: and to say that the testimony is the cause of the thing testified, this is surely absurd, if any thing be, and could not have been said by Mr. Locke, if he had not confounded the testimony with the thing testified.

When a horse that was stolen is found and claimed by the owner, the only evidence he can have, or that a judge or witness can have, that this is the very identical horse which was his property, is similitude.

But would it not be ridiculous from this to infer that the identity of the horse consists in similitude only? The only evidence I have that I am the identical person who did such actions, is, that I remember distinctly I did them; or, as Mr. Locke expresses it, I am conscious I did them. To infer from this, that personal identity consists in consciousness, is an argument, which, if it had any force, would prove the identity of a stolen horse to consist solely in similitude.

. . . Is it not strange that the sameness or identity of a person should consist in a thing which is continually changing, and is not any two minutes the same?

Our consciousness, our memory, and every operation of the mind, are still flowing like the water of a river, or like time itself. The consciousness I have this moment can no more be the same consciousness I had last moment, than this moment can be the last moment. Identity can only be affirmed of things which have a continued existence. Consciousness, and every kind of thought, is transient and momentary, and has no continued existence; and therefore, if personal identity consisted in consciousness, it would certainly follow, that no man is the same person any two moments of his life; and as the right and justice of reward and punishment are founded on personal identity, no man could be responsible for his actions.

Reid's Criticism of Locke

These selections from Reid contain several complaints about Locke's account of personal identity. One complaint deserves special emphasis. Reid's most significant objection to Locke can be outlined as follows: Suppose Alfred, an 80-year-old general, clearly remembers taking a standard from the enemy in battle 40 years ago (when Alfred was known only as "Fred"). Then, on Locke's view, it follows that

1. Alfred = Fred.

Furthermore, 40 years ago Fred clearly remembered being flogged as a 10-year-old child. (He was known then simply as "Freddy"). So, on Locke's view,

2. Fred = Freddy.

By the transitivity of identity, from (1) and (2) we must conclude that

3. Alfred = Freddy.

The problem is that 80-year-old Alfred cannot remember being flogged 70 years ago. In fact, at the age of 80 he no longer remembers anything prior to his twentieth year. Thus, Locke's account of personal identity would require us to conclude that Alfred is Fred, and Fred is Freddy, but Alfred is not Freddy. As Reid says, the consequence of Locke's memory criterion for personal identity seems to be that "the general is, and at the same time is not, the same person with him who was flogged at school." Since this conclusion is impossible, the view that leads us to it must be false.

Reid's argument provides a good example of a ***reductio ad absurdum*** argument. Locke's memory criterion for personal identity requires us to accept statements (1) and (2); the principle of the transitivity of identity then requires us to conclude from these statements that (3) is true. However, his memory criterion also requires us to say that (3) is false. Thus, Locke's theory of personal identity, along with the principle of transitivity of identity, requires us to conclude that (3) is true, and also requires to conclude that (3) is false. As a result of employing Locke's memory criterion and the transitivity of identity, we are led to contradict ourselves and say that Alfred both is and is not Freddy. To avoid this impossible situation, we will need to give up something—either the transitivity of identity, or Locke's memory criterion for personal identity. Reid has no trouble deciding which we should reject.

reductio ad absurdum: In its most common form, a *reductio* argument attempts to establish that some statement is false by showing that unacceptable (false, implausible, or absurd) consequences follow from the statement. A *reductio* argument can also be used to argue for the truth of a statement by showing that an unacceptable consequence follows if we deny the statement.

Logic Box

Reductio Ad Absurdum Argument

A *reductio ad absurdum* argument is called a *reductio* argument for short. In its most common form, a *reductio* argument attempts to establish that some view is false by showing that unacceptable (implausible, contradictory, or absurd) consequences will follow from the view. Alternatively, a *reductio* argument can be used more positively to argue that a view is true by showing that an unacceptable consequence will follow if we attempt to deny the view.

Example: If, as the story says, Santa visits every household on the same night, then his reindeer would have to travel faster than the speed of light. But that's impossible—nothing can travel faster than light, so the story can't be correct in every detail.

It is worth thinking about how Locke might reply to Reid's objection. Are there any relatively minor modifications to Locke's account that might enable it to escape Reid's objection? Or is the problem so great that any revision that would evade Reid's argument would require throwing out Locke's theory altogether? If the memory criterion fails to provide an account of personal identity, is there some other *psychological* criterion for personal identity that might fare better? Reid believes there is, and we turn next to his own account of personal identity.

Reid's Conception of the Self

self: Usually a synonym for *person*; the term is also used to designate an essential metaphysical constituent of persons that is referred to by the pronoun *I*.

Reid's writings suggest an alternative view about the nature of persons, or—as he calls us—selves. The **self** is, on his view, "indivisible," and as such it can never undergo change. (Recall the early atomists' account of atoms as *uncuttable* and therefore immune to change.) Because they are incapable of change, our earlier and later selves have a relation of what Reid calls *perfect identity* to one another: They are what make us the same persons for the duration of our lives (or, perhaps, for the duration of many lives).

Reid accepts that there is some sense in which, very loosely speaking, we can and do undergo significant physical and psychological changes. But those changes must occur without any changes to our selves. If *the same person* really does exist both before and after the change, then it follows that the changes were, strictly speaking, not changes to the person at all. If I shed a hair or lose a limb, but I still exist, then the hair or limb I lost were not any essential part of me. Similarly, if my thoughts and feelings change while I continue to exist, then that only goes to show that those thoughts and feelings were no part of what constitutes *me*. Although I might informally say that "I" change over the duration of my life, what changes is not *me*—I am an indivisible self, incapable of change. In this way, the metaphysical entity that Reid calls the *self* must be completely *featureless*—that is, since any of your features can change over time but your self cannot change, any features you have are not part of your self. You—your self—are aloof and detached from your continually changing physical and psychological characteristics.

Reid insists that there can be no perfect identity of this sort between earlier and later stages of any physical object ("body," or "object of sense"). When a tree undergoes a change by losing a leaf, we may *say* it is still the same tree, but we say this only "for the convenience of speech." We talk in this loose and informal way "because language could not afford a different name for every different state of such a changeable being." In other words, it is a linguistic convenience to call things "the same" even though they are really only continuous with one another. Wherever there is real identity there must be something that persists entirely unchanged and, Reid thinks, the only example each person has of perfect identity is his or her own self.

Why does Reid believe that we must be unchanging selves? His reasoning can be reconstructed in this way:

1. Nothing can change and still be the same.
2. Our physical constituents and psychological traits change throughout our lives.
3. *We* do not change throughout our lives; that is, we remain the same person through the many changes in our physical and psychological traits.
4. Therefore, we are not those physical and psychological traits, and they are not any essential part of us.

The first premise is an ancient and familiar view about the natures of sameness and change—namely, that they are incompatible. The second premise then expresses the plausible idea that we undergo change in our physical and psychological attributes over time, and the third premise holds to the thought that we nonetheless persist through those changes. If our physical and psychological traits do not remain the same, and yet we remain the same person, then it is tempting to conclude that we must be some nonphysical (and non-psychological) thing. That persisting thing is what we each call our "self." Reid was thus in agreement with Plato's idea that the soul "is the very likeness of the divine, and immortal, and intellectual, and uniform, and indissoluble, and unchangeable."

How persuasive is this reasoning for an unchanging self? One potentially serious problem *may* be this: Reid needs to be cautious about what motivates his acceptance of the third premise. Recall in the previous chapter that we saw a reason to believe that Theseus's ship might be the same ship even after the gradual replacement of all of its parts. The view that made this possible required the *continuity* of the ship throughout the voyage to be sufficient for its remaining the *same* ship. It appears that Reid agrees with this idea when he writes that "A ship of war, which has successively changed her anchors, her tackle, her sails, her masts, her planks, and her timbers, while she keeps the same name, is the same." But according to the form of reasoning we reconstructed in the previous paragraph, if (1) no *physical part* of Theseus's ship stays the same, and yet (2) it remains *the same ship*, then (3) Theseus's ship is not physical. So unless we want to concede that wooden ships have unchanging selves (or souls), we may not want to rely on this form of reasoning.

Perhaps Reid thinks he can avoid this objectionable consequence by calling the identity of the ship at different stages in the voyage an "imperfect identity"—in other words, an "identity" of linguistic convenience only. But if we say that the ship is not (*really*, or *strictly speaking*) the "same" ship, because its parts and features change, then we need to know why we should not say the same thing about persons. Why is our identity "perfect," as the third premise requires, and the identity of everything else "imperfect"? The only answer Reid provides is that we get our idea of our own perfect identity "from that natural conviction which every man has from the dawn of reason," and that "we have an invincible belief, that [the thinking being] remains the same when all its thoughts and operations change." But "natural convictions" and "invincible beliefs" are not arguments or evidence.

In the next chapter we will investigate in more detail the view that persons might be unchanging "selves" who persist through physical and psychological flux; in so doing, we will explore famous objections to the idea that we are "selves" of the sort Thomas Reid describes.

CONCLUSION

The problem of personal identity concerns the numerical identity of persons over time: What unifies a human life that extends from infancy to old age in such a way that it can be, despite the countless changes we undergo in body and mind, the life of a single person? John Locke proposed to unify the many and various stages of a person's life by making them all aspects of a single consciousness that extends as far into the past as our memories extend, and no further. Thomas Reid sought to unify the flux of physical and psychological changes that each person undergoes into the life of a single person by conceiving of the person as an indivisible component that runs unchanged through the flux.

It becomes clear as we investigate the problem of personal identity that it is actually a knot of several different problems—about the nature of change and identity, about the nature of persons, and about our prospects for immortality. Each of these problems is so deeply entangled with the others that solving any one of them might require us to unravel the entire knot.

Key Terms and Figures

Diotima p. 45
problem of personal identity p. 48
qualitative identity p. 48
numerical identity p. 48
John Locke p. 49
relativity of identity p. 54
forensic conception of persons p. 55
psychological criterion p. 55
Thomas Reid p. 56
***reductio ad absurdum* p. 59**
self p. 60

Additional readings on personal identity

Korfmacher, C. Personal Identity. *Internet Encyclopedia of Philosophy*. Retrieved July 11, 2014, from http://www.iep.utm.edu/person-i/

Martin, R. & Barnes, J. (Eds.). (2002). *Personal Identity*. Wiley-Blackwell.

Olson, E. T. Personal Identity. *The Stanford Encyclopedia of Philosophy*, Winter 2010. Edward N. Zalta (Ed.). Retrieved July 11, 2014, from http://plato.stanford.edu/archives/win2010/entries/identity-personal.

Perry, J. (1978). *A Dialogue on Personal Identity and Immortality*. Indianapolis: Hackett Publishing Company.

Perry, J. (Ed.) (2008). *Personal Identity*. Oakland: University of California Press.

Chapter 4
Divided Selves

Learning Objectives

- Describe the traditional concept of the self, and explain Hume's reason for thinking there is no such thing as a self.
- Explain the bundle theory of the self.
- Compare and contrast realism, eliminativism, and reductionism.
- Say why Hume might reasonably be classified as an eliminativist about the self, and why he might reasonably be classified as a reductionist about the self.
- Explain the phenomenon of brain fission.
- State how fission, whether of amoeba or of brains, is thought to show that continuity is not the same as identity.
- Identify at least two ways in which continuity differs from identity.
- Describe the relational theory of the self.

Despite their very different views about personal identity, John Locke and Thomas Reid agreed that some essential aspect of a person runs the length of her life and unifies her many different stages into one person. On Locke's view, a single consciousness encompasses both past and present thoughts and actions and provides the unity needed to constitute a person as the same through a lifetime of changes. On this view, the dark corners of the past that are irretrievably beyond the reach of our present consciousness cannot be parts of *our* past. On Reid's view, a featureless and indivisible entity he called the *self* runs the length of a person's life. However dramatic the physical and psychological changes we undergo in a lifetime, our unchanging self ensures that we are one and the same person throughout. Both philosophers see us as having a kind of metaphysical unity, with the many parts of our life bound together by a single consciousness or a single self.

In this chapter we explore the issue of personal identity further by studying the ideas of philosophers who believe we lack this sort of unity—philosophers who reject a metaphysical criterion for personal identity. Novelist and essayist Salman Rushdie nicely summed up this alternative view:

> In the modern age, we have come to understand our own selves as composites, often contradictory, even internally incompatible. We have understood that each of us is many different people. Our younger selves differ from our older selves, we can be bold

in the company of our lovers and timorous before our employers, principled when we instruct our children and corrupt when offered some secret temptation; we are serious and frivolous, loud and quiet, aggressive and easily abashed. The nineteenth century concept of the integrated self has been replaced by this jostling crowd of 'I's.[1]

We saw hints of this view in the words of Diotima, who said we "are preserved, not absolutely the same, but by substitution, the old worn-out mortality leaving another new and similar existence behind."[2] In this chapter we will examine the ideas of philosophers who took this point seriously.

DAVID HUME ON THE SELF

David Hume: Scottish philosopher best known for his radical and skeptical development of empiricism; his writings contain important critiques of the self, personal identity, inductive reasoning, and the evidential status of testimony about miracles.

traditional theory of the self: View that the self is an entity, typically nonphysical, that persists throughout a person's physical and psychological changes; its persistence is normally explained by regarding the self as metaphysically simple or indivisible. It is the referent of the first person pronoun "I" and is what we are thought to be conscious of when we are self-aware. This theory, in part or whole, can be found in Plato's treatment of the soul, René Descartes's theory of the mind, and Thomas Reid's theory of the self.

In the following selection from his writing, Scottish philosopher **David Hume** (1711–1776) criticizes the **traditional theory of the self** to which many of his predecessors and contemporaries subscribed. By *self*, many of Hume's contemporaries meant

a. Something that persists continuously, uninterrupted, the whole course of our lives;
b. Something that is simple—that is, it is not divisible into parts;
c. Something that we are, or can be, conscious of whenever we direct our attention to it ('we feel its existence').

In Chapter 3, we found both (a) and (b) in Plato's description of the soul, as well as in Reid's view of the self; (c) is explicit in Locke's view of the self, and—as we will see below—implicit in Reid's view. Although Reid wrote half a century after Hume published on personal identity, it is useful to see the view of the self defended by Reid as the direct target of Hume's criticisms.

In the selection below, Hume attempts to provide an argument against the idea that we have, or are, a self (as it has traditionally been defined). He also offers a diagnosis of the error that leads us to believe we have a self. Third, Hume sketches an account of what he believes persons actually are, to replace the idea that we are unchanging selves. We will consider each of these aspects of his discussion.

Of Personal Identity (David Hume, 1739)[3]

There are some philosophers who imagine we are every moment intimately conscious of what we call our *self*; that we feel its existence and its continuance in existence; and are certain, beyond the evidence of a demonstration, both of its perfect identity and simplicity. The strongest sensation, the most violent passion, say they, instead of distracting us from this view, only fix it the more intensely, and make us consider their influence on self either by their pain or pleasure. To attempt a farther proof of this were to weaken its evidence; since no proof can be derived from any fact, of which

---

[1] Rushdie, S. (2002). India's Fiftieth Anniversary. *Step Across This Line: Collected Nonfiction 1992–2002*. Toronto: Alfred A. Knopf Canada, 163.

[2] From Plato. (n.d.). *Symposium*. 208. (Benjamin Jowett, Trans.). Retrieved July 19, 2014, from http://www.gutenberg.org/cache/epub/1600/pg1600.txt

[3] Hume, D. (1739). *A Treatise of Human Nature*. Book 1, Part 4, Section 6. Retrieved July 29, 2014, from http://www.gutenberg.org/files/4705/4705-h/4705-h.htm

we are so intimately conscious; nor is there any thing, of which we can be certain, if we doubt of this.

Unluckily all these positive assertions are contrary to that very experience, which is pleaded for them, nor have we any idea of self, after the manner it is here explained. For from what impression could this idea be derived? This question it is impossible to answer without a manifest contradiction and absurdity; and yet it is a question, which must necessarily be answered, if we would have the idea of self pass for clear and intelligible. It must be some one impression, that gives rise to every real idea. But self or person is not any one impression, but that to which our several impressions and ideas are supposed to have a reference. If any impression gives rise to the idea of self, that impression must continue invariably the same, through the whole course of our lives; since self is supposed to exist after that manner. But there is no impression constant and invariable. Pain and pleasure, grief and joy, passions and sensations succeed each other, and never all exist at the same time. It cannot, therefore, be from any of these impressions, or from any other, that the idea of self is derived; and consequently there is no such idea.

But farther, what must become of all our particular perceptions upon this hypothesis? All these are different, and distinguishable, and separable from each other, and may be separately considered, and may exist separately, and have no need of anything to support their existence. After what manner, therefore, do they belong to self; and how are they connected with it? For my part, when I enter most intimately into what I call myself, I always stumble on some particular perception or other, of heat or cold, light or shade, love or hatred, pain or pleasure. I never can catch myself at any time without a perception, and never can observe any thing but the perception. When my perceptions are removed for any time, as by sound sleep; so long am I insensible of myself, and may truly be said not to exist. And were all my perceptions removed by death, and could I neither think, nor feel, nor see, nor love, nor hate after the dissolution of my body, I should be entirely annihilated, nor do I conceive what is farther requisite to make me a perfect non-entity. If any one, upon serious and unprejudiced reflection thinks he has a different notion of himself, I must confess I can reason no longer with him. All I can allow him is, that he may be in the right as well as I, and that we are essentially different in this particular. He may, perhaps, perceive something simple and continued, which he calls himself; though I am certain there is no such principle in me.

But setting aside some metaphysicians of this kind, I may venture to affirm of the rest of mankind, that they are nothing but a bundle or collection of different perceptions, which succeed each other with an inconceivable rapidity, and are in a perpetual flux and movement. Our eyes cannot turn in their sockets without varying our perceptions. Our thought is still more variable than our sight; and all our other senses and faculties contribute to this change; nor is there any single power of the soul, which remains unalterably the same, perhaps for one moment. The mind is a kind of theatre, where several perceptions successively make their appearance; pass, re-pass, glide away, and mingle in an infinite variety of postures and situations. There is properly no simplicity in it at one time, nor identity in different; whatever natural propension we may have to imagine that simplicity and identity. The comparison of the theatre must not mislead us. They are the successive perceptions only, that constitute the mind; nor have we the most distant notion of the place, where these scenes are represented, or of the materials, of which it is composed.

What then gives us so great a propension to ascribe an identity to these successive perceptions, and to suppose ourselves possest of an invariable and uninterrupted existence through the whole course of our lives? In order to answer this question, we must distinguish betwixt personal identity, as it regards our thought or imagination, and as it regards our passions or the concern we take in ourselves. The first is our present subject; and to explain it perfectly we must take the matter pretty deep, and account for that identity, which we attribute to plants and animals; there being a great analogy betwixt it, and the identity of a self or person.

We have a distinct idea of an object, that remains invariable and uninterrupted through a supposed variation of time; and this idea we call that of identity or sameness. We have also a distinct idea of several different objects existing in succession, and connected together by a close relation; and this to an accurate view affords as perfect a notion of diversity, as if there was no manner of relation among the objects. But though these two ideas of identity, and a succession of related objects be in themselves perfectly distinct, and even contrary, yet it is certain, that in our common way of thinking they are generally confounded with each other. That action of the imagination, by which we consider the uninterrupted and invariable object, and that by which we reflect on the succession of related objects, are almost the same to the feeling, nor is there much more effort of thought required in the latter case than in the former. The relation facilitates the transition of the mind from one object to another, and renders its passage as smooth as if it contemplated one continued object. This resemblance is the cause of the confusion and mistake, and makes us substitute the notion of identity, instead of that of related objects. However at one instant we may consider the related succession as variable or interrupted, we are sure the next to ascribe to it a perfect identity, and regard it as enviable and uninterrupted. Our propensity to this mistake is so great from the resemblance above-mentioned, that we fall into it before we are aware; and though we incessantly correct ourselves by reflection, and return to a more accurate method of thinking, yet we cannot long sustain our philosophy, or take off this bias from the imagination. Our last resource is to yield to it, and boldly assert that these different related objects are in effect the same, however interrupted and variable. In order to justify to ourselves this absurdity, we often feign some new and unintelligible principle, that connects the objects together, and prevents their interruption or variation. Thus we feign the continued existence of the perceptions of our senses, to remove the interruption: and run into the notion of a soul, and self, and substance, to disguise the variation. But we may farther observe, that where we do not give rise to such a fiction, our propension to confound identity with relation is so great, that we are apt to imagine something unknown and mysterious, connecting the parts, beside their relation; and this I take to be the case with regard to the identity we ascribe to plants and vegetables. And even when this does not take place, we still feel a propensity to confound these ideas, though we are not able fully to satisfy ourselves in that particular, nor find any thing invariable and uninterrupted to justify our notion of identity.

Thus the controversy concerning identity is not merely a dispute of words. For when we attribute identity, in an improper sense, to variable or interrupted objects, our mistake is not confined to the expression, but is commonly attended with a fiction, either of something invariable and uninterrupted, or of something mysterious and inexplicable, or at least with a propensity to such fictions. What will suffice to prove this hypothesis to the satisfaction of every fair enquirer, is to shew from daily experience and observation, that the objects, which are variable or interrupted, and yet are supposed to continue the same, are such only as consist of a succession of parts, connected together by resemblance, contiguity, or causation. For as such a succession answers evidently to our notion of diversity, it can only be by mistake we ascribe to it an identity; and as the relation of parts, which leads us into this mistake, is really nothing but a quality, which produces an association of ideas, and an easy transition of the imagination from one to another, it can only be from the resemblance, which this act of the mind bears to that, by which we contemplate one continued object, that the error arises. Our chief business, then, must be to prove, that all objects, to which we ascribe identity, without observing their invariableness and uninterruptedness, are such as consist of a succession of related objects. . . .

This may be confirmed by another phenomenon. A change in any considerable part of a body destroys its identity; but it is remarkable, that where the change is produced gradually and insensibly we are less apt to ascribe to it the same effect. The reason can plainly be no other, than that the mind, in following the successive changes of the body, feels an easy passage from the surveying its condition in one moment to the viewing of it in another, and at no particular time perceives any interruption in its actions. From which continued perception, it ascribes a continued existence and identity to the object. . . .

. . . The effect of so strong a relation is, that though every one must allow, that in a very few years both vegetables and animals endure a total change, yet we still attribute identity to them, while their form, size, and substance are entirely altered. An oak, that grows from a small plant to a large tree, is still the same oak; though there be not one particle of matter, or figure of its parts the same. An infant becomes a man, and is sometimes fat, sometimes lean, without any change in his identity. . . .

We now proceed to explain the nature of personal identity, which has become so great a question in philosophy, especially of late years in England, where all the abstruser sciences are studied with a peculiar ardour and application. And here it is evident, the same method of reasoning must be continued, which has so successfully explained the identity of plants, and animals, and ships, and houses, and of all the compounded and changeable productions either of art or nature. The identity, which we ascribe to the mind of man, is only a fictitious one, and of a like kind with that which we ascribe to vegetables and animal bodies. It cannot, therefore, have a different origin, but must proceed from a like operation of the imagination upon like objects. . . .

. . . [T]he true idea of the human mind, is to consider it as a system of different perceptions or different existences, which are linked together by the relation of cause and effect, and mutually produce, destroy, influence, and modify each other. Our impressions give rise to their correspondent ideas; and these ideas in their turn produce other impressions. One thought chases another, and draws after it a third, by which it is expelled in its turn. In this respect, I cannot compare the soul more properly to any thing than to a republic or commonwealth, in which the several members are united by the reciprocal ties of government and subordination, and give rise to other persons, who propagate the same republic in the incessant changes of its parts. And as the same individual republic may not only change its members, but also its laws and constitutions; in like manner the same person may vary his character and disposition, as well as his impressions and ideas, without losing his identity. . . .

The whole of this doctrine leads us to a conclusion, which is of great importance in the present affair, viz. that all the nice and subtle questions concerning personal identity can never possibly be decided, and are to be regarded rather as grammatical than as philosophical difficulties. Identity depends on the relations of ideas; and these relations produce identity, by means of that easy transition they occasion. But as the relations, and the easiness of the transition may diminish by insensible degrees, we have no just standard, by which we can decide any dispute concerning the time, when they acquire or lose a title to the name of identity. All the disputes concerning the identity of connected objects are merely verbal, except so far as the relation of parts gives rise to some fiction or imaginary principle of union, as we have already observed.

What I have said concerning the first origin and uncertainty of our notion of identity, as applied to the human mind, may be extended with little or no variation to that of simplicity. An object, whose different co-existent parts are bound together by a close relation, operates upon the imagination after much the same manner as one perfectly simple and indivisible and requires not a much greater stretch of thought in order to its conception. From this similarity of operation we attribute a simplicity to it, and feign a principle of union as the support of this simplicity, and the center of all the different parts and qualities of the object.

The Theatre of the Mind

Hume claims that when he turned his attention inward to observe his own self, he couldn't find one. What he found was only a succession of changing psychological states: shifting thoughts, feelings, and sensations rapidly replacing one another. He further doubts that others would see anything different when they look into themselves. In short, Hume claims to have no *experience* of any self, and believes that if we take a "serious and unprejudiced" look, we will agree that we have no such experience either. A self is something we are supposed to be aware of whenever we have self-awareness. If attentive inner observation does not uncover a self, then what does it reveal? What do we discover when we turn our gaze inward? According to Hume, we find only "different perceptions, which succeed each other with an inconceivable rapidity, and are in a perpetual flux and movement."

Hume famously compares the mind to "a kind of theatre," where various perceptions, thoughts, feelings, and sensations make an appearance on stage and then glide away to be replaced by others, in continuous succession. As the "audience" to this inner theatre, we sit offstage, in the dark, aware only of what passes before us on the stage. Nothing fitting our earlier description of a "self" ever passes before the mind's eye. Hume's "theatre" suggests a way of strengthening his claim. Employing his image, we might add that we can never see our self pass before our mind's eye because we are always the *audience* to what passes on the stage of the mind, not players in the show. To be observed, the self must go onstage; but if it could do that, it would not be the audience to itself. Perhaps the self can never simultaneously be both the offstage audience and the onstage performer—that would make it unsurprising that we fail to find our self when we turn our gaze inward.

Although we cannot explore the idea in this chapter, we should note a consequence of Hume's view that all our ideas originate in experience. If, as he insists, we never experience our self, then we can have no idea or concept of a self. His conclusion should then state that we don't even understand what philosophers like Reid are talking about when they refer to the mysterious entity called the self.

"I" and My Shadow

If Hume is right that we fail to find our selves when we look for them, why are we so tempted to think that we have (or are) enduring selves? Before turning to Hume's explanation for our error, we should consider one direct argument for the idea that we do indeed have awareness of an enduring self.

Thomas Reid wrote that although "My thoughts, and actions, and feelings, change every moment: they have no continued, but a successive, existence; but that *self*, or *I*, to which they belong, is permanent . . .". He called the idea that the "self" or "I" persists unchanged a "natural conviction" or "invincible belief," and suggested that it is a conviction we all share.

> We probably at first derive our notion of identity from that natural conviction which every man has from the dawn of reason of his own identity and continued existence. The operations of our minds are all successive, and have no continued existence. But the thinking being has a continued existence, and we have an invincible belief, that it remains the same when all its thoughts and operations change.[4]

What could be the source of an "invincible belief" that the self, or "I," is permanent? And why suppose that any such belief can be trusted? One reason might be that *each of us has a uniquely reliable way of identifying him or herself*—this is something we can do successfully no matter how much change we undergo. Even if I awake tomorrow in the body of a gigantic insect, I will recognize that what awakes is still *me*—I only need to close my eyes, fix my attention on myself, and say "Here am *I*, and no one else." I will surely be right about *who* I find.

But, the argument continues, our ability to re-identify *ourselves* at different times requires that we persist—that *we continue the same*—between those different times. And our ability to reliably re-identify ourselves shows that we somehow *recognize ourselves* as the same persons, despite any changes in our bodies or in our thoughts and feelings. In short, our ability to re-identify ourselves successfully, which we do whenever we say or think, "Here *I* am," justifies our belief that *we* persist unchanged through the physical and psychological flux. What does my "I" refer to, if not my *self*? I suspect that ideas like these are the source of Reid's "natural conviction . . . that every man has of his own identity and continued existence."

Twentieth century British philosopher **Gilbert Ryle** (1900–1976) reacts to this line of thought as follows:

Gilbert Ryle: Twentieth century British philosopher whose influential 1949 book *The Concept of Mind* gave rise to the important subdiscipline now referred to as the philosophy of mind.

> 'I', in my use of it, always indicates me and only indicates me. 'You', 'she', and 'they' indicate different people at different times. 'I' is like my own shadow; I can never get away from it, as I can get away from your shadow. There is no mystery about this constancy, but I mention it because it seems to endow 'I' with a mystifying uniqueness and adhesiveness. 'Now' has something of the same besetting feeling.[5]

Ryle's tongue-in-cheek observation about the "adhesiveness" of the pronoun *I* is a response to the idea that we successfully re-identify ourselves, and so we *somehow* recognize ourselves despite the changes we undergo.

To see Ryle's point, we should follow his suggestion that we compare the adhesiveness of *I* to the adhesiveness of *now*—or, better, *here*. To do so, think of *here* as the name of a place, just as we use *Halifax* and *San Francisco* to refer to particular places. Of course, the location *here* is always the place we happen to be, but if *here* names a place, then it

[4] Reid, T. (1969). *Essays on the Intellectual Powers of Man*. Cambridge, Mass.: MIT Press, 343.

[5] Ryle, G. (1949). *The Concept of Mind*. Penguin Classics, London, 189.

will be a mysterious place. *Here* is a place stuck to the bottom of our shoes, from which we cannot escape. No matter how far we travel, it follows us like our shadow, and wherever we stop we will still be *here*. Similarly, *now* is a time that never seems to pass—no matter how long we wait it will still be *now*. Like *I*, *here* and *now* follow us everywhere.

Ryle's point is that the apparent adhesiveness of *here*, *now*, and *I* derives from our erroneous decision to think of those terms as working like names. If they operate like names, then we must first recognize the places, times, or persons to which they refer before we can successfully apply them. But the correct applications of *here*, *now*, and *I* do not require us to recognize the places, times, or selves to which we apply them. If I awoke one morning in a completely unfamiliar environment, I would not think that I *recognize* my location just because I know "I am *here*." And when a gigantic insect awakens in my bed and thinks (correctly), "It is *me*," that does not require that the insect recognize *who* it is. "It is *me* (or *I*)" is true even if it is a different person who thinks it each time. If Ryle's point is right, then the impression that we correctly re-identify ourselves from one occasion to another, as that impression is fostered by our use of the pronoun *I*, is a mirage, and it does not support Reid's conviction that "the thinking being has a continued existence."

Hume's Diagnosis: Identity and Succession

If we can set aside Reid's "natural conviction" or "invincible belief" that the self has a continuous existence, then we are in a better position to appreciate the force of Hume's own diagnosis of the idea that there is an enduring self behind the flux of mental states we observe. Hume's diagnosis is that we have a natural propension—that is, a propensity or tendency—to confuse two things that, in moments of reflection, we know are actually very different from one another. The two things we regularly confuse are these:

1. "Several different objects existing in succession and connected together by a close relation."
2. "An object that remains invariable and uninterrupted through a . . . variation of time."[6]

Sometimes, when confronted by something of the first kind, "the relation [between the successive objects] facilitates the transition of the mind from one . . . to another, and renders its passage smooth as if it contemplated one continued object." So when the mind makes a smooth transition along any sequence of distinct but closely related objects, we have a natural tendency to *mistake* the sequence of related objects for the persistence of a single object. Motion pictures work just that way: We are exposed to a rapid succession of still photos of an object—a stream of discrete snapshots. But the illusion Hume describes takes hold, and where there is only a succession of still photos we seem to see a single picture of an object in smooth, unbroken motion.

This mistake, to which Hume thinks our psychology makes us naturally prone, is repeated whenever we look into the flux of our own minds and observe only a succession of rapidly passing thoughts, feelings, and sensations. The propensity is so powerful that,

[6] Hume, D. (1739). A *Treatise of Human Nature*. Book 1, Part 4, Section 6. Retrieved July 29, 2014, from http://www.gutenberg.org/files/4705/4705-h/4705-h.htm

"though we incessantly correct ourselves by reflection," we continue to make the mistake. And then, as Hume says,

> . . . Our last resource is to yield to it, and boldly assert that these different related objects are in effect the same, however interrupted and variable. In order to justify to ourselves this absurdity, we often feign some new and unintelligible principle, that connects the objects together . . . and run into the notion of a soul, and self, and substance, to disguise the variation.[7]

That mysterious, unchanging entity—what Hume calls an "unintelligible principle" and, later, an "imaginary principle of union"—is a *fiction* to which the confusion of (1) and (2) gives rise. That "unintelligible" and "imaginary principle" is the source of a belief in metaphysical unity—the featureless self, or the unitary overarching consciousness that Reid and Locke thought belonged to persons. Hume appears to think, then, that there is nothing—no metaphysical principle—in virtue of which we are the same persons for the duration of our lives.

Hume's Theory of the Self

After criticizing the conception of an enduring self to which many of his contemporaries subscribed, and after diagnosing the error he believes led his contemporaries to think there was any such thing, Hume offers his own account of the self: "[M]ankind . . . are nothing but a **bundle** or collection of different perceptions, which succeed each other with an inconceivable rapidity, and are in perpetual flux and movement."[8] Elsewhere, he writes that "They are the successive perceptions only, that constitute the mind"; "It is the composition of these [perceptions], therefore, which forms the self"; and "These [perceptions] therefore must be the same with self."[9] In short, a "self" is only a collection of disparate things, bundled together in our thinking because they exist "in succession, and [are] connected together by a close relation." An analogy will help make Hume's idea clear.

bundle theory of the self: A metaphysically reductionist theory of selves or persons attributed to David Hume. It identifies selves with collections ("bundles") of psychological characteristics that change their constituents over time. On this view, selves are *analogous* to teams or nations.

Suppose you remain a lifelong fan of a particular baseball team, the famous Mudville Nine. At different times the team consists of different players, coaches, and owners. Since you first became a fan, some players have been traded; some retired from the sport; one became a manager; another left after the team moved to its new stadium and before it was sold to new owners. The changes have all been gradual, and over any two adjacent seasons there has been significant overlap in personnel—indeed, only an observant fan would notice many of the changes from one season to the next. But over the many years during which you have been a fan of the Mudville Nine, nothing has remained the same—nothing essential and unchanged constitutes the team.

On Hume's view a person is not one unified or indivisible thing, but a collection of disparate things, much like a team. We thus resemble "a republic or commonwealth, in

[7] Hume, D. (1739). *A Treatise of Human Nature*. Book 1, Part 4, Section 6. Retrieved July 29, 2014, from http://www.gutenberg.org/files/4705/4705-h/4705-h.htm

[8] Hume, D. (1739). *A Treatise of Human Nature*. Book 1, Part 4, Section 6. Retrieved July 29, 2014, from http://www.gutenberg.org/files/4705/4705-h/4705-h.htm

[9] Hume, D. (1739). *A Treatise of Human Nature*. Book 1, Part 4, Section 6. Retrieved July 29, 2014, from http://www.gutenberg.org/files/4705/4705-h/4705-h.htm

which the several members are united by the reciprocal ties of government and subordination," and which "may not only change its members, but also its laws and constitutions." In this way, Hume says, "the same person may vary his character and disposition, as well as his impressions and ideas, without losing his identity."[10] What "identity" is Hume referring to here? What makes the Mudville Nine I once followed as a child the *same* team I follow as an adult?

Because Hume thinks the self we described earlier is a mere "fiction," it is tempting to think that he does not believe there are any selves at all, but things are not as clear as we might like. It will be easier to understand Hume's view if we first distinguish among several metaphysical positions.

Three Metaphysical Postures

Setting selves aside for a moment, imagine three metaphysicians arguing about whether *pairs of socks* exist. Their argument is not about whether matching left and right socks exist—all three metaphysicians agree that *those things* exist. The argument is about whether, *in addition to those two socks*, there also exist pairs of socks. There are three distinct positions possible:

Metaphysical Realism Pairs of socks exist—they are real. But pairs of socks cannot be reduced to the matching left and right socks that comprise them. So if I have a pair of socks, then I really have *three* things: (i) a left sock, (ii) a matching right sock, and (iii) a pair of socks.

Metaphysical Reductionism Pairs of socks exist—they are real. But a pair of socks is *nothing in addition* to a left sock and a matching right sock. Instead of saying we have three things when we have a pair of socks, we should say that (i) and (ii) *constitute* the pair of socks—or, alternatively, that the pair of socks *reduces*, without any remainder, *to* the two matching socks.

Metaphysical Eliminativism Pairs of socks do not exist. Only left socks and (matching) right socks really exist. Clearly, the left sock is not a pair of socks; and obviously the right sock is not a pair of socks. So, if the left sock and the right sock are all that exists, and neither of those is a pair of socks, then pairs of socks do not exist—they are mere "fictions."

It is important to see that there are *two* alternatives to the metaphysical realist position. Although the reductionist and the realist agree that pairs of socks exist, the eliminativist and the reductionist both dismiss the realist idea that something more than left and right socks exists. Reductionists seek a middle ground. They want to say that pairs exist, but also that pairs—*as they are conceived by the realist*—do not exist.

realism: A metaphysical view about a class of disputed entities (e.g., selves, minds, values, etc.) according to which such entities are both real and not reducible to entities of another kind.

eliminativism: A metaphysical view about a class of disputed entities according to which the entities do not exist—whether or not we know it, all our talk about the entities is fiction.

There are also three parallel metaphysical options for thinking about selves. According to **realism**, our selves exist, and they are something in addition to the psychological features that make us up. This is the perspective taken by Plato and Reid. According to **eliminativism**, there is no such thing as the self—it is a mere fiction, an illusion generated by our natural tendency to mistake a succession of fleeting things for a single enduring entity. According to

[10] Hume, D. (1739). A *Treatise of Human Nature*. Book 1, Part 4, Section 6. Retrieved July 29, 2014, from http://www.gutenberg.org/files/4705/4705-h/4705-h.htm

reductionism, selves do exist, but they are *nothing in addition* to our successive psychological constituents. A self reduces to, or consists in, a bundle or collection of related and successive psychological states. And so a self is very much like a sports team or, to use Hume's analogy, like a nation. They really do exist, but they are nothing in addition to the fleeting thoughts, feelings, and sensations we are aware of when we turn our gaze inward.

reductionism: A metaphysical view about a class of disputed entities according to which such entities are real, but they are reducible to (constituted by) entities of another kind. A reductive theory provides *generalizations* identifying entities of one kind with entities of another kind (e.g., "All lightening is atmospheric electrical discharge").

Are Verbal Disputes Idle?

Our three metaphysical postures provide a framework within which to understand Hume. When he speaks out against the realist conception of the self, Hume says it is only a fiction—selves *as conceived by the realist* do not exist. When he talks this way he sounds much like an eliminativist about selves. But when he describes persons as *bundles of psychological states*, he sounds much like a reductionist: Selves are real after all, but they are nothing more than a collection of successive stages and parts. Such "bundles" persist, even though all their parts change, *in the same way* that a sports team—or "republic or commonwealth"—stays the same, although its players, managers, owners, and fans change.

But *what way* is that? In *what way* are teams and persons actually the same? Once we remove any underlying "principle" of metaphysical unity of the sort Locke and Reid believed in, persons can easily start to look like a rough assemblage of bits and pieces, whose lives are connected from one moment to another *by nothing real*. Perhaps that is how Hume sees matters in some of his moods:

> The whole of this doctrine leads us to a conclusion, which is of great importance in the present affair, viz. that all the nice and subtle questions concerning personal identity can never possibly be decided, and are to be regarded rather as grammatical than as philosophical difficulties. . . . [W]e have no just standard, by which we can decide any dispute concerning the time, when they acquire or lose a title to the name of identity. All the disputes concerning the identity of connected objects are merely verbal. . . .[11]

Hume's proposal is that we should see disputes about identity over time and through change as "merely verbal" rather than as substantive metaphysical disputes. That is, whether I am *the same person* my mother gave birth to many years ago is not a matter that can be settled on the basis of any facts about persons. There are grounds for saying I am the same person, and also grounds for saying I am not the same person, but there is nothing—"no just standard," as Hume says—in light of which to settle the question whether my infant and adult selves are the "same" person.

Hume would likely think we should feel the same way about whether Theseus and his crew reached their destination on the same ship on which they began their voyage: There is no fact of the matter here. Recall that Reid also says that identity "has no fixed nature when applied to bodies; and questions about the identity of a body are very often questions about words."[12] So concerning the identity of a ship over time, Hume and Reid are in agreement, but while Reid thinks disputes about the identity of *persons* are genuine and not verbal, Hume sees no reason to exempt persons from the problems that beset change and identity elsewhere.

---

[11] Hume, D. (1739). A *Treatise of Human Nature*. Book 1, Part 4, Section 6. Retrieved July 29, 2014, from http://www.gutenberg.org/files/4705/4705-h/4705-h.htm

[12] From Reid, T. (1969). *Essays on the Intellectual Powers of Man*. Cambridge, Mass.: MIT Press, 25.

A conclusion this dramatic should be accompanied by words of caution. First, Hume's claim seems to be that disputes about personal identity are often only *verbal*. This means that when we are deciding whether we are the same persons after suffering traumatic accidents, or the same persons for the duration of our ordinary uninterrupted lives, there are no prior facts that would settle the issue. So we must *decide* what to say without the help of any deep metaphysical principle. This is not because some important facts or principles are *hidden* from us—on Hume's view the facts about our selves parade before the mind's eye and nothing relevant is hidden. His conclusion is not that we don't *know* some important fact that might resolve things. We know all the facts that matter, and they still don't settle our disputes about personal identity.

Second, we need to note that saying a dispute is only verbal does not entitle us to conclude that it is *arbitrary* what we should say, or that any decision about what to say is as good as any another. Nor is it the same as saying that disputes about identity are not genuine or important. If Hume's arguments are successful, all he can conclude is that our disputes about identity—our decisions about what to say in various difficult cases—are not to be settled in light of any underlying metaphysical principles. But there might still be *other considerations* in light of which those disputes can be resolved, and in light of which a "jostling crowd of 'I's" will qualify—or fail to qualify—as one and the same person.

In the final section of this chapter, we consider one account of what those other considerations might be. Before doing so, we turn to a similarly radical view about personal identity, this time from a more contemporary philosopher.

DEREK PARFIT ON BRAIN FISSION

Derek Parfit: A contemporary British philosopher best known for important work on the problem of personal identity and the relevance of personal identity to ethics.

Contemporary British philosopher **Derek Parfit** (1942–) also defends a deeply radical perspective on personal identity. Despite some broad resemblances between their final results, Hume and Parfit arrive at different forms of skepticism about personal identity, and they do so by travelling along very different roads. We first look at Parfit's ideas about troublesome cases for personal identity, and then discuss his own view.

What Happens to Me? (Derek Parfit, 1971)[13]

My targets are two beliefs: one about the nature of personal identity, the other about its importance.

The first is that in these cases the question about identity must have an answer.

No one thinks this about, say, nations or machines. Our criteria for the identity of these do not cover certain cases. No one thinks that in these cases the questions "Is it the same nation?" or "Is it the same machine?" must have answers.

Some people believe that in this respect they are different. They agree that our criteria of personal identity do not cover certain cases, but they believe that the nature of their own identity through time is, somehow, such as to guarantee that in these cases questions about their identity must have answers. This belief might be expressed as follows: "Whatever happens between now and any future time, either I shall still exist, or I shall not. Any future experience will either be *my* experience, or it will not.

[13] Philosophical Review, Vol. 80, No. 1 (Jan. 1971) pp. 3–27, and is presently published by Duke University Press. Used by permission.

. . . [O]ne cause of our concern is the belief which is my second target. This is that unless the question about identity has an answer, we cannot answer certain important questions (questions about such matters as survival, memory, and responsibility).

Against this second belief my claim will be this. Certain important questions do presuppose a question about personal identity. But they can be freed of this presupposition. And when they are, the question about identity has no importance.

I

We can start by considering the much-discussed case of the man who, like an amoeba, divides.

Wiggins has recently dramatized this case.[14] He first referred to the operation imagined by Shoemaker.[15] We suppose that my brain is transplanted into someone else's (brainless) body, and that the resulting person has my character and apparent memories of my life. Most of us would agree, after thought, that the resulting person is me. I shall here assume such agreement.

Wiggins then imagined his own operation. My brain is divided, and each half is housed in a new body. Both resulting people have my character and apparent memories of my life.

What happens to me? There seem only three possibilities: (1) I do not survive; (2) I survive as one of the two people; (3) I survive as both.

The trouble with (1) is this. We agreed that I could survive if my brain were successfully transplanted. And people have in fact survived with half their brains destroyed. It seems to follow that I could survive if half my brain were successfully transplanted and the other half were destroyed. But if this is so, how could I *not* survive if the other half were also successfully transplanted? How could a double success be a failure?

We can move to the second description. Perhaps one success is the maximum score. Perhaps I shall be one of the resulting people.

The trouble here is that in Wiggins' case each half of my brain is exactly similar, and so, to start with, is each resulting person. So how can I survive as only one of the two people? What can make me one of them rather than the other?

It seems clear that both of these descriptions—that I do not survive, and that I survive as one of the people—are highly implausible. Those who have accepted them must have assumed that they were the only possible descriptions.

What about our third description: that I survive as both people?

It might be said, "If 'survive' implies identity, this description makes no sense—you cannot be two people. If it does not, the description is irrelevant to a problem about identity."

. . . The alternative, for which I shall argue, is to give up the language of identity. We can suggest that I survive as two different people without implying that I am these people.

When I first mentioned this alternative, I mentioned this objection: "If your new way of talking does not imply identity, it cannot solve our problem. For that is about identity. The problem is that all the possible answers to the question about identity are highly implausible."

We can now answer this objection.

---

[14] Wiggins, D. (1967). *Identity and Spatio-Temporal Continuity*. Oxford, 50.

[15] Shoemaker, S. (1963). *Self-Knowledge and Self-Identity*. Ithica, NY, 22.

We can start by reminding ourselves that this is an objection only if we have one or both of the beliefs which I mentioned at the start of this paper.

The first was the belief that to any question about personal identity, in any describable case, there must be a true answer. For those with this belief, Wiggins' case is doubly perplexing. If all the possible answers are implausible, it is hard to decide which of them is true, and hard even to keep the belief that one of them must be true. If we give up this belief, as I think we should, these problems disappear. We shall then regard the case as like many others in which, for quite unpuzzling reasons, there *is* no answer to a question about identity. (Consider: "Was England the same nation after 1066?")

. . . My first conclusion, then, is this. The relation of the original person to each of the resulting people contains all that interests us—all that matters—in any ordinary case of survival. This is why we need a sense in which a person can survive as two. . . .

II

Identity is a one-one relation. Wiggins' case serves to show that what matters in survival need not be one-one.

Wiggins' case is of course unlikely to occur. The relations which matter are, in fact, one-one. It is because they are that we can imply the holding of these relations by using the language of identity.

The use of this language is convenient. But it can lead us astray. We may assume that what matters *is* identity and, hence, has the properties of identity.

In the case of the property of being one-one, this mistake is not serious. For what matters is in fact one-one. But in the case of another property, the mistake *is* serious. Identity is all-or-nothing. Most of the relations which matter in survival are, in fact, relations of degree. If we ignore this, we shall be led into quite ill-grounded attitudes and beliefs.

. . . To turn to a recent debate: most of the relations which matter can be provisionally referred to under the heading "psychological continuity" (which includes causal continuity). My claim is thus that we use the language of personal identity in order to imply such continuity. This is close to the view that psychological continuity provides a criterion of identity.

Williams has attacked this view with the following argument. Identity is a one-one relation. So any criterion of identity must appeal to a relation which is logically one-one. Psychological continuity is not logically one-one. So it cannot provide a criterion.[16]

. . . I suggest a slightly different reply. Psychological continuity is a ground for speaking of identity when it is one-one.

If psychological continuity took a one-many or branching form, we should need, I have argued, to abandon the language of identity. . . .

V

. . . This revised way of thinking . . . is also the way in which we ourselves could think about our lives. And it is, I suggest, surprisingly natural.

One of its features, the distinction between successive selves, has already been used by several writers. To give an example from Proust: "we are incapable, while we

[16] Williams, B. (1956–57). Personal Identity and Individuation. *Proceedings of the Aristotelian Society, LVII*, 229–253; also (1960–61). *Analysis, 21*, 43–48.

are in love, of acting as fit predecessors of the next persons who, when we are in love no longer, we shall presently become. . . . "*[17]

Although Proust distinguished between successive selves, he still thought of one person as being these different selves. This would not do on the way of thinking that I propose. If I say, "It will not be me, but one of my future selves," I do not imply that I will be that future self. He is one of my later selves, and I am one of his earlier selves. There is no underlying person who we both are.

We will only be able to scratch the surface of Parfit's curious and novel views about personal identity and person survival. At the heart of his account is a view about the relationship between identity and continuity, which we will describe first. We will then provide a brief summary of his central example and the lesson he thinks we should draw.

Identity vs. Continuity

When changes in an object are sufficiently small and gradual, the resulting object is *continuous* with the original object. This means that the overlap between the two—the aspects in which there is no change at all—overwhelms in degree and importance the differences between the two. One proposal, which we saw in our discussion of Theseus's ship, was that *continuity* between an object at one time and an object at another time might be enough to make them earlier and later stages of *the same* object—that is, that continuity might be all we need for identity over time.

Twentieth-century Austrian philosopher Ludwig Wittgenstein offers a nice metaphor for the idea of continuity:

> ... [I]n spinning a thread we twist fibre on fibre. And the strength of the thread does not reside in the fact that some one fibre runs through its whole length, but in the overlapping of many fibres."[18]

physical continuity: Two things are said to be *physically continuous* with one another when there is only insignificant physical change from one to the other. In other words, there is substantial overlap in the physical material and physical characteristics of the two things at any two adjacent moments.

psychological continuity: Two persons—or one person at two times—are said to be *psychologically continuous* when there is only insignificant psychological change from one to the other. In other words, there is substantial overlap in the psychological characteristics of the two persons or the two stages of one person.

In Wittgenstein's image we see what continuity amounts to: the overlapping of many fibres. In the case of persons, who undergo both physical and psychological changes over the span of their lives, there are two kinds of "fibres" that bind together their earlier and later stages. First, for most people, there is strong **physical continuity**. The cells that compose a person are replaced very gradually, so that, even though all her matter is replaced over a span of seven years, a person consists of almost the same matter, in the same arrangements, from one day to the next. Occasionally, as a result of a traumatic accident, physical continuity can be disrupted or broken, and a person on one day might have significant physical differences from herself on the previous day. There is also strong **psychological continuity** between our earlier and later selves. Most of my current mental states—my beliefs and desires, for example—are the same ones I had yesterday, even if no beliefs and desires survive from my infancy. Psychological continuity can also be disrupted when persons undergo trauma or suffer brain damage, but for most of us the daily psychological changes are relatively small. So we are linked to our past selves by numerous

[17] Proust, M. (1949). *Within a Budding Grove*. London. I–226.

[18] Wittgenstein, L. (1953). *Philosophical Investigations*. (G. E. M. Anscombe, Trans.) The MacMillan Company. Remark §69.

overlapping fibres—both physical and psychological—even if, contrary to Reid's thought, no one fibre runs the entire length of our lives.

Parfit, like most people, thinks that *psychological* continuity with some future person is what we most desire when we desire to survive into the future. Moreover, if we have enough psychological continuity with some past person, then however much she differs physically from us, we will think of that person as our earlier self. Most people will agree with Parfit that if my brain were successfully transplanted into another person's brainless body, so that the resulting person remembered my past and had my personality, then the resulting person would be me and not the person to whom the body originally belonged. Despite this fact, Parfit does not believe that psychological or physical continuity is always enough to ensure identity. That is, although the person after a brain transplant is psychologically continuous with me and also *is* me, the continuity between us is not by itself what makes that person me. To understand why, let us consider how continuity and identity differ.

We should note that, like identity, continuity appears to be *transitive*. If A is continuous with B, and B is continuous with C, then A is continuous with C. (We will leave open here the problem about what to say when we have a long chain of items related by continuity. Even though there is continuity between adjacent links in the chain, there is *no overlap* between two links that are sufficiently remote from one another.)

Continuity, unlike identity, is *a matter of degree*. The continuity one object has with a second thing can be greater than the continuity it has with a third thing—the number of overlapping fibres involved can vary, making one thread or one segment of a thread stronger than another. But identity is *all-or-nothing* and it does not come in degrees. Either A is numerically identical with B or it is not, and it cannot be more numerically identical with B than it is with C.

Finally, numerical identity is always what Parfit calls a *one-one* relation. That is, if A = B, and A = C, then B = C. An object cannot be identical with *two things* that are not identical with each other. But continuity is not always a one-one relation—sometimes it is a *one-many* relation. This means it is possible for B and C to both be continuous with A, even though A and B are not identical to each other. We see this in cases of reproduction by fission. An amoeba reproduces by splitting into two amoebae, both of which are *continuous* with the parent amoeba. But since the offspring are *two* amoebae, they cannot be the same *one*—they are not numerically identical. Parfit's central example in his discussion of personal identity is very like the amoeba: An imaginary (but possible) surgery results in two persons who are psychologically continuous with one person but, because they are *two*, are not numerically identical.

Brain Fission

Parfit's argument, which turns on our response to a case of *brain fission*, is best understood by reflecting on three simpler cases. First, consider a brain transplant: If my brain is transplanted into another person's body (suppose it is a woman's body), will the resulting person be me, or will it be that other person? That is, will the result be *me with a new body*, or will the result be *her with a new brain*? Parfit shares the intuitions of almost every science fiction writer when he maintains that the result will still be me, but with a new body. Perhaps the reason is obvious: Along with my brain go all my psychological characteristics, so the "woman" who remains after the brain transplant will have my personality, memories, thoughts, feelings, and desires. Even if we hesitate to say that the resulting woman is *me*, we must at least admit that she is psychologically continuous with me. The resulting person will not be the same man as me, since she will not be a man, but if she is the same person as me, it will be because she has my memories and other psychological traits.

Second, there are cases of people surviving the destruction of substantial parts of their brains, including the loss of up to half the brain, without suffering significant psychological deficits. When we reflect on someone who has survived the destruction or removal of half of her brain, but who has the original person's memories and personality, we should recognize the remaining person as the original person.

Third, consider what happens when someone who has survived the loss of half her brain then has the remaining half transplanted into another person's brainless body. If we agree that the loss of half the brain leaves us with the same person, and also that brain transplants result in the person whose brain it is, then it seems to follow that the result of transplanting half a brain will be the person whose half-brain it originally was.

Now we are in a position to consider a case of a person undergoing **brain fission**. Suppose half of your brain is transplanted into the brainless head of another body. The other half of your brain is not destroyed but is transplanted into the brainless head of a second body. The two resulting persons will both be psychologically continuous with you—both seem to remember what you did before the surgery, and both have your distinctive pattern of beliefs and preferences. Parfit's question is this: If I am the person whose brain is divided between two different bodies, then what happens to *me* after the procedure? There are only three possible answers:

brain fission: A hypothetical procedure, usually involving the division and transplant of a subject's brain, that results in two recipients, both of whom are psychologically continuous with the original donor. Brain-fission is widely thought to demonstrate that psychological continuity is not sufficient for personal identity.

1. I am *both* of the resulting people.
2. I am *only one* of the resulting people.
3. I am *neither* of the resulting people.

Parfit thinks none of these answers can be right. In summary, his argument is this: *Both* of the resulting people can't be me, since that would mean that they are the same person as each other. But *two* people can't be *one* and the same person. Identity, as we saw, is a one-one relationship, but the relationship between the original (prefission) person and the two resulting persons is a one-many relationship. Furthermore, I can't be *only one* of the resulting people, since each of them has exactly the same relationship to me, and so each has the same claim to be me. It would be completely arbitrary to say that I was one of the resulting people but not the other. Finally, I can't be *neither* of the resulting people, since that would mean I didn't survive the operation. But it seems clear that I did survive. If only one of the two half-brain recipients survives the operation, then that person would be me, since this would simply be the third case we considered earlier. And the fact that another person survives her transplant operation cannot prevent me from surviving my transplant operation. To see this point clearly, imagine that one of the two recipients awakens from surgery before the other. He sits up, engages cheerfully in conversation, and he claims to be me—after all, he has my memories, my personality, my beliefs and desires. It makes no sense to say to him, "If the other person never wakes up then you will have successfully survived the operation; but if he does wake up, I'm sorry to inform you that you haven't survived." If Parfit's reflections on these answers are correct, then none of the answers to "What happens to me?" can be right. But there are no other possible answers.

Although this outcome may seem unpalatable, Parfit thinks there is nothing puzzling about it. We understand exactly why we get this result and why none of the answers are adequate. To make the result palatable, we need to do two things. We must give up our assumption that the question "What happens to me?" has, in every case, an answer. The question about whether some earlier person is numerically identical with some later person may not always be a good question to ask. Parfit believes that we are already content to think this way about other things—for example, about nations or about sports teams. In England, the people, the commerce, the government, the economy, the laws, the language, and much else have all changed beyond recognition in the 500 years that have passed since the reign of Henry VIII. But is it *the same nation*? Parfit thinks we are not troubled by the fact that we can't decisively answer this question. Whether we say it is the same nation seems only a verbal matter—a decision about what to say when the facts themselves leave the matter open. So Parfit's first suggestion is that we see the decision about whether to say some future person is numerically identical with us in the same way.

Second, we must separate questions about whether we *survive* the operation from questions about whether someone who exists after the operation is *numerically identical* with us. Parfit suggests that our future survival requires only that someone exist in the future who is *psychologically continuous* with us; it does not require that someone exist in the future who is *numerically identical* with us. I will naturally say that some future person who is continuous with me *is me*, and that will be harmless so long as there is only one future person who is continuous with me. But if there is more than one future person who is continuous with me, then although I will have survived into the future, no one who exists in the future will *be me*. So we should stop thinking that it matters for our survival whether someone in the future is really numerically identical with us.

We thus find Parfit much in agreement with Diotima when, at the end of his essay, he describes a future person who is continuous with himself: "He is one of my later selves, and I am one of his earlier selves. There is no underlying person who we both are."[19] Although there is no future person who is us, there are many selves—a jostling crowd of them—in a queue that stretches back to our birth and reaches forward into the future. Each of us is, right now, just one self in such a crowd. We are psychologically continuous with our younger selves, but we are not them.[20]

RELATIONAL SELVES

David Hume and Derek Parfit reject the idea that there is some criterion of personal identity, some metaphysical principle of the sort Locke and Reid sought, in light of which there is always a good answer to the question whether an earlier person is the same as some later person. Both recognize that we are comfortable thinking this way about the

[19] Parfit, D. (1971). Personal Identity. *Philosophical Review*, 80, 24.

[20] Partfit's view that there is "no underlying person" and Hume's view that there is no underlying self are sometimes described as versions of the "no-self" or "no-mind" doctrine found in Buddhism. Parfit encourages the comparison when he writes, "Buddha would have agreed" in *Reasons and Persons* (Oxford University Press, 1986, p. 273). But the comparison has been challenged by scholars who reject the eliminativist interpretation of Buddhist theories of the self. In accord with the Buddha's doctrine of the Middle Way, the individual self or soul is to be identified with a continuous but always changing *stream* (*sanatana*) of mental events. That is a reductionist theory and not an eliminativist one. But as reductionist advocates of the bundle theory, Hume and Parfit would have agreed.

identity of nations or teams. But what view about selves or persons could help us to think this way about ourselves? What view of persons could make us comfortable with the thought that *there is not always a fact of the matter* about whether we are the same person as some earlier or later person? The arguments of Hume and Parfit threaten to leave us with only skepticism about the very idea of persons. But it helps to note that their skeptical arguments only target *metaphysical conceptions* of what persons are. One way to escape the skepticism is to see whether other, non-metaphysical ways of thinking about persons are possible. In this section we describe a contemporary theory about the nature of persons that does not require any underlying or overarching metaphysical principles.

Perhaps we have already glimpsed a non-metaphysical view of persons that would make this way of thinking easier. Recall John Locke's suggestion that our concept of a person is a *forensic* concept. Many of the theories we have encountered so far are metaphysical theories of persons in that they conceive of persons as human animals with a special component or ingredient added—an extra ingredient that distinguishes us from animals, machines, or nations. Plato adds to the human animal a soul, and Reid adds a self. But on the forensic conception of persons it is not the addition of any new ingredient that makes a person out of an animal. Persons are human animals that have been assigned *a special status*—the status of bearers of rights and responsibilities. This makes the forensic concept of a person a first step in the direction of a perspective on selves and persons that has come to dominate contemporary feminist philosophy—*the relational theory of the self*.

American feminist philosopher **Annette Baier** (1929–2012) writes that

Annette Baier: An American philosopher, famous for her work in moral psychology and her re-interpretations of Hume. In numerous writings Baier developed and defended a relational theory of persons.

> The term "person" is a status term, and it is *our* term. It is we who have to decide what that status is, and whether we give it to a human fetus, to other animals, to corporations. . . . Sometimes one wishes we could just drop the term, so heavily freighted is it with its theological past and with current controversies. But words are hard to kill. The only realistic strategy is to make do with the old concept, heavily burdened though it is.[21]

When seen from the perspective of metaphysical questions about change and identity, the old idea of the "self" appears to have crumbled under pressure from Hume and Parfit. As Baier says, on the view that *person* is a status term, *we get to decide* what is or is not a person, but our decision is a moral or political one and there is nothing in metaphysics to settle these matters. As Baier hints in this passage, many feminist philosophers have tried to *reconstruct* a new idea of persons or selves. Rather than resuscitate a metaphysical conception, they seek to offer a non-metaphysical, *political conception* of what persons are.

relational theory of persons (or selves): Theory of the self that maintains that our status as persons, as well as the central features required to qualify as selves or persons, are owed to our relations with other persons. Persons are distinguished from non-persons not by any special metaphysical ingredient or special capabilities we might have independent of social settings, but by the social (including moral and political) relations in which they are embedded.

It is only a short distance from the forensic conception of personhood as a status to a relational conception of persons. The moral and legal status that constitutes us as persons on the forensic view is a status we cannot have unless we are embedded in legal and moral practices and institutions and, therefore, in a complex set of *relations with other persons*. According to the **relational theory of persons (or selves)**, we acquire the status of persons from the many and various relations we have to and with other persons, and persons are distinguished from non-persons by the social relations in which they are embedded. A useful analogy might be that an everyday object becomes transformed into a *gift* not by having any

[21] Baier, A. C. (1995). A Naturalist View of Persons. *Moral Prejudice: Essays on Ethics*. Cambridge, Mass.: Harvard University Press, 324.

additional ingredient added, but by being given a particular role in human relationships, practices, and transactions. *Gift*, like *person*, is a social identity, not a metaphysical one.

Relational theories of persons claim that we cannot qualify for the status of persons unless we are embedded in relations with others, but relational theories generally go even further. Note that Locke's view of persons combines metaphysical and relational views of persons: To be a person is to be something that has legal and moral standing, but human animals only qualify for legal and moral status because they have the extra psychological ingredient of consciousness. Consciousness is then understood as an extra metaphysical ingredient that, when added to what would otherwise be mere animals, results in selves or persons. The possession of consciousness is what enables animals to qualify for personhood. So Locke's forensic theory of persons resembles relational theories in making personhood a *status term*, but it also resembles metaphysical theories of persons in so far as it ties our status as persons to the possession of the *extra ingredient* of consciousness. Other theories that count personhood as a status sometimes link that status to possession of other traits—they will say that personhood requires the ability to use language, or rationality, or self-consciousness. If such traits are required to qualify as persons, and these traits are themselves extra metaphysical ingredients added to the human animal, then the relational conception of persons already depends on some prior metaphysical conception of persons. However, this consequence can be avoided, and we can have a purely relational theory, if we do not need to view the traits required to qualify for the status of personhood as extra ingredients needed to make persons out of animals.

Baier argues that the traits needed to acquire the status of persons are themselves *essentially social acquisitions*. That is, they could not be acquired except with and from other persons. Language, rationality, and self-consciousness are, as she says, the "essential arts of personhood." They are the distinctive tools and skills needed to be persons, and they depend on other persons for their existence. On Baier's view, the traits needed to qualify as persons are themselves possible only in social settings: Language is an essentially social art, and rationality is not an innate capacity but the outcome of socially cultivated ways of conducting ourselves in conversations, negotiations, and arguments. Even self-consciousness (of the sort needed to qualify as a person) depends, according to Baier, on our awareness of the awareness that others have of us.[22] As she puts the more general point, "A person, perhaps, is best seen as one who was long enough dependent upon other persons to acquire the essential arts of personhood. Persons essentially are second persons, who grow up with other persons."[23] If she is right, then the relational theory of persons does not *need* to rest on any prior metaphysical theory of persons or selves. On Baier's view, the traits needed to qualify for the moral and legal status of persons are not "extra" ingredients that, when mixed in, elevate the human animal into personhood. They are themselves social arts acquired by being successfully embedded in the very human relationships and practices that constitute us as persons. So it appears that there will be no quick and easy way to make relational theories dependent on any prior metaphysical view of persons.

---

[22] On the social nature of reason and rationality, see Lecture I: Reason, in Baier, A. C. (1997). *The Commons of the Mind: The Paul Carus Lectures*. Chicago: Open Court Publishing Co., 1–19. On the social nature of self-consciousness, see Cartesian Persons, in Baier, A. C. (1985). *Postures of the Mind: Essays on Mind and Morals*. Minneapolis: University of Minnesota Press, 74–92.

[23] Baier, A. C. (1985). Cartesian Persons. *Postures of the Mind: Essays on Mind and Morals*. Minneapolis: University of Minnesota Press, 84.

The metaphysical self described by Plato, Reid, and Locke exists independent of any social or political setting, and so it has no gender, class, or race. Those things are all optional; they are paraphernalia we accumulate during a life in society with others, but they are not any essential part of what it is to be persons. In contrast, the relational theory of persons has the consequence that we could not be the particular persons we are apart from the relationships in which we each are or have been embedded. The relational perspective is one from which

> . . . persons are socially embedded and . . . agents' identities are formed within the context of social relationships and shaped by a complex of intersecting social determinants, such as race, class, gender, and ethnicity.[24]

From this perspective, the metaphysical self of Plato and Reid looks like an abstraction, remote and detached from the details that constitute us as the persons we are and that are central to our self-understandings. The metaphysical self is, as we saw earlier, completely featureless. We now see that this also means that our social contexts and social determinants (gender, race, and so on) are no essential part of what we are. Thus the issues of most concern to feminist thinkers tend to disappear from view when our relations with others are made only incidental to the nature of persons and selves. Similarly, questions about whether those relations have been distorted by oppression or injustice are only questions about the environment in which persons exist, but they never touch who or what we really are. On the relational theory, they are precisely what make us who we are.

What does this conception of persons have to say about the problem of personal identity? We find only a few hints in the writings of relational theorists. Baier claims that because we are "second persons," who acquire from other persons the essential capacities needed to qualify as persons, in becoming persons we also

> . . . acquire a sense of our place in a series of persons, to some of whom we have special responsibilities. We acquire a sense of ourselves as occupying a place in an historical and social order of persons, each of whom has a personal history interwoven with the history of a community.[25]

If we can take the relational view of ourselves, then we might extend the set of relations in which we are embedded—the relations that constitute us as persons—to include the jostling crowd of selves that, if Diotima, Hume, and Parfit are right, make up a "single" person at different times. We should then be able to make some sense of a relational account of the many divided selves that each person is. To see what this would mean, compare the quotation from Salman Rushdie at the beginning of this chapter with the following passage from American philosopher **John Dewey** (1859–1952). Dewey was a lifelong critic of "a belief in the fixity and simplicity of the self" and an early advocate of a relational view of persons:

John Dewey: Leading American pragmatist philosopher during the first half of the twentieth century. Dewey was a lifelong critic of metaphysical theories of the self and one of the earliest advocates of the relational theory of persons.

> . . . selfhood (except as it has encased itself in a shell of routine) is in process of making, and that any self is capable of including within itself a number of inconsistent

[24] Mackenzie, C., & Stoljar, N., Eds. (2000). Introduction: Autonomy Refigured. *Relational Autonomy*. Oxford: Oxford University Press, 4.

[25] Baier, A. C. (1985). Cartesian Persons. *Postures of the Mind: Essays on Mind and Morals*. Minneapolis: University of Minnesota Press, 90.

> selves, of unharmonized dispositions. . . . Inconsistencies and shiftings in character are the commonest things in experience. Only the hold of a traditional conception of the singleness and simplicity of soul and self blinds us to perceiving what they mean: the relative fluidity and diversity of the constituents of selfhood. There is no one ready-made self behind activities. There are complex, unstable, opposing attitudes, habits, impulses which gradually come to terms with one another, and assume a certain consistency of configuration. . . .[26]

On Dewey's picture, persons are not fixed entities. At any given time we are selves in the process of transformation, *en route* from the selves we recently were to those we will soon become. The self each of us is at any given moment is the result of ongoing negotiations with other persons in our community, as well as negotiations between the selves we once were and those we hope to be. That would make selves or persons not so very different from nations or teams. As with nations and teams, the question of whether we are the same person or a different person after some change is a matter for decision—no underlying or overarching metaphysical principle determines what we should say. But that does not mean it is arbitrary what we should say. Consider a simple illustration. A Canadian awaiting execution in the United States has appealed to have his sentence commuted by claiming, among other things, that *he is no longer the same person* as the young man who committed the horrific crimes for which he was convicted more than thirty years ago. The debates surrounding his case are not metaphysical, but legal, moral, and political. According to the non-metaphysical conception of persons described by the relational theory, that is exactly as it should be.

We have not tried to defend the relational theory of selves, but described it in enough detail to illustrate one way to absorb the impact of the skeptical challenges to metaphysical theories of persons found in Hume and Parfit. The skepticism of their arguments threatened to support the idea that there are no such things as selves, on the grounds that there is no fact of the matter about whether there is any self that persists through change. But on the relational theory, we are offered a view of personhood as a "status" that we decide to withhold or confer on grounds that are not metaphysical—they are moral and political.

[26] Dewey, J. (1922). *Human Nature and Conduct: An Introduction to Social Psychology*. New York: Henry Holt and Company. Retrieved July 19, 2014, from http://www.gutenberg.org/cache/epub/41386/pg41386.txt

CONCLUSION

In the previous chapter we examined efforts by John Locke and Thomas Reid to find a metaphysical unity underlying the many transformations that persons undergo, to bind the many different stages a person passes through into the stages of a single person. Both philosophers attempted to do this by identifying a constituent of persons that extends the breadth of our lives unchanged—consciousness, or the self. In this chapter we saw how David Hume and Derek Parfit denied that persons can have the sorts of unity Locke and Reid were seeking.

Hume and Parfit argue that we must settle for continuity—a much weaker relation than identity—to tie together our earlier and later selves. If persons have insufficient unity to form an integrated self, then we will not have the sort of metaphysical status that the metaphysical realists supposed. And, if that is so, persons will either be fictions, as the metaphysical eliminativist says, or we will be a "bundle" of disparate components—a jostling crowd—as the metaphysical reductionist says. Either way, we will be a great deal less than Plato, Locke, or Reid believed.

The relational theory of the self developed by contemporary feminist philosophers is a distant cousin of Locke's forensic concept of persons, and it illustrates what a non-metaphysical view of persons might look like. Some such view seems to be needed to absorb the skeptical arguments of Hume and Parfit. The relational theory offers a way of understanding persons without making them into fictions and without making decisions about personal identity look arbitrary or groundless, but the grounds for those decisions will be moral and political, not metaphysical.

Key Terms and Figures

David Hume p. 64
traditional theory of the self p. 64
Gilbert Ryle p. 69
bundle theory of the self p. 71
realism p. 72
eliminativism p. 72
reductionism p. 72
Derek Parfit p. 74
physical continuity p. 77
psychological continuity p. 77
brain fission p. 79
Annette Baier p. 81
relational theory of persons (or selves) p. 81
John Dewey p. 83

Additional readings on selves and divided selves

Baier, A. C. (1997). *The Commons of the Mind: The Paul Carus Lectures.* Chicago: Open Court Publishing Company.

Meyers, D. (2010). "Feminist Perspectives on the Self." *The Stanford Encyclopedia of Philosophy*, Spring 2010. Edward N. Zalta (Ed.) Available at http://plato.stanford.edu/archives/spr2010/entries/feminism-self

Olson, E. T. (1998). "There is No Problem of the Self." *Journal of Consciousness Studies* 5, 5–6, 645–57.

Parfit, D. (1986). *Reason and Persons.* Oxford: Oxford University Press.

Perry, J. (1978). *A Dialogue on Personal Identity and Immortality.* Cambridge: Hackett Publishing Company.

Chapter 5
Death and Immortality

Learning Objectives

- Contrast being a living thing and having a life, and discuss which matters for the possibility of an afterlife.
- Summarize Plato's argument for the immortality of the soul, and describe at least one problem with the argument.
- Explain the fallacy of equivocation and the fallacy of false dilemma.
- Describe the relevance of the problem of personal identity to doctrines of reincarnation.
- Summarize the Argument from Indivisibility, and identify at least one weakness in the argument.
- Compare and contrast Epicurus and Lucretius on why we should not fear death.
- Identify at least two challenges to the idea that an immortal life would be preferable to a finite life.

In this chapter we explore two questions: *Do persons continue to exist after their deaths?* And *Is a person's death always a bad thing for the person who dies?* Although the first is a question about survival or persistence through change, the second is about values—about whether it is *better* to be immortal than to have a finite existence. As such it may seem to be outside the usual borders of metaphysics or epistemology, but a good way to explore the natures of death and immortality is to ask whether they are inevitably bad.

Most people who give any thought to these questions assume that it would be better to be immortal than to exist for only a finite time. The assumption seems a natural consequence of the idea that death is a bad thing for the person who dies. But that further idea—that our deaths are always or usually misfortunes for us—depends on views about the nature of death. We will explore those views more carefully in this chapter.

TALKING ABOUT THE DEAD

death: Refers either to the cessation of vital biological functions (biological death) or to the permanent end of the life that someone leads (personal death). There are religious and philosophical disagreements about whether the two kinds of death always coincide.

Our concern is with the life, death, and possible immortality of *persons*. To coherently discuss these topics we will need to settle how we will use some important vocabulary.

A person's **death** refers to *the permanent cessation of her existence*—when she dies, she ceases to exist, and she will never exist again. How can we possibly say this with confidence? The objection to such confidence is as follows: A great many people believe that there is a life—an

afterlife—that awaits after death; some even believe that the afterlife is *eternal.* Furthermore, what happens after death is unresolved for a good reason: We cannot know what happens until we are dead. So for all we know, it is possible that we will continue to exist in some form.

afterlife: Any continuation of a person's life, whether finite or eternal, after her biological death.

The objection is a misunderstanding. We have only attempted to *define the word* "death." Think of it as a decision about how we intend to use the word. In doing this, we have not taken a side on the issue of whether there is an afterlife. Those who believe that an afterlife awaits believe that we continue to exist, and so they believe that *we* do not die (as "death" has been defined). They may think something else dies—our bodies, perhaps—but they do not believe that persons die. By defining the word "death" (and, correspondingly, "die" and "dead") as the cessation of existence, we leave open the question of whether we actually die. But as a result of our definition we do know what happens after death: nothing does, since when we are dead we do not exist.

Even under this definition, "death" can still to refer to two different things. First, a person's *death* as refers to an event that marks the end of her life, or the end of the process of dying. My *dying* is an event in my life, and it can be brief or protracted, but my *death* refers to the event of my ceasing to exist. But "death" sometimes also refers to *the state or condition* that follows the event of our death—the state or condition of *being dead.* The "condition" of being dead is not like any other; it is not pleasant or unpleasant, it is not terrifying or boring. We can best see this by comparing it to the condition of being extinct. Dinosaurs are now extinct, but that is not the condition in which they currently exist. It is the condition of no longer existing. To speak paradoxically: There are no extinct species or dead people. There are species and persons who no longer exist, and that explains why they are not suffering, or happy, or bored.

Like the term "death," "life" is also ambiguous. Persons are *living organisms* for at least part of the time we exist. In this respect we are not different than carrots—they are also *alive.* Being alive is a biological or a medical status requiring, in our case, breath, heartbeat, and brain activity. But in addition to being alive, persons also *have*, or *lead*, a life. The lives we lead—our *biographical lives*—are the series of events, activities, feelings, and thoughts in which we play a part. A carrot is just as alive as we are, but it does not lead any kind of life. Because "life" is ambiguous between *being a living thing* and *having a biographical life*, our understanding of when life ends is also ambiguous. A person's *biological death*—sometimes referred to as the death of her body—refers to when she ceases to be a living organism, as marked by the cessation of vital functions. But a *person's death* refers to the end of her biographical life. We can leave open for now whether a person's death must coincide with the end of her biological life, but even if they coincide they are still distinct ideas or concepts—which is why we can understand the idea of vampires: the undead, who continue to lead lives even though they are no longer alive.

Those who believe in an *afterlife* believe that a person's *biographical life* continues after her *biological death.* Some people put this point by saying *the body dies* but *the person* (whom they might even conceive as an immaterial soul, or spirit) continues to exist. Finally, although the two are often treated together, belief in an afterlife is not the same as belief in **immortal**, or *eternal, life.* To have an afterlife is to have an autobiographical life that extends beyond biological life. But that extension might be finite. Those who believe in a finite afterlife eventually need to face their own deaths. Belief in personal immortality, on the other hand, is the belief that we *never* cease to exist, so immortality is the only genuine alternative to eventual death.

immortal: Something is said to be immortal, or to have immortality, when it will *always* exist—there is *never* any end to its existence.

TWO ARGUMENTS FOR IMMORTALITY

In this section, we examine two metaphysical arguments that conclude that persons are immortal. The first, formulated by Plato, uses conceptual tools for describing change that were developed by the ancient idealists. The second argument makes an early appearance in Plato, but it was circulated widely in the seventeenth and eighteen centuries and it employs the ideas about change that were developed by ancient atomists.

Plato and Reincarnation

Although Plato presents a number of arguments designed to justify his belief in the immortality of the soul, many of those arguments presuppose other important Platonic doctrines, for which he offers independent defenses. However, at least one of his arguments for immortality can be kept apart from his other doctrines.

Plato believes that immortality takes the form of *reincarnation*—persons are born, live a human life, die, and then are reborn to live another human life. Some of those who believe in reincarnation think the sequence from birth to death repeats only a limited number of times. On their view, reincarnation means a longer existence for the individual, but it does not amount to immortality. But if the cycle of birth and death is repeated without end, as Plato appears to believe, then it qualifies as a form of immortality. On Plato's view of reincarnation, the individual soul endures as far into the future as we can conceive, and it has also existed as far into the past as we can imagine. Not only do souls not die, but, strictly speaking, souls never come into being—they have always existed. Whether reincarnation is a form of immortality or only extends our finite existence, it is important for any version of the doctrine to maintain that the person who is later reborn is the *same person* who existed earlier. So a view about personal identity that will make this possible is an essential component of doctrines of reincarnation.

The following discussion about the nature of the soul is an excerpt from a dialogue set in the hours leading up to Socrates's execution. Socrates tries to console his disciples, among them a young man named Cebes, by proving that he will not perish.

Proof of Reincarnation (Plato)[1]

> Cebes answered: I agree, Socrates, in the greater part of what you say. But in what concerns the soul, men are apt to be incredulous; they fear that when she has left the body her place may be nowhere, and that on the very day of death she may perish and come to an end—immediately on her release from the body, issuing forth dispersed like smoke or air and in her flight vanishing away into nothingness. If she could only be collected into herself after she has obtained release from the evils of which you are speaking, there would be good reason to hope, Socrates, that what you say is true. But surely it requires a great deal of argument and many proofs to show that when the man is dead his soul yet exists, and has any force or intelligence.
>
> True, Cebes, said Socrates; and shall I suggest that we converse a little of the probabilities of these things?
>
> I am sure, said Cebes, that I should greatly like to know your opinion about them.

[1] From Plato. (n.d.). *Phaedo: The Last Hours of Socrates.* (Benjamin Jowett, Trans.). Retrieved July 20, 2014, from http://www.gutenberg.org/cache/epub/1658/pg1658.txt

I reckon, said Socrates, that no one who heard me now, not even if he were one of my old enemies, the Comic poets, could accuse me of idle talking about matters in which I have no concern:—If you please, then, we will proceed with the inquiry.

Suppose we consider the question whether the souls of men after death are or are not in the world below. There comes into my mind an ancient doctrine which affirms that they go from hence into the other world, and returning hither, are born again from the dead. Now if it be true that the living come from the dead, then our souls must exist in the other world, for if not, how could they have been born again? And this would be conclusive, if there were any real evidence that the living are only born from the dead; but if this is not so, then other arguments will have to be adduced.

Very true, replied Cebes.

Then let us consider the whole question, not in relation to man only, but in relation to animals generally, and to plants, and to everything of which there is generation, and the proof will be easier. Are not all things which have opposites generated out of their opposites? I mean such things as good and evil, just and unjust—and there are innumerable other opposites which are generated out of opposites. And I want to show that in all opposites there is of necessity a similar alternation; I mean to say, for example, that anything which becomes greater must become greater after being less.

True.

And that which becomes less must have been once greater and then have become less.

Yes.

And the weaker is generated from the stronger, and the swifter from the slower.

Very true.

And the worse is from the better, and the more just is from the more unjust.

Of course.

And is this true of all opposites? and are we convinced that all of them are generated out of opposites?

Yes.

And in this universal opposition of all things, are there not also two intermediate processes which are ever going on, from one to the other opposite, and back again; where there is a greater and a less there is also an intermediate process of increase and diminution, and that which grows is said to wax, and that which decays to wane?

Yes, he said.

And there are many other processes, such as division and composition, cooling and heating, which equally involve a passage into and out of one another. And this necessarily holds of all opposites, even though not always expressed in words—they are really generated out of one another, and there is a passing or process from one to the other of them?

Very true, he replied.

Well, and is there not an opposite of life, as sleep is the opposite of waking?

True, he said.

And what is it?

Death, he answered.

And these, if they are opposites, are generated the one from the other, and have there their two intermediate processes also?

Of course.

Now, said Socrates, I will analyze one of the two pairs of opposites which I have mentioned to you, and also its intermediate processes, and you shall analyze the other to me. One of them I term sleep, the other waking. The state of sleep is opposed to the state of waking, and out of sleeping waking is generated, and out of waking, sleeping; and the process of generation is in the one case falling asleep, and in the other waking up. Do you agree?

I entirely agree.

Then, suppose that you analyze life and death to me in the same manner. Is not death opposed to life?

Yes.

And they are generated one from the other?

Yes.

What is generated from the living?

The dead.

And what from the dead?

I can only say in answer—the living.

Then the living, whether things or persons, Cebes, are generated from the dead?

That is clear, he replied.

Then the inference is that our souls exist in the world below?

That is true.

And one of the two processes or generations is visible—for surely the act of dying is visible?

Surely, he said.

What then is to be the result? Shall we exclude the opposite process? And shall we suppose nature to walk on one leg only? Must we not rather assign to death some corresponding process of generation?

Certainly, he replied.

And what is that process?

Return to life.

And return to life, if there be such a thing, is the birth of the dead into the world of the living?

Quite true.

Then here is a new way by which we arrive at the conclusion that the living come from the dead, just as the dead come from the living; and this, if true, affords a most certain proof that the souls of the dead exist in some place out of which they come again.

Yes, Socrates, he said; the conclusion seems to flow necessarily out of our previous admissions.

The Argument from Opposites

We can reconstruct the central argument for immortality and reincarnation in Plato's discussion as follows:

1. Everything that comes to be comes to be from its opposite.
2. The Dead and the Living are opposites.
3. So, the Dead come to be from the Living, and the Living come to be from the Dead.

This, Plato thinks, supports the idea that just as those who are dead must previously have been living, so we who are alive must previously have been dead. This gives rise to a potentially endless cycle of life and death. How good is this argument?

The first premise of this **Argument from Opposites** states a view about change that goes back to Parmenides. If a man becomes an insect, then *something that is an insect* comes to be from *something that is not an insect*—in that way, whatever "comes to be" comes from its opposite. Plato's argument depends crucially on the idea of "opposites," which makes an appearance in both premises. To say that two things are **opposites** means that nothing can be both of the two at the same time. In effect, they exclude one another. But even within the constraints of this definition, we see that there are two different kinds of opposites:

Argument from Opposites: An argument developed by Plato that purports to establish the immortality of the soul and the doctrine of reincarnation using the idea that life and death are opposites, together with the ancient idealist principle that all things come to be from their opposites.

opposites: Two things or properties are said to be opposites if nothing can be (or have) both at the same time.

> **Contradictories:** Opposites such that (i) nothing can be both of them (at the same time) and, furthermore, (ii) whatever is not one of the two contradictories must be the other.

Between them, two **contradictories** must cover all the options. For example, spherical and *non-spherical* (or *not spherical*) are contradictories, since (i) nothing can be both spherical and *non-spherical* (at the same time), and (ii) whatever is not *spherical* is *non-spherical*.

contradictories: Two statements are contradictories if the truth of one ensures the falsity of the other and the falsity of one ensures the truth of the other. In ancient metaphysics, two *things* or *properties* were said to be contradictories if they were opposites such that whatever was not one of them had to be the other.

> **Contraries:** Opposites such that (i) nothing can be both of them (at the same time), but (ii) some things can be neither of the two contraries.

For example, *black* and *white* are **contraries** since (i) nothing can be *black* and *white* (all over, at the same time), but (ii) some things can be neither *black* nor *white*—they might be red or blue. Contradictories and contraries are both species of opposites because of what they share in (i), but they are different kinds of opposites because they differ in (ii).

contraries: Two statements are contraries if they cannot both be true, but they might both be false. In ancient metaphysics, two *things* or *properties* are said to be contraries if they are opposites such that nothing can be both of them but something might be neither of them.

Which of these two kinds of opposites—contradictories or contraries—is employed in Plato's argument for reincarnation? The first premise of his argument seems plausible when we understand it as saying that whatever comes to be must come to be from its contradictory. Thus, nothing can *come to be* spherical unless it was first *not spherical*; nothing can *come to be* green unless earlier it was *not green*, and so on. But the first premise does not seem true, or even plausible, if Plato is referring to contraries. Using black and white as our example, it is clear that something can become white without having been black: Before it became white it might have been red. So if the first premise of the argument is to remain plausible, we need to understand "opposites" in that premise as referring to contradictories and not to contraries.

Let us turn to the second premise of Plato's argument: the claim that the living and the dead are opposites. What sort of opposites are the living and the dead—contraries or contradictories? It is not plausible that the dead are the contradictories of the living, since the living and the dead do not cover all the options. Some things are neither living nor dead, but are simply inanimate. If that is right, then the living and the dead are contraries. But in that case we cannot conclude from the fact that something comes to be living that it must have been dead; it may have been inanimate. Contradictories must come from their contradictories, but contraries do not need to come from their contraries. So one reply to Plato's argument would be that most living things come to be from other living things (for example, parents), but living things in general come to be from inanimate things. In that case, life comes from nonlife, and not from the dead (the deceased).

Logic Box

Fallacy of Equivocation

When taken out of context, most words or sentences are ambiguous: They can have more than one meaning or can be reasonably interpreted in more than one way. But it is a fallacy to support a conclusion by *relying* on the fact that a word or sentence *will be* interpreted in more than one way in order to make the argument appear plausible. When a *single* interpretation of a premise, or of a key term or phrase that occurs more than once in an argument, cannot support the conclusion by itself, then the argument is unsound.

Example: "A pizza is better than *nothing,* and *nothing* is better than sex; so a pizza is better than sex."

fallacy of equivocation: A fallacy that relies on the ambiguity of a word or sentence in order to make the argument appear sound.

Plato's argument then commits the **fallacy of equivocation**: It equivocates by using the single term "opposites" with two different meanings. The first premise is only plausible if "opposites" means "contradictories," but the second premise is only plausible if "opposites" means "contraries." If "opposites" had the same meaning (whether contradictories or contraries) in both premises, then at least one of the premises would be implausible. But if "opposites" means different things in different premises—for example, if it means "contradictory" in the first premise but means "contrary" in the second—then the premises will both be plausible but the argument will be invalid.

There is, in addition, a problem common to most views involving reincarnation, including Plato's. On Plato's account, the souls of the dead drink from the waters of the river *Lethe* (meaning "forgetfulness") before they can be reincarnated, and this erases all memory of the life that has just ended. Plato must say something like this if he wants us to believe that we have had many previous lives when we have no recollection of them. This confronts the doctrine of reincarnation with a **dilemma**.

dilemma: A forced choice between two options, neither of which is acceptable.

false dilemma: Confronting a view with a dilemma—an apparently forced choice between two unacceptable options—when there are actually more than two alternatives.

On the one hand, the fact that we have no knowledge or memory of any previous life suggests that there might be no *psychological continuity* between the person in one life and the person in her next life. According to John Locke, a later self must remember the thoughts and deeds of any earlier self if they are to be different stages of the same person. But even those who think Locke's requirement is too stringent often hold that there must be *some* form of psychological continuity between two selves if they are to qualify as different stages of the same person. Such philosophers will surely look at Plato's doctrine of

Logic Box

Dilemma and False Dilemma

A dilemma is a problem that confronts a statement, doctrine, or theory, in which accepting the statement requires us to choose between two options, both of which are problematic.

A **false dilemma** is a fallacy that represents a doctrine as compelling a choice between two problematic alternatives when, in fact, there are more than two alternatives to choose among. For example, "Either you are with us or you are against us" confronts us with two options, both of which might be unacceptable. This is a false dilemma, since we can reject both options and remain neutral.

reincarnation and say that even if the *same soul* is reborn again, it is not enough for the *same person* to be reborn. According to this criticism, in Plato's account *my soul* continues to exist after my death (or the death of my body), but *I* do not continue to exist. He owes us an account of why we should believe our reincarnated souls are reincarnations of *us*. Unless it is accompanied by an account of personal identity that can ease this worry, it is unlikely that reincarnation can be the basis for a theory of personal immortality.

On the other hand, suppose Plato does somehow satisfy us that we are our reincarnated souls—that their survival is also *our* survival. Plato will then have an account of personal immortality. But, unless his account includes significant psychological ties to my future reincarnations, it is utterly unclear *why I (now) should care* whether I survive. Immortal life loses its attraction if there are no significant psychological connections between our earlier and later selves. David Hume expressed this worry best: "The soul, therefore, if immortal, existed before our birth: And if the former state of existence no wise concerned us, neither will the latter."[2] In other words, we have no interest in our past selves if we have no psychological connections to them, and the same will be true of any future selves with whom we have no psychological connection—their continued survival will not matter to us.

So the dilemma Plato's doctrine of reincarnation poses is that if we have no significant psychological connections to any future incarnations of our souls, then either those future incarnations of our soul are no longer *us*, in which case we do not survive the deaths of our bodies, or they are us, but we have no reason to care whether we survive.

Body Parts

The second argument for immortality we will consider also has ancient origins, but it was revived many times in later millennia. In the same dialogue as the Argument from Opposites, Socrates confronts the worry that on the death of the body the soul might be "dispersed like smoke or air":

> Now the compound or composite may be supposed to be naturally capable, as of being compounded, so also of being dissolved; but that which is uncompounded, and that only, must be, if anything is, indissoluble. . . .
>
> And the uncompounded may be assumed to be the same and unchanging, whereas the compound is always changing and never the same.[3]

Socrates's reply points out that only things consisting of many parts ("compounded") can be decomposed into parts and dispersed in the wind. Things that are not compounded of parts ("uncompounded") are immune to dissolution and dispersal—they are, in effect, indestructible. This was the idea behind ancient atomism: Change, and destruction, consists in the re-arrangement and dispersal of parts, so what has no parts cannot change or be destroyed. We know the body is compounded of parts, and so will be dispersed, but how can we determine if the soul is also divisible into parts? Plato attempts to answer by

[2] Hume, D. (1742). Of the Immortality of the Soul. *Essays, Moral, Political, and Literary*. Retrieved July 20, 2014, from http://www.econlib.org/library/LFBooks/Hume/hmMPL49.html

[3] From Plato. (n.d.). *Phaedo: The Last Hours of Socrates*. (Benjamin Jowett, Trans.). Retrieved July 20, 2014, from http://www.gutenberg.org/cache/epub/1658/pg1658.txt

appealing to the ways in which he thinks souls resemble divine beings, and so we might expect them to also partake of the immortality of divine beings. None of this is which a reason to think the soul is not divisible into parts, but it is easy to discern a simple argument for immortality in Socrates's suggestion:

1. The human body is divisible into parts.
2. The person (or, mind, soul, self, etc.) is not divisible into parts.
3. Whatever is divisible is destructible; whatever is indivisible is indestructible.
4. Therefore, the human body is destructible, but persons (minds, souls, selves, etc.) are not destructible.

Argument from Indivisibility: Argument for the immortality of the soul that depends on the idea that the soul, unlike the body, cannot be divided into parts. Versions appeared as early as Plato, but variations of the argument are widespread in the modern era and can be found in philosophers as diverse as René Descartes and Thomas Reid.

René Descartes: French philosopher and mathematician who made major contributions to seventeenth-century science and philosophy. He is best known for his development and defense of a foundationalist theory of knowledge, his dualist theory of mind, and lasting contributions to geometry.

This argument, which we will call the **Argument from Indivisibility**, seems a good start toward the conclusion that persons are immortal. Variations on the argument were widely promoted in the cause of immortality. It is easy to agree with the first premise, so the challenge is to make the second premise seem plausible. We will look briefly at two attempts to justify the second premise—one from the seventeenth century and one from the eighteenth century.

Seventeenth-century French philosopher **René Descartes** (1596–1640) offers a variant of the Argument from Indivisibility to show that minds and bodies are distinct things, and he sees clearly that it suggests that minds could be immortal. But he also offers a justification for the premise that the mind is not divisible into parts. In his Sixth Meditation[4], Descartes writes:

> [W]hen I consider the mind, that is to say, myself inasmuch as I am only a thinking thing, I cannot distinguish in myself any parts, but apprehend myself to be clearly one and entire; and although the whole mind seems to be united to the whole body, yet if a foot, or an arm, or some other part, is separated from my body, I am aware that nothing has been taken away from my mind. And the faculties of willing, feeling, conceiving, etc. cannot be properly speaking said to be its parts, for it is one and the same mind which employs itself in willing and in feeling and understanding.

We are not likely to find Descartes's central claim persuasive. He may be correct that the loss of my foot does not "take away from" my mind, but that is not, by itself, a good reason to think my mind does not have parts. It can only be a reason for saying that my foot is not a part of my mind. Furthermore, we have ample reason to think that the loss of parts of the brain can "take away from" a person's mind. By Descartes's reasoning, that should suggest that the mind has parts—even physical parts.

We might answer Descartes by saying that the loss of parts of the brain can result in the loss of mental faculties, and the loss of a mental faculty is the loss of part of the mind. But Descartes immediately tries to block this objection: The division of the mind into various mental *faculties* is not, he thinks, a division of the mind into *parts*, and so the loss of a mental faculty is not the loss of *a part of the mind*. The various faculties of the mind—perception, willing, feeling, and so on—are only different tasks that *one and the same mind* performs. In other words, Descartes claims that the will is not one *part* of

[4] Descartes, R. (n.d.). Meditations. In *The Philosophical Works of Descartes*, Elizabeth S. Haldane, Trans. London: Cambridge University Press.

the mind and the imagination another *part*; rather, willing and imagining are different tasks that the same entity performs.

It is not clear how we should evaluate Descartes's claim that mental faculties are different activities of the mind and not different parts, but even if he were right, it would not be a good reason to think that minds lack parts. After all, running and swimming are not different parts, but only different activities. They are performed by *the same parts*—by my arms, legs, muscles, lungs, and so on. We can even say that these various activities are all performed by *one and the same physical body*. But that does not imply that the body that performs those different tasks has no parts. Similarly, if the different mental activities of willing, feeling, and thinking are different tasks performed by the same mind, this would not imply that the mind has no parts.

Decartes's considerations do not appear to show that the mind is indivisible, and so do not successfully support the second premise of the Argument from Indivisibility. In the second half of the eighteenth century, Thomas Reid promoted a closely related attempt to defend the idea that persons are not divisible into parts:

> [A]ll mankind place their personality in something that cannot be divided, or consist of parts. A part of a person is a manifest absurdity.
>
> When a man loses his estate, his health, his strength, he is still the same person, and has lost nothing of his personality. If he has a leg or an arm cut off, he is the same person he was before. The amputated member is no part of his person, otherwise it would have a right to a part of his estate, and be liable for a part of his engagements. It would be entitled to a share of his merit and demerit, which is manifestly absurd. A person is something indivisible . . .[5]

Reid offers two arguments in favour of the idea that persons do not have parts, and so are not divisible and destructible. He first reasons that since we remain the same persons before and after a body part is amputated, the body part is not *a part of the person*. However, although it seems plausible, as Reid says, that my amputated foot is not a part of me, it does not follow that it *was not* a part of me before it was detached from my body. We are not entitled to say anything more than that it is *no longer* a part of me. Notice also that my severed foot is no longer a *part of my body* either, although that doesn't show that it wasn't once a part of my body or that my body lacks parts. Thus, Reid's first consideration does not show that the still-attached and still-functional body parts of persons are not *parts of persons*.

His second argument is that if a person's foot were a part of a person, then it would be entitled to a share of her property. It is not entitled to any share of her property, so, he concludes, it is not a part of her. This argument seems to have nothing to do with whether the foot is amputated or still attached—my still-attached foot has no more claim to a part of my property than my severed foot has. Reid is right that our various body parts are not each entitled to a share of our property. My left foot, which currently rests under my desk, does not own any part of my home, and it is not a partial owner of the whole home, even while it is a fully functional part of me. But this doesn't show that I—the person who does own the property—have no parts. To explain why our parts have no claim to our property we need only two observations. First, only persons can own property. Secondly,

---

[5] Reid, T. (1969). *Essays on the Intellectual Powers of Man*. Cambridge, Mass.: The MIT Press, 340–341.

not all parts of persons are persons. This is unsurprising—parts of vacuum cleaners are not vacuum cleaners, and parts of watches are not watches. It follows, then, that parts of persons—whether attached or detached—cannot own property. It does not follow from the fact that a body part cannot own property that the part is not *part of a person*; it only follows that a part of a person is not a person. Similarly, my watch keeps time, but none of its parts can keep time. That doesn't show that those parts are not parts of my watch; it only shows that the parts of my watch are not also watches.

Many early philosophers suspected that a defense of personal immortality might be found in the Argument from Indivisibility, but to make that argument persuasive we would need a reason believe the second premise—a reason to think persons are not divisible. The arguments we have seen in support of the second premise fail, so unless a better defense of it can be found, it should not persuade us that persons are immortal.

FEARING DEATH

People who reflect seriously on the prospect of their own death—on the possibility that they will cease to exist—usually ask about the *values* we should assign to death and immortality. A natural position to take combines two thoughts: First, that each person's death is a bad thing for her, something to be feared, something to be delayed, and if at all possible something to be avoided entirely. Second, a longer life is better than a shorter life, and so an immortal life would be best of all. Since these thoughts concern the kinds of attitudes we ought to have toward our own deaths, they may seem to lie outside the scope of theories of reality and knowledge. But they do not if, as many philosophers have maintained, our two apparently natural thoughts about death and immortality rest on a failure to appreciate *the nature of death and immortality*. We will accordingly use questions about how we ought to feel about death and immortality to deepen our understanding of their natures.

We will examine two closely related defenses of the view that it is not rational to fear our own deaths, and discuss two related attempts to persuade us that an immortal life would be undesirable. We begin with reflection on the fear of death by ancient Greek atomist **Epicurus** (341–270 BC).

Epicurus: Ancient Greek philosopher who defended a version of atomism; he founded the school known as Epicureanism, which derives guidelines for a better life from the ideas that pleasure is the only good thing and pain is the only bad thing.

Death is Nothing to Us (Epicurus)[6]

> [T]rain yourself to hold that death is nothing to us, because good and evil consist in sensation, and death is the removal of sensation. A correct understanding that death is nothing to us makes the mortality of life enjoyable—not because it gives you an unbounded span of time, but because it removes the desire for immortality. There is nothing terrifying in life to someone who truly understands that there is nothing terrifying in the absence of life.
>
> Only a fool says that he fears death because it causes pain ahead of time, not because it will cause pain when it comes. For something that causes no trouble when present causes only a groundless pain when merely expected. So death, the most terrifying of evils, is nothing to us, because as long as we exist death is not present, whereas

[6] Epicurus. (n.d.). *Letter to Menoeceus*. (Peter Saint-Andre, Trans.). Retrieved July 20, 2014, from http://www.monadnock.net/epicurus/letter.html

when death is present we do not exist. It is nothing to those who live (since to them it does not exist) and it is nothing to those who have died (since they no longer exist).

Most people shrink from death as the greatest of evils, or else extol it as a release from the evils of life. Yet the wise man does not dishonor life (since he is not set against it) and he is not afraid to stop living (since he does not consider that to be a bad thing). Just as he does not choose the greatest amount of food but the most pleasing food, so he savors not the longest time but the span of time that brings the greatest joy. It is simpleminded to advise a young person to live well and an old person to die well, not only because life is so welcome but also because it is through the very same practices that one both lives well and dies well. It is even worse to say that it is good to never have been born, or:

> Having been born, to
> pass through the gates
> of Hades as soon as
> possible.

If he believes what he says, why doesn't he depart from life? It is easily done, if he has truly decided. But if he is joking, it is a worthless remark to those who don't accept it. . . .

Epicurus has two objections to those who fear the prospect of their own deaths. First, death cannot be a *bad thing* for the person who dies, since nothing is bad unless it can be experienced as painful, and the dead person suffers from no pain. Of course, this does not mean that the death of a person is not a bad thing for their loved ones, who will suffer the pain of losing them. But on the view that nothing is bad for someone unless it causes them pain, nothing can be said to be bad for the dead.

We might object that even though we no longer exist after death, and do not have experiences of any kind, it is perfectly rational to fear death *now* while we are alive and face the terrifying prospect of not existing. Epicurus addresses precisely this objection: "Only a fool," he says, would fear death "ahead of time"—that is, only a fool would fear the prospect of her own death. Why?

First, Epicurus tells us, if something will not be a bad thing when it happens, then it makes no sense to fear it in advance of its happening. It is not rational for me to fear the sunrise unless, for some reason, the sunrise will be bad thing for me. Epicurus's central objection, however, is that we will never have to face our own deaths; we will never have any encounter with death. My friends and loved ones will face my death by confronting my absence from their lives, but their doing so requires their continued existence. I do not continue to exist beyond my own death, so when I am alive, *I will not be dead*, and when I am dead, *I will not be*. There is, then, no circumstance in which I will encounter my own death. That is why, as Epicurus says, our own deaths are nothing to us.

Epicurus's reasoning may be a remedy for one misunderstanding of death—as a confrontation with nothingness. The Epicurean point is that there will never be any such confrontation. Our deaths will not bring us face-to-face with nothingness (because we will fail to show up for the meeting). However, there are aspects of his argument that need further thought. Is Epicurus right that nothing can be a bad thing for us if we never experience it, or its consequences, ourselves? If something can be a bad thing for us even though we do not experience it, then it might be reasonable to fear our deaths even though we will never experience them. Is Epicurus right to assume that those who fear their own deaths fear them because they erroneously think they will be there to experience death? It may be that our fear of death has another source altogether. For example, we might legitimately be concerned about our loved ones and worry about how they will cope when we are gone, or we might fear leaving our projects unfinished. I suspect Epicurus would reply that, in that case, it is not really *death* that we fear.

Suppose we recognize Epicurus's point that our own deaths will not be dreadful for us, since there is *nothing at all* that they will be like for us, and also accept that it is not reasonable for us to fear the prospect of being dead. Still, there might be any number of reasons to fear *losing* our lives and all that they contain. To dread the *loss* of one's life is not the same as dreading an *encounter* with nothingness. In the following lines from one of his poems, Philip Larkin responds to Epicurus, whose argument he finds to be only a "trick" consisting of "specious stuff."

> This is a special way of being afraid
> No trick dispels. Religion used to try,
> That vast moth-eaten musical brocade
> Created to pretend we never die,
> And specious stuff that says *No rational being*
> *Can fear a thing it will not feel*, not seeing
> That this is what we fear—no sight, no sound,
> No touch or taste or smell, nothing to think with,
> Nothing to love or link with,
> The anaesthetic from which none come round.[7]

Larkin's disagreement with Epicurus must be developed in more detail than we can attempt here, but perhaps some observations can point us in useful directions for further exploration. Larkin is careful not to discuss death positively, in terms of what we will experience when dead, but only negatively, in terms of what we will have lost. His point seems to be this: Epicurus may be right that death is not at all like an *encounter with nothingness*, so it is unreasonable to fear any such encounter. But death does amount to *not having* any more encounters with anything, and that is something that it is perfectly reasonable to dread.

To explore the apparent disagreement between Larkin and Epicurus further, we might begin by asking whether this is *a real disagreement* at all. Is there is any genuine difference between *experiencing nothing* and *not experiencing anything*? Suppose you are threatened with the future loss of your eyesight. Does it make sense to say that it would not be reasonable to be frightened at the prospect of *seeing nothing*, since when you lose your eyesight you won't be "seeing" at all, but it is perfectly reasonable to be frightened at the prospect of *not seeing anything* again? If there is a real difference between these, we would also need to explore how, if at all, the difference will matter to Epicurus's argument. In particular, is it reasonable *now*, when we are alive, to fear the *loss* of things that will not matter to us when we are dead?

Lucretius: A Roman follower of ancient atomism and defender of many of the ideas of Epicurus. He is best known for his long philosophical poem *On the Nature of Things*.

The following section examines an interesting extrapolation from Epicurus's ideas as presented by one of his Roman followers, **Lucretius** (c. 99–55 BC). The lines come

[7] Larkin, P. (1977). Aubade. In *Philip Larkin: Collected Poems*. Anthony Thwaite, Ed.). Farrar, Straus, and Giroux, 208.

from his long poem *On the Nature of Things*, which Lucretius wrote in part to introduce Romans to the philosophical accomplishments of the ancient Greeks, and especially to the atomists.

"Folly of the Fear of Death" (Lucretius)[8]

Therefore death to us
Is nothing, nor concerns us in the least, . . .
Yet nothing 'tis to us who in the bonds
And wedlock of the soul and body live,
Through which we're fashioned to a single state. . . .

. . . For when in life one pictures to oneself
His body dead by beasts and vultures torn,
He pities his state, dividing not himself
Therefrom, removing not the self enough
From the body flung away, imagining
Himself that body, and projecting there
His own sense, as he stands beside it: hence
He grieves that he is mortal born, nor marks
That in true death there is no second self
Alive and able to sorrow for self destroyed,
Or stand lamenting that the self lies there
Mangled or burning. . . .

. . . But ask the mourner what's the bitterness
That man should waste in an eternal grief,
If, after all, the thing's but sleep and rest?
For when the soul and frame together are sunk
In slumber, no one then demands his self
Or being. Well, this sleep may be forever,
Without desire of any selfhood more,
For all it matters unto us asleep. . . .
Death is, then, to us
Much less—if there can be a less than that
Which is itself a nothing: for there comes
Hard upon death a scattering more great
Of the throng of matter, and no man wakes up
On whom once falls the icy pause of life. . . .

Look back:
Nothing to us was all fore-passed eld
Of time the eternal, ere we had a birth.
And Nature holds this like a mirror up
Of time-to-be when we are dead and gone.

---

[8] Lucretius. (n.d.). *On the Nature of Things*. (William Ellery Leonard, Trans.). Retrieved July 20, 2014, from http://www.gutenberg.org/cache/epub/785/pg785.txt

And what is there so horrible appears?
Now what is there so sad about it all?
Is't not serener far than any sleep? . . .

. . . Nor by prolonging life
Take we the least away from death's own time,
Nor can we pluck one moment off, whereby
To minish the aeons of our state of death.
Therefore, O man, by living on, fulfil
As many generations as thou may:
Eternal death shall there be waiting still;
And he who died with light of yesterday
Shall be no briefer time in death's No-more
Than he who perished months or years before.

This selection begins with the Epicurean idea that death is nothing to us, but Lucretius embellishes it in several ways. First, when we suppose that being dead is terrible, we commonly imagine *ourselves* being torn apart by beasts and vultures, or *ourselves* left mangled and burning. (Apparently these were more common ways of dying in ancient Rome than they are today.)

When we imagine such things we are guilty of a double error. The person who fears death makes a mistake by "imagining / Himself [to be] that body." Since we cease to exist at death, the corpses that are torn and mangled are not us. Although our bodies sometimes outlast us, any indignities done to them are not done to us since we no longer exist. Second, if we find the contemplation of such scenes disturbing, then we have also forgotten that we will not be there to contemplate them: "[I]n true death there is no second self / Alive and able to sorrow for self." So we first suppose it is *us* who must suffer the indignities done to our bodies, and then we imagine that we must helplessly contemplate those indignities. Both errors forget Epicurus's lesson: Since we will not be there, our death will be nothing to us.

Lucretius then compares death to dreamless sleep, in which we are conscious of nothing. If we do not find the prospect of sleep terrifying then we should not find the prospect of being dead terrifying. The analogy between death and dreamless sleep seems appropriate in this respect: In both cases, we are not conscious of anything. The analogy between being asleep and being dead is of less help, however, if (like Larkin) it is not the prospect of facing nothing that frightens us, but the prospect of not facing anything. I can even fear falling asleep if it means I will miss out on something that is important. There is, in addition, one obvious difference between the unconsciousness of sleep and the unconsciousness of death: We go to sleep with the full anticipation of seeing the next day, but we do not go to our deaths with any such expectation. Unconsciousness is much easier to face when we believe it to be temporary.

Symmetry Argument: An argument given by Lucretius that we should not fear death since it is only a mirror image of the period of nonexistence preceding birth. Since contemplation of the latter does not occasion fear, neither should contemplation of death.

The **Symmetry Argument** then follows, when Lucretius says, "Look back: Nothing to us was all fore-passed eld / Of time the eternal, ere we had a birth." To paraphrase, Lucretius says when we look back at the time that elapsed before our births—effectively, an *eternity* in which we did not exist—we find nothing horrifying to contemplate. But, he continues, "Nature holds this like a mirror up / Of time-to-be when we are dead and gone." That is, the time before our births is a mirror image of what awaits us when we are dead. The time before we came into existence (a period of *prenatal* nonexistence) is a mirror image of the time after which we cease to exist (a period of *posthumous* non-existence), and if the one is not frightening, then the other should not be frightening. Nonexistence is something we have already been through. It was not horrible before, so it will not be horrible the next time. Because they are perfectly symmetrical, we should have the same attitude to our own deaths that we have to the eternity of nonexistence that preceded our births.

Again, we will let Philip Larkin object to the Symmetry Argument. There is, he suggests, an important asymmetry between our posthumous nonexistence and our prenatal nonexistence that Lucretius overlooks. In one brief section of a poem about the very elderly[9], Larkin writes,

> At death, you break up: the bits that were you
> Start speeding away from each other for ever
> With no one to see. It's only oblivion, true:
> We had it before, but then it was going to end,
> And was all the time merging with a unique endeavour
> To bring to bloom the million-petalled flower
> Of being here. Next time you can't pretend
> There'll be anything else. . . .

The Symmetry Argument requires that there be no relevant difference between prenatal nonexistence and posthumous nonexistence—no difference that is relevant to how we ought to feel about them. But Larkin claims there is a difference that should matter to us, so the symmetry between the two breaks down.

It is true, as Lucretius says, that both are cases of not existing for an eternity; both are "only oblivion." In retrospect we know that the long stretch of prenatal nonexistence "was going to end" with the unique and mysteriously many-faceted life each of us lives. From the perspective we come to occupy at the centre of our biographical lives, the past is a history that *converges* ("merging") on where we are now, and out of which we come into being. Parts of the past during which we did not exist eventually became parts of *our* past. But our posthumous nonexistence has no such culmination. Apart from a few very minor ripples we might make, which settle down soon after we sink into oblivion, in the future everything *diverges* ("speeding away from each other") in directions that have nothing to do with us.

We can legitimately understand the time before our birth in terms of *what is still to come for us*, but we can only understand the time after our death in terms of *what has been lost to us*. This is a real difference, and it matters to how we ought to feel about our deaths. The poet still believes a bad end awaits us all.

EROSION OF BODY AND SOUL

Most of us believe that dying too soon would be bad, and that living longer would be better. Then it seems that living forever would be best of all—an immortal life would be good. Whether that is true is something we should explore. We will begin by examining the case for thinking that an immortal life would be bad for us.

---

[9] Larkin, P. (1977). The Old Fools. In *Philip Larkin: Collected Poems*. Anthony Thwaite, Ed.). Farrar, Straus, and Giroux, 196.

An immortal life, as we understand it, is a biographical life that *never* ends. We seldom take the trouble to think what it would mean to continue our lives after our sun has dimmed and cooled, after the earth is a cold and airless cinder drifting in the darkness of space, even after our galaxy has been stripped of its spiral arms and cannibalized for parts by larger neighbouring galaxies, and even after the probable heat death of the known universe. And yet, we are supposed to think we will continue through all that. Fortunately, the *problems* that are thought to be associated with immortality will arrive long before then—a few hundred years, or at most a couple of millennia, will suffice for the cracks to show.

Tithonus: A character from Greek mythology who was a lover of Aurora, the goddess of the dawn, and who was granted immortality without eternal youth.

The following lines are from an Alfred Lord Tennyson poem in which one immortal, **Tithonus**, describes his unfortunate plight. According to classical myth Tithonus was a beautiful young man who caught the eye of Aurora, the goddess of the dawn, as she arose each morning in the east. Tithonus became Aurora's lover, but, as goddesses are inclined to do, she soon tired of him. When Aurora departed, she granted him one wish, and Tithonus recklessly asked for immortality, but he forgot to ask for *eternal youth*. In Tennyson's lines we hear from Tithonus after many centuries have passed, and he has become little more than a pile of human rubble on the horizon, where he watches the still youthful goddess reappear each morning and longs for his own death.

Tithonus (Alfred Lord Tennyson, 1859)[10]

The woods decay, the woods decay and fall,
The vapors weep their burthen to the ground,
Man comes and tills the field and lies beneath,
And after many a summer dies the swan.
Me only cruel immortality
Consumes: I wither slowly in thine arms,
Here at the quiet limit of the world, . . .

. . . I ask'd thee, 'Give me immortality.'
Then didst thou grant mine asking with a smile,
Like wealthy men who care not how they give.
But thy strong Hours indignant work'd their wills,
And beat me down and marr'd and wasted me,
And tho' they could not end me, left me maim'd
To dwell in presence of immortal youth,
Immortal age beside immortal youth,
And all I was, in ashes. . . .
Let me go: take back thy gift:
Why should a man desire in any way
To vary from the kindly race of men,
Or pass beyond the goal of ordinance
Where all should pause, as is most meet for all? . . .

[10] Tennyson, A. (1859). *Enoch Arden*. Retrieved July 20, 2014, from http://www.gutenberg.org/cache/epub/1358/pg1358.html

Ay me! ay me! with what another heart
In days far-off, and with what other eyes
I used to watch—if I be he that watch'd—
The lucid outline forming round thee; . . .

Yet hold me not for ever in thine East:
How can my nature longer mix with thine?
Coldly thy rosy shadows bathe me, cold
Are all thy lights, and cold my wrinkled feet
Upon thy glimmering thresholds, when the steam
Floats up from those dim fields about the homes
Of happy men that have the power to die,
And grassy barrows of the happier dead.
Release me, and restore me to the ground;
Thou seest all things, thou wilt see my grave:
Thou wilt renew thy beauty morn by morn;
I earth in earth forget these empty courts,
And thee returning on thy silver wheels.

The famous opening lines of this poem describe death as an event that is both as natural and as inevitable as the cycle of seasons. But death is also something from which Tithonus has been excluded—he is an onlooker rather than a participant in natural events. For him, immortality is "only cruel." How can ancient mythology tell us anything about immortality?

Our initial reaction may be that Tithonus represents a problem with eternal aging, not with immortality. He made a mistake in not asking for eternal youth. Let's see if we can improve on Tithonus's request to the goddess: Having learned from his mistake, what would we ask as a parting gift from her? We would perhaps ask her to grant an immortal life in which we do not age, where we stay forever at some preferred physiological age. We'll need to select a *fixed* physiological age, with no aging whatsoever, since in a life that lasts *forever* even glacially slow aging will eventually put us in Tithonus's situation. Of course, we won't want to stay too young or too old, but somewhere between the extremes we should find an age at which to exist forever—perhaps 21 years, 30 years, or 40 years.

Next we'll need to sort out *what kind of body* (of the relevant age) we're going to have. We might, for sentimental reasons, wish to keep our own bodies, but this shouldn't matter. Any new body will become "our own" once we become accustomed to it in a few years or decades. But we'll need to do something about the fact that we are mere creatures of flesh and blood. We are frail, and over enough time we are sure to accumulate a great many nicks and cuts and to damage or even lose body parts. Even granite erodes from exposure to air and water given enough time, and granite is vastly more durable than we are. The physical world is full of dangers. As things now stand, odds are that most of us will not be struck by lightning, mauled by grizzly bears, or severely injured in a traffic accident. But the only reason the odds favour us is that our lifespan is relatively short. In a world anything like our current world, if we are around long enough it is *extremely likely* that there will be serious damage inflicted—over and over again—on our chosen bodies.

These considerations suggest that Tithonus's problem was not merely that he neglected to ask for eternal youth. Even if we managed to stay youthful, the normal wear and tear of being an embodied human being in a sharp-edged world could only be endured for a finite time. If we seek genuine immortality, we should not want a body of flesh and bone; we should not want to exist in any *human body*. We will not escape Tithonus's problems in bodies anything like our current ones. Of course, we might ask the goddess to change *the kind of world* we exist in so that it cannot do us any damage. She might soften the hard edges and dull the sharp ones, remove the bears that might maul us and the seas that might drown us. Our present universe won't serve for immortals with human bodies. Eventually, even Aurora will need to change her position in the hierarchy of gods since she cannot continue to be the goddess of *the dawn* after the sun expires in roughly 4 billion years. Our imaginative exercise so far points in one direction: For physical beings that are *anything like us*, a physical world *anything like ours* would not be a good place to live forever.

The story of Tithonus helps focus our attention on the many changes needed to make immortality bearable. This leads to a dilemma. Unless the changes we undergo are quite significant, immortal life will not be pleasant—we will encounter some variation of the problems that afflicted Tithonus. But if those problems are addressed by making significant changes, the resulting immortal person might no longer be us. The dilemma is that without enough change immortality is undesirable; but with the needed changes what survives might no longer be us. The aging, immortal Tithonus expresses understandable doubts about whether he is the same person who once lived as a mortal: "[W]ith what another heart/. . . and with what other eyes/I used to watch –/if I be he that watch'd." That worry should be prominent for anyone who imagines a desirable but immortal life.

One response to our dilemma might be to follow Locke and Parfit in the view that what matters for our survival is only psychological continuity. However much physical change might be needed to make immortality attractive, if we can preserve enough psychological continuity with our past selves then the persons who survive those changes might still be us. Our next exercise in imagination will therefore consider the psychology of immortality.

Death and Desire

Bernard Williams: Distinguished twentieth-century English moral philosopher.

English philosopher **Bernard Williams** (1929–2003) maintains, against Lucretius, that a person's death is a bad thing for her. The reason is that we have desires to satisfy, and death prevents us from satisfying them. Williams's response to Lucretius makes use of a classification of desires into two categories.

First, there are some things we desire to do but *only if* we live long enough. Those desires are *conditional* on our being alive. For example, I desire to travel to Paraguay when I retire—if I live that long. It's one of the things I would like to do if I'm still around, but *it is not my reason for wanting to be around*. I would have the same degree of interest in existing even if travel to Paraguay was ruled out. With no prospect of ever visiting Paraguay, my interest in living would not decrease. Some of our desires, however, are *categorical* (unconditional) desires. These desires give us *our reasons for wanting to live*—we want to live in order to fulfill them. For example, I want to spend time with the people I love, to gaze at the stars, and to discuss philosophy with friends. These are not things I merely desire to do *if* I happen to be around; they are my reasons for wanting to still be around. Unlike conditional desires, our categorical desires are our reasons for wanting to live; they are the source of our interest in continuing to exist. If I learned that I could never do the things I categorically desire, then my interest in living would diminish.

It is because some of our desires are categorical that Williams thinks Lucretius is wrong about death. Death will prevent our doing what we categorically desire, and this makes it perfectly rational to regard death as a bad thing and to struggle against its approach. So long as we have such desires, it is perfectly reasonable to hope we will continue to exist—to have what Williams calls the "anti-Lucretian hope."

Despite believing that death is a bad thing for us, Williams does not believe it is *always* a bad thing, so he does not believe that immortality would be preferable to death. In the following selection, he reflects on the case of a woman—a fictional character known as EM—who, after over 300 years of life, passes up the chance of immortality. Unlike Tithonus she stays the same age and remains physically healthy. But, like the goddess Aurora, she has grown cold and indifferent to life. Williams defends the view that the problems that lead EM to give up on further life are not mere *contingencies*—that is, they are not problems that are peculiar to her own case or to her special circumstance. They are, he thinks, problems that are unavoidable in any human life that continues for too long. If that is right, then the problems that lead EM to refuse immortality are problems that would make immortality undesirable for any of us.

Reflections on the Tedium of Immortality (Bernard Williams, 1973)[11]

Immortality, or a state without death, would be meaningless, I shall suggest; so, in a sense, death gives meaning to life. That does not mean we should not fear death (whatever force that injunction might be taken to have, anyway). Indeed, there are several very different ways in which it could be true at once that death gave the meaning to life and that death was, other things being equal, something to be feared. Some existentialists, for instance, seem to have said that death is what gave meaning to life, if anything did, just because it was the fear of death that gave meaning to life; I shall not follow them. I shall rather pursue the idea that from facts about human desire and happiness and what a human life is, it follows both that immortality would be, where conceivable at all, intolerable, and that (other things being equal) death is reasonably regarded as an evil. Considering whether death can reasonably be regarded as an evil is in fact as near as I shall get to considering whether it should be feared: they are not quite the same question.

My title is that, as it is usually translated into English, of a play by Karel Čapek which was made into an opera by Janaček and which tells of a woman called Elina Makropulos, *alias* Emilia Marty, *alias* Ellian Mcgregor, alias a number of other things with the intials 'EM', on whom her father, the Court physician to a sixteenth-century Emperor, tried out an elixir of life. At the time of the action she is aged 342. Her unending life has come to a state of boredom, indifference and coldness. Everything is joyless: 'in the end it is the same', she says, 'singing and silence'. She refuses to take the elixir again; she dies; and the formula is deliberately destroyed by a young woman among the protests of some older men.

EM's state suggests at least this, that death is not necessarily an evil, and not just in the sense in which almost everybody would agree to that, where death provides an end to great suffering, but in the more intimate sense that it can be a good thing not to live too long. It suggests more than that, for it suggests that it was not a peculiarity

---

[11] "Problems of the Self," by Bernard Williams. Copyright (c) 1973 Cambridge University Press. Reprinted with the permission of Cambridge University Press.

of EM's that an endless life was meaningless. That is something I shall follow out later. First, though, we should put together the suggestion of EM's case, that death is not necessarily an evil, with the claim of some philosophies and religions that death is necessarily not an evil. Notoriously, there have been found two contrary bases on which that claim can be mounted: death is said by some not to be an evil because it is not the end, and by others, because it is. There is perhaps some profound temperamental difference between those who find consolation for the fact of death in the hope that it is only the start of another life, and those who equally find comfort in the conviction that it is the end of the only life there is. . . .

. . . No-one need deny that since, for instance, we grow old and our powers decline, much may happen to increase the reasons for thinking death a good thing. But these are contingencies. We might not age; perhaps, one day, it will be possible for some of us not to age. If that were so, would it not follow then that, more life being *per se* better than less life, we should have reasons so far as that went (but not necessarily in terms of other inhabitants) to live for ever? EM indeed bears strong, if fictional, witness against the desirability of that; but perhaps she still laboured under some contingent limitations, social or psychological, which might once more be eliminated to bring it about that really other things were equal. Against this, I am going to suggest that the supposed contingencies are not really contingencies; that an endless life would be a meaningless one; and that we could have no reason for living eternally a human life. There is no desirable or significant property which life would have more of, or have more unqualifiedly, if we lasted for ever. In some part, we can apply to life Aristotle's marvellous remark about Plato's Form of the Good:[12] 'nor will it be any the more good for being eternal: that which lasts long is no whiter than that which perishes in a day'. But only in part; for, rejecting Lucretius, we have already admitted that more days may give us more than one day can.

If one pictures living for ever as living as an embodied person in the world rather as it is, it will be a question, and not so trivial as may seem, of what age one eternally is. EM was 342; because for 300 years she had been 42. This choice (if it was a choice) I am personally, and at present, well disposed to salute—if one had to spend eternity at any age, that seems an admirable age to spend it at. Nor would it necessarily be a less good age for a woman: that at least was not EM's problem, that she was too old at the age she continued to be at. Her problem lay in having been at it for too long. Her trouble was it seems, boredom: a boredom connected with the fact that everything that could happen and make sense to one particular human being of 42 had already happened to her. Or, rather, all the sorts of things that could make sense to one woman of a certain character; for EM has a certain character, and indeed, except for her accumulating memories of earlier times, and no doubt some changes of style to suit the passing centuries, seems always to have been much the same sort of person.

There are difficult questions, if one presses the issue, about this constancy of character. How is this accumulation of memories related to this character which she eternally has, and to the character of her existence? Are they much the same kind of events repeated? Then it is itself strange that she allows them to be repeated, accepting the same repetitions, the same limitations—indeed, *accepting* is what it later becomes, when earlier it would not, or even could not, have been that. The repeated patterns of personal relations, for instance, must take on a character of being inescapable. Or is the pattern of her experiences not repetitious in this way, but varied?

[12] *Ethica Nicomachea* 1096 4.

> Then the problem shifts, to the relation between these varied experiences, and the fixed character: how can it remain fixed, through an endless series of very various experiences? The experiences must surely happen to her without really affecting her; she must be, as EM is, detached and withdrawn.
>
> EM, of course, is in a world of people who do not share her condition, and that determines certain features of the life she has to lead, as that any personal relationship requires peculiar kinds of concealment. That, at least, is a form of isolation which would disappear if her condition were generalised. But to suppose more generally that boredom and inner death would be eliminated if everyone were similarly becalmed, is an empty hope: it would be a world of Bourbons, learning nothing and forgetting nothing, and it is unclear how much could even happen.
>
> The more one reflects to any realistic degree on the conditions of EM's unending life, the less it seems a mere contingency that it froze up as it did. That it is not a contingency, is suggested also by the fact that the reflections can sustain themselves independently of any question of the particular character that EM had; it is enough, almost, that she has a human character at all. Perhaps not quite. One sort of character for which the difficulties of unending life would have less significance than they proved to have for EM might be one who at the beginning is more like she is at the end: cold, withdrawn, already frozen. For him, the prospect of unending cold is presumably less bleak in that he is used to it. But with him, the question can shift to a different place, as to why he wants the unending life at all; for, the more he is at the beginning like EM is at the end, the less place there is for categorical desire to keep him going, and to resist the desire for death. In EM's case, her boredom and distance from life both kill desire and consist in the death of it; one who is already enough like that to sustain life in those conditions may well be one who had nothing to make him want to do so. But even if he has, and we conceive of a person who is stonily resolved to sustain for ever an already stony existence, his possibility will be of no comfort to those, one hopes a larger party, who want to live longer because they want to live more.
>
> To meet the basic anti-Lucretian hope for continuing life which is grounded in categorical desire, EM's unending life in this world is inadequate, and necessarily so relative to just those desires and conceptions of character which go into the hope. That is very important, since it is the most direct response, that which should have been adequate if the hope is both coherent and what it initially seemed to be. It also satisfied one of two important conditions which must be satisfied by anything which is to be adequate as a fulfillment of my anti-Lucretian hope, namely that it should clearly be *me* who lives for ever. The second important condition is that the state in which I survive should be one which, to me looking forward, will be adequately related, in the life it presents, to those aims which I now have in wanting to survive at all. That is a vague formula, and necessarily so, for what exactly that relation will be must depend to some extent on what kinds of aims and (as one might say) prospects for myself I now have. What we can say is that since I am propelled forward into longer life by categorical desires, what is promised must hold out some hopes for those desires.

On William's view we are kept going by our categorical desires. But EM has already fulfilled her categorical desires again and again, to the point where even their satisfaction now bores her. Her 300 years has proven adequate for satisfying all her desires, but also for tiring of them. Since her reasons for wanting to live were to satisfy those categorical desires, any further continuation of her life is only tedious. When the strength of her categorical desires diminishes, or when she has lost those desires entirely, the strength of her interest in life diminishes and she will have lost any reason to struggle against the approach of death or to think of its arrival as a bad thing.

Williams must persuade us that EM's eventual boredom is not a reflection of her character—that *any* person would eventually experience the same loss of interest in life. His argument rests in part on a belief that any desire will diminish in strength, or eventually disappear, if we occupy ourselves long enough with its satisfaction. The argument requires that there is nothing we could happily do *forever*. It's unclear how one should decide whether this is true, but one route for exploring the claim might be to simply recall something you found endlessly fascinating when you were four years old, but in which you no longer have the slightest interest. Pick something you would now find tiresome. Of course, those where childish things, and you are no longer a child, so it is not surprising that the same things would bore you now. Now ask yourself whether the same thing could eventually happen to your *present* interests. Part of Williams's claim is that in the span of a normal human life you will experience the same loss of interest in the things that engage you now, and the same can be said of the things that engage your interest at any stage in your life. We would all be horrified at the prospect of living with the same interests, knowledge, and capabilities we had at four years of age. That is not because there was anything wrong with those interests and capabilities, it is because a lifetime is too long to have only them. We change, and the desires we seek to fulfil are very different at different stages in our lives. That helps us sustain an ongoing interest in life, but, on William's view, it only helps for a lifespan of relatively short duration.

It might be thought that EM need only change her categorical desires on a regular basis. Even if the pursuit of satisfaction for one set of desires grows tiresome in, say, 50 years, she can replace that set of desires with another, and so on, continually renewing her interest in living. There is no obvious reason that the kind of psychological changes we undergo could not be continued for the long run. To see how Williams might respond to this suggestion, note that there is an important connection between the set of desires that a person has at any given time and her personality or character at that time. The categorical desires that ground a person's interest in living are even more central to her character—to *who* she is—than her conditional desires, for they are what give her life meaning. Williams mentions that the accumulation of memories and experiences also affects our characters. So to imagine an immortal life in which a person's categorical desires—not to mention her memories and experiences—undergo regular change is to imagine a life in which her character and personality also undergo regular change. The objection to Williams that we are considering suggests that, in order to make immortality bearable, EM must undergo very important changes. She will need to change what she wants most, and what most matters to her, over and over again. She will need to change the kind of person she is on an ongoing basis. Once again, the attempt to make an immortal life attractive places great pressure on us to say what would make those immortal persons who persist into the remote future *still us*.

There are two ways to ensure that some person in the remote future is me. On the one hand, they might *overlap with me psychologically*, sharing many of my psychological traits. They might continue to have some of the beliefs and passions that are most important to me. This is the scenario Williams thinks will ensure tedium—the same categorical desires, over a long enough time, can only result in a life that grows tiresome. On the other hand, perhaps the person who exists in the remote future might share none of my current psychological traits but will at least *be psychologically continuous with me*, in the same way that I am psychologically continuous with my four-year-old self even though we have little in common. For this, there must be a long, unbroken line of selves, leading from me to that future person, in which each self is psychologically very similar to the ones adjacent to it in time. The selves in the queue naturally view the selves directly ahead of them as their future editions—they notice common interests and concerns, and so they understandably see them as continuations of their present selves. But as we look further ahead in the queue, we will find persons with whom we have less and less in common, and whose personalities are increasing remote from our own. Nonetheless, if psychological continuity is enough for survival, those future persons with whom we will eventually have nothing in common will still be us. They will still be us even if they are the sorts of persons we would now despise and would rather not become. Naturally, when I do become those people, I won't despise myself, but I *now* despise that sort of person, and so I *now* have no interest in becoming them. If psychological continuity is enough for personal identity, and if I live for long enough, then I and my future selves will be, at best, indifferent strangers. Whether there is some deep metaphysical sense in which that future person still qualifies as *me*, it is difficult to see how it can *matter to me* whether he ever exists.

Perhaps our earlier dilemma has grown an additional branch: If we don't change enough from what we now are, (i) immortality will be unbearable. But if we do change enough to make immortality bearable, then either (ii) the persons who survive the change won't be *us* anymore, or (iii) they will be future versions of ourselves that we are indifferent to becoming. If those are the options, then our own deaths, so long as they don't come too soon, will either be preferable to more life or, at the very least, will be a matter of indifference to us. Whether we find such considerations compelling, they should at least give us pause and encourage us to consider that even if a long life is better than one that is too short, it may not be that an immortal life is better than a finite one.

CONCLUSION

We have looked at two metaphysical arguments for the immortality of persons: the ancient Argument from Opposites and the more modern Argument from Indivisibility. Both made use of a distinction between bodies and persons, with the latter conceived of as nonphysical minds, spirits, or souls. And both arguments were found lacking. We asked whether it is rational to fear our own deaths, and whether immortality—the only alternative to eventual death—might be good or bad. We emphasized two arguments, one focusing on the physical problems associated with immortality, and the other on the psychological problems. The two arguments we emphasized concluded that the idea of immortality faces a difficult dilemma. As human beings are, an immortal life looks to be unbearable, so we would need to undergo changes—both physical and psychological. But the needed changes would be so significant that they raise doubts about whether the immortal persons who survive us would still be "us," and whether they would be anyone who would matter to us.

In our discussion of death and immortality, we took for granted that it makes sense to think of ourselves as beings that have both mental, or psychological, lives and bodily, or physical, lives. In the chapters ahead we will ask how these aspects of ourselves are related, whether both bodies and minds exist, and whether they are separable aspects of persons.

Key Terms and Figures

- **death p. 86**
- **afterlife p. 87**
- **immortal p. 87**
- **opposites p. 91**
- **Argument from Opposites p. 91**
- **contradictories p. 91**
- **contraries p. 91**
- **fallacy of equivocation p. 92**
- **dilemma p. 92**
- **false dilemma p. 92**
- **Argument from Indivisibility p. 94**
- **Rene Descartes p. 94**
- **Epicurus p. 96**
- **Lucretius p. 98**
- **Symmetry Argument p. 100**
- **Tithonus p. 102**
- **Bernard Williams p. 104**

Additional readings on death and immortality

Hasker, W. (2014). Afterlife. *The Stanford Encyclopedia of Philosophy*, Spring 2014. (Edward N. Zalta, Ed.). Retrieved on July 20, 2015, from http://plato.stanford.edu/archives/spr2014/entries/afterlife

Luper-Foy, S. (1993). Annihilation. In *The Metaphysics of Death*, John Martin Fischer, Ed. Stanford, California: Stanford University Press, 269–90.

Nagel, T. (1979). Death. *Mortal Questions*. New York: Cambridge University Press, 1–10.

Perry, J. (1978). *A Dialogue on Personal Identity and Immortality*. Cambridge: Hackett Publishing Company.

Plato. (n.d.). *Phaedo*. (Benjamin Jowett, Trans.). Available at http://www.gutenberg.org/cache/epub/1658/pg1658.txt

Chapter 6

Minds and Bodies

Learning Objectives

- Articulate the challenges of absorbing the impact of the scientific world view on our understanding of ourselves.
- Define the concept of the "physical."
- Compare and contrast two distinct dualist theories of mind and one materialist theory of mind.
- Apply Leibniz's Law to formulate a range of possible challenges to materialist theories of mind.
- Identify two versions of the interaction problem that dualist theories will need to address.
- Explain why epiphenomenalism seems a viable option to those unconvinced by the materialist theory.

During the scientific revolution of the seventeenth century, dramatic new views of the world—ones that are now quite familiar to us—began to take shape. As our conception of the natural world and our place in it changed, so did our conception of ourselves. This is the first of three chapters that will explore how our understanding of ourselves changed as a result of the scientific revolution.

Threats to earlier conceptions of persons presented by the newly emerging sciences were noticed even while the scientific revolution was getting underway, and measures were taken to oppose it. The result was a *dualistic* view of persons that maintains a wide and popular following today. According to this view, our bodies are part of the physical world but our minds are nonphysical entities. In this chapter, we look at the proposed metaphysical gap between minds and bodies, and we consider how some philosophers have proposed to close that gap. The questions we will explore are metaphysical, and sometimes epistemological, but we should be alert to the fact that significant changes in our understanding of ourselves have implications for our understanding of the social, moral, and political world we inhabit. Although we cannot attempt any exploration of those implications here, we cannot avoid encountering them.

THEORIES OF MIND

In this chapter and the next we will encounter several theories about the nature of the mind and its relationship to the body. Those views include two forms of dualism and three materialist views. Before exploring these theories in detail, some brief definitions will help us understand the range of options.

Dualism

dualism: The view that the body is a physical thing or substance, and the mind is a nonphysical thing or substance.

Dualism is the view that body and mind are two different kinds of substances—the body is material (physical), and the mind is immaterial (nonphysical). We will encounter two varieties of dualism in our studies:

> **Interactionist Dualism:** A form of dualism in which minds can affect bodies, and bodies can affect minds.

epiphenomenalism: The dualist view of mind and bodies according to which bodies can affect minds, but minds cannot affect bodies.

> **Epiphenomenalism: Epiphenomalism** is a form of dualism in which bodies can affect minds, but minds cannot affect bodies.

Materialism

materialist theory of mind (also, **materialism**): The view that the mind is a physical entity and that all mental states and events are physical states and events.

Materialism is the view that both minds and bodies are material or physical things. We will examine the first two materialist theories of mind in some detail, but will only briefly discuss the third form of materialism:

> **Mind-Brain Identity Theory** Mind-brain identity theory identifies the mind with the brain, and identifies mental states, processes, and events with the physical (i.e., neurological and electrochemical) states, processes, and events occurring in the brain.

> **Functionalism** Functionalism identifies our mental states with the functional roles occupied by, or jobs performed by, physical states of the brain.

> **Eliminative Materialism** According to eliminative materialism, advances in the neurosciences will eventually prove that there really are no minds, no mental states, and no mental events; talk about our mental lives is a fiction that serves to explain behaviour only until improved neuroscientific theories can replace the fiction.

nonphysical: Defined by contrast to *physical*, a nonphysical thing or substance is thought to be anything that lacks physical properties and, so, is not governed by the laws of physics.

physical: Although the best characterization of the *physical* (in contrast to the *nonphysical*) is a matter of philosophical disagreement, an important definition of a physical entity—owed to Descartes in the seventeenth century—says that it is any entity that is subject to the laws of physics.

Before considering arguments for dualism, two important matters need clarification. The contrast between dualist and materialist theories depends on a distinction between physical and nonphysical things, so we will need a better understanding of that distinction. We will also need to become familiar with a form of reasoning that plays a central role in the debates between dualist and materialist theories of mind.

Physical vs. Nonphysical

According to the dualist theory of mind, the mind is a **nonphysical** substance (entity), and the body is a **physical** substance (entity). But what is meant by a *nonphysical* substance? For example, can we say whether a rainbow is a physical object or a nonphysical object? And what should we say about a shadow? Is energy physical? How can we begin to look for answers to such questions as these? If we hope to argue meaningfully about whether the mind is physical or nonphysical, we must be clear about the line between the two.

First, notice that the term *nonphysical* (as well as its synonyms, such as *immaterial* or *non-corporeal*) is understood only *by contrast* to *physical*. That is, *nonphysical* means simply *not physical*. So if we want to understand what *nonphysical* means, we'll need to understand what is meant by *physical*.

Second, although dualist theories of persons have been around a long time (recall Plato), our understanding of what constitutes the *physical* world underwent a dramatic change in the seventeenth century, thanks largely to such thinkers as Galileo Galilei and René Descartes. Although the physical world had long been understood as subject to laws, it was only in the early seventeenth century that physical laws began to be articulated in the language of mathematics. The result was a revolutionary new way of understanding physical law and, hence, the physical world. In effect, a new conception of the physical realm appeared, and that conception has stayed with us. Once physical laws could be stated in the language of mathematics, physical objects were seen as governed by **strict laws**: that is, laws that were precise or exact, and that allowed for no exceptions. Just as there are no exceptions to the rules of arithmetic or geometry, there are no exceptions to the mathematical laws of nature.

strict laws: Laws that are precise and that allow no exceptions; physical laws are believed to be *strict* in this sense.

Consequently, people came to understand the physical world and physical substances (entities) as *those things that are subject the strict laws of physics*. By contrast, then, nonphysical substances were understood as substances that are not subject to such laws. So when a dualist says that the mind is nonphysical, part of what is meant is that the mind is not subject to physical laws. This view of the mind will naturally be appealing to anyone who wants to portray aspects of the mind—say, the imagination, or our decision-making faculty—as free. When understood in this way, the dualist view of the mind might have the consequence that nonphysical minds do not have *any* physical properties or characteristics. If an object has any physical characteristic—say, a physical magnitude such as mass, length, or size—then the object will be subject to whatever physical laws apply to objects with that physical magnitude. It is worth noting that we have defined *physical entities* in terms of *physical laws*. But which laws are those? However we answer the question, we cannot say that physical laws are those that govern the behaviour of physical entities, for that would leave us with a **circular definition** that defines *physical entities* in terms of *physical entities*. To complete this account of the physical realm, we will eventually need an understanding of *what physical laws are* that does not make use of the idea of a physical entity.

circular definition: A definition that uses a term to define itself. Such definitions are useless, since they serve to explain the meaning of a term only to those who already understand it.

On this view of the physical world, rainbows and shadows are easily seen as physical entities, since they conform strictly to well-known physical laws of light and optics. They

Logic Box

Circular Definitions

A circular definition uses a term to define itself. Circular definitions of a term are useless, since they can only explain the meaning of a term to someone who already knows it. They fail to explain anything we don't already understand.

Example: A *predator* is an animal that engages in predatory behaviour.

are, in short, *physical* because we can expect to fully explain them and their behaviour in terms of physical laws. It is useful to recognize that, on this conception of *physical*, *energy* also qualifies as physical. There are physical laws to which all forms of energy are subject—laws concerning the transformation of energy from one form to another (e.g., from mechanical to electrical, potential to kinetic, etc.) as well as laws concerning the conversion of energy to mass. So if someone entertains the idea that the mind might be "a form of energy," they are saying that the mind is physical, and so they are advocating materialism, not dualism.

Leibniz's Law

Philosophical arguments about the nature of mind invariably make use of an important metaphysical principle that was first explicitly formulated in the seventeenth century. It is sometimes referred to as **Leibniz's Law** after the philosopher who formulated it—Gottfried Leibniz (1646–1716). Leibniz formulated many metaphysical and logical principles, and we will encounter others later, but the one that concerns now us is this:

Leibniz's Law (or the **indiscernibility of identicals**): A metaphysical principle that says if A=B, then if A has a certain property or characteristic at a given time, B must also have that property or characteristic at that time.

> The Indiscernibility of Identicals: If A=B, then if A has a certain property (characteristic) at a given time, B must also have that property (characteristic) at that time.

In different words, if A is the same thing as B, then A cannot be different from B in any way. Whatever is true about A is also true about B, and vice versa. On one way of looking at it, the law is stating the obvious: *Nothing can be different from itself in any way.*

To make sure we understand Leibniz's Law, consider an example. The real name of writer Mark Twain was Samuel Clemens. So, Mark Twain and Samuel Clemens are one and the same person—that is, Mark Twain = Samuel Clemens. Leibniz's Law tells us that if Samuel Clemens smoked cigars, then Mark Twain smoked cigars. And if Samuel Clemens smoked a Cuban cigar on New Year's Eve in 1900, then it follows that Mark Twain smoked a Cuban cigar on New Year's Eve in 1900. Why? Because they are the same person—Mark Twain can't do anything that Samuel Clemens doesn't do.

Notice that Leibniz's Law does not say that nothing can change or *become different* than it is. It does not say that something, when considered at one time, cannot be different from itself when considered at another time. Rather, it says that if Samuel Clemens changes, then Mark Twain changes at the same time and in the same way. So, if Samuel Clemens quit smoking last night, then Mark Twain quit smoking last night. Leibniz's Law, in effect, concerns *identity at a time*—it tells us that if A=B, then whatever is true of A *at a given time* is also true of B *at that time*.

Leibniz's Law also applies to substances and kinds of things as well as particular things. For example, if table salt is the same substance as sodium chloride, then if table salt is mined in Death Valley, dissolves in warm water, and causes high blood pressure, then sodium chloride is mined in Death Valley, dissolves in warm water, and causes high blood pressure.

Leibniz's Law is a crucial tool in efforts to defend dualist theories of mind. The reason it is so important is that it follows directly from Leibniz's Law that if A (whatever it is) is *different from* B (whatever it is) *in any way at all*, then A is not B (that is, A is not identical to B). In that case, all that a successful defense of dualism needs to show is that minds have some characteristic that physical objects can't have, or that physical objects have some characteristic that minds can't have. Then, from Leibniz's Law, it will immediately follow that minds can't be physical objects. This is, in fact, the central strategy employed by attempts to defend dualist theories of mind.

It is precisely the strategy that seventeenth century philosopher René Descartes follows in his defense of dualism: He thinks he can locate several characteristics of minds that no physical objects have, and concludes that minds can't be physical objects. One of Descartes's distinguishing characteristics is that minds are *knowable with certainty*, but physical objects are *not knowable with certainty*. In effect, Descartes defends an epistemological difference between the mind and the external world of physical bodies, and uses that difference to argue for the metaphysical conclusion that minds and bodies are distinct kinds of substances.

In a discussion we will examine more carefully in a different context, Descartes famously says, "I think, therefore I am." He is saying that because he thinks he exists, he can be absolutely certain he exists. Nothing else can be known to exist so easily; I can't conclude that there must be leprechauns from the fact that I think there are leprechauns, and from the fact that I think there are trees I can't conclude that there are trees. But if I think I exist, that is enough to establish with complete certainty that I do exist. After all, I can't *think* that I exist unless I have a thought; but I can't have any thoughts unless I exist. So I can't possibly have the thought that I exist and still be mistaken. Of course, I can only have such certainty about my own existence—my thinking that you exist doesn't assure me that you do. Descartes's argument for dualism proceeds from this point.

CARTESIAN DUALISM

"A Thing Which Thinks" (Descartes, 1641)[1]

> But I do not yet know clearly enough what I am, I who am certain that I am; and hence I must be careful to see that I do not imprudently take some other object in place of myself, and thus that I do not go astray in respect of this knowledge that I hold to be the most certain and most evident of all that I have formerly learned. That is why I shall now consider anew what I believed myself to be before I embarked upon these last reflections . . .
>
> What then did I formerly believe myself to be? Undoubtedly I believed myself to be a man. But what is a man? Shall I say a reasonable animal? Certainly not; for then I should have to inquire what an animal is, and what is reasonable; and thus from a single question I should insensibly fall into an infinitude of others more difficult; and I should not wish to waste the little time and leisure remaining to me in trying to unravel subtleties like these. But I shall rather stop here to consider the thoughts which of themselves spring up in my mind . . . In the first place, then, I considered myself as having a face, hands, arms, and all that system of members composed on bones and flesh as seen in a corpse which I designated by the name of body. In addition to this I considered that I was nourished, that I walked, that I felt, and that I thought, and I referred all these actions to the soul: but I did not stop to consider what the soul was, or if I did stop, I imagined that it was something extremely rare and subtle like a wind, a flame, or an ether, which was spread throughout my grosser parts. As to body I had no manner of doubt about its nature, but thought I had a very clear knowledge of it;

[1] Descartes, R. (1641). *Meditations on First Philosophy*, Meditation II.

and if I had desired to explain it according to the notions that I had then formed of it, I should have described it thus: By the body I understand all that which can be defined by a certain figure: something which can be confined in a certain place, and which can fill a given space in such a way that every other body will be excluded from it; which can be perceived either by touch, or by sight, or by hearing, or by taste, or by smell . . .

But what am I, now that I suppose that there is a certain genius which is extremely powerful, and, if I may say so, malicious, who employs all his powers in deceiving me? Can I affirm that I possess the least of all those things which I have just said pertain to the nature of body? I pause to consider, I revolve all these things in my mind, and I find none of which I can say that it pertains to me. It would be tedious to stop to enumerate them. Let us pass to the attributes of soul and see if there is any one which is in me? What of nutrition or walking [the first mentioned]? But if it is so that I have no body it is also true that I can neither walk nor take nourishment. Another attribute is sensation. But one cannot feel without body, and besides I have thought I perceived many things during sleep that I recognized in my waking moments as not having been experienced at all. What of thinking? I find here that thought is an attribute that belongs to me; it alone cannot be separated from me. I am, I exist, that is certain. But how often? Just when I think; for it might possibly be the case if I ceased entirely to think, that I should likewise cease altogether to exist. I do not now admit anything which is not necessarily true: to speak accurately I am not more than a thing which thinks, that is to say a mind or a soul, or an understanding, or a reason, which are terms whose significance was formerly unknown to me. I am, however, a real thing and really exist; but what thing? I have answered: a thing which thinks.

And what more? I shall exercise my imagination [in order to see if I am not something more]. I am not a collection of members which we call the human body: I am not a subtle air distributed through these members, I am not a wind, a fire, a vapor, a breath, nor anything at all which I can imagine or conceive; because I have assumed that all these were nothing. Without changing that supposition I find that I only leave myself certain of the fact that I am somewhat. But perhaps it is true that these same things which I supposed were non-existent because they are unknown to me, are really not different from the self which I know. I am not sure about this, I shall not dispute about it now; I can only give judgment on things that are known to me. I know that I exist, and I inquire what I am, I whom I know to exist. But it is very certain that the knowledge of my existence taken in its precise significance does not depend on things whose existence is not yet known to me; consequently it does not depend on those which I can feign in imagination. . . . But I already know for certain that I am, and that it may be that all these images, and, speaking generally, all things that relate to the nature of body are nothing but dreams [and chimeras]. . . .

But what then am I? A thing which thinks. What is a thing which thinks? It is a thing which doubts, understands, [conceives], affirms, denies, wills, refuses, which also imagines and feels.

Certainly it is no small matter if all these things pertain to my nature. But why should they not so pertain? Am I not that being who now doubts nearly everything, who nevertheless understands certain things, who affirms that one only is true, who denies all the others, who desires to know more, is averse from being deceived, who imagines many things, sometimes indeed despite his will, and who perceives many likewise, as by the intervention of the bodily organs? Is there nothing in all this which is as true as it is certain that I exist, even though I should always sleep and though he who has given me being employed all his ingenuity in deceiving me? Is there likewise any one of these attributes which can be distinguished from my thought, or which

> might be said to be separated from myself? For it is so evident of itself that it is I who doubts, who understands, and who desires, that there is no reason here to add anything to explain it. And I have certainly the power of imagining likewise; for although it may happen (as I formerly supposed) that none of the things which I imagine are true, nevertheless this power of imagining does not cease to be really in use, and it forms part of my thought. Finally, I am the same who feels, that is to say, who perceives certain things, as by the organs of sense, since in truth I see light, I hear noise, I feel heat. But it will be said that these phenomena are false and that I am dreaming. Let it be so; still it is at least quite certain that it seems to me that I see light, that I hear noise and that I feel heat. That cannot be false; properly speaking it is what is in me called feeling; and used in this precise sense that is no other thing than thinking.

Descarte's Argument for Dualism

There is much going on in this complicated passage, but we can isolate for our consideration one strand of Descartes's reasoning—his core argument for dualism. We can summarize the relevant core in four steps:

1. *That I exist* can be known with complete certainty.
2. *That any physical object exists* cannot be known with complete certainty (there is always some possibility for error, however slight).

Now, Descartes need only apply Leibniz's Law to reach his conclusion:

3. So, I cannot be any physical object.

From (3), it seems natural enough for Descartes to move directly to the conclusion that

4. I am a nonphysical object.

This argument locates a difference between myself and all physical objects—my existence is known by me with certainty, but the existence of physical objects, including my own body, is not known with certainty. By what seems a straightforward application of Leibniz's Law, Descartes then concludes that I am not any physical object—not even my own physical body. This application of Leibniz's Law seems at first glance to be analogous to the following:

1. I am red.
2. No physical object is red (suppose they are all green).

It would follow from these premises that

3. I am not a physical object.

Descartes thus adopted a dualist theory: Minds are nonphysical (immaterial), and bodies are physical (material).

But Descartes's critics complain that in order to establish the truth of dualism using Leibniz's Law, Descartes must locate a characteristic of minds that physical things do not have. The characteristic he settles on is that the existence of my mind can be known (by me) with complete certainty, but this is not true of any physical object. But is the fact (if it is one) that *we cannot know* the existence of physical objects with certainty really a characteristic of physical objects, or is it only a characteristic of us? Critics might reply that, although the colours of objects are characteristics of those objects, the fact (if it is one) that things are knowable (or not knowable) by me is not a characteristic of those things. If I suddenly acquire knowledge or lose knowledge about an object, it will not result in change to the object. It will only be a change in me. And that suggests that my knowing something about the object (or my having certainty about it) is not a characteristic of the object itself, but only a characteristic of me. If that is right, then Descartes's argument for dualism is not a legitimate application of Leibniz's Law, which requires that he use characteristics of the objects he is reasoning about.

To clarify the point, critics can offer arguments such as the following, which works exactly like Descartes's argument, but is clearly a bad argument. Suppose Sherlock Holmes reasons as follows:

1. That the person who murdered Obadiah is Obadiah's murderer is something I can know with complete certainty.

Holmes can know this even if he doesn't know who murdered Obadiah. Holmes then adds a second premise:

2. That the person who murdered Obadiah is Professor Moriarty is not something I can know with complete certainty.

In this premise, Holmes is talking about his villainous arch enemy, to whom the strong (but inconclusive) evidence at the scene of Obadiah's murder points. So Holmes can't be *completely certain* that Moriarty is Obadiah's murderer. By reasoning from (1) and (2) exactly as Descartes does in his argument for dualism, Holmes will arrive at the following conclusion:

3. So, Professor Moriarty can't be Obadiah's murderer.

This argument has the same form as Descartes's argument for dualism. But, surely, Holmes cannot *prove* in this way that Professor Moriarty is innocent. After all, the available evidence points to Moriarty; no available evidence exonerates him. According to Holmes's conclusion, Moriarty *cannot possibly be* the killer. That is simply not something he should be able to find out without consulting the facts at the crime scene. Worse yet, however, Holmes's argument does not merely apply to Professor Moriarty—it will apply equally to *anyone whose name Holmes puts into the second premise*. If we take it seriously, then, Holmes's argument will prove that no one murdered Obadiah! For that reason alone, we should not take the argument seriously.

Descartes's argument for the distinction between mind and body takes the same form as Holmes's argument.[2] Since that argument is bad, but it has the same form as Descartes's, there must also be something wrong with Descartes's argument. We already know what is wrong with it: It is not a genuine application of Leibniz's Law. Holmes's analogous argument fails because his knowing (or not knowing) something about Moriarty is not a characteristic *of Moriarty*, but only *of Holmes*. Descartes's argument for dualism fails because whether we have or lack certainty about physical objects is a characteristic of us, not a characteristic of physical objects.

[2] For the idea of an argument's form, see Appendix A.

Of course, if Descartes's argument fails to prove that dualism is true, it will not show that dualism is false—there could be other good reasons for believing it is true. We will turn now to an argument that purports to show that dualism is false. It only purports to show that one form of dualism—*interactionist dualism*—is false, so before proceeding we need to understand that form of dualism better.

INTERACTIONISM

Interactionism labels the view that minds and bodies can causally interact with one another. The interaction goes both ways:

interactionism: The view that there are causal interactions in both directions between minds and bodies—bodies affect minds, and minds affect bodies.

> *The body affects the mind.* If I take a peculiar chemical, it alters my brain's chemistry, and I begin to have hallucinations. If I stab myself with a pin, stimulating nerve endings, I feel pain, and so on.

and

> *The mind affects the body.* If I imagine biting into a lemon, then my mouth waters. If I decide to pick up my cup, my hand moves toward the cup, and so on.

The combination of interactionism with dualism is called **interactionist dualism**: As the name suggests, the dualist view that the mind is nonphysical and the body physical is simply conjoined to the idea that the two interact. On this view of the mind-body relation, a nonphysical entity can, and does, interact with a physical entity. It seems obvious—just common sense—that minds and bodies do affect one another in these ways, and so interactionist dualism is the most attractive form of dualism. Unfortunately, there appears to be a very serious problem with this commonsense view—a problem so serious that it has led most philosophers to abandon interactionist dualism.

interactionist dualism: A theory of the mind that combines dualism and interactionism. On this view even though bodies are physical and minds are nonphysical, there is still two-way causal traffic between them.

The difficulties for interactionist dualism surfaced very early, as several of Descartes's contemporaries challenged his attempt to combine dualism with interactionism. Notably, Princess **Elizabeth of Bohemia** (1618–1680) initiated a philosophical correspondence with him in which she sought clarification of his views and raised several objections to his dualist interactionism. In her first letter to Descartes in May 1643, Elizabeth wrote:

Elizabeth of Bohemia: Daughter of the King of Bohemia, Elizabeth conducted an extensive philosophical correspondence with René Descartes from 1643 until his death in 1650. Her letters contain early criticisms of Descartes's attempts to combine dualism and interactionism; she ultimately recommends abandoning dualism in order to preserve mind-body interactions.

> For the determination of movement seems always to come about from the moving body's being propelled—to depend on the kind of impulse it gets from what sets it in motion, or again, on the nature and shape of this latter thing's surface. Now the first two conditions involve contact, and the third involves that the impelling thing has extension; but you utterly exclude extension from your notion of soul, and contact seem to me incompatible with a thing's being immaterial.[3]

Elizabeth observes that the precise angle and direction ("the determination") of movement after one object interacts with another always depend on the details ("the nature and shape") of the surfaces of the interacting objects. But nonphysical objects have no surfaces and no shapes, and there are no differences among them of the kind that

[3] Descartes, R. Correspondence with Princess Elizabeth. *Philosophical Writings*. (E. Anscombe & P. T. Geach, Trans.) Indianapolis: Bobs-Merrill. 1971: 274–75.

normally explain different effects. So what, then, determines the details of our actions when they result from nonphysical causes? Furthermore, Elizabeth sees no possibility of interaction between body and soul if the soul has no *spatial dimensions* ("extension"). Finally, she doubts that entities can interact if there is no contact between them, but she doubts that any sense can be made of "contact" between two entities if one of them has no spatial dimensions or other physical properties.

In another letter, from June 1643, Elizabeth confesses that she "could more readily allow that the soul has matter and extension than that an immaterial being has the capacity of moving a body and being affected by it."[4] So she believes Descartes cannot coherently be *both* a dualist and an interactionist, and she recommends that he give up his dualism in order to save his interactionism. Elizabeth is only the first in a long line of critics who have challenged the combination of dualism and interactionism. In the next section, we will look at two ways of articulating the problems that dualism and interactionism pose for each other.

The Interaction Problem

interaction problem: The problem of explaining how the mind can influence the body. This is a problem that afflicts dualist theories, since they require that the mind have no physical properties while the body has only physical properties.

The challenge faced by interactionist dualism is to explain how a nonphysical mind can affect a physical body. The general problem of explaining this is called the **interaction problem**. Interactionist dualism requires that the mind affect the body—this is one half of the two-way interaction between them. And that means that an entity with *no physical properties* will have to be able to cause changes in the *physical properties* of other objects. We can approach the central problem in two phases. First, we will ask whether nonphysical minds can cause things to happen in the physical world without themselves having any location in the physical world—this might be called the *location problem*. Second, we will ask whether their doing so would result in violations of the laws of physics—this problem takes the form of an *inconsistent triad*.

Consider the reasoning one contemporary philosopher gives for thinking that nonphysical minds would be impotent to produce changes in the physical world.

Locating the Mind (Richard Taylor)[5]

> However natural it may seem to conceive a person in such terms, as a dual complex of two wholly disparate things, body and mind, it is nonetheless an impossible conception, on the simplest metaphysical grounds. For on this view, the body and the mind *are* wholly disparate things, so that any bodily change wrought by the mind or by some nonphysical occurrence transpiring therein is a change that lies quite outside the realm of physical law. This means that human behavior is veritably miraculous. . . .
>
> Consider some clear and simple case of what would on this theory constitute the action of the mind upon the body. Suppose, for example, that I am dwelling in my thought upon high and precarious places, all the while knowing that I am really safely ensconced in my armchair. I imagine, perhaps, that I am picking my way along a precipice and visualize the destruction that awaits me far below in case I make the smallest slip. Soon, simply as the result of these thoughts and images, which are not for

[4] *Ibid.*, p. 278

[5] Taylor, Richard, Metaphysics, 4th. Ed., (c) 1992, pp. 19-23. Reprinted and Electronically reproduced by permission of Pearson Education, Inc., Upper Saddle River, New Jersey.

a moment attended by any belief that I am in the slightest danger, perspiration appears on the palms of my hands. Now here is surely a case, if there is any, of something purely mental, unobservable, and wholly outside the realm of physical nature bringing about observable physical changes. . . .

But what actually happens, alas, is not nearly so simple as this. To say that thoughts in the mind produce sweat on the hands is to simplify the situation so grossly as hardly to approximate any truth at all of what actually happens. A complete account of the complexities involved here cannot be given, for it is unknown, but some elaboration is possible, in light of which it is far from obvious that we have, even in this case, an instance of the mind acting on the body.

The perspiration, everyone knows, is secreted by tiny, complex glands in the skin. They are caused to secret this substance, not by any mind acting on them, but by the contraction of little unstriated muscles. These tiny muscles are composed of numerous minute cells, wherein occur chemical reactions of the most baffling complexity. It is believed, however, that the energy required for their activity is derived from the oxidation of fatty acids, or perhaps of acetoacetate. Their contraction in any case generates electrical current of small but measurable amounts. It might be supposed that these muscles are enervated by the mind, which by some mysterious alchemy produces the chemical reactions within their cells; but this, even if it makes any sense, is certainly not true. The muscles are activated by hormones produced by the adrenal medulla in response to impulses of the autonomic nervous system, probably by the hormones epinephrine or norepinephrine, or, more likely in the present case, by an epinephrine-like substance that is produced in the minute quantities by andrenergic fibers, that is, certain post-ganglionic neurons of the sympathetic nervous system. . . . Stimulation of a neuron increases the permeability of the neuron membrane, causing a diffusion of sodium ions into the neuron itself, . . . with a resultant flow of current. Such currents are easily detected and fairly accurately measured by a physiologist. The diffused fibers of the sympathetic nervous system coalesce and center about two chains of ganglia that are arranged along the sides of the spinal cord. . . . These, in turn, connect eventually, and in the most dreadfully complicated way, with the hypothalamus, a delicate part of the brain that is centrally involved in the emotional reactions of the organism, and in the so-called homeostasis of the organism, *i.e.*, in the self-regulation of its internal environment. . . . The hypothalamus, in turn, is closely connected with the cortex and subcortical areas of the brain, so that physical and chemical changes within these areas produce corresponding physical effects within the hypothalamus, which in turn, by a series of physical processes whose complexity has only barely been suggested, produces such remote effects as the secretion of perspiration on the surface of the hands.

Such, in the barest outline, is something of the chemistry and physics of emotional perspiration. What is involved is an enormously complex causal chain of physical processes. For each part of this causal chain that is understood, there are doubtless a hundred that are not. The important point, however, is that in describing it as best we can, there is no need, at any stage, to introduce mental or nonphysical substances or reactions. The diffusion of sodium ions into a neuron, for instance, with the resultant flow of current, is not perfectly understood, but no one supposes that the understanding of this would be enhanced by reference to nonphysical or mental events, nor is it even possible to imagine how such nonphysical events could ever bring about, abet, or inhibit any such ion diffusion. . . .

But how exactly are we to conceive of this action of the mind upon that portion of the brain? Presumably, thoughts—that is, ideas or images—occur "within the mind." This must not for a moment be thought to mean that these occur within the brain or any part of it, for they are, according to the view we have been considering, strictly non-

> physical entities having no location in space, either within the heads or elsewhere, and no physical property whatever that would render them susceptible to observation or even to any detection by microscopes, probes, or any other physical apparatus. Yet these nonphysical things do, according to this view, act upon a physical object: the brain. . . . Conceive, then, if possible, how an *idea* can effect such a change as this, how an idea can render more permeable the membranes of certain brain cells, how an idea can enter into a chemical reaction whose effect is the diffusion of sodium ions at a certain place, or how an idea can move the particles of the cortical cells or otherwise aid or inhibit chemical reactions occurring therein. Try, I say, to form a conception of this, and then confess that, as soon as the smallest attempt at any description is made, the description becomes unintelligible and the conception an impossible one. . . .
>
> . . . Interactionism becomes quite unintelligible as soon as one endeavors to spell out, in some considerable detail, some bodily change, and then to show how mental or nonphysical processes can in any way be involved in such a change. It is not enough to say that the mind acts upon the body or that some particular mental thing, like an idea, acts upon some particular part of the body, such as the sweat glands. It is the precise *localization* of such activity that presents a great difficulty; as of course it must, since mental processes are, by the very description that is usually given of them, not localizable in the first place.

Taylor provides a detailed description of some of the many links in the complex physical chain of events leading up to the appearance of perspiration on the palms of his hands. His initial thought—that he was caused to perspire *by his vividly imagining* himself in a terrifying situation and, therefore, *by a mental event*—suggests that by tracing backward along the chain of events leading to his sweaty palms we will find a causally responsible act of imagining. But if, as the dualist claims, that act of imagining was a nonphysical act, then somewhere in the chain of physical events there will need to be a physical event without a physical cause—there will need to be a gap in the chain of physical causes and effects that is filled by a nonphysical entity.

The first thing Taylor's description of the cause of perspiration suggests is that there is no such place—no event in the chain of events—that cannot be assigned a physical cause. Wherever we have a physical event, we find—if our search is sufficiently thorough—another physical cause that suffices to explain it. But, as Taylor freely admits, there are many parts of the causal chain he describes that we do not fully understand. So why aren't those the locations where a nonphysical event—an imagining—might be hidden, and from which it might intervene in the sequence of physical causes and effects? One problem is that this suggestion is vulnerable to being overturned each time our scientific understanding of the brain advances. If dualists can only locate nonphysical events where our knowledge is incomplete, then dualism will always be in retreat from the advance of scientific knowledge.

Taylor thinks, however, that the problem for the dualist is even greater. He thinks we cannot make sense of the suggestion that a nonphysical cause intervenes to produce a physical effect—it is, he says, "unintelligible." His reason is that we can only hope to locate a nonphysical event somewhere in, or at the beginning of, our sequence of physical and chemical events if it makes sense to assign *locations* to nonphysical events. But we cannot assign a location to a mental event without thereby assigning to it a physical property. To have a location in space is *already* to have a physical property, and nonphysical events cannot have physical properties. If this is correct, then nonphysical minds can have no locations—they are nowhere. The problem for the dualist idea that an act of imagining is nonphysical is not that we cannot discover where the nonphysical act is located in the causal chain leading to sweaty palms. Taylor thinks the real problem is that nonphysical acts of imagining cannot have locations. And, he implies, if they have no location in space, they cannot enter into causal interactions with physical events that are located in space.

To explore Taylor's argument further, we might ask whether assigning a location to an event in space or time is, as he believes, to assign it a physical property, or whether something merely having a location in space is simply too little to constitute it as physical. After all, if there are nonphysical entities of any kind—minds, mental events, ghosts, or fairies—then they will need to be located *somewhere* in the universe. (Is there anywhere else for them to be?) "In the universe" is hardly a precise location, but why should that matter for Taylor's objection? So if we suppose that (1) to be "somewhere in the universe" is to have a spatial location, and also agree that (2) to have a spatial location is to have a physical property, then Taylor's objection to interactionist dualism is an objection to the idea that there could be any sort of nonphysical object anywhere. But this seems too quick! Should we be satisfied that thinking, imagining, and feeling bored are all *physical* phenomena merely because they are all *things that I do in my study*? Dualists, and not only interactionist dualists, will want to consider carefully which of Taylor's premises to question.

The Closure of the Physical Realm

The physical realm is widely thought to be "closed" or, put another way, physical quantities are "conserved" in nature. The idea is that very basic, very general physical laws require that certain physical quantities be conserved (preserved) in any interaction involving physical objects. For example, the law of conservation of momentum says that the *momentum* of physical objects, which is obtained by multiplying the mass of an object and its velocity, is conserved whenever they interact with each other. Consider a simple example, in which a moving billiard ball hurls toward a stationary billiard ball. Before they interact, the two billiard balls have the mass and velocity shown in Table 6.1:

Table 6.1

Ball One:	Ball Two:
Mass: 1 kg	Mass: 1 kg
Velocity: 10 m/s	Velocity: 0 m/s (not moving)

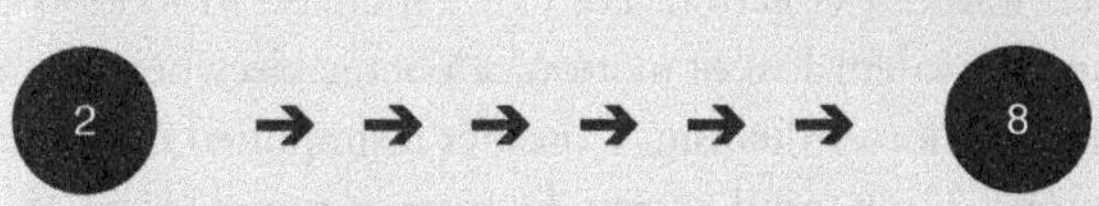

In Motion	Stationary

The momentum of each ball is calculated by multiplying its mass times its velocity, so the momentum of ball one is 10 kgm/s and the momentum of ball two is 0 kgm/s. The *total*, or combined, momentum of the two balls *before* they interact is 10—that is, 10 + 0. The law of conservation of momentum says that *before and after they interact, the two balls must have exactly the same total, or combined, momentum.* (We are supposing that no other forces are acting on the billiard balls—if there are other forces, then the same principle still applies, but the story becomes more complicated.) For example, suppose that after the interaction, the moving ball rebounds from the stationary ball, which is sent rolling across the table so that both balls are now moving. After the interaction, our two balls might have the following momenta (Table 6.2):

Table 6.2

Ball One:	Ball Two:
Mass: 1 kg	Mass: 1 kg
Velocity: 4 m/s	Velocity: 6 m/s
Momentum = 4 kgm/s	Momentum = 6 kgm/s

The total momentum after the collision in this interaction is 4 + 6 = 10, which is the same total momentum they had before the interaction. This is exactly what the conservation of momentum requires. The momentum has been redistributed: The first ball originally had it all, and the second ball had none, but now each ball has some of the momentum. The total amount of momentum before and after the interaction must always be the same. In effect, we cannot create momentum out of nothing.

The law of conservation of momentum is just one example of a conservation law. Many other physical quantities are conserved in nature. We can also view the law of conservation of momentum, and all conservation laws, as saying that all physical changes or events will have a completely adequate physical explanation. For example, if some object (e.g., one of our billiard balls, or the coffee cup on my desk) suddenly acquires momentum, going from zero momentum to some positive momentum, then something else must have contributed that amount of energy to it. But whatever contributed the energy must have had energy to contribute, and therefore it must have been physical. Energy, and momentum, can't just appear out of nowhere without violating a fundamental physical law. If some physical event occurs that is not explained by other physical events, and is not in accord with physical laws, then some important physical quantity will not be conserved. To prevent this, there must always be physical explanations for physical events. As this idea is sometimes expressed, the physical realm, or the realm of physical laws, has **closure**—in short, we never have to go outside the physical realm to find the explanations of physical events.

closure: (or **closure of the physical realm**) The general idea that any physical event can be completely explained by appealing only to other physical events. *Closure* is thought to be a consequence of conservation laws in physics, according to which certain basic physical quantities (e.g., momentum, mass, energy) are always conserved in nature.

It is important to recognize that claims about conservation laws have been checked countless times, and no one has found a violation. For every increase in motion or energy in one thing, we always find an equivalent loss of motion or energy elsewhere to explain it. This point causes trouble for interactionist dualism. Consider a simplified example: I *decide* to move my arm, and it does move. If my mind, or my decision, is nonphysical, then it will have no mass, and so it will have no momentum. My arm has mass, but since it was not moving before I decided to move it, it also had no momentum, like the second billiard ball just before the collision. Before the interaction the total momentum of mind and body combined was, then, zero. But once my arm is set in motion, it will have some positive momentum. According to the dualist, what sets my arm in motion (my decision, a nonphysical event in a nonphysical mind) has no mass and, so, it contributed no momentum to the interaction. My moving arm has somehow acquired momentum that did not exist before my mind interacted with it. *Momentum is not conserved in the interaction between nonphysical minds and physical bodies*. A basic law of physics is violated each time a nonphysical mind moves a physical body.

Logic Box

Inconsistent Triads

Two statements are **logically inconsistent** when it is not possible for both be true; that is, if one of them is true, then the other *must* be false. An **inconsistent triad** is then a set of three statements or doctrines that are related to each other in such a way that *it is not possible for all* of them to be true. Thus, if any two are true, then the third *must* be false. In an inconsistent triad, it is logically impossible for all three statements to be true, so *at least one* of them is false. But it is also possible that *more than one* of them is false.

Example: The following three statements form an inconsistent triad: (1) Either Samara or Dahlia took the last cookie from the jar; (2) Samara did not take the last cookie from the jar; (3) Dahlia did not take the last cookie from the jar.

Taking into account the closure of physical laws—or, alternatively expressed, of the physical realm—we can restate the interaction problem in the form of an inconsistent triad. Here is our trio of doctrines:

1. *Dualism:* The body is physical and the mind is nonphysical.
2. *Interactionism:* The mind affects the body and the body affects the mind.
3. *Closure of Physical Laws*: All physical changes can be completely explained by their physical causes.

By reflecting on what follows when we suppose that any two statements in the triad are true, we can see that these doctrines form an inconsistent triad.

First, if (1) dualism and (2) interactionism are true, then (3) the closure of physical laws must be false. We can see this in the following way: If a nonphysical mind affects the physical body, then there is a physical change for which there is not an adequate *physical* explanation. The physical change is not then explained by its physical causes, so its occurrence violates a basic law of physics.

Second, if (1) dualism and (3) the closure of physical laws both are true, then (2) interactionism must be false. That is, if the mind is nonphysical, but every physical (bodily) change has a completely physical explanation, then the mind does not contribute to the explanation of the behaviour of the body. We then have a view called *epiphenomenalism*, which maintains that minds are nonphysical but they cannot affect bodies.

Third, if (2) interactionism and (3) the closure of physical laws are true, then (1) dualism must be false. That is, if the mind does affect the body, but what the body does has a completely physical explanation, then *the mind must be physical.* We then have some form of materialism, not dualism.

The inconsistent triad purports to show that we must give up at least one of our three doctrines. Which one? Consider the options:

I. We can keep interactionism and dualism, and give up our belief in the closure of physical law.

There are two problems with this choice. First, if we give up the closure of physical law, we have to give up the conservation laws of physics, and we if give them up, we have to give up physics. We then need to learn to live without believing that the physical world is governed

logically inconsistent: Two statements are logically inconsistent or contradictory when the truth of one guarantees the falsity of the other and the falsity of one guarantees the truth of the other.

inconsistent triad: A set of three statements or doctrines related to one another in such a way that it is not possible for all of them to be true. Although it is logically impossible for all three statements in an inconsistent triad to be true, and so at least one of them *must* be false, it is also possible that more than one of them is false.

by strict laws. Second, to give up the closure of physical law *because* it conflicts with interactionist dualism will get us into trouble, because interactionist dualism has the consequence that a law of physics is violated each and every time a mind has an effect on a body. That happens literally hundreds of billions of times every single day: Each time any one of the billions of people on this planet performs an intentional action (e.g., decides to move her arm) a law of physics is violated. So (1) and (2) together do not merely imply that there will be *occasional* violations of physical law—violations that might be overlooked by us—they entail that such violations are occurring all around us, hundreds of billions of times every day. Why, then, can't we find any when we look for them? When we look long enough, we are able to find physical explanations for physical events. So, to give up (3) because it conflicts with (1) and (2) flies directly in the face of *easily checkable facts* about the behaviour of physical objects. Perhaps we should first consider the alternatives for escaping the inconsistency among our three doctrines.

II. We can give up the idea that the immaterial mind affects the body; that is, give up interactionism.

If we give up the idea that immaterial minds affect material bodies, we will have only physical explanations for everything physical bodies do. But physical bodies can still affect immaterial minds if we want them to—that won't wreak any havoc with the laws of physics. Why not accept this? The doctrine that our physical bodies are unaffected by our minds is called *epiphenomenalism*. The problem with this view is obvious to some critics: If it is true, then minds become useless things to have. They will be useless things to have, first, because nothing we do or say is explained by the fact that we have minds; and, second, because we would still do all the same things we now do, and say all the same things we now say, even if we didn't have minds—since, on this view, our minds have nothing do with our behaviour. Minds would be useless because they would contribute nothing to the explanation of what we do or say, and because taking our minds away will not change what we do or say.

III. We can give up the idea that minds are immaterial—that is, give up dualism.

The result would be a materialist theory of mind. The advantages of such a theory are now, hopefully, obvious: A physical mind would be a *useful* thing to have, since physical minds can interact with our bodies and can do so without violating the basic laws of physics. Physical minds would be minds that participate in bringing about our actions.

Given these apparent choices, it is not surprising that by the second half of the twentieth century, dualism had all but disappeared from the philosophy of mind, and most contemporary philosophical and scientific accounts of the mind are now materialist theories. Later, we will look at different versions of materialist theories of mind. First, however, we need to understand why many people resist materialist theories of mind, and see if materialists can ease the worries we might have about being reduced to merely physical things.

INDIRECT WORRIES ABOUT MATERIALISM

Materialism is the view that the mind and all of its contents—our beliefs, desires, hopes, wishes, perceptions, and feelings—are physical phenomena. On this view, we are completely physical entities, with no nonphysical parts or components. The most obvious form of materialism is **mind-brain identity theory**, according to which the mind is just the brain, and our thoughts, desires, and feelings are just neurological or electrochemical events occurring in the brain. In effect, every mental event *is* a physical event in the brain.

mind-brain identity theory: A materialist theory of mind that identifies mental states and events with physical (e.g., neurological and electrochemical) states and events in the brain. It is often formulated as a reductionist theory, and so it claims to reduce all mental phenomena to physical phenomena involving the brain.

Although this idea addresses the interaction problem and explains how minds can affect behaviour, resistance to it is still widespread. We will start by looking at some relatively indirect challenges to materialist theories of mind. These challenges are indirect because they don't attend to the metaphysical arguments surrounding the materialist theory itself. Instead, they point to the wider implications of materialism for our view of ourselves. We'll consider two such indirect challenges: The first claims that materialist theories of mind undermine morality; the second that materialist theories of mind conflict with religious doctrine.

A Moral Objection to Materialism

Some people believe there is a clash between regarding persons as purely physical, and regarding them as worthy of the special moral status they have. We might capture their reasoning as follows:

1. If materialism is true, then persons are only complex organisms—complicated biological "machines" made of flesh and blood—differing from cattle, rats, and spiders only in their degree of physical complexity.
2. If persons are only complex biological machines, then they are not things of special moral value—they are not worthy of the sort of love, respect, and praise we bestow upon them. They will lack that special human dignity or worth that makes them deserving of moral respect and moral treatment.
3. But persons *are* worthy of love and respect, and they *do* have the special dignity or worth that requires us to treat them with moral respect.
4. So, persons are not merely complex biological mechanisms, and the materialist theory of mind must be false.

Materialists respond to this complaint two ways: The more cynical response is that this reasoning doesn't show that materialism is *false*; it only shows that if materialism is true, then human life is more bleak than we generally admit, and our pretensions about our "special worth" are only myths. In effect, this response rejects premise (3) of the moral objection. This cynical response might even add that we only need to look with an unbiased eye at human history, or at contemporary human affairs, to see that we can't believe the inflated drivel about the "special dignity" and "moral worth" of human beings. How are we to explain the atrocities, the abuse, the lies, the death and suffering that human beings are continually inflicting on one another? There has never been a species as murderous, as cruel, and as indifferent to the suffering of its own kind as human beings. So, once we put aside our self-congratulatory fairy tales, the facts bear out the ugly materialist story. Of course, this is not how *most* materialists would reply; there is a far less cynical way to reconcile the materialist conception of human beings with morality.

Perhaps a better, or more politic, response is to deny premise (2) of the argument: A materialist can insist that at least some complex biological mechanisms are worthy of love and respect, and do have special moral value. They will reason as follows:

1. Human beings have moral value, and they are worthy of love and respect.
2. Human beings are merely complex biological organisms.
3. So, at least some complex biological organisms have moral value and are worthy of love and respect.

Indeed, this response can go even further and say that a failure to recognize this conclusion is a form of chauvinism that invites abuse. For example, when we wish to regard some class of human beings as unworthy of minimally decent moral treatment—to enslave them, for example—the standard move has been to deny that they have souls or minds, or to regard them as *mere animals*. Furthermore, our treatment of other species has not been exemplary. Once we see that we, too, are mere animals, however cunning and clever we think we are, and that therefore *mere animals can be morally significant*, we are then in a position to extend morality further—perhaps to include dolphins, orangutans, gorillas, or even dogs. These animals are also, like us, complicated biological mechanisms, with very sophisticated brains. So the materialist reply to the moral objection is that rather than deprive human beings of moral worth, materialism helps extend our moral sympathies more widely. This counts as moral progress.

A Theological Objection to Materialism

Not surprisingly, some think there may be serious conflicts between materialist theories of mind and religious doctrines. If one subscribes to those religious doctrines, and believes they conflict with materialism, then one will believe materialism to be false. But noting a conflict between two beliefs only tells us that one of them is false; it doesn't tell us which. It may be that these concerns can only show that materialism has unwelcome consequences for certain religious beliefs; for example, for some recent versions of Christianity. One theological objection to materialism takes the following form:

1. If materialism is true, then there is no life after death.
2. But, there is life after death.
3. So, materialism is not true.

The materialist response can take two forms: First, materialists can simply deny premise (2). We need to give up the mythology of life after death. This response can go even further: Since there is already an independent argument—the inconsistent triad—for the conclusion that materialism is true, then if materialism does conflict with immortality, it simply follows that no immortal life awaits us.

However, there is no reason someone who believes in an afterlife must believe premise (1). It is not obvious that belief in materialism is incompatible with belief in an immortal afterlife. In fact, historically a great many Christians who believed in an afterlife have been materialists. That is why they placed so much importance on *the resurrection of the body* on judgment day. On their view, God gathers up all your material parts and reassembles *you* on judgment day. If God reassembles you by reassembling your *physical* parts, the implication is that *you* are physical. So there is no essential conflict between materialism and belief in an afterlife. The conflict between materialism and dualism will have to be resolved on its own terms.

MIND-BRAIN IDENTITY THEORY

correlation: A regular association of two things or events—when one appears, the other appears according to some regular pattern. In a *perfect correlation* between two events, one event will *always* be associated with the other.

If, in order to address the interaction problem, we need to identify the mind with a physical entity, then the brain is the best candidate. There is much evidence that mental functions are directly correlated with brain functions. The relevant evidence takes the form of **correlations** that have been observed between brain events and mental events: Particular forms of brain damage result in particular mental deficits, or particular electrochemical interventions in the brain result in particular thoughts, feelings, or imagery. Two things are *correlated* when they regularly occur together, as smoke and fire are strongly correlated. But correlation is not the same as identity—smoke is not the same as fire. Even if smoke and fire were perfectly correlated, so that we never found one without the other, it would not make smoke and fire the same things.

Discovered correlations between mental events and brain events are only part of the story for thinking that mental events just *are* brain events. Those correlations need to be seen in light of the conclusion we reached earlier—namely, that if mental events matter to our behaviour at all, they will need to be physical events. So the mind-brain identity theory requires that we find a certain kind of physical event in the brain that is always correlated with a certain kind of mental event. For example, whenever we have a particular feeling—say, a feeling of amusement—there must be a particular brain event present. Without such correlations we can't take the further step of *identifying* feelings of amusement with brain events. In fact, neuroscientists believe they have located a physical event that is correlated with being amused:

> A *mind-brain correlation*: Whenever we are amused or find something funny, there is an increase in electrochemical activity in a region of the brain called the inferior temporal gyrus.

This is a *correlation* between one kind of mental state or mental event (our being amused) and one kind of brain event (increased activity in the inferior temporal gyrus). Dualists will still insist that *two completely distinct things* may be perfectly correlated with one another, and so they may insist that, despite their correlation, the electrical events in our brain are one thing, and the feelings of amusement are another. But if we address the interaction problem by giving up dualism for a materialist theory of mind, we will need to suppose that our feelings of amusement just are physical states. Since we find no other physical states that are correlated with our feelings of amusement, the electrochemical events in our inferior temporal gyrus seem the best candidates.

Notice, now, that if this particular kind of brain event—increased activity in the temporal gyrus—really *is* a feeling of amusement, then whatever causes us to feel amused (e.g., a joke) will cause increased activity in the temporal gyrus, and whatever behaviour (e.g., smiles and laughter) is caused by our feelings of amusement will be caused by increased activity in the temporal gyrus. In other words, if a mental state is identical with some brain state, then that mental state and that brain state will have the same causes and effects—they will play the same causal role. This is a consequence of Leibniz's Law. So mind-brain identity theory claims that when we find a physical state that has the same causal role as our feelings of amusement, then we can reasonably believe that our discovered correlation is a discovered identity. We can thus say,

> A *mind-brain identity:* Feelings of amusement just are (=) increased electrochemical activity in the inferior temporal gyrus.

As various scientific studies of the brain progress, the mind-brain identity theory says we will find these sorts of relationships between mental states and brain states for all our mental states. That is what entitles us to say that the mind is the brain.

Epiphenomenalism

A die-hard dualist might not, however, be persuaded. Suppose, she might say, we accept that the increased activity in the temporal gyrus always causes laughter; furthermore, let us also suppose that things we find amusing—jokes and comedy—always cause the relevant kind of increased electrochemical activity. So the things we thought were the causes and effects of our feelings of amusement are, in fact, the causes and effects of electrochemical activity in the brain. But that doesn't mean that feelings of amusement *are* electrochemical events in the brain. It could equally mean that feelings of amusement are the constant, but nonphysical, *accompaniments* of increased activity in the inferior temporal gyrus. For all that the evidence suggests, nonphysical feelings of amusement might be the epiphenomenal accompaniments of events in the brain. The idea is best explained in a simple diagram, in which arrows connect causes to their effects:

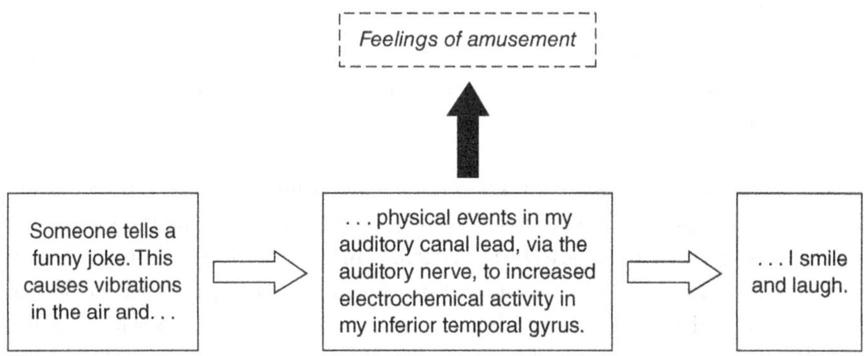

Figure 6.1

As Figure 6.1 shows, the nonphysical feelings of amusement are *epiphenomenal*—that is, although they are caused by physical events in my brain, the feelings themselves do not cause any of the physical behaviour (e.g., laughter, etc.) that follow from my hearing the joke. Since my feelings of amusement are nonphysical, they are causally impotent, and the electrochemical activity in the brain is fully responsible for all the physical and behavioural effects from my hearing the joke. But, as Figure 6.1 also shows, the feelings of amusement are not identical to the electrochemical activity in my brain. They are consequences of it, like shadows cast by my brain activity. In our example, my laughter is not a result of my feeling amused. It is a result of brain activity that also has feelings of amusement as a side effect. On the epiphenomenalist view of mind and body, our mental lives are side effects of the stream of causes and effects—not part of that stream.

We saw earlier that the obvious objection to epiphenomenalism is that it makes minds useless things to have, since it represents our minds as powerless to explain what we do or say, and because what we do or say would not change if we didn't have minds. At this stage of the argument between dualists and materialists, the defender of the mind-brain identity theory is likely to raise a version of this objection by invoking an important metaphysical principle called **Ockham's Razor**. Ockham's Razor says that we should not have unnecessary components in an explanation. That is, when we have two equally plausible explanations of the same thing, the simpler explanation is the better one. An explanation that requires only *one* thing to explain something is better than an explanation that requires two or three things to explain the same phenomenon, providing that both explain the phenomenon equally well. The simpler explanation will be better because the more complicated explanation will contain components that are *redundant or superfluous*. So the materialist's reply is that the addition to the diagram of the nonphysical, and causally impotent, feeling of amusement is superfluous—all that needs explaining is already explained without it. In effect, the vertical arrow in Figure 6.1 should be replaced with a sign of identity.

Ockham's Razor: A methodological and metaphysical principle that says we should not have any more components in an explanation than are needed. Thus, when we have two equally plausible explanations of something, the simpler of the two explanations is the better one.

How well does Ockham's Razor work as a reply to the epiphenomenalist? That will depend on whether the addition of the nonphysical and epiphenomenal feeling of amusement is really a redundant or superfluous addition to Figure 6.1. You will need to think this through carefully: Is there anything left unexplained if we leave out the nonphysical feeling? This is a matter to which we will return in the following chapter, where we will encounter a contemporary revival of epiphenomenal dualism.

Reduction and Elimination

We have largely used one example, but, in general, mind-brain identity theory says that each type of mental state or event is identical with a particular type of brain state or brain event. Exactly *which type* of brain event is identical with *which type* of mental event is left for neuroscientists to discover. On this view, our mental lives are appropriate matters for scientific investigation and study, and we can hope to one day discover enough mind-brain correlations to enable us to construct a properly scientific account of our mental lives. In that event, our mental lives will be *reduced* to aspects of our physical lives.

The mind-brain identity theory of mind is called a **reductionist theory of mind**—that is, it *reduces* minds and mental states to brains and brain states. A reductionist theory is one that claims that one kind of entity *really just is* (i.e., reduces to) another kind of entity. A great many successful scientific discoveries have taken this form. For example, we have discovered that

reductionist theory of mind: A materialist theory of mind that maintains that we can have true generalizations identifying mental states of the same type with physical states of the same type.

a. Water is H_2O.

b. Lightning is an atmospheric electrical discharge.

c. Heat is the kinetic energy of molecules.

It is important to notice that these reductionist claims do not deny that water, lightning, or heat exist. Rather, they purport to tell us more about what those things really are. Sometimes, in the effort to understand some puzzling phenomenon, it helps if we know that it is really just an aspect of another phenomenon we already understand. For example, suppose we have a good understanding of kinetic energy and how it works, but the phenomenon of heat remains mysterious. If we can *reduce* heat to kinetic energy—that is, if we can *identify* heat with one kind of kinetic energy—then we will have a better understanding of heat. Although the brain sciences are still very young, and there is a great deal we don't yet understand about how the brain functions, we know exactly how to go about learning more. So if we can reduce minds to brains and mental events to brain events, then we will know how to go about learning more about minds and mental events.

This is a simple point, but it is easily misunderstood. Misunderstandings arise because there can be a very uncertain boundary between (1) *reducing* a phenomenon that is mysterious to another phenomenon that is less mysterious, and (2) *eliminating* the mysterious first phenomenon—that is, denying that the first phenomenon exists. For example, someone might say that

a. UFOs are really just swamp gas; or

b. witches are really just delusional people; or

c. Santa Claus is really just the spirit of giving.

But someone who says these things doesn't intend to announce *a discovery about the true constitution of* UFOs, witches, or Santa Claus. What they mean is that *there are no such things* as UFOs—belief in UFOs is a mistake that results from misidentifying what is really only swamp gas. They are saying that UFOs don't exist. They are eliminating them from their view of what the world contains.

Reduction and elimination are sometimes confused, since when we reduce one phenomenon (X) to another phenomenon (Y), we can express the result as "Xs really are Ys" (minds are really just brains); and when we eliminate one phenomenon, we sometimes also say "Xs really are Ys" (UFOs are really just swamp gas). When reductionist materialists deny that there are nonphysical minds, then someone who is accustomed to thinking of minds as nonphysical might *mis*-hear that as a way of saying that there are no minds. This is a misunderstanding of the reductionist view—a confusion of *reduction* with *elimination*. Similarly, if you are accustomed to thinking of UFOs as alien spacecraft, then the discovery that what we have been calling UFOs are really only glowing methane gases from a nearby swamp will not sound like a discovery about the nature of UFOs. It will—in this case, rightly—only sound like the discovery that there are no UFOs. For this reason it is important to remember that when mind-brain identity theorists say that mental events are really just electrochemical events in the brain, they are *not denying the reality of mental events*. Instead, they are *reducing* mental events to physical events: They are, they think, explaining mental events in terms we can better understand.

eliminative materialism: A form of materialism that sees the discoveries and explanatory successes of modern neuroscience as showing that minds and mental states are fictions; when the neurosciences are complete and we can provide physical explanations for all behaviour, then talking about minds and mental states will no longer serve any explanatory purpose.

It is worth mentioning, however, that there is one form of materialism, called **eliminative materialism**, that understands the discoveries of modern neuroscience in a very different way. Eliminative materialists think that what modern neuroscience has discovered is that there really are no minds, and so there are no feelings of amusement, no thoughts, no desires, and so on. There are *only* such things as electrochemical events in the inferior temporal gyrus. Although we won't explore eliminative materialism here, you need to be aware of it so that you avoid confusing what mind-brain identity theorists say with what eliminative materialists say. The distinction between the three metaphysical postures of realism, reductionism, and eliminativism will help. Dualism is a form of metaphysical realism about minds—it holds that minds and mental states are real, but that they are something in addition to the brain and brain states. The mind-brain identity theorist believes that mental states and events—our beliefs, desires, hopes, wishes, and so on—are *very real things*: They are physical states and events involving our brains. For the eliminative materialist, brains are very real things, but minds are fictional or mythological entities. We should not confuse the latter two views, despite the fact that both views can say that minds are really just brains. Remembering the distinction between them requires a good grasp of the distinction between reduction and elimination.

CONCLUSION

In this chapter we asked whether the mind is physical or nonphysical. We encountered two dualist theories that distinguish nonphysical minds from physical bodies, but only one of those—interactionist dualism—allows that minds can affect or control bodies. The second dualist theory, epiphenomenalism, maintains that, although physical things can indeed affect nonphysical things, nonphysical things cannot affect physical things.

The great advantage of materialist theories of mind is that they face no problems explaining how minds can interact with the physical world. After all, according to such theories, minds are themselves among the entities of the physical world, so they are linked to other physical entities in all the usual ways—by cause and effect, and in accord with physical laws. Mind-brain identity theories argue that we will only be able to explain the causal powers of the mind by identifying the mind with the brain and by reducing mental events to physical changes in the brain.

Surprisingly, the reductionist aspect of mind-brain identity theory that allows mind-brain identity theory to avoid interaction problems actually creates some important problems for the theory. The next chapter looks at criticisms of the mind-brain identity theory, and presents a sophisticated but non-reductionist form of materialism that has risen to prominence among contemporary theories of the mind.

Key Terms and Figures

dualism p. 112
epiphenomenalism p. 112
materialism p. 112
nonphysical p. 112
physical p. 112
strict laws p. 113
circular definition p. 113
Leibniz's Law p. 114
indiscernibility of identicals p. 114
interactionism p. 119
interactionist dualism p. 119
Elizabeth of Bohemia p. 119
interaction problem p. 120
closure (closure of the physical realm) p. 124
logically inconsistent p. 125
inconsistent triad p. 125
mind-brain identity theory p. 126
correlation p. 128
Ockham's Razor p. 131
reductionist theory of mind p. 131
eliminative materialism p. 132

Additional readings on dualism, interactionism, and mind-brain identity theory

Churchland, P. (2013). Chapter 2: The Ontological Problem (the Mind-Body Problem). *Matter and Consciousness*, Third Edition. MIT Press, 11–36.

Gertler. B. (2007). In Defense of Mind-Body Dualism. In J. Feinberg and R. Shafer-Landau (Eds.), *Reason and Responsibility*, Thirteenth edition. Wadsworth, 285–96.

Heil, J. (2004). *Philosophy of Mind: A Contemporary Introduction*, Second edition. New York: Routledge, 15–40.

Place, U. T. (1956). Is Consciousness a Brain Process? *The British Journal of Psychology*, *47*: 44–50, 1956. Widely reprinted, including in Chalmers, D. J. (2002). *Philosophy of Mind: Classical and Contemporary Readings*. Oxford: Oxford University Press, 55–60.

Robinson, H. Dualism. *Stanford Encyclopedia of Philosophy*. Retrieved July 26, 2014, from http://plato.stanford.edu/entries/dualism

Tollefsen, D. (1999). Princess Elizabeth and the Problem of Mind-Body Interaction. *Hypatia 14.3*, 59–77.

Chapter 7

Minds and Machines

Learning Objectives

- Contrast reductive and non-reductive theories of mind.
- Construct at least two objections to reductive materialism.
- Define functionalist theories of mind, and clarify how functionalism addresses the problems that confront reductive materialism.
- Show why functionalism implies the possibility of genuine artificial intelligence.
- Describe the Turing Test for artificial intelligence.
- Describe Searle's Chinese Room thought experiment and explain why it is thought to expose a problem with the Turing Test.
- Explain what reversed spectra and zombies are, and why each is thought to be a problem for functionalist theories and for materialist theories of mind.

Two things explain the success of materialist theories of mind in the twentieth century. First, the obvious alternative—dualism—appeared to have a fatal weakness: It was unable to allow for minds to affect or control bodies. But if nonphysical minds cannot have effects on bodies, they cannot have effects on our behaviour, and then they aren't worth having. Second, the developing neurosciences offered suggestive evidence for the mind-brain identity theory version of materialism through the discovery of numerous correlations between mental states and brain states. Although such correlations are not proof of identities between mental and physical states, they point clearly in that direction.

Nonetheless, in the second half of the twentieth century disagreements surfaced within the materialist school, and a number of philosophers began to offer challenges to the mind-brain identity theory. The result was not a return to dualism, but a move to a more sophisticated form of materialism, one that came to dominate contemporary thinking about the mind. The new developments were found especially congenial when philosophers saw that increasingly sophisticated computers provide a better model for understanding both brains and minds. In this chapter, we explore these more recent developments in the philosophy of mind.

REDUCTIONISM AND MULTIPLE REALIZABILITY

Mind-brain identity theory seemed the most viable theory of mind only for a relatively short period of the mid-twentieth century; it was quickly challenged by other materialist theories. What caused trouble for mind-brain identity theory was its *reductionism*. The theories that challenged it were *non-reductionist*, or non-reductive, versions of materialism. To better understand why many materialists grew dissatisfied with the mind-brain identity theory, we must better understand the reductionism that shaped it.

Modelled after successful reductions in the sciences, reductive theories of mind hold that entities of one sort, such as mental states, are really just entities of another sort, such as physical states of the brain. That is what it means to say that things of the first kind are *reduced to* things of the second kind. For example, feelings of amusement are electrochemical events of a certain sort occurring in a specific part of the brain. Reductive materialism holds that we can make such claims about *all* mental states and events. For example, as they investigate the brain further, perhaps neuroscientists will discover such things as these:

- A belief that it is raining is a specific electrochemical potential of the cerebral cortex.
- Sensations of pain are excitations of the C-fibres in our nervous systems.
- Feelings of love are excess accumulations of potassium ions in the hypothalamus.

In each of these claims, a particular *kind of mental state* (e.g., a certain belief, sensation, or feeling) is identified with a particular *kind of physical state* of the brain or nervous system. So a reductive form of materialism, such as the mind-brain identity theory, offers *generalizations* that identify mental states and brain states, just as a chemist might offer the generalization "All table salt is sodium chloride," or a physicist might offer the generalization "All ambient heat is kinetic energy."

A consequence of such generalizations is that if you and I have the same belief, or the same kind of sensation or feeling, then we will be in the same kind of physical state. So if a feeling of love is just an excess of potassium ions in the hypothalamus region of the brain, and we both feel love, then we will both have an excess of potassium ions in that part of our brains. Similarly, if we *all* feel love, we will *all* have that particular type of brain state. If a reductivist form of materialism is true, then *all those who have the same kind of mental state will also have the same kind of brain state*. Put the other way around, if you do *not* have the same brain states as someone else, then you do *not* have the same mental states they have. If the hypothalamus region of your brain is not flooded with an excess of potassium ions, then you are not currently experiencing a feeling of love. This is the consequence of reductive materialism about the mind that eventually led to concerns within the materialist camp.

chauvinistic (or chauvinism): In the philosophy of mind, this refers to a presumption that any creature with a radically different physical structure than humans cannot have the same kinds of mental states as humans. Chauvinism of this sort is thought to be a consequence of generalizations about mind-brain identities that are standard in reductionist theories of mind: If our minds are *our* brains, then nothing can have a mind unless it has a brain *like ours*.

Suspicions about mind-brain identity theory take two closely related forms. The first criticism is that reductive mind-brain identity theory is **chauvinistic**: The theory has the consequence that any creature that is not physically very like us (i.e., who does not have the same sort of brain, or is not capable of having the same sort of brain states) cannot have any of the same mental states we have.

Why should this consequence be a problem for the theory? Suppose there are intelligent life forms on other planets whose evolution has followed different trajectories than ours. For example, they might have brains, but do not have brains that work anatomically, neurologically, or chemically in the same way as ours. (Some people have speculated about the possibility of life forms with silicon-based chemistry, quite unlike our carbon-based chemistry.) Now, according to the mind-brain identity theory, we can already be sure that any such alien creatures will not have beliefs, desires, and feelings of the sort that we have, since *those kinds mental states* are identical with particular kinds of states of our distinctively human brains. So if alien brains are physically very different than ours, the mind-brain identity theory dictates that their mental states, if they have any, will also have to be very different than ours. If the mind-brain identity theory is true, we have to conclude that we could never understand—or be understood by—aliens who are physically different from us. After all, if their brains are not like ours, then they could not have any of the same beliefs, desires, or feelings we have and, so, will be unintelligible to us.

Similarly, we can conclude in advance, without ever building one, that no future supercomputer will be able to have thoughts, beliefs, or intentions. After all, computers will not have biological brains with the physiology or chemistry of our brains, so they will never have the same kinds of brain states we have. If the mind-brain identity theory is right, computers will never have thoughts, desires, or feelings. In general, if minds are just *brains like ours*, we must conclude that nothing could have a mind at all unless it has a brain *like ours*.

Of course, it may be true that there are no intelligent life forms that are physically very different from us or, if there are life forms physically quite unlike us, perhaps they do not have anything like thoughts and feelings. But the problem is that we should not be able to decide this in advance of actual space exploration or in advance of actually meeting them. The question of whether a creature that is physiologically and neurologically very different from us is capable of thinking that it is raining or of feeling wonder or pain seems to be an empirical one, and not a question we should let our theory of mind settle in advance of the relevant investigations. Reductive materialism, as represented by mind-brain identity theory, seems to do exactly that, and this makes it an unattractive theory of mind.

A second problem looks even worse for reductive materialism. We already have good reason to believe that people can perform a lot of the same mental operations, and have a lot of the same beliefs, desires, and feelings, without being in the same physical (brain) states. For example, partially brain-damaged patients, who lose certain mental abilities when portions of their brains are damaged or even removed, have in many cases been able to recover those same mental abilities later *by using different parts their brains*. The fact that, in different people, different regions of the brain can perform the same mental tasks, or that two different brains can perform the same tasks in two different ways, is referred to as the **multiple realizability** of mental states. In short, it means that different brains can physically "realize," or actualize, the same mental states in different ways.

multiple realizability: Mental states are *multiply realizable* when the same types of mental states can be actualized, or realized, in physically different ways by the brain.

The phenomenon of multiple realizability has struck some philosophers as a devastating problem for the reductive mind-brain identity theory of mind. If, for example, feelings of love can be realized in one way by my brain—by a flood of potassium ions into my hypothalamus—but in another way by your brain—by a flood of alcohol molecules into your cerebral cortex—then we can no longer accept the generalization that feelings of love are identical with, or "reduce to," a brain state of a particular kind. This doesn't mean that "feelings of love" are nonphysical—it only means that they can take *many different physical forms*, in something like the way modes of transportation can take many different physical forms (e.g., cars, boats, planes, horses, and so on).

Philosophers who find these criticisms of the reductionist aspect of the mind-brain identity theory compelling have developed *non-reductive* forms of materialism. To see what this means, we'll consider the best-known example of non-reductive materialism: the *functionalist* theory of the mind.

FUNCTIONALIST THEORIES OF MIND

Reductive materialism claims that all mental states of the same kind must be physical states of the same kind, but that pre-judges whether there might be aliens and, one day, supercomputers endowed with minds. Its critics also doubt that it accords well with what we already know about how the human brain works. Materialists therefore need a way of identifying mental states with physical states of the brain that allows them to identify different instances of the *same type of mental state* with *different types of physical states* of the brain. For example, it should be possible for your belief that today is Thursday, and my belief that today is Thursday, to be identical with different physical states. When I believe it is Thursday, perhaps I am in brain state number 278, but when you have that same belief, perhaps you are in brain state number 146. At the same time, the new theory must be able to tell us why your brain state number 146 and my brain state number 278, as *different* as they are physically, can still be the *same* belief.

It is not difficult to see how this might be possible—after all, there are lots of examples of *things of the same kind* that have *very different physical constitutions*. Consider three examples:

1. A *carburetor* is the component of an internal combustion engine that regulates the mixture of fuel and air. But carburetors come in many different designs, and they can be made from very different materials (e.g., metal, glass, or plastic) and still serve that function.
2. The *bait* is the component of a mouse trap that entices a mouse into the trap. But we can use a piece of cheese, a piece of apple, or a piece of cracker in the mouse trap and they can all be *bait*, despite their very different physical compositions.
3. A *coffee table* is a piece of furniture that serves the purpose of keeping magazines, the remote control, and coffee cups off the living room floor. But coffee tables come in many different designs and materials—one might be constructed of wood, another of metal, and a third of glass.

In each of these examples, things of *the same kind*—carburetors, bait, and coffee tables—are "realized" in multiple ways; the same sort of thing can be physically constituted from a variety of materials in a variety of shapes. In each case, we can see what makes this possible: Being a coffee table doesn't consist in having a special material composition—it consists in serving a certain function in our homes. Similarly, being bait, or being a carburetor, doesn't require having some particular physical composition; it only requires that the object fill a certain role or perform a certain function. There are many examples of objects that are identified, or defined, by the functions they perform and not by the materials from which they are made.

functional role: The causal role that something occupies in a wider system; in other words, the contribution it makes in taking us from inputs, or causes, to outputs, or effects.

If I describe something as "bait," as a "carburetor," or as a "coffee table," I am describing it by mentioning its function—its **functional role** or job—not by mentioning what it is composed of or how it is constructed. From knowing only that something is a coffee table, you can't infer much about what it is made from or how it is constructed, but you will know what job it is meant to perform. Similarly, when I call something "bait," I am labelling it in terms of its function—I am describing it in a vocabulary that indicates the job it performs within the mouse trap of which it is a functioning part. But my description of it as "bait" tells you nothing about its material composition. Some things can, in this way, be given *functional descriptions*. When someone calls me "Professor," they are giving me a functional description. "Professor" names my job or role, not my physical characteristics or composition. The lessons we are meant to take from these examples are as follows:

> Some things can be identified or described in terms of their function (i.e., job or role) rather than in terms of their physical make-up.
>
> Things with the same functional description can have different physical constitutions—they can be physically very different from each other despite having the same function.

functionalism: A form of materialist theory of mind that identifies *types* of mental states with the *functional roles* occupied by physical states of the brain. Functionalism is a *materialist* theory because it holds that each mental state—the occupants of functional roles—is a physical state; but it is also a *nonreductionist* theory since it allows different instances of the same type of mental state to have different physical constitutions.

With this in mind it's easy to state the functionalist theory of mind—for short, **functionalism**. Functionalism says, simply, that when we talk about people's mental states we are giving functional descriptions of them. Even more simply: Mental states are states of our brain or central nervous system identified in terms of their functional roles. So, when I say that you and I both believe that today is Thursday, I am saying that you and I each have a brain state that plays the same functional role—a state that does the same job in explaining and controlling your behavior and mine. Although you and I have physical states that perform the same function, and so we have the same belief, this does not mean we have the states of the same physical kind.

It is important to keep in mind that when functionalists speak of something's "function" or "functional role," they need not mean the purpose for which it was designed or intended. Our ears serve a function even if no one planned or intended for them to have that function. (Mother nature doesn't plan ahead.) Broadly speaking, functionalists use the term "function" for *the causal role* that an object occupies—for *what it does*, whether or not it was designed or intended for that purpose. Thus, the belief that it is raining might have as its causal role that it is normally produced by looking out the window on a rainy day, and it normally causes us to pick up our umbrellas on the way out the door.

When we understand functional states in this way, we can see that they don't just cause behaviour—they can also cause, or be caused by, other mental states. My glimpse out the window might cause a belief that it is raining, but it might also cause me to feel gloomy and to have the additional thought that I should cancel the picnic. Furthermore, it helps to notice that the behaviour or "output" that a mental state produces is not generally caused by that mental state acting alone—it is also determined by the other mental states that are already there and that work in concert with it to produce our behaviour. Thus, the *belief* that it is raining will cause us to pick up our umbrellas if we also have, among our mental states, a *desire* to stay dry. But in the presence of very different desires, the belief that it is raining can cause us to act in very different ways. So functional roles are causal roles, but those can be intricately interconnected and so quite difficult to describe.

Non-reductive Materialism

non-reductive materialism: Any materialist theory of mind that denies that we can have true generalizations that identify mental states with physical states. Although it holds that mental states are always physical states, it allows that mental states of the same kind are not always physical states of the same kind. Functionalism is the best known non-reductive materialist theory.

Our functionalist theory of mind no longer prevents aliens, or dogs, or future supercomputers from having at least some of the same mental states we have, even if we are all physically constituted in very different ways. And it no longer prevents two people from using different parts of their brains to realize the same mental state; indeed, even a single person might, at different times, realize the same mental state in different physical ways. Functionalism is, then, a form of **non-reductive materialism**. It remains a form of materialism, since mental states remain physical states. If they weren't, they couldn't do the jobs or occupy the causal roles that make them the states they are. But it is also "non-reductionist" because, on the functionalist view, *no generalizations can be made about the physical basis or constitution of any type of mental state*. Although we can reduce heat to the kinetic energy of particles, or water to H_2O, we cannot reduce love to an excess of potassium ions the hypothalamus, even if that is exactly how love is constituted in my brain. Generalizations of another sort can still be made: For example, if we both have the belief that it is raining, then we will both have physical states of our brains with similar functions—we will both have states of our brains that regulate our behaviour in similar ways, such as getting us to cancel the picnic or to collect our umbrellas before we go outdoors.

The central difference between reductive materialism, such as the mind-brain identity theory, and the non-reductive functionalist theory can be put this way: Suppose we are mentally equivalent in some way. The mind-brain identity theory then says we must be physically equivalent in some way. But the functionalist theory denies this, and says that if we are *mentally equivalent* in some way, then we only need to be *functionally equivalent* in some way. According to functionalist theories, it doesn't matter what something is made of or what it looks like—it will have a mind if it has something that does the jobs that minds do. So nothing in the functionalist theory prevents us from encountering aliens who think and feel, or from one day building machines—supercomputers, for example—that think. If the alien or the supercomputer have parts that perform the same jobs that parts of our brains perform when we are thinking, then the alien or the supercomputer is also thinking. It should now be obvious that functionalism not only allows for the possibility of intelligent but nonhuman life forms, it also makes artificial intelligence a very real possibility.

Functionalism and Artificial Intelligence

> . . . [F]or we may easily conceive a machine to be so constructed that it emits vocables . . . but not that it should arrange them variously so as appositely to reply to what is said in its presence, as men of the lowest grade of intellect can do.[1]

To sharpen our appreciation of the functionalist theory, we will look at how functionalists answer the question of whether we could in principle (even if not in practice) build a machine that thinks. We will also need to explore how we would know if we succeeded.

Could a machine really think? If by "machine" we mean merely a complex physical object, then the answer has to be yes. After all, *we* think, and we are machines

[1] Descartes, R. (1637). *Discourse on Method*, Part V. (John Veitch, Trans.). Retrieved on July 30, 2014, from http://www.gutenberg.org/cache/epub/59/pg59.txt

of that sort. As inventor Thomas Edison is reported to have said, we are machines made of meat. To make our question more interesting, we should restrict the term "machine" to *an artifact manufactured from inorganic materials*. If that is what we mean by a "machine," then could a machine think? It's easy to see how dualists or reductive materialists will answer our question: Both must give a resounding no. Dualism requires that thinking things be made of the right sort of nonphysical stuff, and reductive materialism requires that thinking things be made of the same sort of physical stuff we are made of.

Since the functionalist idea is that something will have a mind if it has parts that do whatever minds do, we need only check to see if something does the right things in order to determine if it has a mind. But what is it that minds do? What *function(s)* do minds have? This is a tough question, and fortunately we don't need to answer it.[2] We can simply proceed in this way: Since we assume we have minds, we can say that a machine that does what our minds do also has a mind. In particular, if a machine could do what we do when we think—if it could perform the same tasks—then that machine would be thinking. This is a direct consequence of functionalism, since functionalism says that to be thinking is to be performing certain sorts of tasks. So if a machine performs the tasks that qualify us as "thinking" when we perform them, then it also thinks; and if it thinks, it is fair to say that it has, at least to that extent, a mind.

Of course, few people, if any, believe that we have already succeeded in building machines that can think. Nonetheless, many of those engaged in research on artificial intelligence hold out hope that, with enough time and ingenuity, it could be done. Others engaged in such research doubt the possibility. These two groups of researchers view their *research programs* in different ways. Those who believe we could in principle design a machine—a sufficiently fast and complex piece of hardware with a sufficiently complex program—that *actually thinks* subscribe to the program of **strong artificial intelligence** (strong AI). On the other side, there are those who concede that a machine might one day perform the same tasks that we perform when we are thinking, but still doubt that any such machine would really be thinking. They say instead that the machine would only **simulate** thinking—that is, imitate thinking or duplicate the output of thinking beings without actually doing any thinking. This second group of researchers subscribe to the more modest program of **weak artificial intelligence** (weak AI).

strong artificial intelligence: A program of research in artificial intelligence that believes that a sufficiently fast and complex piece of hardware with a sufficiently complex program could in principle duplicate—in other words, actually possess—mental states and mental processes.

simulate: In the philosophy of mind, to simulate is to give a behavioural imitation—a mock presentation—of mental states without actually having mental states.

weak artificial intelligence: A program of research in artificial intelligence that believes that no piece of hardware, however fast, complex, or sophisticated, can ever do more than merely *simulate* mental states and mental processes.

Since functionalists say that something that is functionally equivalent to us is therefore mentally equivalent to us, they think that having components that can do what our minds do is all there is to having a mind like ours. They dismiss the idea that we might build a supercomputer that could do what our minds do but that would not have a mind. Whatever does what minds do *is* a mind. In other words, functionalists accept the strong AI program.

[2] A plausible (but rough) functionalist answer might begin with the idea that minds mediate between information that a creature takes in from its environment and the behaviour that it puts out–they mediate between informational input and behavioural output. Then, *mental states are just those physical states, identified in terms of their functional roles*—that is, in terms of their particular jobs within a system (organism, machine, etc.)–that mediate between informational input from the system's environment and its behavioural output. This remains only a very crude beginning until we have a better understanding of what "information" and "behaviour" mean.

The Turing Test

How can we tell if something is actually thinking or is only *simulating*, or imitating, thinking? It is useful to remember how miserably some have failed to handle similar questions in the past. At one time, questions like the following were sometimes taken seriously: "Do women (or people of other races, people of other ethnic groups, and so on) think?" "Do women really have minds, or do they only simulate having minds?" "Could they one day be taught to think?" Suppose, in order to answer this question, we propose a relatively simple empirical test: If they can carry on intelligent conversations that are indistinguishable from conversations that men carry on, then women also think. Alternatively put: *If they can do things that qualify as thinking when men do them*, then *they also think*. To refuse to allow some such test could hardly do more than reveal an ugly bias.

To design a fair test for whether a machine is actually thinking and not merely simulating thinking, we will need to ensure that our test meets a few minimal conditions:

1. We must be careful not to impose on machines requirements that are *too strong*.

A requirement will be too strong if we—or at least persons whom we count as thinking—don't meet the requirement. For example, we can't have the requirements that the test subject must be able to write or understand poetry; or that the subject be capable of feeling love; or that the subject be able to understand the novels of James Joyce. These requirements are too strong because we all know people who don't meet them.

2. We must be careful not to make the requirements for a thinking machine *too weak*.

A requirement will be too weak if things that we already agree do not think—for example, stones or waterfalls—can easily pass the test. Such a test won't successfully sort the thinkers from the non-thinkers.

3. We must not impose on machines requirements that *are not understood well enough* to decide if something actually meets them.

An example of a requirement for a thinking thing that fails to meet this condition might be "The test subject must have self-awareness." We might require that a subject have self-awareness before it qualifies as having a mind, but only if we can first make clear exactly what we require for self-awareness and if we can say exactly how we know that other people have it. But without such refinements, we will only disagree about whether something passes the test. For example, some infants can recognize themselves in a mirror. Is that self-awareness? The same infants lack the ability to feel embarrassment. Doesn't that demonstrate a lack of self-awareness? Do such infants have or lack self-awareness?

4. Our requirement for machines should *not assume in advance that "having a mind" is an all-or-nothing affair*.

That is, we should not assume that either something has no mind at all or has a full-blown intellect and a complex emotional life just like normal adult humans. Minds might come in degrees, from relatively simple minds to much fancier minds like ours. If that is so, then the fact that something does not have a mind as fancy as ours is not a reason to conclude that it has no mind at all.

In 1950, British mathematician **Alan Turing** (1912–1954) proposed a simple test for whether a computer is capable of thought. His test, which he called the **Imitation Game**,

Alan Turing: British mathematician, logician, and computing theorist who led the team of cryptographers that cracked the Enigma code, developed the idea of a universal Turing machine (the foundation for all modern computing), and established the first research program on artificial intelligence.

Imitation Game: Alan Turing's original name for what we now know as the *Turing Test*.

was a test for artificial intelligence. In his honour, it is now usually referred to as the **Turing Test**. Turing proposed a way to judge whether something has a mind without allowing our prior biases or prejudices to determine the outcome of the test.

Turing Test: A test to detect artificial intelligence originally proposed by Alan Turing, who referred to it as the *Imitation Game*. The test looks for functional equivalence between machines and persons—specifically, equivalence in how each conducts conversations—and supposes that whenever a machine is functionally equivalent to persons, then it is mentally equivalent as well.

The Imitation Game (Alan Turing)[3]

I propose to consider the question, 'Can machines think?' This should begin with definitions of the meaning of the terms 'machine' and 'think'. The definitions might be framed so as to reflect so far as possible the normal use of the words, but this attitude is dangerous. If the meaning of the words 'machine' and 'think' are to be found by examining how they are commonly used it is difficult to escape the conclusion that the meaning and the answer to the question, 'Can machines think?' is to be sought in a statistical survey such as a Gallup poll. But this is absurd. Instead of attempting such a definition I shall replace the question by another, which is closely related to it and is expressed in relatively unambiguous words.

The new form of the problem can be described in terms of a game which we call the 'imitation game'. It is played with three people, a man (A), a woman (B), and an interrogator (C) who may be of either sex. The interrogator stays in a room apart from the other two. The object of the game for the interrogator is to determine which of the other two is the man and which is the woman. He knows them by labels X and Y, and at the end of the game he says either 'X is A and Y is B' or 'X is B and Y is A'. The interrogator is allowed to put questions to A and B thus:

C: Will X please tell me the length of his or her hair?

Now suppose X is actually A, then A must answer. It is A's object in the game to try and cause C to make the wrong identification. His answer might therefore be

'My hair is shingled, and the longest strands, are about nine inches long.'

In order that tones of voice may not help the interrogator the answers should be written, or better still, typewritten. The ideal arrangement is to have a teleprinter communicating between the two rooms. Alternatively the question and answers can be repeated by an intermediary. . . .

We now ask the question, 'What will happen when a machine takes the part of A in this game?' Will the interrogator decide wrongly as often when the game is played like this as he does when the game is played between a man and a woman? These questions replace our original, 'Can machines think?'

2. Critique of the New Problem.

. . . The new problem has the advantage of drawing a fairly sharp line between the physical and the intellectual capacities of a man. No engineer or chemist claims to be able to produce a material which is indistinguishable from the human skin. It is possible that at some time this might be done, but even supposing this invention available we should feel there was little point in trying to make a 'thinking machine' more

[3] A.M. Turing, 'Computing Machinery and Intelligence', Mind Vol LIX, no. 236, Oct 1950. Reprinted by permission.

human by dressing it up in such artificial flesh. The form in which we have set the problem reflects this fact in the condition which prevents the interrogator from seeing or touching the other competitors, or hearing their voices. Some other advantages of the proposed criterion may be shown up by specimen questions and answers. Thus:

Q: Please write me a sonnet on the subject of the Forth Bridge.
A: Count me out on this one. I never could write poetry.
Q: Add 34957 to 70764.
A: (Pause about 30 seconds and then give as answer) 105621.
Q: Do you play chess?
A: Yes.
Q: I have K at my K1, and no other pieces. You have only K at K6 and R at R1. It is your move. What do you play?
A: (After a pause of 15 seconds) R-R8 mate.

The question and answer method seems to be suitable for introducing almost any one of the fields of human endeavour that we wish to include. We do not wish to penalise the machine for its inability to shine in beauty competitions, nor to penalise a man for losing in a race against an aeroplane. The conditions of our game make these disabilities irrelevant. The 'witnesses' can brag, if they consider it advisable, as much as they please about their charms, strength or heroism, but the interrogator cannot demand practical demonstrations. . . .

6. *Contrary Views on the Main Question.*

We may now consider the ground to have been cleared and we are ready to proceed to the debate on our question, 'Can machines think?' and the variant of it quoted at the end of the last section. We cannot altogether abandon the original form of the problem, for opinions will differ as to the appropriateness of the substitution and we must at least listen to what has to be said in this connexion.

It will simplify matters for the reader if I explain first my own beliefs in the matter. Consider first the more accurate form of the question. I believe that in about fifty years' time it will be possible to programme computers with a storage capacity of about 10^9, to make them play the imitation game so well that an average interrogator will not have more than 70 per cent. chance of making the right identification after five minutes of questioning. The original question, 'Can machines think?' I believe to be too meaningless to deserve discussion. Nevertheless I believe that at the end of the century the use of words and general educated opinion will have altered so much that one will be able to speak of machines thinking without expecting to be contradicted. I believe further that no useful purpose is served by concealing these beliefs. The popular view that scientists proceed inexorably from well-established fact to well-established fact, never being influenced by any unproved conjecture, is quite mistaken. Provided it is made clear which are proved facts and which are conjectures, no harm can result. Conjectures are of great importance since they suggest useful lines of research.

I now proceed to consider opinions opposed to my own.

(1) *The Theological Objection.* Thinking is a function of man's immortal soul. God has given an immortal soul to every man and woman, but not to any other animal or to machines. Hence no animal or machine can think.

I am unable to accept any part of this, but will attempt to reply in theological terms. I should find the argument more convincing if animals were classed with men, for there is a greater difference, to my mind, between the typical animate and the inanimate than there is between man and the other animals. The arbitrary character of the orthodox view becomes clearer if we consider how it might appear to a member of some other religious community. How do Christians regard the Moslem view that women have no souls? But let us leave this point aside and return to the main argument. It appears to me that the argument quoted above implies a serious restriction of the omnipotence of the Almighty. It is admitted that there are certain things that He cannot do such as making one equal to two, but should we not believe that He has freedom to confer a soul on an elephant if He sees fit? We might expect that He would only exercise this power in conjunction with a mutation which provided the elephant with an appropriately improved brain to minister to the needs of this soul. An argument of exactly similar form may be made for the case of machines. It may seem different because it is more difficult to "swallow". But this really only means that we think it would be less likely that He would consider the circumstances suitable for conferring a soul. The circumstances in question are discussed in the rest of this paper. In attempting to construct such machines we should not be irreverently usurping His power of creating souls, any more than we are in the procreation of children: rather we are, in either case, instruments of His will providing mansions for the souls that He creates.

However, this is mere speculation. I am not very impressed with theological arguments whatever they may be used to support. Such arguments have often been found unsatisfactory in the past. In the time of Galileo it was argued that the texts, "And the sun stood still . . . and hasted not to go down about a whole day" (Joshua x. 13) and "He laid the foundations of the earth, that it should not move at any time" (Psalm cv. 5) were an adequate refutation of the Copernican theory. With our present knowledge such an argument appears futile. When that knowledge was not available it made a quite different impression.

(2) *The 'Heads in the Sand' Objection*. "The consequences of machines thinking would be too dreadful. Let us hope and believe that they cannot do so."

This argument is seldom expressed quite so openly as in the form above. But it affects most of us who think about it at all. We like to believe that Man is in some subtle way superior to the rest of creation. It is best if he can be shown to be *necessarily* superior, for then there is no danger of him losing his commanding position. The popularity of the theological argument is clearly connected with this feeling. It is likely to be quite strong in intellectual people, since they value the power of thinking more highly than others, and are more inclined to base their belief in the superiority of Man on this power.

I do not think that this argument is sufficiently substantial to require refutation. Consolation would be more appropriate: perhaps this should be sought in the transmigration of souls.

According to Turing's Imitation Game, something qualifies as a machine with a mind—or, more specifically, as a machine capable of understanding and thinking—if its performance in response to questions in extensive "blind" interviews are indistinguishable from the performance of persons. A *blind* test is used to overcome chauvinism (e.g., our prejudices against shiny metal things), and the test requires of a machine only that it be able to do in conversations what we do in conversations. So the test claims, in effect, that whatever can perfectly imitate something with a mind also has a mind.

We have already seen that the functionalist theory of mind claims that if anything is **functionally equivalent** to something with a mind—that is, if it has components with

functional equivalence: Something that does the same job as, or occupies the same causal role as, something else. Something is functionally equivalent to another thing with a mind if it has components with the same causal roles as minds and, so, can do whatever things with minds can do.

the same causal roles as minds and can do whatever things with minds do—then it also has a mind. The Turing Test looks for functional equivalence between machines and persons—specifically, equivalence in how each conducts conversations—and it supposes that whenever functional equivalence is found, there is mental equivalence. If the functionalist theory of mind is right, the Turing Test ought to successfully reveal whether a machine has genuine thought and understanding.

CHALLENGES TO FUNCTIONALISM

Functionalism offers an attractive solution to problems that seemed devastating for earlier theories. First, because it is a materialist theory, functionalism can allow for mental states to interact with the physical world and to control our bodies and behaviour. So, unlike dualist theories, functionalism makes minds useful things to have. Second, because it is not reductionist, functionalism allows for the multiple realizability of mental states and, thereby, it avoids the pitfalls of chauvinism. But all is not clear sailing. In the following sections we look at objections to functionalism that have arisen from a few different directions. Because functionalism implies the possibility of genuine artificial intelligence, objections to the possibility of artificial intelligence will also be objections to functionalism. After setting aside some common misunderstandings of artificial intelligence, we will look at one famous objection to the idea of strong AI. Then, in the closing sections, we will turn to objections to functionalism—indeed, to materialist theories of any sort—that arise from the curious way that the external, or objective, point of view on persons seems to overlook the inside, or subjective, points of view.

Initial Misgivings

Some people doubt that any machine could ever do what Turing imagines, and it will be helpful to remove some of the most common misunderstandings before we proceed. Here are two frequently heard objections to the idea that machines might think:

A. A machine can only reply to our questions with answers that we have already programmed it to give.

B. We, the programmers, can predict in advance the answers that a machine would give.

But (A) is false. Notice that we don't program even a simple pocket calculator by giving it the *answers* to sums, multiplications, and so on. There are simply too many answers for us to program them all into pocket calculators in advance. So instead we program the calculator with the means for calculating the answers. Even with a simple pocket calculator, the answers to the "questions" we "ask" it are not merely programmed into it.

And (B) is *in one way* false, and *in another way* true. To see that it is false, consider the case of a pocket calculator—I can't predict what answer it will give to a multiplication problem that is too difficult for me to do. If I could already predict its answer, why would I bother to use a pocket calculator? And I certainly can't predict the responses of a good chess program. If I could, I would be able to defeat it every time. Objection (B) is true, however, in that I can predict its answers to *the very easy questions*. But this won't show that something lacks a mind, since I can also do this with people. If I am playing chess with another person, and we are roughly equally matched, then when I suddenly see an opening for my opponent—say, a move that will allow her to checkmate me—I can predict with a very high degree of success that she will also see the move, and I can predict that if she does see the move she will almost certainly make it. We can't do any better than this with chess-playing computers.

It is always dangerous to think we can know in advance what some future machine will be capable of doing. The ingenuity of designers and programmers has already surprised us too often. We now work daily on computers with a level of sophistication that, only 50 years ago, no one would have imagined possible. So it might be wise to wait and see whether a future machine will pass the Turing Test. Instead, we might investigate further what a machine's passing the Turing Test really tells us about the machine.

In the following section we will see an ingenious thought experiment designed by American philosopher **John Searle** that purports to show that passing the Turing Test fails to establish that a machine has thought and understanding.

John Searle: American philosopher known for his early work on speech acts and his later work on theories of consciousness, especially his Chinese Room thought experiment, which he proposed as a counterexample to strong AI and functionalism.

The Chinese Room (John Searle)[4]

What psychological and philosophical significance should we attach to recent efforts at computer simulations of human cognitive capacities? In answering this question, I find it useful to distinguish what I will call "strong" AI from "weak" or "cautious" AI (Artificial Intelligence). According to weak AI, the principal value of the computer in the study of the mind is that it gives us a very powerful tool. For example, it enables us to formulate and test hypotheses in a more rigorous and precise fashion. But according to strong AI, the computer is not merely a tool in the study of the mind; rather, the appropriately programmed computer really *is* a mind, in the sense that computers given the right programs can be literally said to *understand* and have other cognitive states. In strong AI, because the programmed computer has cognitive states, the programs are not mere tools that enable us to test psychological explanations; rather, the programs are themselves the explanations.

. . . My discussion here will be directed at the claims I have defined as those of strong AI, specifically the claim that the appropriately programmed computer literally has the cognitive states and that the programs thereby explain human cognition. When I hereafter refer to AI, I have in mind the strong version, as expressed by these two claims.

I will consider the work of Roger Schank and his colleagues at Yale (Schank & Abelson 1977), because I am more familiar with it than I am with any other similar claims, and because it provides a very clear example of the sort of work I wish to examine. But nothing that follows depends upon the details of Schank's programs. The same arguments would apply to . . . any Turing machine simulation of human mental phenomena.

Very briefly, and leaving out the various details, one can describe Schank's program as follows: the aim of the program is to simulate the human ability to understand stories. It is characteristic of human beings' story-understanding capacity that they can answer questions about the story even though the information that they give was never explicitly stated in the story. Thus, for example, suppose you are given the following story: "A man went into a restaurant and ordered a hamburger. When the hamburger arrived it was burned to a crisp, and the man stormed out of

[4] "Minds, Brains, and Programs," by John R. Searle in "Behavioral and Brain Sciences, Volume 3, Issue 03 (September 1980), pp. 417-457.

the restaurant angrily, without paying for the hamburger or leaving a tip." Now, if you are asked "Did the man eat the hamburger?" you will presumably answer, "No, he did not." Similarly, if you are given the following story: "A man went into a restaurant and ordered a hamburger; when the hamburger came he was very pleased with it; and as he left the restaurant he gave the waitress a large tip before paying his bill," and you are asked the question, "Did the man eat the hamburger?," you will presumably answer, "Yes, he ate the hamburger." Now Schank's machines can similarly answer questions about restaurants in this fashion. . . . When the machine is given the story and then asked the question, the machine will print out answers of the sort that we would expect human beings to give if told similar stories. Partisans of strong AI claim that in this question and answer sequence the machine is not only simulating a human ability but also

1. that the machine can literally be said to *understand* the story and provide the answers to questions, and
2. that what the machine and its program do *explains* the human ability to understand the story and answer questions about it.

Both claims seem to me to be totally unsupported by Schank's work, as I will attempt to show in what follows.

. . . Suppose that I'm locked in a room and given a large batch of Chinese writing. Suppose furthermore (as is indeed the case) that I know no Chinese, either written or spoken, and that I'm not even confident that I could recognize Chinese writing as Chinese writing distinct from, say, Japanese writing or meaningless squiggles. To me, Chinese writing is just so many meaningless squiggles. Now suppose further that after this first batch of Chinese writing I am given a second batch of Chinese script together with a set of rules for correlating the second batch with the first batch. The rules are in English, and I understand these rules as well as any other native speaker of English. They enable me to correlate one set of formal symbols with another set of formal symbols, and all that "formal" means here is that I can identify the symbols entirely by their shapes. Now suppose also that I am given a third batch of Chinese symbols together with some instructions, again in English, that enable me to correlate elements of this third batch with the first two batches, and these rules instruct me how to give back certain Chinese symbols with certain sorts of shapes in response to certain sorts of shapes given me in the third batch. Unknown to me, the people who are giving me all of these symbols call the first batch "a script," they call the second batch a "story," and they call the third batch "questions." Furthermore, they call the symbols I give them back in response to the third batch "answers to the questions," and the set of rules in English that they gave me, they call "the program." Now just to complicate the story a little, imagine that these people also give me stories in English, which I understand, and they then ask me questions in English about these stories, and I give them back answers in English. Suppose also that after a while I get so good at following the instructions for manipulating the Chinese symbols and the programmers get so good at writing the programs that from the external point of view—that is, from the point of view of somebody outside the room in which I am locked—my answers to the questions are absolutely indistinguishable from those of native Chinese speakers. Nobody just looking at my answers can tell that I don't speak a word of Chinese. Let us also suppose that my answers to the English questions are, as they no doubt would be, indistinguishable from those of other native English speakers, for the simple reason that I am a native English speaker. From the external point of view—from the point

> of view of someone reading my "answers"—the answers to the Chinese questions and the English questions are equally good. But in the Chinese case, unlike the English case, I produce the answers by manipulating uninterpreted formal symbols. As far as the Chinese is concerned, I simply behave like a computer; I perform computational operations on formally specified elements. For the purposes of the Chinese, I am simply an instantiation of the computer program.
>
> Now the claims made by strong AI are that the programmed computer understands the stories and that the program in some sense explains human understanding. But we are now in a position to examine these claims in light of our thought experiment.
>
> 1. As regards the first claim, it seems to me quite obvious in the example that I do not understand a word of the Chinese stories. I have inputs and outputs that are indistinguishable from those of the native Chinese speaker, and I can have any formal program you like, but I still understand nothing. For the same reasons, Schank's computer understands nothing of any stories, whether in Chinese, English, or whatever . . .
> 2. As regards the second claim, that the program explains human understanding, we can see that the computer and its program do not provide sufficient conditions of understanding since the computer and the program are functioning, and there is no understanding. . . . In the Chinese case I have everything that artificial intelligence can put into me by way of a program, and I understand nothing; in the English case I understand everything, and there is so far no reason at all to suppose that my understanding has anything to do with computer programs, that is, with computational operations on purely formally specified elements. . . . Notice that the force of the argument is not simply that different machines can have the same input and output while operating on different formal principles—that is not the point at all. Rather, whatever purely formal principles you put into the computer, they will not be sufficient for understanding, since a human will be able to follow the formal principles without understanding anything. . . .
>
> Well, then, what is it that I have in the case of the English sentences that I do not have in the case of the Chinese sentences? The obvious answer is that I know what the former mean, while I haven't the faintest idea what the latter mean. But in what does this consist and why couldn't we give it to a machine, whatever it is?

We won't explore Searle's answer to his final question. However, it is easy to see that the target of his thought experiment is the functionalist theory of mind. The **Chinese Room** is clearly an embellished Turing Test, intended to show that something could perfectly *simulate* understanding and yet not actually understand. If a machine only simulates having that mental state, then it provides a good imitation of something that has that state, but without actually having that state; if it actually has some mental state that we have, then it *duplicates* that mental state. The Chinese Room is meant to simulate understanding without duplicating it. But then, Searle thinks, he can pass the Turing Test for understanding Chinese even though he doesn't understand the language. If that is right, then the Turing Test *fails* as a test for whether something has understanding. And if the Turing Test fails, then the functionalist theory of mind is in trouble.

Chinese Room: A thought experiment designed by John Searle that purports to demonstrate that it is possible to produce a perfect simulation of understanding the Chinese language without understanding any Chinese. The thought experiment is a form of a Turing Test, and is intended as a counter to *strong AI* and to the *functionalist theory of mind.*

We can put Searle's point more generally. Functionalism is committed to strong AI, and so maintains that something will have understanding if, in response to the same inputs, it gives the same outputs as a person who has understanding. But against this,

Searle claims in his thought experiment that "I have inputs and outputs that are indistinguishable from those of the native Chinese speaker . . . but I still understand nothing." If this is possible, then the Chinese Room is functionally equivalent to a person who understands Chinese, and yet the Chinese Room understands no Chinese. Recall, however, that the functionalist theory says that if anything is functionally equivalent to a person who has understanding, then it is mentally equivalent to a person who has understanding. In other words, if Searle is right about the Chinese Room thought experiment, the functionalist theory of mind must be false.

This line of thought leaves much to explore, but we will content ourselves here with a look at only one of the objections that the defenders of strong AI have to the Chinese Room thought experiment, and the reply that Searle gives to that objection. In the following paragraphs, Searle continues by summarizing what he calls the "Systems Reply" to his argument:

> **I. The systems reply (Berkeley).** "While it is true that the individual person who is locked in the room does not understand the story, the fact is that he is merely part of a whole system, and the system does understand the story. The person has a large ledger in front of him in which are written the rules, he has a lot of scratch paper and pencils for doing calculations, he has 'data banks' of sets of Chinese symbols. Now, understanding is not being ascribed to the mere individual; rather it is being ascribed to this whole system of which he is a part."
>
> My response to the systems theory is quite simple: let the individual internalize all of these elements of the system. He memorizes the rules in the ledger and the data banks of Chinese symbols, and he does all the calculations in his head. The individual then incorporates the entire system. There isn't anything at all to the system that he does not encompass. We can even get rid of the room and suppose he works outdoors. All the same, he understands nothing of Chinese, and a fortiori neither does the system, because there isn't anything in the system that isn't in him. If he doesn't understand, then there is no way the system could understand because the system is just a part of him.[5]

In the original version of the thought experiment, in which Searle is hidden in a room with symbols and rule books that tell him how to manipulate the symbols, Searle's argument seems plausible. But does it seem plausible in the variation of the thought experiment that Searle describes here? On this variation, we are asked to imagine that Searle has committed to memory all the symbols, and all the rules for manipulating them, so he no longer needs to be hidden. We are then to imagine that he comes out in the open and writes down appropriate answers to questions native Chinese speakers pass him on slips of paper. Even in this case, Searle maintains, he can, in principle, succeed without understanding a word of Chinese.

If Searle can do all that without understanding Chinese, then he can surely proceed as just described, but without using the paper or without writing down responses. He can instead form and store mental images of written Chinese, which will be images of symbols he will insist he does not understand. He can also memorize the rules for reading Chinese aloud from a written script, as well as the rules for inscribing spoken Chinese symbols on paper. With these two additions to his repertoire of skills, he can carry on what appear

---

[5] From Searle, J. (1980). Minds, Brains, and Programs. *Behavioral and Brain Sciences*, 3: 419.

to be conversations with native Chinese speakers. When someone says something in Chinese, he transforms those sounds, using the rules he has learned, into sentences that he visualizes as written on his mental tablet; he then visualizes writing next to them appropriate responses, which he reads off his mental tablet to provide a spoken response in Chinese. In this way, he can successfully "pass" at a party as someone who understands Chinese, carrying on what seem to be conversations about the weather, sports, or politics—all without understanding a word of Chinese. It is precisely here that some defenders of functionalism and strong AI dig in their heels; for, they respond, if Searle can do all this, then he has done all that is required for understanding Chinese, and he is simply wrong to think that *something more* is needed.

There is a lot to explore in Searle's Chinese Room argument, but in response to it, and to a number of similar arguments, philosophers of mind divide into roughly two camps: (1) those who are persuaded by Searle, and so conclude that *something more* needs to be added to the functionalist story to explain what minds are; and (2) those who think that if Searle, inside the Chinese Room, has a sufficiently sophisticated rule book, and if he operates quickly enough so that he, or the room, passes the Turing Test, then Searle—or the Chinese Room—already *does* understand Chinese. Searle's response to the Systems Reply encourages this second group, since they believe that if Searle "internalizes" everything he needs to pass undetected in a Chinese conversation, then he will have passed the only test we have for whether someone understands Chinese. He will have passed the same test we require students of the Chinese language to pass in order to demonstrate their understanding. But if there is no other test for whether someone understands Chinese, it would be pointless to deny that Searle understands it. We might as well deny that a native Chinese speaker understands Chinese, and insist that she is only *simulating* understanding the language.

Have Thinking Machines Already Arrived?

We have only reached the point from which disagreements about functionalism and AI begin. Both sides on this issue still have much to say. Before we leave this topic let us consider, as an exercise, the following questions:

1. When we add two numbers—without the aid of a calculator, and without pencil and paper, but in our heads—is that an example of thinking (albeit, an example of very simple thinking)?

and

2. Does a calculator add numbers?

If the answer to both questions is yes, then shouldn't we say that calculators already "think"? It won't follow that they think very much or very well, or that they think imaginatively or creatively. Nor does it follow that they know that they are thinking. But if "adding" is an example of thinking when we do it in our heads, and pocket calculators also add, then shouldn't we say that we have *already* created some very simple—and very boring—minds? Why not?

Consider three possible responses. First, we could insist that calculators don't actually *add* the numbers we give them as input, but only simulate adding. To make this stick, we will need a better understanding of the contrast between *duplicating* some activity—that is, really doing it—and *merely simulating* it. Alternatively, we might say that, although calculators actually do add numbers, adding—even when we do it in our heads—is not an example of *thinking*. To make this claim seem plausible, we owe a better account of what "thinking" really is. Finally, we could grant our pocket calculators admission to the club of Thinking Beings, but concede that it is not a very elite club. Along this route, we may need to rethink our views about what, if anything, makes having a mind or being a person special. These are not easy matters to decide, but they are exactly the sorts of issues that need further exploration if we want a better understanding of what it is to have a mind.

THE VIEW FROM INSIDE

Functionalism holds that mental states and events are physical states and events of the brain in so far as they occupy causal roles in which they mediate between the information we take in from our environment and our behaviour. As we have already seen, this has the consequence that *if two "systems" are functionally equivalent, then they must be mentally equivalent*. This means that if we can show that it is possible for two systems to be functionally equivalent without being mentally equivalent, then we will have identified a serious problem for the functionalist theory of mind. This is precisely what Searle's Chinese Room thought experiment tries to demonstrate: The Chinese Room is meant to be functionally equivalent to someone who understands Chinese but, since it is thought to lack understanding, it is not mentally equivalent to someone who understands Chinese.

Once we see the basic structure of Searle's objection, we can also see how to construct other possible objections to functionalism. All we need to do is look for possible cases of systems that are functionally equivalent to persons with minds but that are not mentally equivalent. What functionalism's critics hope to find are plausible cases of people whose mental or "inner lives" are clearly different, even though their "outer lives"—the behaviour they exhibit in response to information they take in from their surroundings—are indistinguishable. While critics suspect that such cases are possible, functionalists think the attempt to devise such cases will always end in failure. In the next section, we examine two examples of this strategy for criticizing functionalism.

The Reversed Spectrum

Consider the following.

1. Because of an abnormality of the cones in my retina (my colour receptors), everything that looks red to you looks green to me, and everything that looks green to you looks red to me. In short, my colour *experiences* are red-green reversed.
2. I have learned to label things that look green to me "red," and to label things that look red to me "green." In short, my colour *vocabulary* is "red"-"green" reversed.

As a result, we will appear to agree in judgments about the colours of things. We will respond to ripe tomatoes in similar ways ("They're red"), the sight of ripe tomatoes will remind us both of "red" roses, and so on. In short, there is nothing in our behaviour, including our speech, that could reveal the difference in our experiences—my red-green colour reversal is undetectable. So, despite our very different experiences, we are functionally equivalent.

This is probably a familiar thought experiment, but now we are prepared to see that, if it really is possible, it serves as a challenge to functionalism. The undetectable reversal of colour experience illustrates two people who are mentally very different (i.e., the reversal of our colour experiences) but who are functionally equivalent—as the undetectability indicates. So this appears to be exactly what functionalism says is impossible. But why should the scenario described in (1) and (2) be impossible?

It will help kick-start our reflections on this problem to consider a parallel scenario. Suppose everything *looks twice as long* to me as it does to you, including, of course, our measuring sticks. A table that looks one metre long to you looks two metres long to me, but when we each measure it we will get the same result. Since the one-metre measuring stick also looks two metres long to me, when I use it to measure the table, I will agree that the table is one metre in length. We will never detect my visual doubling of lengths. Does this scenario resemble the reversed spectrum case in useful ways? There may be some reason to suspect that visual doubling is not possible and, if it is not possible, we might have to reconsider whether a reversed spectrum is possible.

What does it mean to say, as we have, that a table that looks one metre long to you looks two metres long to me? In particular, how can it be that the table looks two metres long to me and yet *looks the same in length (to me)* as the one metre measuring stick? These questions are not easy to answer in a way that makes our scenario seem possible. One natural answer to the first question is that when we say that something *looks two metres in length*, we just mean that it *looks twice as long as a one-metre measuring stick*. We then define the look (in length) of things by comparing them to the metre stick. But, if that is right, then a table that looks one metre long to you and two metres long to me would need to *look the same* as the metre stick to you, but would need to *look twice as long* as the metre stick to me. If that were a consequence of my visual doubling of lengths, then we would easily detect it by noticing that *our comparisons* between the metre stick and other objects would disagree—that is, if something looked one metre long to you but looked two metres long to me, then it would look (to you) the same length as the metre stick, but would look (to me) twice as long as the metre stick. *That* is a difference we will easily detect! It does no good to object that, in this scenario, if the one-metre stick *also* looks two metres long to me, then the table will look the same length as the metre stick and still look two metres long. The point is that to look one metre long *is* to look the same length as the standard one-metre measuring stick—*however that measuring stick looks*. If that is right, then the table can't look two metres long and also look the same length as a one-metre measuring stick.

Is the case of red-green colour reversal different in ways that protect it from similar detection? That will depend. Is there a comparative method of defining what it is for something to look red or to look green, such as we used for looking one metre in length? Suppose, for example, when we say that something "looks red" we mean that it "looks the way ripe tomatoes look" (*however* they look), and when something "looks green," it "looks the way summer grass looks" (*however* that looks). Perhaps then the reversal of our colour experiences will be detectable when we make the right comparisons between objects. For example, we are supposing that if some test object looks red to you, then it looks green to me; so you will say that it looks the same as ripe tomatoes (since that is what "looking red" means), and I will say it looks the same as summer grass (since that is what "looking green" means). We would find ourselves disagreeing in our *comparisons* of the colours of objects, and so our reversed colour experiences will be detected.

Perhaps, however, this is not at all what it means for something to "look red" or "look green." There is clearly much work to be done before we can say whether undetectable colour reversals are possible, and whether they present a serious challenge to functionalist theories of mind. But it is not obvious that our imagined colour reversals are possible, and so all options remain on the table.

The Zombie Threat: Further Adventures in Epiphenomenalism

The preceding objection to functionalism claimed that two persons might be functionally identical but have *different* mental states. Our second objection claims that we can have functional equivalence between two people even though one of them *lacks* a mental state that the other has. We encountered a similar claim in Searle's Chinese Room thought experiment, where we were asked to entertain the possibility that Searle successfully passes as someone who understands Chinese, but he lacks any understanding of the language. If we can imagine this for the state of understanding, then why not for *all* mental states?

Consider a challenge to materialism first suggested by Leibniz early in the eighteenth century:

> Moreover, it must be confessed that *perception* and that which depends upon it are *inexplicable on mechanical grounds*, that is to say, by means of figures and motions. And supposing there were a machine, so constructed as to think, feel, and have perception, it might be conceived as increased in size, while keeping the same proportions, so that one might go into it as into a mill. That being so, we should, on examining its interior, find only parts which work one upon another, and never anything by which to explain a perception.[6]

Leibniz points to an important distinction between the physical events in the brain and our conscious experiences. Suppose we build a functioning brain—as he puts it, a mill or factory that produces thoughts and feelings—that is large enough for us to stroll through and examine in detail. (We will get the same result if we imagine shrinking ourselves so that we can explore someone's brain.) Leibniz's claim is that our search will reveal only physical objects and events, and we will not find mental states—we find nothing that even resembles a mental state. From our perspective as outsiders exploring the brain of another person, her mental life will be invisible to us. But how could that be if, as materialists insist, mental states are physical states? If they are just physical states, why should mental states look any different from the "inside" than they do from the "outside"? Unlike eighteenth century thinkers, neuroscience has advanced far enough to allow something equivalent to taking a stroll through the brains of others. Modern surgeries, lesioning, electrical stimulation, and a variety of scanning technologies (e.g., MRI, CT, EEG, and PET) enable us to examine functioning brains in significant detail. What do we find there?

---

[6] Leibniz, G. F. W. (1714). *Mondalogy*. Section 17. (Robert Latta, Trans.). London: The Claredon Press. 227–228.

Let us suppose we have an organic being—call her Zelda—who is physically indistinguishable from a normal human being but, alas, is incapable of feeling amusement. Zelda's brain has been very cleverly designed to do the following sorts of things: When we tell her funny jokes, auditory inputs send electrochemical messages, via other parts of her brain, to her inferior temporal gyrus, where they produce an increase in electrochemical activity. That increased activity triggers a cascade of further physical events that result in the contraction of specific muscles in her vocal chords, and those movements then produce vibrations in the air that sound exactly like laughter. Her brain is also wired so that if we give her visual input from a high precipice, physical changes occur within her hypothalamus, which, by an exceedingly complex chain of events, leads to the contraction of tiny, unstriated muscles that causes glands in her palms to secrete perspiration. But Zelda is also incapable of forming mental imagery or feeling fear. Nor, we should add, is she able to feel pain. The damage caused whenever her doctor pierces her skin with a hypodermic needle sends a series of electrical and chemical events racing through her nervous system. Those events cause various muscles to contract, which cause Zelda to flinch and cry out. Despite her perfect display of behaviour that normally indicates pain, and despite the fact that she undergoes the very same internal *physical* events that we undergo when we feel pain, Zelda feels nothing at all.

We can continue the story as far as we like, describing the physical and chemical events that connect Zelda's environmental inputs to her behavioural outputs, and we will find that from our outsider perspective—that includes the perspective of the scientists who examine her brain in detail—Zelda is indistinguishable from us. But she feels no amusement, fear, or pain; there are no mental states intervening between her inputs and her outputs. Zelda is wired to process and respond to the world exactly as we are wired, and yet she has no mental interior. From the inside, everything is blank. Zelda is functionally indistinguishable from us, but she lacks our rich interior life—she is what philosophers refer to in thought experiments as a **zombie**: a perfect simulation of a conscious being, but without any consciousness.[7] And if zombies are even *possible*, then functionalism must be false.

zombie: In philosophy, *zombie* refers to a perfect simulation of a conscious being that lacks any consciousness. Zombies have the full range of non-conscious mental states, but they have no conscious mental states. The very idea of zombies, which is much disputed, is thought to show that functionalism is false.

But why believe that Zelda is even possible? Recall the epiphenomenalist view from Chapter 6, where we illustrated how feelings of amusement can be the effect of physical events in our environments and in our brains (e.g., increased activity in the temporal gyrus), and those same physical events in the brain also cause our behaviour (e.g., laughing). However, as they were shown in Figure 6.1, feelings of amusement floated uselessly above the sequence of physical events—they were inert side effects, and the physical events did all the work. The feelings are, on this view, both nonphysical and epiphenomenal. Now if, as the epiphenomenalist says, that is how things are with us, then Zelda already works exactly like us, except that she doesn't have the useless epiphenomenal side effects that are, in us, feelings. From this perspective, Zelda is only a more streamlined version of us—she has been stripped of the components that don't do anything anyway. This "streamlining" is what we should expect if we insist on a materialist view of the mind. The epiphenomenalist view of our mental lives now sees an opening through which it might return to respectability.

[7] Philosophical zombies are meant to be functionally indistinguishable from us. This means that we can never detect the ones who, like Zelda, live apparently normal lives in our midst. They should not be confused with Hollywood zombies, who, because they walk stiffly and gorge on the brains of the living, are easily detectable.

We saw earlier that epiphenomenalism has been criticized because it contains components that are useless or superfluous—everything that needs explaining is already explained without mentioning causally inert feelings. The metaphysical principle of Ockham's Razor says that we can improve our theory by simply cutting them out. Now we see a possible response to this criticism of epiphenomenalism. Perhaps there *is* something left unexplained if we leave out the nonphysical feelings. Even if epiphenomenal feelings cannot help explain our behaviour, such as flinching in response to the stab of a needle, nonphysical feelings will not be redundant or superfluous if they explain why, when we flinch, we also *feel* pain, or why, when we hear a good joke, we not only laugh, but we *feel* amused. If we cut away those feelings, we would be just like Zelda, who really is nothing but a "machine made of meat." In short, the epiphenomenal side effects of our physical lives might be needed to explain feelings and experiences; why amusement, fear, or pain *feel* a certain way from the inside—they might be needed to explain why we have an "inner" life at all. Nonphysical and epiphenomenal feelings and experiences might be all that stands between us and zombies.

The materialist critics will not be satisfied by this. The mind-brain identity theorist will certainly object that, despite our denials, Zelda actually *does* feel amusement. After all, she has increased electrochemical activity in her inferior temporal gyrus, and those events in her brain *are* feelings of amusement; furthermore, pains *are* activated C-fibres, so when her C-fibres are activated she *feels* pain. So Zelda can't possibly be physically equivalent to us and not have the same feelings we have. We also know what functionalists will say about Zelda: She has internal physical states that occupy the very same causal roles occupied by our feelings of amusement, fear, and pain, and *that is all there is* to having feelings of amusement, fear, and pain. So Zelda can't possibly be functionally equivalent to us and not have the feelings we have. By the standards of both mind-brain identity theory and functionalism, Zelda is simply not a possibility.

Once again, there is much to be said before we get to the bottom of these matters. Nonetheless we have arrived at a good place to begin. But the waters are already getting deep, and we have other places to visit nearer to shore.

CONCLUSION

In this chapter we explored functionalism, a leading non-reductionist version of the materialist theory of mind. Functionalism's tolerance of physical variations among the sorts of things that are capable of having minds extends all the way to machines; so functionalism allows for artificial intelligence, and it helps explain how it might one day be achieved. Ever since the early work in computing theory by Alan Turing, we have even had a test for AI that seems designed in the spirit of functionalism. The Turing Test, however, also becomes one target for functionalism's critics. John Searle's famous Chinese Room thought experiment brings out what critics perceive as a weakness in the Turing Test, and so in the functionalist theory of mind. In the thought experiment, being able to see what goes on inside the room—the gears and levers at work in producing answers to Chinese questions—seems to diminish our confidence that understanding must be involved.

Similarly, when we look closely at the processes in our brain that connect our incoming perceptions of the world with our outgoing actions, it can easily begin to look as though this perspective is one from which minds simply cannot be found. Materialist theories of mind seem content to settle for that objective point of view, but their critics seem equally confident that this leaves out what is most important about minds. Critics of mind-brain identity theory and functionalism think that the internal or subjective point of view—the point of view that each person has of her own mind—is ignored by materialism. The internal point of view, which prevents us from becoming philosophical zombies, is even thought by some to make epiphenomenal dualism respectable.

Key Terms and Figures

chauvinistic p. 136
multiple realizability p. 137
functional role p. 138
functionalism p. 139
non-reductive materialism p. 140
strong artificial intelligence p. 141
simulate p. 141
weak artificial intelligence p. 141
Alan Turing p. 142
Imitation Game p. 142
Turing Test p. 143
functional equivalence p. 145
John Searle p. 147
Chinese Room p. 149
zombie p. 155

Additional readings on functionalism

Dennett, D. (1985). Can Machines Think? In M. Shafto (Ed.), *How we Know*. San Francisco: Harper and Row,121–145.

Fodor, J. (1981). The Mind-Body Problem. In John Heil (Ed.), *Philosophy of Mind: A Guide and Anthology*. Oxford: Oxford University Press, 168–82.

Hauser, L. The Chinese Room Argument. *Internet Encyclopedia of Philosophy*. Retrieved July 27, 2014, from http://www.iep.utm.edu/chineser

Levin, J. (2013). Functionalism. In E. N. Zalta (Ed.), *The Stanford Encyclopedia of Philosophy*, Fall 2013. Retrieved July 27, 2014, from http://plato.stanford.edu/archives/fall2013/entries/functionalism

Chapter 8

Freedom and Determinism

Learning Objectives

- Define *determinism* and discuss how it differs from compatibilism and libertarianism.
- Describe the relationships among the ideas of necessity and possibility.
- Explain the difference between determinism and fatalism.
- Clarify how the predictability of future events is relevant to whether they are determined.
- Summarize the relevance, if any, of indeterminacy in quantum mechanics for freedom.
- Explain what a scope fallacy is, and provide examples of your own.
- Identify the scope fallacy that determinists are sometimes accused of committing.
- Explain two different ways that philosophers have tried to make freedom compatible with determinism.

In preceding chapters we examined arguments for the idea that minds are physical entities, and that mental states such as beliefs and desires are physical states of the brain. We also saw that a common way to distinguish between physical and nonphysical entities involves the laws of physics. Physical entities are subject to physical laws, while nonphysical entities are not. Together, these two ideas—that we are physical, and that physical entities are subject to strict physical laws—raise a new question about our place in nature.

When we think of ourselves as subject to strict physical laws, an obvious question is whether this view of ourselves is consistent with the ideas that we are free and that we are responsible for our actions. We do not normally hold people responsible for actions they cannot help performing. If you are pushed into the vase by someone else, you don't get the blame for its breaking. But when there are options available, and you freely choose one course of action over another, then you can be held morally and legally responsible. If we accept that we are purely physical, and so are bound by physical laws, we threaten the idea that we are free, and without the idea that we are free, the idea that we are morally responsible is in jeopardy.

Accordingly, this chapter explores two questions: *Is everything, including our actions, determined?* And *is free will possible* for purely physical beings? (We won't examine the idea of responsibility, which deserves its own extended treatment.) As we will see, neither question is simple enough for a simple answer, but by looking at some of the work of previous philosophers who have grappled with these questions, we can put ourselves in a better position to think them through on our own.

FATALISM AND DETERMINISM

Any examination of freedom and determinism must make use of the ideas of *necessity* and *possibility* in order to define the various positions one can take in the debates. They also play an essential role in nearly every argument we consider.

Possibility and Necessity

What is *possible*, what is *actual*, and what is *necessary* are related in complex ways, and those complex relations are the subject of an entire branch of logic. For our purposes, however, we only need to recognize the following connections:

> Principle I. *If something is necessary, then it is actual; if it is actual, then it is possible.*

We can illustrate this first set of relationships with a simple diagram:

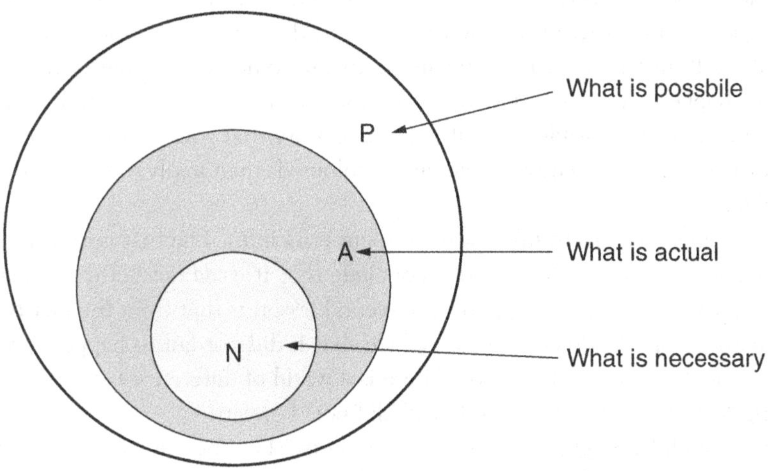

Figure 8.1

Figure 8.1 shows that the set of possible things includes the set of actual things. There is room for something to be in the set of possible things (P) but not be actual (i.e., not be in A); for example, purple aardvarks are possible but they are not actual. We can also see that the set of actual things includes the set of necessary things. From the fact that something is actual (i.e., it is in A), we cannot conclude that it is necessary (i.e., it is in N)—it might be in the part of A that lies outside N. If there is anything in the part of A that lies outside N, then some of what actually happens isn't necessary—it doesn't *have to* happen, it just *does*. For example, although aardvarks are born tawny coloured, perhaps it didn't *have* to be that way; they might have been born purple instead. In that case, purple aardvarks are located in the part of P that is outside A, and tawny aardvarks are located in the part of A that is outside N.

Consider a single toss of a fair coin, which can result in heads or tails. There are two *possible* outcomes, heads or tails, but only one of those two possibilities will *actually* turn up. (Both heads and tails are inside P, but only one of them can be inside A.) On a single toss of an ordinary coin, it is *necessary* that we get *either heads or tails*—there is no other option. But even though it is necessary that we get one or the other, it is not necessary that we get heads, and it is not necessary that we get tails. (Neither heads nor tails is inside N.) It isn't necessary that we get heads, since tails is also possible, and it isn't necessary that we get tails, since heads is also possible. In other words, something is not necessary if some alternative to it is possible. This takes us to our second principle: If something is necessary, then no alternative to it is possible.

Principle II: 'Necessary' *is equivalent to* 'not possible not'.

necessary: Equivalent to "not possible not." Necessary things are things that could not fail to exist; a necessary statement is one that could not fail to be true.

possible: A thing or event is possible when it can exist or occur. Alternatively put, if a thing or event is possible, it is not necessary that it not exist or occur. All necessary things are possible, but not all possible things are necessary.

This principle defines *necessary* in terms of what is possible: If an event is **necessary**, then it is not **possible** that the event does not occur—that is, there is no alternative to it. Consider our coin toss again, but this time we will use a special coin that has heads on both sides—tails is no longer a possibility. Now it is *necessary* that the outcome be heads; there is no other alternative. And that's an important idea: If it is *not possible* that an event *not* occur, since there is no alternative to it, then the event is *necessary*. But principle II also tells us that if there is any alternative to some event—that is, if it is possible that it not happen—then it is not necessary for it to happen. For example, if aardvarks of another colour are possible, then it is not necessary that they be tawny coloured, and if it is not necessary that aardvarks be tawny coloured, then aardvarks of another colour are possible.

There are two lessons to take away from our principles. The first is that if something that happens is necessary, then we can conclude that it *could not* fail to happen—there is no alternative but for it to happen. The second lesson is that from the fact that something actually happens, we can only conclude that it did not fail to happen—we cannot conclude that there is no alternative. There is a world of difference between saying that something "could not" happen and that it "did not" happen.

These principles might tie your head in "nots," but they are well worth thinking through. You will need them to understand determinism and to appreciate the debates concerning freedom and determinism.

Foreknowledge and Fate

fatalism: The metaphysical doctrine that everything we do is necessary, fated, so there is never any possibility of doing anything different. *Psychological fatalism* refers to the feeling of helplessness or powerlessness in determining what happens to oneself.

We begin with an idea that is more general than determinism: the idea that everything that happens, including everything we do, is *fated*. **Fatalism** is the idea that everything we do is necessary—there is no possibility of doing anything else. This is a metaphysical doctrine, not a psychological thesis, but the term is sometimes used for a psychological attitude—a feeling of powerlessness to determine how one's life will go. Our concern is only with the metaphysical doctrine.

Consider one rationale for fatalism. Some theologians believe that there is an omniscient, or all-knowing, God, who knows from the beginning of time everything that will ever happen. But God's *foreknowledge*, they think, has the consequence that everything is fated. Here is how they reason:

1. God knows I will have a salad for lunch tomorrow.
2. If God knows I will have the salad, then I cannot not have the salad.
3. Therefore, it is necessary (*it is fated*) that I will have a salad for lunch tomorrow.

Here, (3) follows from (1) and (2) when we use the definition of "necessary" in principle II. The fatalist is not saying that God *makes me* order the salad, only that He *knows* I will order it. Some theologians also believe that God has *pre-ordained*, or pre-arranged, everything that happens. Early Christian theologian St. Augustine, for example, describes pre-ordination as the idea that "the universe is directed down to the whirling leaves of trees."[1] Here we are only interested in whether His *foreknowledge* of events implies that they *must* happen, not whether God has pre-arranged for them to happen. The fatalist reasons that if what I do has already been written—in this case, written in the thoughts of an all-knowing God—then *I can't do otherwise*.

If foreknowledge of events means they are fated, then they are necessary, and that means there is no possibility that they will not occur—recall principle II. The argument tries to establish fatalism by reasoning from the premise that God knows what I *will* do tomorrow to the conclusion that what I do tomorrow is necessary. And certainly, if God knows in advance that I will order a salad tomorrow, then I *will* order a salad. I *won't* do otherwise. But to show that what I do tomorrow is fated, it must be shown that I *cannot* do otherwise. What is there in our argument for fatalism that justifies concluding that I *must* order the salad?

The source of the fatalist conclusion is premise (2), which *assumes* the truth of fatalism—that is, it *begs the question* in favour of fatalism. We are entitled to say that if God knows I will have the salad for lunch, then I *won't not* have it—God won't be wrong. But God's foreknowledge does not, by itself, entitle us to say that I *cannot not* have the salad. Saying I cannot not have the salad is equivalent to saying it is *necessary* that I have the salad. The "cannot" in premise (2) unjustifiably smuggles fatalism into one premise of the argument for fatalism.

The point that foreknowledge of an event implies that it *will* happen, but not that it *must* happen, is sometimes difficult to see. Let us consider a fanciful example. Assume for a moment that we really are free—that there are alternatives among which we can choose, and our choices among them are free. Then, because your critical reasoning skills are so highly valued, you are invited to join the team of courageous specialists who will test our first time machine. On the first experimental test, you travel only a short distance into the future, where you observe and take careful notes about what others are doing tomorrow. You then return to the present with detailed knowledge of things that will happen the next day. For example, because you observed it, you know today what I will freely choose to have for lunch tomorrow, even though I haven't decided yet. So you have foreknowledge of what I will *freely* do in the future. Your knowing in advance what I will choose does not prevent my choice from being free, and its being free does not prevent you from knowing what my choice will be. So foreknowledge of some event does not *by itself* show that the event is fated, necessary—foreknowledge can be knowledge of what someone freely does.

---

[1] From Saint Augustine. (n.d.). *The Confessions of Saint Augustine*. (E. B. Pusey, Trans.) Retrieved August 1, 2014, from http://www.gutenberg.org/cache/epub/3296/pg3296.txt

Defining Determinism

Fatalism is closely related to the determinist doctrine. Indeed, it would not be wrong to think of determinism as a special kind of fatalism—fatalism with a twist.

determinism: The metaphysical doctrine that all events are *determined*—that is, necessitated, or made necessary—*by prior causes.* Some philosophers use *determinism* for the doctrine that all events have causes, but when they do so they usually assume that causes always determine their effects.

Determinism is the view that everything that happens is determined. An event is determined when its occurrence is *made necessary by preceding events*—that is, there is no option but for it to occur *given what happened in the past.* Determinism, like fatalism, holds that all events and actions are necessary, but determinism differs because it adds the crucial idea that events are *made necessary by what preceded them.* If determinism is true, then my choosing the salad for lunch today was not really optional—it was made inevitable by something that happened in the past. The freedom I felt when choosing from the menu was only an illusion.

causal determinism: The doctrine that events are determined (i.e., necessitated, or made necessary) by their causes. The doctrine can take different forms—biological or social determinism, for example—depending on what sorts of causes are emphasized.

Although there are many forms of determinism, they all agree that when an event is determined, something that happened earlier makes it inevitable. **Causal determinism** is the view that present and future events are made inevitable by the past events that cause them. Once a particular causal background is in place, what happens next is no longer left open—it can no longer fail to happen. This form of determinism will occupy most of our attention.

Most people agree that our causal backgrounds—whether our genetic inheritance or our family upbringing—have an influence on our lives. Almost everyone accepts this. But the belief that the past *influences* the present is not the same as the belief that the past *determines* the present. Although it can sometimes be very difficult to do, and we may fail in the attempt, we can, in principle, resist or overcome influences. What influences us may push us in one direction, but it does not make it *impossible* for us to go in a different direction. If what happens is determined by the past, then how things go is not something that can be altered, even with the most superhuman effort. As our earlier definition of necessity, from principle II, tells us, if something is determined, or necessary, then there is *no possibility* that it will fail to happen.

CAUSAL DETERMINISM

Causal determinism first appeared in the seventeenth century as a by-product of the newly emerging physical sciences. We begin our exploration of the doctrine by reflecting on a "vast intelligence"—usually referred to as *Laplace's demon*—that makes a brief appearance in the writings of eighteenth century French astronomer and mathematician **Pierre Simon de Laplace** (1749–1827). As you read this short selection, take note of how Laplace's demon makes successful predictions of future events.

Pierre Simon de Laplace: French mathematician and astronomer who did important work in celestial mechanics and in probability theory.

Determinism and Predictability (Laplace, 1812)[2]

> All events, even those which on account of their insignificance do not seem to follow the great laws of nature, are a result of it just as necessarily as the revolutions of the sun. In ignorance of the ties which unite such events to the entire system of the

[2] From Laplace, P. S. (n.d.). *A Philosophical Essay on Probabilities.* (F. W. Truscott & F. L. Emory, Trans., 1902). Retrieved August 1, 2014, from http://archive.org/stream/philosophicaless00lapliala/philosophicaless00lapliala_djvu.txt

universe, they have been made to depend upon final causes or upon hazard, according as they occur and are repeated with regularity, or appear without regard to order; but these imaginary causes have gradually receded with the widening bounds of knowledge and disappear entirely before sound philosophy, which sees in them only the expression of our ignorance of the true causes.

Present events are connected with preceding ones by a tie based upon the evident principle that a thing cannot occur without a cause which produces it. This axiom, known by the name of *the principle of sufficient reason*, extends even to actions which are considered indifferent; the freest will is unable without a determinative motive to give them birth; if we assume two positions with exactly similar circumstances and find that the will is active in the one and inactive in the other, we say that its choice is an effect without a cause. . . . The contrary opinion is an illusion of the mind, which, losing sight of the evasive reasons of the choice of the will in indifferent things, believes that choice is determined of itself and without motives.

We ought then to regard the present state of the universe as the effect of its anterior state and as the cause of the one which is to follow. Given for one instant an intelligence which could comprehend all the forces by which nature is animated and the respective situation of the beings who compose it—an intelligence sufficiently vast to submit these data to analysis—it would embrace in the same formula the movements of the greatest bodies of the universe and those of the lightest atom; for it, nothing would be uncertain and the future, as the past, would be present to its eyes. The human mind offers, in the perfection which it has been able to give to astronomy, a feeble idea of this intelligence. Its discoveries in mechanics and geometry, added to that of universal gravity, have enabled it to comprehend in the same analytical expressions the past and future states of the system of the world. Applying the same method to some other objects of its knowledge, it has succeeded in referring to general laws observed phenomena and in foreseeing those which given circumstances ought to produce. All these efforts in the search for truth tend to lead it back continually to the vast intelligence which we have just mentioned, but from which it will always remain infinitely removed. This tendency, peculiar to the human race, is that which renders it superior to animals; and their progress in this respect distinguishes nations and ages and constitutes their true glory.

Let us recall that formerly, and at no remote epoch, an unusual rain or an extreme drought, a comet having in train a very long tail, the eclipses, the aurora borealis, and in general all the unusual phenomena were regarded as so many signs of celestial wrath. Heaven was invoked in order to avert their baneful influence. No one prayed to have the planets and the sun arrested in their courses: observation had soon made apparent the futility of such prayers. But as these phenomena, occurring and disappearing at long intervals, seemed to oppose the order of nature, it was supposed that Heaven, irritated by the crimes of the earth, had created them to announce its vengeance. Thus the long tail of the comet of 1456 spread terror through Europe, already thrown into consternation by the rapid successes of the Turks, who had just overthrown the Lower Empire. This star after four revolutions has excited among us a very different interest. The knowledge of the laws of the system of the world acquired in the interval had dissipated the fears begotten by the ignorance of the true relationship of man to the universe; and Halley, having recognized the identity of this comet with those of the years 1531, 1607, and 1682, announced its next return for the end of the year 1758 or the beginning of the year 1759. The learned world awaited with impatience this return which was to confirm one of the greatest discoveries that have been made in the sciences, and fulfil the prediction of Seneca when he said, in speaking of the revolutions of those stars which fall from an enormous height: "The day will come when, by study pursued through several ages, the things now concealed will appear with evidence; and posterity will be astonished that truths so clear had escaped us." Clairaut then undertook to submit to analysis the perturbations which the comet had experienced by the action of the two great planets, Jupiter and Saturn; after immense calculations he fixed its next passage at the perihelion toward the beginning of April, 1759, which was actually verified by observation. The regularity which astronomy shows us in the movements of the comets doubtless exists also in all phenomena.

> The curve described by a simple molecule of air or vapor is regulated in a manner just as certain as the planetary orbits; the only difference between them is that which comes from our ignorance.

One of Laplace's central claims is that whenever an action or event does not appear to be determined, that appearance only reflects our ignorance of its causes. So long as we are ignorant of the causes of things, we are unable to predict what will happen next, and that unpredictability creates the illusion that the future is open. But with growing knowledge of the laws of nature comes an increased ability to predict natural phenomena, and as we successfully predict more things, "chance" begins to disappear from our world. If all things become predictable, we will see through the illusion that some things only happen by chance.

Laplace suggests a thought experiment involving a simple extrapolation of our present scientific knowledge—that is, our knowledge of the physical causes of things. If a sufficiently vast intelligence, with knowledge of all the operations of the physical world, were to look upon the universe, he would see "the present state of the universe as the effect of its anterior state and as the cause of the one which is to follow." **Laplace's demon** is a hypothetical intelligence that possesses the vast quantities of information and the immense computational powers needed to predict the future state of the universe from its present state. The demon would not have the illusion that anything occurs by chance or that anything is undetermined.

Laplace's demon: A hypothetical intelligence that possesses all the information about physical laws and initial conditions and the immense computational powers needed to predict the future state of the universe from its present state. Although Laplace never refers to him as a "demon," he first appears in Laplace's work *A Philosophical Essay on Probabilities.*

As Laplace and his contemporaries could, with enough information, predict the path of a comet, so Laplace's demon could predict even "[t]he curve described by a simple molecule of air or vapor." If he can predict the motions of each air molecule, then the demon will even be able to predict the apparently "random" results of a coin toss. That the outcome of a coin toss could, with enough information, be predicted only shows that the outcome is not random after all. If Laplace's demon can predict the future, will that show that the future is determined? And will it show that we are not free?

Predictions and Causes

Exactly how is Laplace's demon able to predict the future state of the universe? He makes his predictions using the same method we use to predict future events, but he does so with vastly more information and vastly greater powers of calculation. We already predict some future events—such as the return of a comet or the position of a planet in its orbit—by, in Laplace's words, "referring to general laws observed phenomena and in foreseeing those which given circumstances ought to produce." On this view predictions of the future require two kinds of information: information about the "general laws," and information about the "given circumstances."

First, we need to be familiar with some of the laws or regularities found in nature. Unlike us, the demon knows *all* the laws of nature—those that govern "the movements of the greatest bodies of the universe and those of the lightest atom." But our predictions also depend on information about the **initial conditions** of the things that are governed by the laws of nature—that is, the physical properties things have that are relevant to what they will do in the future. To predict the future state of the universe, the demon will need to know the initial, or present, state of everything in the universe—of every planet, every molecule, and so on. He will need to know the exact physical properties (e.g., position, velocity, mass, and so on) each particle of matter currently has. With this information—all the laws plus the initial conditions of all things—Laplace's demon is able to calculate exactly where every particle will be at any time in the future and, so, he will be able to predict the future state of the entire universe.

initial conditions: The properties or characteristics of things that are relevant to predicting how they will behave in accordance with the laws of nature.

We get a glimpse into how Laplace's demon works with a simple example of how we make the same sort of predictions on a much smaller scale. We will use the law of conservation of momentum, which states that the total momentum possessed by objects after they interact will be the same as the total momentum they had before they interacted. Simply expressed, *the total momentum before and after an interaction is the same.* Now imagine we stage an interaction between two objects that have a combined *initial* momentum of 10 units, and then try to predict what their combined momentum will be *after* they interact. Of course, we predict they will have a total momentum of 10 units after they interact. It's easy to see how we do this—we use our knowledge of the law, plus our knowledge of the initial conditions—which, in our simplified example, consists in the objects' pre-interaction momenta—to predict what the total momentum will be after the interaction. Our reasoning might be represented as follows:

Predictions: Deducing the Future

1. *Law*: The total momentum before and after an interaction is always the same.
2. *Initial conditions*: The total momentum before the interaction is 10 units.
3. *Prediction*: The total momentum after the interaction will be 10 units.

The reasoning used by Laplace's hypothetical demon is vastly more complicated, but the logical principles involved are the same. What intrigues Laplace is that from our knowledge of the present or past and of the physical laws, we are predicting the future by *deducing* it. If this is possible, then the causal determinist concludes that the future is *determined by the past.* In our example, the determinist would say that given the total momentum before the interaction plus the law of conservation of momentum, the momentum after the interaction *has to be* 10 units—it is not possible for the final momentum to be anything else. So the future total momentum is determined.

It is important to note that this style of reasoning can also be used to *explain* past and present phenomena. Some philosophers think the reasoning we use to make predictions also illustrates how causal explanations proceed. Suppose something has been observed to happen—say, we saw two objects racing away from one another with a total momentum of 10 units—and we want to know *why* they had that momentum. The explanation is given using the law of conservation of momentum together with the information that the objects had 10 units of momentum before they interacted. Our causal explanation of the observed momentum then looks like this:

Retrodictions: Causal Explanations

1. *Law*: The total momentum before and after an interaction is always the same.
2. *Initial conditions*: The total momentum before the interaction was 10 units.
3. *To be explained*: The total momentum after the interaction was 10 units.

retrodiction: A prediction of something that has already happened. *Retrodiction* can be used as a causal explanation of a phenomenon that employs the same information and style of reasoning that could also have been used to predict it.

This gives us a model for how causal explanations work that links them to how predictions work. Causal explanations use the same style of reasoning and make use of the same information that predictions of future events use. We might even say that causal explanations of events are just **retrodictions**—that is, they are "predictions" of what has already happened. This is only an artful way of saying that predictions of the future also work by showing the route from causes to their effects. It is the causal structure or order of the universe that makes it predictable.

The reasoning that supports determinism can now be expressed simply: *If we can validly deduce future states of the universe from physical laws and initial conditions, then those future states of the universe are determined by the earlier states of the universe*. And the close relation between predictions and causal explanations helps us understand why this is called *causal* determinism. The future is determined by the past because, given the initial conditions of things in the past plus the laws that govern how things behave, the future *cannot* turn out any other way. If, given the present state of the universe, there were more than one way the future could turn out, then we would not be able to deduce future states of the universe from present states of the universe. But we do that all the time—just look at our simple example. Laplace's demon, who is much better informed than we are, simply does it much better. When he predicts the future from the past or present, he is only tracing the many lines of causation that lead inexorably from the past into the future.

Many philosophers find the case for causal determinism persuasive, but not everyone is on board. In the following two sections, we look at two strategies for objecting to the argument for causal determinism.

First Objection: Quantum Indeterminacy

The first objection to causal determinism says that Laplace is mistaken in thinking that the physical world is governed by the kinds of laws that his demon requires in order to deduce future events from past events. It is understandable that he would have thought this—at the time Laplace was writing, Newton's deterministic laws were thought to govern the complete physical world. We now know that is wrong. According to contemporary physics, the behaviour of elementary particles—the particles that make up the atoms that make up the molecules that make up the objects all around us—are accurately described by a branch of physics called *quantum mechanics*. And unlike Newton's physics, quantum mechanics is not deterministic—the laws of quantum mechanics are *indeterministic*. Let's see what this means.[3]

If, as Newton thought, nature is governed by deterministic laws, then two perfectly identical experiments will give identical results. That is, the same past conditions plus the same laws will result in the same future. But in quantum mechanics, two identical experiments can

[3] Although physicists agree about what the mathematical principles of quantum mechanics are, they do not agree about how to interpret them. In order to examine the implications of quantum mechanics for free will, we assume the majority view here that *nature is not deterministic at the level of elementary particles*. Although this is the majority view, it is disputed among physicists.

have different results—the same past plus the same laws can result in different futures, and which future we get is a matter of chance. Instead of allowing us to say precisely what will happen on each occasion, indeterministic laws only allow us to give a range of possible outcomes, along with information about how likely each kind of outcome in that range is. If this is what laws of nature are like, then critics can object that causal determinism relies on an outdated scientific theory. The sort of reasoning that Laplace's demon depends on is simply not possible.

The determinist, however, has two rebuttals to this objection. First, the objection assumes that because elementary particles do not obey deterministic laws, then larger objects composed of those particles—including objects as large as persons—do not obey deterministic laws. But that is an assumption to which we might not be entitled by quantum mechanics. It is a matter of some dispute whether indeterminism "trickles upward" from elementary particles to the much larger objects composed of those particles. *Somehow*, predictions of the sort in our example of predictive reasoning are made daily—and made successfully. It may be that quantum indeterminacy does not trickle upward, in which case large objects might still obey deterministic laws. Or it may be that indeterminacy does trickle upward, but that it gets so *diluted* in the process that it is undetectable—for example, perhaps an immeasurably small amount of momentum is lost in one out of a trillion interactions. In either case, quantum indeterminacy does not provide large cumbersome beings like ourselves with freedom from deterministic laws. From the indeterministic laws of quantum mechanics, we acquire only the same liberty that a falling stone—which is also made of elementary particles—has. And stones are not free to disobey physical laws.

Second, any holiday that quantum indeterminacy grants us from strict determinist laws will not give us free will. To have a free will, we need to be in charge of our own actions—what we do must somehow be *up to us*. Put another way, free will does not require our actions to be uncaused or undetermined, but it requires that they be caused or determined *by us*. Unlike the deterministic laws of earlier physics, the laws of quantum mechanics plus a set of initial conditions do not strictly determine what will happen. That is because, within the range of possible outcomes permitted by the laws, *what happens next is a matter of chance*. So the unpredictability at the quantum level arises because individual events at that level—for example, whether a particular atom will decay—are entirely random. If quantum mechanics made our actions unpredictable exceptions to strict laws, then our actions would also be random: We couldn't predict or control what we will do from one moment to the next. Indeterminism would have the result that what we do is *not up to us*. Therefore, the indeterminacy of quantum mechanics is not able to give us freedom of will.

Second Objection: The Scope Fallacy

Any attempt to evaluate the reasoning offered to support causal determinism quickly takes us into deep waters. Nonetheless, we will attempt an objection to the central argument for causal determinism, and thus leave the next move in the debate up to the determinist.

The argument for causal determinism, as summarized earlier, takes the following form:

Argument for Causal Determinism

1. If future states of the universe can be validly deduced from physical laws and initial conditions, then those future states of the universe are determined by the earlier states of the universe.

2. But future states of the universe can be validly deduced from physical laws and initial conditions.
3. Therefore, future states of the universe are determined by the earlier states of the universe.

The objection to this reasoning has two parts. First, critics will challenge the first premise of the argument by taking a closer look at the actual reasoning we use to predict future events. Second, the objection offers a diagnosis of causal determinism by exposing the fallacy on which it rests. So the objection first aims to convince us that a premise is flawed, and then to explain why we might find the premise tempting despite its flaws. We will proceed in two stages.

Stage One The first component of the objection takes aim at premise (1), which summarizes the significance of our predictive and explanatory styles of reasoning. The objection is that, contrary to the claim made in premise (1), the reasoning we use when we make predictions based on laws and initial conditions does not support any *deterministic conclusions*.

We can grant that, in our previous example, we correctly deduce the future momentum of interacting objects using only the laws of physics and the initial conditions of the objects. But look carefully at the conclusion: It says that the total momentum after the interaction *will be* 10 units, not that it *must be* 10 units. If our conclusion was that the momentum after the interaction *must be* 10 units, or that it *necessarily is* 10 units, or that it is *not possible for it to not be* 10 units, then the laws plus the initial conditions would show that the predicted result of the interaction is determined. But none of those things follows from the premises used to make the prediction. The conclusion that follows is, exactly as we have stated, that the post-interaction momentum *will*—not *must*—be 10 units. According to the objection we are considering, this is true about all inferences of the sort employed by us or by Laplace's demon when we predict a future event using knowledge of physical laws. The laws of physics tell us only how things *will* behave in certain conditions, not how they *must* behave.

We saw earlier that past events can be used to predict future events because future events are caused by past events. This provides another way to state our objection to determinism. Put in terms of causation, the first premise of the argument for determinism says that if future states of the universe are *caused* by earlier states of the universe, then those future states of the universe are *determined*, or *made necessary, by* the earlier states of the universe. But the critic of determinism says we are only entitled to say that if future states of the universe are caused by earlier states, then those future states are *brought about by* the earlier states. We can put the difference in how each side understands causes and effects as follows:

> *Determinism*: If A causes B, then when we have A, B will *necessarily* occur.
>
> *Determinism's critics*: If A causes B, then when we have A, B will *actually* occur.

So determinists believe that effects are *made necessary*—necessitated—by their causes; determinism's critics believe that effects are only *made actual* by their causes. The objection to the argument for causal determinism is that the first premise is false—it gives an interpretation of predictions and causal explanations (or predictive and retrodictive reasoning) that is not justified by our actual predictions and explanations. The critic's view of causation should not be confused with indeterminacy of the kind we saw in quantum mechanics—the criticism is *not* saying that effects are random or unpredictable. It is only saying that effects are not *necessitated* by their causes, and that still allows us to say exactly which effects *will* follow from which causes.

To many people, the style of deductive reasoning employed when making predictions and giving explanations *feels* like it ought to support the stronger conclusion that future events are determined by past events. Perhaps a diagnosis of the error in the argument for determinism—which we will attempt next—can help make that feeling go away.

Stage Two According to our objection, the view that physical laws plus initial conditions determine future events rests on a **scope fallacy**.[4] The fallacy is well concealed, so we'll need to do some digging to uncover it. We should first notice that the argument for causal determinism has been carelessly formulated. Both premises say that future states of the universe can be validly deduced from laws and initial conditions. But any deductive argument or reasoning is always a series of statements, in which statements (i.e., conclusions) are deduced from other statements (i.e., premises). Furthermore, validity is itself a relationship between statements (i.e., premises and conclusions). So, strictly speaking, *states of the universe* cannot be *validly deduced* from other states of the universe. Only statements can be deduced from statements. Perhaps our expression of the argument is convenient shorthand, but we must be careful not to let it mislead us. Determinism is concerned with the kind of necessity that belongs to *events*, not with the kind of necessity that belongs to *statements* about events.

scope fallacy: An inference that results from misidentifying the range of things that a term covers (that is, its scope), so that it is treated as covering, or applying to, the wrong things.

With this in mind, we can turn to the scope fallacy that critics accuse determinists of committing. Recall that a valid argument is defined as one in which it is not possible for the conclusion to be false if its premises were true. Put another way, if an argument is valid, then *it is necessary for the conclusion to be true if the premises are.* But precisely *what*

Logic Box

Scope Fallacies

A scope fallacy is an inference that results from a failure to appreciate the range of things that a term is being applied to, so it is treated as covering, or applying to, the wrong things. For example,

- Premise: I bought my car at the world's biggest automobile auction.
- Conclusion: Therefore, I bought the world's biggest automobile.

In the premise the phrase "the world's biggest" applies to automobile *auctions*—that's the interpretation that makes the premise plausible; but the conclusion treats the phrase as applying to *automobiles*. Grammatically the premise can be read either way, and that might leave unclear the actual range of things, or the *scope*, to which the phrase is intended to apply. This ambiguity is what makes the fallacious inference tempting.

[4] There are many scope fallacies. The one we are concerned with here is usually called a *modal scope fallacy*. Since this is the only scope fallacy we are concerned with, we can simplify the name.

is "necessary" in a valid argument? That is, *to what* does the "necessary" apply—what is its proper scope? Consider a sample valid deduction concerning a fair toss of a fair coin:

1. If the coin toss does not result in heads, then it will result in tails.
2. The coin toss will not result in heads.
3. Therefore, the coin toss will result in tails.

Note that the conclusion that follows from (1) and (2) is not that the toss *must* result in tails. That would mean that it was *not possible* for heads to result from the toss. But heads *was* a possible outcome of our fair coin toss—it just isn't the *actual* outcome. So there is nothing in the argument that shows one particular outcome to be necessary. On the contrary, because there are two possible outcomes, *neither is necessary*. But if it is not the conclusion of a valid argument that is required to be necessary, then what is? The answer can be seen in the definition of a valid argument:

i. *In a valid argument, it is necessary that if premises (1) and (2) were both true, then conclusion (3) would be true.*

This comes straight from our definition of *validity*. As we can see in (i), the necessity lies in *the relationship* between the premises and the conclusion. That is, *the entire "if . . . then" statement* that connects the premises to the conclusion is necessary. But this does not mean that the conclusion of the argument is itself necessary. To say that, we would need to write

ii. *In a valid argument, if premises (1) and (2) were both true, then it is necessary that conclusion (3) be true.*

Here, it is only the conclusion of the argument that is necessary. Do you see the difference? The first formulation says that what is necessary is that *given (1) and (2), then (3)*. That's just the definition of a valid argument. The second formulation says that *given (1) and (2), then (3) is necessary*. But that misrepresents the definition of a valid argument by putting the "necessary" in the wrong place. It's exactly as though we were to say that *if the coin doesn't come up heads then it has to come up tails*. That's correct if it means that what is necessary is that *if* it doesn't come up heads, *then* it will come up tails. It's not correct if it means that what is necessary is that the coin comes up tails. The latter would mean that heads wasn't even a possibility, and so either the coin or the toss wasn't fair.

If we were to confuse (i) for (ii), we would be committing a scope fallacy. In this case, our fallacy would consist in applying the "necessary" to the wrong thing. It is properly placed in (i) but misplaced in (ii). To someone who regularly confuses (i) and (ii), or who thinks they say the same thing, it will look as though every conclusion of a valid argument says that *something* is necessary. According to determinism's critics, this is precisely what the determinist has done—the metaphysical doctrine that everything is determined rests on a scope fallacy. A scope fallacy makes it look as though the conclusions of predictive and explanatory reasoning are all necessary. This then entices determinists to think that future events are made necessary by earlier states of the universe. But all that is necessary is that, given certain laws and certain initial conditions, a certain future event *will* occur. We can still rely on our knowledge of physical laws and initial conditions to deduce what *will* happen—reasoning of the sort used by Laplace's demon is just fine. But such reasoning does not provide grounds for thinking that the events we predict *must* happen.

If the objection is right, it shows that the earlier defense of determinism fails. Of course, that isn't enough to show that determinism is false—there may be other arguments for the view. But the burden now falls squarely with determinists to provide such an argument, and until they do we are justified in having doubts.

LIBERTARIANISM AND COMPATIBILISM

So far we have not addressed directly the idea of *a free choice* or *a free action*. What optional positions can we take on whether our choices or actions are free? Naturally, many determinists—sometimes called *hard determinists*—believe determinism rules out free choice. If everything is determined, then our choices and actions are determined, and if they are determined, they are not free. But there is a second kind of determinism called **compatibilism**—sometimes called *soft determinism*—that holds that freedom and determinism are compatible. Because compatibilists agree that everything is determined, they are properly viewed as one kind of determinist. On the other hand, many philosophers who think we are free do not think that determinism and freedom can be reconciled. If no reconciliation is possible, but our actions are free, then our actions are not determined. **Libertarianism** is the view that our actions are free *because* they are not determined.[5]

compatibilism (of freedom and determinism): The view that actions can be free even though they are determined by prior causes. Compatibilists typically distinguish free and unfree actions by drawing a distinction between the sorts of causes that determine them.

libertarianism: The doctrine that human actions are not determined and, for that reason, are free. (Not to be confused with the political ideology of the same name.)

It is not uncommon for these three positions—hard determinism, compatibilism, and libertarianism—to generate some confusion. Table 8.1 distinguishes the positions. We have been using the label *determinism* for the view that all effects are made necessary by their causes. Some philosophers prefer a much broader definition of determinism—as the view that *everything has a prior cause*. However, philosophers who use this broader definition also believe events are made necessary by their causes. Their definition of determinism thus ends up agreeing with ours—on either way of defining determinism, it is the view that prior causes make events necessary.

Table 8.1 Free Will and Determinism

	Q1: Is every action and event *caused*?	Q2: Do causes make their effects *necessary* (i.e., necessitate them)?	Q3: Are at least some of our actions *free*?
Determinism (Hard determinism)	Yes	Yes	No
Compatibilism (Soft determinism)	Yes	Yes	Yes
Libertarianism: Option 1	No	Yes	Yes
Libertarianism: Option 2	Yes	No	Yes

[5] *Libertarianism*, as the term is used in the debate about free will, has *nothing* to do with the political movements or parties of the same name.

In Table 8.1, both forms of determinism give yes answers to *both* questions Q1 and Q2. This makes room for at least two kinds of libertarians: those who answer no to Q1, and those who answer no to Q2. The first sort of libertarian thinks our actions are *uncaused*, and this is what prevents them from being determined. Someone who thinks that the laws of physics are indeterministic might be a libertarian of this sort. But, as we saw earlier, this also appears to mean that we cannot cause our own actions. So if our actions need to be *up to us* in order to be free, then this option fails to give a satisfactory account of free action. But libertarians do not need to take that position. The second sort of libertarian thinks our actions have causes, but she does not accept that causes *determine* (i.e., necessitate, or make necessary) their effects. This makes it possible for our actions to be caused by us without our actions being necessary. And if they are not necessary, that means that there are alternative actions possible. Our earlier objection to the argument for causal determinism creates space for the second form of libertarian by arguing that causal explanations of events do not necessitate them. Does this allow for freedom?

A. J. Ayer: British philosopher who was important for his role in transplanting the logical positivist school of thought from Germany to England in the 1930s. Ayer published widely read works in epistemology, metaphysics, ethics, logic, and the philosophy of language.

British philosopher **A. J. Ayer** (1910–1989) believes it does. Ayer defends the view that causes do not necessitate their effects—that is, that causal explanations tell us only what *will* happen, not what *must* happen. This is just what the critic of causal determinism claimed in the previous section. In light of this view, Ayer provides an account of what it means to be free.

Freedom and Causation (A. J. Ayer, 1946)[6]

When I am said to have done something of my own free will it is implied that I could have acted otherwise; and it is only when it is believed that I could have acted otherwise that I am held to be morally responsible for what I have done. For a man is not thought to be morally responsible for an action that it was not in his power to avoid. But if human behaviour is entirely governed by causal laws, it is not clear how any action that is done could ever have been avoided. It may be said of the agent that he would have acted otherwise if the causes of his action had been different, but they being what they were, it seems to follow that he was bound to act as he did. Now it is commonly assumed both that men are capable of acting freely, in the sense that is required to make them morally responsible, and that human behaviour is entirely governed by causal laws: and it is the apparent conflict between these two assumptions that gives rise to the philosophical problem of the freedom of the will. . . .

But now we must ask how it is that I come to make my choice. Either it is an accident that I choose to act as I do or it is not. If it is an accident, then it is merely a matter of chance that I did not choose otherwise; and if it is merely a matter of chance that I did not choose otherwise, it is surely irrational to hold me morally responsible for choosing as I did. But if it is not an accident that I choose to do one thing rather than another, then presumably there is some causal explanation of my choice: and in that case we are led back to determinism. . . .

Let it be granted, then, that when we speak of reconciling freedom with determinism we are using the word 'freedom' in an ordinary sense. It still remains for us to make this usage clear: and perhaps the best way to make it clear is to show what it is that freedom, in this sense, is contrasted with. Now we began with the assumption that freedom is contrasted with causality: so that a man cannot be said to be acting freely

[6] Ayer, A. J. 'Freedom and Necessity' in Philosophical Essays, 1965. Macmillan, London. Reproduced with permission of Palgrave Macmillan.

if his action is causally determined. But this assumption has led us into difficulties and I now wish to suggest that it is mistaken. For it is not, I think, causality that freedom is to be contrasted with, but constraint. And while it is true that being constrained to do an action entails being caused to do it, I shall try to show that the converse does not hold. I shall try to show that from the fact that my action is causally determined it does not necessarily follow that I am constrained to do it: and this is equivalent to saying that it does not necessarily follow that I am not free. . . .

. . . [I]t may be true that no one now compels me to get up and walk across the room: but if my doing so can be causally explained in terms of my history or my environment, or whatever it may be, then how am I any more free than if some other person had compelled me? I do not have the feeling of constraint that I have when a pistol is manifestly pointed at my head; but the chains of causation by which I am bound are no less effective for being invisible.

. . . If I suffered from a compulsion neurosis, so that I got up and walked across the room, whether I wanted to or not, or if I did so because somebody else compelled me, then I should not be acting freely. But if I do it now, I shall be acting freely, just because these conditions do not obtain; and the fact that my action may nevertheless have a cause is, from this point of view, irrelevant. For it is not when my action has any cause at all, but only when it has a special sort of cause, that it is reckoned not to be free.

But here it may be objected that, even if this distinction corresponds to ordinary usage, it is still very irrational. For why should we distinguish, with regard to a person's freedom, between the operations of one sort of cause and those of another? Do not all causes equally necessitate? And is it not therefore arbitrary to say that a person is free when he is necessitated in one fashion but not when he is necessitated in another?

That all causes equally necessitate is indeed a tautology, if the word 'necessitate' is taken merely as equivalent to 'cause'; but if, as the objection requires, it is taken as equivalent to 'constrain' or 'compel', then I do not think that this proposition is true. For all that is needed for one event to be the cause of another is that, in the given circumstances, the event which is said to be the effect would not have occurred if it had not been for the occurrence of the event which is said to be the cause . . . and this fact is usually deducible from some causal law which states that whenever an event of the one kind occurs then, given suitable conditions, an event of the other kind will occur in a certain temporal or spatiotemporal relationship to it. In short, there is an invariable concomitance between the two classes of events; but there is no compulsion, in any but a metaphorical sense. . . . It is in this way indeed that my behaviour is explained. But from the fact that my behaviour is capable of being explained, in the sense that it can be subsumed under some natural law, it does not follow that I am acting under constraint. . . .

. . . [T]he very word 'determinism' is in some degree misleading. For it tends to suggest that one event is somehow in the power of another, whereas the truth is merely that they are factually correlated. And the same applies to the use, in this context, of the word 'necessity' and even of the word 'cause' itself. . . . As a result we tend to form an imaginative picture of an unhappy effect trying vainly to escape from the clutches of an overmastering cause. But, I repeat, the fact is simply that when an event of one type occurs, an event of another type occurs also, in a certain temporal or spatio-temporal relation to the first. The rest is only metaphor. And it is because of the metaphor, and not because of the fact, that we come to think that there is an antithesis between causality and freedom.

Nevertheless, it may be said, if the postulate of determinism is valid, then the future can be explained in terms of the past: and this means that if one knew enough about the past one would be able to predict the future. But in that case what will happen in the future is already decided. And how then can I be said to be free? What is going to happen is going to happen and nothing that I do can prevent it. If the determinist is right, I am a helpless prisoner of fate.

But what is meant by saying that the future course of events is already decided? If the implication is that some person has arranged it, then the proposition is false. But if all that is meant is that it is possible, in principle, to deduce it from a set of particular facts about the past, together with the appropriate general laws, then, even if this is true, it does not in the least entail that I am a helpless prisoner of fate. It does not even entail that my actions make no difference to the future: for they are causes as well as effect; so that if they were different their consequences would be different also. What it does entail is that my behaviour can be predicted: but to say that my behaviour can be predicted is not to say that I am acting under constrain. It is indeed true that I cannot escape my destiny if this is taken to mean no more than that I shall do what I shall do. But this is a tautology, just as it is a tautology that what is going to happen is going to happen. And such tautologies as these prove nothing whatsoever about the freedom of the will.

Freedom from Compulsion

Ayer is explicitly concerned with the tension between two ideas: the idea that our actions are *caused*, and the idea that they are *free*. He agrees that our actions, and the choices that lead to them, have causes. If they did not, then it would only be "an accident that I choose to do one thing rather than another." But the tension between causes and freedom only arises because, as Ayer states, we start off assuming that "freedom is contrasted with causality"—that is, that to be free is to be uncaused, or that to be caused is to be unfree. This, he claims, is a mistake.

Ayer's proposal is that only very special kinds of causes will pose a threat to our freedom. When a cause *compels or constrains* us, it leaves us without options, and then we are not free to do otherwise. I am compelled to act in certain ways if I suffer from a compulsive disorder—I *can't control* what I do. And I am compelled to give you my wallet if you point a gun at my head. In this second case I *can* disobey you and die, but I am still not free since you leave me only two undesirable options—give you my wallet or die—and only one of those is reasonable to choose. But these sorts of cases are not typical, and most causes neither compel nor constrain us. Ayer's view is that an action will be free—open to us to perform or not perform—so long as it doesn't have the sort of cause that compels it to happen or the sort that prevents it from happening. So freedom is possible for us since, although all actions have causes, not all causes make their effects compulsory.

What does Ayer think the *causes* of our actions are like if they don't compel or constrain us? An answer can be found in his closing paragraphs: We are told that the idea that the future is determined by causes only means that "if one knew enough about the past one would be able to predict the future," and this in turn only means that "it is possible, in principle, to deduce it [the future] from a set of particular facts about the past, together with the appropriate general laws." Ayer is suggesting that when we say something has a cause, we only mean that it can be deduced from earlier conditions and general laws. As we discussed earlier, the critics of determinism think this view of causes does not permit us to say that effects are necessitated by their causes. As Ayer puts it, "[f]rom the fact that my behaviour is capable of being explained . . . it does not follow that I am acting under constraint." Causes, on Ayer's view, serve well enough to explain why things happen, but the further idea that they somehow compel their effects, or make them necessary, is a misleading metaphor.

We saw that some philosophers define *determinism* as the view that everything has a cause. Ayer agrees that all actions have causes, so he agrees that they are "determined" *in that sense*. But he also thinks that at least some actions—those that are not compelled or constrained by their causes—are free. For these reasons, Ayer is often described as a *compatibilist*—someone who accepts that actions can be both determined and free. But although Ayer accepts that all events, including our actions, are fully explained by their prior causes, he does not accept that all events are made necessary by their causes. If that idea—that their causes make events necessary—is needed to qualify him as a proper determinist, then Ayer does not qualify. From this perspective, Ayer wants to reconcile freedom with causation, not with determinism. It is more accurate to see Ayer as a *libertarian*, who maintains that some of our actions are free precisely because they are not determined—they are not necessitated even though they are caused. It shouldn't surprise us that the way Ayer is classified depends on which definition of determinism we use.

Freedom from External Causes

Ayer's position derives from his agreement with our earlier complaint about the Argument for Causal Determinism. That complaint was, first, that successful predictions of events tell us only what events *will* occur, but not that those events *must* occur, and, second, that causal explanations of events tell us why an event *does* happen, but not why it *must* happen. Because Ayer accepts this, he does not accept the usual determinist doctrine that events are necessitated by their causes. As a result, freedom comes very easily for us. For Ayer, our choices and actions are caused but not determined (i.e., their causes don't compel them), and so other choices and actions are possible. On this view, an action is free if there are genuine alternatives to performing it. But there is a second, and very different, idea of what freedom requires.

Strictly speaking, compatibilists must take the hard road and accept that everything that has a cause is determined and occurs of necessity. Although compatibilists believe that everything we do is necessitated by past conditions and events, they also believe that at least some of what we do is free. How could that be possible? The central idea of this form of compatibilism is that some of the causes that make our actions necessary are *internal to us*. For example, sometimes the causes of my actions are my own deliberations, desires, and motives (which are, let us suppose, physical states of my brain). As a result, those actions are determined, but they are determined *by us*—or, more precisely, by our desires, beliefs, and so on. So according to this school of compatibilists, free actions are not *undetermined* actions—they are actions that are *determined by us*. And what could "free will" be if not the ability to determine ourselves what we will do? On this view, if an action has *the right sort of internal causes* and is determined by those causes, then it will be a free action. An unfree action of mine is one that has an *external cause*, and so it is not determined by me. Freedom and determinism then go hand-in-hand.

To work out the details of this form of compatibilism we will need to decide what sort of internal cause an action or choice must have in order to qualify as free. Not every cause internal to the body or brain will serve to make an action free. For example, if a lesion on my brain causes me to burst uncontrollably into song whenever the sun comes out, then my singing will not be a free action. The lesion in my brain is, *in some important sense*, "external" to me—it is not part of who I am. The distinction between causes that are internal to us and those that are external cannot, then, be a distinction between causes with different spatial locations (inside and outside our skin, for example). Most compatibilists say that an action is free if its causes are the person's own reasons and motives. These details are important, but however they are worked out, the central idea remains: Being caused—even being necessitated—by *the right sort of cause* is precisely what freedom consists in. So an action can be free only if it is determined—*in the right way*. Freedom and determinism are not only compatible; they are complimentary.

Baron d'Holbach: A philosopher of the French Enlightenment who developed and defended a materialistic and atheistic system of thought.

This form of compatibilism was a central target of the unflinching determinism advocated by French Enlightenment philosopher **Baron d'Holbach** (c.1723–1789). d'Holbach was critical of all efforts to evade what he saw as the radical implications of causal determinism. The following extract from his work focuses on his response to the form of compatibilism we have just described.

Against Compatibilism (Baron d'Holbach, 1770)[7]

[M]an is a being purely physical; in whatever manner he is considered, he is connected to universal Nature: submitted to the necessary, to the immutable laws that she imposes on all the beings she contains, according to their peculiar essences; conformable to the respective properties with which, without consulting them, she endows each particular species. Man's life is a line that Nature commands him to describe upon the surface of the earth: without his ever being able to swerve from it even for an instant. He is born without his own consent; his organizations does in no wise depend upon himself; his ideas come to him involuntarily; his habits are in the power of those who cause him to contract them; he is unceasingly modified by causes, whether visible or concealed, over which he has no control; give the hue to his way of thinking, and determine his manner of acting. . . .

As a part, subordinate to the great whole, man is obliged to experience its influence. To be a free agent it were needful that each individual was of greater strength than the entire of Nature; or, that he was out of this Nature: . . . In short, man would be an unnatural being; totally incapable of acting in the manner we behold. . . .

The will, as we have elsewhere said, is a modification of the brain, by which it is disposed to action or prepared to give play to the organs. . . . In consequence, he acts necessarily; his action is the result of the impulse he receives either from the motive, from the object, or from the idea, which has modified his brain, or disposed his will. . . . In all this he always acts according to necessary laws, from which he has no means of emancipating himself. . . .

The errors of philosophers on the free-agency of man, have arisen from their regarding his will as the *primum mobile*, the original motive of his actions; for want of recurring back, they have not perceived the multiplied, the complicated causes, which, independently of him, give motion to the will itself, or which dispose and modify his brain, whilst he himself is purely passive in the motion he receives. . . .

In short, the actions of man are never free; they are always the necessary consequence of his temperament, of the received ideas, of the notions, either true or

[7] From d'Holbach. (n.d.). *The System of Nature*. Retrieved August 1, 2014, from http://www.gutenberg.org/cache/epub/8909/pg8909.txt

false, which he has formed to himself of happiness: of his opinions, strengthened by example, forfeited by education, consolidated by daily experience. . . .

. . . [I]f in the heat of the dispute he insists and asks, "Am I not the master of throwing myself out of the window?" I shall answer him, no; that whilst he preserves his reason, there is not even a probability that the desire of proving his free-agency, will become a motive sufficiently powerful, to make him sacrifice his life to the attempt; if, notwithstanding this, to prove he is a free agent, he should actually precipitate himself from the window, it would not be a sufficient warrantry to conclude he acted freely, but rather that it was the violence of his temperament which spurred him on to this folly. Madness is a state that depends upon the heat of the blood, not upon the will. A fanatic or a hero, braves death as necessarily as a more phlegmatic man or a coward flies from it. There is, in point of fact, no difference between the man who is cast out of the window by another, and the man who throws himself out of it, except that the impulse in the first instance comes immediately from without, whilst that which determines the fall in the second case, springs from within his own peculiar machine, having its more remote cause also exterior. When Mutius Scaevola held his hand in the fire, he was as much acting under the influence of necessity, caused by interior motives, that urged him to this strange action, as if his arm had been held by strong men; pride, despair, the desire of braving his enemy, a wish to astonish him, an anxiety to intimidate him, &c. were the invisible chains that held his hand bound to the fire. . . .

Man may therefore cease to be restrained, without, for that reason, becoming a free agent: in whatever manner he acts, he will act necessarily; according to motives by which he shall be determined. . . . The virtuous Socrates submitted to the laws of his country, although they were unjust; notwithstanding the doors of his gaol were left open to him he would not save himself; but in this he did not act as a free agent; the invisible chains of opinion, the secret love of decorum, the inward respect for the laws, even when they were iniquitous, the fear of tarnishing his glory, kept him in his prison: they were motives sufficiently powerful, with this enthusiast for virtue, to induce him to wait death with tranquillity; it was not in his power to save himself, because he could find no potential motive to bring him to depart, even for an instant, from those principles to which his mind was accustomed.

Man, says he, frequently acts against his inclination, from whence he has falsely concluded he is a free agent; when he appears to act contrary to his inclination, he is determined to it by some motive sufficiently efficacious to vanquish this inclination. A sick man, with a view to his cure, arrives at conquering his repugnance to the most disgusting remedies: the fear of pain, the dread of death, then become necessary and intelligent motives; consequently, this sick man cannot be said, with truth, by any means, to act freely.

When it is said, that man is not a free agent, it is not pretended to compare him to a body moved by a simple impulsive cause: he contains within himself causes inherent to his existence; he is moved by an interior organ, which has its own peculiar laws; which is itself necessarily determined, in consequence of ideas formed from perceptions, resulting from sensations, which it receives from exterior objects. As the mechanism of these sensations, of these perceptions, and the manner they engrave ideas on the brain of man, are not known to him, because he is unable to unravel all these motions; because he cannot perceive the chain of operations in his soul, or the motive-principle that acts within him, he supposes himself a free agent; which, literally translated, signifies that he moves himself by himself; that he determines himself without cause; when he rather ought to say, he is ignorant how or for why he acts in the manner he does. . . .

It is the great complication of motion in man, it is the variety of his action, it is the multiplicity of causes that move him, whether simultaneously or in continual succession, that persuades him he is a free agent: . . . if his machine was less complicated, he would perceive that all his actions were necessary, because he would be enabled to recur instantly to the cause that made him act. . . .

Nevertheless, it must be acknowledged that the multiplicity, the diversity of the causes which continually act upon man, frequently without even his knowledge, render it impossible, or at least extremely difficult, for him to recur to the true principles of his own peculiar actions, much less the actions of others; they frequently depend upon causes so fugitive, so remote from their effects, and which, superficially examined, appear to have so little analogy, so slender a relation with them, that it requires singular sagacity to bring them into light. This is what renders the study of the moral man a task of such difficulty; this is the reason why his heart is an abyss, of which it is frequently impossible for him to fathom the depth. . . .

. . . Man, in running over, frequently without his own knowledge, often in despite of himself, the route which Nature has marked out for him, resembles a swimmer who is obliged to follow the current that carries him along; he believes himself a free agent, because he sometimes consents, sometimes does not consent, to glide with the stream; which, notwithstanding, always hurries him forward; he believes himself the master of his condition, because he is obliged to use his arms under the fear of sinking.

"The Heart is an Abyss"

The compatibilist thinks her actions are free because they are determined by herself—by her own reasons and motives. This amounts to saying that an action of ours is free if we do it *because* it is what we want to do. In d'Holbach's vocabulary, this says that our actions are free when they are determined by our own "wills." But, he thinks, this view fails to ask what determines our wills, and so it mistakenly treats our "will" as if it were at the very *beginning* of the chain of causes and effects that lead to our action. D'Holbach argues that this is a mistake: Our wills might determine our actions, but something else determines our wills, so they are not free. And if our wills are not free, then the actions that are determined by our wills are not free. In order to be free it is not enough that we get to do what we want if our wants are themselves determined by something "external" to us.

Compatibilists may have a simple rejoinder to d'Holbach's objection. It starts with the idea that even though our actions are caused, it matters what their cause is: With the right sort of cause, our actions will be free. D'Holbach objects that the cause of our actions—even the right sort of internal cause—will itself have another cause, and that cause won't be compatible with freedom of action. But perhaps compatibilists can simply repeat their first move: Just as my action is free if it has the right sort of cause (e.g., my will), so my will could also be free if it has the right sort of cause. The debate will then involve compatibilists saying that my action is free because it is what I want to do; d'Holbach would object that something else caused me to have the want, so my action isn't free after all. The compatibilist would then respond that my action would still be free if I wanted to have the want that caused my action. Perhaps you can see where d'Holbach thinks this would lead. He would next ask about the cause of my second want—my want to have the first want. Although it is open to the compatibilist to say that the second want was caused by a third want—a want to have the want to want to perform the actions—it is unlikely that the compatibilists could win this argument. D'Holbach could keep moving back along the chain of causes until he eventually found causes that are clearly "external" to us.

It is for this reason that d'Holbach thinks the compatibilist's distinction between internal and external causes of actions fails to reconcile freedom with determinism. There is, he thinks, only a very superficial distinction between the man who is thrown out the window by others and the man who throws himself out the window. In either case, if we follow the chain of causes and effects back far enough, we will always discover that the causal origins of the man's leap through the window are outside his control. Because the internal causes of our actions will themselves always have external causes, the distinction between internal and external causes cannot help us reconcile freedom and determinism.

D'Holbach recognizes that, in the normal case, the causes of the motives and reasons that move us to action are themselves multiple and complicated, so that our own motives will ultimately be mysterious to us. Even if our decision to act is the result of careful and conscious deliberation, our deliberation makes use of beliefs, preferences, and reasons, each of which has a cause that is buried somewhere in the past. For this reason, a person's "heart is an abyss, of which it is frequently impossible for him to fathom the depth."

On d'Holbach's view, there is simply no way for us to be free without stepping "out of this Nature," becoming "an unnatural being." In short, to be free we would have to step outside the causal order of things—our actions would have to be entirely uncaused. But we could only do that if the dualist theory of persons were true. The ideas that our minds are physical entities, and that physical entities are governed by natural laws, forces us to face the problem of freedom and determinism. At any rate, stepping "out of this Nature," and outside the stream of cause and effect, won't help. As we have seen, a free action cannot be an uncaused action, since our uncaused actions are not controlled by us. They would not be free, but only random and unpredictable.

In all likelihood, because d'Holbach assumes that causes make their effects necessary, he overlooked another possibility—the one explored by Ayer. If Ayer's suggestion is plausible, free actions might be caused—and so not at all "unnatural"—even without being determined.

CONCLUSION

In this chapter we examined in detail a central argument for causal determinism, and we also considered two objections to the doctrine. The first objection, which rejects the view that the laws of nature are deterministic, did not appear to help us recover our freedom. The second objection—that the argument for causal determinism rests on a well-concealed scope fallacy—will, even if successful, only show that the defense of determinism fails. That is not the same as showing that the doctrine is false. We also explored two ways of trying to preserve freedom in a universe of law-governed causes and effects. Ayer argues that causation is not deterministic—that is, causes make their effects happen, but they don't thereby make them necessary. He can then hold that some of our actions are free because they are caused without being compelled or determined. A second effort to preserve freedom is resigned to the view that our actions are determined, and that it is not possible for us to do otherwise. But, according to this compatibilist view, our actions are free whenever their determining causes are our own reasons and motives.

We end our exploration of freedom and determinism by putting a heavy burden on determinists. They must either show that their central argument is not guilty of the scope fallacy, or they must provide another argument for determinism.

Key Terms and Figures

necessary p. 160
possible p. 160
fatalism p. 160
determinism p. 162
causal determinism p. 162
Pierre Simon de Laplace p. 162
Laplace's demon p. 164
initial conditions p. 165
retrodiction p. 166
scope fallacy p. 169
compatibilism (of freedom and determinism) p. 171
libertarianism p. 171
A. J. Ayer p. 172
Baron d'Holbach p. 176

Additional readings on freedom and determinism

Hoefer, C. (2010). Causal Determinism. *The Stanford Encyclopedia of Philosophy*. Spring 2010. (Edward N. Zalta, Ed.). Available at http://plato.stanford.edu/archives/spr2010/entries/determinism-causal

Honderich, T. (1993). *Are You Free? The Determinism Problem*. New York: Oxford University Press.

Kane, R. (2005). *A Contemporary Introduction to Free Will*. New York: Oxford University Press.

Strawson, G. (2002). The Bounds of Freedom. In Robert Kane, Ed., *The Oxford Handbook of Free Will*. New York: Oxford University Press.

Timpe, K. (n.d.). Free Will. *Internet Encyclopedia of Philosophy*. Available at http://www.iep.utm.edu/freewill

Chapter 9
Certainty and Doubt

Learning Objectives

- Describe the appeal the geometric method had for Descartes.
- Explain the infinite regress of justification and how it leads to global skepticism.
- Clarify the foundationalist theory of justification, and describe the distinction between basic and non-basic beliefs used by the theory.
- Show how Descartes uses skeptical doubts to help discover certainties.
- Explain why the Cogito was thought to be suited to serve in the foundations of knowledge.
- Describe at least two important differences between coherentism and foundationalism.
- Summarize at least two objections to coherentism, and say how coherentists might reply.
- Contrast epistemological individualism and social epistemology.

This chapter and the two that follow explore some of the central questions in epistemology. Our concern is with the nature and sources of knowledge and justification, and with the prospects for acquiring knowledge and certainty. In the present chapter we examine the relationships between certainty and doubt, especially those described by Descartes. We also introduce the idea of justification, and look carefully at two very different theories of justification—foundationalism and coherentism.

In the sixteenth and seventeenth centuries literacy spread throughout Europe, decades of religious wars were fought, and horrific plagues swept through villages and cities. In the world of ideas, Copernicus decentred the earth, the scientific revolution was stirring in centres of learning, and important new discoveries—especially in astronomy and physics—were eroding the world view of the preceding millennium. It was an environment of uncertainty, in which questions about what we could trust and what we could believe urgently needed new answers. It was in this environment that René Descartes undertook his quest for certainty.

Descartes developed one of the most ambitious epistemological programs of any philosopher, and his work has influenced all who have followed. Although earlier philosophers discussed the same issues, Descartes moved questions about the possibility of knowledge from the periphery of philosophy to its centre. An appreciation of Descartes' epistemology is essential to understanding the reactions against him that followed.

KNOWLEDGE AND METHOD

A philosophical theory about the nature of knowledge will have at its heart a theory about the nature of justification, and we will examine two such theories. To understand why a *theory of justification* should be central to a theory of knowledge, we need to impose some tentative organization on the relevant vocabulary, beginning with the ideas of *belief* and *justification*, and their place in an account of knowledge.

Belief To *believe* something is to accept it as true. Beliefs can be true or false, and justified or unjustified. When a belief is not true, it does not qualify as knowledge—it is then only a false opinion. We do not need a theory about what "truth" is in order to say this, any more than we would need a theory about the nature of oxygen in order to understand that water is H_2O.

Justification When a person's belief is *justified*, she has reasons or evidence for thinking the belief is more likely to be true than it is to be false. Justification comes in degrees related to the strength of our reasons for the belief. You have *weak* justification for a belief when the evidence indicates that it is slightly more likely to be true than it is to be false; you have *strong* justification for a belief when the evidence indicates that it is much more likely to be true than false. If you have *conclusive* justification for a belief, then the evidence leaves no reason to suspect that you might be in error. If a belief is true but it is not justified, it does not qualify as knowledge—you may guess correctly where the money is hidden, but making a lucky guess is not the same as knowing.

Knowledge A simple way to think of "knowledge" combines the two previous ideas: that a belief must be true to qualify as knowledge, and that it must be justified to qualify as knowledge. This suggests that a person *knows* something—and doesn't *merely believe* it—if she has a belief that is both true and justified. In other words, ***knowledge** is justified true belief.*

knowledge: Although the right philosophical account of knowledge is contested, the term *knowledge* is generally used in philosophy to refer to beliefs that are both true and conclusively justified—that is, knowledge is justified true belief.

Although many philosophers think this definition flawed, many also believe it at least points us in the right direction. But there is little agreement about how to best complete or repair the definition. That it is flawed is suggested by examples like this one offered by Bertrand Russell[1]:

> It is very easy to give examples of true beliefs that are not knowledge. There is the man who looks at a clock which is not going, though he thinks it is, and who happens to look at it at the moment when it is right; this man acquires a true belief as to the time of day, but cannot be said to have knowledge.

Russell describes a belief that fails to qualify as knowledge despite being *true*, but the example illustrates more than that. The man has a true belief that it is, say, 6:00 p.m., and, furthermore, he is *justified* in believing that is 6:00 p.m. After all, his belief about the time derives from, and is supported by, what the clock says. We can even strengthen his

[1] Russell, B. (1948). *Human Knowledge: Its Scope and Limits.* New York: Simon and Schuster: 155.

justification by adding that the clock has been in his family for decades, and it has never stopped before—it is a famously reliable clock. So his belief that it is 6:00 p.m. is both true and justified—perhaps even highly justified. Nonetheless, it is a fluke. If he had looked at the clock earlier or later, he would have arrived at the same belief, but then his belief would have been false.

Russell's example suggests that when a true belief, or the grounds for it, are the result of accident or luck, then we are reluctant to count it as *knowledge*. Knowledge is not something we can bungle our way into. But how should the definition of knowledge be amended, or with what should it be replaced? One possibility is that the element of luck should be removed from our theory of knowledge. We might do this by requiring a reliable *method* for producing true beliefs before they qualify as knowledge. Another possibility is that we should require a true belief to have the *strongest* or most *conclusive* form of justification before it qualifies as knowledge. The man in Russell's example would need much stronger justification to *know* that it is 6:00 p.m. How strong does our justification for believing something need to be before we can properly *know* it?

Consider the example of lottery tickets. (This example and others like it are widely discussed by contemporary epistemologists.) If you hold one ticket out of, say, a billion that have been sold, then the belief that you hold a losing ticket is *very highly* justified. Nonetheless, you still do not *know* you will lose. If, on this basis, you could know you will lose, then each of the one-billion ticket holders could also know that they will lose—their odds are the same as yours. But if you *all* know you will not win, then it follows that none of you will win. But that is wrong: We can be sure that one of you will win. This line of reasoning suggests to some epistemologists that unless our justification for a belief is perfect, leaving *no* chance that our belief is mistaken, we do not qualify as having knowledge.

In the pages that follow we will look at an important theory of knowledge and justification developed by René Descartes. Descartes agrees with two central points already mentioned: First, that genuine knowledge cannot be true belief arrived at by luck. We need, he thinks, a *method* that can assure us that it results in true beliefs. Second, Descartes thinks that if a true belief is to qualify as knowledge, then our justification for the belief must rise to the level of complete certainty. In autobiographical writings, Descartes describes how he struggled with questions about what to believe and sought a reliable method to guide him toward the truth. The following passage describes how he arrived at a method for overcoming his many doubts.

"Discourse on Method" (René Descartes, 1637)[2]

> From my childhood, I have been familiar with letters; and as I was given to believe that by their help a clear and certain knowledge of all that is useful in life might be acquired, I was ardently desirous of instruction. But as soon as I had finished the entire course of study, at the close of which it is customary to be admitted into the order of the learned, I completely changed my opinion. For I found myself involved in so many doubts and errors, that I was convinced I had advanced no farther in all my attempts at learning, than the discovery at every turn of my own ignorance. . . .

[2] From Descartes, R. (1901). *Discourse on the Method of Rightly Conducting the Reason*, Parts I and II. (John Veitch, Trans.). Retrieved from www.gutenberg.org/cache/epub/59/pg59.txt

Of philosophy I will say nothing, except that when I saw that it had been cultivated for many ages by the most distinguished men, and that yet there is not a single matter within its sphere which is not still in dispute, and nothing, therefore, which is above doubt, I did not presume to anticipate that my success would be greater in it than that of others; and further, when I considered the number of conflicting opinions touching a single matter that may be upheld by learned men, while there can be but one true, I reckoned as well-nigh false all that was only probable.

As to the other sciences, inasmuch as these borrow their principles from philosophy, I judged that no solid superstructures could be reared on foundations so infirm; and neither the honor nor the gain held out by them was sufficient to determine me to their cultivation: . . .

For these reasons, as soon as my age permitted me to pass from under the control of my instructors, I entirely abandoned the study of letters, and resolved no longer to seek any other science than the knowledge of myself, or of the great book of the world. I spent the remainder of my youth in traveling, in visiting courts and armies, in holding intercourse with men of different dispositions and ranks, in collecting varied experience, in proving myself in the different situations into which fortune threw me, and, above all, in making such reflection on the matter of my experience as to secure my improvement. . . .

It is true that, while busied only in considering the manners of other men, I found here, too, scarce any ground for settled conviction, and remarked hardly less contradiction among them than in the opinions of the philosophers. So that the greatest advantage I derived from the study consisted in this, that, observing many things which, however extravagant and ridiculous to our apprehension, are yet by common consent received and approved by other great nations, I learned to entertain too decided a belief in regard to nothing of the truth of which I had been persuaded merely by example and custom; and thus I gradually extricated myself from many errors powerful enough to darken our natural intelligence, and incapacitate us in great measure from listening to reason. . . .

. . . [B]ut as for the opinions which up to that time I had embraced, I thought that I could not do better than resolve at once to sweep them wholly away, that I might afterwards be in a position to admit either others more correct, or even perhaps the same when they had undergone the scrutiny of reason. I firmly believed that in this way I should much better succeed in the conduct of my life, than if I built only upon old foundations, and leaned upon principles which, in my youth, I had taken upon trust. . . .

. . . But I had become aware, even so early as during my college life, that no opinion, however absurd and incredible, can be imagined, which has not been maintained by some one of the philosophers; and afterwards in the course of my travels I remarked that all those whose opinions are decidedly repugnant to ours are not in that account barbarians and savages, but on the contrary that many of these nations make an equally good, if not better, use of their reason than we do. . . . I was thus led to infer that the ground of our opinions is far more custom and example than any certain knowledge. And, finally, although such be the ground of our opinions, I remarked that a plurality of suffrages is no guarantee of truth where it is at all of difficult discovery, as in such cases it is much more likely that it will be found by one than by many. I could, however, select from the crowd no one whose opinions seemed worthy of preference, and thus I found myself constrained, as it were, to use my own reason in the conduct of my life.

But like one walking alone and in the dark, I resolved to proceed so slowly and with such circumspection, that if I did not advance far, I would at least guard against falling. . . .

> The long chains of simple and easy reasonings by means of which geometers are accustomed to reach the conclusions of their most difficult demonstrations, had led me to imagine that all things, to the knowledge of which man is competent, are mutually connected in the same way, and that there is nothing so far removed from us as to be beyond our reach, or so hidden that we cannot discover it, provided only we abstain from accepting the false for the true, and always preserve in our thoughts the order necessary for the deduction of one truth from another. And I had little difficulty in determining the objects with which it was necessary to commence, for I was already persuaded that it must be with the simplest and easiest to know, and, considering that of all those who have hitherto sought truth in the sciences, the mathematicians alone have been able to find any demonstrations, that is, any certain and evident reasons, I did not doubt but that such must have been the rule of their investigations. I resolved to commence, therefore, with the examination of the simplest objects, not anticipating, however, from this any other advantage than that to be found in accustoming my mind to the love and nourishment of truth, and to a distaste for all such reasonings as were unsound.

Descartes models his "method of rightly conducting the reason" on geometry, the discipline he thinks has the best claim to producing secure and indisputable truths. He notes that the considerable success of geometry is owed to the fact that it begins with simple and secure truths—called *axioms*—from which geometers then reason deductively to more complex truths, called *theorems*. By carefully following this method, geometry eventually arrives at new insights into more complicated geometric matters, with the result that geometers can place as much confidence in their new discoveries as they have in their original axioms.

The plan Descartes laid out is extremely ambitious: He intends to reconstruct all of human knowledge on a secure foundation, using the same method that had proven so successful in geometry. If we can locate secure starting points that are beyond dispute, comparable to the axioms of geometry, and if we reason carefully and methodically from those starting points, we can be assured that we will arrive at truths. Those truths will be justified by the axioms and deductions that lead us to them. Descartes' proposal is that whatever can be established by his **geometric method** deserves the title of "knowledge," and whatever cannot be deduced from indisputable axioms is only opinion.

geometric method: A method of arriving at knowledge by deduction from self-evident starting points, such as axioms in geometry or basic beliefs in epistemology.

foundationalism: A theory of justification that maintains that beliefs are justified by showing how they are supported by a special class of basic or foundational beliefs (which are self-justifying and do not themselves depend on any other beliefs for justification).

FOUNDATIONALISM: THE GEOMETRIC METHOD

The geometric style into which Descartes reorganizes knowledge is called **foundationalism**, a theory of justification that maintains that all beliefs can be divided into two kinds: *basic beliefs*, or those that do not receive their justification from any other beliefs; and *non-basic beliefs*, or those that receive their justification indirectly from basic beliefs. Let us see what makes this view appealing.

skepticism: The view that we have no knowledge. Skepticism can be local, or limited, as when someone doubts that it is possible to know anything about, for example, the future or morality, or it can be global, or unlimited, as when someone doubts is it possible to know anything through sense experience—or to know anything at all.

The Infinite Regress of Justification

Foundationalism is motivated by the idea that it is our only alternative to **skepticism**, the view that knowledge is not possible for us. There are both local and global forms of skepticism. *Local skeptics* believe that there are some topics about which we might never have knowledge—for example, about whether there is a God, or whether there is intelligent life in other galaxies. But a few philosophers have entertained more *global forms of skepticism*, and doubt that we have any knowledge at all.

One global form of skepticism emerges from reflection on two ideas that appear to be only common sense. The first is that *in order to justify a belief we must have other beliefs to support it*—in other words, a belief is not justified unless it has the support of other things we believe. For example, if I believe the earth is spherical, and you ask what justifies my belief, I might offer the following support: (i) The earth casts a round shadow on the moon when it passes between the sun and moon during a lunar eclipse; and (ii) the sails of ships disappear below the horizon as they move farther from shore. The facts in (i) and (ii) are evidence that the earth is spherical, but I am not justified in believing that the earth is spherical by (i) and (ii) *unless I believe* those facts. If my belief is to be justified by evidence, I need to believe the evidence that supports it.

Second, suppose I believe (i) and (ii), and I offer them to justify my belief that the earth is spherical. You might now ask what justifies me in believing (i) and (ii). If it turns out that I have *no reason at all* to believe them, and yet they are the only support I have for my belief, then I am not justified in believing that the earth is spherical. A *belief that is not justified cannot provide justification for another belief*.

Putting the preceding points together, a belief is justified only if it is supported by other beliefs, and those other beliefs can justify the original belief only if they are already justified. Perhaps you see that trouble is coming. A belief, B_1, cannot be justified by another belief, B_2, unless B_2 is also justified. But B_2 cannot be justified unless it is justified by another belief, B_3; but B_3 cannot justify B_2 unless it is justified by B_4, which will need to be justified by B_5, and so on. We are set out upon an **infinite regress of justification**—an infinite series of prior justified beliefs, each of which needs other prior beliefs in order to be justified. The justification of any one belief now seems to require an infinite number of justified beliefs.

infinite regress of justification: An infinite series of justified beliefs, in which each belief is justified by beliefs that are epistemologically prior to it in the series. The infinite regress is thought to be the consequence of two ideas: (i) that a belief can only be justified by other beliefs, and (ii) that a belief can only justify another belief if it is already justified. Since no one has an infinite number of beliefs, the regress threatens to lead into global skepticism about knowledge and justification.

Obviously none of us has an infinite number of beliefs. If an infinite number of beliefs are required for the justification of even a single belief, and no one has an infinite number of justified beliefs, then it follows that none of us has *any* justified beliefs. And, of course, if knowledge is justified true belief, and none of our beliefs is justified, then none of our beliefs will qualify as knowledge. This would be devastating if true. It would mean that no one can know anything, but also that no one has any justification—not even weak justification—for believing anything. The infinite regress of justification plunges us into global skepticism.

Foundationalism offers a way to escape the regress that threatens to plunge us into total skepticism by rejecting the starting point of the skeptical argument. A simple analogy illustrates the central idea behind foundationalism. Consider the following two rules:

i. In order to be a teacher, you must be certified to teach.

ii. The only way to become certified to teach is to be certified by another teacher.

With a little reflection, we can see that strict adherence to our rules has the consequence that no one will become a teacher. If I want to be a teacher, I must be certified by someone who is already a teacher; but for that person to be a teacher, she must already have been certified by someone who was a teacher, and so on. You can see where this goes. Our rules (i) and (ii) require an infinite regression of certifiers. If we don't have an infinite number of teachers (i.e., certifiers), then we cannot have *any* teachers.

An easy way to deal with our teacher shortage is to change one of the rules that created it. We could relax the first rule and permit a *first generation* of teachers to teach without certification. They can then certify later generations of teachers even though they are not themselves certified. Alternatively, we could relax the second rule and allow a first generation of teachers to receive certification without having to receive it from previous teachers—perhaps the first generation of teachers could be certified by the Minister of Education. Either way, we avoid both the teacher shortage and the infinite regress that caused it by permitting a generation of certifiers who have not been certified by a previously certified generation.

Similarly, we can escape global skepticism and the infinite regress of justification if there is a generation of justified beliefs that can be used to justify other beliefs, but that does not require justification from any previous generation of beliefs. Foundationalism is the theory of justification that says that we can avoid global skepticism by recognizing the existence of a special class of beliefs—a first generation of beliefs called **basic beliefs**—that support, or justify, other beliefs, but that do not themselves need the support of any further beliefs.

basic beliefs: An important class of beliefs in a foundationalist system of knowledge or justification. Basic beliefs are used to justify other, non-basic beliefs, and they are usually treated as justified even though they do not owe their own justification to the support of other beliefs. Basic beliefs are usually described as self-justifying or self-evident, and classical foundationalism holds that they must be certain.

The idea behind foundationalism is simple: If we think the world rests on the back of a turtle, we should ask what holds up the turtle. If the answer is that it rests on the back of another turtle, then we should ask what holds up the second turtle. If we think this can't go on forever, with an infinite number of turtles stacked all the way down, then there will have to be a foundational turtle—the basic turtle—who holds up all the turtles piled on his back, but who does not rest on the back of a turtle himself. A foundational or basic turtle, if there was one, would prevent the need for an infinite number of turtles.

Basic beliefs, if there are any, could bring the infinite regress of justification to a halt in two ways:

a. Basic beliefs might be used to justify other non-basic, or non-foundational, beliefs even though the basic beliefs are not themselves justified. In this case, basic beliefs would be *unjustified justifiers*. (A basic turtle could support other turtles, but nothing at all supports him—he is an unsupported supporter.)

or

b. Basic beliefs might be justified so that they can be used to support, or justify, other beliefs, but they do not acquire their own justification from any other beliefs. In that case, basic beliefs would have to be *self-justifying*. (The basic turtle at the bottom of the pile is supported, but *he supports himself*—he is self-supporting.)

If there is a class of basic beliefs, then we can avoid the infinite regress and global skepticism. Foundationalists usually put this point the other way around: Since some of our beliefs *are* justified, and since we do know *some* things, there can't be an infinite regress of justification. But if there is no infinite regress of justification, there must be basic beliefs. There must be some unjustified justifiers or some self-justifying beliefs.

The Need for Certainty

Descartes defends the view that some beliefs are self-justifying or self-evident, but on his view basic beliefs are not merely justified. They are known with *complete certainty* to be true. Like the self-evident axioms of geometry from which geometric theorems are derived, the basic beliefs from which knowledge is derived must be beyond doubt. There is a reason to insist we have *certainty* at the foundations of knowledge.

certainty: A belief is *certain* when it is not possible for it to be false.

A belief is **certain** when (and only when) it is not possible that it is false. This definition captures the intuitive idea that when there is any chance that a belief is false, then we are not certain that it is true. To establish that we know something with certainty we will need to show that there is *no possibility* that we are mistaken. So why must the foundations of knowledge be certain?

Consider what happens if we deduce new information from the following statements, each of which has only a 70 percent chance of being true:

1. If Renée parked in a red zone, then her car has been towed.
2. Renée did park in a red zone.
3. So, Renée's car has been towed.

Since each of our premises (1) and (2) has only a 70 percent chance of being true, there is only a 49 percent chance that *both* premises are true. This is calculated in the same way we calculate the odds of two coins coming up heads on a fair toss. If *each* coin has a 50 percent chance of coming up heads, then the chance that *both* will come up heads is determined by multiplying 50 × 50 percent, leaving a 25 percent chance that both will come up heads. Since the truth of our conclusion depends on the truth of *both* premises, our conclusion (3) has only a 49 percent chance of being true. Suppose we now extend our line of reasoning, adding new information that also has a 70 percent chance of being true.

4. If Renée's car has been towed, then she will be forced to pay towing fees.
5. So, Renée will be forced to pay towing fees. [From (3) and (4)]

Our new conclusion has only a 34.3 percent chance of being true—70 percent of 49 percent. In other words, if the basic beliefs we use to support our other beliefs are *less than certain* (i.e., less than 100 percent), and so are only *probably* true, then the non-basic beliefs they support will be even less likely to be true. In any line of reasoning employing multiple premises, the probability that our conclusion is true rapidly decreases. Uncertainty in the starting points can easily accumulate to undermine our justification for our conclusions. So if we want to have confidence in our conclusions, we need to begin our reasoning with beliefs that are known with certainty.

When Descartes set off in search of basic or foundational beliefs from which to derive the rest of knowledge, he was searching for beliefs that are certain. The success of his plan depended on locating foundational propositions—axioms—that are so secure that they can eventually support the weight of all of human knowledge, just as the axioms of geometry support all of geometrical knowledge. Where can such propositions be found?

THE NEED FOR DOUBT: METHODOLOGICAL SKEPTICISM

Descartes realized that by the time he began to reflect seriously he had already acquired some beliefs—perhaps many—that were false, and some that might have been true but that were unjustified. He also understood that once our beliefs are infected with errors, those errors tend to spread. So Descartes decided that the first step needed in his search for truth was to eliminate the false and unjustified opinions he had already accumulated.

Unfortunately, this is more challenging than it appears. Our beliefs do not come *labelled* as true or false. To believe something is to think that *it is true*. So even if our beliefs did come labelled, they would all be labelled as true, even the false ones. Given this situation, how do we eliminate the false beliefs that have taken root in our thinking? In the selection from his writings that follows, Descartes makes a radical proposal. If we know the basket contains some poisoned apples, but we can't tell the poisoned apples from the good ones, then we need to throw out the whole basket. Similarly, Descartes proposes *to rid himself of all beliefs and start over*. If he can find a way to do this, then he can "commence to build anew from the foundations."

To sweep his head clear of previous opinions, Descartes enlists his *method of doubt*. **Methodological skepticism**, as we now call it, tries to create widespread doubt in order to help rid us of any beliefs that might be false. As a methodological skeptic, Descartes is not a true skeptic. The point of methodological skepticism is not to plunge us into doubt and then leave us there. Instead, it plunges us into doubt in order to cleanse us of error, so that we are then in the appropriate condition to proceed down the path to knowledge. Descartes believes that doubting is an essential first step since it rids us of the prejudices and errors that stand in the way of acquiring genuine knowledge. Let us see how he implements methodological skepticism.

methodological skepticism: The use of skeptical doubts and arguments to help rid inquirers of any false beliefs that might stand in the way of acquiring knowledge. Not a true form of skepticism, since it does not deny that knowledge is possible; instead it sees skepticism as one tool to use *en route* to knowledge.

The General Upheaval (René Descartes, 1643)[3]

It is now some years since I detected how many were the false beliefs that I had from my earliest youth admitted as true, and how doubtful was everything I had since constructed on this basis; and from that time I was convinced that I must once for all seriously undertake to rid myself of all the opinions which I had formerly accepted, and commence to build anew from the foundation, if I wanted to establish any firm and permanent structure in the sciences. . . . To-day, then, . . . I shall at last seriously and freely address myself to the general upheaval of all my former opinions.

Now for this object it is not necessary that I should show that all of these are false—I shall perhaps never arrive at this end. But inasmuch as reason already persuades me that I ought no less carefully to withhold my assent from matters which are not entirely certain and indubitable than from those which appear to me manifestly to be false, if I am able to find in each one some reason to doubt, this will suffice to justify my rejecting the whole. And for that end it will not be requisite that I should examine each in particular, which would be an endless undertaking; for owing to the fact that the destruction of the foundations of necessity brings with it the downfall of the rest of the edifice, I shall only in the first place attack those principles upon which all my former opinions rested.

All that up to the present time I have accepted as most true and certain I have learned either from the senses or through the senses; but it is sometimes proved to me that these senses are deceptive, and it is wiser not to trust entirely anything by which we have once been deceived.

But it may be that although the senses sometimes deceive us concerning things which are hardly perceptible, or very far away, there are yet many others to be met with as to which we cannot reasonably have any doubt, although we recognize them by their means. For example, there is the fact that I am here, seated by the fire, attired in a dressing gown, having this paper in my hands and other similar matters. . . .

---

[3] From Descartes, R. (1911). *Meditations on First Philosophy*, in *The Philosophical Works of Descartes*, translated by Elizabeth S. Haldane (Cambridge University Press).

At the same time I must remember that I am a man, and that consequently I am in the habit of sleeping, and in my dreams representing to myself the same things or sometimes even less probable things, than do those who are insane in their waking moments. How often has it happened to me that in the night I dreamt that I found myself in this particular place, that I was dressed and seated near the fire, whilst in reality I was lying undressed in bed! At this moment it does indeed seem to me that it is with eyes awake that I am looking at this paper; that this head which I move is not asleep, that it is deliberately and of set purpose that I extend my hand and perceive it; what happens in sleep does not appear so clear nor so distinct as does all this. But in thinking over this I remind myself that on many occasions I have in sleep been deceived by similar illusions, and in dwelling carefully on this reflection I see so manifestly that there are no certain indications by which we may clearly distinguish wakefulness from sleep that I am lost in astonishment. And my astonishment is such that it is almost capable of persuading me that I now dream.

Now let us assume that we are asleep and that all these particulars, e.g. that we open our eyes, shake our head, extend our hands, and so on, are but false delusions; and let us reflect that possibly neither our hands nor our whole body are such as they appear to us to be. At the same time we must at least confess that the things which are represented to us in sleep are like painted representations . . .

. . . For whether I am awake or asleep, two and three together always form five, and the square can never have more than four sides, and it does not seem possible that truths so clear and apparent can be suspected of any falsity [or uncertainty].

Nevertheless I have long had fixed in my mind the belief that an all-powerful God existed by whom I have been created such as I am. But how do I know that He has not brought it to pass that there is no earth, no heaven, no extended body, no magnitude, no place, and that nevertheless [I possess the perceptions of all these things and that] they seem to me to exist just exactly as I now see them? And, besides, as I sometimes imagine that others deceive themselves in the things which they think they know best, how do I know that I am not deceived every time that I add two and three, or count the sides of a square, or judge of things yet simpler, if anything simpler can be imagined? . . .

. . . To these reasons I have certainly nothing to reply, but at the end I feel constrained to confess that there is nothing in all that I formerly believed to be true, of which I cannot in some measure doubt, and that not merely through want of thought or through levity, but for reasons which are very powerful and maturely considered; so that henceforth I ought not the less carefully to refrain from giving credence to these opinions than to that which is manifestly false, if I desire to arrive at any certainty [in the sciences].

But it is not sufficient to have made these remarks, we must also be careful to keep them in mind. For these ancient and commonly held opinions still revert frequently to my mind, long and familiar custom having given them the right to occupy my mind against my inclination and rendered them almost masters of my belief; nor will I ever lose the habit of deferring to them or of placing my confidence in them, so long as I consider them as they really are, i.e. opinions in some measure doubtful, as I have just shown, and at the same time highly probable, so that there is much more reason to believe in than to deny them. That is why I consider that I shall not be acting amiss, if, taking of set purpose a contrary belief, I allow myself to be deceived, and for a certain time pretend that all these opinions are entirely false and imaginary, until at last, having thus balanced my former prejudices with my latter [so that they cannot divert my opinions more to one side than to the other], my judgment will no longer be dominated by bad usage or turned away from the right knowledge of the truth. For I am assured that there can be neither peril nor error in this course, and that I cannot at present yield too much to distrust, since I am not considering the question of action, but only of knowledge.

I shall then suppose, not that God who is supremely good and the fountain of truth, but some evil genius not less powerful than deceitful, has employed his whole energies in deceiving me; I shall consider that the heavens, the earth, colours, figures, sound, and all other external things are nought but the illusions and dreams of which this genius has availed himself in order to lay traps for my credulity; I shall consider myself as having no hands, no eyes, no flesh, no blood, nor any senses, yet falsely believing myself to possess all these things; I shall remain obstinately attached to this idea, and if by this means it is not in my power to arrive at the knowledge of any truth, I may at least do what is in my power [i.e. suspend my judgment], and with firm purpose avoid giving credence to any false thing, or being imposed upon by this arch deceiver, however powerful and deceptive he may be. But this task is a laborious one, and insensibly a certain lassitude leads me into the course of my ordinary life. And just as a captive who in sleep enjoys an imaginary liberty, when he begins to suspect that his liberty is but a dream, fears to awaken, and conspires with these agreeable illusions that the deception may be prolonged, so insensibly of my own accord I fall back into my former opinions, and I dread awakening from this slumber, lest the laborious wakefulness which would follow the tranquility of this repose should have to be spent not in daylight, but in the excessive darkness of the difficulties which have just been discussed.

Manufacturing Doubt

In this selection from his writings, Descartes implements his methodological skepticism by examining the *sources* of his beliefs and manufacturing doubts about all beliefs that have unreliable origins. He first considers all those beliefs—which might be a majority of our beliefs—that originate in perception (i.e., sense experience) of the world. Descartes finds that sense experience can never give us certainty, so he concludes that no belief acquired through the senses is suited to serve in the foundations of knowledge. He gives several reasons for this, beginning with commonplace reservations and then escalating the severity of his suspicions.

1. *Error and Illusion:* "It is sometimes proved to me that these senses are deceptive, and it is wiser not to trust entirely to anything by which we have once been deceived."[4]

Descartes' first reason for believing the senses do not provide complete certainty is that we are familiar with cases in which our senses have already misled us. But, he thinks, what sometimes misleads us cannot be trusted to provide certainty.

Perhaps this conclusion is too hasty. After all, we only know that our senses sometimes mislead us because we have discovered—*by relying on our senses*—that they have done so. I discover that my eyes mislead me when the lighting is poor by relying on my eyes when the lighting is better. This suggests that occasional failures of our senses only show that they are not to be trusted in *poor viewing conditions*. And that is no reason to think we cannot put complete trust in our senses when we are in *optimal viewing conditions*.

[4] *Ibid.*

Descartes then offers a further objection to trusting our senses that applies even to optimal conditions.

2. *Dreams:* "I remind myself that on many occasions I have in sleep been deceived . . . I see so manifestly that there are no certain indications by which we may clearly distinguish wakefulness from sleep."[5]

Descartes makes the modest claim that for all we know *right now*, we might be dreaming *at this very moment*—and this will be true at any moment we care to consider. Clearly, if we cannot tell whether we are awake or dreaming at any moment, then we cannot be certain that our experiences at any moment reflect reality. But Descartes also claims that no test ("indications") can tell us whether we are awake at the moment we apply the test. Why is there no test that can distinguish waking from dreaming? Can't we pinch ourselves?

Notice that although a litmus test can establish that a substance is an acid, dreaming of applying a litmus test doesn't establish anything about the substance. Similarly, if there is a test to prove we are awake *when we apply the test*, it won't show that we are awake *if we only dream that we apply it*. So although there may be tests—the "pinch test" or some other—that can successfully distinguish waking from dreaming, any such test always assumes what it tries to show—namely, that we are awake when we apply it. If Descartes is right that we cannot distinguish waking from dreaming with any certainty, then we cannot trust our senses to give us certainty even in what appear to be ideal viewing conditions. To secure his conclusion that we cannot have complete confidence in any belief acquired through experience, Descartes enlists a final skeptical device: the hypothesis that there might be a deceptive evil genius.

3. *The Evil Genius:* "I shall then suppose, [that] some evil genius not less powerful than deceitful, has employed his whole energies in deceiving me; I shall consider that the heavens, the earth, colors, figures, sound, and all other external things are nothing but the illusions and dreams of which this genius has availed himself in order to lay traps for my credulity."[6]

A sufficiently powerful opponent determined to mislead you about as much as possible could easily manufacture a perfect illusion—say, a multidimensional hallucination that you are a student reading this sentence. However extraordinarily unlikely this is, it remains a *possibility*, and even the most remote possibility that we are being misled prevents us from being certain about anything we experience.

Descartes believes these fantastical doubts show that our senses do not give us certainty, and so cannot provide beliefs suited for the foundations of knowledge. We must turn elsewhere. Below, we see Descartes' first proposal for basic beliefs.

The Cogito (René Descartes, 1643)[7]

> The Meditation of yesterday filled my mind with so many doubts that it is no longer in my power to forget them. And yet I do not see in what manner I can resolve them; and, just as if I had all of a sudden fallen into very deep water, I am so disconcerted

[5] *Ibid.*

[6] *Ibid.*

[7] *Ibid.*

that I can neither make certain of setting my feet on the bottom, nor can I swim and so support myself on the surface. I shall nevertheless make an effort and follow anew the same path as that on which I yesterday entered, i.e. I shall proceed by setting aside all that in which the least doubt could be supposed to exist, just as if I had discovered that it was absolutely false; and I shall ever follow in this road until I have met with something which is certain, or at least, if I can do nothing else, until I have learned for certain that there is nothing in the world that is certain. Archimedes, in order that he might draw the terrestrial globe out of its place, and transport it elsewhere, demanded only that one point should be fixed and immovable; in the same way I shall have the right to conceive high hopes if I am happy enough to discover one thing only which is certain and indubitable.

I suppose, then, that all the things that I see are false; I persuade myself that nothing has ever existed of all that my fallacious memory represents to me. I consider that I possess no senses; I imagine that body, figure, extension, movement and place are but the fictions of my mind. What, then, can be esteemed as true? Perhaps nothing at all, unless that there is nothing in the world that is certain.

But how can I know there is not something different from those things that I have just considered, of which one cannot have the slightest doubt? Is there not some God, or some other being by whatever name we call it, who puts these reflections into my mind? That is not necessary, for is it not possible that I am capable of producing them myself? I myself, am I not at least something? But I have already denied that I had senses and body. Yet I hesitate, for what follows from that? Am I so dependent on body and senses that I cannot exist without these? But I was persuaded that there was nothing in all the world, that there was no heaven, no earth, that there were no minds, nor any bodies: was I not then likewise persuaded that I did not exist? Not at all; of a surety I myself did exist since I persuaded myself of something [or merely because I thought of something]. But there is some deceiver or other, very powerful and very cunning, who ever employs his ingenuity in deceiving me. Then without doubt I exist also if he deceives me, and let him deceive me as much as he will, he can never cause me to be nothing so long as I think that I am something. So that after having reflected well and carefully examined all things, we must come to the definite conclusion that this proposition: I am, I exist, is necessarily true each time that I pronounce it, or that I mentally conceive it.

Descartes' first, and most important, basic belief is "I am, I exist." Elsewhere he famously expresses this as "I think, therefore I am" (in its well-known Latin formulation: *Cogito ergo sum*); this idea is usually referred to simply as the **Cogito**.

Cogito: Short for Descartes' famous "I think, therefore I am" (*cogito ergo sum* in Latin).

To understand the Cogito properly, we must contrast it with similar propositions, such as "I walk, therefore I am." Although, in this simple line of reasoning, the conclusion "I am" follows from the premise "I walk," doubt about sense experience always leaves us uncertain that the premise is really true. From this uncertain premise we cannot acquire certainty that we exist. The case is different for these two lines of reasoning:

i. I think that I think, therefore I do think.
ii. I think that I exist, therefore I do exist.

In these examples, we *can* know the premises with complete certainty, and our certainty does not depend on any experience we have of ourselves or our thoughts. Consider why: Suppose I do not exist. Then I cannot mistakenly think I exist. Therefore, if I do think I exist, then I exist. Similarly, if I do not think, then I cannot mistakenly think I do think. So if I do think that I think, then I think. In short, I can know that I exist and that I think even while doubting *everything* my senses tell me, and even though a powerful and evil genius is working hard to deceive me.

Each of these thoughts—that *I exist* and that *I think*—are self-justifying: They need no other beliefs from which to receive their justification, since to merely think them is already to have justification for believing they are true. Furthermore, these are things we know with certainty. If we think them at all, then there is *no possibility* that they are false. These are exactly what *basic* beliefs ought to be—self-justifying and known with certainty. Both "I think" and "I am" are perfectly suited to serve as *axioms* in Descartes' geometrical restructuring of knowledge.

Recall that Descartes' plan was to locate basic beliefs that can be known with complete certainty, like the axioms in a geometrical system, and then to deduce other beliefs from them, just as geometers deduce theorems from axioms. Only our basic beliefs, or axioms, and any beliefs—the theorems—that are validly deduced from them qualify as *knowledge*. All the rest are opinions. To escape from doubt and recover knowledge, Descartes will eventually need additional basic beliefs to supplement the Cogito. He will also need to undertake long chains of careful reasoning to get from those basic beliefs to other beliefs. Until that work is done, we do not know which among the things we now believe will eventually qualify as knowledge.

We won't explore the extent to which Descartes succeeded in his ambitious epistemological program. He did, however, believe he could locate many additional basic beliefs, thus providing a much wider foundation for knowledge than is provided by the Cogito alone. And he believed he could, through a series of careful deductions from those basic beliefs, rebuild the edifice of human knowledge—at the very least, he thought he could recover those parts that were worth salvaging. Not everyone agrees that we can overcome the severe doubts with which Descartes begins, so few have attempted to follow in his footsteps.

COHERENTISM

Critics have drawn attention to two problems in Descartes' epistemology. Some have challenged the foundationalist approach to justification, arguing that the distinction between basic and non-basic beliefs does not accurately reflect our practice of providing justification for beliefs. Critics in this first group propose alternative theories of justification to replace foundationalism. A second group focuses on the strikingly *individualistic* form in which Descartes arranges his theory of knowledge, taking him to task for failing to give credit to the social contexts in which knowledge is actually produced. We will look at each of these complaints in turn.

Coherence and Justification

The best known alternative to foundationalism is the *coherence theory of justification*, also known as *coherentism*. Coherentism accepts the foundationalist starting point: In order to justify a belief we must offer other beliefs in its support, and those beliefs are also in need of justification. Foundationalists see this as the start of an inevitable regress that will lead us into global skepticism. Although the potential for an infinite regress is there, coherentists do not think the right way to avoid it is to adopt the style of justification used in geometry. Descartes was right to recognize that in order to justify a mathematical theorem one needs to show how it can be deduced from a set of self-evident axioms, but this highly regimented procedure does not reflect our best practices in justifying other kinds of beliefs.

When called upon to justify a belief, we draw on a variety of supports, and which one we emphasize depends on what the belief is about. If I am asked to justify my belief that tomorrow will be a good day for a hike, I will cite recent weather reports and the fact that the trails won't be crowded because tomorrow is Tuesday. When asked to justify my belief that eggs should not be fried without removing them from the shell, I will describe my failed attempts to make hard fried eggs and cite passages from Snopes's classic *Manual for the Preparation of Avian Eggs*.

Two aspects of these examples should be noted: First, each belief I offer in support of my original opinions remains open to doubt—you can easily bring yourself to doubt any one of them by introducing skeptical considerations. Nonetheless, if called upon to do so I know how to go about offering support for those supporting beliefs. I can confirm the weather report I saw on television by checking the newspaper and several independent online sources. Second, I have no idea how to ground my beliefs by tracing them back to any self-verifying axioms from which they can be validly deduced. Instead, I justify a belief by showing how it *harmonizes* or *fits together* with other pieces of information in my possession—that is, with my other beliefs and with those I can easily acquire if I am pressed for justification. However, showing how one belief "fits" or "coheres" with other beliefs is not the same as deducing it from a foundation of basic beliefs.

According to the **coherence theory of justification (coherentism)**, a belief is justified by showing how it *coheres* with other beliefs, when those other beliefs already make up a largely coherent body of beliefs. We begin our inquiries with a substantial *collection* of beliefs that is already justified—because it is already a largely coherent collection. Only then are individual beliefs justified by showing how they cohere with this larger body of beliefs. Unless our view of the world is already deeply confused and incoherent, any new belief will count as justified if it hangs together with the many other things we already believe. If any new candidate for belief does not fit with our expectations about how the world is, it will initially be suspect, and our level of scrutiny will be raised until we either find a way to dismiss it (e.g., "I was hallucinating") or to fit it together with the other things we believe, even if that means we must make some adjustments in our earlier beliefs.

coherence theory of justification: A theory of justification according to which a belief is justified by showing that it "fits" or "coheres" with other beliefs that make up a largely coherent system of beliefs.

American philosopher **William James** (1842–1910) describes the process of adding new beliefs while requiring them to fit with old beliefs before they qualify as justified.

William James: American philosopher and psychologist who, along with Charles S. Peirce, founded the American pragmatist movement in philosophy. His work touched on almost every area of philosophy and continues to be influential. He is known as the founder of modern American psychology, where his work, especially his theory of emotions, continues to have defenders.

Minds That Grow Like Grease Spots (William James, 1907)[8]

Lecture II

What Pragmatism Means

. . . The process here is always the same. The individual has a stock of old opinions already, but he meets a new experience that puts them to a strain. Somebody contradicts them; or in a reflective moment he discovers that they contradict each other;

[8] From James, W. (1907). *Pragmatism; A New Name for Some Old Ways of Thinking*. Retrieved from http://www.gutenberg.org/cache/epub/5116/pg5116.txt

or he hears of facts with which they are incompatible; or desires arise in him which they cease to satisfy. The result is an inward trouble to which his mind till then had been a stranger, and from which he seeks to escape by modifying his previous mass of opinions. He saves as much of it as he can, for in this matter of belief we are all extreme conservatives. So he tries to change first this opinion, and then that (for they resist change very variously), until at last some new idea comes up which he can graft upon the ancient stock with a minimum of disturbance of the latter, some idea that mediates between the stock and the new experience and runs them into one another most felicitously and expediently.

This new idea is then adopted as the true one. It preserves the older stock of truths with a minimum of modification, stretching them just enough to make them admit the novelty, but conceiving that in ways as familiar as the case leaves possible. An outree explanation, violating all our preconceptions, would never pass for a true account of a novelty. We should scratch round industriously till we found something less eccentric. The most violent revolutions in an individual's beliefs leave most of his old order standing. Time and space, cause and effect, nature and history, and one's own biography remain untouched. New truth is always a go-between, a smoother-over of transitions. It marries old opinion to new fact so as ever to show a minimum of jolt, a maximum of continuity. We hold a theory true just in proportion to its success in solving this 'problem of maxima and minima.' But success in solving this problem is eminently a matter of approximation. . . .

The point I now urge you to observe particularly is the part played by the older truths. . . . Their influence is absolutely controlling. Loyalty to them is the first principle—in most cases it is the only principle; for by far the most usual way of handling phenomena so novel that they would make for a serious rearrangement of our preconceptions is to ignore them altogether, or to abuse those who bear witness for them. . . .

But often the day's contents oblige a rearrangement. If I should now utter piercing shrieks and act like a maniac on this platform, it would make many of you revise your ideas as to the probable worth of my philosophy. . . .

Lecture V

Pragmatism and Common Sense

. . . To take the nearest possible example, consider these lectures of mine. What you first gain from them is probably a small amount of new information, a few new definitions, or distinctions, or points of view. But while these special ideas are being added, the rest of your knowledge stands still, and only gradually will you 'line up' your previous opinions with the novelties I am trying to instil, and modify to some slight degree their mass.

You listen to me now, I suppose, with certain prepossessions as to my competency, and these affect your reception of what I say, but were I suddenly to break off lecturing, and to begin to sing 'We won't go home till morning' in a rich baritone voice, not only would that new fact be added to your stock, but it would oblige you to define me differently, and that might alter your opinion of the pragmatic philosophy, and in general bring about a rearrangement of a number of your ideas. Your mind in such processes is strained, and sometimes painfully so, between its older beliefs and the novelties which experience brings along.

Our minds thus grow in spots; and like grease-spots, the spots spread. But we let them spread as little as possible: we keep unaltered as much of our old knowledge, as many of our old prejudices and beliefs, as we can. We patch and tinker more than we

> renew. The novelty soaks in; it stains the ancient mass; but it is also tinged by what absorbs it. Our past apperceives and co-operates; and in the new equilibrium in which each step forward in the process of learning terminates, it happens relatively seldom that the new fact is added raw. More usually it is embedded cooked, as one might say, or stewed down in the sauce of the old.

On James's account, we are only justified in provisionally adopting a new belief when it can be made to cohere with our old beliefs. This encourages us to preserve our old system of beliefs as far as possible. *By itself*, this very conservative strategy would require us to discard any ideas that contradicted our present view of the world, and it would prevent our body of knowledge from growing. But the conservative element is balanced by the recognition that what really matters is *coherence*, and often the best way to achieve coherence is to make adjustments to previous beliefs. For the sake of coherence, we are prepared to modify or discard some of our old opinions. We thus look for a way to incorporate new ideas that will maximize coherence in our total set of beliefs while minimizing disruptions in our old ways of thinking.

The coherence theory of justification differs from foundationalism in several important ways. First, according to Descartes' foundationalism, a single belief is justified if it can be deduced from a self-verifying axiom. But a single belief cannot "cohere"—only collections of beliefs can do that. So what is justified by coherence is, in the first instance, a *collection of beliefs*—perhaps theories or world views. Individual beliefs can then be justified indirectly by being shown to cohere with an already justified—that is, coherent—set of beliefs. Second, since according to the coherence theory knowledge does not rest on any foundation, there is no place for self-justifying beliefs and no need for a category of beliefs that are known with certainty. No justified belief is justified by anything other than the support it receives from other beliefs. The body of knowledge is woven from countless strands, all of them fragile in varying degrees.

Objections to Coherentism

Three common objections to coherentism are worth noting. The first claims that coherentism provides a circular account of justification; the second objection says that coherentism generates too many incompatible systems of knowledge; and the third is that coherent sets of beliefs can lack contact with reality. We will take up each objection briefly.

Circularity According to coherentism, my belief that dragons are extinct depends for its justification on a coherent system of beliefs to which it belongs. By fitting into that coherent system of beliefs, my belief about dragons qualifies as justified. But my larger system of beliefs is coherent, and so is justified, in part because it contains the belief that dragons are extinct—that is, my belief about dragons contributes to the overall coherence of the whole. The result is that my belief about dragons is justified by cohering with a set of beliefs that is justified, in part, because other beliefs in the set cohere with my belief about dragons. That amounts to indirectly using a belief to justify itself, which is a case of reasoning in a circle.

The coherentist replies that each particular belief is justified by its coherence with the whole system of beliefs to which it also belongs, but that is not the same thing as being justified by itself—even if it contributes to the coherence of the whole system. A better, alternative way to see it is that the various beliefs in the system *mutually support* one another. In an old joke, a policeman finds a drunk leaning against a lamppost and tells him to go home. The drunk is hesitant to move, and claims to be holding up the lamppost. The policeman sends him staggering away, and both the drunk and the lamppost fall over. The drunk was holding up the lamppost that held him up. This is not an impossible form of circular support, but simply mutual support. Similarly, my belief about dragons lends support to the system of beliefs from which it receives justification.

Relativism It is possible to construct a large number of equally coherent systems of belief where those systems are not consistent *with one another*. You may have a coherent system of beliefs that contains the belief that Elvis is dead, while my equally coherent system of beliefs contains the belief that Elvis is alive. The objection is, then, that our systems of belief are *mutually incompatible*, despite the fact that both are, by the standards of the coherence theory, *justified to the same degree*. Justification will then be relative: Whether a belief is justified will depend on which system of beliefs it is evaluated in.

Coherentists might not see this as a problem at all. Coherentism is a theory of *justification*, not a theory of *truth*. Although two inconsistent beliefs cannot both be *true*, there is no reason that two inconsistent beliefs cannot both be *justified*. If I am justified in believing that Elvis is alive and you are justified in believing he is dead, then our systems of belief must differ in other ways in order for both to remain internally coherent. Perhaps we also have different beliefs about the available evidence or about the reliability and trustworthiness of people who claim to have seen Elvis recently. We cannot both be right about Elvis, but there is no reason we cannot not both be justified in our respective opinions.

Delusions A justified belief is supposed to be one that is likely to be true. However, a person suffering from delusions may have *coherent delusions*—that is, a perfectly coherent but delusional set of beliefs that has nothing to do with reality. A coherence theory of justification must say that a highly coherent delusion is highly justified, so the theory fails to explain why being justified, or cohering, increases the likelihood that a belief is true.

One response coherentists might attempt says that highly delusional systems of belief tend to be weeded out over time, some by natural selection and most by the practical pressures of daily life. Any coherent but delusional systems of belief that prevent us from avoiding predators or finding food will tend to disappear quickly, leaving behind only those coherent systems of belief that enable us to successfully cope with the world. This ensures that any systems of belief that survive in the long run have important connections with reality.

The critic of coherentism has a rejoinder to the coherentist's reply: According to a coherence theory, considerations affecting the long-term survival of systems of belief have nothing to do with whether those systems of belief are coherent, and so they should be irrelevant to whether they are justified. Of two *equally coherent* belief systems, one may enable me to cope successfully with my environment, while the other is delusional and results in my being eaten by tigers. But since they are equally coherent, coherentists must count the two systems of belief as *equally justified*. Although it may be true that the pressures of coping with the world will weed out non-adaptive systems of belief, the coherence theory cannot say that systems of belief that survive are more *justified* than those that become extinct.

Some philosophers—William James is one example—think that how well a system of beliefs enables us to cope with the world *is* relevant to how justified that system of beliefs is, but such philosophers are not pure coherentists about justification. Purists, for whom coherence is *all* that matters for justification, cannot consistently think that way.

THE SOCIAL DIMENSIONS OF KNOWLEDGE

A second complaint about Descartes' foundationalist program criticizes the highly individualistic form Descartes gives to his theory of knowledge. According to this second line of criticism, Descartes, and traditional epistemology in general, fails to give sufficient credit to the social contexts in which individual knowers are embedded. Indeed, Descartes does not merely *fail to notice* the role played by his social location, he makes every effort to *escape* from his social context, which he believes provides him only with prejudices that will deflect him from the pursuit of truth.

Descartes' second class of critics claim that escape from social context is impossible, and that there is no perspective for the individual to occupy that is not already shaped by the way she is socially embedded. Fantasizing about an escape from prior biases, they claim, only leads us to ignore them, when we should instead try to identify our biases and work to correct those that are harmful.

Going it Alone: Solitary Knowers

Consider two of the ways that Descartes' epistemology is *individualistic.* In keeping with his methodological skepticism, Descartes' first step in the pursuit of truth required him to discard the entire body of inherited opinion. The influence of others on his thinking was seen as a corrupting influence, so he deliberately made his own search for truth a solitary endeavour. As Descartes tells us, when he finally arrived at the age to undertake his project,

> . . . the setting in of winter arrested me in a locality where, as I found no society to interest me, and was besides fortunately undisturbed by any cares or passions, I remained the whole day in seclusion, with full opportunity to occupy my attention with my own thoughts. Of these one of the very first that occurred to me was, that there is seldom so much perfection in works composed of many separate parts, upon which different hands have been employed, as in those completed by a single master.[9]

After Descartes uses the method of doubt to sweep away his social inheritance of previous opinions, he then identifies a foundation on which to "build anew," and the central component of that foundation is the Cogito—his own certainty of his own existence. This introduces a second form of individualism to his epistemology. Descartes' "I think, therefore I am" is a thought each of us can have, and by doing so we each acquire a foundation for our own knowledge. But the Cogito cannot make me certain that *you* exist, or make you certain that I exist, so each of us must construct our own knowledge only

[9] Descartes, R. (n.d.). *Discourse on Method*, Part II. (John Veitch, Trans.). Retrieved from www.gutenberg.org/cache/epub/59/pg59.txt

on the foundation of our own existence. Descartes' methodological skepticism was an attempt to escape from his own time and place, to cut away ties to his family, teachers, and society, in the hope that he would be able to start over on his own. In the same way, his epistemology requires each person to commence the search for knowledge from the beginning and, proceeding without the company of others, to erect all of knowledge on our own backs—truly a task for Hercules.

Although Descartes' foundationalism provides a clear illustration of *epistemological individualism*, his views are not alone in ignoring or dismissing the social contexts of knowers. Our discussion of coherentism assumed that what matters for justification is coherence among the beliefs belonging to individual knowers. According to coherentists, *my beliefs* are justified if they cohere with *my other beliefs*. Understood this way, traditional forms of coherentism are also forms of epistemological individualism. **Epistemological individualism** is the view that the faculties of individuals—their individual reason, perception, and judgment—are not dependent on social interactions, yet they are sufficient for acquiring knowledge and justification. The alternative view—the perspective taken by **social epistemology**—is that knowledge and justification depend on social interactions, practices, and institutions.

epistemological individualism: The view that the faculties of individuals—their individual reason, perception, and judgment—are sufficient for acquiring knowledge and justification independently of any social contexts or social interactions in which the individual knower is embedded.

social epistemology: The study of the role of social contexts, interactions, practices, and institutions in the development and transmission of knowledge. It is also used to label the theory that these social factors are essential for knowledge and justification, in contrast with *epistemological individualism.*

Charles S. Peirce: Highly regarded American philosopher and logician who is usually credited with founding the philosophical school of thought known as *pragmatism* and the discipline of *semiotics* (the general study of signs).

To illustrate a social epistemology, in the next sections we look at a version of the coherence theory of justification that recognizes a role for social context in knowledge and justification.

Travelling Together

Descartes' method of doubt—his idea that the construction of genuine knowledge should begin by discarding our prior opinions—was dismissed by the nineteenth-century American philosopher **Charles S. Peirce** (1839–1914). Peirce wrote

> We cannot begin with complete doubt. We must begin with all the prejudices which we actually have when we enter upon the study of philosophy. Those prejudices are not to be dispelled by a maxim, for they are things which it does not occur to us *can* be questioned. Hence this initial skepticism will be a mere self-deception, and not real doubt; and no one who follows the Cartesian method will ever be satisfied until he has formally recovered all those beliefs which in form he has given up. . . . Let us not pretend to doubt in philosophy what we do not doubt in our hearts.[10]

If Pierce is right, we cannot begin by doubting everything. Where should we begin? From what starting point should we set out on our quest for certainty? Peirce believes the following:

> . . . But in truth, there is only one state of mind from which you can "set out," namely, the very state of mind in which you actually find yourself at the time you do "set out"—a state in which you are laden with an immense mass of cognition already formed, of which you cannot divest yourself if you would; . . .[11]

His idea is that we have no realistic alternative but to start from where we are—that is, from whatever beliefs we happen to have when we begin our search for knowledge.

[10] From Peirce, C. (1868). Some Consequences of Four Incapacities. *Journal of Speculative Philosophy* 2: 140–157.

[11] From Peirce, C. (1905). What Pragmatism Is. *The Monist*, 15:2: 161–181.

This can be combined with the acknowledgement that the source of a great many of our pre-reflective beliefs are other persons—family, friends, teachers, and authors have all contributed to the beliefs that compose our starting points in the search for knowledge. No believer is an island, and the beliefs with which we set out are largely a social inheritance. If we suppose a coherence theory of justification, the system of beliefs we must try to make coherent are the beliefs of a *community of believers* to which we belong and on which we are dependent. They are not the beliefs of an isolated individual. The attempt to justify one of my beliefs then is, in at least one component, the attempt to justify my beliefs to others.

Acknowledging social inheritance, epistemology then needs to change its focus from an exclusive emphasis on individual knowers to a wider perspective that includes the many relationships among knowers that might be relevant to knowledge. The roles played by testimony, by experts and authorities, and by the social practices and institutions that are involved in the acquisition and transmission of knowledge are all important topics to investigate under the heading of epistemology. This is one way that epistemology becomes social epistemology.

Among those who have emphasized this point in their approach to epistemology are contemporary feminist philosophers. We will turn next to the writings of a leading feminist epistemologist. **Helen Longino** (1944–) explains and defends a close cousin of the coherence theory of justification that makes knowledge a social possession rather than an individual one.

Helen Longino: American feminist philosopher of science and epistemology, best known for her defense of the view that social values and diverse perspectives make essential contributions to objectivity in knowledge, including scientific knowledge.

Knowledge and Social Location (Helen E. Longino, 1999)[12]

> Each of the . . . ways of contextualizing justification has a different bearing on the sociality of knowledge. The first, which treats context as the background of assumptions each agent brings to epistemic justification, poses the following problem. If there is no place outside of some set of assumptions from which to judge independently the relative merits of different sets of assumptions, how can we avoid subjectivism? I have argued that subjectivism can only be avoided by incorporating critical interaction into one's notion of justification.[13] Knowledge is the outcome not just of the cognitive agent's encounter with the world, but of cognitive agents' encounters with one another. The latter encounters bring assumptions to the surface for criticism and then endorsement, rejection, or modification. A recalcitrant agent will not defend or modify her beliefs in response to criticism. Such recalcitrance amounts to opting out of membership in an epistemic community. A parallel point can be made in relation to the second form of contextualization. This treats as context the shared values, assumptions, and social experiences in light of which members of a community engage in critical interaction, the background sharing of which is constitutive of community membership. . . . The approach I favor sees the dependence of justification on contextual factors not as itself an alternative to traditional normative approaches like foundationalism or coherentism, but as requiring a new formulation of normative questions—one that begins with contextual dependence. In particular, I argue that the role of shared values, etc.,

[12] Helen Longino, "Feminist Epistemology", in The Blackwell Companion to Epistemology, ed. by John Greco and Ernest Sosa (Oxford: Blackwell Publishers, 1999). Reprinted by permission.

[13] Here Longino refers to the fourth chapter of her book *Science as Social Knowledge*.

means that the knowledge produced in communities is at best partial and that communities must themselves develop sites of critical discourse about their assumptions both through incorporating diverse perspectives within themselves as internal resources for criticism and by engaging with communities whose background is different. That is, the community must open itself to the kind of critical interactions that (ideally) occur within it. This level of shared interaction requires some shared values or assumptions, appeal to which grounds criticism across communities, but it does not require a fully shared set of values. . . .

. . . Feminist scholars have argued that traditional epistemological theories have served to legitimate, by masking, the role that assumptions about gender play in scientific theorizing and in the construction of epistemological concepts like reason. Contextualism, especially the first two kinds discussed, incorporates or is suborned in feminist insights into the situated or conditioned character of cognitive agency. The individualist response to contextualism is relativism—either endorsed or presented as a *reductio ad absurdum* of the contextualist analysis. Grounding justification in dialogic interaction, in critical discursive interaction, socializes justification, making the full exercise of cognitive agency dependent on relations with others. Thus social epistemology restores a measure of normative prescription to contextual theories of justification. . . .

. . . Louise Antony . . . argued against the social turn in feminist epistemology. Antony rejects the turn in general and as an epistemological approach distinctive of or uniquely valuable to feminists. Antony, however, writes as a feminist epistemologist who endorses a different approach. . . .

Antony's rejection takes the form of a defense of epistemological individualism against a series of challenges. Distinguishing various forms of individualism, she takes methodological individualism to be under attack in arguments I have offered in various papers about the sociality of knowledge. Methodological individualism is the claim that the individual is the primary epistemic subject. This seems to mean both that the individual is the primary cognitive agent and that individuals are the primary objects or targets of epistemic norms. Antony advances several considerations intended to save methodological individualism from socializing arguments.

1. Even if objectivity requires critical interaction, she says, an individual can achieve some degree of objectivity by being reflective about her beliefs, assumptions, etc., i.e. the critical interaction can be internal to the individual, so the individual can to some extent meet the criterion of objectivity without social interaction. To this point the social epistemologist can respond that such reflectivity on the part of individuals (a) is limited in its scope only to those assumptions of which the individual is aware and (b) is in any case the internal rehearsal of a social practice of criticism. It is therefore dependent on and derivative from those patterns of interaction through which individuals learns to reason.
2. Social knowledge presupposes individual epistemic agency. No individual can leave their subjective position, and epistemic processes involve individualistic judgment and perception, so individuals are epistemologically basic. The social epistemologist can agree with all this, but note that the kind of individual agency described is necessary but not sufficient. Of course social knowledge involves individuals; the social is constituted of individuals in interaction, but the interaction is as necessary as the individuals. In the case of scientific inquiry, what is being claimed is that interactive practices (a) make personal, individual beliefs [NB:

not private sensations or experiences] into knowledge and (b) transform belief in the process of challenge and response either because the content changes through that process or because the content becomes more firmly anchored in a network of experiential and doxastic states.

3. Antony proposes that the sociality thesis properly understood amounts to nothing more than the claim that human beings use each other to enhance their own individual epistemic situations. This is no challenge to epistemological individualism. But there are at least two meanings of "enhancement." In one, quantitative, sense it means increasing the range of epistemic capacity. So we are one another's cognitive prostheses—extending one another's cognitive range as telescopes and stethoscopes do. In this sense social interaction is not necessary for knowledge *per se*, though we could not know as much without each other. In a second, qualitative, sense, however, the enhancement means the transformation of belief into knowledge. In this sense the sociality thesis is a challenge to epistemic individualism. It is not (nor is it intended as) a challenge to psychological individualism. The claim is not that we could not have the beliefs we have absent our critical interactions with others. The claim is rather about the status of those beliefs, in particular whether or not they qualify as knowledge. This is a function of social interaction. In rejecting individualism, I am not claiming with Nelson that the community is the primary subject of knowledge, but rather that the ratification of belief which warrants labeling it knowledge is an interactive process.

Ever-Widening Perspectives

In this selection Longino discusses two ways that taking a knower's context into account in our theory of justification helps reveal the essentially social nature of knowledge. She begins by observing that if we limit the context that matters for justification to "the background of assumptions each agent brings to *epistemic* justification," then our beliefs will remain subjective—that is, they never become more than personal opinions. Put differently, Longino believes that if we only use our own beliefs and values to evaluate, or justify, our own beliefs—as epistemological individualism requires—then we will never have genuine knowledge. Her remedy for subjectivism is to acknowledge that justification and knowledge do not result only from interactions among an individual's own thoughts, or even from interactions between individual thoughts and the external world. The justification of beliefs always involves our "encounters with one another": We must, for example, meet the challenges and objections of others. It is only by surviving open and critical encounters with the ideas available in a wider "**epistemic** community"—a community of inquirers and knowers—that our opinions can become justified. In effect, the justification of a belief needs to come *from a perspective that is not limited to the person whose belief it is*—it requires a perspective that is wider than that of the solitary individual. The different beliefs and values of the members of a community, not the contents of a single individual's mind, are what we must struggle to make coherent.

epistemic: Having to do with knowledge. An *epistemic community* is a community of inquirers seeking knowledge; an *epistemic policy* is a policy for acquiring knowledge, and so on.

Longino then takes the contextualization of knowledge one step further. It is easy to understand an "epistemic community" as a group of individual inquirers who have a large number of *shared* values and beliefs. It is what they share that makes them into an epistemic *community*. Widening the context in which justification takes place from the contents of a solitary mind to a community of different but relatively like-minded people is a big improvement of perspective, but it does not go nearly far enough. By limiting the context in which beliefs are evaluated to a community that already shares a great many opinions and values, we risk reproducing on a larger scale the problems that result from limiting the context of justification to a single mind. For example, if a single individual can have a coherent but delusional set of beliefs, then so can an insular community. But now, instead of finding that justification is personal or *subjective*, we find that it is *relative* to a community of like-thinking people. We haven't yet acquired a fully objective perspective from which to justify beliefs. Longino therefore adds two components to the context from which justification is acquired. First, communities of genuine inquirers must incorporate "diverse perspectives within themselves"—that is, the communities must tolerate and encourage internal diversity, so that dominant opinions are regularly subjected to scrutiny and regularly face challenges. Second, a community of genuine inquirers must always be "engaging with communities whose background is different." That is, the borders of our epistemic communities must be left wide open, and we should be actively seeking engagements with communities with whom we share fewer assumptions.

What may seem for some people to be only political concerns—for example, the need for increasing diversity and greater inclusiveness—are, on Longino's view, also epistemological necessities. On her account of epistemology, it is only by contextualizing justification—by giving due credit to our social interactions, practices, and institutions—that we can see how mere opinions become justified and thereby transformed into knowledge.

CONCLUSION

Noting the tremendous security of knowledge in mathematics, Descartes modelled all of human knowledge after geometry. In doing so he developed a foundationalist account of justification and knowledge. Descartes thought he saw a route to certainty that took him directly through the most radical forms of doubt he could imagine, and on the other side of doubt he thought he found certainty in the Cogito.

The coherence theory of justification offers an alternative to Descartes' highly regimented geometric model. Coherentism claims to more accurately represent our actual practices when we justify beliefs, and it does not require any distinction between basic or foundational beliefs and others. But coherentists have problems of their own to address. They especially need to explain why justified beliefs are more likely than unjustified beliefs to be true or to represent reality.

Feminist philosophers and others have also criticized traditional epistemologists—both foundationalist and coherentist varieties—for being implausibly individualistic in their treatment of justification. Epistemological individualism fails to take into account the kinds of epistemic resources that other people—perhaps especially people with whom we already disagree—can become in our pursuit of knowledge. A social epistemology attends to the many ways in which our critical interactions with others make it possible to justify what would otherwise be only personal opinions, and to transform opinions into knowledge.

Key Terms and Figures

- knowledge p. 182
- geometric method p. 185
- foundationalism p. 185
- skepticism p. 185
- infinite regress of justification p. 186
- basic beliefs p. 187
- certainty p. 188
- methodological skepticism p. 189
- Cogito p. 193
- coherence theory of justification (coherentism) p. 195
- William James p. 195
- epistemological individualism p. 200
- social epistemology p. 200
- Charles S. Peirce p. 200
- Helen Longino p. 201
- epistemic p. 203

Additional readings on theories of knowledge and justification

Dancy, J. (1985). *Introduction to Contemporary Epistemology*. Oxford: Basil Blackwell Ltd. See especially Chapters 2 ("Knowledge"), 4 ("Foundationalism"), and 8 ("Coherentism").

Grasswick, H. (2013). Feminist Social Epistemology. *The Stanford Encyclopedia of Philosophy*. Spring, (Edward N. Zalta Ed.). Available at http://plato.stanford.edu/archives/spr2013/entries/feminist-social-epistemology.

O'Brien, D. (2006). *An Introduction to the Theory of Knowledge*. Cambridge: Polity Press. See Especially Chapters 2 ("What is Knowledge?"), 6 ("Foundationalism"), and 7 ("Coherentism").

Plato. (n.d.). *Theatetus*. Available at http://www.gutenberg.org/cache/epub/1726/pg1726.txt

Rosenberg, J. (2000). *Three Conversations About Knowing*. Indianapolis: Hackett Publishing Co.

Williams, M. (2001). *Problems of Knowledge: A Critical Introduction to Epistemology*. Oxford: Oxfrod University Press. See especially Chapters 1 ("The Standard Analysis"), 7 ("Foundations"), and 10 ("Coherence").

Chapter 10
Living Without Certainty

Learning Objectives

- Explain the distinction between rationalism and empiricism—both as theories of concepts and as theories of justification.
- Summarize how empiricists explain our possession of ideas of things that cannot be experienced.
- Outline Locke's distinctions among intuitive, demonstrative, and sensitive forms of knowledge, and provide illustrations of each.
- Contrast Descartes and Locke on whether knowledge depends on certainty.
- Summarize David Hume's argument for skepticism about inferences based on past experience.
- Discuss Hume's *remedy* for skepticism about inferences based on past experience, and explain why it is not an attempted *refutation* of skepticism.
- Contrast skepticism and fallibilism.

Descartes requires all knowledge to rest on a foundation of certainty and, since he believes sense experience never provides certainty, he holds that experience is never a source of genuine knowledge. In this chapter we explore the ideas of philosophers who believe that if we want to know the world, experience is the only possible source of such knowledge.

The philosophers we examine—*empiricists*—think that any knowledge must ultimately depend on experience, so the range of experiences available sets limits to what we can know or be justified in believing. But they also agree with Descartes that sensory experience does not deliver the kind of certainty he requires before we have knowledge; empiricists hold that we can have knowledge even without certainty.

What would a theory of knowledge look like that settled for less than certainty? In this chapter we examine several ways of knowing and living without certainty.

RATIONALISM AND EMPIRICISM

No belief constitutes genuine knowledge unless it has sufficient justification. In Descartes's final epistemological theory, a belief can be justified in only two ways: Either it is self-justifying or it can be deduced by careful reasoning from beliefs that are themselves self-justifying. This foundationalist picture, modelled after geometry, is the heart of Descartes's theory of justification and knowledge. Another feature of his theory also deserves emphasis: He thinks reason, but not experience, is the source of knowledge. Descartes requires basic beliefs that can be known with certainty even if we cannot tell whether we are awake or dreaming, and even if we cannot know whether there is an all-powerful demon working to mislead us about what we experience. Given the unreliability of sense experience, Descartes maintains that the basic beliefs at the foundations of knowledge are knowable through the use of reason alone. But if all basic beliefs can be known independent of experience, then any knowledge we later derive from them by deductive reasoning will also be independent of experience. This idea qualifies Descartes as a *rationalist*.

Rationalism privileges reason over experience in the quest for knowledge. Descartes subscribed to the **rationalist theory of knowledge**: Only reason can provide the sort of justification needed for beliefs to be genuine knowledge. Descartes's basic beliefs are self-justifying, so they are justified independent of any experience. Other, non-basic beliefs are justified only by being rationally deduced from basic beliefs. Descartes therefore qualifies as a rationalist about justification and knowledge. Two points should be noted about this theory.

rationalism: The doctrine that not all ideas and justification can come from experience alone. It usually combines a *rationalist theory of concepts* with a *rationalist theory of justification*, but the term is used for either of those doctrines as well as for the combination of them.

rationalist theory of knowledge: The view that only reason can provide adequate justification for beliefs to qualify them as genuine knowledge; experience will always be insufficient for knowledge.

First, the view seems most plausible when we consider special kinds of beliefs. For example, consider our belief that 2+3 *always* equals 5. This is something we think we know to be true, and yet our experience cannot confirm or justify it. We have simply not had the range of experience that would be needed to assure us that 2+3 *always*, and *everywhere*, equals 5. We appear to have a justified belief—indeed, knowledge—for which we lack the sort of experience that could back it up.

There is a second side to rationalism. In the seventeenth century, our **ideas**—or, as we now refer to them, our *concepts*—were understood as the components or constituents from which we form our beliefs, in something like the way words are the components from which we form sentences. Thus, if I believe that *grass is green*, I first need to have the idea, or concept, of *grass* and the idea, or concept, of *green*, just as I must have the words *grass* and *green* before I can construct the sentence "Grass is green." Where do we get the simpler ideas, such as *grass* and *green*, that we use to form beliefs? For part of his answer to this question, Descartes defended a second aspect of rationalism:

idea: Apart from its common contemporary use, in which it refers indifferently to beliefs, concepts, theories, plans, and more, *idea* had a technical use in seventeenth- and eighteenth-century epistemology, where it refers to *thoughts* or their simple constituents (roughly the equivalent of *concepts*).

> **Rationalist Theory of Concepts**: At least *some* ideas or concepts are *innate*—that is, they are not acquired from experience, but are inborn.

rationalist theory of concepts: At least *some* ideas (concepts) are *innate*—that is, they are not acquired from experience, but are inborn.

On this view, there are some ideas we cannot acquire from experience, but we have them nonetheless, since they have been built into our minds from birth. Descartes did not deny that we acquire *some* ideas from experience (e.g., you need visual experience to acquire the idea of *green*), but he did deny that we could acquire *all* our ideas from experience. Thus, for example, he believed that our geometric idea of *triangle* cannot come from experience, since it is part of our idea, or concept, of a triangle that it will have exactly 180° in its interior angles. Since every triangle we can draw or see will have slightly more or less than 180° in its interior angles, we could not have acquired this idea from experience of actual triangles. Similarly, Descartes thought we have an idea of God, and part of that idea is that God, if there is one, is infinitely powerful.

Even atheists must have the *idea* or concept of God, since they have formed the belief *there is no God*, and they can't do that if they don't have the ideas—including the idea of *God*—needed to form the belief. But, Descartes thinks, the idea of God is quite complex, containing many constituents, and we could never get all the constituents of our idea of God from experience. In particular, we have no experience of anything infinite, and part of our idea of God is that He is infinitely powerful. Since we do have such ideas, but we cannot acquire them from experience, they must, he thinks, be **innate**.

innate ideas: Ideas or concepts that cannot be acquired from experience, so that they must, if we have them, be acquired independently of any experience of the world. Often referred to as *inborn*.

empiricism: The doctrine that all ideas and all justifications come from experience. Empiricism usually combines an *empiricist theory of concepts* with an *empiricist theory of justification*, but the term is used for either of those doctrines as well as for the combination of them.

empiricist theory of knowledge: The view that all *justification* for beliefs comes from sensory experience; no belief that lacks the support of experience can be justified or qualify as knowledge.

empiricist theory of concepts: The view that all ideas, or concepts, *originate* in experience. On the traditional form of the theory, some simple ideas, such as "blue," or "tangy," are thought to come directly from experience, while other, more complex ideas, such as "cat," or "electron," are thought to be constructed from the ideas that come directly from experience.

Even in the seventeenth century, rationalism was not the only game in town. A starkly contrasting approach was **empiricism**: the view that all ideas for forming beliefs and all justification for beliefs are derived from sense experience, or perception. Most empiricists accepted Descartes's view that the senses cannot deliver complete certainty; however, since they also believed justification for our beliefs can only come from experience, they concluded that we simply cannot have the kind of certainty that Descartes was looking for. So if we do have any genuine knowledge, that knowledge cannot require certainty. Like rationalism, empiricism can be divided into two doctrines:

> **Empiricist Theory of Knowledge:** All justification for beliefs comes from experience;

and

> **Empiricist Theory of Concepts:** All ideas, or concepts, originate in experience.

It is useful to note that the decision to adopt rationalism or empiricism does not settle whether one will be a foundationalist or a coherentist about justification. Descartes was a foundationalist about justification because he accepted the important foundationalist distinction between basic and non-basic beliefs. But his rationalism demonstrates his contention that we are justified in accepting basic beliefs, like the Cogito, on the basis of reason alone, with no support from experience.

In the sections that follow, we explore the two empiricist doctrines in more detail as we examine the views of two famous empiricists, John Locke and David Hume. Neither Locke nor Hume thinks we can have the sort of certainty that Descartes maintains we need to overcome doubt, but both believe we get by just fine without it.

EMPIRICISM AND THE LIMITS OF KNOWLEDGE AND THOUGHT

John Locke defends the empiricist theory of concepts, according to which *all* ideas are derived from experience (i.e., *none* are innate). There is an immediate objection to the view that all our ideas come from experience—namely, we seem to have some ideas that could not be derived from any experience of the objects they represent (e.g., our ideas of fictional objects like *unicorns*, or of "invisible" objects like *God*, or of objects that are too small to perceive, like *electrons*). To explain how such ideas can be obtained from experience alone, empiricists distinguish between "simple ideas" and "complex ideas."

"Of Ideas" (John Locke, 1689)[1]

1. . . . it is past doubt that men have in their minds several ideas,—such as are those expressed by the words whiteness, hardness, sweetness, thinking, motion, man, elephant, army, drunkenness, and others: it is in the first place then to be inquired, *how he comes by them*? . . .
2. . . . Let us then suppose the mind to be, as we say, white paper, void of all characters, without any ideas:—How comes it to be furnished? Whence comes it by that vast store which the busy and boundless fancy of man has painted on it with an almost endless variety? Whence has it all the *materials* of reason and knowledge? To this I answer, in one word, from *experience*. In that all our knowledge is founded; and from that it ultimately derives itself. Our observation employed either, about external sensible objects, or about the internal operations of our minds perceived and reflected on by ourselves, is that which supplies our understandings with all the *materials* of thinking. These two are the fountains of knowledge, from whence all the ideas we have, or can naturally have, do spring. . . .

Of Complex Ideas.

1. Made by the Mind out of simple Ones.

   We have hitherto considered those ideas, in the reception whereof the mind is only passive, which are those simple ones received from sensation and reflection before mentioned, whereof the mind cannot make one to itself, nor have any idea which does not wholly consist of them. But as the mind is wholly passive in the reception of all its simple ideas, so it exerts several acts of its own, whereby out of its simple ideas, as the materials and foundations of the rest, the others are framed. The acts of the mind, wherein it exerts its power over its simple ideas, are chiefly these three: (1) Combining several simple ideas into one compound one; and thus all complex ideas are made. (2) The second is bringing two ideas, whether simple or complex, together, and setting them by one another, so as to take a view of them at once, without uniting them into one; by which way it gets all its ideas of relations. (3) The third is separating them from all other ideas that accompany them in their real existence: this is called abstraction: and thus all its general ideas are made. This shows man's power, and its ways of operation, to be much the same in the material and intellectual world. For the materials in both being such as he has no power over, either to make or destroy, all that man can do is either to unite them together, or to set them by one another, or wholly separate them. . . . Ideas thus made up of several simple ones put together, I call *complex*;—such as are beauty, gratitude, a man, an army, the universe; which, though complicated of various simple ideas, or complex ideas made up of simple ones, yet are, when the mind pleases, considered each by itself, as one entire thing, and signified by one name.

Even though we cannot acquire the idea of *unicorn* from an experience of unicorns, we can *construct* the entire complex idea from simpler ideas—for example, from our idea of horses and our idea of horns, which were themselves acquired from experiences of horses and horned animals. This explains how we come to have at least some ideas that we cannot acquire directly from experience. Since, on Locke's empiricist view, all ideas

[1] Locke, J. (1690). *An Essay Concerning Humane Understanding*, Volume One, Book II, Chapters I and XII. Retrieved on August 3, 2014, from http://oll.libertyfund.org/titles/761

simple ideas: In the empiricist theory of concepts, ideas that are acquired directly from experience; they are also usually conceived of as uncompounded—as ideas that cannot be constructed from other ideas.

complex ideas: In the empiricist theory of concepts, ideas that cannot be acquired directly from experience, but can be constructed from *simple ideas* that are acquired directly from experience.

come from experience, we cannot have any **simple ideas** that are not derived directly from some experience, and we cannot have any **complex ideas** whose constituent parts cannot be traced back to such simple ideas.

Empiricism, Meaning, and Nonsense

In addition to being the constituents of our beliefs, ideas were thought by early empiricists and rationalists alike to serve as the *meanings* of our words. Their view about linguistic meaning is relatively simple: We use language to communicate ideas; so if we use any words that do not have ideas associated with them, then those words have no meanings. It is probably not appropriate to call the sounds we make that have no ideas or meanings associated with them *words*. As Locke says, "He that hath names without ideas, wants [lacks] meaning in his words, and speaks only empty sounds."[2]

This view leaves empiricists with two ways of handling words like "God," "unicorn," "electron," or any other words that appear to be associated with ideas we cannot acquire directly from sense experience. First, as we have seen, empiricists might show how the idea we associate with the word can be compounded out of other ideas we have received from experience—so the idea expressed by the word is really a *complex* idea. But, second, if they fail to find a way that we could have acquired the relevant idea from sense experience, directly or indirectly, they must insist that we have no such idea, so the word actually has no meaning. Empiricists therefore hold the view that some of what we say—even some things that might *appear* on the surface to be perfectly meaningful—turn out on closer examination to be meaningless sounds. Despite appearances to the contrary, sometimes we don't know what we are talking about when we use words for things that are too remote from experience.

Rationalists, however, have a third option that is not available to empiricists. Upon finding that an idea cannot not be derived from experience and that it cannot be constructed from other ideas that are derived from experience, rationalists can say that we still have the idea that is associated with the word. But, they say, it is an innate idea. Whenever our understanding of what words mean extends beyond what we could have gleaned from experience alone, then our capacity of understanding—our idea—must be innate. They can insist that the word still has meaning and that we can understand what it means even if we could not have acquired that idea from experience.

Consider how this difference between empiricists and rationalists is manifested. Suppose a rationalist like Descartes successfully convinces empiricists that some idea—say, the idea of God—could not have been derived from experience. Descartes would use this fact to establish that his rationalist theory of concepts is right—our idea of God must therefore be innate. But an empiricist would use the fact that the idea of God cannot be derived from experience to show only that the word is meaningless—that we have no such idea, so we don't know what we are talking about when we use the word *God*. We go through the motions of someone who understands what she is saying when we talk about *God*, but our word means nothing.

Locke also subscribes to the empiricist theory of knowledge. Let us now see how he explains the acquisition of *knowledge* of the world within the constraints of an empiricist theory. Locke's theory of knowledge describes three kinds of knowledge, each having a different level or degree of certainty.

---

[2] Locke, J. (1690). *An Essay Concerning Humane Understanding*, Volume One, Book III, Chapter X. Retrieved August 3, 2014, from http://www.gutenberg.org/cache/epub/10615/pg10615.txt

"Degrees of Knowledge" (John Locke, 1689)[3]

I. Intuitive

. . . For if we will reflect on our own ways of thinking, we will find, that sometimes the mind perceives the agreement or disagreement of two ideas *immediately by themselves*, without the intervention of any other: and this I think we may call *intuitive knowledge*. For in this the mind is at no pains of proving or examining, but perceives the truth as the eye doth light, only by being directed towards it. Thus the mind perceives that *white* is not *black*, that a *circle* is not a *triangle*, that *three* are more than *two* and equal to *one and two*. Such kinds of truths the mind perceives at the first sight of the ideas together, by bare intuition; without the intervention of any other idea: and this kind of knowledge is the clearest and most certain that human frailty is capable of. This part of knowledge is irresistible, and, like bright sunshine, forces itself immediately to be perceived, as soon as ever the mind turns its view that way; and leaves no room for hesitation, doubt, or examination, but the mind is presently filled with the clear light of it. *It is on this intuition that depends all the certainty and evidence of all our knowledge*; which certainty every one finds to be so great, that he cannot imagine, and therefore not require a greater: for a man cannot conceive himself capable of a greater certainty than to know that any idea in his mind is such as he perceives it to be; and that two ideas, wherein he perceives a difference, are different and not precisely the same. He that demands a greater certainty than this, demands he knows not what, and shows only that he has a mind to be a sceptic, without being able to be so. Certainty depends so wholly on this intuition, that, in the next degree of knowledge which I call demonstrative, this intuition is necessary in all the connexions of the intermediate ideas, without which we cannot attain knowledge and certainty.

II. Demonstrative.

The next degree of knowledge is, where the mind perceives the agreement or disagreement of any ideas, but not immediately. Though wherever the mind perceives the agreement or disagreement of any of its ideas, there be certain knowledge; yet it does not always happen, that the mind sees that agreement or disagreement, which there is between them, even where it is discoverable; and in that case remains in ignorance, and at most gets no further than a probable conjecture. The reason why the mind cannot always perceive presently the agreement or disagreement of two ideas, is, because those ideas, concerning whose agreement or disagreement the inquiry is made, cannot by the mind be so put together as to show it. In this case then, when the mind cannot so bring its ideas together as by their immediate comparison, and as it were juxta-position or application one to another, to perceive their agreement or disagreement, it is fain, *by the invention of other ideas*, (one or more, as it happens) to discover the agreement or disagreement which it searches; and this is that which we call *reasoning*. . . .

Those intervening ideas, which serve to show the agreement of any two others, are called *proofs*; and where the agreement and disagreement is by this means plainly and clearly perceived, it is called *demonstration*; it being *shown* to the understanding, and the mind made to see that it is so. . . .

This knowledge, by intervening proofs, though it be certain, yet the evidence of it is not altogether so clear and bright, nor the assent so ready, as in intuitive knowledge. For, though in demonstration the mind does at last perceive the agreement

[3] From Locke, J. (1689). *An Essay Concerning Human Understanding*, Volume Two, Book IV, Chapters II and XI. Retrieved August 3, 2014, from http://www.gutenberg.org/cache/epub/10616/pg10616.txt

or disagreement of the ideas it considers; yet it is not without pains and attention: there must be more than one transient view to find it. A steady application and pursuit are required to this discovery: and there must be a progression by steps and degrees, before the mind can in this way arrive at certainty, and come to perceive the agreement or repugnancy between two ideas that need proofs and the use of reason to show it. . . .

III. Sensitive Knowledge of the particular Existence of finite beings without us.

These two, viz. intuition and demonstration, are the degrees of our *knowledge*; whatever comes short of one of these, with what assurance soever embraced, is but *faith* or *opinion*, but not knowledge, at least in all general truths. There is, indeed, another perception of the mind, employed about *the particular existence of finite beings without us*, which, going beyond bare probability, and yet not reaching perfectly to either of the foregoing degrees of certainty, passes under the name of *knowledge*. There can be nothing more certain than that the idea we receive from an external object is in our minds: this is intuitive knowledge. But whether there be anything more than barely that idea in our minds; whether we can thence certainly infer the existence of anything without us, which corresponds to that idea, is that whereof some men think there may be a question made; because men may have such ideas in their minds, when no such thing exists, no such object affects their senses. But yet here I think we are provided with an evidence that puts us past doubting. For I ask any one, Whether he be not invincibly conscious to himself of a different perception, when he looks on the sun by day, and thinks on it by night; when he actually tastes wormwood, or smells a rose, or only thinks on that savour or odour? We as plainly find the difference there is between any idea revived in our minds by our own memory, and actually coming into our minds by our senses, as we do between any two distinct ideas. If any one say, a dream may do the same thing, and all these ideas may be produced, in us without any external objects; he may please to dream that I make him this answer:—1. That it is no great matter, whether I remove his scruple or no: where all is but dream, reasoning and arguments are of no use, truth and knowledge nothing. 2. That I believe he will allow a very manifest difference between dreaming of being in the fire, and being actually in it. But yet if he be resolved to appear so sceptical as to maintain, that what I call being actually in the fire is nothing but a dream; and that we cannot thereby certainly know, that any such thing as fire actually exists without us: I answer, That we certainly finding that pleasure or pain follows upon the application of certain objects to us, whose existence we perceive, or dream that we perceive, by our senses; this certainty is as great as our happiness or misery, beyond which we have no concernment to know or to be. So that, I think, we may add to the two former sorts of knowledge this also, of the existence of particular external objects, by that perception and consciousness we have of the actual entrance of ideas from them, and allow these three degrees of knowledge, viz. *intuitive, demonstrative, and sensitive*; in each of which there are different degrees and ways of evidence and certainty. . . .

This notice by our Senses, though not so certain as Demonstration, yet may be called Knowledge, and proves the Existence of Things without us.

The notice we have by our senses of the existing of things without us, though it be not altogether so certain as our intuitive knowledge, or the deductions of our reason employed about the clear abstract ideas of our own minds; yet it is an assurance that deserves the name of *knowledge*. If we persuade ourselves that our faculties act and inform us right concerning the existence of those objects that affect them, it cannot pass for an ill-grounded confidence: for I think nobody can, in earnest, be so sceptical as to be uncertain of the existence of those things which he sees and feels. At least, he that can doubt so far, (whatever he may have with his own thoughts,) will never have any controversy with me; since he can never be sure I say anything contrary to his own opinion. . . .

This Certainty is as great as our Condition needs.

But yet, if after all this any one will be so sceptical as to distrust his senses, and to affirm that all we see and hear, feel and taste, think and do, during our whole being, is but the series and deluding appearances of a long dream, whereof there is no reality; and therefore will question the existence of all things, or our knowledge of anything: I must desire him to consider, that, if all be a dream, then he doth but dream that he makes the question, and so it is not much matter that a waking man should answer him. But yet, if he pleases, he may dream that I make him this answer, That the certainty of things existing in *rerum natura* [in the nature of things] when we have the testimony of our senses for it is not only as great as our frame can attain to, but as our condition needs. For, our faculties being suited not to the full extent of being, nor to a perfect, clear, comprehensive knowledge of things free from all doubt and scruple; but to the preservation of us, in whom they are; and accommodated to the use of life: they serve to our purpose well enough, if they will but give us certain notice of those things, which are convenient or inconvenient to us. For he that sees a candle burning, and hath experimented the force of its flame by putting his finger in it, will little doubt that this is something existing without him, which does him harm, and puts him to great pain: which is assurance enough, when no man requires greater certainty to govern his actions by than what is as certain as his actions themselves. And if our dreamer pleases to try whether the glowing heat of a glass furnace be barely a wandering imagination in a drowsy man's fancy, by putting his hand into it, he may perhaps be wakened into a certainty greater than he could wish, that it is something more than bare imagination. So that this evidence is as great as we can desire, being as certain to us as our pleasure or pain, i.e. happiness or misery; beyond which we have no concernment, either of knowing or being. Such an assurance of the existence of things without us is sufficient to direct us in the attaining the good and avoiding the evil which is caused by them, which is the important concernment we have of being made acquainted with them.

Knowledge: With and Without Certainty

Locke recognizes three kinds of knowledge that differ, among other ways, in kind or degree of certainty. First, Locke recognizes something he calls "intuitive knowledge," by which he means the knowledge we have of our own ideas, their characteristics, and their similarities and differences. Even if Descartes is right and I cannot know whether there is a blue flower before me—because, for example, I can't know if I am awake or dreaming—I can still know with certainty that *I have the idea* that there is a flower before me, that it is *the idea of a flower that is blue*, and that *it is different from my idea of the red vase* that the flower appears to be in. Similarly, even if I don't know whether anything triangular really exists, I can know—again, with certainty—that my idea of a triangle is the idea of a three-sided figure. In each case, what I have is knowledge about my own ideas—Locke's *intuitive knowledge*. Such knowledge is, Locke thinks, "the clearest and most certain that human frailty is capable of," and the kind of certainty we have about our own ideas is such that "a man cannot conceive himself capable of a greater certainty."

Second, Locke identifies what he calls "demonstrative knowledge," which has the same degree of certainty as intuitive knowledge, but is not so easy to come by. It refers to what we can know by careful reasoning or proofs whenever our reasoning begins with premises, or axioms, of which we already have intuitive knowledge. Although I cannot know intuitively that my idea of a triangle is the idea of a figure with 180° in its interior angles, this is something that can be *demonstrated.* Locke thinks a demonstration consists in placing ideas next to one another in a series or chain so that they constitute the individual steps in a proof, and then, relying on intuitive knowledge of the differences and similarities between the ideas in adjacent steps of the proof, eventually arriving at a conclusion. Between them, Locke's intuitive and demonstrative knowledge represent everything Descartes would be prepared to count as "knowledge."

Locke is willing to go one step further than Descartes to count some of what we believe about the world around us, on the basis of our senses, as genuine knowledge. So, as a third category of knowledge, Locke recognizes the existence of something he calls "sensitive knowledge." This is knowledge we have about the existence of particular things in the world, or knowledge of particular facts, insofar as that knowledge is acquired through sensory experience. My knowledge that there is a flower in front of me—based on seeing it—and my knowledge that the flower in front of me is blue, are examples of sensitive knowledge. Locke agrees with Descartes that our beliefs about the world around us, insofar as those beliefs derive from our sensory experience, will not have the same degree of certainty as intuitive and demonstrative knowledge, so they will not have the certainty Descartes requires for genuine knowledge. Locke holds that sensitive knowledge nonetheless sometimes "deserves the name of knowledge."

Before he will count a belief as *knowledge*, Locke requires that it have as much certainty as we need to conduct our lives by it—as much as we need to successfully pursue happiness or to avoid misery when we act on the belief. Any certainty beyond that will be certainty for which we have no need. On Locke's view, from "the testimony of our senses" alone, we get just as much justification "as our frame can attain to"—that is, as much as we are *capable* of acquiring. That amount of justification is also as much as "our condition needs." Our faculties—our senses—are designed to preserve us, to enable us to avoid pain and seek happiness. The information our senses provide about the world is perfectly adequate for *those* purposes and, on Locke's view, this is good enough for the information to "deserve the name of knowledge." Because we are limited to whatever justification we can get from experience, the certainty that Descartes desires is not within our reach.

In effect, Locke does not disagree with Descartes that it is remotely *possible* that we are, at this very moment, only dreaming we are engaged in philosophy, or only dreaming we are caught in a fire. But Locke thinks that the *mere possibility* that we are dreaming does not prevent us from having the degree of justification for our beliefs that we need for our daily purposes. Perhaps our lives would be less risky and less fragile if we had certainties, but what we do have is enough to get by. Although Descartes would no doubt believe Locke is settling for too little justification, Locke thinks it is all the justification we can get—and that it is enough. In other writings, Descartes recognizes a category of beliefs or ideas he calls "morally certain, that is, as having sufficient certainty for application to ordinary life."[4] Descartes's "moral certainties" appear to coincide with what Locke counts as sensitive *knowledge*. Both agree, however, that sense experience cannot provide the certainty that Descartes wants for his epistemological project of establishing all human knowledge on new foundations. Both also agree that sense experience provides enough justification "for application to ordinary life." What they disagree about is whether the justification provided by our senses qualifies us as having knowledge.

As an empiricist, Locke is content to live on a smaller budget of justification than Descartes. The question remains, however, whether Locke is right to believe that the justification we can get from experience is enough for the conduct of life. David Hume, as we will see next, does not believe it is.

HUME AND THE LIMITS OF REASON

Like Locke, Hume accepts both the empiricist theory of justification and the empiricist theory of concepts, but he draws much more radical consequences from his empiricism. In this section we examine one of the most radical and famous implications that Hume drew from empiricist beginnings.

Hume's writings clearly assert his commitment to the empiricist theory of concepts: "All our simple ideas in their first appearance are derived from simple impressions . . ."[5] Following Locke's lead, Hume distinguishes between simple and complex ideas. Simple ideas are received directly from experience, while complex ideas are constructed from simple ideas. But Hume also introduces a distinction between our *ideas* and the *experiences* from which our ideas are directly acquired. He refers to those experiences as *impressions*. According to Hume, our impressions—our experiences—are more vivid (i.e., forceful and lively) than the ideas we retain after the perceptual experience has passed. Put simply, ideas are only the faint images left by impressions. All ideas ultimately derive from experience, so unless a purported idea can be traced back to a perceptual experience—an impression—we do not have the idea.

In his effort to remain faithful to his empiricist principles, Hume notes that there are distinctions among (i) what we directly *experience* at a given moment, (ii) what we *remember* having experienced at an earlier time, and (iii) what we *infer* from our past and present experiences. If I now see the sun begin to set, I may get the idea that the sky is *about to* darken. Similarly, when I see a man falling toward the water, I get the idea that he *will* get wet. I do not yet experience the darkening of the sky or the wetness of the water—these are matters for the immediate future that go beyond my current experience. But that does not mean these ideas are entirely independent of my experience. I remember the sky darkening *yesterday*—and the day before and the day before that—immediately after the sun set, and I remember from many previous encounters that water makes things wet. But since it hasn't yet happened, I haven't yet experienced that the sky *will darken tonight*. And I certainly can't *remember* it happening tonight since it hasn't happened yet. What, then, is the source of my idea that the sky is about to darken, or my idea that *this* man will get wet when he splashes through the surface of the water? The ideas must have derived from some inference.

---

[4] *The Philosophical Writings of Descartes*. (1984). Volume 1. John Cottingham, Robert Stoothoff, & Dugal Murdoch (Eds.) Cambridge: Cambridge University Press: 289–90.

[5] Hume, D. (n.d.). Of the Origin of Our Ideas. A *Treatise of Human Nature*, Part I. Retrieved August 3, 2014, from http://www.gutenberg.org/cache/epub/4705/pg4705.txt

According to empiricism, all knowledge comes from experience, yet I seem to have knowledge of things that have yet to happen—things that lie beyond what I have so far experienced. If I do know things that go beyond my past and present experience, I must know them by *reasoning from past experiences*, by *inferring* what will happen next on the basis of what has happened in the past. This is precisely the sort of reasoning—*inductive reasoning*—we use every day. I don't merely *believe* that the sun will come up tomorrow; I think I am *justified in believing* it will. And to justify my belief, I can point out that the sun has consistently risen each morning for thousands upon thousands of mornings. Even if, on the basis of my past experience, I cannot be completely certain that it will rise tomorrow—after all, a meteor strike might destroy the earth—I can be *very* confident that it will, and my confidence is justified. *Inductive reasoning from past experience* is the process by which we think we become justified in believing such things. Remarkably, Hume thinks this is all wrong.

What follows is Hume's famous attack on the idea that inductive reasoning from past experience empowers us to know, or to justifiably believe, things beyond our current experience, or beyond what we remember from past experience. When Hume refers to "arguments from experience," he means reasoning in which we try to infer *what will happen* from past experiences of *what has happened*. Hume's argument is thus a challenge to most of what we think of as inductive reasoning.

Reasoning from Experience (David Hume, 1748)[6]

31. In reality, all arguments from experience are founded on the similarity which we discover among natural objects, and by which we are induced to expect effects similar to those which we have found to follow from such objects. And though none but a fool or madman will ever pretend to dispute the authority of experience, or to reject that great guide of human life, it may surely be allowed a philosopher to have so much curiosity at least as to examine the principle of human nature, which gives this mighty authority to experience, . . . From causes which appear *similar* we expect similar effects. This is the sum of all our experimental conclusions. Now it seems evident that, if this conclusion were formed by reason, it would be as perfect at first, and upon one instance, as after ever so long a course of experience. But the case is far otherwise. Nothing so like as eggs; yet no one, on account of this appearing similarity, expects the same taste and relish in all of them. It is only after a long course of uniform experiments in any kind, that we attain a firm reliance and security with regard to a particular event. Now where is that process of reasoning which, from one instance, draws a conclusion, so different from that which it infers from a hundred instances that are nowise different from that single one? This question I propose as much for the sake of information, as with an intention of raising difficulties. I cannot find, I cannot imagine any such reasoning. But I keep my mind still open to instruction, if any one will vouchsafe to bestow it on me.

32. Should it be said that, from a number of uniform experiments, we *infer* a connexion between the sensible qualities and the secret powers; this, I must confess, seems the same difficulty, couched in different terms. The question still recurs, on what process of argument this *inference* is founded? . . . How is this remedied by experience? It only shows us a number of uniform effects, resulting from certain objects, and teaches us that those particular objects, at that particular time, were endowed with such powers and forces. When a new object, endowed with similar sensible

[6] Hume, D. (n.d.). *Enquiry Concerning Human Understanding*, Section IV, Part II. Retrieved on August 3, 2014, from http://www.gutenberg.org/cache/epub/9662/pg9662.txt

qualities, is produced, we expect similar powers and forces, and look for a like effect. From a body of like colour and consistence with bread we expect like nourishment and support. But this surely is a step or progress of the mind, which wants to be explained. . . . Of what nature is it, then? To say it is experimental, is begging the question. For all inferences from experience suppose, as their foundation, that the future will resemble the past, and that similar powers will be conjoined with similar sensible qualities. If there be any suspicion that the course of nature may change, and that the past may be no rule for the future, all experience becomes useless, and can give rise to no inference or conclusion. It is impossible, therefore, that any arguments from experience can prove this resemblance of the past to the future; since all these arguments are founded on the supposition of that resemblance. Let the course of things be allowed hitherto ever so regular; that alone, without some new argument or inference, proves not that, for the future, it will continue so. In vain do you pretend to have learned the nature of bodies from your past experience. Their secret nature, and consequently all their effects and influence, may change, without any change in their sensible qualities. This happens sometimes, and with regard to some objects: Why may it not happen always, and with regard to all objects? What logic, what process of argument secures you against this supposition? My practice, you say, refutes my doubts. But you mistake the purport of my question. As an agent, I am quite satisfied in the point; but as a philosopher, who has some share of curiosity, I will not say scepticism, I want to learn the foundation of this inference. . . .

33. I must confess that a man is guilty of unpardonable arrogance who concludes, because an argument has escaped his own investigation, that therefore it does not really exist. . . . But with regard to the present subject, there are some considerations which seem to remove all this accusation of arrogance or suspicion of mistake.

It is certain that the most ignorant and stupid peasants—nay infants, nay even brute beasts—improve by experience, and learn the qualities of natural objects, by observing the effects which result from them. When a child has felt the sensation of pain from touching the flame of a candle, he will be careful not to put his hand near any candle; but will expect a similar effect from a cause which is similar in its sensible qualities and appearance. If you assert, therefore, that the understanding of the child is led into this conclusion by any process of argument or ratiocination, I may justly require you to produce that argument; nor have you any pretence to refuse so equitable a demand. You cannot say that the argument is abstruse, and may possibly escape your enquiry; since you confess that it is obvious to the capacity of a mere infant. If you hesitate, therefore, a moment, or if, after reflection, you produce any intricate or profound argument, you, in a manner, give up the question, and confess that it is not reasoning which engages us to suppose the past resembling the future, and to expect similar effects from causes which are, to appearance, similar. This is the proposition which I intended to enforce in the present section. If I be right, I pretend not to have made any mighty discovery. And if I be wrong, I must acknowledge myself to be indeed a very backward scholar; since I cannot now discover an argument which, it seems, was perfectly familiar to me long before I was out of my cradle.

Hume's Argument

Hume's argument has been very influential, and it is worth the effort to understand it. We can summarize the core of the argument as follows:

1. All knowledge of matters of fact beyond our present experience depends on our knowledge of cause and effect.

For example, where we see smoke we *infer* that there is probably a fire, because we know from past experience that smoke is caused by fire. If we didn't know that fire causes smoke, seeing the smoke would not be reason to infer that there is a fire. Hume wants to know just how good such inferences are. He introduces his second premise:

2. All knowledge of cause and effect depends on our knowledge that nature is uniform—that is, that the future will resemble the past.

Countless times, when we have seen smoke and investigated, we have found fire, so when we see smoke now, we conclude that there is *probably* a fire. But why? Why do we suppose that just because *smoke was a reliable indicator of fire in the past*, the smoke we see *now* is also a reliable indicator of fire? When we think this way, we must make a crucial assumption, often referred to as the assumption of the **uniformity of nature**. This is the assumption that because nature has operated in a certain way in the past—because, for example, nature followed certain laws in the past, and because certain kinds of causes invariably had certain kinds of effects in the past—then nature will continue to operate in those same ways in the future.

uniformity of nature: The principle that nature behaves in the same ways (i.e., follows the same laws and exhibits the same causal regularities) at all times and throughout the extent of the universe. We don't need different sets of physical laws for different times and places.

From our premises it follows that

3. All knowledge of matters of fact beyond our present experience depends on our knowledge that nature is uniform—that the future will resemble the past.

The reasoning from premises (1) and (2) to the conclusion (3) has this form: A depends on B, and B depends on C, so A depends on C. So far the argument shows that our ability to know *what will happen* in the future on the basis of *what has happened* in the past depends on our assumptions that nature will continue to follow the same laws and that the same causes will have the same effects. But according to Hume, we do not have justification for the assumption of the uniformity of nature. Before we look at his rationale, let's see where accepting his view will take us. Hume's rejection of our assumption of the uniformity of nature can be expressed in the additional premise:

4. We cannot know that the future will resemble the past.

Notice that the premise does not say that the future will not resemble the past. It only says we cannot *know* that it will. This is a crucial step in Hume's reasoning, and we will consider his defense of it momentarily. We can already see what will follow from his premises: From (3) and (4) it follows that

5. We can have no knowledge of matters of fact beyond our present experience.

If Hume's conclusion is right, then what we can know on the basis of experience is far more limited than what most have thought: Our knowledge at a given moment cannot reach, by the use of inference, beyond what we are experiencing at that moment and what we remember having experienced in the past. In particular, our beliefs about what lies beyond our immediate experiences cannot be justified, so they cannot qualify as knowledge. Our belief that the food on our plate will nourish us, or that the solid floor beneath our feet will support our weight, or countless more beliefs about the future cannot be justified. From an empiricist perspective, reasoning from past experience is our only possible justification for such beliefs, so if that form of reasoning is, as Hume argues, illegitimate, then we have no justification for such beliefs. If we cannot know what the future might be like on the basis of experience, then an empiricist like Hume, who thinks there is no alternative source for justification, must conclude that we have *no reasons* for holding any beliefs about what might happen in the future. If that is right, we have no *knowledge* of such matters.

At the centre of Hume's argument is the all-important premise (4)—that we cannot know that the future will resemble the past. This amounts to saying that we cannot justify our belief in the uniformity of nature. *Why not?*

Will the Future Be Like the Past?

If, like empiricists, we believe that genuine knowledge must be grounded in experience, then there is only one way we can be justified in thinking that things will behave in the future as they behaved in the past—namely, by experience. But why can't we know on the basis of experience that nature behaves uniformly? After all,

(1') *In the past*, we have seen that the future has always been like the past.

As cryptic as it initially sounds, this premise records an obvious fact: Every past event is a future event to some event located even further in the past. Everything that happened yesterday happened in the future to everything that happened the day before yesterday. On the day before yesterday, yesterday was in the future. From our past experience, then, we learn that the future *has always been* like the past. From this it seems reasonable to conclude that

(2') *In the future*, the future will probably be like the past.

There is, however, a serious problem with this thought: (2') follows from (1') only if we *assume* that the future will be like the past. How else could the fact that the future always *was* like the past be made relevant to deciding whether the future *will be* like the past? This assumption—which is required to make the argument work—is just the conclusion that the argument was intended to establish. Any argument for the conclusion that the future will resemble that past, *if based on past experience*, will have to assume that the future will resemble the past. Such reasoning is therefore circular—it commits the **fallacy of begging the question**. So, on Hume's view, a great many of our beliefs—all those that rely on inferences from past and present experiences—are ultimately incapable of being justified.

fallacy of begging the question: Also known as *circular reasoning*, this is the fallacy of assuming or presupposing, in the premises of an argument, the truth of the conclusion that is supposed to be supported by those premises. Such arguments can only persuade someone of a conclusion if she already believes the conclusion.

To reason beyond our present experience, we must first *assume* the uniformity of nature; but that is an assumption that experience itself can never justify. Nothing in what we experience now, or that we remember having experienced in the past, can be

Logic Box

Fallacy of Begging the Question

It is a fallacy to assume or presuppose, in the premises of your argument, the truth of the conclusion that is supposed to be supported by those premises. If your premises could only be found plausible by people who *already* accept your conclusion, you should worry that you might be reasoning in a circle. To avoid circular reasoning, try to reason from premises that would be acceptable to someone who doesn't already accept the conclusion you want to establish.

Example: "There must be a God, since the Bible and the Quran both say there is, and the Bible and the Quran are both reliable since they were divinely inspired."

a legitimate reason to think that nature will behave in the same way tomorrow, or even one minute from now.

Hume's conclusion is deeply skeptical: We cannot know, or be justified in believing, that the future will be like the past, so we cannot make reasonable inferences from our present experiences and memories to conclusions about things beyond our present experiences. For all we can know or justifiably believe, Yogi Berra, former sage of the New York Yankees, might have been right when he said, "The future ain't what it used to be."

Hume's Response to Skepticism

Hume believes his skeptical argument cannot be answered—we cannot escape from the skepticism to which it gives rise. But nor can we live in a constant state of uncertainty about whether the floor will support our weight, whether smoke is a sign of fire, or whether water will quench our thirst. For such potentially disabling doubts, Hume thinks we already have a good remedy[7]:

> This sceptical doubt, both with respect to reason and the senses, is a malady, which can never be radically cured, but must return upon us every moment, however we may chase it away . . . Carelessness and in-attention alone can afford us any remedy. . . .
>
> . . . The intense view of these manifold contradictions and imperfections in human reason has so wrought upon me, and heated my brain, that I am ready to reject all belief and reasoning, and can look upon no opinion even as more probable or likely than another. Where am I, or what? From what causes do I derive my existence, and to what condition shall I return? Whose favour shall I court, and whose anger must I dread? What beings surround me? and on whom have, I any influence, or who have any influence on me? I am confounded with all these questions, and begin to fancy myself in the most deplorable condition imaginable, environed with the deepest darkness, and utterly deprived of the use of every member and faculty.
>
> Most fortunately it happens, that since reason is incapable of dispelling these clouds, nature herself suffices to that purpose, and cures me of this philosophical melancholy and delirium, either by relaxing this bent of mind, or by some avocation, and lively impression of my senses, which obliterate all these chimeras. I dine, I play a game of backgammon, I converse, and am merry with my friends; and when after three or four hours' amusement, I would return to these speculations, they appear so cold, and strained, and ridiculous, that I cannot find in my heart to enter into them any farther.

In effect, Hume believes we must resign to living without *any* justification for most of our beliefs. He does not see this as a reason to despair, since "nature" will provide the "remedy" for skepticism by distracting us from our doubts and plunging us back into the midst of our busy and active lives, where we will live contently without certainty, knowledge, or justification.

Hume's solution never overcomes skepticism about the reasons for our beliefs, but instead suggests that we can cheerfully carry on without good reasons. Hume is not suggesting that we should avoid forming ideas about the future. When I see the sun begin

[7] Hume, D. (1739). *A Treatise of Human Nature*, Part IV, Sections II and VII. Retrieved August 3, 2014, from http://www.gutenberg.org/cache/epub/4705/pg4705.txt

to set, I still get the idea that the sky is about to grow dark, and when I see the man falling toward the water, I still get the idea that he will soon be wet. I cannot, however, base these ideas on any legitimate inference, so I have no justification for them. As the following passages show, Hume believes we have something else that does the work our reason fails to do.

"Skeptical Solution of these Doubts" (David Hume, 1748)[8]

34. Nor need we fear that this philosophy, while it endeavours to limit our enquiries to common life, should ever undermine the reasonings of common life, and carry its doubts so far as to destroy all action, as well as speculation. Nature will always maintain her rights, and prevail in the end over any abstract reasoning whatsoever. Though we should conclude, for instance, as in the foregoing section, that, in all reasonings from experience, there is a step taken by the mind which is not supported by any argument or process of the understanding; there is no danger that these reasonings, on which almost all knowledge depends, will ever be affected by such a discovery. If the mind be not engaged by argument to make this step, it must be induced by some other principle of equal weight and authority; and that principle will preserve its influence as long as human nature remains the same. What that principle is may well be worth the pains of enquiry. . . .

36. This principle is Custom or Habit. For wherever the repetition of any particular act or operation produces a propensity to renew the same act or operation, without being impelled by any reasoning or process of the understanding, we always say, that this propensity is the effect of *Custom*. . . .

    Custom, then, is the great guide of human life. It is that principle alone which renders our experience useful to us, and makes us expect, for the future, a similar train of events with those which have appeared in the past.

    Without the influence of custom, we should be entirely ignorant of every matter of fact beyond what is immediately present to the memory and senses. . . .

38. What, then, is the conclusion of the whole matter? A simple one; though, it must be confessed, pretty remote from the common theories of philosophy. All belief of matter of fact or real existence is derived merely from some object, present to the memory or senses, and a customary conjunction between that and some other object. Or in other words; having found, in many instances, that any two kinds of objects—flame and heat, snow and cold—have always been conjoined together; if flame or snow be presented anew to the senses, the mind is carried by custom to expect heat or cold, and to *believe* that such a quality does exist, and will discover itself upon a nearer approach. This belief is the necessary result of placing the mind in such circumstances. It is an operation of the soul, when we are so situated, as unavoidable as to feel the passion of love, when we receive benefits; or hatred, when we meet with injuries. All these operations are a species of natural instincts, which no reasoning or process of the thought and understanding is able either to produce or to prevent. . . .

---

[8] Hume, D. *Enquiry Concerning Human Understanding*, Section V, Part I. Retrieved August 3, 2014, from http://www.gutenberg.org/cache/epub/9662/pg9662.txt

> 85. But though animals learn many parts of their knowledge from observation, there are also many parts of it, which they derive from the original hand of nature; which much exceed the share of capacity they possess on ordinary occasions; and in which they improve, little or nothing, by the longest practice and experience. These we denominate Instincts, and are so apt to admire as something very extraordinary, and inexplicable by all the disquisitions of human understanding. But our wonder will, perhaps, cease or diminish, when we consider, that the experimental reasoning itself, which we possess in common with beasts, and on which the whole conduct of life depends, is nothing but a species of instinct or mechanical power, that acts in us unknown to ourselves; . . . Though the instinct be different, yet still it is an instinct, which teaches a man to avoid the fire; as much as that, which teaches a bird, with such exactness, the art of incubation, and the whole economy and order of its nursery.

If the empiricists are right, and our ideas and opinions are limited to what we can acquire through sense perception, then where are the limits of what we can know? Hume contends that we can *know nothing* beyond what we are experiencing at each moment or what we can remember having experienced in the past. We can know nothing about things that are not currently in sight—we cannot, for example, know that the bread we eat will provide us with nourishment merely because previous pieces of bread have nourished us; we cannot know that the object in our hand will fall to the floor if we release it, or that the neighbour's house is on fire when we see smoke billowing from the windows. These things could only be known by inference from what we have previously experienced, but such inferences are always illegitimate.

Even though we cannot legitimately *infer* that there is fire where we see smoke, Hume maintains that with enough experience we will soon develop the (completely unjustifiable) psychological *habit* of thinking that there is a fire whenever we see smoke. That is, we develop habits of thought that take us from the things we experience to conclusions about things that lie beyond what we experience. We then act out of habit, *just as if we had certainty*, even though further reflection convinces us that we don't have any certainty. Our "nature"—as creatures of custom, habit, and instinct—*explains* why we think and act as we do, but nothing does, or could, *justify* it. As creatures of reason, we simply could not function in the world; but as creatures of custom and habit we get by well enough. So on Hume's view, we have very little genuine knowledge; but we don't suffer from the lack of it.

FALLIBILISM: LIVING WITHIN OUR MEANS

Locke and Hume agree that the only justification for our beliefs must come from experience. Because of this, they agree, we cannot have the sort of certainty on which Descartes thinks we depend—experience doesn't provide such certainty about the world in which we live and struggle to survive. But neither philosopher is troubled by this in the way that Descartes was. Both believe we can get by well enough on a much smaller budget of justification than Descartes wants.

Locke thinks we can cope with the world adequately and successfully pursue our own happiness using the limited and uncertain resources of sense experience. If we broaden our range of experiences and make careful inferences from the experiences we do have, the odds that we are right about the world are pretty good. But they still fall far short of being certain.

Hume also settles for less than Descartes thinks is needed. He thinks we can have no knowledge or justification for beliefs about matters that lie beyond our present experiences and memories. Hume recognizes that this does not stop us from forming unjustified beliefs about such things, and he agrees that those unjustified beliefs might be suitable for the conduct of our lives. Although we will never have the epistemological security that Descartes seeks, Hume thinks that our nature—that is, our logically illegitimate movements of thought that arise from instinct, custom, and habit—will guide us well enough.

Although the empiricists believe perfect immunity to error lies beyond our reach, they are not troubled since they do not think that leading a human life requires such immunity. On this point Descartes appears to agree—he allows that experience will give us "moral certainty," which is "sufficient certainty for application to ordinary life." But Descartes has larger ambitions. He wants to establish a foundation capable of sustaining the entire body of human knowledge—a foundation for all the sciences—and that requires more certainty than we need "for application to ordinary life."

Perhaps this gives us another way to understand the difference between Descartes and the empiricists: Descartes had other objectives than successfully leading his daily life and, he thought, those further objectives require complete certainty. It may turn out that what we need to successfully cope in our daily lives is less certainty than we need for constructing a scientific theory about the world. According to this suggestion, Locke and Hume want only the *practical certainty* that we can acquire from experience, but Descartes wants a *theoretical certainty* that experience cannot provide. If Descartes requires beliefs to meet higher standards of justification than the empiricists require, perhaps that is because he needs those beliefs to serve for more demanding purposes.

Empiricists contend that the theoretical certainty that Descartes wanted is simply not available. But do our efforts to construct a properly scientific or theoretical account of the world really require such certainty? There are some philosophers—and also some scientists—who think that certainty, or the quest for it, can only get in the way of progress. *Fallibilism* is the view that no belief or theory requires certainty. Sometimes the fallibilist view is completely general, and claims that we cannot have and do not need certainty *about anything at all*. More often, though, fallibilism is the more limited view that there can be no certainty *about matters of fact*. In this form, fallibilism is the idea that *any* belief or *any* theory might eventually be shown wrong and might need to be revised or overturned in light of some unanticipated future experience.

Fallibilism differs from skepticism since, while fallibilists say that *any* of our beliefs might be false, skeptics say that *all* of our beliefs might be false. These are importantly different claims: From the fact that any belief (e.g., *either* B_1 *or* B_2 *or* B_3) might be false, we cannot infer that they might all be false. That would be like inferring from the fact that *any one* of us might have been the person who took the last cookie to the conclusion that we might *all* have been the person who took it. Similarly, *any* coin in a series of 100 tosses has a 50 percent chance of coming up heads, but it does not follow from this that there is a 50 percent chance that they might *all* come up heads. Although fallibilists say we should be prepared to give up any belief, they don't think it follows that we should be prepared to give them all up. Thus, fallibilists are not skeptics.

fallibilism: The view that no idea should be treated as certain, since any belief or any theory might be overturned in light of some future experience.

Fallibilism is best thought of as recommending that *we treat all ideas as hypotheses*—nothing should be treated as immune to possible revision in the future. But they do not doubt that our opinions are often justified—even strongly justified. The most common motivations for fallibilism have empiricist beginnings. Hume argued that our belief in the uniformity of nature is an assumption that no amount of experience can justify—there are no compelling reasons to think that our past experiences will be a reliable guide to the future, which always has the potential to surprise us and overturn our most secure beliefs. In the same vein, a common thought for fallibilists is that some future experience—something we do not foresee or anticipate—may yet contradict even our most strongly held beliefs or our best supported theories. One fallibilist, William James, expresses this idea colourfully when he says,

> . . . Experience, as we know, has ways of *boiling over*, and making us correct our present formulas. . . .
>
> . . . Meanwhile we have to live to-day by what truth we can get to-day, and be ready to-morrow to call it falsehood. Ptolemaic astronomy, euclidean space, aristotelian logic, scholastic metaphysics, were expedient for centuries, but human experience has boiled over those limits . . .[9]

Empiricists hold that the fate of our theories is always hostage to the evidence of experience, and this provides one argument for fallibilism. Experience is never complete or finished—we can't know today what surprises tomorrow may hold. Therefore, even our very best theories are always vulnerable to being overturned by some unanticipated future experience—that is the core idea of fallibilism. In James's comments we also see a second argument for adopting the fallibilist position—this time a *historical argument*. The historical evidence suggests that even our most deeply entrenched ideas—ideas so firmly established as to be beyond any realistic doubt—are eventually revised or discarded in light of new discoveries. Our most secure and successful theories have again and again turned out to be only temporary beliefs. So, in light of the evidence of history, it would be unwise, and very unempirical, to treat any theory as more than a temporary hypothesis.

Finally, Charles Peirce, who is responsible for coining the term *fallibilism* for his epistemological theory—thinks there is a good *methodological reason* to be a fallibilist. According to Peirce, the idea that some theory or opinion is known with complete certainty can only be an obstacle to intellectual and scientific progress. A theory that we regard as so secure it cannot be overturned will never receive the sort of scrutiny needed to improve it, and it will not give us any motivation to explore alternative ideas. An idea that is not tinged with uncertainty leaves us with no motivation to expend the effort needed to improve it. Peirce believed that certainty, if we think we can have it, only serves to block intellectual progress. He holds that any philosophy that claims to have certainty is "a philosophy which barricades the road of further advance toward the truth," and so violates the one rule that he thinks "deserves to be inscribed upon every wall of the city of philosophy: *Do not block the way of inquiry*."[10]

[9] James, W. (1906). *Pragmatism; A New Name for Some Old Ways of Thinking*. Retrieved August 3, 2014, from http://www.gutenberg.org/cache/epub/5116/pg5116.txt

[10] Peirce, C. S. (n.d.). The First Rule of Logic. In (1998) *The Essential Peirce: Selected Philosophical Writings, Volume 2 (1893–1913)*. Peirce Edition Project (Ed.). Bloomington: Indiana Press: 48.

Empiricism—the idea that we have no justification for our beliefs but what we can get from experience—is thought by its best defenders unable to give us certainty. For Locke and Hume this is not a problem, for, they think, we can and do live without certainty. Fallibilists like James and Peirce believe uncertainty is not only inevitable, but good. They hold that the kind of certainty Descartes seeks is not empirically realistic, and that desire for it blocks the road to truth.

CONCLUSION

We examined epistemological theories that do not hold that knowledge must rest on a foundation of certainty. Locke thinks we cannot acquire from experience any certainty about what exists beyond our own thoughts or about what the facts are, but he does not think this prevents us from acquiring knowledge. Knowledge of the world does not, on his view, require certainty. Hume believes that we cannot acquire justification from experience—even weak justification—for many of our more important beliefs. Neither the lack of certainty nor the lack of justification is thought by these philosophers to interfere with our ability to live a successful human life. If our ideas or beliefs serve us well enough in the conduct of our lives, and yet we do not have certainty, then empiricists think this only shows that we have no need for certainty. Descartes's ambition to rebuild the entire system of human knowledge on secure foundations may have influenced his thought that certainty is required for theoretical and scientific knowledge. Even that thought is challenged by fallibilists, who think that certainty—or, at least, the idea that we might have some certainty—is only an obstacle to future progress in the direction of truth.

Descartes's rationalism and foundationalism had their origins in his doubts about the reliability of our sense experiences. The empiricists who followed Descartes in the attempt to understand the nature and limits of justification, knowledge, and certainty agreed that sense experience alone provides little in the way of certainty or knowledge. Unlike Descartes, the empiricists thought this should not trouble us, since we get by well enough without them.

Whether our senses can deliver knowledge about the world surely depends on how sense perception works. In the next chapter, we examine philosophical theories about the nature of perception in order to help us understand whether experience could be a reliable source of knowledge or certainty about the world.

Key Terms and Figures

rationalism p. 207
rationalist theory of knowledge p. 207
idea p. 207
rationalist theory of concepts p. 207
innate ideas p. 208
empiricism p. 208
empiricist theory of knowledge p. 208
empiricist theory of concepts p. 208
simple ideas p. 210
complex ideas p. 210
uniformity of nature p. 218
fallacy of begging the question p. 219
fallibilism p. 224

Additional readings on empiricism, induction, and fallibilism

Heatherington, S. Fallibilism. *Internet Encyclopedia of Philosophy*. Available at http://www.iep.utm.edu/fallibil/

Morris, W. E. (2013). David Hume. *The Stanford Encyclopedia of Philosophy*, Spring Edition. (Edward N. Zalta, Ed.). Available at http://plato.stanford.edu/archives/spr2013/entries/hume/

Russell, B. (1959). On Induction. *The Problems of Philosophy*. Oxford: Oxford University Press: 33–38. Available at http://www.gutenberg.org/cache/epub/5827/pg5827.txt

William, M. (2001). Induction. *Problems of Knowledge: A Critical Introduction to Epistemology*. Oxford: Oxford University Press: 201–210.

Chapter 11

The Veil of Perception

Learning Objectives

- Describe the supposed tension between scientific and common sense views of the world.
- Outline Descartes' dream argument for skepticism about the senses, and summarize at least two possible objections to it.
- Contrast the representational and direct realist theories of perception.
- Explain the idea that there is a veil of perception, and say why it leads to skepticism about the external world.
- Outline the argument from the relativity of perception, and summarize some possible objections to it.

Early epistemologists thought they saw an unresolvable tension between the newly emerging sciences and our common sense understanding of reality. When we find ourselves with two opposing views of the world and our place in it, it becomes important to see if they can co-exist, or if one perspective must be discarded. If both the scientific and common sense views cannot be merged into a single coherent vision, then we are under pressure to give up aspects of one or the other, and in doing so will need to give up something important to ourselves. However, as the scientific picture of the world has taken shape around us, it has become obvious to many philosophers that it cannot be reconciled with our common sense view. Something, they think, will have to give—one or the other of these world views will need to be relegated to the realm of illusion.

One focal point of the dispute between science and common sense concerns the nature and reliability of sense perception. It is widely believed that the physical sciences provide a picture of the world very unlike the everyday world revealed by our senses. In this chapter we examine the reasons many have offered for doubting the reliability of our sense experiences, and we will explore those doubts in the context of the purported clash between the scientific and common sense pictures of the world.

TWO PERSPECTIVES ON REALITY

A conflict between our common sense and our scientific pictures of the world was suggested by Descartes in the seventeenth century, and it continues to concern contemporary thinkers. We begin with two presentations of the supposed conflict, from several centuries apart. Descartes thought that a choice between the two views of the world would be a choice between trusting experience and trusting reason. Consider how he frames the disagreement.

Two Ideas of the Sun (René Descartes, 1641)[1]

> . . . I have noticed that in many cases there was a great difference between the object and its idea. I find, for example, two completely diverse ideas of the sun in my mind; the one derives its origin from the senses, . . . according to this idea the sun seems to be extremely small; but the other is derived from astronomical reasoning, i.e. is elicited from certain notions that are innate in me, or else it is formed by me in some other manner; in accordance with it the sun appears to be several times greater than the earth. These two ideas cannot, indeed, both resemble the same sun, and reason makes me believe that the one which seems to have originated directly from the sun itself, is the one which is most dissimilar to it.

On Descartes' view, our pre-scientific and common sense picture of reality is a blend of custom, prejudice, and untutored sense experience, while our scientific picture is the result of careful reasoning and a willingness to suspend trust in our senses.

In this brief passage Descartes aligns a pre-scientific theory of the sun with sense experience: The idea that the sun is very small and close to the earth is an idea that "derives its origin from the senses," and is an idea that "seems to have originated directly from the sun itself." The later, more scientific idea of the sun is aligned with reason: that the sun is far away and is much larger than the earth is "derived from astronomical reasoning," which depends on innate mathematic ideas. The idea of the sun that is derived from the senses is the "most dissimilar to it"; but the idea of the sun derived from "astronomical reasoning" better represents the actual sun. Here, our pre-scientific and common sense view of the sun is the result of sense experience, but our scientific view is arrived at by allowing what our reason tells us to overrule what our senses tell us.

One might hesitate to accept Descartes' way of aligning the errors of common sense with sense experience and the truths of science with reason. After all, isn't our scientific view of the world one that has evolved by letting our beliefs become better informed by experience—and experiment? Even in Descartes' example of astronomy, the size and distance to the sun could not have been known by mathematical reasoning alone. It required us to feed our mathematical calculations with numbers drawn from precise observations and measurements. So perhaps the right way to express the conflict between common sense and science is not by contrasting sense experience with reason, but by contrasting informal or careless observations with more refined and careful observations. We will return to this suggestion later, but in case you think such worries belong only to the seventeenth century, or to philosophers alone, consider the following passage from distinguished twentieth-century physicist **Sir Arthur Eddington** (1882–1944).

Sir Arthur Eddington: A distinguished British physicist and astronomer best known for his work on stellar physics, his 1919 observations of the deflection of starlight by gravity (which was the first experimental confirmation of Einstein's general theory of relativity), and his popular lectures on the philosophy of science.

[1] From Descartes, R. (1911). *Meditations on First Philosophy*, Meditation III. (Elizabeth Haldane, Trans.)

"The Two Tables" Arthur Eddington (1928)[2]

I have settled down to the task of writing these lectures and have drawn up my chairs to my two tables. Two tables! Yes; there are duplicates of every object about me—two tables, two chairs, two pens.

This is not a very profound beginning to a course which ought to reach transcendent levels of scientific philosophy. But we cannot touch bedrock immediately; we must scratch a bit at the surface of things first. And whenever I begin to scratch the first thing I strike is—my two tables.

One of them has been familiar to me from earliest years. It is a commonplace object of that environment which I call the world. How shall I describe it? It has extension; it is comparatively permanent; it is coloured; above all it is *substantial.* By substantial I do not merely mean that it does not collapse when I lean upon it; I mean that it is constituted of "substance" and by that word I am trying to convey to you some conception of its intrinsic nature. It is a *thing*; not like space, which is a mere negation; nor like time, which is—Heaven knows what! But that will not help you to my meaning because it is the distinctive characteristic of a "thing" to have this substantiality, and I do not think substantiality can be described better than by saying that it is the kind of nature exemplified by an ordinary table. And so we go round in circles. After all if you are a plain commonsense man, not too much worried with scientific scruples, you will be confident that you understand the nature of an ordinary table. I have even heard of plain men who had the idea that they could better understand the mystery of their own nature if scientists would discover a way of explaining it in terms of the easily comprehensible nature of a table.

Table No. 2 is my scientific table. It is a more recent acquaintance and I do not feel so familiar with it. It does not belong to the world previously mentioned—that world which spontaneously appears around me when I open my eyes, though how much of it is objective and how much subjective I do not here consider. It is part of a world which in more devious ways has forced itself on my attention. My scientific table is mostly emptiness. Sparsely scattered in that emptiness are numerous electric charges rushing about with great speed; but their combined bulk amounts to less than a billionth of the bulk of the table itself. Notwithstanding its strange construction it turns out to be an entirely efficient table. It supports my writing paper as satisfactorily as table No. 1; for when I lay the paper on it the little electric particles with their headlong speed keep on hitting the underside, so that the paper is maintained in shuttlecock fashion at a nearly steady level. If I lean upon this table I shall not go through; or, to be strictly accurate, the chance of my scientific elbow going through my scientific table is so excessively small that it can be neglected in practical life. Reviewing their properties one by one, there seems to be nothing to choose between the two tables for ordinary purposes; but when abnormal circumstances befall, then my scientific table shows to advantage. If the house catches fire my scientific table will dissolve quite naturally into scientific smoke, whereas my familiar table undergoes a metamorphosis of its substantial nature which I can only regard as miraculous.

There is nothing *substantial* about my second table. It is nearly all empty space—space pervaded, it is true, by fields of force, but these are assigned to the category of "influences", not of "things". Even in the minute part which is not empty we must not

[2] From Eddington, A. S. (1928). *The Nature of the Physical World.* Retrieved on August 4, 2014, from http://www.gutenberg.ca/ebooks/eddingtona-physicalworld/eddingtona-physicalworld-01-h-dir/eddingtona-physicalworld-01-h.html

> transfer the old notion of substance. In dissecting matter into electric charges we have travelled far from that picture of it which first gave rise to the conception of substance, and the meaning of that conception—if it ever had any—has been lost by the way. . . .
>
> I will not here stress further the non-substantiality of electrons, since it is scarcely necessary to the present line of thought. Conceive them as substantially as you will, there is a vast difference between my scientific table with its substance (if any) thinly scattered in specks in a region mostly empty and the table of everyday conception which we regard as the type of solid reality . . . It makes all the difference in the world whether the paper before me is poised as it were on a swarm of flies and sustained in shuttlecock fashion by a series of tiny blows from the swarm underneath, or whether it is supported because there is substance below it, it being the intrinsic nature of substance to occupy space to the exclusion of other substance; all the difference in conception at least, but no difference to my practical task of writing on the paper.
>
> I need not tell you that modern physics has by delicate test and remorseless logic assured me that my second scientific table is the only one which is really there—wherever "there" may be. On the other hand I need not tell you that modern physics will never succeed in exorcising that first table—strange compound of external nature, mental imagery and inherited prejudice—which lies visible to my eyes and tangible to my grasp.

Descartes's two ideas of the sun and Eddington's two tables illustrate a much broader conflict between our common sense and scientific world views. Both suppose that when our common sense view of the world differs from a scientifically informed view, then preference must be given to the scientific picture. This need not be merely the expression of a pro-science bias. Our best scientific theories have earned their prestige by passing a wide range of experimental tests that our common sense views regularly fail, so it is not bias, but evidence and argument that lead Descartes and Eddington to prefer the scientific pictures of the sun or table.

But what do we see with our untrained eyes if it is not the real sun or the real table? In broad terms, Descartes and Eddington share a common view about how perception works: Our senses provide a faulty representation of the world—a distorted picture of reality. Therefore we must *reason* our way beyond the faulty representation to a more accurate understanding of reality. Perception itself imposes a veil between us and reality. Eddington expresses this point in his closing sentence: What lies visible to our eyes is a "strange compound of external nature, mental imagery and inherited prejudice."

We should be careful not to misunderstand this point. It can seem a plausible idea that how things appear before we take accurate measurements or before we reason carefully about what we see may eventually need correction by further reflection or more careful observations. But, curiously, this doesn't seem to be the point Descartes and Eddington are making. Because our common sense view of the world clashes with our scientific view, and because our common sense view is derived from sense experience, then—they think—sense experience itself clashes with our scientific view of reality. They are not saying that we need to *observe things more carefully*; rather, they are saying that *observing* isn't the right way to get to know reality. A key assumption they make in order to reach this conclusion is that *the erroneous but common sense view of the world* is *the view of the world derived directly from sense experience*. As we become more scientifically sophisticated and recognize that our common sense views are wrong, both thinkers assume that sense experience is the culprit.

To see why they think this way, we will first need to closely examine Descartes's rationale for being suspicious of sense experience. We can then examine more recent views about the nature of perception that have descended from Descartes.

DESCARTES ON SENSE EXPERIENCE

We saw earlier that Descartes did not trust in sense experience. Two of the reasons for his mistrust tell us something useful about how he understood the operations of the senses. A brief reminder is in order. Descartes first noted that "It is sometimes proved to me that these senses are deceptive, and it is wiser not to trust entirely to anything by which we have once been deceived."[3] However, the fact that our senses *sometimes* "deceive us" (for example, in poor perceptual conditions) is itself something we only learn by *relying on* our senses in better perceptual conditions. It is by turning on the light that we sometimes correct our errors. Thus, the fact that we are sometimes misled by our senses only shows that we should not trust them in poor lighting or at great distances. This cannot be a reason for doubting sense experience altogether, but only a reason for using our senses more carefully. Our senses appear to be self-correcting—that is, sensory information acquired in poor conditions is corrected by sensory information acquired in better conditions. Similarly, information acquired by one sense—say, by touch—might be corrected by information acquired by another—say, by sight. None of this seems to be a reason for *mistrusting the senses* rather than a reason for *mistrusting hasty or careless observations*.

In order to make his doubts about sense experience more extensive, Descartes offers his **argument from dreams**: "I remind myself that on many occasions I have in sleep been deceived . . . I see so manifestly that there are no certain indications by which we may clearly distinguish wakefulness from sleep."[4] Recall the reason that "there are no certain indications"—no tests—to distinguish dreaming states from waking states. Even if there were a good test for establishing that we are awake, *dreaming that we are applying the test* won't yield reliable results, so the test must assume that we are not dreaming and cannot be used to establish it.

argument from dreams: An argument from Descartes's *Meditations* that purports to show that we cannot acquire any knowledge or certainty from sensory experience (on the grounds that there is no reliable way to distinguish waking experiences from dream experiences).

The fact that we have previously been "deceived" in sleep, together with our inability to distinguish, at this moment, waking and dreaming states, raises doubt about the reliability of sense perception even in the best viewing conditions. Simply being a more careful observer won't help with *this* problem. If we have sometimes—in dreams—acquired false beliefs about what is directly in front of us, even in what seem to be optimal viewing conditions, then we should not trust our senses in *any* perceptual conditions.

The Argument from Dreams: A Closer Look

The first thing to keep track of in any attempt to understand Descartes's argument from dreams is that he is *not* claiming that it is possible that everything is a dream, or that there is no real difference between dreams and waking life. Others have entertained such ideas,

[3] From Descartes, R. (1911). *Meditations on First Philosophy*, Meditation I. (Elizabeth Haldane, Trans.), Cambridge University Press.

[4] *Ibid.*

and one of its better known formulations comes from the fourth century BC Chinese skeptical philosopher Chuang Chou[5]:

> "Those who dream of the banquet may weep the next morning, and those who dream of weeping may go out to hunt after dawn. When we dream we do not know that we are dreaming. In our dreams we may even interpret our dreams. Only after we are awake do we know we have dreamed. Finally, there comes a great awakening, and then we know life is a great dream. But the stupid think they are awake all the time, and believe they know it distinctly. Are we (honorable) rulers? Are we (humble) shepherds? How vulgar! Both Confucius and you were dreaming. When I say you were dreaming, I am also dreaming. . . .
>
> Once I, Chuang Chou, dreamed I was a butterfly and was happy as a butterfly. I was conscious that I was quite pleased with myself, but I did not know that I was Chou. Suddenly I awoke, and there I was, visibly Chou. I do not know whether it was Chou dreaming that he was a butterfly or the butterfly dreaming that it was Chou. Between Chou and the butterfly there must be some distinction.

Like Descartes, Chuang Chou was skeptical about our ability to tell waking from dreaming states. But, unlike Descartes, he entertained the possibility that all waking life was an extended dream. In that event, our distinction between waking and dreaming is only a distinction we have drawn *within a dream*—between, for example, *your dreaming* that you are a butterfly and *your dreaming* that you are someone who has awakened from a dream about being a butterfly.

A common objection to Chou's idea is that it seems to erase the very distinction between waking and dreaming upon which it depends. If everything is a dream, then we have only the distinction between *dreaming* (that we are awake) and *dreaming* (that we are asleep and dreaming). But this is a distinction drawn *within the realm of dreams*, so it requires that there actually be such a state of dreaming. But what could *that* be unless there is such a thing as a contrasting state of wakefulness? This may be what Chou hints at in his final sentence: If there is not a real distinction—as opposed to only a dreamed distinction—between Chou and the butterfly, then there is no distinction between being the butterfly dreaming that he is Chou, and being Chou dreaming that he is the butterfly.

However this turns out, Descartes does not follow Chuang Chou in proposing that it is possible that we are always dreaming. What sorts of errors, then, does Descartes think dreams lead us into?

A. I might have false beliefs about something *while I am wide awake*, because I mistake a dream that I had last night for something that happened yesterday.

For example, last night I dreamed I repaid the money I owe you and, as a result, today I mistakenly believe that I no longer owe you any money. This might show that my *memory* is unreliable—I don't *remember* whether I repaid the loan or only dreamed it—but nothing about this sort of error shows that my *senses* are unreliable. This is not the sort of error Descartes has in mind.

[5] Also *Zhuang Zhou*, or *Zhuangzi*. Chou's exact dates are uncertain. Appropriately, it is also uncertain whether he really existed. Selection from CHAN, WING-TSIT; A SOURCE BOOK IN CHINESE PHILOSOPHY. (C) 1963 Princeton University Press, 1991 renewed PUP. Reprinted by permission of Princeton University Press.

B. I might mistakenly think, *while I'm awake* and I see a table before me, that I'm actually sound asleep and dreaming.

Here, I mistake my current waking state for a dreaming state. However, this does not seem to be an error in which I am misled *by a dream*, since I am not dreaming at all. If there really are mistakes of this sort, they would show something about the unreliability of waking experience. Notice also that if there is any "test" to distinguish waking from dreaming (e.g., pinching oneself), then nothing prevents me from applying the test successfully *in this case*. The problem with such tests, as we have seen, is that dreaming we apply the test does not give reliable results; but in the sorts of cases we are considering now we are awake, and cannot be dreaming that we are applying the test. Therefore, there is no obvious reason to expect the test to give false results. But, again, these are not the sorts of cases Descartes is concerned with. The cases on which his argument depends are better described this way:

C. I mistakenly think, *while I am asleep and dreaming*, that I see a table before me, when there is no table there.

Here, I mistake my current dreaming state for a current waking state. Since it is dreaming that misleads us—as Descartes says, "I have in sleep been deceived"—it will be this case that interests Descartes. That is, his argument for doubting our senses does not turn on the claim that our senses are unreliable in optimal viewing conditions—that is what he wants to prove, not what he assumes. Rather, his argument depends on the idea that *if we are dreaming right now*, then (a) we cannot know that we are dreaming, and (b) our senses are misleading us.

Two Responses to the Argument from Dreams

How does the fact (if, as Descartes believes, it is a fact) that we have false beliefs about the world *while we are dreaming* indicate that *our senses* are an unreliable source for knowledge of reality? There are two reasons for doubting that it does.

First Response Descartes's dream argument for skepticism about the senses depends on the assumption that there is symmetry between dreaming and waking. It assumes that because

a. *When I am dreaming*, I cannot always know that I am dreaming;

then it is also true that

b. *When I am wide awake*, I cannot always know that I am awake.

This is like supposing that since

a'. *When I'm dead*, I cannot know that I am dead;

then it is also true that

b'. *When I am alive*, I cannot know that I am alive.[6]

[6] This analogy is from William, B. (2002). *Truth and Truthfulness*. Princeton University Press: 130.

Descartes' argument appeals to the fact that we are deceived when we are asleep and dreaming. But it is not clear that Descartes has provided any reason to think we are similarly deceived when we are awake. Even if it is true that *when I am dreaming* I cannot always tell that I am dreaming, that does not by itself give reason to think that *when I am awake* I cannot usually tell that I am awake. But if we can, or usually can, tell that we are awake when we are awake, then we have no grounds for skepticism about beliefs based on our senses in optimal viewing conditions. A possible challenge to Descartes' argument from dreams, then, is that just because I form unreliable beliefs when I am asleep and dreaming, that is *no reason* for thinking that I form unreliable beliefs when I am wide awake and in optimal viewing conditions.

Second Response When I am asleep and dreaming, I am typically in darkness, where I can see little or nothing; furthermore, my eyes are closed—and I cannot *see* when my eyes are closed. What this suggests is that when I am asleep and dreaming, any errors I make should not be blamed on my sense of sight—*I'm not even using my eyes.* If we have false beliefs about the world when we are asleep and dreaming, but we are not acquiring those beliefs through our senses, then the false beliefs we have in dreams cannot show that sense experience is an unreliable means of acquiring information about the world. In the same way, we cannot conclude that horses are an unreliable mode of transportation because we have problems riding our donkey. Therefore, the argument from dreams doesn't support skepticism *about the senses*. If this objection is right, all that the argument from dreams shows is that *we can't trust our dreams* for reliable information about the world. But most of us already know that.

Perhaps we can imagine Descartes replying as follows: When I am asleep and dreaming, I *do see* things. For example, if I dream I have a pizza on the table before me, then although I do not see *an actual pizza*, I do see *a mental image of a pizza*. Even though I am in complete darkness and my "outer eyes" are closed, I am still *seeing mental imagery* with my "inner eyes." Very well—suppose this is true. Then the argument from dreams would show that we cannot trust our "inner eyes" to provide reliable information about the outer world. It still fails to show that our "outer eyes"—our senses—are unreliable. If Descartes hopes to show that our *sensory experience* is unreliable as a source of knowledge, he needs to answer these responses to his argument from dreams.

Before the Mind's Eye

Do dreamers really see mental images with an "inner eye"—images that pass before "the mind's eye"? Descartes appears to think so. In his First Meditation, he describes dreams in this way: "the things which are represented to us in sleep are like painted representations."[7] Dreaming is like having a series of mental images passing before the mind's eye. Let's think about some of the consequences of understanding dreams this way.

---

[7] From Descartes, R. (1911). *Meditations on First Philosophy*, Meditation I. (Elizabeth Haldane, Trans.), Cambridge University Press.

Suppose I am in bed, sound asleep with my eyes closed, and I am having a vivid dream about eating a pizza. Suppose that in my dream I have all of the following thoughts:

a. "I *see* a pizza—it looks delicious."

b. "I *smell* a pizza—it smells like cheese and pepperoni."

c. "I am *eating* a slice of the pizza—it feels warm and tastes salty."

If I believe, while dreaming, that I am actually doing any of these things, then I am making a mistake of the kind that Descartes suggests dreams can cause, and I have three false beliefs. But what errors have I made to lead me to hold these false beliefs? Here is one kind of answer:

> *Error (a)*: I falsely believe that I see *a pizza*, but I am *actually seeing something else*—namely, a mental image, or representation, of a pizza.

This makes sense if we think of dreaming as Descartes does, as seeing images before the mind's eye. When I mistake my dreaming state for a waking state, I am mistaken about what I see—is it a pizza, or a very life-like image of a pizza? But if this is the right way to explain the error I make in (a), consider how we will need to explain the errors I make in (b) and (c):

> *Error (b)*: I falsely believe that I smell *a pizza*, but I am *actually smelling something else*—namely, a mental image, or a mental odour, of a pizza.

If we smell things in dreams as well as see them, then we must have a mind's nose as well as a mind's eye. Similarly, the warmth of the pizza that I dream I feel requires whatever mental organ is needed for touch—perhaps mental fingers.

> *Error (c)*: I falsely believe that I am eating *a pizza*, but I am *actually eating something else*.

To continue this pattern of explanation, we need to say that I am eating a mental image of a pizza, since there is no actual pizza present for me to eat. Apparently, then, I am eating the mental pizza with my mind's mouth—my "inner mouth"—since my "outer mouth" is eating nothing while I sleep. If, in our dreams, we eat as well as see and smell, then we need a "mind's mouth" as well as a mind's eye and a mind's nose.

Recall that we are looking for an explanation of the mistake that leads me to hold the false beliefs in (a)–(c). The explanation we are considering is this: When, in Descartes' words, "I have in sleep been deceived," I mistake *the object of my perception* (e.g., seeing, smelling, feeling, and so on)—which, in dreams, is only mental imagery—with the actual things represented by the mental images. This is the explanation we get of our false beliefs when we understand dreaming as *the perception of mental images*. In kind, it is no different than mistaking a store mannequin for a real person. The explanation requires that, when we are asleep and dreaming, we are perceiving inner things—mental images. Therefore, we will need to have *inner organs of sense* with which to do the perceiving.

homunculus: An "inner" person. When we refer to our mind's eye, analogous to the eye in the human body, we are describing our mind as if it were a homunculus.

This might seem plausible when we focus on dreams of visual experiences, as in (a), but the same explanation becomes increasing suspect when applied to smell, touch, or other modes of perception, as in (b) or (c). We interact in our dreams and fantasies in other ways than merely by "seeing" things. If we make love in our dreams, this pattern of explanation will require us to have "inner bodies." If dreamers actually see, but with their mind's eye, and make love, but with their mind's body, we will need to have an entire "inner person" to explain dreams and the sorts of errors Descartes think we make in dreams. Philosophers refer to this "inner person," whose eyes are our "mind's eyes," as a **homunculus**. That a homunculus dwells in each of us is a consequence of understanding dreaming, and imagining, and so on, as *the perception of mental images*. As metaphor, this way of understanding dreams might be useful, but as metaphor it cannot support Descartes' skeptical idea that *perception* is shown to be unreliable by any false beliefs we acquire in our dreams.

Fortunately, it is not mandatory to think of dreams as Descartes does. Consider the difference between two people who *mistakenly* think they have just kicked a soccer ball. The first person is mistaken because it wasn't a soccer ball she kicked, but a volleyball. She is right about what she did—she *kicked* a ball; but she is wrong about what she did it to—it was a volleyball, not a soccer ball. *She is wrong about the object of her action, not about her action*. The second person also mistakenly thinks she kicked a soccer ball, but she is mistaken because she didn't actually *kick* the soccer ball, she only *tripped over it*. This is a case of being mistaken about what she did, not about what she did it to. *She is wrong about her action, not about the object of her action*.

In our Cartesian explanations of my errors in (a)–(c), I was wrong about the object, but not about the act—I misidentified *what* I was perceiving, but I really was perceiving. This is precisely why I must have inner organs of sense. But a second view of dreams explains the false beliefs in (a)–(c) by saying that I am mistaken about the act I am engaged in, not about the object of my act. According to this second view, I'm not seeing, smelling, or eating anything—I'm only dreaming that I'm seeing, smelling, and eating. But it really is a pizza that I dream I am seeing, smelling, and eating, not an image of a pizza. On this view the mistake I make when I acquire a false belief while dreaming is

> *Error (d)*: I falsely believe that I am seeing (and smelling, and eating, and so on) a pizza, but what I am *actually doing* is something else—I am *dreaming* that I am seeing (and smelling, and eating, and so on) a pizza.

Dreaming that we are seeing a pizza, unlike seeing a mental image of a pizza, does not require that we have inner eyes to do the "seeing," any more than dreaming that we are flying requires us to have inner wings. This second view of the errors we might be prone to while dreaming does not require a homunculus—we aren't really doing the things we only dream we are doing, and neither are our homunculi.

Descartes appears to believe that when we dream we are actually perceiving things, but the "things" we perceive are only mental images or representations. That is why he supposes that the false beliefs we have while dreaming establish that *perception*, and not merely dreaming, cannot be trusted. What is more, the following selection from his Second Meditation suggests that he thinks *all* perceiving—even when we are wide awake—is only the perception of images or representations.

The Piece of Wax (Descartes, 1641)[8]

Let us begin by considering the commonest matters, those which we believe to be the most distinctly comprehended, to wit, the bodies which we touch and see; not indeed bodies in general, for these general ideas are usually a little more confused, but let us consider one body in particular. Let us take, for example, this piece of wax: it has been taken quite freshly from the hive, and it has not yet lost the sweetness of the honey which it contains; it still retains somewhat of the odor of the flowers from which it has been culled; its colour, its figure, its size are apparent; it is hard, cold, easily handled, and if you strike it with the finger, it will emit a sound. Finally all the things which are requisite to cause us distinctly to recognize a body are met with in it. But notice that while I speak and approach the fire what remained of the taste is exhaled, the smell evaporates, the colour alters, the figure is destroyed, the size increases, it becomes liquid, it heats, scarcely can one handle it, and when one strikes it, no sound is emitted. Does the same wax remain after this change? We must confess that it remains; none would judge otherwise. What then did I know so distinctly in this piece of wax? It could certainly be nothing of all that the senses brought to my notice, since all these things which fall under taste, smell, sight, touch, and hearing, are found to be changed, and yet the same wax remains.

Perhaps it was what I now think, viz. that this wax was not that sweetness of honey, nor that agreeable scent of flowers, nor that particular whiteness, nor that figure, nor that sound, but simply a body which a little while before appeared to me as perceptible under these forms, and which is now perceptible under others. But what, precisely, is it that I imagine when I form such conceptions? Let us attentively consider this and, abstracting from all that does not belong to the wax, let us see what remains. Certainly nothing remains except a certain extended thing which is flexible and movable. But what is the meaning of flexible and movable? Is it not that I imagine that this piece of wax being round is capable of becoming square and of passing from a square to a triangular figure? No, certainly it is not that, since I imagine it admits of an infinitude of similar changes, and I nevertheless do not know how to compass the infinitude by my imagination, and consequently this conception which I have of the wax is not brought about by the faculty of imagination. What now is this extension? Is it not also unknown? For it becomes greater when the wax is melted, greater when it is boiled, and greater still when the heat increases; and I should not conceive [clearly] according to truth what wax is, if I did not think that even this piece that we are considering is capable of receiving more variations in extension than I have ever imagined. We must then grant that I could not even understand through the imagination what this piece of wax is, and that it is my mind alone which perceives it. I say this piece of wax in particular, for as to wax in general it is yet clearer. But what is this piece of wax which cannot be understood except by the [understanding or] mind? It is certainly the same that I see, touch, imagine, and finally it is the same which I have always believed it to be from the beginning. But what must particularly be observed is that its perception is neither an act of vision, nor of touch, nor of imagination, and has never been such although it may have appeared formerly to be so, but only an intuition of the mind, which may be imperfect and confused as it was formerly, or clear and distinct as it is at present, according as my attention is more or less directed to the elements which are found in it, and of which it is composed.

[8] *Ibid.*

Yet in the meantime I am greatly astonished when I consider [the great feebleness of mind] and its proneness to fall [insensibly] into error; for although without giving expression to my thought I consider all this in my own mind, words often impede me and I am almost deceived by the terms of ordinary language. For we say that we see the same wax, if it is present, and not that we simply judge that it is the same from its having the same colour and figure. From this I should conclude that I knew the wax by means of vision and not simply by the intuition of the mind; unless by chance I remember that, when looking from a window and saying I see men who pass in the street, I really do not see them, but infer that what I see is men, just as I say that I see wax. And yet what do I see from the window but hats and coats which may cover automatic machines? Yet I judge these to be men. And similarly solely by the faculty of judgment which rests in my mind, I comprehend that which I believed I saw with my eyes.

A man who makes it his aim to raise his knowledge above the common should be ashamed to derive the occasion for doubting from the forms of speech invented by the vulgar; I prefer to pass on and consider whether I had a more evident and perfect conception of what the wax was when I first perceived it, and when I believed I knew it by means of the external senses or at least by the common sense as it is called, that is to say by the imaginative faculty, or whether my present conception is clearer now that I have most carefully examined what it is, and in what way it can be known. It would certainly be absurd to doubt as to this. For what was there in this first perception which was distinct? What was there which might not as well have been perceived by any of the animals? But when I distinguish the wax from its external forms, and when, just as if I had taken from it its vestments, I consider it quite naked, it is certain that although some error may still be found in my judgment, I can nevertheless not perceive it thus without a human mind.

But finally what shall I say of this mind, that is, of myself, for up to this point I do not admit in myself anything but mind? What then, I who seem to perceive this piece of wax so distinctly, do I not know myself, not only with much more truth and certainty, but also with much more distinctness and clearness? For if I judge that the wax is or exists from the fact that I see it, it certainly follows much more clearly that I am or that I exist myself from the fact that I see it. For it may be that what I see is not really wax, it may also be that I do not possess eyes with which to see anything; but it cannot be that when I see, or (for I no longer take account of the distinction) when I think I see, that I myself who think am naught. So if I judge that the wax exists from the fact that I touch it, the same thing will follow, to wit, that I am; and if I judge that my imagination, or some other cause, whatever it is, persuades me that the wax exists, I shall still conclude the same. And what I have here remarked of wax may be applied to all other things which are external to me [and which are met with outside of me]. And further, if the [notion or] perception of wax has seemed to me clearer and more distinct, not only after the sight or the touch, but also after many other causes have rendered it quite manifest to me, with how much more [evidence] and distinctness must it be said that I now know myself, since all the reasons which contribute to the knowledge of wax, or any other body whatever, are yet better proofs of the nature of my mind! And there are so many other things in the mind itself which may contribute to the elucidation of its nature, that those which depend on body such as these just mentioned, hardly merit being taken into account.

But finally here I am, having insensibly reverted to the point I desired, for, since it is now manifest to me that even bodies are not properly speaking known by the senses or by the faculty of imagination, but by the understanding only, and since they are not known from the fact that they are seen or touched, but only because they are understood, I see clearly that there is nothing which is easier for me to know than my mind.

Loose Talk About Perception

Descartes's discussion of his sensory experience of a piece of wax illustrates his views about our perception of the world external to the mind. By examining a piece of wax both before and after it is brought near a fire, he notes the information he receives from each of his five senses (see Table 11.1):

Table 11.1

The Sense	Information Received Before the Transformation of the Wax	Information Received After the Transformation of the Wax
Sight	yellow colour, square shape	white-ish colour, irregular shape
Smell	odour of flowers	odourless
Taste	sweetness of honey	tasteless
Touch	hard, cold	soft, warm
Hearing	emits a sharp sound	emits a squishy sound

Watching the wax undergo gradual change, we happily say we perceive the same piece of wax before and after the transformation. But nothing with which we are acquainted *via* our five senses is the same before and after the change; there is no overlap between the second and third columns of Table 11.1. Therefore, although we *say* we perceive the same wax, nothing we actually perceive is the same before and after the change. So, Descartes concludes, we don't, strictly speaking, perceive the underlying and enduring substance of the wax. We perceive only its properties or qualities, which Descartes compares to garments worn by the underlying substance, and those garments have changed.

Although we commonly say such things as "I see the wax" or even "I see the same piece of wax," Descartes concludes that this is misleading. We *understand* that the wax is the same, but we don't *perceive* anything that stays the same. Descartes believes that our common but careless way of speaking about perception misleads us into thinking we can perceive "things which are external" to us. However, we should not be confused by our common ways of speaking. We also say, "I see what you mean," but we don't think we can literally *see* meanings. "I see what you mean" is only our informal way of saying we *understand* what someone means. It is not always easy to avoid such confusion. Consider the following dialogue:

Sarah: Can you taste the difference between these two brands of beer?
Tim: No problem. I'm an experienced and discerning drinker, and I never confuse different brands of beer.
Sarah: Very well, then, taste this beer.
Tim (taking a sip, and savouring it carefully): That's pretty good stuff—you can really taste the hops.
Sarah: Okay, now taste this one.

Tim (savouring slowly the second bottle of beer): This isn't bad, but it's much sweeter than the first beer. It's far too sweet for me.
Sarah: Very well, now taste the difference.
Tim: What?
Sarah: You did say you could *taste the difference*, didn't you?[9]

Although Tim said he could *taste the difference*, it turns out he couldn't. What he really meant is that he could *tell* the difference between two beers (by tasting them). Descartes thinks that all of our talk about *perceiving physical objects* is "careless talk" of just this sort. What we perceive are not the objects themselves, but their properties or characteristics, as indicated in the second and third columns of Table 11.1. If we have any knowledge of objects at all, it is only by making *inferences about them* from what we do perceive—from the perceptible garments under which they are hidden. As for the physical objects themselves, they might be very different from anything we actually perceive with our senses. We have already seen that Descartes and Eddington agree on this point.

TWO THEORIES OF PERCEPTION

direct realist theory of perception: A theory of perception that says we directly—without intermediaries—perceive ordinary physical objects that exist independently of our perception of them.

representational theory of perception: The theory that we can only directly perceive mental representations, or sense-data, of physical objects—representations that cannot exist apart from our awareness of them.

sense-data: The hypothetical mental representations of objects that some philosophers believe we are directly aware of in perceptual experience. According to defenders of the representational theory of perception, sense-data are the directly perceived intermediaries between us and the unperceived external world.

Descartes' theory of perception was one predecessor to a theory that plays an important role in thinking about perception to this day. The best way to understand it is by contrast to the common sense idea that we perceive ordinary physical objects that exist independently of our perception of them. This is the **direct realist theory of perception**. It is also sometimes called the *naive realist theory of perception* to hint that it expresses the views of uninformed common sense. On this view we can see, smell, hear, taste, and feel just what common sense says we do—the tables, books, roses, trees, and many other physical objects around us. The alternative view, which we find in Descartes' thinking, is the **representational theory of perception**, which says that we directly perceive only mental representations of physical objects, and that the "external" objects that cause our experiences are known to us (if they are known at all) only indirectly by inference from perceived representations.

In the selection that follows, Bertrand Russell provides an explanation and defense of the representational theory of perception. In his terminology, the "representations" or "images" of which we are directly aware are called **sense-data**—that is, data given directly to us in sense experience.

"Appearance and Reality" (Bertrand Russell, 1912)[10]

In daily life, we assume as certain many things which, on a closer scrutiny, are found to be so full of apparent contradictions that only a great amount of thought enables us to know what it is that we really may believe. In the search for certainty, it is natural to begin with our present experiences, and in some sense, no doubt, knowledge is to be derived from them. But any statement as to what it is that our immediate experiences

[9] Thanks to the late Herman Tennessen for relating a version of this to me.

[10] From Russell, B. (1912). *The Problems of Philosophy*. Retrieved August 4, 2014, from http://www.gutenberg.org/cache/epub/5827/pg5827.txt

make us know is very likely to be wrong. It seems to me that I am now sitting in a chair, at a table of a certain shape, on which I see sheets of paper with writing or print. By turning my head I see out of the window buildings and clouds and the sun. I believe that the sun is about ninety-three million miles from the earth; that it is a hot globe many times bigger than the earth; that, owing to the earth's rotation, it rises every morning, and will continue to do so for an indefinite time in the future. I believe that, if any other normal person comes into my room, he will see the same chairs and tables and books and papers as I see, and that the table which I see is the same as the table which I feel pressing against my arm. All this seems to be so evident as to be hardly worth stating, except in answer to a man who doubts whether I know anything. Yet all this may be reasonably doubted, and all of it requires much careful discussion before we can be sure that we have stated it in a form that is wholly true.

To make our difficulties plain, let us concentrate attention on the table. To the eye it is oblong, brown and shiny, to the touch it is smooth and cool and hard; when I tap it, it gives out a wooden sound. Anyone else who sees and feels and hears the table will agree with this description, so that it might seem as if no difficulty would arise; but as soon as we try to be more precise our troubles begin. Although I believe that the table is 'really' of the same colour all over, the parts that reflect the light look much brighter than the other parts, and some parts look white because of reflected light. I know that, if I move, the parts that reflect the light will be different, so that the apparent distribution of colours on the table will change. It follows that if several people are looking at the table at the same moment, no two of them will see exactly the same distribution of colours, because no two can see it from exactly the same point of view, and any change in the point of view makes some change in the way the light is reflected.

For most practical purposes these differences are unimportant, but to the painter they are all-important: the painter has to unlearn the habit of thinking that things seem to have the colour which common sense says they 'really' have, and to learn the habit of seeing things as they appear. Here we have already the beginning of one of the distinctions that cause most trouble in philosophy—the distinction between 'appearance' and 'reality', between what things seem to be and what they are. The painter wants to know what things seem to be, the practical man and the philosopher want to know what they are; but the philosopher's wish to know this is stronger than the practical man's, and is more troubled by knowledge as to the difficulties of answering the question.

To return to the table. It is evident from what we have found, that there is no colour which pre-eminently appears to be *the* colour of the table, or even of any one particular part of the table—it appears to be of different colours from different points of view, and there is no reason for regarding some of these as more really its colour than others. And we know that even from a given point of view the colour will seem different by artificial light, or to a colour-blind man, or to a man wearing blue spectacles, while in the dark there will be no colour at all, though to touch and hearing the table will be unchanged. This colour is not something which is inherent in the table, but something depending upon the table and the spectator and the way the light falls on the table. When, in ordinary life, we speak of *the* colour of the table, we only mean the sort of colour which it will seem to have to a normal spectator from an ordinary point of view under usual conditions of light. But the other colours which appear under other conditions have just as good a right to be considered real; and therefore, to avoid favouritism, we are compelled to deny that, in itself, the table has any one particular colour.

The same thing applies to the texture. With the naked eye one can see the grain, but otherwise the table looks smooth and even. If we looked at it through a microscope, we should see roughnesses and hills and valleys, and all sorts of differences that are imperceptible to the naked eye. Which of these is the 'real' table? We are naturally tempted to say that what we see through the microscope is more real, but that in turn would be changed by a still more powerful microscope. If, then, we cannot trust what we see with the naked eye, why should we trust what we see through a microscope? Thus, again, the confidence in our senses with which we began deserts us.

The shape of the table is no better. We are all in the habit of judging as to the 'real' shapes of things, and we do this so unreflectingly that we come to think we actually see the real shapes. But, in fact, as we all have to learn if we try to draw, a given thing looks different in shape from every different point of view. If our table is 'really' rectangular, it will look, from almost all points of view, as if it had two acute angles and two obtuse angles. If opposite sides are parallel, they will look as if they converged to a point away from the spectator; if they are of equal length, they will look as if the nearer side were longer. All these things are not commonly noticed in looking at a table, because experience has taught us to construct the 'real' shape from the apparent shape, and the 'real' shape is what interests us as practical men. But the 'real' shape is not what we see; it is something inferred from what we see. And what we see is constantly changing in shape as we move about the room; so that here again the senses seem not to give us the truth about the table itself, but only about the appearance of the table.

Similar difficulties arise when we consider the sense of touch. It is true that the table always gives us a sensation of hardness, and we feel that it resists pressure. But the sensation we obtain depends upon how hard we press the table and also upon what part of the body we press with; thus the various sensations due to various pressures or various parts of the body cannot be supposed to reveal *directly* any definite property of the table, but at most to be *signs* of some property which perhaps *causes* all the sensations, but is not actually apparent in any of them. And the same applies still more obviously to the sounds which can be elicited by rapping the table.

Thus it becomes evident that the real table, if there is one, is not the same as what we immediately experience by sight or touch or hearing. The real table, if there is one, is not *immediately* known to us at all, but must be an inference from what is immediately known. Hence, two very difficult questions at once arise; namely, (1) Is there a real table at all? (2) If so, what sort of object can it be?

It will help us in considering these questions to have a few simple terms of which the meaning is definite and clear. Let us give the name of 'sense-data' to the things that are immediately known in sensation: such things as colours, sounds, smells, hardnesses, roughnesses, and so on. . . . It is plain that if we are to know anything about the table, it must be by means of the sense-data—brown colour, oblong shape, smoothness, etc.—which we associate with the table; but, for the reasons which have been given, we cannot say that the table is the sense-data, or even that the sense-data are directly properties of the table. Thus a problem arises as to the relation of the sense-data to the real table, supposing there is such a thing.

argument from the relativity of perception: An argument from the premise that objects of perception appear different to different observers to the conclusion that different observers perceive different things.

Russell subscribes to a version of the representational theory of perception. Several times in this selection, Russell repeats a version of the **argument from the relativity of perception**. The central idea in the argument is that what we each experience is always relative to, or dependent on, our condition and perspective, and this leads Russell and others to the conclusion that what we perceive are mental representations or sense-data. Since the argument from the relativity of perception is one of the key arguments on behalf of the representational theory, it will be examined more closely later. Referring to the table in his study, Russell employs the following example of the argument from the relativity of perception:

1. The apparent colour (or shape, or texture, etc.) of the table varies with the condition or perspective of the observer.
2. So, the directly perceived colour of the table varies with the condition or perspective of the observer.
3. Thus, what is perceived is not the real table, nor is it "something which is inherent in the table"—what we directly see is merely "appearance."

As for the real table, if we know it at all, it will be known only by inference from the appearances or sense-data we perceive. We will revisit this argument shortly, and consider challenges to it, but before doing so we should consider its consequences for our knowledge of the world.

SKEPTICISM ABOUT THE EXTERNAL WORLD

The representational theory of perception has been so widely and popularly held that it is easy to overlook the threat it poses to the possibility of knowledge about the world. The nature of that threat emerges clearly in Russell's continued development of his views about the role of perception in our knowledge of the world.

"The Existence of Matter" (Bertrand Russell, 1912)[11]

> The problem we have to consider is this: Granted that we are certain of our own sense-data, have we any reason for regarding them as signs of the existence of something else, which we can call the physical object? When we have enumerated all the sense-data which we should naturally regard as connected with the table, have we said all there is to say about the table, or is there still something else—something not a sense-datum, something which persists when we go out of the room? Common sense unhesitatingly answers that there is. What can be bought and sold and pushed about and have a cloth laid on it, and so on, cannot be a *mere* collection of sense-data. If the cloth completely hides the table, we shall derive no sense-data from the table, and therefore, if the table were merely sense-data, it would have ceased to exist, and the cloth would be suspended in empty air, resting, by a miracle, in the place where the table formerly was. This seems plainly absurd; but whoever wishes to become a philosopher must learn not to be frightened by absurdities.
>
> One great reason why it is felt that we must secure a physical object in addition to the sense-data, is that we want the same object for different people. When ten people are sitting round a dinner-table, it seems preposterous to maintain that they are not seeing the same tablecloth, the same knives and forks and spoons and glasses. But the sense-data are private to each separate person; what is immediately present to

[11] *Ibid.*

the sight of one is not immediately present to the sight of another: they all see things from slightly different points of view, and therefore see them slightly differently. Thus, if there are to be public neutral objects, which can be in some sense known to many different people, there must be something over and above the private and particular sense-data which appear to various people. What reason, then, have we for believing that there are such public neutral objects? . . .

Of course it is not by argument that we originally come by our belief in an independent external world. We find this belief ready in ourselves as soon as we begin to reflect: it is what may be called an *instinctive* belief. We should never have been led to question this belief but for the fact that, at any rate in the case of sight, it seems as if the sense-datum itself were instinctively believed to be the independent object, whereas argument shows that the object cannot be identical with the sense-datum. This discovery, however—which is not at all paradoxical in the case of taste and smell and sound, and only slightly so in the case of touch—leaves undiminished our instinctive belief that there *are* objects *corresponding* to our sense-data. Since this belief does not lead to any difficulties, but on the contrary tends to simplify and systematize our account of our experiences, there seems no good reason for rejecting it. We may therefore admit—though with a slight doubt derived from dreams—that the external world does really exist, and is not wholly dependent for its existence upon our continuing to perceive it.

The argument which has led us to this conclusion is doubtless less strong than we could wish, but it is typical of many philosophical arguments, and it is therefore worth while to consider briefly its general character and validity. All knowledge, we find, must be built up upon our instinctive beliefs, and if these are rejected, nothing is left. But among our instinctive beliefs some are much stronger than others, while many have, by habit and association, become entangled with other beliefs, not really instinctive, but falsely supposed to be part of what is believed instinctively.

Philosophy should show us the hierarchy of our instinctive beliefs, beginning with those we hold most strongly, and presenting each as much isolated and as free from irrelevant additions as possible. It should take care to show that, in the form in which they are finally set forth, our instinctive beliefs do not clash, but form a harmonious system. There can never be any reason for rejecting one instinctive belief except that it clashes with others; thus, if they are found to harmonize, the whole system becomes worthy of acceptance.

It is of course *possible* that all or any of our beliefs may be mistaken, and therefore all ought to be held with at least some slight element of doubt. But we cannot have *reason* to reject a belief except on the ground of some other belief. Hence, by organizing our instinctive beliefs and their consequences, by considering which among them is most possible, if necessary, to modify or abandon, we can arrive, on the basis of accepting as our sole data what we instinctively believe, at an orderly systematic organization of our knowledge, in which, though the *possibility* of error remains, its likelihood is diminished by the interrelation of the parts and by the critical scrutiny which has preceded acquiescence.

Russell notes that we "instinctively"—that is, pre-reflectively—believe that there are physical objects existing independent of us. After our "discovery," to which we are led by the argument from the relativity of perception—that we perceive only sense-data, our intuitive belief in the physical table persists. But if we can never perceive the table, what reason do we have for thinking that it—or any other physical object—exists independent of us? What justifies our pre-reflective belief in a world of physical objects?

Russell suggests, first, that our pre-reflective belief in an external world causes no difficulties. We *can* retain it until we are compelled, by argument or evidence, to give it up. Second, the belief that there is an external world "tends to simplify and systematize our account of our experiences." For example, the belief that there is an independent, physical table before us helps explain why you and I both have *similar* experiences—similar sense-data—when we look in the same direction. It also helps to explain why table-like sense-data recur when I turn to look back in this direction after looking away. In other words, there are persistent patterns or regularities in my experience, and those are explained by the *hypothesis* that my experiences are caused by some relatively stable physical objects that exist external to the mind.

Russell therefore thinks that our belief in a world of physical objects external to the mind is an intellectual *hypothesis* that is justified because it helps explain regularities in our experience that would otherwise be mysterious. We might reconstruct this sort of reasoning as follows:

1. There are persistent, observable regularities in our sense-data.
2. Those regularities are best explained by supposing, or hypothesizing, that our sense-data are caused by relatively stable objects that exist external to our minds.
3. Therefore, there are probably relatively stable objects that exist external to our minds.

Russell's reasoning for the existence of an external world is a form of *inductive reasoning* called **inference to the best explanation**. According to this kind of inductive reasoning, our belief in the existence of a world of physical objects external to our minds is justified because the existence of such a world would provide the best explanation of the patterns we observe in our experience. If Russell's reasoning is to be persuasive, he needs to convince us that the existence of mind-independent physical objects can explain the regularities we discover in our sense-data, but also that no alternative explanation will work as well or better. His argument requires, for example, that our experience is *not* better explained by the hypothesis that an evil genius is determined to deceive us, or by the hypothesis that we are experiencing a simulation created by machines that wish to enslave us, or by the hypothesis that nothing exists outside our minds but a dizzying high-velocity whirl of subatomic particles behaving in indeterminate ways.

inference to the best explanation: An inductive argument that reasons from the premise that some hypothesis provides the best explanation of some phenomena to the conclusion that the hypothesis is probably true. The strength of such inferences depends on the success of the hypothesis in explaining the phenomenon and on the lack of any better or equally good alternative explanation of the phenomenon.

Logic Box

Inference to the Best Explanation

In this inductive style of reasoning, one infers from the existence of some phenomena or data that is in need of an explanation, plus the premise that a particular hypothesis gives the best explanation of the phenomena, to the conclusion that the hypothesis is *probably* true. The hypothesis is only justified if it successfully explains the phenomenon and if no other hypothesis explains the phenomenon as well.

Example: The rabbit must have returned last night, since there is now a rabbit-sized hole under the garden fence and partially eaten carrots scattered around the garden.

It is worth emphasizing the enormous intellectual shift Russell's argument asks us to make. The argument places our belief in tables on the same epistemological level as our belief in subatomic particles: Belief in the existence of tables is an intellectual hypothesis to help us make sense of observable phenomena, but tables are no more observable than are neutrinos or quarks.

Behind the Veil

veil of perception: The idea that the external world is inaccessible to sense perception on the grounds that perceptual awareness can only be awareness of mental representations. Since it implies that no comparison can be made between our mental representations of objects and the objects themselves (to serve as a check on the accuracy of our representations), it is thought to be grounds for skepticism about the nature and existence of the external world.

As Descartes, Eddington, and Russell understood perception, all we can ever perceive are mental representations of physical objects; we never perceive the physical objects themselves. But some philosophers believe this has an immediate and startling consequence: If it is true that we can never perceive any physical objects external to our mental representations of them, then no *comparison* of our representations of objects with the objects themselves will ever be possible. Consequently, there can be no check on whether or our perceptual representations of external objects are *accurate*. The physical world then lies permanently hidden behind a **veil of perception**. The problem was noted earlier by John Locke, who included what Russell calls "sense-data" under the general heading of "ideas":

> It is evident the mind knows not things immediately, but only by the intervention of the ideas it has of them. Our knowledge, therefore is real only so far as there is a *conformity* between our ideas and the reality of things. But what shall be here the criterion? How shall the mind, when it perceives nothing but its own ideas, know that they agree with things themselves?[12]

Locke clearly sees that the representation theory of perception can lead to deep skeptical worries. If we subscribe to this theory, then observing things *more carefully* won't help us correct or improve our view of the physical world. The "external world" is hidden from us behind a veil of perception, and more careful or attentive observation will only show further details in the weave of the veil. No observations, however careful, can provide a glimpse of what lies on the other side of the veil. Therefore, we can never know if the external world actually resembles our mental representation of it.

Optimists, like Descartes, Russell, and Eddington, think we can make *inferences* from the sense-data we directly perceive and, with enough care and ingenuity, we might draw some valuable conclusions about the nature of reality. Eddington writes that "no one can deny that mind is the first and most direct thing in our experience, and all else is remote inference."[13] But to others this hope appears excessively optimistic, and they point out that our sense-data could, in principle, have a wide variety of causes—perhaps the cause is Descartes's evil genius. More important, the point of the veil of perception is that we can *never* check to see if we've got an accurate account of the external world, so even if

[12] Locke, J. (1690). *An Essay Concerning Human Understanding*, Volume Two, Book IV, Chapter IV, Section 3. Retrieved August 4, 2014, from http://www.gutenberg.org/cache/epub/10616/pg10616.html

[13] Eddington, A. S. (1928). *The Nature of the Physical World*. Retrieved on August 4, 2014, from http://www.gutenberg.ca/ebooks/eddingtona-physicalworld/eddingtona-physicalworld-01-h-dir/eddingtona-physicalworld-01-h.html

we do make inferences about the external causes of our experiences, we will never be able to directly determine if our inferences are correct.

The empiricist theory of knowledge and concepts says that all knowledge and ideas derive from perceptual experience; the representational theory of perception says that all perceptual experience is only awareness of mental images. Together, these theories appear to lead directly to the conclusion that all we can know are our own mental representations. Once we reach that conclusion, a world of independently existing physical objects might easily seem a pointless speculation. This is a difficult consequence to live with. If the representational theory of perception, when combined with empiricism, really does have this consequence, then perhaps we should look for alternatives to one or both of these theories. One way to recover knowledge of the external world might be to give up the empiricist theory of knowledge and to argue that we have, as Descartes thought, some innate ideas, or some knowledge based on reason alone. By supplementing our sensory experiences with the right innate ideas, perhaps we can find a way to piece together knowledge of the external world. This route to escape from the dire consequences outlined above gives up empiricism but retains the representational theory of perception.

A second possibility would be to show that the representational theory of perception is mistaken. We have already seen that one important argument for the theory of perception comes from the relativity of perception. If that argument is no good, then perhaps we can find a route back to direct realism, which puts us in direct perceptual contact with a world external to our minds. We might then hope to recover knowledge of independently existing tables and trees without having to give up empiricism. But what grounds are there for challenging the argument from the relativity of perception?

Revisiting the Relativity of Perception

If we could successfully challenge the argument from the relativity of perception, we might be able to undermine the argument against the direct realist theory of perception. And if we can do that, we might thereby recover solid grounds for belief in the world of physical objects.

The argument from the relativity of perception takes the following general form:

1. How things appear depends on the condition or perspective of the perceiver, which varies from one perceiver to another.
2. Therefore, what is directly perceived depends on the condition or perspective of the perceiver, so varies from one perceiver to another.
3. Therefore, what is directly perceived is in the mind of the perceiver—it is a mental representation, or a sense-datum.

Let us consider two objections to the argument.

Objection One The first movement of the argument reasons from the premise that *how things appear* depends on the observer, and varies from one observer to another, to the conclusion that *what is perceived* depends on the observer and varies from one observer to another. Is this good reasoning? That depends on what we mean by "what is perceived." One response to the argument from the relativity of perception claims that it relies on an ambiguity in the phrase "what is perceived." Consider an example.

Suppose you and I both look at a white rose, and it looks white to you, but it looks pink to me—because, naturally, I am on drugs. Russell takes this to show that *what we see* depends on the condition of the observer. But why are we required to say, as Russell does, that *we see different things*? An alternative—and more natural—description of the example is that *we see the same thing* (the rose) but *how it looks* (white or pink) differs from one observer to the other. How something looks might vary, depending on our condition or perspective, even if what we see is the same thing. Indeed, it is only if we see the same thing that *it*—the thing we both see—can look different: If you and I see different things, then there is no thing that looks different to both of us. Therefore, from the fact that something looks countless different ways, it does not follow that there are countless different things that are perceived. And if *how something looks* can vary without *what we see* varying, then (2) does not follow from (1).

Objection Two The conclusion (3) of the argument from the relativity of perception is that the real objects of perception are *in our minds*—they are "sense-data," "mental images," or "mental representations." How is this established? The inference from (2) to (3) supposes that if what is perceived depends upon the condition of the perceiver, and if it varies from one perceiver to another, then what is perceived exists *in* the perceiver's mind. But just because something varies in ways that depend on my condition does not show that it exists in my mind. The speed at which I walk varies with my condition—it depends on whether I am tired or feeling energetic. But it doesn't follow that the speed at which I walk is "in my mind." The inference from the first conclusion of the argument from the relativity of perception—that what is perceived depends on the condition of the perceiver—to the final conclusion—that what is perceived exists in the mind of the perceiver—is a ***non sequitur***: There is no connection between premise and conclusion to take us from one to the other.

***non sequitur*:** An argument that is invalid and for which there is no discernible connection between the premises and the conclusion.

Before we are fully persuaded by the argument from the relativity of perception, we will need to hear how its defenders would reply to these objections. Unless they have good responses, we should not let the argument convince us of the representational theory of perception. And if we are not convinced of the representational theory of perception, we cannot be led into the skeptical problems presented by the veil of perception.

Of course, this is only the beginning of the discussion. If the argument from relativity fails, there may still be other and better arguments for the representational theory of perception. Until we see those arguments, however, we should not be quick to give up

Logic Box

Non Sequitur

An argument is a *non sequitur* whenever the conclusion does not follow from the premises. Strictly speaking, this would make any invalid argument a *non sequitur*. However, the term is usually only employed to describe an invalid argument or inference in which *there is no apparent connection* between the premise(s) and the conclusion. Even in common fallacies, such as a fallacy of equivocation, there is *some apparent connection* between premises and conclusion that tempts the logically unwary to think they are good arguments. The term *non sequitur* should be saved for those arguments where no connection can be discerned.

the common sense or direct realist theory of perception. According to that theory, we can directly perceive the independently existing contents of our surrounding world. If we can directly perceive those things, then we may be in a good position to do what the veil of perception suggests is impossible: We may be able to test our theories of the world by looking to the world itself. If reality is not hopelessly lost behind an opaque veil of perceptions, then skepticism about the external world will not remain a serious threat to common sense.

CONCLUSION

The representational theory of perception leads thinkers like Descartes and Eddington to hold that there is a gap between the common sense world of our experience and the world that science tells us about. They treat the distinction between common sense and science as the distinction between views of the world that naively rely on the senses and more sophisticated views that hold sense experience to be always suspect. The direct realist view of perception maintains, however, that our senses put us in contact with the world itself rather than with subjective representations of it. On that view of perception the distinction between common sense and science is better understood through the contrast between our initial, and usually inattentive, observations and our more careful and refined observations. There is, on the direct realist view, no insurmountable obstacle—no veil—that cuts us off from the world or prevents us from turning to the world to test our theories about it.

The veil of perception threatens to produce skepticism about the nature and even the existence of a world of physical objects outside our minds. It does so by combining the empiricist thought that knowledge of the external world can only come from perception with the idea that perception only makes us aware of our own mental representations. Together these ideas open an epistemological gap between the mind and the world of physical objects.

This has further curious implications when we recall that our bodies are among the physical objects that lie on the far side of the veil of perception. It was *that* epistemological gap—between mind and body—that led Descartes to a problematic form of dualism. Both the representational theory of perception and the dualist theory of mind give rise to a contrast between the "inner" and "outer" lives of persons, and both theories give rise to deep problems for understanding our place in the world revealed by modern science.

Key Terms and Figures

Sir Arthur Eddington p. 228
argument from dreams p. 231
homunculus p. 236
direct realist theory of perception p. 240
representational theory of perception p. 240
sense-data p. 240
argument from the relativity of perception p. 242
inference to the best explanation p. 245
veil of perception p. 246
***non sequitur* p. 248**

Additional readings on the philosophy of perception and our knowledge of the external world

BonJour, L. (2013). Epistemological Problems of Perception. *The Stanford Encyclopedia of Philosophy*, Spring Edition. (Edward N. Zalta, Ed.). Available at http://plato.stanford.edu/archives/spr2013/entries/perception-episprob

Dancy, J. 1985). Theories of Perception. *Introduction to Contemporary Epistemology*. Oxford: Basil Blackwell Ltd.: 143–59.

Maclachlan, D. L. C. (1989). *Philosophy of Perception*. Englewood Cliffs, New Jersey: Prentice Hall.

O'Brien, D. (2006). Perception. *An Introduction to the Theory of Knowledge*. Cambridge: Polity Press: 36–49.

William, M. (2001). Experience and Reality. *Problems of Knowledge: A Critical Introduction to Epistemology*. Oxford: Oxford University Press: 201–210.

Chapter 12

Creators and Designers

Learning Objectives

- Compare and contrast the following views about the existence of God: theism, deism, fideism, atheism, and agnosticism.
- Explain what a *cosmological argument* is, and describe the logical form all cosmological arguments share.
- Outline four different cosmological arguments, including the moral argument, the first cause argument, the argument from contingency, and the argument from design.
- Describe at least two versions of the argument from design, including the fine-tuning argument.
- Summarize two or more objections to each of the four cosmological arguments, and try to formulate replies to those objections.

There are many aspects of the philosophy of religion worth exploring, but here and in the following chapters we will restrict ourselves to some common metaphysical debates about the existence of God and some central epistemological debates about the rationality of belief in God. Although there is much more to the philosophy of religion than these limited preoccupations, our purpose is only to extend our explorations in metaphysics and epistemology. Even from this narrow perspective, the philosophy of religion stimulates fruitful philosophical investigations into the nature of causes, explanations, natural laws, testimony, the relationship between metaphysical views and moral values, and questions about the relationships between our beliefs and our wishes.

The present chapter asks whether it is *rational* to believe that God exists. Since the rationality of belief in God is tied to the existence of good arguments or evidence for belief, this chapter considers one class of arguments for answering in the affirmative. (Chapter 13 is concerned with more direct experiential evidence for the existence of God.) The arguments examined in this chapter all point to observable "signs" or "indications" in the world, and then reason from the presence of those signs to the existence of a God who explains their presence. They are thus all versions of *cosmological arguments* for the existence of God. There are many arguments of this form, but our discussion is restricted to a few you are likely to have already encountered.

OPTIONS FOR BELIEF

We begin by distinguishing two closely related questions; only the second of these concerns us in this chapter:

Q1: Does God exist?

Q2: Is it reasonable (rational) to believe that God exists?

To see the difference between the questions, notice that one could answer them differently: Someone might believe God exists, but insist that her belief in God is not rational. This is a curious feature of arguments about the existence of God. In almost no other arena do we find some people who will admit—or even *insist*—that their beliefs are non-rational or irrational. The distinction between the questions helps us describe four distinct positions with respect to God's existence.

theist: Theism is belief in the existence of God.

deist: Deists hold that belief in God is rational and has a rational justification. Deists regard belief in God that depends on faith as a form of superstition.

fideist: Fideists reject the idea that belief in God can have a rational foundation or can be supported by evidence. Fideists think religious belief requires faith.

atheist: Atheists believe that God does not exist. Atheism requires *disbelief*, and should not be confused with simply *not believing* in God.

agnostic: Agnostics believe there is no adequate reason to either believe or disbelieve in the existence of God, so they abstain from both.

First, consider **theists**—those who answer *yes* to Q1; in other words, those who believe God does exist. Theists fall into two groups depending on how they answer Q2. Some hold that their belief can be given a rational justification. These persons, classified as **deists**, usually reject belief in God that depends on faith, revelation, prophecy, miracles, or dogma, since they think such things make otherwise respectable religious beliefs into superstitions and therefore unworthy of respect. Their theism rests on their conviction that it is perfectly rational to believe in God.[1] Still other theists—classified as **fideists**—reject the idea that it could be rational to believe in God. Fideists think belief in God requires faith, and they are usually critical of attempts to pursue religious truths armed only with reason.

On the other side of the debate are **atheists**—those who believe there is no God. It is important to remember that to qualify as an atheist, one must have the belief that God does not exist; it is not enough to abstain from taking any position. Finally, there are those who believe the only reasonable thing to do is abstain from taking any position on whether there is a God—these people are **agnostic**. Agnostics do not believe there is a God, nor do they believe that God does not exist. They abstain from both belief and disbelief: Since they think the evidence and arguments are inconclusive, they have no opinion on the issue of God's existence.

Our present concern is only with Q2: Is it *reasonable* to believe God exists? We are concerned, then, with the plausibility of deism. To keep things uncluttered, we will present the arguments as if we were concerned with a disagreement between deists and atheists, but it is useful to keep in mind that even fideists might agree with atheists' objections to deistic attempts to prove the existence of God. Before we can explore the question of whether it is reasonable to believe God exists, two matters are in need of clarification. First, what does "reasonable" or "rational" mean in this debate? Second, what do we mean by "God"?

We can be a little casual about the terms "reasonable" or "rational," so long as we insist that a belief is not rational merely because there is a *good explanation* for why someone would hold it. There are also good explanations for completely unreasonable

[1] The term *deist* has been used with other connotations than this definition indicates. We will restrict ourselves to the meaning given here.

beliefs. We will use "reasonable" or "rational" to mean that if it is *reasonable* to believe God exists, then

(i) There are good reasons (i.e., evidence and/or arguments) for believing God exists; and

(ii) There are not, on balance, stronger reasons for thinking God does not exist.

Answering Q2 then requires that we evaluate the arguments for or against the belief that God exists, that we determine whether there are any grounds for the belief, and that we determine whether any such grounds are outweighed by stronger grounds for believing that God does not exist.

What do we mean by "God"? What, that is, is the sort of being whose existence we are concerned with here? Given the wide range of beings that persons have referred to as a "God," there is no reason to suppose that all those who believe there is a God will believe in the same, or even similar, things. For example, if I worship the sun and believe the sun is a God, then it is extremely easy (but entirely uninteresting) to establish the existence of the God whom I worship—there is lots of evidence that the sun exists. There is simply no sensible way to address all the many varieties of theism in one fell swoop, so we will restrict our discussion to one important and widely held conception of what "God" refers to. After we have decided what sort of thing we are talking about, we can then usefully ask whether any being of *that sort* exists. But we should not assume that there are no other conceptions of what "God" is or might be.

For the purposes of our discussion, "God" is defined as *an all-powerful, all-knowing, all-good creator of everything*. In different terms: God is an *omnipotent, omniscient, omni-benevolent* creator of everything.[2] This definition of God refers to four attributes that are usually thought to belong uniquely to God; nothing else is thought to be either omnipotent, omniscient, omni-benevolent, or the creator of everything. As a result, if it can be established that there is a being with one or more of these four attributes, then it will at least be reasonable to think that being is God. The reason for considering this particular definition is that it has a long and lofty history, and it is widely thought to capture the core of the Christian, Jewish, and Muslim conceptions of God. All these religious traditions are monotheistic (i.e., the belief in a single God); we will not be considering any polytheistic (i.e., the belief in multiple gods) religious traditions.

With these clarifications in mind, our question whether it is rational to believe that God exists then becomes: Are there good arguments or evidence that make it more likely than not that an all-powerful, all-knowing, all-good creator of everything exists? We turn now to the most common form of argument for thinking that a God, defined in this way, exists.

THE LOGIC OF COSMOLOGICAL ARGUMENTS

cosmological argument: An argument for the existence of God that reasons from observable effects back to their causes, and tries to establish that certain existing effects had to have a divine cause.

A **cosmological argument** is an argument for the existence of God that *reasons from observable effects back to their causes*. Such arguments begin by locating some phenomenon, the effect (call it "E"), and arguing that from the fact that E exists, it follows that

[2] God is said to create *everything* even though He does not create everything directly. God is usually thought to create at least some things indirectly, by creating something else that becomes the cause of those things.

Logic Box

Modus Ponens

Modus ponens refers to a valid *form* of argument that can be distilled in the following template (where "P" and "Q" each represent statements):

If P, then Q
P
Therefore Q

Replacing "P" and "Q" with any statements whatsoever will result in a valid argument. For example, if in our template "P" is replaced by "Bullet holes exist" and "Q" is replaced by "Bullets exist," the result will be the valid argument in (1′)–(3′).

there must be a God to serve as the cause of E. Such arguments thus tend to focus on establishing the existence of God as *the creator*. There are many varieties of cosmological argument, but they all have the following form:

1. If E exists, then there is a God.
2. E does exist.
3. So, there is a God.

What is needed to construct a good, persuasive cosmological argument?

It is easy to see that cosmological arguments, at least in the very general form just outlined, are logically valid. Compare the general form of cosmological argument above to this argument:

1'. If bullet holes exist, then there are bullets.
2'. Bullet holes do exist.
3'. So, there are bullets.

modus ponens: The valid argument form: If P, then Q, and P, therefore Q. In *modus ponens* reasoning a *conditional* statement (if P, then Q) serves as one premise; a second premise *affirms* the *antecedent* portion (P) of the conditional statement, and the *consequence* portion (Q) of the conditional statement is the conclusion.

Both arguments share a single valid form that is so common that it has a name: ***modus ponens***. We should also note that the first premise in any argument of this form can be written in a few different ways without affecting the reasoning. Table 12.1 illustrates several ways of saying the same thing.

From the point of view of their logic, the statements in the right-hand column of Table 12.1 all say the same thing: that *bullets are necessary for bullet holes*. In any of these formulations, the statement says that if there are bullet holes there will be bullets, and if there are no bullets there will be no bullet holes. It will sometimes make a cosmological

Table 12.1 Some Equivalences

	General Form	Examples
A	If P, then Q	*If there are bullet holes, then there are bullets.*
B	P only if Q	*There are bullet holes only if there are bullets.*
C	Not P unless Q	*There are no bullet holes unless there are bullets.*

argument clearer if we use one of the alternative (B or C) expressions of the first premise. In any of these formulations of our first premise, the argument will have the form of *modus ponens*, and will be valid.

If the form of reasoning that cosmological arguments employ is valid, we only need to consider whether the premises of any version of the argument are acceptable. In particular, so that our argument does not commit the fallacy of *begging the question*, we should always make a point of asking: Could the premises of a particular cosmological argument be *acceptable to an atheist?* After all, that is the person to whom the argument is addressed, and whom the argument is designed to persuade. How can we ensure this and *still be fair to theists?*

First, no such argument will be persuasive unless it employs some "E" in the second premise ("E does exist") that *both theists and atheists* can be expected to agree exists. For example, the following might be a *valid* argument, but is unlikely to persuade anyone who does not already accept the conclusion:

1". *Angels* can exist only if there is a God.

2". *Angels* do exist.

3". So, there is a God.

Any atheist worth her salt will almost certainly deny the second premise (although she might accept the first premise). If the theist is to turn this into a persuasive argument, she will need to provide grounds for believing the second premise. However, establishing the existence of angels might be just as difficult as establishing the existence of God.

Second, no cosmological argument will be persuasive unless a plausible case can be made for saying that the "E" will not exist *unless there is a God.* This is where the deist has her work cut out for her: She must locate something (i.e., some observable phenomenon, E) that not only obviously exists but that requires God in order to exist. Unsurprisingly, then, most of the work in proving the existence of God *via* a cosmological argument goes into defending the first premise. The difficulty faced by the theist is that she must find something that the atheist will agree exists, but for which we cannot provide an alternative but non-theistic explanation. Thus, if there are plausible alternative explanations of, for example, the existence of angels, then the theist cannot persuasively use the existence of angels to argue for the existence of God.

We have characterized cosmological arguments as a valid form of *deductive* argument. However, there is another form that cosmological arguments sometimes take: They can be *inferences to the best explanation*, and therefore *inductive* arguments. Thus, the following is also a cosmological argument:

1. E is *best explained* as something created by God.
2. E exists.
3. Therefore, there *probably* is a God.

Even though the premises of these inductive versions of cosmological arguments cannot *guarantee* there is a God, they make His existence probable—that is, more likely than not. So if the premises of arguments having this form are true, then we are justified in believing there is a God.

We will look at four cosmological arguments, all of which have been repeated for many centuries. Some version of each is probably already familiar to you: the moral argument, the first cause argument, the argument from contingency, and the argument from design. Even if they are familiar, you should make the effort to think them through further than you already have.

THE MORAL ARGUMENT

moral argument: A cosmological argument for the existence of God that claims there can be no moral values unless there is a God to provide and enforce them.

The **moral argument** is a version of the cosmological argument, which claims that the existence of morality provides us with reason to believe that God exists. Consider the following formulation of the moral argument:

1. Morality, or the difference between right and wrong, can exist only if there is a God.
2. Morality does exist.
3. So, there is a God.

A common theistic view of morality is that it consists in a set of rules or commandments for conduct, and God is needed to lay down the rules that morality requires us to follow, and also to enforce the rules by handing out rewards for obedience and punishments for disobedience. On this view, nothing would be morally right or wrong unless there were a God. Since the general form of argument is valid, we need only concern ourselves with whether the premises are true.

Some atheists have denied the second premise, and so have denied that there really is any difference between right and wrong. A character in the Fyodor Dostoyevsky novel *The Brothers Karamazov* famously says that if there is no God, then anything is permitted.[3] This suggests that he accepts the first premise of the moral argument. A committed atheist who also accepts the first premise should draw the conclusion that, since morality depends on God, and there is no God, then there is no morality ("anything is permitted"). She would therefore be led to deny the second premise of the moral argument. However, it is highly unlikely that any dyed-in-the-wool atheist would accept the first premise. Consider three criticisms of the first premise.

First, it is relatively easy to supply sources other than God for morality. For example, some people hold that morality consists of a set of tacit, or unspoken, agreements or contracts devised and voluntarily entered into by human beings in order to increase their individual prospects of happiness or decrease their prospects for misery. We don't need an omniscient God to tell us that stealing and murder are wrong—we can see for ourselves that they create suffering and impede happiness, and we understand that we could ourselves become victims of theft or murder if we do not agree to rules that forbid such behaviour. We need only a bit of common sense and a modicum of self-interest to see the need to devise moral rules and principles forbidding such practices.

Second, critics of the first premise might point out that even if we accepted that moral chaos would ensue if people did not believe in God—because then "anything is permitted"—this would not show that morality depends on God. It would only show that morality depends on *widespread belief* in God. But a *false* belief will serve just as well: The myth of a vengeful God could suffice to keep us in line even if there were no God. If we

[3] For clear expression of this idea, see Dostoyevsky, F. (1880). *The Brothers Karamazov*. Part One, Book II, Chapter VI, and also Part Four, Book XI, Chapter IV. Available at http://www.gutenberg.org/files/28054/28054-0.txt. We will hear more from Dostoyevsky in a later chapter.

wanted to promote good behaviour and discourage bad behaviour, we might tell people there is a God who will punish or reward them for their behaviour. But there doesn't actually have to be a God for this to work. After all, parents successfully regulate the behaviour of their children by reminding them that Santa is not generous to children who misbehave. On this view, morality does not depend on there being a God, but only on getting people to *believe* there is a God.

Third, in a far more subtle manoeuver, eighteenth-century philosopher **Immanuel Kant** (1724–1804) argued that if we have the belief that morality depends on God, that will *make morality impossible*. Kant is the greatest philosophical representative of the period in European history some refer to as the *Enlightenment*. When asked what "enlightenment" means, Kant replied:

Immanuel Kant: German philosopher who wrote important works on epistemology, metaphysics, ethics, and aesthetics. Kant was the greatest philosophical representative of the *Enlightenment* period in European history; he argued that the view that morality depends on God's rewards and punishments is a reflection of moral immaturity.

> *Enlightenment is the human being's emergence from his self-incurred minority* [immaturity]. *Minority* is inability to make use of one's own understanding without direction from another. This minority is *self-incurred* when its cause lies not in lack of understanding but in lack of resolution and courage to use it without direction from another. *Sapere aude!* ["Dare to be wise"!] Have courage to make use of your *own* understanding! is thus the motto of the enlightenment.[4]

His idea was that Europeans were just beginning to emerge from a stage of self-imposed immaturity—they had the ability to understand, but they were only very slowly acquiring the courage to use that ability. Kant's claim is that if we believe God is needed for morality, our belief makes it impossible for us to be moral. He sees this as a reflection of his contrast between maturity and immaturity. Kant writes,

> Suppose we were to attain to scientific knowledge of God's existence . . . all our morality would break down. In his every action, man would represent God to himself as rewarder or avenger. This image would force itself on his soul, and his hope for reward and fear of punishment would take the place of moral motives.[5]

Kant proposes that belief in a God who hands out rewards and punishments for our actions would render us incapable of doing something *simply because it is the morally right thing to do*. Instead, we would act in order to collect rewards or escape punishments. But persons who need external rewards and punishments to regulate their behaviour are, from a moral point of view, immature. We can all understand the difference, in degree of moral maturity, between someone who refrains from stealing your money or killing you *because it is wrong* and someone whose only reason for refraining is *a fear of getting caught and punished*. Kant believes the latter person lacks any mature understanding of morality, and so is incapable of genuinely moral action. Rather than accept that morality depends on God or on belief in God, Kant argues that belief in a God who regulates our behaviour by meting out rewards and punishments makes it impossible for us to do the right things for the right reasons.

---

[4] From Kant, I. (1784). *An answer to the question: What is Enlightenment?*. In Mary J. Gregory (Trans. & Ed.). (1999). *Practical Philosophy*. Cambridge: Cambridge University Press: 17.

[5] From Kant, I. (1986). *Lectures on Philosophical Theology*. (Allen Wood & Gertrude M. Clark, Trans.). Cornell University Press: 40.

Although, as we have seen, it is possible to reject the second premise of the moral argument, it is not necessary to do so. In light of the three considerations just raised, an atheist is not likely to find the crucial first premise plausible. As the moral argument illustrates, it is usually the first premise of a cosmological argument that presents the most scope for critics to raise objections. We turn next to a famous and purely metaphysical version of a cosmological argument.

THE FIRST CAUSE ARGUMENT

The first cause argument has ancient roots, and versions of it can be found in the works of medieval Christian philosophers, Jewish philosophers (e.g., Moses Maimonides), and Muslim philosophers (e.g., Al-Ghazali). The version we will examine here comes from the Catholic theologian and philosopher **St. Thomas Aquinas** (1225–1274).

St. Thomas Aquinas: A Dominican friar and philosopher, Aquinas is the most important and influential theologian of the Catholic Church. Aquinas produced an extensive synthesis of Aristotle's philosophy and Christian doctrine.

Aquinas attempted a series of five proofs for the existence of God, including a famous version of the first cause argument. Each of his proofs is worth close examination. Versions of his third proof, the argument from contingency, and his fourth proof, the argument from design, were further developed by later thinkers. We will encounter those shortly. As you read Aquinas's five proofs, consider whether the fourth proof seems familiar.[6]

Five Ways to Know God (Thomas Aquinas, c.1266)[7]

> . . . The existence of God can be proved in five ways.
>
> The first and more manifest way is the argument from motion. It is certain, and evident to our senses, that in the world some things are in motion. Now whatever is in motion is put in motion by another, for nothing can be in motion except it is in potentiality to that towards which it is in motion; whereas a thing moves inasmuch as it is in act. For motion is nothing else than the reduction of something from potentiality to actuality. But nothing can be reduced from potentiality to actuality, except by something in a state of actuality. Thus that which is actually hot, as fire, makes wood, which is potentially hot, to be actually hot, and thereby moves and changes it. Now it is not possible that the same thing should be at once in actuality and potentiality in the same respect, but only in different respects. For what is actually hot cannot simultaneously be potentially hot; but it is simultaneously potentially cold. It is therefore impossible that in the same respect and in the same way a thing should be both mover and moved, i.e. that it should move itself. Therefore, whatever is in motion must be put in motion by another. If that by which it is put in motion be itself put in motion, then this also must needs be put in motion by another, and that by another again. But this cannot go on to infinity, because then there would be no first mover, and, consequently, no other mover; seeing that subsequent movers move only inasmuch as they are put in motion by the first mover; as the staff moves only because it is put in motion by the hand. Therefore it is necessary to arrive at a first mover, put in motion by no other; and this everyone understands to be God.

[6] Hint: Compare Plato's argument for the reality of Forms in Chapter 2.

[7] Aquinas, St. Thomas. (n.d.). *Summa Theologica*. Part I, Question Two. (Fathers of the English Dominican Province, Trans.). Retrieved August 8, 2014, from http://www.gutenberg.org/cache/epub/17611/pg17611.txt

The second way is from the nature of the efficient cause. In the world of sense we find there is an order of efficient causes. There is no case known (neither is it, indeed, possible) in which a thing is found to be the efficient cause of itself; for so it would be prior to itself, which is impossible. Now in efficient causes it is not possible to go on to infinity, because in all efficient causes following in order, the first is the cause of the intermediate cause, and the intermediate is the cause of the ultimate cause, whether the intermediate cause be several, or only one. Now to take away the cause is to take away the effect. Therefore, if there be no first cause among efficient causes, there will be no ultimate, nor any intermediate cause. But if in efficient causes it is possible to go on to infinity, there will be no first efficient cause, neither will there be an ultimate effect, nor any intermediate efficient causes; all of which is plainly false. Therefore it is necessary to admit a first efficient cause, to which everyone gives the name of God.

The third way is taken from possibility and necessity, and runs thus. We find in nature things that are possible to be and not to be, since they are found to be generated, and to corrupt, and consequently, they are possible to be and not to be. But it is impossible for these always to exist, for that which is possible not to be at some time is not. Therefore, if everything is possible not to be, then at one time there could have been nothing in existence. Now if this were true, even now there would be nothing in existence, because that which does not exist only begins to exist by something already existing. Therefore, if at one time nothing was in existence, it would have been impossible for anything to have begun to exist; and thus even now nothing would be in existence—which is absurd. Therefore, not all beings are merely possible, but there must exist something the existence of which is necessary. But every necessary thing either has its necessity caused by another, or not. Now it is impossible to go on to infinity in necessary things which have their necessity caused by another, as has been already proved in regard to efficient causes. Therefore we cannot but postulate the existence of some being having of itself its own necessity, and not receiving it from another, but rather causing in others their necessity. This all men speak of as God.

The fourth way is taken from the gradation to be found in things. Among beings there are some more and some less good, true, noble and the like. But *more* and *less* are predicated of different things, according as they resemble in their different ways something which is the maximum, as a thing is said to be hotter according as it more nearly resembles that which is hottest; so that there is something which is truest, something best, something noblest and, consequently, something which is uttermost being; for those things that are greatest in truth are greatest in being, as it is written in *Metaph.* ii [Aristotle]. Now the maximum in any genus is the cause of all in that genus; as fire, which is the maximum heat, is the cause of all hot things. Therefore there must also be something which is to all beings the cause of their being, goodness, and every other perfection; and this we call God.

The fifth way is taken from the governance of the world. We see that things which lack intelligence, such as natural bodies, act for an end, and this is evident from their acting always, or nearly always, in the same way, so as to obtain the best result. Hence it is plain that not fortuitously, but designedly, do they achieve their end. Now whatever lacks intelligence cannot move towards an end, unless it be directed by some being endowed with knowledge and intelligence; as the arrow is shot to its mark by the archer. Therefore some intelligent being exists by whom all natural things are directed to their end; and this being we call God.

In his second proof, Aquinas speaks of "efficient causes." By this, he means pretty much what we mean by "cause" today. To give the efficient *cause* of something is to give what we now call a causal explanation of it. Using our general form for cosmological arguments, Aquinas's first cause argument would look like this:

1. *Cause and effect* can exist only if there is a God.
2. *Cause and effect* do exist.
3. So, there is a God.

The second premise ought to be acceptable to theists and atheists alike. But why should an atheist find the first premise plausible? An independent argument is needed to support it, which is what Aquinas tries to provide.

first cause argument: A cosmological argument for the existence of God that claims there could be no cause and effect unless there is an uncaused cause (i.e., a "first" cause) at the beginning of the chain of causes and effects.

Some have argued for the existence of a Creator by contending that everything must have a cause. But, they reason, since *everything* has a cause, each cause must also have a cause. These thoughts quickly lead to a series of prior causes and effects, stretching to infinity. And that, they say, is impossible. They conclude that there must be a **first cause**—a cause that stands at the beginning of the chain of cause and effect, which itself has no cause. As we have just stated it, this argument has two serious problems. First, it begins with the premise that *everything* must have a cause. That premise, if it is true, requires that any candidate for the first cause will also have a cause, so it cannot actually be a *first* cause. Second, the argument flatly asserts that an infinite series of causes and effects is impossible. *Why* should anyone believe that? If we don't find this claim obvious, we need some reason for accepting it. That is just what Aquinas attempts.

If the series of causes is not infinite, then it must have a beginning. There are two ways this might happen. If we think that (i) *everything must have a cause*, but also that (ii) *the series of causes must have a beginning*, then we will need a *self-caused cause* at the beginning of the series. A self-caused event has a cause—namely, itself—so it satisfies our requirement that everything have a cause. But it also constitutes a *beginning* to the series of causes, so it prevents the series from being infinite. Aquinas finds this incoherent: A self-caused cause would need to exist prior to itself, just as a woman who gave birth to herself would need to already exist in order to bring herself into existence. And that is impossible. So if the series of causes is not infinite, there is only one metaphysical option: A first *uncaused cause* must stand at the beginning of the series. To establish that there is a first cause, all Aquinas needs to show is that the series of prior causes cannot be infinite. He attempts to do so with the following argument:

1. If there is an infinite series of causes and effects, then there will be no first cause in the series.
2. If there is no *first* cause in the series of causes, then there will be no *later* causes and effects in the series; and
3. If there were no *later* causes and effects in the series, there would be no causes and effects *now*.
4. But clearly there are causes and effects now.
5. Therefore, there cannot be an infinite series of causes.

Aquinas therefore thinks an infinite series of causes and effect is not possible: If the series were infinite, it would mean that the series of causes and effects does not have a beginning, and if it never began, it couldn't be going on now. However, we can clearly see it *is* going on now.

A helpful way to understand Aquinas's argument might be this: When we reflect on the obvious fact that we find causes for things going on around us, it is natural to ask whether everything has a cause. If *everything* has a cause, then we are threatened with the prospect of an infinite regress of prior causes. (And then there would be no "Creator," since any purported Creator would also have a cause and, therefore, would not really be *the* Creator.) However, the preceding argument shows that the series of prior causes cannot be infinite—it must have a beginning. If the series of causes and effects has a beginning, what could the beginning be? There are only two possibilities: Either it was something that caused itself, or it was something that had no cause at all. But since, Aquinas argues, nothing can cause itself, the only reasonable option is a first uncaused cause in the series. An uncaused cause at the beginning of the series of causes would be the cause of everything else—that is, it would be the Creator of everything.

An Objection to the First Cause Argument

As expressed above, Aquinas's attempt to show that there can be no infinite series of causes and effects is invalid. It relies on an ambiguity in its second premise, which says that if there is no *first* cause in the series of causes, then there will be no *later* causes and effects in the series. (Aquinas's own words were " . . . to take away the cause is to take away the effect. Therefore, if there be no first cause among efficient causes, there will be no ultimate, nor any intermediate cause."[8]) But this seems plainly false. Aquinas's reason for excluding an infinite series of causes and effects seems to be that an infinite series *has no beginning*; but if something has no beginning then *it never began*, and if it never began it wouldn't be underway now.

However, just because something has no beginning does not mean it can't be underway now. When we say that something never began, we can mean two different things: We might mean *it has always been going on*, or we might mean it *hasn't started yet*. But the reason an infinite series has no beginning isn't that it *hasn't started yet*; the reason an infinite series has no beginning is that it *has always been underway*—that's what is implied by *infinite*. And, of course, if it has always been underway, it can still be continuing now. So Aquinas's argument fails to show that the series of prior causes cannot be infinite.

Even if Aquinas's argument worked better than it does, it is worth noting that nothing in it suggests that there is only *one* thing that is uncaused. If uncaused causes are possible, nothing Aquinas says prevents multiple uncaused causes. If there are many uncaused causes, we aren't likely to think of God as a candidate for all of them.

THE ARGUMENT FROM CONTINGENCY

This next version of the cosmological argument may be the least familiar of the four we are considering, but you will likely recognize the question that motivates it: *Why is there anything at all?* or *Why is there something rather than nothing?* The **argument from contingency** asks why *anything at all* exists, and that seems a perfectly good question. After all,

argument from contingency: A cosmological argument that reasons that only the existence of God, understood as a necessary and self-explanatory being, explains why there is something rather than nothing.

[8] Aquinas, St. Thomas. (n.d.). *Summa Theologica*. Part I, Question Two. (Fathers of the English Dominican Province, Trans.). Retrieved August 8, 2014, from http://www.gutenberg.org/cache/epub/17611/pg17611.txt

things might have turned out differently, so that nothing existed. If this could have happened, there must be some reason, some explanation, for there being something rather than nothing. The argument from contingency says that God is the only possible explanation. We'll look at a version of the argument that was formulated by the eighteenth-century clergyman and philosopher **Samuel Clarke**. Two ideas will help us understand Clarke's argument.

Samuel Clarke: English philosopher and clergyman who developed sophisticated versions of several proofs for the existence of God, most famously his version of the *argument from contingency*.

First, Clarke makes use of a distinction between two types of beings or entities: dependent beings (or, as he elsewhere calls them, contingent beings) and independent beings (or necessary beings). **Contingent beings** are things that exist, but could have not existed—they didn't *have to* exist. For example, toothpicks and aardvarks exist, but events could have unfolded differently, and there could have been no toothpicks or aardvarks. These things don't have to exist, but they do anyway, so they are *contingent* beings. Each thing in the universe seems to be contingent: our sun exists, but there was no necessity that it exist. The same is true of maple trees and toenails: There could have been a universe without them. Are there any entities that are not contingent in this way? That is, are there any **necessary beings**—things that simply *had to* exist, or that *couldn't not exist*? The argument from contingency contends that there is at least one necessary being: God.

contingent beings: Things that exist, but don't *have to* exist; they might have not existed.

necessary beings: Things that could not fail to exist.

principle of sufficient reason: The principle that says there is always an adequate explanation for each thing that occurs.

Second, Clarke employs the **principle of sufficient reason**[9], which says there is an adequate explanation, whether known or unknown, for each thing that happens. We assume this principle whenever we set out looking for an explanation—if we didn't assume there was an explanation, we wouldn't bother looking for one. We have a good track record at finding explanations if we look long and hard enough, but we also recognize that there is an explanation for something that happens even when we can't find it. The principle of sufficient reason bars us from rejecting the question "Why are there toothpicks?" by simply saying that *there is no reason whatsoever*. According to the principle of sufficient reason, we can accept that an explanation has eluded us, but not that there is no explanation.

These two ideas are connected. Dependent or contingent beings don't have to exist—they could have not existed. Thus if they do exist, there must be some reason or explanation for that fact. The matter is quite different with independent or necessary beings, if there are any: If not existing is not an option for something—that is, if it simply *cannot not exist*—then we don't need an explanation for its existence. In short, the principle of sufficient reason applies to contingent beings but not to necessary beings. If we can show that something is a necessary being, we will have shown that no other explanation for its existence is needed—its existence is *self-explanatory*.

A Chain Suspended from Heaven (Samuel Clarke, 1704)[10]

Clarke's argument is challenging, but worth the trouble. We'll take it one piece at a time. Clarke begins by stating the conclusion he hopes to establish, and then provides the first step he wants us to take.

[9] This principle was formulated by G. W. Leibniz, who was also responsible for the principle of the indiscernibility of identicals, discussed in Chapter 6.

[10] Clarke, S. (1704). *A Discourse Concerning the Being and Attributes of God*. Retrieved on August 8, 2014, from http://www.ccel.org/ccel/clarke_s/being.iii.iii.html

> There has existed from eternity, some one unchangeable and independent being. For since something must needs have been from eternity, as has been already proved, and is granted on all hands, either there has always existed some one unchangeable and independent being, from which all other beings that are or ever were in the universe have received their original; or else there has been an infinite succession of changeable and dependent beings, produced one from another, in an endless progression, without any original cause at all. . . .

Clarke is relying here on something he argued earlier—that *something* must have always ("from eternity") existed. His rationale is that if there was a time at which there was nothing at all, then things could not have come into existence later without coming from nothing. But something cannot come from nothing. Therefore, something must always have existed.

The question Clarke now wants to answer is, What sorts of thing or things could have *always existed?* One possibility is that there might be an endless succession of beings, each of which depends for its existence on the things that came before it. In that case, each of the things in the endless succession could be explained by its predecessors in the succession. Then, when we ask the question *why do toothpicks, or aardvarks, exist?* we can always answer by pointing to prior things on which they depend. Now, could these sorts of things—dependent things—be *all* there is? Clarke thinks not:

> . . . But, if we consider such an infinite progression, as one entire endless series of dependent beings, it is plain this whole series of beings can have no cause from without, of its existence; because in it are supposed to be included all things that are or ever were in the universe: And it is plain it can have no reason within itself, of its existence; because no one being in this infinite succession is supposed to be self-existent or necessary, . . . but every one dependent on the foregoing: and where no part is necessary, it is manifest the whole cannot be necessary: . . . An infinite succession, therefore, of merely dependent beings, without any original independent cause, is a series of beings that has neither necessity, nor cause, nor any reason or ground at all of its existence, either within itself or from without . . . [11]

Suppose *everything* that exists is part of this endless succession of contingent or dependent beings. Then there is nothing left over to explain why the succession itself exists—that is, there is nothing to explain why there is something rather than nothing at all. After all, we can't explain why the endless succession exists by pointing to anything *outside* it, since we are supposing that everything is included within the succession. Nor can we explain why the endless succession exists by pointing to anything *contained within* it: Since those things are part of what we are trying to explain, they can't be used to do the explaining. Thus, Clarke thinks, the idea that everything that exists might belong to some endless chain, in which each thing is explained by prior things, merely evades the real question: Why does *anything at all* exist? This is a question about the existence of the entire succession of dependent beings. Why does *it* exist? Clarke provides an analogy from a "late able writer" to show why we cannot responsibly evade this important question:

[11] *Ibid.*

> To suppose an infinite succession of changeable and dependent beings produced one from another in an endless progression, without any original cause at all, is only a driving back from one step to another, and (as it were) removing out of sight, the question concerning the ground or reason of the existence of things. . . .
>
> This matter has been well illustrated by a late able writer.—"Suppose a chain hung down out of the heavens, from an unknown height; and, though every link of it gravitated toward the earth, and what it hung upon was not visible, yet it did not descend, but kept its situation: And, upon this, a question should arise, What supported or kept up this chain? Would it be a sufficient answer to say, that the first or lowest link hung upon the second, or that next above it; the second, or rather the first and second together, upon the third; and so on *in infinitum?* For, what holds up the whole? A chain of ten links, would fall down, unless something able to bear it hindered: One of twenty, if not stayed by something of a yet greater strength, in proportion to the increase of weight. And therefore one of infinite links, certainly; if not sustained by something infinitely strong, and capable to bear up an infinite weight: And thus it is in a chain of causes and effects, tending, or (as it were) gravitating, towards some end. The last, or lowest, depends, or, (as one may say) is suspended upon the cause above it. This, again, if it be not the first cause, is suspended, as an effect, upon something above it, &c. And if they should be infinite, unless (agreeably to what has been said) there is some cause, upon which all hang or depend, they would be but an infinite effect without an efficient [cause]: and to assert there is any such thing, would be as great an absurdity as to say, that a finite or little weight wants something to sustain it, but an infinite one (or the greatest) does not."—*The Religion of Nature Delineated.*[12]

According to the analogy, each contingent being in the universe is like a single link in a chain suspended from the sky. Although we can explain what holds up each link by pointing to the link directly above it, that leaves no explanation of what holds up the chain itself. Similarly, even if we can explain the existence of *each thing in the universe* by pointing to the several things that directly caused it, we still need an explanation of why there is any universe at all. What sort of explanation could possibly satisfy us?

> . . . Either there has always existed some one unchangeable and independent being, from which all other beings have received their original; or else there has been an infinite succession of changeable and dependent beings, produced one from another, in an endless progression, without any original cause at all. According to this latter supposition, there is nothing in the universe self-existent or necessarily-existing: and, if so, then it was originally equally possible, that from eternity there should never have existed any thing at all, as that there should from eternity have existed a succession of changeable and dependent beings: which being supposed, then, what is it that has from eternity determined such a succession of beings to exist, rather than that from eternity there should never have existed any thing at all? Necessity it was not; because it was equally possible, in this supposition, that they should not have existed at all. Chance is nothing but a mere word, without any signification: And other being it is supposed there was none, to determine the existence of these. Their existence, therefore, was deter-

[12] *Ibid.*

> mined by nothing; neither by any necessity in the nature of the things themselves, because it is supposed that none of them are self-existent; nor by any other being, because no other is supposed to exist. That is to say; of two equally possible things, (viz. whether any thing or nothing should from eternity have existed,) the one is determined, rather than the other, absolutely by nothing; which is an express contradiction.[13]

If all the things that make up the universe are contingent beings, then each of them might not have existed, so it is possible for no universe to have existed. If that is right, then there must be some explanation for why the universe does exist—this is required by the principle of sufficient reason. If there is nothing left *outside* the universe to explain it, and the existence of the universe cannot be explained by any of the beings *within* it, then the universe must be explained by something that is not part of the normal succession of dependent things. It must be created by something that is independent of other beings (and which has always existed).

> And, consequently, as before, there must on the contrary, of necessity, have existed, from eternity, some one immutable and independent being, which, what it is, remains in the next place to be inquired.[14]

As we saw earlier, an independent or necessary being is not in need of explanation—it cannot not exist, so there is nothing that needs to be explained when it does exist. It must, in some sense, be *self-explanatory*. In effect, the argument from contingency says that the universe of contingent things is itself a contingent thing, so it must depend for its existence on something that is *not* part of the contingent universe. But since the universe includes every contingent thing, there is nothing contingent left over to explain its existence. Therefore, the explanation of the universe as a whole must be a necessary or self-explanatory being. And, of course, God nicely fits this description.

Objections to Clarke's Argument

We will consider three criticisms of Clarke's argument. They point to an answer—a very different answer than Clarke gives—to our question about why there is something rather than nothing.

Objection One Clarke believes the universe is a contingent thing, so like all contingent things, it requires some explanation. Why does he believe the universe is contingent? He reasons that if each constituent of the universe is contingent—and, therefore, is in need of some explanation—then the universe itself is contingent—and, therefore, is in need of some explanation. This is clear when he writes, "[w]here no part is necessary, it is manifest the whole cannot be necessary."[15] In making this inference, Clarke commits the fallacy of composition.

---

[13] *Ibid.*
[14] *Ibid.*
[15] *Ibid.*

Logic Box

Fallacies of Composition and Division

Fallacy of Composition:

It is a fallacy to infer from the premise that (i) all the parts of a whole, or all the members of a group, have some characteristic, to the conclusion that (ii) the whole, or the group, also has that characteristic.

Example: "Since all the atoms making up this table are too small to see, it must be an illusion that we can see the table. After all, nothing visible can be composed entirely of invisible parts."

It helps to keep the fallacy of composition straight by seeing it together with its mirror image: the fallacy of division.

Fallacy of Division:

It is a fallacy to infer from the premise that (i) a whole, or a group, has some characteristic, to the conclusion that (ii) the parts of the whole, or the members of the group, also have that characteristic. This is the inverse of the fallacy of composition.

Example: "Human existence serves no purpose at all, so there is no purpose served by my going to class today."

fallacy of composition: The fallacy of inferring from the possession of a property by the parts or members to the possession of that property by the whole or group.

fallacy of division: The fallacy of inferring from the possession of a property by the whole or group to the possession of that property by the parts or members.

From the fact that each being in the universe is contingent, we cannot conclude that the universe itself is contingent. And if we have no reason for thinking that the universe as a whole is contingent, then we have no grounds for assuming there must be an explanation for its existence. In effect, the principle of sufficient reason may be a perfectly good principle to apply to each entity in the universe, but even if it is, we are not obliged to apply it to the entire collection of entities—that is, to the universe itself.

Objection Two If Clarke fails to establish that the universe as a whole is contingent, then the possibility remains that it is necessary. Notice that Clarke's conclusion holds that God is an independent, necessary, and self-explanatory being: That is why we do not need to look for any explanation of God. But if something can be self-explanatory, we need a reason to think *the universe as a whole* is not self-explanatory.

Objection Three Clarke's account suffers from *explanatory redundancy*. The principle of sufficient reason says that there is an adequate explanation for each thing in the universe. If that is so, an explanation of the universe—the collection of all things—would be superfluous. If there is a non-divine explanation for *each* thing in the universe, and the universe is everything there is, then there is *nothing left* for God to explain. Consider this example: There is an explanation for the fruit bowl (the potter made it), and another explanation for each piece of fruit in the bowl (each grew on a different tree). Then an explanation for *the whole bowl of fruit* has been given—there is nothing left to explain. This third objection, you might notice, is a rejection of Clarke's analogy of the chain suspended from the heavens. If the objection is right, then since we already have an adequate explanation for why each link stays up (i.e., the preceding link holds it up), there is no need for an explanation of why the whole chain stays up. If none of the links can fall, then the chain cannot fall.

So *why is there something rather than nothing?* If we accept that there are separate explanations for the various things that make up the universe (toothpicks, aardvarks, and maple trees each have their own explanations), then we already know why there is something rather than nothing—we know why there are toothpicks, aardvarks, and maple trees. By explaining the existence of those things, we will have explained why there is something rather than nothing. As you might expect, some philosophers might find this answer unsatisfactory—it seems awfully thin gruel to those who think our question hungers for something deeper and more substantial. But if we are content with our explanations of the many contingent things that make up the universe, then perhaps the great mystery is not why there is something rather than nothing, but only why we continue to ask the question to which we already know the answer.

DESIGN AND THE TELEOLOGICAL ARGUMENT

A final version of cosmological argument we will consider—the **argument from design** or, as it is also known, the **teleological argument**—is probably already familiar to you. This argument claims that there is intelligent design in nature, and concludes that nature must be the work of an intelligent designer. A classic example was formulated by eighteenth- and nineteenth-century British theologian and philosopher **William Paley** (1743–1805), but new forms of the argument continue to emerge. We will use Paley's formulation as our starting point.

argument from design (teleological argument): A cosmological argument that claims there is intelligent, purposive design in nature, and argues that only the existence of an intelligent designer can explain it.

William Paley: English philosopher and clergyman, best known for his formulation of the argument from design (employing the analogy of a watchmaker).

The Watchmaker (William Paley, 1802)[16]

> In crossing a heath, suppose I pitched my foot against a *stone*, and were asked how the stone came to be there, I might possibly answer, that, for any thing I knew to the contrary, it had lain there forever; nor would it, perhaps, be very easy to [show] the absurdity of this answer. But suppose I had found a *watch* upon the ground, and it should be inquired how the watch happened to be in that place, I should hardly think of the answer which I had before given – that, for any thing I knew, the watch might have always been there. Yet, why should not this answer serve for the watch, as well as for the stone? Why is it not as admissible in the second case, as in the first? For this reason, and for no other, viz. that, when we come to inspect the watch, we perceive (what we could not discover in the stone) that its several parts are framed and put together for a purpose . . . This mechanism being observed . . . the inference, we think, is inevitable; that the watch must have had a maker; that there must have existed, at some time and at some place or other, an artificer or artificers, who formed it for the purpose which we find it actually to answer; who comprehended its construction, and designed its use. . . .
>
> There cannot be design without a designer; contrivance without a contriver; order without choice; arrangement without any thing capable of arranging; subserviency and relation to a purpose, without that which could intend a purpose; means suitable to an end, and executing their office in accomplishing that end, without the end ever having been contemplated or the means accommodated to it. . . .
>
> The conclusion which the *first* examination of the watch, of its works, construction, and movement suggested, was, that it must have had, for the cause and author of that construction, an artificer, who understood its mechanism, and designed its use. . . . [E]very indication of contrivance, every manifestation of design, which existed in the

[16] William Paley, Natural Theology (Oxford University Press, Reprint Edition 2008). Reprinted by permission.

> watch, exists in the works of nature; with the difference, on the side of nature, of being greater and more, and that in a degree which exceeds all computation.

At the heart of Paley's reasoning is this simple inference:

1. Wherever there is intelligent purpose or design, there is an intelligent designer responsible for it.
2. Nature exhibits intelligent purpose or design.
3. So, there must be an intelligent designer responsible for nature.

Again, this is just one version of a cosmological argument. It is a *valid* form of reasoning, so we need to focus on the plausibility of the premises. Critics of the argument from design have denied one or both of the premises.

Consider the claim that there is *intelligent purpose* or *design* in nature. The initial difficulty this presents is that too much of what passes for *design* may just be in the eye of the beholder rather than in nature. One person's randomness may be another person's intricate pattern. So we need to clarify the idea of *design* if we expect the atheist to agree that there is design in nature. Without such clarification, it is too easy for the atheist to dismiss the second premise by saying, as David Hume did, that

> The whole [universe] presents nothing but the idea of a blind Nature, impregnated by a great vivifying principle, and pouring forth from her lap, without discernment or parental care, her maimed and abortive children![17]

Why should we prefer Paley's description of nature as exhibiting intelligent design to Hume's description of nature as a botched mess? We can attempt to clarify the *design* that some claim to see in nature in more ways than one, and each kind of design suggests a different variant of the teleological argument.

Small Designs

We might consider the many examples of *decorative* or *patterned* designs among objects in nature. Items can easily be found that exhibit order, regularities, or patterns. For example, crystals seem to grow in very precise arrangements; we find a curiously regular arrangement among the pebbles on a beach, where rows of larger stones are found closer to the water, with parallel rows of increasingly smaller stones as we move inland from the shoreline. But these are patterns or regularities that too easily submit to other explanations (e.g., the physical chemistry of substances that form crystals; the wave action on shorelines), so such "designs" will not need to invoke God in their explanation.

A second and better way of seeing design in nature might be to focus on what can seem quite remarkable: So many things appear to be constructed in order to achieve some particular result or to fulfill some definite purpose. (Hence the title *teleological argument*—*teleological* means "purposeful" or "goal directed.") For example, the eye seems ideally designed to achieve its purpose of vision; fish, which live in water, just happen to

[17] Hume, D. (1779). *Dialogues Concerning Natural Religion.* Retrieved on August 9, 2014, from http://www.gutenberg.org/cache/epub/4583/pg4583.txt

be ideally designed for swimming (if they were cubical, they would all starve to death).[18] This way of understanding design in nature—as *purposefulness*—confronts two serious challenges.

First, as Hume once said, "There are many inexplicable difficulties in the works of Nature."[19] His point is that the purposeful design, such as it is, of a great many things is far from perfect. Indeed, many things in nature are very poorly designed for the purposes they serve. We wouldn't need eyeglasses, or have so many lower-back problems, if our eyes or our lower backs had been better designed. In many cases, it is even plausible to think that things in nature are *poorly designed* for the jobs they do—we have very poor night vision even though the night holds many dangers for us. So whatever the explanation of the apparently purposive design in nature, it is such poor design that it does not justify our thinking that it is the work of an all-powerful and all-good Creator.

Second, the atheist can too easily provide *alternative* explanations of the purposive designs we discern in nature. If any plausible alternative is available, then God is not *needed* to explain the many designs in nature, and the first premise of the argument from design is false. That premise cannot be persuasive when there are other, even better, explanations for nature's apparently "purposive design." The most obvious and far reaching explanations of purposive design rely on Charles Darwin's *theory of natural selection*. Even Hume, 100 years before **Charles Darwin** developed his theory, saw the central point clearly. Hume discusses the surprise some people might feel upon learning about the process by which the wonderfully designed ships of their era came about:

Charles Darwin: English naturalist who developed the theory of natural selection; the theory is significant for, among *much* else, demonstrating how apparently purposive design emerges in organisms as an inevitable result of selective pressures.

> [W]hat surprise we must feel when we find him [the carpenter who built a ship] a stupid mechanic, who imitated others, and copied an art, which, through a long succession of ages, after multiplied trials, mistakes, corrections, deliberations, and controversies, had been gradually improving? Many worlds might have been botched and bungled, throughout an eternity, ere this system was struck out . . .[20]

In other words, a long and gradual process of copying, with minor modifications made to each new generation of copies, while discarding countless mistakes along the way, produces a result that looks as if it were the product of great intelligence.

That, of course, is also how natural selection explains the apparently purposive design of much that we see in nature: Some living things are better suited than others for surviving and reproducing in their environments. Those that are less well-suited fail to get "copied" as frequently as those that are more successful and, after many generations, those that remain appear very cleverly adapted to their environments. Along the way, many botched and bungled organisms are discarded.

The most spectacular instances of purposive design in nature show up in the ways that living things are wonderfully adapted to their environments, or in the ways that the

---

[18] Georg Lichtenberg writes of a man who "marveled at the fact that cats had two holes cut in their fur at precisely the spot where their eyes were." In G. C. Lichtenberg, The Wastebooks *The Waste Books*. (R. J. Hollingdale, Trans.) New York: *New York Review Books*, 2000: 113, G26.

[19] Hume, D. (1779). *Dialogues Concerning Natural Religion*. Retrieved on August 9, 2014, from http://www.gutenberg.org/cache/epub/4583/pg4583.txt

[20] *Ibid*.

parts of organisms are beautifully suited to perform their specific functions. However, the theory of evolution by natural selection has proven remarkably successful in explaining the emergence of such traits. Purposeful design in living things is the result of many blind and stupid steps, each taken without foresight or intelligence. Thus no justification for the first premise of the teleological argument can be found in the purposeful design of living organisms.

Large Designs

In response to these challenges to the argument from design, the deist may wish to broaden the scope of the "designs" that are appealed to in the argument. For example, the deist might point to the fact that nature *as a whole* seems to be strictly governed by laws: The laws of physics describe a kind of pattern, order, or design that runs through all things. The physical universe needn't exhibit law and order of this sort, but it does, so that must indicate intelligence at work.

To the claim that natural laws are themselves a sign of an intelligent designer, the atheist can make the following reply. The laws of physics come in more or less basic, or fundamental, forms, and the less basic laws are explained by the more basic laws, not by the operation of an intelligent designer. For example, the formation of crystals can be explained by the more basic (and more general) laws of chemical interactions, and these are in turn explained by the more basic (and more general) laws of quantum mechanics. If this strategy is to be useful for the deist, she will need to locate design in the most fundamental of physical laws. The problem, however, is that we know very little about those laws. The supposed design at the bottom of physical law so far eludes us. If there is any unexplained design or pattern in fundamental physics, we don't know what it is, so we can hardly use it to argue for the existence of a designer. Furthermore, even if we assume we will one day stumble upon the most fundamental laws, there is no reason to suppose they will display anything purposive or intelligent that calls for a designer.

In a similar vein, the deist might grant that although the theory of natural selection can explain how eyes come to be, natural selection is itself an extremely ingenious process, so its very operation shows great intelligence at work. Natural selection, it might be said, is God's wonderful design for producing the delightful diversity and purposefulness among living things. The problem with this strategy is that natural selection is such a poor choice of mechanisms that it cannot plausibly be attributed to an *intelligent* designer. Recall Hume's point about a designer who discards multiple botched attempts before arriving at a tolerable draft of things—this is exactly how natural selection operates. Natural selection not only discards generation after generation of attempts before producing eyes that can see the stars, it also produces cataracts, glaucoma, macular degeneration, and children who are born blind. These are only a few aspects of nature's "delightful diversity"; natural selection fails to produce helpful traits far more often than it succeeds. The designer of an evolutionary process that works in this way does not seem either beneficent or intelligent.[21]

---

[21] In a later chapter, we will consider the possibility that God might have deliberately chosen to create a world with a few blemishes.

These versions of the argument from design are not likely to persuade the atheist or agnostic that God exists. The arguments depend on there being *no better or equally good alternative explanation* of the natural order. As we have seen, however, there clearly are such alternatives. The argument also implies that there should be only perfect design—the sort of design for which an all-good, all-knowing, and all-powerful being might be responsible; instead we find deeply flawed designs throughout nature.

Fine-Tuning the Universe

The most recent version of the argument from design can be found in the idea that laws of nature have been very precisely "tuned" to make it possible for us to exist. Our best explanation of the operations of the physical world makes use of a relatively small number of basic physical forces and a somewhat larger number of basic physical particles. The different forces and particles have distinctive properties, or values, and each contributes something important to the operations of the physical world. For example, the weak and strong nuclear forces have very precise strengths that we can measure with tremendous accuracy, and various particles—protons, for example—have precisely measured masses.

A problem arises because of two facts: First, there is no apparent reason why the masses of protons or the strengths of nuclear forces must have the precise values they have. Although physical laws and theories incorporate these precise values in their formulations as mathematical constants, nothing in those theories explains *why* the universe has precisely *these* values and not some other values. Second, if those values were different by only the tiniest amount, the universe would be a very different place. In particular, if these fundamental values differed ever so slightly, stars, galaxies, planets, and the living things that inhabit them could never have come into existence. That we are even here to wonder about our existence depends on the *very unlikely coincidence* that each of these physical values is precisely set to make it possible for us to exist. The obvious explanation of this remarkable and unlikely coincidence is that fundamental physical values have been *preset*—in other words, the universe has been tuned—by an intelligent being who is interested in our existence and survival. And, naturally, God is a good candidate for this role. Distinguished philosopher of religion Alvin Plantinga summarizes this idea:

> It's as if there are a large number of dials that have to be tuned to within extremely narrow limits for life to be possible in our universe. It is extremely unlikely that this should happen by chance, but much more likely that this should happen if there is such a person as God.[22]

fine-tuning argument: A version of the argument from design that claims that fundamental physical constants can only have acquired the values needed to make the universe hospitable to intelligent life if those values were deliberately preset by an intelligent designer.

This version of the argument from design could only be formulated after we acquired a good understanding of physical laws and the fundamental properties those laws invoke. It may be that an even better understanding of physical laws is required before we can fully evaluate the argument.

Some critics point out that the **fine-tuning argument** relies crucially on the fact that our current physics contains *no explanation* of the particular values that fundamental

[22] Plantinga, A. (2007). The Dawkins Confusion; Naturalism ad absurdum. *Christianity Today*, March/April. Retrieved on August 9, 2014, from http://www.philvaz.com/apologetics/DawkinsGodDelusionPlantingaReview.pdf

particles and forces have. But that might be a temporary state of affairs. For all their phenomenal successes, our current physical theories are still incomplete, and we are not yet in possession of a Final Theory of the physical universe. The objection, then, is that the fine-tuning argument for the existence of God is *premature*—for all we can say at this stage of our knowledge, a Final Theory might yet explain the precise values of fundamental forces and particles. From the perspective of a complete physical theory, the "settings" of those fundamental values will no longer be an unlikely coincidence, but will be seen as the inevitable consequence of deeper underlying physical laws. According to this objection, the fine-tuning argument is another attempt to fill a temporary gap in our knowledge with the idea of God. In the past such uses of God were proven dismal failures as science proceeded to fill in the gaps. Whether this reply to the fine-tuning argument is adequate depends on whether a Final Theory is possible, and whether the laws of the Final Theory contain any significant unexplained physical values. If they do, we will still need to explain why *those* values are accurately tuned to favour the emergence of intelligent life.

A second objection challenges the claim that the current values for fundamental physical properties are *unlikely*. Theists contend that an intelligent designer has carefully tuned the universe only because it is very unlikely that fundamental physical properties needed for intelligent life could have arisen in any other way. But a universe friendly to human life is only improbable if we assume that the universe is not infinite in extent or duration. Consider that you will never get 20 heads in a row in any series of coin tosses. There is no physical law that *prevents* it from happening, but it is so unlikely that we can be sure it *will not* happen. It will not happen because your lifetime allows you only a relatively small and finite number of coin tosses. In an infinite series of tosses, 20 consecutive heads is *certain* to show up—even certain to show up an infinite number of times. Similarly, the odds that the fundamental physical properties would all be precisely tuned to allow for life are poor in a finite universe with only a finite number of opportunities for setting those values. If, however, the universe turns out to be infinite in extent and duration, and if the fundamental physical values can vary from one part of the universe to another, then the current values will inevitably show up. Even if the universe is not infinite, but is significantly more extensive than the observable portions we are familiar with, the odds may be reasonably good that some portion of the universe will be congenial to intelligent life. In that case, there is no need to invoke God to explain why the universe is tuned to our channel.

Consider the *multiverse* reply to the fine-tuning argument. Suppose there is a *huge* number of "pocket universes" that are physically isolated from one another. Suppose further that the fundamental physical values differ from one universe to another, so that different physical laws apply in different pocket universes. Then the great improbability of life-friendly physical laws will mean that in the *vast majority* of pocket universes, the physical laws will make it impossible for intelligent life to emerge. But it will also mean that in a *very few* universes, such as ours, the physical laws will allow life to emerge. Now, if the number of pocket universes is sufficiently large, then the probability of there being a universe that is congenial to humans is high. The multiverse response explains the existence of a human-friendly universe by supposing that there is an extremely large number of universes, each governed by different physical laws. No divine designer is then called for.

Whether there is a multitude of universes is something on which physicists are not in agreement. It would be highly suspicious for atheists to offer the suggestion that there is a vast number of universes if the *only* reason for the suggestion is that it rebuts the fine-tuning argument. In that case, the theists' argument would rest on *what we know* about the laws of physics, but the atheists' reply would rest on what appears to be only a *convenient speculation*. The multiverse response will not rest on a mere speculation only if there are already independent reasons for suspecting that there are many universes.[23]

[23] The theory of the multiverse and other similar theories have been proposed on independent grounds in both cosmology and quantum mechanics.

CONCLUSION

We have examined four cosmological arguments for the existence of God, and more than one variation of some of those. Despite important differences among them, they share a common form: Each argues that there exists something—morality, causation, design, or the universe itself—that could not exist unless there were a creator with the properties that only God is thought to have.

Some cosmological arguments may already be familiar, but you should now be able to formulate them more clearly, and you can better discern the challenges each will need to address. The objections to each formulation of the cosmological argument are designed to raise doubts about the rationality of belief in God. Of course, once again, this does not take us to the end of these topics, but only to a point from which you will need to think things through on your own.

Cosmological arguments maintain that God has left signs, traces, evidence, or clues in his creation, from which we can deduce his existence. Any knowledge of God's existence based on such arguments would be, at best, *indirect*—just as our knowledge of the deer in the woods is indirect if we can only deduce his presence from his spoor. However, there are some deists who think it is rational to believe in God because they, or others whose testimony they are justified in accepting, have had *direct* encounters with or direct experiences of God. We will examine such claims in Chapter 13.

Key terms and Figures

theist p. 252
deist p. 252
fideist p. 252
atheist p. 252
agnostic p. 252
cosmological argument p. 253
***modus ponens* p. 254**
moral argument p. 256
Immanuel Kant p. 257
St. Thomas Aquinas p. 258
first cause argument p. 260
argument from contingency p. 261
Samuel Clarke p. 262
contingent beings p. 262
necessary beings p. 262
principle of sufficient reason p. 262
fallacy of composition p. 266
fallacy of division p. 266
argument from design (teleological argument) p. 267
William Paley p. 267
Charles Darwin p. 269
fine-tuning argument p. 271

Additional readings about cosmological arguments

Davies, P. (2008). *The Goldilocks Dilemma: Why the Universe is Just Right for Life?* New York: Mariner Press.

Himma, K. E. (n.d.). Design Arguments for the Existence of God. (James Fieser, Ph.D., founder and general editor; Bradley Dowden, Ph.D., general editor). *Internet Encyclopedia of Philosophy*. Available at http://www.iep.utm.edu/design

Mackie, J. L. (1982). *The Miracle of Theism: Arguments for and Against the Existence of God*. Oxford: Clarendon Press.

Reichenbach, B. (2013). Cosmological Argument. *The Stanford Encyclopedia of Philosophy*, Spring Edition. (Edward N. Zalta, Ed.). Available at http://plato.stanford.edu/archives/spr2013/entries/cosmological-argument

Chapter 13

Religious Experience and Miraculous Events

Learning Objectives

- Explain the contrast between religious experiences and mystical experiences.
- Summarize some of the factors that are relevant to deciding when it is rational to accept testimony at face value.
- Explain how an event's likelihood is relevant to the strength of the justification that can be provided by testimony of the event.
- Apply general criteria for evaluating testimony to the special cases of religious experience and miracles.
- Outline the distinctions between "marvels" and miracles.
- Summarize Hume's famous objection to the rationality of accepting testimony concerning miracles.

In Chapter 12, we began our exploration of whether it is rational to believe in the existence of God by examining arguments based on observable phenomena in the world—signs or manifestations from which the existence of God can be rationally inferred. Such arguments are always *indirect*, in the sense that they draw inferences from observed effects to an unobserved cause or creator. This chapter explores more direct forms of justification, and our concerns are epistemological rather than metaphysical. Some theists hold that belief in God can be justified by direct experiences of God; still others believe it can be justified by experiences of miracles. Are they right?

At first glance, those who claim that the existence of God can be inferred from the occurrence of miracles appear to be offering another version of a cosmological argument—they point to some miraculous phenomenon, and argue that nothing less than God could have been responsible for it. But there are two significant differences between cosmological arguments and arguments based on miracles. First, cosmological arguments tend to claim that the existence of God can be inferred from the presence of something in nature, such as causation or design, or something that is a normal part of everyone's experience of the world, such as morality. But if there are miracles they are *violations of nature's laws*, so they are anything but a normal part of our world. Unsurprisingly then, the central question is not whether it is reasonable to infer the existence of God from the occurrence of miracles, but whether it is reasonable to believe that there are miracles. Second, cosmological arguments reason from the existence of phenomena (e.g., design in nature, causation, morality, something rather than nothing) that are assumed to be available for all to observe. However, miracles are not events that everyone is presumed to witness—they are meant to be rare and unusual, and are observed by only very few. Much the same can be said about direct experiences of God. If there are any such experiences, very few people have them.

Since the experiential evidence—whether it consists in purported direct experience of the divine or an encounter with a miraculous event—is available to very few witnesses, the central epistemological question is whether we can be justified in taking those witnesses at their word. This chapter is therefore concerned with questions about the rationality of relying on the testimony of others.

RELIGIOUS EXPERIENCE

mystical experience: An experience typically characterized by those who have it as an experience of some "higher" or "ultimate" reality; such experiences are often described as experiences of "unity" with a higher being, or of the dissolution of boundaries between the self and other things.

religious experience: Not to be confused with mystical experiences, religious experiences are described by those who have them as direct experiential encounters with God.

We should be clear about the specific phenomenon we are concerned with when we talk about "religious experiences." Many people claim to have had **mystical experiences**, which they find it appropriate to describe as an experience of "the unity of all things," of "transcending the boundaries of the self," or of an "inner light" that "emanates" from all things. These experiences are certainly interesting, but they are not our present topic. Even atheists can and do have experiences they are prepared to describe in these and similar ways—that is, even atheists have mystical experiences. But an experience of "the unity of the self with all things" is not an experience of an all-knowing, all-powerful Creator.

Mystical experiences are distinct from **religious experiences**—experiences that are described by those who have them as *experiential encounters with, or of, God.* Those who have had religious experiences describe them by saying, for example, that they have *seen* God, perhaps in a vision, or that God has spoken directly to them—in which case, they have presumably *heard* God. Of course, atheists will want to deny that anyone could actually see God or hear God's voice, since they will say there is no God to be seen or heard. For this reason, we have characterized religious experiences as ones that are *described as* experiential encounters with God: Both theists and atheists can accept that there are experiences that are described in that way, even if they disagree about how to understand them or what conclusions can be drawn from them.

Some people have claimed to have experiential encounters with God, and there are some whose sincerity we have no reason to doubt. What needs to be explored is how we should *understand* such claims, and whether the experiences or the testimony of those who claim to have them can *justify* a belief that there is a God. It will be useful at the outset to distinguish two views about the justification that might be derived from religious experiences by asking two questions:

A. Does the *testimony* given by others of their religious experience give *us* (who have not shared the experience) reason to believe that there is a God?

testimony: Reports or claims based on first-hand experience that are offered as inductive evidence for others who have not themselves had the relevant experience.

This question asks about the reliability of the **testimony**—the claims or reports of those who purport to have had first-hand experiences. In particular, if we have not had the relevant experiences ourselves, can we regard other people as reliable witnesses to the existence of God and use their testimony to justify our belief? There is a second kind of justification we will also need to consider:

B. Are religious experiences a good reason for the *subjects* of the experiences—the persons who have them—to believe that there is a God?

Our second question asks whether, if we have religious experiences ourselves—experiences we are inclined to describe as encounters with God—we then have good reason to believe that there is a God. Even if it turns out that we cannot take the word of others, that does not mean we cannot trust our own experiences. I may have a good reason to believe that God exists even if I cannot provide you with a good reason to believe it.

Both of these questions can be asked about the religious experiences of **St. Teresa of Avila** (1515–1582). Her report of her experiences provides a useful case study for a number of the epistemological issues that arise in this chapter.

St. Teresa of Avila: A religious mystic, theologian, and Catholic reformer who founded numerous convents throughout Spain. Teresa was canonized, in part because her religious experiences were given credence by her followers.

The Visions of Teresa (St. Teresa)[1]

At the end of two years, during the whole of which time both other people and myself were continually praying for what I have described—that the Lord would either lead me by another way or make plain the truth: . . . I had the following experience. I was at prayer on a festival of the glorious Saint Peter when I saw Christ at my side—or, to put it better, I was conscious of Him, for neither with the eyes of the body nor those of the soul did I see anything. I thought He was quite close to me and I saw that it was He Who, as I thought, was speaking to me. Being completely ignorant that visions of this kind could occur, I was at first very much afraid, and did nothing but weep, though, as soon as He addressed a single word to me to reassure me, I became quiet again, . . .

Sorely troubled, I went at once to my confessor, to tell him about it. He asked me in what form I had seen Him. I told him that I had not seen Him at all. He then asked me how I knew it was Christ. I told him that I did not know how, but that I could not help realizing that He was beside me, and that I saw and felt this clearly; . . . I did nothing, in my efforts to make myself understood, but draw comparisons—though really, for describing this kind of vision, there is no comparison which is very much to the point, for it is one of the highest kinds of vision possible. . . .

. . . One day, when I was at prayer, the Lord was pleased to reveal to me nothing but His hands, the beauty of which was so great as to be indescribable. . . .

Of all impossibilities, the most impossible is that these true visions should be the work of the imagination. There is no way in which this could be so: by the mere beauty and whiteness of a single one of the hands which we are shown the imagination is completely transcended. In any case, there is no other way in which it would be possible for us to see in a moment things of which we have no recollection, which we have never thought of, and which, even in a long period of time, we could not invent with our imagination, because, as I have already said, they far transcend what we can comprehend on earth.

Explaining Conviction

Is Teresa's honest testimony *a reason for us to believe* there is a God? Is her experience *a reason for her to believe* there is a God? Answering these questions involves deciding whether religious experiences accurately present an independent or objective reality—that is,

---

[1] From Chapter XXVII. *The Life of Teresa of Jesus*. (E. A. Peters, Trans., 1960). Chapter XXVII. Retrieved August 9, 2014, from http://catholicfirst.com/thefaith/catholicclassics/stteresa/life/teresaofavila07.html#CHAPTER%20XXVII

veridical experience: An experience that accurately presents or represents an independent reality; an experience in which how things appear is how they actually are. Opposite of *non-veridical experience.*

non-veridical experience: An experience in which how things seem is not how they actually are; an experience that does not accurately present or represent reality. Opposite of *veridical experience.*

whether they are **veridical experiences**—or if they are merely illusions or delusions—that is, **non-veridical experiences**, or experiences that do not accurately present any independent reality. Many who have had religious experiences insist that they had such vivacity and power that it is impossible not to believe they are veridical. The intensity of religious experiences, signalled by the inability of those who have them to doubt what they see, is one of their common features. Thus, Teresa says, "Of all impossibilities, the most impossible is that these true visions should be the work of the imagination."[2] But this cannot resolve the issue of whether religious experiences are veridical, since many delusions have the same overwhelming power to compel the belief of the deluded person. Because the feeling of absolute conviction is common to both religious experiences and delusions, that feeling cannot be relied on to determine whether an experience is veridical or only a delusion.

Atheists cannot simply dismiss the testimony of persons who claim to have had experiences of God as mere delusions solely because they have *religious* experiences. To do so would be to *beg the question* against theism. If someone tells me she saw a unicorn, and I already know that there are no such things, then I am entitled to classify her testimony as mistaken. If she is sincere in her belief, then, assuming I already know there are no unicorns, I may be curious about the possible causes of her erroneous belief. Similarly, if *we already know* there is no God, then we are entitled to dismiss every sincere claim to have experienced God as error or delusion. But, in the present context, we cannot dismiss sincere claims to have experienced God on *these* grounds, since that would require the prior assumption that there is no God. But that is precisely what is now in question.

Sigmund Freud: Famous Austrian psychologist, the founder of psychoanalysis, and the inventor of the concept of the unconscious mind. Freud developed well-known accounts of dreams, delusions, and neuroses, and proposed psychoanalytic techniques for their analysis and treatment.

Sigmund Freud (1856–1939) famously said that people suffer from illusions that derive from or express their wishes. That is, he claimed that people sometimes have very powerful conscious or unconscious motiviations for believing they see things they don't. We sometimes cling passionately to a belief because it fulfills our wishes, or because it is an important source of comfort or security. Freud explained sincere accounts of religious experience and religious belief as the products of wish fulfillment. He wrote that

> . . . religious ideas . . . are illusions, fulfillments of the oldest, strongest and most urgent wishes of mankind. The secret of their strength lies in the strength of those wishes. . . .
>
> When I say these things are illusions, I must define the meaning of the word. An illusion is not the same thing as an error; nor is it necessarily an error. Aristotle's belief that vermin are developed out of dung (a belief to which ignorant people still cling) was an error; . . . On the other hand, it was an illusion of Columbus's that he had discovered a new sea-route to the Indies. The part played by his wish in this error is very clear. . . . What is characteristic of illusions is that they are derived from human wishes. . . . Thus we call a belief an illusion when a wish-fulfillment is a prominent factor in its motivation, and in so doing we disregard its relations to reality, just as the illusion itself sets no store by verification.[3]

illusion: Usually used to refer to any perceptual misrepresentation of reality, but also used (by Sigmund Freud) to refer to any beliefs or experiences, whether veridical or non-veridical, that are caused by our wishes rather than by evidence.

Notice that although he supposed religious beliefs are *irrational*, Freud did not say they are *false*. In this respect, Freud used the term **illusion** in a novel way. According to his usage,

---

[2] *Ibid.*

[3] From Freud, S. (1961). *The Future of an Illusion.* (James Strachey, Trans.) New York: W.W. Norton & Co. Inc.: 30–31.

if a belief is derived from wish fulfillment rather than from evidence, then it is "illusory"—*even though it might still be true*. Freud classified religious experiences as illusions because he believed they are caused by our desires for security and comfort. However, his confidence that all religious experiences are illusions motivated by wishes derived from his prior assumption that it is not reasonable to believe that God exists. In this context we cannot make that same assumption. A diagnosis of religious experience as *always* having a non-rational explanation would only be appropriate after it were established that it is not rational to believe in God. If religious experience is not to be trusted, then we need other, independent reasons for doubting it.

Even if it were true that we are strongly motivated to believe in God because we suffer from deep fears and insecurities, that would not be a good reason to think those beliefs are false. This is a point to which Freud's discussion is sensitive—he does not attempt to move from his idea that religious beliefs and experiences have irrational origins to the conclusion that such beliefs or experiences are false or non-veridical. Freud accepts that even a true belief might have unsavoury origins.

EVALUATING TESTIMONY

Testimony of religious experience poses an epistemological problem for the simple reason that we must all, atheists included, rely heavily on the testimony of others for much of our information about the world. This can be a precarious way to get by, but we could hardly do otherwise. Thankfully, others are often reliable witnesses who give honest reports of what they have observed. In many cases there is nothing wrong with relying on the testimony of others, but we also know that there are times when it is not reasonable to believe others. There are even times when we cannot trust our own experiences. Because we are content to rely on the testimony of others for so much else, we cannot abstain from belief in religious experiences or miracles merely on the grounds that we have not had such experiences ourselves. That principle, if we took it seriously, would eliminate a great many of our beliefs. So we need to look more closely at the factors that make it rational to accept the testimony of others on some occasions but rational to reject their testimony on others.

In many cases we rely on the testimony of others to inform us about things that we might, with some investment of time and trouble, have learned for ourselves. In such cases, if the truth of the information we receive second-hand is important to us, we can take the time and trouble to check it ourselves. We may be content to make use of the testimony of others, but we are not *dependent* on it. In special cases, where matters of great importance turn on the reliability and trustworthiness of those from who we receive our information, we have put in place institutions and practices designed to encourage truth-telling and to discourage misrepresentation. Thus, there are severe penalties for lying in a court of law, and the sciences rely on peer corroboration and review. Such mechanisms help discourage careless observation and insincere reports and thereby make it more reasonable to rely on the testimony of others. But in the unique sorts of cases that concern us here—the testimony of witnesses to God or miracles—we generally cannot independently check the truth of witnesses' reports, and so *we have nothing to go on but the testimony itself*. Under what circumstances are we justified in taking people at their word if there is no prospect of checking their claims?

There is no hard and fast rule for when it is reasonable to take the statements of others at face value. There are, however, some guidelines we all follow. Consider the following factors that most of us already take into account when deciding whether to believe the testimony of others:

1. *Is the witness morally trustworthy?* At a minimum, we take into account a person's reputation for honesty or dishonesty, and any known motive for misleading us. For example, when someone stands to profit from having us believe them, we don't usually take what they say at face value. Many people in sales have strong incentives to lie, so we seldom take them at their word.
2. *Does the witness have the needed perceptual abilities?* Are their senses in good working order, and are they using them in conditions in which they function reliably? When people are blind drunk, when the lighting is very poor, or when the event they claim to witness is very distant, we are rightly hesitant to rely on their testimony.
3. *Is the witness a competent judge of what she claims to see?* Normally, we want to know whether the witness has an adequate understanding of the things and events she reports. For example, if someone who has very little knowledge of scientific instruments claims to have seen a particle accelerator in the next room, we might want to ask whether she can tell a particle accelerator from a particle detector. Under the heading of competent judgment we might add considerations about the witness's degree of gullibility: Is the witness someone who is taken in by every simple card trick or slight of hand?
4. *How likely is the event our witness is testifying about?* The claim to have seen a grizzly bear roaming the streets at night carries more weight when reported in Banff than when reported in Miami, simply because the likelihood of a grizzly wandering into downtown Banff is considerably higher than the likelihood that one would find its way to Miami. Highly improbable events do sometimes happen, and they can be witnessed and accurately reported. But we ought to be, and are, more cautious about accepting reports of such events. When we evaluate someone's testimony along this dimension, we are not evaluating the testifier, but only the event to which she testifies. That distinguishes this factor from the others, all of which focus on traits of the testifier.

Our list of considerations is not complete—perhaps you can think of additional factors. But each of these considerations is *relevant* to determining the probability that a person's testimony is true, and so is relevant to determining the extent to which we would be justified in believing it. Scoring well on all these tests does not ensure true testimony, and failing to satisfy one or more of them does not show that the testimony is false. But the failure to satisfy any one of these conditions *greatly weakens the case for believing* a witness's testimony, and if their testimony fares poorly in enough of these ways, we are not justified in believing it.

Furthermore, our satisfaction with a particular piece of testimony when it is considered along any one of these dimensions will always be a matter of degree. One honest person may be more diligent about telling the truth than another honest person, and even though we both have good eyesight, yours might still be sharper than mine. So although none of these considerations is intended to be decisive, any of them can be relevant to our justification for believing or disbelieving testimony.

Evaluating Testimony about Religious Experience

Despite the qualifications we must place on the use of the four factors discussed above, they already reveal enough to help us appreciate the magnitude of the problem facing testimony about religious experience. It is usual in such cases that there can be no independent confirmation of what we are told. But, even worse, religious experiences are often connected to altered states of consciousness, induced by fasting, the ingestion of peyote, and so on. When these features are present, they will not show that the testimony is false, but they do tend to make acceptance of the testimony reckless, and it ceases to be reasonable to use such testimony to justify our beliefs. This is not to give special treatment to testimony about religious experiences—it is simply to apply the same standards we apply elsewhere, whenever we wonder whether to rely on the word of others. We should not relax our standards for testimony about religious experience.

There is a much deeper problem for testimony of religious experiences—that is, of experiences of God. When someone claims to have seen a grizzly bear, we know what questions to ask in order to determine if what they saw was really a bear, and if the bear was really a grizzly. When someone claims to have seen God, we generally do not know what questions to ask in order to determine if the witness is a *reliable judge* of what she saw. Did the being look all-powerful, all-knowing, and all-good? What does an all-knowing being look like? The problem with claims about religious experience is that we do not know enough to determine whether, or how well, experiences of God fulfill the requirements in conditions (2) and (3) above. Consider condition (2). What experiential conditions are optimal for experiencing God? Is it better at night or in broad daylight? If we want to be assured that what we experience is God, is it better to be straight and sober, better to fast for a week, or better to be high on peyote? Condition (3) is even harder to satisfy. Exactly what sort of knowledge or understanding of God must someone have in order to reliably *identify* what they have experienced as God? What, for example, does God look or sound like? If a voice spoke to you from a burning bush, could you really tell if it was the voice of God? If you think God can appear in any form He desires, then such testimony only becomes more problematic—if George can appear in any form he desires, we have no way of knowing whether the person stealing vegetables in the garden is George.

We cannot begin to evaluate someone's claim to have experienced God unless we ourselves have an adequate conception of how God would appear. But we have no such conception. The usual ways we have of distinguishing reliable testimony from unreliable testimony then appear to be unhelpful when applied to the testimony of those who claim to have witnessed God. In light of these considerations, it is unlikely that we can use the testimony of others who claim to have experienced God to justify our belief in the existence of God.

God's Penmanship

If we cannot regard the testimony of those who sincerely report experiences of God as strong reason to believe there is a God, how *should* we regard it? Should we dismiss all such people as delusional? We need not be so dismissive, for there may be other ways to appreciate what they are saying.

A man I knew some years ago claimed that God occasionally spoke to him. Skeptical but intrigued, I asked some rather obvious questions: In what language does God speak to him? (My acquaintance was fluent in both English and German.) What sort of voice does God have—a man's voice or a woman's voice? Is His voice deep or high pitched? Does God have an accent? Does He prefer the vocabulary of a medieval scholar, sprinkled with Latin phrases, or that of an uneducated person? Not surprisingly, my acquaintance brushed off such questions as simply *missing the point*. "God," he told me, "isn't like that." God didn't speak to him in a particular "language," and didn't use what we ordinarily think of as a "voice."

If we allow that our ways of describing our verbal communications with each other might not be the most appropriate way of describing God's communications, the right question to ask is, Why did my acquaintance say God *spoke* to him? Is "speaking" the right way to describe what God was doing? Recall Teresa's words: "I saw Christ at my side—or, to put it better, I was conscious of Him, for *neither with the eyes of the body nor those of the soul did I see anything*."[4] Although Teresa was at first tempted to describe her experience as *seeing* Christ, she immediately withdrew that characterization—she recognized that "seeing" wasn't the right word to describe her experience, since it had nothing to do with the use of her eyes.

To appreciate this line of questioning, compare my friend's case (or Teresa's) with this one: Suppose I tell you I occasionally receive letters from God: He *writes* to me. You are understandably skeptical, and ask to see one of the letters. You have lots of questions—Are His letters handwritten or typed? If handwritten, does He print or use cursive script? Suppose I respond that "He doesn't use the postal service, He doesn't use stamps, and He doesn't use paper or ink. Furthermore, He doesn't have what we normally think of as a style of 'penmanship,' and He doesn't write in any 'language.'" If you press the matter further, I will perhaps say, "His letters can't be read by others—they aren't *that sort* of letter." At some point, it should be clear that it is not *literally* true that God writes me letters; perhaps I was speaking in metaphors. Perhaps something is happening in my life that I can't find the means to express literally, and I think this metaphor best expresses my experience. Remember how Teresa evaluates her descriptions of her experiences: "I did nothing, in my efforts to make myself understood, but draw comparisons—though really, for describing this kind of vision, there is no comparison which is very much to the point . . ."[5] Teresa recognizes that she cannot be understood as *literally* having seen Christ, so she appears to view her own account as a woefully inadequate simile.

This problem often arises when people say they have had an experience of God. If we take their words literally, we are perhaps distorting or trivializing the experience for which they are struggling to find an expression. But if we don't take their words literally, we may have to conclude that we don't understand them well enough to evaluate them. This is not to suggest that what they say is *false*—we can't suspect someone of being mistaken if we aren't sure what they mean. It might be important to understand what people are attempting to express when they speak, in all sincerity, about "experiences of God." But to take them seriously is not the same as taking them to be reliable witnesses. It is an important fact that sincere people claim to have

---

[4] From Chapter XXVII. *The Life of Teresa of Jesus*. (E. A. Peters, Trans., 1960). Chapter XXVII. Retrieved August 9, 2014, from http://catholicfirst.com/thefaith/catholicclassics/stteresa/life/teresaofavila07.html#CHAPTER%20XXVII

[5] *Ibid*.

such experiences, and it might be useful to understand the phenomenon better. So far, however, we have found no way to use the experiences they describe as *evidence* for the existence of God.

Despite the initial obstacles to viewing religious experiences as veridical, British philosopher **C. D. Broad** (1887–1971) believes we are sometimes justified in believing the testimony of those who claim to have had religious experiences. He defends this conclusion with an ingenious *argument from analogy*.

C. D. Broad: British philosopher who did important work in the first half of the twentieth century on problems in the philosophy of science, epistemology, and ethics. He is known for his examination of claims made in psychic research and their relevance to epistemology and metaphysics.

Experiences of God (C. D. Broad, 1939)[6]

. . . The Argument from Design and the arguments from ethical premisses start from facts which are common to every one. But some people seem to be almost wholly devoid of any specifically religious experience; and among those who have it the differences of kind and degree are enormous. Founders of religions and saints, e.g., often claim to have been in direct contact with God, to have seen and spoken with Him, and so on. An ordinary religious man would certainly not make any such claim, though he might say that he had had experiences which assured him of the existence and presence of God. So the first thing that we have to notice is that capacity for religious experience is in certain respects like an ear for music. There are a few people who are unable to recognize and distinguish the simplest tune. But they are in a minority like the people who have absolutely no kind of religious experience. Most people have some slight appreciation of music. But the differences of degree in this respect are enormous, and those who have not much gift for music have to take the statements of accomplished musicians very largely on trust. Let us, then, compare tone-deaf persons to those who have no recognizable religious experience at all; the ordinary followers of a religion to men who have some taste for music but can neither appreciate the more difficult kinds nor compose; highly religious men and saints to persons with an exceptionally fine ear for music who may yet be unable to compose it; and the founders of religions to great musical composers, such as Bach and Beethoven.

This analogy is, of course, incomplete in certain important respects. . . . Granted that religious experience exists, that it has such-and-such a history and conditions, that it seems vitally important to those who have it, and that it produces all kinds of effects which would not otherwise happen, is it *veridical*? Are the claims to knowledge or well-founded belief about the nature of reality, which are an integral part of the experience, *true or probable*? . . .

Now I think it must be admitted that, if we compare and contrast the statements made by religious mystics of various times, races, and religions, we find a common nucleus combined with very great differences of detail. Of course the interpretations which they have put on their experiences are much more varied than the experiences themselves. It is obvious that the interpretations will depend in a large measure on the traditional religious beliefs in which various mystics have been brought up. I think that such traditions probably act in two different ways.

(i) The tradition no doubt affects the theoretical interpretation of experiences which would have taken place even if the mystic had been brought up in a different tradition. A feeling of unity with the rest of the universe will be interpreted very dif-

[6] Selection from "Arguments for the Existence of God", by C.D. Broad. In C. D. Broad, Religion, Philosophy and Psychical Research (Routledge & Keagan Paul, 1953), pp.156–67. [Originally published in the Journal of Theological Studies 40 (1939): 16–30]. Reprinted by permission.

ferently by a Christian who has been brought up to believe in a personal God and by a Hindu mystic who has been trained in a quite different metaphysical tradition.

(ii) The traditional beliefs, on the other hand, probably determine many of the details of the experience itself. A Roman Catholic mystic may have visions of the Virgin and the saints, whilst a Protestant mystic pretty certainly will not. . . .

Such explanations, however, plainly do not account for the first origin of religious beliefs, or for the features which are common to the religious experiences of persons of widely different times, races, and traditions.

Now, when we find that there are certain experiences which, though never very frequent in a high degree of intensity, have happened in a high degree among a few men at all times and places; and when we find that, in spite of differences in detail which we can explain, they involve certain fundamental conditions which are common and peculiar to them; two alternatives are open to us. (i) We may suppose that these men are in contact with an aspect of reality which is not revealed to ordinary persons in their everyday experience. And we may suppose that the characteristics which they agree in ascribing to reality on the basis of these experiences probably do belong to it. Or (ii) we may suppose that they are all subject to a delusion from which other men are free. . . .

. . . Let us now imagine a race of beings who can walk about and touch things but cannot see. Suppose that eventually a few of them developed the power of sight. All that they might tell their still blind friends about colour would be wholly unintelligible to and unverifiable by the latter. But they would also be able to tell their blind friends a great deal about what the latter would feel if they were to walk in certain directions. These statements would be verified. This would not, of course, *prove* to the blind ones that the unintelligible statements about colour correspond to certain aspects of the world which they cannot perceive. But it would [show] that the seeing persons had a source of additional information about matters which the blind ones could understand and test for themselves. It would not be unreasonable then for the blind ones to believe that probably the seeing ones are also able to perceive other aspects of reality which they are describing correctly when they make their unintelligible statements containing colour-names. The question then is whether it is reasonable to regard the agreement between the experiences of religious mystics as more like the agreement among trained microscopists about the minute structure of cells, or as more like the agreement among habitual drunkards about the infestation of their rooms by pink rats or snakes, or as more like the agreement about colours which the seeing men would express in their statements to the blind men. . . .

Is there any analogy between the facts about religious experience and the fable about the blind men some of whom gained the power of sight? It might be said that many ideals of conduct and ways of life, which we can all recognize now to be good and useful, have been introduced into human history by the founders of religions. These persons have made actual ethical discoveries which others can afterwards recognize to be true. It might be said that this is at least roughly analogous to the case of the seeing men telling the still blind men of facts which the latter could and did verify for themselves. And it might be said that this makes it reasonable for us to attach some weight to what founders of religions tell us about things which we cannot understand or verify for ourselves; just as it would have been reasonable for the blind men to attach some weight to the unintelligible statements which the seeing men made to them about colours.

I think that this argument deserves a certain amount of respect, though I should find it hard to estimate how much weight to attach to it. I should be inclined to sum up as follows. When there is a nucleus of agreement between the experiences of men in different places, times, and traditions, and when they all tend to put much the same kind of interpretation on the cognitive content of these experiences, it is reasonable to ascribe this agreement to their all being in contact with a certain objective aspect of reality *unless* there be some positive reason to think otherwise. The practical postulate which we go upon everywhere else is to treat cognitive claims as veridical unless there be some positive reason to think them delusive. . . . I think it would be inconsistent to treat the experiences of religious mystics on different principles. So far as they agree they should be provisionally accepted as veridical unless there be some positive ground for thinking that they are not. . . .

It is plain that this argument has considerable plausibility. . . . There has obviously been a gradual refinement and purification of religious beliefs and concepts in the course of history, just as there has been in the beliefs and concepts of science. Certain persons of religious genius, such as some of the Hebrew prophets and the founders of Christianity and of Buddhism, do seem to have introduced new ethico-religious concepts and beliefs which have won wide acceptance, just as certain men of scientific genius, such as Galileo, Newton, and Einstein, have done in the sphere of science. It seems somewhat arbitrary to count this process as a continual approximation to true knowledge of the material aspect of the world in the case of science, and to refuse to regard is as at all similar in the case of religion. . . .

Broad provides a clever **argument from analogy** to help us understand how justification could be provided by the testimony of people who have had religious experiences. According to the analogy, those who have not had religious experiences are like a race of blind people, and those who have had religious experiences are to be compared to members of that race who have suddenly acquired sight. The "sighted ones" can then report two sorts of things:

argument from analogy: A form of *inductive reasoning* in which the premises state that two things are similar in certain initial respects and the conclusion states that the things are *probably* similar in some further respect. Arguments from analogy vary in strength depending on the number of similarities in the premises and the relevance of those initial similarities to the further similarities mentioned in the conclusion.

a. The colours of objects around us

Those of us who are blind will never be able to directly confirm these reports for ourselves, and we may not even be sure that we understand them. If we believe such reports, it will be because we take others—those who claim to have sight—at their word. What justifies us in taking them at their word is that they also give reports of

b. The shapes and locations of distant objects

Those of us who are blind will be able to check these reports for ourselves, since we can move to the locations where the sighted people report the presence of objects

Logic Box

Argument from Analogy

A form of *inductive reasoning* in which the premises state that two things are similar in certain initial respects, and the conclusion is drawn that they are *probably* similar in some further respect. The strength of an argument from analogy depends on *how many* initial similarities there are between the two things, and *how relevant* those initial similarities are to any further similarity that the conclusion says they probably have.

Example: Apples and plums are both fruit, both grow on trees, and both red and spherical. Apples are sweet, so plums are probably also sweet.

and we can feel their shapes. Broad suggests that because the few who claim to be "sighted" can successfully deliver reports of the second kind, this gives "the blind" a reason, or justification, to believe reports of the first kind. That is, because we can confirm that some of the reports they give are true, even if we can't confirm it in the same direct way they do, we have good reason to suspect they have veridical experiences of a kind we don't have. If they have experiences of a sort we don't also have, we should seriously entertain the possibility that they have experiences of things we know nothing about. Therefore, we should take their reports of colours seriously, even if we can never confirm those reports for ourselves and even if we don't really understand them.

For this to be a convincing analogy for religious experience, it is crucial that those who report having had religious experiences *also* give reports of things that the rest of us—those of us who are "blind" to God—can confirm, even if we cannot do so in the same direct way that they do. Only in this way can they demonstrate that they have experiences of a kind that the rest of us do not have, and also that experiences of that kind are veridical. So what information of that kind do those who claim to have religious experiences "bring back" from their experiences? According to Broad, "These persons have made actual ethical discoveries which others can afterwards recognize to be true."[7] On Broad's analogy between persons who are sighted and persons who have religious experiences, the new moral doctrines reported by people who have religious experiences are intended to be analogous to the reports of shapes and locations given by sighted people. Both kinds of reports provide information the blind can check and use to confirm that others have veridical experiences of a sort that they—the blind—do not have. To evaluate Broad's argument, we must ask whether this is really so.

The Doubts of the Blind

Broad's crucial claim is that those who have had religious experiences make "ethical discoveries" that those of us who lack religious experience cannot make for ourselves, but that we can nonetheless confirm to be true. Grounds for suspicion about this claim are difficult to avoid. We need only ask, How would we recognize or confirm an ethical discovery of this sort if one were made? The problem is that those who claim to have experienced God, and to have received moral truths or moral guidance directly from God, offer moral "truths" of two kinds:

i. Those moral "discoveries" that are only *moral platitudes*—things we already know or already think we know to be moral truths. The purported discoveries are then *things we might easily have discovered on our own*, without any divine assistance.

Consider the moral principle "Thou shalt not kill." Do we really need to hear from an omniscient being that killing others is a bad idea? If this is something we might have figured out on our own, it provides no evidence that the person who "discovers" it had any encounter with God. But there is a second kind of moral discovery that might be derived from an encounter with God—moral discoveries we could *not* have made on our own.

---

[7] *Ibid.*

ii. Those moral "discoveries" that do not *appear to be* moral truths at all. In general, these purported discoveries strike us as moral falsehoods or, at the very least, they are things we cannot recognize to be moral truths.

Any moral discovery that falls in this category is not obvious, and it *is not anything we could have figured out on our own*. This amounts to saying that it is something we would not already recognize as a moral truth when it is reported, and it is not something we can confirm to be true. Consider the authors of *Leviticus* and *Exodus*, who provide such surprising moral propositions as these: eating shellfish is a moral "abomination" (*Leviticus* 11:10); and it is morally permissible for me to sell my daughter into slavery (*Exodus* 21:7). Perhaps they are right, but unless we can find some way of independently establishing that these surprising claims are moral *truths*, we cannot use them as evidence that their authors were inspired by the voice of God.

Anything that qualifies as the genuine *discovery* of an ethical truth *via* a religious experience will (a) need to be a *novel* ethical principle, not something already ascertainable by those who do not have religious experiences, and (b) need to be an ethical principle we can independently establish to be true, even if we ourselves do not have religious experiences. If condition (a) is not met, we have no reason to think the experience is one from which *anything new* can be learned. But in Broad's analogy, the only evidence that someone has had a veridical religious experience consists in the new moral truths they claim to have learned from the experience. On the other hand, if condition (b) is not met, we have no reason to think that the moral discovery they claim to have made is a *truth* rather than a falsehood—in which case, we again have no reason to trust that they have had a veridical experience.

The problem with Broad's argument is that it is highly doubtful that anything can satisfy both (a) and (b) at the same time. Any genuinely novel moral truth that *could only* have been acquired directly from God will be one that we (who are "blind") *cannot* already discover and recognize on our own. If it satisfies condition (a), and it is so novel that we could not have uncovered it without divine assistance, then it is unlikely that it could satisfy condition (b) and be a moral discovery that we can confirm on our own. Furthermore, if it satisfies condition (b), then it is unlikely that it could satisfy condition (a)—any moral claim we can confirm to be true on our own does not require divine help to discover. But unless *both* conditions can be met, then the person who has a religious experience cannot offer any information comparable to the information about the shapes and locations of objects that the sighted offer to the blind in Broad's analogy. The new moral doctrines reported by those who claim to have religious experiences, and the shapes and locations of distant objects reported by those who have sight, are not similar in the ways that Broad's argument from analogy requires.

MIRACLES

A second form of experiential evidence for the existence of God is thought to be provided by miracles. Like those who claim to have religious experiences of God, those who purport to have witnessed miracles also take their experience to be powerful and compelling evidence for the existence of God. Miracles are events that occur in violation of natural laws, and so they need to be explained by something that is not bound by such laws—and this, plausibly, is an all-powerful being. But very few claim to have witnessed a miracle, so the central epistemological question that remains concerns the reliability of those who provide testimony for miracles. For this reason, many of the considerations that arose in our discussion of religious experiences continue to be relevant. In the following selection from his writings, David Hume gives a famous argument for the conclusion that it is *never rational* to believe testimony about miracles. Some of the components of his argument should be familiar.

"Of Miracles" David Hume (1748)[8]

Part I.

Though experience be our only guide in reasoning concerning matters of fact; it must be acknowledged, that this guide is not altogether infallible, but in some cases is apt to lead us into errors. . . .

A wise man, therefore, proportions his belief to the evidence. In such conclusions as are founded on an infallible experience, he expects the event with the last degree of assurance, and regards his past experience as a full *proof* of the future existence of that event. In other cases, he proceeds with more caution: He weighs the opposite experiments: He considers which side is supported by the greater number of experiments: to that side he inclines, with doubt and hesitation; and when at last he fixes his judgement, the evidence exceeds not what we properly call *probability*. . . .

To apply these principles to a particular instance; we may observe, that there is no species of reasoning more common, more useful, and even necessary to human life, than that which is derived from the testimony of men, and the reports of eye-witnesses and spectators. This species of reasoning, perhaps, one may deny to be founded on the relation of cause and effect. I shall not dispute about a word. It will be sufficient to observe that our assurance in any argument of this kind is derived from no other principle than our observation of the veracity of human testimony, and of the usual conformity of facts to the reports of witnesses. It being a general maxim, that no objects have any discoverable connexion together, and that all the inferences, which we can draw from one to another, are founded merely on our experience of their constant and regular conjunction; it is evident, that we ought not to make an exception to this maxim in favour of human testimony, whose connexion with any event seems, in itself, as little necessary as any other. Were not the memory tenacious to a certain degree, had not men commonly an inclination to truth and a principle of probity; were they not sensible to shame, when detected in a falsehood: Were not these, I say, discovered by experience to be qualities, inherent in human nature, we should never repose the least confidence in human testimony. A man delirious, or noted for falsehood and villany, has no manner of authority with us.

. . . There are a number of circumstances to be taken into consideration in all judgements of this kind; and the ultimate standard, by which we determine all disputes, that may arise concerning them, is always derived from experience and observation. . . .

. . . We entertain a suspicion concerning any matter of fact, when the witnesses contradict each other; when they are but few, or of a doubtful character; when they have an interest in what they affirm; when they deliver their testimony with hesitation, or on the contrary, with too violent asseverations. There are many other particulars of the same kind, which may diminish or destroy the force of any argument, derived from human testimony.

---

[8] From Hume, D. (1777). *An Enquiry Concerning Human Understanding.* Retrieved August 9, 2014, from http://www.gutenberg.org/cache/epub/9662/pg9662.txt

Suppose, for instance, that the fact, which the testimony endeavours to establish, partakes of the extraordinary and the marvellous; in that case, the evidence, resulting from the testimony, admits of a diminution, greater or less, in proportion as the fact is more or less unusual. The reason why we place any credit in witnesses and historians, is not derived from any *connexion*, which we perceive *a priori*, between testimony and reality, but because we are accustomed to find a conformity between them. . . . The very same principle of experience, which gives us a certain degree of assurance in the testimony of witnesses, gives us also, in this case, another degree of assurance against the fact, which they endeavour to establish; from which contradiction there necessarily arises a [counterpoise], and mutual destruction of belief and authority. . . .

The Indian prince, who refused to believe the first relations concerning the effects of frost, reasoned justly; and it naturally required very strong testimony to engage his assent to facts, that arose from a state of nature, with which he was unacquainted, and which bore so little analogy to those events, of which he had had constant and uniform experience. . . .

But in order to [increase] the probability against the testimony of witnesses, let us suppose, that the fact, which they affirm, instead of being only marvellous, is really miraculous; and suppose also, that the testimony considered apart and in itself, amounts to an entire proof; in that case, there is proof against proof, of which the strongest must prevail, but still with a diminution of its force, in proportion to that of its antagonist.

A miracle is a violation of the laws of nature; and as a firm and unalterable experience has established these laws, the proof against a miracle, from the very nature of the fact, is as entire as any argument from experience can possibly be imagined. Why is it more than probable, that all men must die; that lead cannot, of itself, remain suspended in the air; that fire consumes wood, and is extinguished by water; unless it be, that these events are found agreeable to the laws of nature, and there is required a violation of these laws, or in other words, a miracle to prevent them? Nothing is esteemed a miracle, if it ever happen in the common course of nature. It is no miracle that a man, seemingly in good health, should die on a sudden: because such a kind of death, though more unusual than any other, has yet been frequently observed to happen. But it is a miracle, that a dead man should come to life; because that has never been observed in any age or country. There must, therefore, be a uniform experience against every miraculous event, otherwise the event would not merit that appellation. And as a uniform experience amounts to a proof, there is here a direct and full *proof*, from the nature of the fact, against the existence of any miracle; nor can such a proof be destroyed, or the miracle rendered credible, but by an opposite proof, which is superior.

. . . When anyone tells me, that he saw a dead man restored to life, I immediately consider with myself, whether it be more probable, that this person should either deceive or be deceived, or that the fact, which he relates, should really have happened. I weigh the one miracle against the other; and according to the superiority, which I discover, I pronounce my decision, and always reject the greater miracle. If the falsehood of his testimony would be more miraculous, than the event which he relates; then, and not till then, can he pretend to command my belief or opinion.

Part II.

In the foregoing reasoning we have supposed, that the testimony, upon which a miracle is founded, may possibly amount to an entire proof, and that the falsehood of that testimony would be a real prodigy: But it is easy to show, that we have been a great deal too liberal in our concession, and that there never was a miraculous event established on so full an evidence.

For *first*, there is not to be found, in all history, any miracle attested by a sufficient number of men, of such unquestioned good-sense, education, and learning, as to secure us against all delusion in themselves; of such undoubted integrity, as to place them beyond all suspicion of any design to deceive others; of such credit and reputation in the eyes of mankind, as to have a great deal to lose in case of their being detected in any falsehood; and at the same time, attesting facts performed in such a public manner and in so celebrated a part of the world, as to render the detection unavoidable: All which circumstances are requisite to give us a full assurance in the testimony of men. . . .

The many instances of forged miracles, and prophecies, and supernatural events, which, in all ages, have either been detected by contrary evidence, or which detect themselves by their absurdity, prove sufficiently the strong propensity of mankind to the extraordinary and the marvellous, and ought reasonably to beget a suspicion against all relations of this kind. This is our natural way of thinking, even with regard to the most common and most credible events. . . .

How many stories of this nature have, in all ages, been detected and exploded in their infancy? How many more have been celebrated for a time, and have afterwards sunk into neglect and oblivion? Where such reports, therefore, fly about, the solution of the phenomenon is obvious; and we judge in conformity to regular experience and observation, when we account for it by the known and natural principles of credulity and delusion. And shall we, rather than have a recourse to so natural a solution, allow of a miraculous violation of the most established laws of nature? . . .

Upon the whole, then, it appears, that no testimony for any kind of miracle has ever amounted to a probability, much less to a proof; and that, even supposing it amounted to a proof, it would be opposed by another proof; derived from the very nature of the fact, which it would endeavour to establish. It is experience only, which gives authority to human testimony; and it is the same experience, which assures us of the laws of nature. When, therefore, these two kinds of experience are contrary, we have nothing to do but substract the one from the other, and embrace an opinion, either on one side or the other, with that assurance which arises from the remainder. But according to the principle here explained, this substraction, with regard to all popular religions, amounts to an entire annihilation; and therefore we may establish it as a maxim, that no human testimony can have such force as to prove a miracle, and make it a just foundation for any such system of religion.

I beg the limitations here made may be remarked, when I say, that a miracle can never be proved, so as to be the foundation of a system of religion. For I own, that otherwise, there may possibly be miracles, or violations of the usual course of nature, of such a kind as to admit of proof from human testimony; though, perhaps, it will be impossible to find any such in all the records of history. Thus, suppose, all authors, in all languages, agree, that, from the first of January 1600, there was a total darkness over the whole earth for eight days: suppose that the tradition of this extraordinary event is still strong and lively among the people: that all travellers, who return from foreign countries, bring us accounts of the same tradition, without the least variation or contradiction: it is evident, that our present philosophers, instead of doubting the fact, ought to receive it as certain, and ought to search for the causes whence it might be derived. The decay, corruption, and dissolution of nature, is an event rendered probable by so many analogies, that any phenomenon, which seems to have a tendency towards that catastrophe, comes within the reach of human testimony, if that testimony be very extensive and uniform. . . .

. . . All this might astonish me; but I would still reply, that the knavery and folly of men are such common phenomena, that I should rather believe the most extraordinary events to arise from their concurrence, than admit of so signal a violation of the laws of nature. . . .

I am the better pleased with the method of reasoning here delivered, as I think it may serve to confound those dangerous friends or disguised enemies to the *Christian Religion*, who have undertaken to defend it by the principles of human reason. Our most holy religion is founded on *Faith*, not on reason; and it is a sure method of exposing it to put it to such a trial as it is, by no means, fitted to endure.

The Marvelous and the Miraculous

Hume begins by reminding us that the strength of a belief or conviction ought to be proportional to the evidence for it: The stronger the evidence, the more rational our belief. He further recognizes that we already have considerable evidence to support "the veracity of human testimony." Hume thinks our justification for accepting testimony comes from the relatively high degree of "conformity of facts to the reports of witnesses" that we have already observed. That is, people have largely proven themselves to be reliable witnesses, and that makes it legitimate for us to accept testimony from them. At the same time, we are not completely naive about testimony—we have also observed that witnesses sometimes contradict one another, that some witnesses are "of a doubtful character," and so on. Therefore the decision to take testimony at face value is always a tricky balancing act—some of the evidence may lean in one direction while other evidence leans in the opposite direction. When that happens, we must judge "which side is supported by the greater number of experiments [experiential evidence]," and take that side. When the reasons for and against accepting someone's testimony are put on the scale, the *rational* thing to do is side with the preponderance of evidence.

Our earlier considerations (1) through (4) are among the factors that must be taken into account when deciding whether to believe someone's testimony. Of utmost importance for Hume's argument is consideration (4), which says that when the event reported is already exceedingly unlikely to have occurred, we ought to give less credence to the testimony. In short, when someone reports the occurrence of a highly improbable event, we need additional evidence for the event before it is reasonable to believe it occurred. Depending on the case, that might mean an additional witness, physical evidence, a photograph, or a lie-detector test. However, it is not rational to simply take someone's word when the event she reports is exceedingly unlikely to have happened—even if our witness is someone we think is honest, she is still capable of making mistakes about what she saw. Hume describes such cases as "marvels." When events are "extraordinary and marvellous," he says, then we already have "another degree of assurance against the fact" that is reported. But, as Hume is careful to illustrate—with the example of an Indian prince who rejects reports of frost—such reports might be true even if it is not rational to believe them on the basis of testimony from one or two witnesses.

"Marvels" are events that are exceedingly unlikely to occur, but they are not impossible. When there are enough trustworthy corroborating witnesses to, for example, a grizzly bear wandering the streets of Miami at night, or enough physical evidence to back up the testimony of a single witness, it can be rational to accept testimony to the occurrence

miracle: An event or occurrence that violates natural physical laws and is, therefore, thought to be a result of divine intervention in the natural realm.

of marvels. **Miracles** are another matter altogether, for they are, by definition, events that violate a law of nature and, in that sense, are not merely improbable but physically impossible. When no law of nature is violated by the occurrence of a highly unusual event, there is always a possible natural explanation for it, and there is no need to see the event as a manifestation of the hand of God. Only when an event violates a law of nature do we have grounds to suspect divine intervention—that is why miracles are counted as powerfully direct evidence for the existence of God.

For Hume this means that when we assess the likelihood that a miracle has occurred, we must balance the testimony of a witness against the experiential evidence for the law of nature that is thought to be violated. But nothing will qualify as a law of nature unless it is supported by "firm and unalterable experience"—evidence that is "as entire as any argument from experience can possibly be imagined." In short, when weighing the evidence for and against a miracle, we must put on one side of the scale vast amounts of highly corroborated and carefully verified observations of a large number of witnesses to the truth of the natural law. On the other side is the unverifiable testimony of one or a few witnesses to a miraculous event. In such cases, the rational thing to believe—that is, the thing that is supported by the greatest preponderance of evidence—is that the testimony is simply mistaken. As Hume concludes, "Upon the whole, then, it appears, that no testimony for any kind of miracle has even amounted to a probability, much less to a proof."[9]

The case for miracles is even worse than the argument so far suggests. We must also add to the totality of evidence to be weighed the evidence we already have for "the knavery and folly of men"—and that evidence is considerable. In other words, not only does the weight of evidence for the natural law that is allegedly violated by the miracle hopelessly overpower the unverifiable testimony of one or two witnesses, but we must also factor in our considerable experiential evidence that persons are capable of, and even prone to, deception and error. When the evidence pointing to the existence of human "knavery and folly" is also taken into account, it becomes even more irrational to believe the testimony. In other words, we have plenty of evidence for the inviolability of the natural law, and we also have plenty of evidence that human beings can be knaves or fools. When we are asked to believe someone's testimony to a miracle, we are being asked to take the word of a possible knave or fool over the well-verified observations that support the natural law. It deserves emphasis that, once again, *this is not to say that the testimony is false, or that the miracle never occurred*—it is only to say that *it is not rational to believe the testimony*. If that is right, then the testimony of witnesses to miracles will not constitute good grounds for believing in the existence of God.

It is important to keep track of the fact that Hume offers an *inductive argument* against belief in the existence of God on the basis of testimony. He does not intend to show that miracles are impossible; he only intends to show that, on empirical grounds, it is irrational to believe that miracles occur. This is why, near the end of his argument, he can consistently give an illustration—his example of eight days of worldwide darkness—of the sort of empirical evidence needed before it becomes rational to believe in a miracle. With enough testimonial corroboration from the right kind of witnesses, we *can* be justified in believing a miracle occurred. But Hume feels confident saying is that no report of a

[9] *Ibid.*

miracle has ever come close to meeting the very high standards needed for it to be rational for us to believe the report.

Earlier, we distinguished the question of whether God exists from the question of whether it is rational to believe He exists. Hume's argument is only intended to address the latter, and to that question he gives a firm no. But Hume ends his critique of testimony about miracles by suggesting that his criticisms may actually help theists defend themselves against the "dangerous friends or disguised enemies" of their religious beliefs. For, he says, the "disguised enemies" of religious belief are those who have "undertaken to defend it by the principles of human reason." Hume suspects that to attempt a rational defense of religious belief is to play directly into the hands of the enemies of religion. The strategy can only end up exposing religion to "such a trial as it is, by no means, fitted to endure." In other words, Hume suggests that religious belief is not rational, and that the attempt to make it look rational only sets it up for failure—it only serves the atheist's purpose, since religion is to be "founded on *Faith*, not reason." So Hume insists that even if the merits of his arguments are accepted, religious belief should not be shaken by them.

Grounds for Self-Doubt

Perhaps we cannot use the testimony of others who claim to have directly experienced God or a miracle as good grounds for belief that there is a God. But what about the other question we began with: If we were to have such experiences ourselves, would we then have good reason to believe there is a God?

We should first notice that if the testimony of other people is not a good reason for us to believe there is a God, then our own testimony cannot be a good reason for others to believe there is a God. Our word is only as good for them as theirs is for us. But this doesn't tell us whether we can believe our own eyes, so that even if our testimony does not give *others* a reason to believe there is a God, our experiences may nonetheless give *us* a reason to believe it. Similarly, even if Teresa's *testimony* about her own experience does not justify *us* in believing there is a God, her *experience* might justify *her* belief.

Of course, we all recognize that there are *some* experiences that can't be trusted. Drug- or fever-induced hallucinations are good examples of non-veridical experiences that are likely to produce false beliefs. When other people relate visions that result from experiments with peyote, we do not generally take their experience as a reliable guide to reality, and for the same reason we cannot take our own peyote-induced experiences as veridical. This obvious point can be generalized: Our own experiences, and our own understanding of our experiences, must confront any challenges that can be legitimately posed for the experiences of others. Most of the grounds for being suspicious of the religious experiences of others are also grounds for being suspicious of our own experiences. If we cannot answer the questions we expect others to answer on the "witness stand," then we cannot, in fairness, regard our own experiences any differently than theirs.

It may be true that, as Teresa says, it is impossible to have a religious experience and believe that it was only imagined. But even if a powerful experience makes a belief very compelling, we can still have strong contrary reasons for doubting ourselves. And those grounds ought to at least keep us open to alternative ways of understanding our own experiences.

CONCLUSION

In Chapter 12 we examined arguments that purport to establish the existence of God on the basis of indirect evidence—attempts to deduce the existence of God the Creator from aspects of His creation. In this chapter, we examined two kinds of experiential evidence for the existence of God. Some persons claim to have had direct experiences of God, and others to have witnessed miracles. But neither religious experiences nor miracles are widely shared, so the important epistemological questions concern whether we are justified in accepting the word of the few who claim to be "witnesses" to the existence of God. Our primary purpose in this chapter has been to explore whether, and when, it is rational to believe in God on the basis of testimony. We examined purported cases of direct experiences of God, and an argument, from C. D. Broad, for why testimony of such experiences ought to be taken seriously. We also encountered a famous argument by David Hume for the conclusion that we cannot use the testimony of miracles to give rational support for belief in God.

Once again, we leave off in a place where theists face significant challenges in overcoming the doubts of agnostics and atheists. Having explored defenses of theism, we will use the next chapter to allow atheists to mount their best defense for their position. Our discussion continues, then, to explore the debate between the atheist and the deist, both of whom assume that the question of God's existence can be settled by using reason. We will then be in a better position to consider the fideist's view that we are getting nowhere precisely because we are demanding reasons rather than opening ourselves up to faith.

Key Terms and Figures

mystical experience p. 276
religious experience p. 276
testimony p. 276
St. Teresa of Avila p. 277
veridical experience p. 278
non-veridical experience p. 278
Sigmund Freud p. 278
illusion p. 278
C. D. Broad p. 283
argument from analogy p. 285
miracle p. 292

Additional readings on miracles, religious experience, and testimony

Alston, W. P. (1991). *Perceiving God: The Epistemology of Religious Expereince*. Ithaca: Cornell University Press.

Fogelin, R. (2003). *A Defense of Hume on Miracles*. Princeton, NJ: Princeton University Press.

James, W. (1982). *The Varieties of Religious Experience*. Viking Penguin Inc. Originally published by Longmans, Green, & Co. (1902).

Mackie, J. L. (1982). Miracles and Testimony. In *The Miracle of Theism*. Oxford: Oxford University Press: 13–29.

Mackie, J. L. (1982). Religious Experience and Natural Histories of Religion. In *The Miracle of Theism*. Oxford: Oxford University Press: 177–98.

Webb, M. (2011). Religious Experience. *The Stanford Encyclopedia of Philosophy*, Winter Edition. (Edward N. Zalta, Ed.). Available at http://plato.stanford.edu/archives/win2011/entries/religious-experience

Chapter 14
The Problem of Evil

Learning Objectives

- Formulate the problem of evil and clarify the concept of "evil" that is involved.
- State some common objections to each premise of the problem of evil, and summarize common responses to those objections.
- Contrast power and logical possibility, and explore paradoxes involving the idea of omnipotence.
- Explain Hannah Arendt's doctrine of the banality of evil.
- Give examples of *ad hominem* fallacies, and explain why they are a fallacious form of reasoning.
- Describe a theodicy, and explain why some writers think that belief in a theodicy is both a metaphysical and a moral error.

In this chapter we examine a famous problem that is frequently cited by atheists as a proof that there is no God: the problem of evil or, as it is sometimes called, the problem of suffering. Since you are likely to have some familiarity with the problem of evil, and even with the most common theistic replies to it, we will attempt to take our reflections further by emphasizing the atheist's objections to the most familiar theistic replies. Naturally, theists will have much more to say about where the argument should go next.

From the perspective of the deist, this chapter is intended to end on a sour note—with the idea in ascendant that it is not *rational* to believe in God. Although this conclusion is necessarily premature—after all, we have not considered *every possible reason* for belief in God, only the most commonly entertained ones—the conclusion nonetheless takes us to a useful juncture, where fideism often parts ways with deism and atheism. Deists and atheists share an important assumption: both assume that the question of whether God exists can and should be settled on the basis of evidence and rational argument. In the chapter that follows, we will examine this assumption by exploring the views of theists who dismiss the very *relevance* of evidence or reason for belief in God.

THE SHAPE OF THE PROBLEM

A simple argument has long haunted deists, and has always been a mainstay in the defense of atheism. The argument purports to prove that God, as we have defined Him, does not exist. It does so in a way that claims to show that it is *not rational* to believe there is a God.

The argument has the following form:

1. If there is a God, then there would be no evil.
2. But, there is evil.
3. Therefore, there is no God.

modus tollens: The valid argument form: If P, then Q, and not-Q, so not-P. *Modus tollens* reasoning consists of a *conditional* statement (If P, then Q) for one premise, which tells us that if a certain antecedent condition (P) is satisfied, then a certain consequent condition (Q) will arise. The second premise then *denies* (i.e., not-Q) that the consequent condition has arisen, and so requires us to conclude that the antecedent condition is not satisfied (i.e., not-P).

This is a valid deductive argument with the form of ***modus tollens***, so the theist's response must challenge one, or both, of the premises. Although this formulation makes the existence of any amount of evil a problem for theism, the problem can also be given a weaker formulation that makes the *quantity* of evil a problem for theism. On this second version, it is claimed that, even if the existence of God can be reconciled with the existence of some amount of evil, it cannot be reconciled with the gratuitous amount of evil in the world. More than half the world's people, at this moment, are hungry. An estimated 27 million people live in slavery—that's the largest absolute number of people living in slavery in human history. There are entire ethnic groups for whom the average lifespan is less than 40 years. Since the causes of their low life expectancy are poverty, malnutrition, and associated diseases, their relatively short lives are, on average, full of struggle and suffering. The *sheer numbers* add force to the problem of evil. Finally, along with the existence of evil and its quantity, an additional challenge is posed by how evil gets *distributed*. Great evils can happen to good people, while very bad people can live lives of pleasure and ease; the kinds and quantities of the evils that befall us do not appear to be any reflection of what we deserve. In summary, if we suppose the world was created by a being who is all powerful, all-knowing, and all-good, then we need some explanation of why there is evil, why there is so much evil, and why evil is distributed as it is.

problem of evil: An objection to theism that uses the existence, quantity, or distribution of natural and moral evils to argue that the universe cannot be the work of a divine creator.

There is an obvious resemblance between this argument, which constitutes the **problem of evil**, and the cosmological arguments for God's existence we considered earlier. The problem of evil and cosmological arguments might arrive at opposite conclusions, but both work from the assumption that an artisan's character and abilities are reflected in her creations, so we can infer some things about her from the work she creates. An artist's paintings might reveal something about how she sees the subjects she portrays, and the

Logic Box

Modus Tollens

A valid *form* of argument that can be distilled in the following template, where P and Q each represent statements:

If P, then Q
Not-Q
Therefore, not-P

The first premise says that if a certain antecedent condition (P) is satisfied, then a certain consequent condition (Q) will arise. The second premise then *denies* that the consequent condition has arisen, and so requires us to conclude that the antecedent condition was *not* satisfied. Replacing P and Q with any statements whatsoever will result in a valid argument. For example, if P is replaced in our template with "He did the assigned readings," and Q is replaced with "He passed the exam," the result will be the following valid argument:

i. If he did the assigned readings, then he passed the exam.
ii. He did *not* pass the exam.
iii. Therefore, he did *not* do the assigned readings.

cabinetmaker's cabinets might reveal something about her skills or talents. Cosmological arguments, as we saw, suggested that morality, or the design we find in nature, show us something important about their creator. Similarly, in the problem of evil it is supposed that the presence of evil in the world reveals something about the world's creator, but this time what it reveals is that the world was *not* created by an all-powerful, all-knowing, and all-good being. Before we examine some of the ways theists attempt to rebut the premises of the argument, we will need to better understand some features of those premises.

Three Clarifications

I. Two Kinds of Evil Our brief statement of the argument uses the broad term *evil,* which needs clarification. First, *evil* is typically a term of judgment or appraisal that is reserved for religious contexts. It is used to imply that something is bad or wrong from the perspective of some religious system. The word *sin* is similar—we don't generally call a wrongdoing a *sin* unless it is perceived as an offense against God or God's commands. Non-theists are more likely to use other terms of moral appraisal, and words like *sin* and *evil* do not often appear in their vocabulary. In our discussion, *evil* is used without religious connotations—it is simply shorthand for any very bad thing.

Second, it is important to know that two sorts of *evils* are intended by the term: On the one hand, there are **natural evils**. These are primarily natural disasters or catastrophes, big or small, resulting in suffering or death, which are not dependent on anyone's moral wrongdoings. In the other hand, there are also **moral evils**—moral wrongs resulting in suffering and harm to others. There are hybrids of natural and moral evil: For example, a drought, caused by lack of rain, may result in great human tragedy, but suffering might be greatly reduced or even eliminated but for the fact that others withhold assistance. In such cases, natural and moral evils jointly conspire to produce great human suffering.

natural evil: Suffering and harm that befall people as a result of natural phenomena—bad things that are not caused by morally responsible agents.

moral evil: Despite the usual religious connotation of the term *evil,* in the problem of evil, *moral evil* refers to any harm or wrong done to someone by the deliberate actions of other persons—these are the wrongs that we do to others.

II. God's Character The heart of the argument for atheism lies in the definition of God: If God is all-knowing, all-powerful, and all-good, He would not have created a world in which there is evil. Since this world does contain much evil, no God *of that sort* could have created it. If we deviate from the definition of God with which we have been working, it becomes easy to explain the existence of evil, but for most theists this is an unacceptable form of evasion. Consider why.

Suppose God is all-powerful and all-good, but *He doesn't know everything.* Then He could have made a mess of things from simple ignorance. Creating a universe is a challenging task, requiring a great deal of specialized knowledge, so if we believe God didn't know what he was doing, we won't be surprised to find serious problems with His work. Alternatively, if God is all-powerful and all-knowing, but *He is not all-good,* then He could have created a word containing evil out of wickedness or malice. For a God who is malicious or cruel, the temptation to embellish his work with a few touches of evil would have been irresistible. And, finally, if God is all-good and all-knowing, but *not very powerful,* then He might have bungled things out of weakness or incompetence. The wisest and best-intentioned Creator might be powerless to prevent flaws from appearing in His work. So the problem of evil is only a problem for the sort of God we have defined. This still makes the argument sufficiently far-reaching to pose a serious challenge to theism, since very few theists want to evade the problem of evil by supposing that God is ignorant, malicious, or incompetent. If by "God" we mean a being who is all-knowing, all-good, and all-powerful, then the problem of evil has to be faced head on.

III. Power and Possibility A subtle point about the nature of power can be made to play a large role in the problem of evil. In general, theists who believe that God is *all-powerful* do not believe He can do *everything*. Rather, they accept that even though there are no limits to the power of an all-powerful being, there may nonetheless be limits on what an all-powerful being can do. Most theists believe that even an all-powerful being will be unable to do something that is logically impossible. (Not everyone agrees—Descartes, for example, thought God has the power to do logically impossible things.)

contradiction: Two statements are contradictories if the truth of one ensures the falsity of the other and the falsity of one ensures the truth of the other. We have a contradiction (of the form "P and not-P") when we conjoin with "and" contradictory statements.

logical impossibility: An object or event is logically impossible when it has a logically inconsistent description.

omnipotence paradox: A paradox that purports to show that omnipotence is logically impossible. In its most popular form, it poses the question: *Can God make a stone so big that He can't lift it?*

Consider a simple example: If God cannot do things that are logically impossible, then He cannot create a four-sided triangle. Similarly, *we* cannot *draw* a four-sided triangle. In our case, working out in the gym and taking advanced drafting courses won't help. No increase in our strength or skills will enable us to draw four-sided triangles, and this is so for a very simple reason: Our inability to draw a four-sided triangle is not owed to any deficiency in our powers or talents. Similarly, the reason God cannot create four-sided triangles has nothing to do with any deficiency in His power. To express the central point somewhat paradoxically: God cannot create four-sided triangles because there are no such things for Him to create. The problem is that a four-sided triangle is a **contradiction** in terms: It is **logically impossible**. When theists say God is all-powerful, they usually mean that *God can do anything that is logically possible*—anything that can be described without contradiction. There may still be some things God cannot do, but that He cannot do them is not owed to any limitation of His power.

With the distinction between power and logical possibility in mind, it might be a useful exercise to think through the so-called **omnipotence paradox**, which is sometimes offered as a proof that no omnipotent being—and therefore no God—could exist. The paradox begins by posing a *dilemma* for omnipotent beings: *Can God, or any omnipotent being, make a stone so big that He can't lift it?* If the theist answers yes, then there is something God cannot do—He can't *lift* the stone. If the theist answers no, then there is something God cannot do—He can't *make* the stone. Either way, there is something God

Logic Box

Contradiction and Logical Impossibility

Two statements are *contradictories* whenever the truth of one *requires* that the other be false, and the falsity of one requires that the other be true. It is not possible for both of two contradictory statements to be true, or for both to be false. We have a contradiction (the form P and not-P) whenever we conjoin with "and" two statements that contradict each other, thus ensuring that the conjunction of the two is false. The contradiction is *explicit* when we both assert and deny the same thing (e.g., "All snow is white, but not all snow is white"). We have an *implicit* contradiction when we conjoin two statements that, because of what they mean or imply, contradict one another. For example, "George is a married bachelor" contains a concealed contradiction that is brought out by examining its meaning. Since "bachelor" means "unmarried man," the statement implies both that George is married and that George is not married. Finally, some thing or event is logically impossible if a statement or description of it is a contradiction. Thus, married bachelors and four-sided triangles are logical impossibilities.

cannot do. But, the conclusion then says, this amounts to an admission that nothing can really be omnipotent—that an omnipotent being is impossible.

How good is this argument? If an omnipotent being is possible, then He will have the power to make a stone of *any* size or *any* mass, but he will not have the power to make a stone that is logically impossible—that is, a stone for which the description is contradictory. For example, an omnipotent being will not be able to make, or lift, a six-sided spherical stone, any more than He might make or lift a married bachelor. Is there anything logically impossible about the stone that God is challenged by the omnipotence paradox to make and lift?

One argument for saying that the stone is logically impossible comes from trying to answer both questions in the affirmative—trying to grasp both horns of the dilemma. We would then need to say, "*Yes*, God can make a stone so big he can't lift it," and "*Yes*, God can lift *that stone*." Notice that in answering yes to the second question, we have to say that God *can lift* a stone that is so big He *can't lift* it. That would be a logically impossible stone. So according to this line of reasoning, the omnipotence paradox does not show that *an omnipotent being* is logically impossible; it only shows that *a stone that cannot be lifted by an omnipotent being* is logically impossible.

In light of our clarifications of the notion of evil, of the role of the defining traits of God in the problem, and of the distinction between power and logical possibility, we are in a good position to examine some common theistic objections to the problem of evil, as well as atheists' replies to those objections.

CONTINUING THE ARGUMENT: PREMISE ONE

In much of what follows, we will examine attempts by theists to construct a **theodicy**—a rational defense of God's omnipotence and goodness in the face of evil.[1] We begin by considering objections of theists to the first premise of the argument for atheism, along with expected replies from atheists to those objections. Recall that the first premise of the atheist's argument is that *if there is a God (an all-knowing, all-good, all-powerful creator of everything), there would be no evil.* How might a theist object to this premise? We will consider three theistic objections and three replies to each of those objections.

theodicy: A theory, usually concerning the metaphysics of good and evil, that attempts to reconcile the existence of evil with the idea of an omnipotent, omniscient, and omnibenevolent Creator.

The Existence of Opposites

> *Theist's first objection: Good and evil are opposites, so the existence of evil is required for the existence of good.*

Here, the theist's idea is that good and evil are opposites and, in general, in order to create a world containing one of a pair of opposites (good), God had to create the other (evil) as well. So although God did create evil, it was necessary for Him to do so in order to create good.

This is probably a familiar response to the problem of evil, but the atheist has several replies that should be equally familiar. First, the theist's objection assumes that something

[1] The term was coined by G. W. Leibniz, who also formulated the principle of sufficient reason and the principle of the indiscernibility of identicals.

cannot exist unless its opposite also exists. This is far from obvious. The existence of something does not generally require the existence of its opposite; indeed, some things can exist only if their opposites do not exist. For example, a state of universal peace exists only when a state of war does not exist. No reason has been given to think that good and evil are any different in this respect than war and peace.

Second, even if it were true that good could not exist without evil, that is no justification for *the vast quantity of evil* that exists. If the existence of good really depends on the existence of evil, God could have allowed one very minor evil and left everything else to be good. Perhaps this misses the theist's point, and he intended us to understand that there must be exactly *as much* evil as there is good—that the creation of one must always be balanced by the creation of an equal amount of the other. In order to create a vast amount of good, God needed to create a vast amount of evil. This would mean we cannot do any amount of good without also creating an equal amount of evil, so that *our moral accounts are always balanced, whether we do good or evil.* An unsavoury consequence that has been drawn from the view that good and evil must be in balance is that if we want to create good, then an excellent way to do so is to create evil. According to famous eighteenth-century sadist the **Marquis de Sade**, "this being the case, they can give themselves over to evil since, indeed, it is but one of the fashions of producing good."[2]

Marquis de Sade: A French sexual libertine and sadist who spent much of his life in prisons and mental asylums; he was the author of numerous volumes of sophisticated philosophical pornography and eroticism.

Third, the requirement that God must make at least some evil in order to create any amount of good is either (i) a limitation on God's power (He lacks the power to do it any other way); or it is (ii) a logical requirement (just as he can't make a triangle without making three sides). But there is no reason at all to suspect (ii), since there is no *logical impossibility* in the idea that someone does a good thing without an evil following from it. But if the reason God is required to make evil is that He lacks the *power* to make good without evil, then theism is false.

Knowledge of Good and Evil

> *Theist's second objection: Knowledge, or understanding, or appreciation of what is good requires knowledge, or understanding, or appreciation of evil.*

According to this objection to the first premise of the problem of evil, we must have knowledge of evil in order to have knowledge of good. Alternatively, if we did not know about evil we would fail to appreciate the good we have. So God created evil in order that we could *know*, or understand, or appreciate good things. But even if we need knowledge of evil in order to have knowledge of good, that does not require God to create evil; it requires only that *knowledge* of evil exist. God could easily have given us knowledge of evil, or made it possible for us to acquire such knowledge, without having to create or permit evil. Perhaps this reply misses the theist's central point, which is that *knowledge* of good requires the *existence* of evil. This combines elements of both replies so far: It says that in order to *know* good, we first need to know evil, and in order to come to know evil, evil must actually exist. Again, the theist concedes that God did indeed create evil, but insists that He needed to do so for our benefit. Once again the atheist has three rejoinders.

[2] From de Sade, Marquis. (n.d.). *Justine, Philosophy in the Bedroom and Other Writings.* (Compiled and edited by R. Seaver & A. Wainhouse). New York, NY, 1965: Grove Press: 457.

First, knowledge, or understanding, or appreciation of something does not normally require the existence of that thing, let alone the existence of its opposite. For example, we know what unicorns are, and neither unicorns nor anti-unicorns needed to exist for us to know that. No reason has been provided for thinking that things are any different for our knowledge of what is good. Second, even if knowledge of what something is required the existence of its opposite, then knowledge of what is good would still not require the existence of *so much evil*. God would be a poor teacher if he needed to arrange things so that millions of people suffer just so that others can be taught what is good. Why not create a very small amount of evil, and make knowledge of it widely available? Third, the atheist once again wants to know what "requires" means in the theist's objection. It cannot be logically impossible to teach us about evil—and, thereby, about good—without creating any evil. We often teach moral lessons by telling children fictional stories in which evil makes an appearance. It should, then, at least be logically possible for God to teach us about good in the same way. Does God then lack the *power* to give us knowledge of what is good without having to create evil? If so, then he is not all-powerful, and theism is false.

Choosing Evil

Theist's third objection: Human free will, not God, is responsible for creating evil.

Unlike the previous objections to the first premise of the problem of evil, this one does not concede that God created evil. Instead, the responsibility for the existence of evil is shifted onto us. The central idea is that God would have been negligent to have created us without free will, but once we have free will, we are free to do evil. Then evil is entirely a consequence of our own exercise of freedom, and the responsibility for it is ours, not His.

Again, we consider three replies on behalf of the atheist. First, the atheist will point out that free will cannot explain a great deal of evil, since human free will is not responsible for natural evils. Unless, of course, natural evil is a form of retribution, or punishment, inflicted on us by God for the moral evils we do. In that case, we need to know why earthquakes and floods don't spare the innocent. One theistic answer is that *there are no innocents*, but that claim moves from philosophical argument into the realm of religious doctrine and dogma. It may be true that even the smallest baby is not innocent, but, if that were so, it would be a matter for faith and not something that has any place in a *rational critique* of the problem of evil. This response to the atheist—that there are no innocents—also risks putting us in grave moral danger, for it requires us to look at the suffering and death of small children from natural causes and to always think *they had it coming*. We may be reluctant to become the sort of person who is willing to think that.

Second, it is far from obvious that free will, by itself, can explain moral evil. Merely having a free will cannot *require* anyone to choose evil over good; if it did, it would not be "free" will. So our freedom *allows* us to choose to do evil, and also allows us to choose to do good. But if human beings were created both free *and good*, then when we are given a choice between doing good and doing evil, we would freely choose to do good. If we choose to do evil when we are also free to choose to do good, a plausible explanation of why we would make that choice is that *we are evil*. But, whatever the complete explanation, we cannot explain the moral evils we do simply by saying that we are free. If we freely choose evil, some other explanation is needed.

Hannah Arendt: A German-American political philosopher who did important work on totalitarianism, power, and violence, Arendt reported on the trial and execution of Adolph Eichmann for his role in the genocide of the Jews.

Third, it will be said that many of the greatest moral evils for which human beings are responsible are not a result of our freely *choosing evil* over good—at least, not in any meaningful sense of *choosing evil*. In her famous study of the trial and execution of Adolph Eichmann in Jerusalem (for his role in the genocide of the Jews), German-American political philosopher **Hannah Arendt** (1906–1975) described what she called the *banality of evil*: "the dilemma between the unspeakable horror of the deeds and the undeniable ludicrousness of the man who perpetrated them."[3] Eichmann was a mid-level bureaucrat assigned the complex and challenging task of arranging the transportation of the Jews to the death camps. He was efficient, took pride in doing his job well, and thought of little more than earning his next promotion. He was too preoccupied with shuffling papers and arranging train schedules to give much thought to what awaited passengers on the trains or to his own complicity in bringing about their fates.

banality of evil: The view, formulated by Hannah Arendt, that the greatest of evils arise from mundane sources—usually from the everyday thoughtlessness of ordinary people—and not from evil or demonic intentions or powers.

Arendt was both surprised and terrified to discover that Eichmann was not a monster at all—he had no cruel or sadistic motives "[e]xcept for an extraordinary diligence in looking out for his personal advancement, he had no motives at all."[4] Instead, she found that he was just like most of us, trying to do his job and stay uninvolved. Arendt concluded that evil "possesses neither depth nor any demonic dimension . . . That is its 'banality.'"[5] The **banality of evil** lies in its utterly mundane origins—we need not have evil motives, nor need we have demonic and sadistic personalities, to do our share in bringing about even the greatest of evils. Simply keeping our heads down and not causing waves, and perhaps occasionally averting our eyes—these are the real sources of many of the greatest evils. But there is no realistic sense in which people who live largely thoughtless, unimaginative, and uninvolved lives are *choosing evil* over good. We do not need to *choose to do evil* in order to play our part in bringing it about.

We have so far been considering the theist's objections to the first premise of the problem of evil, and the atheist's replies to those objections. In the following section, we turn to theistic objections to the second premise.

CONTINUING THE ARGUMENT: PREMISE TWO

St. Augustine: An early Christian theologian and philosopher, one of the intellectual founders of Catholicism, and bishop of the province of Hippo in North Africa. Under the influence of ideas descended from Plato, Augustine shaped early Christian teachings into a systematic philosophy.

The second premise of the atheist's argument says simply "There is evil." In order to disagree with this premise, the theist will need to deny that evil exists. This has been attempted in two closely related ways. Both strategies are employed by **St. Augustine** (354–430) in the following paragraphs.

"No Nature at All is Evil" (St. Augustine, c. 427)[6]

> This cause, however, of a good creation, namely, the goodness of God,—this cause, I say, so just and fit, which, when piously and carefully weighed, terminates all the controversies of those who inquire into the origin of the world, has not been recognized by some heretics, because there are, forsooth, many things, such as fire, frost, wild beasts,

[3] From Baehr, P. (Ed.) (2000). *The Portable Hannah Arendt*. New York: Penguin Books: 328.
[4] *Ibid.* p. 379.
[5] *Ibid.* p. 396.
[6] St. Augustine, *The Works of Aurelius Augustine, Bishop of Hippo*, Marcus Dods, Ed. (1913). Vol. I. *The City of God*; Ediinburgh: T. & T. Clark, 38, George Street: pp. 461–64.

and so forth, which do not suit but injure this thin blooded and frail mortality of our flesh, which is at present under just punishment. They do not consider how admirable these things are in their own places, how excellent in their own natures, how beautifully adjusted to the rest of creation, and how much grace they contribute to the universe by their own contributions as to a commonwealth; and how serviceable they are even to ourselves, if we use them with a knowledge of their fit adaptations,—so that even poisons, which are destructive when used injudiciously, become wholesome and medicinal when used in conformity with their qualities and design; just as, on the other hand, those things which give us pleasure, such as food, drink, and the light of the sun, are found to be hurtful when immoderately or unseasonably used. And thus divine providence admonishes us not foolishly to vituperate things, but to investigate their utility with care; and, where our mental capacity or infirmity is at fault, to believe that there is a utility, though hidden, as we have experienced that there were other things which we all but failed to discover. For this concealment of the use of things is itself either an exercise of our humility or a levelling of our pride; for no nature at all is evil, and this is a name for nothing but the want of good. But from things earthly to things heavenly, from the visible to the invisible, there are some things better than others; and for this purpose are they unequal, in order that they might all exist. . . .

But it is much more surprising that some even of those who, with ourselves, believe that there is one only source of all things, and that no nature which is not divine can exist unless originated by that Creator, have yet refused to accept with a good and simple faith this so good and simple a reason of the world's creation, that a good God made it good; and that the things created, being different from God, were inferior to Him, and yet were good, being created by none other than He. . . . Was it not obviously meant to be understood that there was no other cause of the world's creation than that good creatures should be made by a good God? In this creation, had no one sinned, the world would have been filled and beautified with natures good without exception; and though there is sin, all things are not therefore full of sin, for the great majority of the heavenly inhabitants preserve their nature's integrity. And the sinful will, though it violated the order of its own nature, did not on that account escape the laws of God, who justly orders all things for good. For as the beauty of a picture is increased by well-managed shadows, so, to the eye that has skill to discern it, the universe is beautified even by sinners, though, considered by themselves, their deformity is a sad blemish.

Initially, Augustine appears only to be denying that there are *natural evils* ("no nature at all is evil") while conceding that there are moral evils ("there is sin"). But when Augustine gives his reasons for thinking there is no natural evil, his rationale applies equally to moral evils. Augustine's objections to the existence of evil are found in two claims that will occupy our attention next.

First, Augustine holds that what appears to be evil is not really evil but only the absence of good—evil is, he says, "a name for nothing." In this case, only good things exist, and when we refer to evil we are referring to an absence of something good. Second, Augustine claims that the universe is made better by what only *appears* to be evil. Thus he says that the universe is "beautified even by sinners," and he provides an analogy that says that "the beauty of a picture is increased by well-managed shadows." But Augustine's claim, and his analogy, can be understood in two ways. On the one hand, he may be saying that some evil actually does exist (i.e., there really are sinners and dark shadows) but that the existence of evil *contributes* to the beauty of the whole work, as a little salt might contribute to the flavour of the soup. On this interpretation, if some sin did not exist, then the world as a whole would be less beautiful. Alternatively, Augustine may mean that what are taken as "sins" only *appear* to be evil, but they are not really evil *because their presence makes the universe a better place*. It is only when sins are seen out of context ("considered by themselves") that they *appear* to be blemishes. But to "the eye that has skill to discern it," it would be obvious that sins are not blemishes, or evils, at all. For the purposes of this section, which is concerned with the possibility of *denying the existence of evil*, we will consider only this second interpretation.

Both of Augustine's claims are strategies for denying that evil exists, so both are strategies for denying the second premise of the problem of evil. We will consider each of Augustine's proposals.

A Name for Nothing

Augustine's first objection: Evil has no positive reality—it is merely the privation, or absence of good.

In some pairs of opposites, one member of the pair is plausibly understood as only an absence or lack of the other member. For example, perhaps darkness doesn't exist, but there are some places where light is absent. It will only seem that light and darkness both exist if we fail to appreciate that darkness is merely the absence of light. Augustine's first point is that good and evil are like this. We do not need both good and evil to exist in order to fill out the details of reality. If that is right, God cannot be responsible for creating evil since there is none—there is only an absence, in some places, of good.

The atheist will surely want to know how we are to decide which member of a pair of opposites has "positive reality" and which is only a privation of a positive reality. Is the *presence* of a virus—a plague, for example—that indiscriminately kills millions of people the *absence* of a good? Of course we *can* always think of hunger as merely the absence of food, poverty as the absence of wealth, disease as the absence of health, and war as the absence of peace. We can even stretch the idea further and think of drought as the absence of rain and a flood as the absence of drier conditions. But this only exposes the arbitrariness of our decision about what is a positive reality and what is its privation.

Nonetheless, the atheist's central reply to Augustine's objection is that it is unclear how casting hunger, poverty, disease, war, drought, and floods in the role of privations can prevent them from being evils. If war is an absence of peace, and war is an evil, then absences can be evils. Now, if the absence of a good is responsible for suffering and death, then the problem of evil will simply be restated as a problem about God's negligence. Knowing, as He surely did, what the consequences would be, God mysteriously *neglected* to create the goods whose absence is evil. God would not have created a world with defects in it, even if those defects are merely privations or absences. We still need to understand why God permits them.

Beautiful Sinners

Augustine's second objection: Evil is only apparent; from a wider perspective, what appears to us as evil would be seen as good.

Augustine's second objection, as we are interpreting it here, concedes that some things do *seem* to be evil, but they only seem that way from our very limited human perspective. If we could see the larger picture—of which these apparent evils are but a part—or if we knew the divine rationale for the things that appear evil, we would see that they are both necessary and good. On this view, the existence of evil is an illusion of perspective, and everything that exists is actually good. Leibniz nicely puts this point as follows:

> . . . You have known the world only since the day before yesterday, you see scarce farther than your nose, and you carp at the world. Wait until you know more of the world . . . and you will find there [only] a contrivance and a beauty transcending all imagination.[7]

A first atheistic reply focuses on the idea that the human perspective is too limited for us to be able to see things as they really are. Anyone who tells us that things appear evil from a human perspective, but that those same things would appear good if seen from the divine perspective, thereby tells us something that, by her own admission, she cannot know. If we are limited by our human perspective, we can't know what things will look like from the divine perspective. When Augustine and Leibniz tell us that from the divine perspective everything will be seen to be good, they are telling us something they cannot know to be true.

Perhaps Augustine and Leibniz have a response: They can simply say we *can* know from our limited perspective just how things will look from God's perspective. The relevant knowledge that there is, in reality, no evil can be obtained by performing a simple, and very human deduction: The Creator of everything is all-powerful, all-knowing, and all-good; *therefore*, His creation will not contain any evil. Unfortunately, this response tries to *show* that the conclusion of the atheist's argument is false by *assuming* it is false. The "simple deduction" begins with the premise that everything was created by an all-powerful, all-knowing, and all-good Creator, so it *begs the question* against the argument for the conclusion that there is no God.

Second, if taken seriously, Augustine's view should result in moral paralysis. Theists should abandon their so-called "good works," since efforts to alleviate poverty and hunger, for example, are either efforts to *prevent* good things from happening or efforts to *undo* the good things that have already been done. Limited as we are by our merely human sensibilities, we are unable to understand how slavery and the starvation of children—which *seem to us* so obviously awful—could be *good* things. Augustine says that whenever something looks evil to us finite creatures, "our mental capacity or infirmity is at fault."[8] But if our own capacity for moral judgment deviates *this far* from the moral truth, we ought to conclude that we are simply incompetent to make moral judgments of any kind.

This last complaint points in the direction of a completely different line of argument for atheists to explore. The theodicies of Augustine and Leibniz seem to say that famine, murder, and so on are actually good things, and that they would be seen as such from

[7] From Leibniz, G. (1985). *Theodicy*. Retrieved on August 10, 2014, from http://www.gutenberg.org/cache/epub/17147/pg17147.txt

[8] From *The Works of Aurelius Augustine, Bishop of Hippo*, ed. by Marcus Dods, Vol. I. *The City of God*; Edinburgh: T. & T. Clark, 38, George Street. 1913, pp. 461–64.

God's perspective. But the point of view from which genocide and slavery look like good things is precisely the point of view of those who participate in genocides or condone slavery. And, speaking now from our all-too-human perspective, that is a moral point of view we should not defend.

We need to consider the moral implications of such theodicies, and ask whether those implications are harmless. In the next section we examine two attempts to treat the problem of evil from a moral perspective.

MORAL CALLOUSNESS

There is more than one way to conceive of a world in which there is no evil, and it matters how we go about it. On the one hand, we can imagine a world in which many of the things that happen in our actual world never happen—a world in which children never suffer from hunger, genocides never occur, and no one tortures animals for amusement. In short, we can conceive of a world in which evil does not exist as a world in which the things we now consider evil never happen. On the other hand, we might try to conceive of a world in which everything that happens in our world continues to happen, but in which those same things are no longer evil. There are still starving children and genocides, and animals are still tortured for amusement. In this scenario, however, we are asked to suppose that those are good things or, at the very least, not bad things. In the first case we imagine an evil-free world by imagining a world that is very different from ours; in the second we imagine that everything in our world—just as it is—is good.

It is important to recognize that those who want to defend a theodicy and also want to be faithful to the facts are only left with the second alternative—the strategy of denying that these things are evil. This is why what began as a metaphysical disagreement about what really exists ends up resembling a moral disagreement about whether the things that exist are good or evil. This is exactly how some critics of theodicies see the disagreement: They charge theists who are willing to construct a theodicy with a grave moral error and with callous indifference to the suffering of others. The charge is not that theodicies are bad metaphysics, but that they are bad morals.

The accusation is usefully coupled with the problem of how evil is *distributed*. Try a simple thought experiment. Suppose there exists a race of morally superficial, morally shallow creatures. They like to think very highly of themselves, but in truth they don't care much about the suffering of others. Suppose furthermore that they also recognize that there is a remedy for much of the world's suffering, requiring only a little effort on their part. But because they are so distracted by and preoccupied with their relatively enjoyable lives they are unwilling to lift a finger to help others. In order to continue to think highly of themselves, they are motivated to believe that there is nothing they can do about the suffering of others. They might even tell themselves that there are important "metaphysical" reasons why such suffering is required, or that there is a point of view from which the suffering of others doesn't look so bad. As one theologian wrote, "A theodicy justifies the happiness of the powerful and the suffering of the powerless."[9] From one perspective, such superficial creatures look like moral monsters. From another, they look a lot like us.

---

[9] Gunnerman, J. P. (1979). *The Moral Meaning of Revolution*. New Haven: Yale University Press: p. 43.

The urgent challenge to those who defend a theodicy is to explain why they are not the moral monsters we have just imagined. By insisting on either the necessity or the unreality of evil, theists risk promoting moral passivity and encouraging acquiescence in the suffering of others.

But metaphysical theories are attempts to describe the contents and contours of reality, not attempts to judge them. And since our theodicies are metaphysical theories, how can the moral complaints we are considering be relevant to evaluating them? William James thought that the moral implications of adopting metaphysical theories *are* relevant to how we should evaluate them. In the following passages, he quotes extensively from Leibniz's theodicy and from the writings of the "anarchist"[10] social theorist Morrison I. Swift (1856–1946).

Metaphysics or Morals? (William James, 1907)[11]

> *Refinement* is what characterizes our intellectualist philosophies. They exquisitely satisfy that craving for a refined object of contemplation which is so powerful an appetite of the mind. But I ask you in all seriousness to look abroad on this colossal universe of concrete facts, on their awful bewilderments, their surprises and cruelties, on the wildness which they show, and then to tell me whether 'refined' is the one inevitable descriptive adjective that springs to your lips.
>
> Refinement has its place in things, true enough. But a philosophy that breathes out nothing but refinement will never satisfy the empiricist temper of mind. It will seem rather a monument of artificiality. So we find men of science preferring to turn their backs on metaphysics as on something altogether cloistered and spectral, and practical men shaking philosophy's dust off their feet and following the call of the wild.
>
> Truly there is something a little ghastly in the satisfaction with which a pure but unreal system will fill a rationalist mind. Leibniz was a rationalist mind, with infinitely more interest in facts than most rationalist minds can show. Yet if you wish for superficiality incarnate, you have only to read that charmingly written 'Theodicee' of his, in which he sought to justify the ways of God to man, and to prove that the world we live in is the best of possible worlds. Let me quote a specimen of what I mean.
>
> Among other obstacles to his optimistic philosophy, it falls to Leibniz to consider the number of the eternally damned. That it is infinitely greater, in our human case, than that of those saved he assumes as a premise from the theologians, and then proceeds to argue in this way. Even then, he says:
>
> "The evil will appear as almost nothing in comparison with the good, if we once consider the real magnitude of the City of God. . . . Our earth is only one among the six principal satellites of our sun. As all the fixed stars are suns, one sees how small a place among visible things our earth takes up, since it is only a satellite of one among them. Now all these suns *may* be inhabited by none but happy creatures; and nothing obliges us to believe that the number of damned persons is very great; for a *very few instances and samples suffice for the utility which good draws from evil.* Moreover, since there is no reason to suppose that there are stars everywhere, may there not be

[10] In fact, Swift was a socialist, not an anarchist.

[11] From James, W. (1907). *Pragmatism; A New Name for Some Old Ways of Thinking.* Retrieved on August 10, 2014, from http://www.gutenberg.org/cache/epub/5116/pg5116.txt

a great space beyond the region of the stars? And this immense space, surrounding all this region, . . . may be replete with happiness and glory. . . . Thus the part of the Universe which we know, being almost lost in nothingness compared with that which is unknown to us, but which we are yet obliged to admit; and all the evils that we know lying in this almost-nothing; it follows that the evils may be almost-nothing in comparison with the goods that the Universe contains."

Leibniz continues elsewhere: "There is a kind of justice which aims neither at the amendment of the criminal, nor at furnishing an example to others, nor at the reparation of the injury. . . . It is always founded in the fitness of things, and satisfies not only the offended party, but all wise lookers-on, even as beautiful music or a fine piece of architecture satisfies a well-constituted mind. It is thus that the torments of the damned continue, even [though] they serve no longer to turn anyone away from sin, and that the rewards of the blest continue, even [though] they confirm no one in good ways. . . . for God has made all things harmonious in perfection as I have already said."

Leibniz's feeble grasp of reality is too obvious to need comment from me. It is evident that no realistic image of the experience of a damned soul had ever approached the portals of his mind. Nor had it occurred to him that the smaller is the number of 'samples' of the genus 'lost-soul' whom God throws as a sop to the eternal fitness, the more unequitably grounded is the glory of the blest. What he gives us is a cold literary exercise, whose cheerful substance even hell-fire does not warm. . . .

I find a fine example of revolt against the airy and shallow optimism of current religious philosophy in a publication of that valiant anarchistic writer Morrison I. Swift. Mr. Swift's anarchism goes a little farther than mine does, but I confess that I sympathize a good deal, and some of you, I know, will sympathize heartily with his dissatisfaction with the idealistic optimisms now in vogue. He begins his pamphlet on 'Human Submission' with a series of city reporter's items from newspapers (suicides, deaths from starvation and the like) as specimens of our civilized regime. For instance:

"'After trudging through the snow from one end of the city to the other in the vain hope of securing employment, and with his wife and six children without food and ordered to leave their home in an upper east side tenement house because of nonpayment of rent, John Corcoran, a clerk, to-day ended his life by drinking carbolic acid. Corcoran lost his position three weeks ago through illness, and during the period of idleness his scanty savings disappeared. Yesterday he obtained work with a gang of city snow shovelers, but he was too weak from illness and was forced to quit after an hour's trial with the shovel. Then the weary task of looking for employment was again resumed. Thoroughly discouraged, Corcoran returned to his home late last night to find his wife and children without food and the notice of dispossession on the door.' On the following morning he drank the poison.

"The records of many more such cases lie before me [Mr. Swift goes on]; an encyclopedia might easily be filled with their kind. These few I cite as an interpretation of the universe. 'We are aware of the presence of God in His world,' says a writer in a recent English Review. [The very presence of ill in the temporal order is the condition of the perfection of the eternal order, writes Professor Royce ('*The World and the Individual*,' II, 385).] 'The Absolute is the richer for every discord, and for all diversity which it embraces,' says F. H. Bradley (*Appearance and Reality*, 204). He means that these slain men make the universe richer, and that is Philosophy. But while Professors Royce and Bradley and a whole host of guileless thoroughfed thinkers are unveiling Reality and the Absolute and explaining away evil and pain, this is the condition of the only beings known to us anywhere in the universe with a developed consciousness

Logic Box

Ad Hominem Arguments

An ***ad hominem* argument** commits the fallacy of attacking the person who makes a claim or who presents an argument, instead of evaluating their claim or argument on its own terms. Some *ad hominem* arguments cite a person's character or profession, special circumstances, or some possible conflict of interest as grounds for not considering her views or arguments. This is a fallacy because if someone's claims and arguments really are problematic, they will be problematic regardless of *who* expresses them. One way to gauge whether you might be guilty of an *ad hominem* attack on a person's arguments is to consider whether you would have the same objections if her arguments had been made by someone else. If not, then you are probably guilty of an *ad hominem* fallacy.

Example: "His arguments for the existence of God are suspect. After all, he is a member of the clergy. What would you expect him to argue?"

***ad hominem* argument:** An *ad hominem* is an argument that commits the fallacy of attacking the person who makes a claim or who presents the argument instead of evaluating the claim or argument itself.

> of what the universe is. What these people experience *is* Reality. . . . The philosophers are dealing in shades, while those who live and feel know truth. . . .
>
> "This Cleveland workingman, killing his children and himself [another of the cited cases], is one of the elemental, stupendous facts of this modern world and of this universe. It cannot be glozed over or minimized away by all the treatises on God, and Love, and Being, helplessly existing in their haughty monumental vacuity. . . . These facts invincibly prove religion a nullity. Man will not give religion two thousand centuries or twenty centuries more to try itself and waste human time; its time is up, its probation is ended. Its own record ends it. Mankind has not sons and eternities to spare for trying out discredited systems. . . ."[12]
>
> Such is the reaction of an empiricist mind upon the rationalist bill of fare. It is an absolute 'No, I thank you.' "Religion," says Mr. Swift, "is like a sleep-walker to whom actual things are blank." And such, though possibly less tensely charged with feeling, is the verdict of every seriously inquiring amateur in philosophy to-day who turns to the philosophy-professors for the wherewithal to satisfy the [fullness] of his nature's needs.

Leibniz's response to the problem of evil, when it emphasizes the excessive quantity of evil that exists, is to say that the universe is vast and most of it is unknown to us. Our idea that there is too much evil is a result of our very limited perspective. *For all we know* "the evils may be almost-nothing in comparison with the goods." Leibniz agrees that the suffering of the damned continues far beyond the point at which they serve any useful purpose, such as preventing further sins or deterring others from sin. But they must continue because, as he says, they are needed to keep "all things harmonious in perfection." From the perspective of morality, James sees this only as a demonstration that Leibniz's "feeble grasp of reality is too obvious to need comment," and his philosophy is "superficiality incarnate."

We should pause here to consider whether James and Swift are simply guilty of ***ad hominem*** fallacies—of mere name-calling, or attacks on their opponent's characters—or

[12] Swift, M. I. (1905). *Human Submission*. Part Second. Philadelphia: Liberty Press: 4–10.

whether there is another way to understand their complaints about theodicies. If James's reasoning takes this first form, then he commits an *ad hominem* fallacy:

1. Leibniz is morally superficial, and he has a feeble grasp of reality.

2. Therefore, we *should not* believe his theodicy.

If, on the other hand, his reasoning takes this second form, it does not commit an *ad hominem* fallacy (which is not to say that it is free from other logical errors):

1'. Believing Leibniz's theodicy requires holding morally callous views.

2'. Therefore, we *should not* believe his theodicy.

If this second reconstruction is James's argument, we arrive at a tangled nest of questions. First, the argument seems strong if we interpret the "should not" in conclusion (2') as saying that we are *morally obliged* not to believe Leibniz's theodicy. But it seems less plausible if it is intended to suggest that his theodicy is *not true*. After all, what does whether a metaphysical theory is *immoral* have to do with whether it is *true or false*? We would never decide the truth or falsity of a scientific theory on the basis of any moral consequences that followed from believing the theory, so why should it be any different for a metaphysical theory?

There are other ways to understand what James and Swift are up to in these emotionally charged passages. One possibility is that they begin with the premise that *it is just a fact* that the starvation of children, the practice of slavery, and so on are morally bad. This interpretation is supported by Swift's blunt claim that "These facts invincibly prove religion a nullity." Then, if it can be shown that theodicies deny these facts, they will be shown to fail because they are contradicted by the facts, not—or not *only*—because they are immoral. On this interpretation of James and Swift, theodicies fail for the same reason that bad scientific theories often fail—because they contradict known facts.

On behalf of the theist it might be objected that this requires James and Swift to suppose that there are such things as *moral facts*—facts about what is good or evil. If one is skeptical about the existence of moral facts, the argument will not be found compelling. But a theist who wishes to defend a theodicy is not entitled to skepticism about the existence of moral facts. After all, the theist is insisting that slavery, when seen from God's perspective, is actually good—that slavery is *in fact* good and not evil. So the defenders of a theodicy cannot deny their critics the use of the idea of moral facts without pulling the rug out from under themselves. From the perspective offered by James and Swift, the questions that divide the atheist and the theist concern what the moral facts *are*, not whether there are any.

Although the arguments surrounding the problem of evil are intended to be metaphysical, they seem unable to stay that way for long. Theists commonly respond to the problem of evil by either justifying the evil that does exist, or by denying that any evil exists. This amounts to saying that the things we take to be evil—slavery, famine, and so on—are either *justified* evils or are *not evil*. Our question about whether evil is real becomes a question of whether slavery, famine, and so on are evil. James's point is that this is not a metaphysical question but a moral one.

James's charge is that to defend a theodicy is to deny, to excuse, or even to glorify terrible evils. What response is available to a still-committed theist who is not willing to do any of these things? One strategy for theists to escape the charge of moral callousness is illustrated by **Ivan Karamazov**, a character in Fyodor Dostoyevsky's great novel *The Brothers Karamazov*. In the following paragraphs, Ivan explains to his brother Alyosha, who is a novice monk, something that has been troubling him. He begins by relating a story he had recently read.

Ivan Karamazov: A fictional character in Fyodor Dostoyevsky's *The Brothers Karamazov*, Ivan is portrayed as a cold intellectual who nonetheless brings a deeply philosophical perspective to many of the novel's most memorable scenes.

Fyodor Dostoyevsky: One of Russia's greatest novelists; his many novels and short stories explored philosophical questions about the human condition.

Rebellion (Fyodor Dostoyevsky, 1880)[13]

. . . There was in those days a general of aristocratic connections, the owner of great estates, one of those men—somewhat exceptional, I believe, even then—who, retiring from the service into a life of leisure, are convinced that they've earned absolute power over the lives of their subjects. There were such men then. So our general, settled on his property of two thousand souls, lives in pomp, and domineers over his poor neighbors as though they were dependents and buffoons. He has kennels of hundreds of hounds and nearly a hundred dog-boys—all mounted, and in uniform. One day a serf-boy, a little child of eight, threw a stone in play and hurt the paw of the general's favourite hound. 'Why is my favorite dog lame?' He is told that the boy threw a stone that hurt the dog's paw. 'So you did it.' The general looked the child up and down. 'Take him.' He was taken—taken from his mother and kept shut up all night. Early that morning the general comes out on horseback, with the hounds, his dependents, dog-boys, and huntsmen, all mounted around him in full hunting parade. The servants are summoned for their edification, and in front of them all stands the mother of the child. The child is brought from the lock-up. It's a gloomy, cold, foggy autumn day, a capital day for hunting. The general orders the child to be undressed; the child is stripped naked. He shivers, numb with terror, not daring to cry. . . . 'Make him run,' commands the general. 'Run! run!' shout the dog-boys. The boy runs. . . . 'At him!' yells the general, and he sets the whole pack of hounds on the child. The hounds catch him, and tear him to pieces before his mother's eyes! . . . .

"I understand nothing," Ivan went on, as though in delirium. "I don't want to understand anything now. I want to stick to the fact. I made up my mind long ago not to understand. If I try to understand anything, I shall be false to the fact, and I have determined to stick to the fact." . . .

"Listen! I took the case of children only to make my case clearer. Of the other tears of humanity with which the earth is soaked from its crust to its center, I will say nothing. I have narrowed my subject on purpose. I am a bug, and I recognize in all humility that I cannot understand why the world is arranged as it is. . . . With my pitiful, earthly, Euclidian understanding, all I know is that there is suffering . . . and I can't consent to live by it! . . . Surely I haven't suffered simply that I, my crimes and my sufferings, may manure the soil of the future harmony for somebody else. I want to see with my own eyes the hind lie down with the lion and the victim rise up and embrace his murderer. I want to be there when every one suddenly understands what it has all been for. All the religions of the world are built on this longing, and I am a believer. But then there are the children, and what am I to do about them? That's a question I can't answer. For the hundredth time I repeat, there are numbers of questions, but I've only taken the children, because in their case what I mean is so unanswerably clear. Listen! If all must suffer to pay for the eternal harmony, what have children to do with it, tell me, please? It's beyond all comprehension why they should suffer, and why they

[13] From Dostoyevsky, F. (1880). *The Brothers Karamazov*. (Constance Garnett, Trans.). Retrieved on August 10, 2014, from http://www.gutenberg.org/files/28054/28054-0.txt

should pay for the harmony. Why should they, too, furnish material to enrich the soil for the harmony of the future? . . . [W]hat pulls me up here is that I can't accept that harmony. And while I am on earth, I make haste to take my own measures. . . . While there is still time, I hasten to protect myself, and so I renounce the higher harmony altogether. It's not worth the tears of that one tortured child who beat itself on the breast with its little fist and prayed in its stinking outhouse, with its unexpiated tears to 'dear, kind God'! . . . And if the sufferings of children go to swell the sum of sufferings which was necessary to pay for truth, then I protest that the truth is not worth such a price. . . . I don't want harmony. From love for humanity I don't want it. I would rather be left with the unavenged suffering. I would rather remain with my unavenged suffering and unsatisfied indignation, even if I were wrong. Besides, too high a price is asked for harmony; it's beyond our means to pay so much to enter on it. And so I hasten to give back my entrance ticket, and if I am an honest man I am bound to give it back as soon as possible. And that I am doing. It's not God that I don't accept, Alyosha, only I most respectfully return him the ticket."

"That's rebellion," murmured Alyosha, looking down.

"Rebellion? I am sorry you call it that," said Ivan earnestly. "One can hardly live in rebellion, and I want to live. Tell me yourself, I challenge you—answer. Imagine that you are creating a fabric of human destiny with the object of making men happy in the end, giving them peace and rest at last, but that it was essential and inevitable to torture to death only one tiny creature—that baby beating its breast with its fist, for instance—and to found that edifice on its unavenged tears, would you consent to be the architect on those conditions? Tell me, and tell the truth."

"No, I wouldn't consent," said Alyosha softly.

Throughout his attempts to grapple with the problem of evil, Ivan remains committed to theism. As he tells his brother, "It's not God that I don't accept." Ivan also believes that in order to make the existence of God consistent with the existence of evil, it would be necessary to defend the torture and suffering of children, or to diminish its importance. This is something he refuses to do—he will not succumb to the temptations of a theodicy. Ivan holds fast to the belief that the suffering of children is an unjustifiable evil: It is, he thinks, *a fact* that their suffering is morally inexcusable, and Ivan has decided that he will "stick to the facts."

If Ivan is not prepared to give up his belief in an all-good Creator, and he is not prepared to justify the suffering of the children, then he sees only one alternative. He says simply, "I made up my mind long ago not to understand. If I try to understand anything, I shall be false to the fact." In other words, Ivan gives up any hope of understanding or making sense of the world. The existence of evil would make sense if it were needed for some "higher harmony," but retaining his belief in a "higher harmony" requires Ivan to justify the suffering of children, and this he flatly refuses to do. Ivan's rebellion is not against God, but against any higher harmony that pretends to make the suffering of children morally acceptable. It is useful to note three things about Ivan's reaction to the problem of evil.

First, he is not expressing bafflement or incomprehension in the face of evil; he is expressing a refusal to turn his back on it. Rather than diminish or deny the significance of evil, he chooses instead to give up the idea that the world is comprehensible. This requires him to rebel against any theodicy that tries to make the suffering of the children part of some "higher harmony." Ivan chooses to live in a world that makes no sense rather than believe a theory that can only make sense of it by treating the torture and suffering of a child as necessary or insignificant. If that is what it costs to make sense of things, then, Ivan thinks, the price is too high.

Second, Ivan is not saying that God's ways are mysterious and so we cannot comprehend them—though that may well be true. That would imply that God has some good reason for allowing children to suffer, and that we don't—or can't—comprehend His reason. But Ivan recognizes that this is merely another way of saying there is a good reason for the evil after all, so it is a way to justify indifference to the suffering. For Ivan, saying that the world is incomprehensible is to state *a metaphysical fact about the world*, not merely to give expression to our ignorance about it. The world is not incomprehensible because we fail to grasp its meaning or purpose; it is incomprehensible because it has no meaning or purpose for us to grasp: There is no higher harmony in which the evil of suffering will be diluted.

Third, the incomprehensibility of the world, as Ivan sees it, is a direct consequence of two beliefs he is not prepared to give up: One belief is that the torture and suffering of children is indefensible; the other is that there is an all-good, all-knowing, all-powerful God. So Ivan's reaction to the problem of evil results from what he sees as a forced choice between three options:

i. We can try to deny or to justify evil.

ii. We can give up belief in God.

iii. We can give up the belief that the world and our place in it make sense.

To defend a theodicy is to opt for (i); the atheist opts for (ii); Ivan opts for (iii). This is a surprising consequence, since theists often maintain that belief in God is needed to give meaning to the world and to our lives. Ivan's story tries to illustrate that, in the face of evil, a belief in God could prevent the world from having any meaning.

Ivan Karamazov and William James share the idea that to deny or diminish the significance of certain kinds of suffering is to deny obvious facts. Theodicies are, they think, theories that attempt to do precisely that, so they fail *as theories*—they fail because they fail to fit the facts. But, more importantly, because our theodicies require us to deny facts about the evils of human suffering—to deny *moral facts*—both thinkers agree that defending a theodicy is also a serious moral failing.

CONCLUSION

In this chapter we examined a central argument for atheism. The problem of evil presents a challenge to belief in God that theists have long recognized and wrestled with. The characteristics of God Himself seem to make the existence of evil impossible. Some theists try to reconcile the existence of God and the existence of evil by arguing that evil is necessary for good, while others do so by denying that evil exists.

We examined some of the common metaphysical objections to the problem of evil, and we let the atheists respond to those objections. The next move belongs to the theist, who now needs to supply new metaphysical arguments or to rebut the atheists' responses. Finally, we explored a different kind of objection to the very idea of a theodicy and to any attempt to justify or deny the reality of evil. According to that objection, expressed by William James, the strategy of denying or justifying evil is suspect on moral grounds. Although theodicies are intended to be metaphysical theories, James believes they are only particularly callous moral views.

In Chapter 15, we will explore an idea that many theists, like Ivan Karamazov, have turned to when faced with the problem of evil: the idea of *faith*. Earlier we separated the question of whether God exists from the question of whether it is reasonable to believe God exists. It is the notion of faith that allows us to separate the two questions. It allows theists to go so far as to say that there is a God, but *there is no good reason to believe there is a God*, or even that *there is very good reason to believe there is no God*. Faith clips the wings of any arguments, reasons, or evidence by allowing theists to separate what they think it is reasonable to believe and what they do believe. In Chapter 15, we explore whether this separation comes at an acceptable price.

Key Terms and Figures

modus tollens p. 296
problem of evil p. 296
natural evil p. 297
moral evil p. 297
contradiction p. 298
logical impossibility p. 298
omnipotence paradox p. 298
theodicy p. 299
Marquis de Sade p. 300
Hannah Arendt p. 302
banality of evil p. 302
St. Augustine p. 302
ad hominen argument p. 309
Ivan Karamazov p. 311
Fyodor Dostoyevsky p. 311

Additional readings on the problem of evil

Beebe, J. R. (n.d.). Logical Problem of Evil. (James Fieser, Ph.D., founder and general editor; Bradley Dowden, Ph.D., general editor). *Internet Encyclopedia of Philosophy*. Available at http://www.iep.utm.edu/evil-log

Hick, J. (1990). The Problem of Evil. *Philosophy of Religion*. Fourth edition. Englewood Cliffs, N. J. : Prentice Hall.

Hume, D. (n.d.). *Dialogues Concerning Natural Religion*, Part X. Available at http://www.gutenberg.org/cache/epub/4583/pg4583.txt

Mackie, J. L. (1955). Evil and Omnipotence. *Mind*, *64*: 200–212.

Neiman, S. (2002). *Evil in Modern Thought: An Alternative History of Philosophy*. Princeton University Press, Princeton and Oxford.

Chapter 15

Faith, Revelation, and the Will

Learning Objectives

- Explain the contrast between faith as revelation and faith as willed belief, and distinguish three views about the relationship between faith and reason.
- Describe transrational fideism and summarize at least one objection to it.
- Explain Locke's reasons for thinking that strength of conviction cannot be a way of recognizing genuine faith.
- Describe two ways, both direct and indirect, that belief might result from voluntary acts of will.
- Contrast justifying reasons and prudential reasons, and use Pascal's wager to illustrate prudential reasoning.
- Summarize Clifford's argument for the conclusion that we have a moral duty to believe only on the basis of the evidence.
- Explain William James's definition of faith, and say why it makes faith more widespread than Locke's view.

In an earlier chapter we distinguished two questions: (i) Does God exist? and (ii) Is it reasonable, or rational, to believe that God exists? The second question has so far occupied all our attention. In pursuit of an answer, we examined a variety of attempts to give rational proofs of the existence of God by reasoning from His purported "signs" or effects. We then considered whether religious experiences or miracles, or the testimony of those who claim to have had or witnessed them, can justify belief in God. Finally, we explored an argument that purports to show that it is rational to believe God does not exist. By examining these topics, we identified numerous reasons why many people, *atheists and theists alike*, believe the answer to the second question is: "No. On balance, it is not rational to believe that God exists."

Surprisingly, the conclusion that it is not reasonable to believe God exists is accepted by many theists as well as by atheists. All that theists and atheists need to agree on is that, inconclusive though they may be, the evidence and arguments by themselves do not, on balance, favour belief in the existence of God. The gap between questions (i) and (ii) then encourages theists to think that, although it is not *rational* for them to believe God exists, it is nonetheless true that He exists.

Theists who allow that their belief in God is not reasonable will typically claim that their belief is *a matter of faith*, not a matter of reason. In this chapter, we will search for a better understanding of what that means, and explore whether faith has a legitimate role in determining what we believe.

FAITH: WHAT IS IT?

Theists and atheists can both entertain and understand the proposition "God exists." The difference between the two lies in the attitude each has to that proposition: The theist *accepts* it or *assents* to it, but the atheist *rejects* it or *dissents* from it. So we can say that they have *different attitudes* to the *same proposition*. People can have a wide variety of "attitudes" to the same proposition—I can *assent* to its truth, while you *doubt* it, and someone else *hopes* it is true—but belief requires us to accept or assent to the truth of some proposition.

On this view, what distinguishes faith from other forms of belief is *the source or basis of the assent*. The word *faith* is usually reserved for assent that is not a result of ordinary reason (i.e., evidence or argument). If my assent to the proposition that grass is green is a result of my observations of grass, then my belief that grass is green is not an example of faith. Similarly, if my assent to the proposition that God exists is based on a cosmological argument, then my belief is not an example of faith.

This account of faith is still too broad, since it does not yet identify the *source* our assent must have before it qualifies as faith. Various theists have filled in that detail in two quite different ways. On the one hand, there are those who think that "faith" is belief—assent to a proposition—that is justified by or grounded on **revelation**. That is, they hold that we believe something on faith whenever it has been directly revealed by God; usually these are not things we can know in the ordinary ways. But there are other theists—perhaps more common today—who contend that when we believe something on faith our assent derives from a voluntary act of will. According to them, we believe something on faith only when we have freely chosen to believe it—in other words, faith is *willed belief*. As we proceed we will look in detail at both views.

revelation: A proposition that has been revealed or disclosed by God; believed by some theists to be a possible source of knowledge or justification.

Relationships between Faith and Reason

We will distinguish three views about the relationship between faith and reason:[1] Each has its advocates.

1. **Compatibilism**: *Faith and reason are compatible*.

compatibilism (of faith and reason): The view that whatever is knowable on the basis of faith is also knowable on the basis of reason, and that faith and reason will never impart conflicting beliefs.

On this view, whatever can be known on the basis of faith can also be known on the basis of reason and, furthermore, faith and reason will never give different or conflicting results. A consequence of this view is that if reason soundly *opposes* belief in the existence of God, then a belief in God cannot legitimately be based on faith. Our primary concern is not with compatibilism of this sort, which seems to only make faith superfluous. Instead, we will focus on two fideistic views about faith. Recall that fideism is the doctrine that it is impossible or inappropriate to hold religious beliefs accountable to reason or evidence. There are two forms of fideism:

[1] In an earlier chapter, when discussing the sources of knowledge, we used a *contrast* between reason and experience. But in the debate between reason and faith, "reason" refers to whatever makes it rational to hold a belief, and so includes both *rational arguments* and *experiential evidence*.

2. Transrationalist fideism: *Faith transcends, or goes beyond, reason.*

transrationalist fideism: The view that faith transcends, or goes beyond, reason. Faith is a way of arriving at true beliefs on matters that reason must remain silent about, since they are beyond the reach of reason.

This is the idea that faith has a greater "reach" than reason. On this view, to have faith is to have a way of arriving at true beliefs that reason, even when used to its fullest potential, cannot arrive at. Beliefs held on faith will then never conflict with anything reason tells us, since reason will have *nothing* to tell us on matters that are the proper concern of faith. On all such matters reason is silent. Reason continues to rule *within its own domain*, so no belief that conflicts with reason can be accepted as true on faith. Within reason's proper domain, all appeals to faith are illegitimate. The idea that faith transcends reason has the consequence that it is never possible to use reason to confirm or disprove claims made on the basis of faith. Central to transrational fideism is the idea that reason and faith each operate in separate domains. If that is so, exactly what sort of things can be believed on faith needs to be determined by first locating the boundaries of what reason can legitimately concern itself with.

3. Irrationalist fideism: *Faith and reason are incompatible.*

irrationalist fideism: The view that faith and reason are incompatible—that is, faith can and does provide beliefs that conflict with what our reason tells us. Furthermore, when faith and reason do come into conflict, faith always takes precedence.

According to irrationalist fideism, the beliefs we hold on faith are different from those we hold on the basis of reason, and they can and do conflict with the beliefs that reason supports. What makes this view *radical* is that it also holds that when faith and reason conflict, faith always *takes precedence* over reason. There is, then, no boundary separating the proper domains of reason and faith—they might both have something to say about whether God exists, or about whether broccoli is good for you. But if they say different things, we should always listen to faith. Of course, this cannot be because it is *more reasonable* to listen to faith—it is not, since on this view faith does not provide us with any reasons.

LOCKE ON REASON AND REVELATION

John Locke viewed faith as revelation, and he advocated a version of transrational fideism. Thus, he combined the thought that to accept something on faith requires that it be revealed to us by God, with the idea that God's knowledge extends into realms that we finite knowers cannot hope to explore on our own. Within those realms there are things knowable to God but not to us, and we can only learn of them if God chooses to reveal them to us. Like many of his predecessors in the Christian tradition, Locke understood faith to be a special kind of knowledge—knowledge that is *divinely revealed* rather than based on reason or experience of the world. Given the characteristics of God—that He is all-good and all-knowing—if God reveals something to us then we can be sure of its truth. To have faith is then to have a source of *justification* for beliefs that we could not otherwise have any grounds for holding.

In the passages that follow, Locke is concerned with locating the limits within which faith is legitimate, and he warns us about the dangers of transgressing those limits. Locke lived in a time of horrific religious wars, and was acutely sensitive to the fact that there are often impostors who declare themselves to be in possession of divine revelations. We can also sometimes convince ourselves that some conviction or belief that we hold has been revealed by God when it has not. Since, according to transrational fideists, we cannot use reason to check the truth or falsity of a revelation, errors of this kind are especially dangerous. If we are to rely on faith or revelation, it is crucial to distinguish those things that are genuinely revealed by God from those that are not. This is Locke's primary concern.

Revelation and Reason (John Locke)[2]

Chapter XVIII.

Of Faith and Reason, and their Distinct Provinces. . . .

2. I find every sect, as far as reason will help them, make use of it gladly: and where it fails them, they cry out, It is matter of faith, and above reason. And I do not see how they can argue with any one, or ever convince a gainsayer who makes use of the same plea, without setting down strict boundaries between faith and reason; which ought to be the first point established in all questions where faith has anything to do.

Reason, therefore, here, as contradistinguished to *faith*, I take to be the discovery of the certainty or probability of such propositions or truths, which the mind arrives at by deduction made from such ideas, which it has got by the use of its natural faculties; viz. by sensation or reflection.

Faith, on the other side, is the assent to any proposition, not thus made out by the deductions of reason, but upon the credit of the proposer, as coming from God, in some extraordinary way of communication. This way of discovering truths to men, we call *revelation*.

3. *First*, then I say, that *no man inspired by God can by any revelation communicate to others any new simple ideas which they had not before from sensation or reflection*. . . .

. . . I say, *traditional revelation*, in distinction to *original revelation*. By the one, I mean that first impression which is made immediately by God on the mind of any man, to which we cannot set any bounds; and by the other, those impressions delivered over to others in words, and the ordinary ways of conveying our conceptions one to another.

4. *Secondly*, I say that *the same truths may be discovered, and conveyed down from revelation, which are discernable to use by reason, and by those ideas we naturally may have*. So God might, by revelation, discover the truth of any proposition in Euclid; as well as men, by the natural use of their faculties, come to make the discovery themselves. In all things of this kind there is little need or use of revelation, God having furnished us with natural and surer means to arrive at the knowledge of them. For whatsoever truth we come to the clear discovery of, from the knowledge and contemplation of our own ideas, will always be certainer to us than those which are conveyed to us by *traditional revelation*. For the knowledge we have that this revelation came at first from God can never be so sure as the knowledge we have from the clear and distinct perception of the agreement or disagreement of our own ideas . . . the assurance of its being a revelation is less still than the assurance of [our] senses.

5. Even Original Revelation cannot be admitted against the clear Evidence of Reason.

. . . [A]nd there too our assurance can be no greater than our knowledge is, that it *is* a revelation from God. . . . Since the whole strength of the certainty depends upon our knowledge that God revealed it; which, in this case, where the proposition supposed revealed contradicts our knowledge or reason, will always have this objection hanging to it, viz. that we cannot tell how to conceive that to come from God, . . .

[2] From Locke, J. *An Essay Concerning Human Understanding*, Vol. 2, Book IV, Chapters XVIII and XIX. Retrieved on August 10, 2014, from http://oll.libertyfund.org/titles/locke-the-works-vol-2-an-essay-concerning-human-understanding-part-2-and-other-writings

6. . . . But to all those who pretend not to immediate revelation, but are required to pay obedience, and to receive the truths revealed to others, which, by the tradition of writings, or word of mouth, are conveyed down to them, reason has a great deal more to do, . . . the believing, or not believing, that proposition, or book, to be of divine authority, can never be matter of faith, but matter of reason; and such as I must come to an assent to only by the use of my reason, which can never require or enable me to believe that which is contrary to itself: it being impossible for reason ever to procure any assent to that which to itself appears unreasonable.

In all things, therefore, where we have clear evidence from our ideas, and those principles of knowledge I have above mentioned, reason is the proper judge; and revelation, though it may, in consenting with it, confirm its dictates, yet cannot in such cases invalidate its decrees: nor can we be obliged, where we have the clear and evident sentience of reason, to quit it for the contrary opinion, under a pretence that it is matter of faith: which can have no authority against the plain and clear dictates of reason. . . .

10. . . . Whatever God hath revealed is certainly true: no doubt can be made of it. This is the proper object of faith: but whether it be a *divine* revelation or no, reason must judge; . . .

11. If the Boundaries be not set between Faith and Reason, no Enthusiasm or Extravagancy in Religion can be contradicted.

If the provinces of faith and reason are not kept distinct by these boundaries, there will, in matters of religion, be no room for reason at all; and those extravagant opinions and ceremonies that are to be found in the several religions of the world will not deserve to be blamed. For, to this crying up of faith in *opposition* to reason, we may, I think, in good measure ascribe those absurdities that fill almost all the religions which possess and divide mankind. For men having been principled with an opinion, that they must not consult reason in the things of religion, however apparently contradictory to common sense and the very principles of all their knowledge, have let loose their fancies and natural superstition; and have been by them led into so strange opinions, and extravagant practices in religion, that a considerate man cannot but stand amazed at their follies, . . . So that, in effect, religion, which should most distinguish us from beasts, and ought most peculiarly to elevate us, as rational creatures, above brutes, is that wherein men often appear most irrational, and more senseless than beasts themselves. . . .

Chapter XIX

Of Enthusiasm

1. He that would seriously set upon the search of truth, ought in the first place to prepare his mind with a love of it. For he that loves it not, will not take much pains to get it, nor be much concerned when he misses it. There is nobody in the commonwealth of learning, who does not profess himself a lover of truth; and there is not a rational creature that would not take it amiss to be thought otherwise of. And yet for all this, one may truly say, that there are very few lovers of truth for truth's sake, even amongst those who persuade themselves that they are so. How a man may know whether he be so in earnest, is worth inquiry: and I think there is one unerring mark of it, viz. the not entertaining any proposition with greater assurance, than the proofs it is built upon will warrant. . . . For the evidence that any proposition is true (except such as are self-evident) lying only in the proofs a man has of it, whatsoever degrees

of assent he affords it beyond the degrees of that evidence, it is plain that all the surplusage of assurance is owing to some other affection, and not to the love of truth. . . .

3. Upon this occasion I shall take the liberty to consider a third ground of assent, which with some men has the same authority, and is as confidently relied on as either faith or reason; I mean enthusiasm: which laying by reason, would set up revelation without it. Whereby in effect it takes away both reason and revelation, and substitutes in the room of it the ungrounded fancies of a man's own brain, and assumes them for a foundation both of opinion and conduct.

4. . . . [R]evelation is natural reason enlarged by a new set of discoveries communicated by God immediately, which reason vouches the truth of, by the testimony and proofs it gives, that they come from God. So that he that takes away reason, to make way for revelation, puts out the light of both, and does much-what the same, as if he would persuade a man to put out his eyes, the better to receive the remote light of an invisible star by a telescope. . . .

7. This I take to be properly enthusiasm, which, though founded neither on reason nor divine revelation, but rising from the conceits of a warmed or overweening brain, works yet, where it once gets footing, more powerfully on the persuasions and actions of men, than either of those two, or both together . . .

8. Though the odd opinions and extravagant actions enthusiasm has run men into, were enough to warn them against this wrong principle, so apt to misguide them both in their belief and conduct; yet the love of something extraordinary, the ease and glory it is to be inspired, and be above the common and natural ways of knowledge, so flatters many men's laziness, ignorance, and vanity, that when once they are got into this way of immediate revelation, of illumination without search, and of certainty without proof and without examination; it is a hard matter to get them out of it. Reason is lost upon them, they are above it: they see the light infused into their understandings, and cannot be mistaken; it is clear and visible there, like the light of bright sunshine; shows itself, and needs no other proof but its own evidence: they feel the hand of God moving them within, and the impulses of the spirit, and cannot be mistaken in what they feel. . . . When the spirit brings light into our minds, it dispels darkness. We see it, as we do that of the sun at noon, and need not the twilight of reason to show it us. . . .

9. This is the way of talking of these men: they are sure, because they are sure: and their persuasions are right, because they are strong in them. For, when what they say is stripped of the metaphor of seeing and feeling, this is all it amounts to: and yet these similes so impose on them, that they serve them for certainty in themselves, and demonstration to others.

10. . . . But here let me ask: this seeing, is it the perception of the truth of the proposition, or of this, that it is a revelation from God? This feeling, is it a perception of an inclination or fancy to do something, or of the spirit of God moving that inclination? These are two very different perceptions, and must be carefully distinguished, if we would not impose upon ourselves. I may perceive the truth of a proposition, and yet not perceive that it is an immediate revelation from God. . . . So that the knowledge of any proposition coming into my mind, I know not

how, is not a perception that it is from God. Much less is a strong persuasion, that it is true, a perception that it is from God, or so much as true. . . . I must see that it is God that reveals this to me, or else I see nothing. . . . For if I mistake not, these men receive it for true, because they presume God revealed it. Does it not then stand them upon, to examine upon what grounds they presume it to be a revelation from God? or else all their confidence is mere presumption: and this light, they are so dazzled with, is nothing but an *ignis fatuus* [illusion] that leads them constantly round in this circle; it is a revelation, because they firmly believe it, and they believe it, because it is a revelation.

11. In all that is of divine revelation, there is need of no other proof but that it is an inspiration from God: for he can neither deceive nor be deceived. But how shall it be known that any proposition in our minds is a truth infused by God; a truth that is revealed to us by him, which he declares to us, and therefore we ought to believe? Here it is that enthusiasm fails of the evidence it pretends to. . . . If they say they know it to be true, because it is a revelation from God, the reason is good: but then it will be demanded how they know it to be a revelation from God. If they say, by the light it brings with it, which shines bright in their minds, and they cannot resist: I beseech them to consider whether this be any more than what we have taken notice of already, viz. that it is a revelation, because they strongly believe it to be true. For all the light they speak of is but a strong, though ungrounded persuasion of their own minds, that it is a truth. . . . [A]nd if they believe it to be true, because it is a revelation, and have no other reason for its being a revelation, but because they are fully persuaded without any other reason that it is true; they believe it to be a revelation, only because they strongly believe it to be a revelation; which is a very unsafe ground to proceed on, either in our tenets or actions. And what readier way can there be to run ourselves into the most extravagant errors and miscarriages, than thus to set up fancy for our supreme and sole guide, and to believe any proposition to be true, any action to be right, only because we believe it to be so? The strength of our persuasions is no evidence at all of their own rectitude: crooked things may be as stiff and inflexible as straight: and men may be as positive and peremptory in error as in truth. . . .

13. Light, true light, in the mind is, or can be nothing else but the evidence of the truth of any proposition . . . To talk of any other light in the understanding is to put ourselves in the dark, or in the power of the Prince of Darkness, and by our own consent to give ourselves up to delusion to believe a lie. For if strength of persuasion be the light, which must guide us; I ask how shall any one distinguish between the delusions of Satan, and the inspirations of the Holy Ghost? . . .

14. He therefore that will not give himself up to all the extravagances of delusion and error, must bring this guide of his light within to the trial. God, when he makes the prophet, does not unmake the man. He leaves all his faculties in the natural state, to enable him to judge of his inspirations, whether they be of divine original or no. When he illuminates the mind with supernatural light, he does not extinguish that which is natural. If he would have us assent to the truth of any proposition, he either evidences that truth by the usual methods of natural reason, or else makes it known to be a truth which he would have us assent to by his authority; and convinces us that it is from him, by some marks which reason cannot be mistaken in. Reason must be our last judge and guide in every thing.

Recognizing Genuine Faith

Two closely related themes dominate Locke's discussion of faith:

A. *Genuine faith is recognizable only by reason.*
Locke defines *faith* as the assent to a proposition, when our assent is owed to our belief that the proposition has been revealed to us by God. But how do we decide which propositions are revealed by God and which are not? Locke's central concern is to understand how we can distinguish a genuine revelation from its impostors. He arrives at one principle to guide this decision: "[F]aith can never convince of anything that contradicts our knowledge [reason]." To understand why Locke thinks we need this principle, we should distinguish two distinct beliefs we have whenever we accept something as a matter of faith:

i. Assent to the proposition that (we think) God reveals to us; and
ii. Assent to the proposition that this first proposition is *a revelation from God.*

For example, perhaps I believe that (i) *Angels watch over us*, and also that (ii) *This has been revealed to me by God.* Locke agrees that if God reveals something to us, then it is certainly true. Thus, we can know something on the basis of faith, or revelation, only if we also know God revealed it to us. That is, we can know (i) only if we also know (ii). So the question Locke explores is: What is the basis for our conviction in (ii) that some proposition was revealed by God?

We can't ground our conviction in (ii) on faith, since we need to rely on *something other than faith* to test something's claim to be faith. If we are wondering whether someone is a liar, we cannot simply ask him—a liar and a truth teller will give the same answer. Similarly, if we only accept *on faith* that our belief is genuine faith, the impostors won't be exposed. That only leaves reason to test for genuine revelations . But, then, if the proposition that God is purported to reveal to us in (i) contradicts what we can know on the basis of reason, it will fail to qualify as genuine faith. It must be an impostor to genuine faith—"it being impossible for reason ever to procure any assent to that which to itself appears unreasonable."[3] To accept something on the basis of faith, or revelation, is, for Locke, always the right thing to do, providing that revelation really is the basis for our belief. But only reason can decide whether that is so, and therefore "Reason must be our last judge and guide in everything."[4]

B. *The strength of our conviction is no sign that our faith is genuine.*
Enthusiasm is Locke's label for the *unshakably strong conviction of rightness* that we often associate with fanatics or zealots. Here is how Locke sees someone afflicted with enthusiasm—an "enthusiast"—as reasoning:

enthusiasm: A seventeenth- and eighteenth-century term for *fanaticism* or *zealotry.* It is John Locke's term for an unshakable conviction of rightness that accompanies certain forms of religious belief.

i. I strongly believe, with complete conviction, that some proposition is true.
ii. But this proposition cannot be known, or known with such certainty, by reason or observation.
iii. So, this proposition could only be known with such certainty by faith.

---

[3] *Ibid.*

[4] *Ibid.*

iv. So, my strong conviction must be a matter of faith; it is divinely revealed.

v. But, if something is revealed by God, then it is true.

vi. So, my strong conviction is not misplaced—the proposition is true.

This amounts to declaring that our belief is true solely on the grounds that we hold it with strong conviction—as Locke says, their "confidence of being right is made an argument of truth."[5] In this line of thought, the mistake is in thinking that because we so strongly believe something, it cannot be false. This assumption is evident in how the argument reaches step (iv), which follows from (iii) only if we first rule out the possibility that our strong conviction is simply misplaced or unwarranted. Those infected with enthusiasm can give no reason to think the proposition is actually revealed other than their strong conviction of its truth. In that case, their confidence is no longer based on the assumption that God is infallible, but on the assumption that their strong feelings of conviction are infallible. In effect, they are supposing that the test for whether some proposition comes from God has to be whether *they feel confident* that the proposition is true. This, Locke thinks, is the root of fanaticism.

By taking seriously the question of how to distinguish genuine revelation from its many impostors, Locke makes faith subservient to our "natural" ways of knowing—namely, reason and observation. Not all theists are so bold as to claim they have personally received a revelation directly from God. Indeed, as the numbers of those who make such claims increases, so do our suspicions about them. There may be, however, more indirect ways to access revealed truths.

Revelation and the Authority of Books

Some persons claim to derive many of their moral and religious beliefs from a holy book or text (the book varies from one tradition to another). On the most common of such views, the holy book was itself divinely inspired, or its authorship divinely directed, so it contains *revealed* truths that are beyond the capacity of human reason to discover. On the natural assumption that God is all-knowing and all-good, it follows that whatever is said in the holy book, or its revealed parts, is true. The fact that something is said in the holy book then suffices to *justify* our believing it. If one wants to know what to believe about some difficult moral or religious matter, the obvious place to seek guidance is the holy book.

There are several well-known worries about appeals to such texts as a source for knowledge or justification. For example, in many traditions, the texts are largely known only in translation, and different translators make different strategic choices that affect the meaning of the text. Even in their original languages, the texts are open to multiple interpretations; different people will, and have, understood them differently. These sorts of concerns can certainly be serious, but there are two problems with the use of a holy book to *justify* beliefs that go deeper. We will consider each of these in turn.

First, consider a problem parallel to the one Locke raised for revelation: We can presumably trust genuine revelations, but only if we can first distinguish genuine revelations

[5] *Ibid.*

from their impostors. Similarly, if a book is divinely inspired, then what it says is certainly true—God does not make mistakes, and He does not lie. But how can we decide if a book is divinely inspired? This important decision—the decision as to which books, or which parts thereof, are divinely inspired is naturally a human decision, and so is vulnerable to all the sorts of errors to which human decisions are generally prone. There is, however, one sure test we might apply to distinguish divinely inspired texts from those that are not: Nothing that is divinely inspired will be false. More precisely, each divinely inspired thing that a book says will be true, and any false thing it says could not have been divinely inspired. For example, if a book says it is an abomination to eat shellfish, but it is not actually an abomination, then the book, or that portion of the book, could not have been divinely inspired. Naturally, this requires us to determine on our own, and without appeal to the holy book, whether eating shellfish really is an abomination. This procedure for judging whether a book really contains the word of God has a consequence: We need to know if what the book, or some part of it, says is true before we can assure ourselves that what it says is divinely inspired. If we can't do that, we can't distinguish revealed truths from impostors. But if we can do that, then what the book reveals cannot be beyond the reach of our natural reason and observation. What need, then, do we have for revelations?

Second, the question of whether there are holy books that contain revealed truths may, at any rate, be moot. It is highly doubtful that anyone *actually* relies on what such texts say in order to decide whether they should hold some belief. Of course, many people *say* they do this, and many of those people are completely sincere, but there is a reason to believe they are often mistaken: Persons who appeal to the authority of a holy book are usually *selective* in what they accept from the book. However, if their belief that the book is divinely inspired really were their reason for accepting what it says, they would have exactly the same reason to assent to *every* proposition in the book. Consider a familiar illustration of this point. I know of no theists today who defend the view that they are permitted to sell their daughters. And yet the *Old Testament*, a book accepted as divinely revealed by some theists, states that it is permissible to do so (*Exodus*, 21:7). At the same time, some of those who would be morally outraged at the suggestion that they could sell their daughters continue to cite the *Old Testament* to justify their belief that homosexuality is a sin (*Leviticus*, 18:22). They are, then, *selective readers*: They take what they want from the *Old Testament* and ignore what they don't like. This can best be explained in one way: The selective reader's criterion for which propositions to believe is not whether the proposition appears in the book. If that were their reason, it would also be a completely sufficient reason for them to contemplate selling their daughters. If they believe it unacceptable to sell their daughters, but think that homosexuality is a sin, then the say-so of the holy book is not their reason for disapproving of homosexuality. They have other reasons—or no reasons at all—for thinking those things.

Our reasons for our actions and beliefs often operate in the dark, and it can sometimes be difficult to recognize the grounds for them. Whenever people appeal to the authority of a revealed text to justify a belief, but use the text selectively, then the reason for their belief is not the holy text after all. Their real reasons, whatever they are, might be good or bad, but they should be brought out into the open and evaluated like any other.

FAITH AND THE WILL

If belief in God is justified by revelation, then faith is a kind of super-rational insight, and those few who have genuine faith have a kind of knowledge that others lack. John Locke exposed limits to faith when it is understood in this way: Only reason can legitimately judge whether a particular revelation is genuine or is an impostor, and that means that whenever faith and reason come into conflict, we must listen to reason. To do otherwise is to fall prey to one of revelation's many impostors. If the atheist were right that it is not *rational* to believe God exists, then *any* revelation would ultimately conflict with what it is rational to believe, so if we applied Locke's standard, *no* purported revelation would pass the test of authenticity.

Any theist who does not want reason to be the final judge of her beliefs will perhaps fare better if she adopts a different view about the nature of faith itself—a view that makes no use of the idea of "revelation." In the nineteenth century, a different way of understanding faith rose to prominence that might better express what many contemporary fideists have in mind when they appeal to faith.

Faith and Voluntarism

If faith is not a special, super-rational form of insight or knowledge, what is it? Danish philosopher and theologian **Søren Kierkegaard** (1813–1855) points toward an answer when he says, "Belief is not so much a conclusion, as a resolution . . . Belief is not a form of knowledge, but a free act, an expression of the will." "[6] Kierkegaard's idea is that faith—what he calls simply "belief"—is not the conclusion of a line of reasoning, or a conclusion based on evidence, but a matter of personal resolve. To have faith is to have made a *firm but voluntary decision* to believe something. Faith is not a result of argument or evidence—not even super-rational or revealed evidence; we believe something on faith by *willing* ourselves to believe it. In short, faith is **willed belief**—belief that derives from an act of will or desire.

Søren Kierkegaard: Danish philosopher and theologian who maintained that faith is belief owed to a free act of will—a matter of personal resolve. He advocated a form of irrationalist fideism. On his view, faith calls upon us to believe things that are absurd from the perspective of reason.

willed belief: A belief that results from free choice, decision, or desire; something that is believed only because we *want* it to be true.

An apparent obstacle stands in the way of thinking about faith as Kierkegaard recommends. On his understanding of faith, we need to be able to come to believe something by an act of will—that is, by merely choosing to believe it. But can we really do this? The view that we *can* bring ourselves to believe something by choosing to is called **voluntarism**, and it comes in two forms. First, there is **direct voluntarism**, which says that we can get ourselves to believe something directly, by an act of will alone, simply by willing ourselves (deciding or choosing) to believe it. Direct voluntarism seems implausible if it is applied to beliefs in general, rather than limited to special cases. It seems implausible, for example, to think I can get myself to believe I have eight fingers on each hand just by deciding to believe it. The evidence that stares me in the face whenever I look at my hand *somehow prevents me* from believing I have eight fingers. It might be slightly easier to believe it if I could always successfully avert my attention from my hands, or if I always wore boxing gloves. So if direct voluntarism is to be plausible, it might have to be limited to cases where no overpowering contrary evidence confronts the beliefs that I "will" myself to have. In short, it may be necessary to find ways to *insulate* my beliefs from any

voluntarism: The view that we can bring ourselves to believe something by willing or choosing to believe it.

direct voluntarism: We can get ourselves to believe something directly, by an act of will alone, simply by willing ourselves to believe it.

[6] Yee, S. (Ed.). (2009). Philosophical Fragments 83. In *The Portable Kiekegaard*. (D. F. Swenson, Trans.). British Columbia: Emerald Knight Publishing, 174–75.

direct confrontations with threatening facts. Where we cannot do this, a weaker form of voluntarism may be more plausible.

indirect voluntarism: The view that we can get ourselves to believe what we want to believe, but only by willing ourselves to do other things that will indirectly result in our acquiring the beliefs we want to have.

Indirect voluntarism is the view that we can get ourselves to believe something indirectly, by an act of will alone, simply by willing ourselves to believe it. Human beings are extraordinarily flexible, and we can be brought to believe almost anything if the right "techniques" are applied. I can be brought to believe I am William Shakespeare if I am hypnotized; I can believe that an elephant lives in my closet if I am under the influence of a powerful hallucinogenic drug; and I might come to believe that the earth is flat if I am held captive and brain-washed by the Flat Earth Society. I cannot simply *will myself to believe* these things, but I can freely choose to have myself hypnotized, decide to take an hallucinogenic drug, or voluntarily submit to re-education by the Flat Earth Society. With the right incentives, perhaps we can *indirectly* get ourselves to believe almost anything by choosing to submit to the necessary "techniques."

If faith is belief that results from a voluntary act of will—from choosing to believe—then we need to consider which form of voluntarism is associated with faith: Does faith arise directly from the decision to believe, or does it arise from the decision to do other things that will eventually result in the belief? In fact, fideists have answered both ways. We'll consider an example of each sort of voluntarism below.

Two Kinds of Reasons

We will first consider a view about faith as willed belief that relies on indirect voluntarism. To understand this view, we need to employ a distinction between two kinds of "reasons" for holding a belief.

justifying reasons: Reasons for believing that a proposition is true or is likely to be true.

Justifying reasons are reasons for thinking or believing a proposition is true. We have already seen that an explanation for a belief differs from a justification in that an explanation of the belief need not have any bearing on whether it is true or false. Both false beliefs and true beliefs have perfectly good explanations. But a justification for a belief has everything to do with whether it is true: A successful justification is one that makes the belief more likely to be true than not. We might put it this way: A *justifying reason* for believing something is always a reason for believing *that it is true*. But there is a second kind of "reason" for having a belief that has nothing to do with whether it is true.

prudential reasons: The practical advantages or benefits to be gained from holding a belief; reasons why a belief is advantageous, rather than why the belief is true.

Prudential reasons for holding a belief are the practical advantages or benefits to be gained from having the belief. These are reasons for thinking a belief is advantageous, not reasons for thinking it is true. Prudential, or pragmatic, reasons for having a particular belief are indifferent to whether it is true or false—they concern only whether it "pays" to have the belief.

Consider one reason for believing something that appeals to its practical benefits, but does not justify us in thinking it is true: Suppose you are offered $1 million to believe the earth is flat. If you need the money, it would be eminently practical—and, in that sense, "rational"—for you to acquire the belief that it is flat. Believing the earth is flat would enable you to achieve your financial goals, so it might be prudent for you to acquire the belief even if the evidence convinces you that it is not flat.

It can be prudentially rational for you to believe God exists if believing it will make you feel better—perhaps it will make you feel less alone, more secure, or more hopeful. Similarly, it would be prudentially rational for you to believe God exists if having the belief would prevent you from being burned at the stake by fanatics. If you want to feel better, or if you want to avoid being burned at the stake, then you have a very strong *reason* to believe God exists.

French philosopher and mathematician **Blaise Pascal** (1623–1662) offered a famous *prudential argument* for believing God exists. The reason he provides has nothing to do with whether the belief is true or false. That is, Pascal's argument for believing God exists is an argument for why it is prudent to believe God exists *even if He does not.*

Blaise Pascal: French philosopher and mathematician who developed a famous prudential argument for believing God exists.

The Wager (Blaise Pascal, 1670)[7]

> Let us then examine this point, and say, "God is, or He is not." But to which side shall we incline? Reason can decide nothing here. . . . What will you wager? According to reason, you can do neither the one thing nor the other; according to reason, you can defend neither of the propositions.
>
> Do not then reprove for error those who have made a choice; for you know nothing about it. "No, but I blame them for having made, not this choice, but a choice; for again both he who chooses heads and he who chooses tails are equally at fault, they are both in the wrong. The true course is not to wager at all."
>
> Yes; but you must wager. It is not optional. You are embarked. Which will you choose then? . . . Let us weigh the gain and the loss in wagering that God is. Let us estimate these two chances. If you gain, you gain all; if you lose, you lose nothing. Wager, then, without hesitation that He is. . . .
>
> . . . "Yes, but I have my hands tied and my mouth closed; I am forced to wager, and am not free. I am not released, and am so made that I cannot believe. What, then, would you have me do?"
>
> . . . Endeavour then to convince yourself, not by increase of proofs of God, but by the abatement of your passions. You would like to attain faith and do not know the way; you would like to cure yourself of unbelief and ask the remedy for it. Learn of those who have been bound like you, and who now stake all their possessions. These are people who know the way which you would follow, and who are cured of an ill of which you would be cured. Follow the way by which they began; by acting as if they believed, taking the holy water, having masses said, etc. Even this will naturally make you believe, and deaden your acuteness. . . .

Pascal's argument takes the form of a bet ("wager"). To understand his wager, first consider an analogous bet. Suppose you are given a choice between taking one of two bets (you cannot refuse the choice):

> *Bet One*: You wager \$1 on a toss of a fair coin; if tails comes up, you get to keep your dollar; if heads comes up, you will be tortured and executed.
>
> *Bet Two*: You wager \$1 on a toss of a fair coin; if tails comes up, you get to keep your dollar; if heads comes up, you will win \$10 million.

Now, which is the rational wager to take? The answer is pretty easy: If you take Bet One, you will either gain nothing or you will lose your life; if you take Bet Two, you will either lose nothing or you will gain \$10 million. Clearly, it is rational to accept Bet Two.

---

[7] From Pascal, B. (1670). *Pensées*. Retrieved August 10, 2014, from http://www.gutenberg.org/files/18269/18269-0.txt

Now, let's change the outcomes or "stakes" of the two bets:

Bet One: You wager that God *does not* exist; if you are right, then you go on with your life; if you are wrong, you will burn in hell for eternity.

Bet Two: You wager that God *does* exist; if you are wrong, then you go on with your life; if you are right, you will get an eternity of bliss.

Once again, if you take Bet One, you will either gain nothing or lose everything; if you take Bet Two, you will either lose nothing or gain everything. Clearly, a rational gambler will take the second bet. This is **Pascal's wager**: We are to "weigh the gain and loss in wagering that God is. If you gain, you gain all. If you lose, you lose nothing. Wager, then, without hesitation, that He is".

Pascal's wager: An argument developed by Blaise Pascal to show that it is prudent to believe there is a God, even though there is no justification for the belief.

According to Pascal's wager, it is *prudent to believe* God exists whether or not He does. If the theist's belief that God exists is false, it costs her nothing; but if her belief turns out to be true, an infinite reward awaits her. The atheist, however, pays an infinite price if she is wrong, and she will gain nothing if she is right. So clearly the prudent—that is, *safe*—thing to do is believe that God exists.

A small difficulty immediately arises: It does not seem possible to believe something merely because we can see some benefit in believing it. I can't just *decide* to believe in God. Pascal recognizes this, but he thinks we can get ourselves to believe whatever we want if we do it *indirectly*, by putting ourselves through a process of self-indoctrination. He recommends that we voluntarily participate in religious life and rituals. This, he thinks, will eventually bring us around. Pascal is therefore an *indirect voluntarist* about beliefs.

Declining the Wager

Pascal's conclusions are that (a) it is prudent for us to believe that God exists, whether or not He does, and (b) once we recognize this, we can get ourselves to believe in God by subjecting ourselves to a gradual process of indoctrination. Both ideas give rise to worries.

1. *Pascal's wager has nothing to do with whether there really is a God.* He is only saying that it would be prudent to brainwash ourselves into thinking there is a God, whether or not God exists. So his wager is only of interest to someone who wants to avoid hell-fire or acquire bliss, *more than they want to know the truth.* It will have no appeal to anyone who values knowing the truth about whether God exists more than they value those other things.
2. *Pascal is wrong to think we stand "to lose nothing" if we take his wager.* If we accept Pascal's wager, we must then get ourselves to believe God exists. But our beliefs affect how we act, and a belief this fundamental will dramatically impact how we live the rest of our lives. So if we follow Pascal's advice and get ourselves to believe there is a God, we cannot simply go on with *our* lives—we must go on to live very different lives. If we are wrong, and God does not exist, *we will have lost the life we would otherwise have chosen to lead.* So Pascal is wrong to say that we stand to lose nothing by taking the wager—it requires us to surrender our freedom to choose the only life we will ever have, so we stand to lose a great deal. To take the bet is to resign ourselves to the lives of indoctrinated subjects.

3. *A belief for which we have only prudential grounds will be inherently unstable*. Among self-reflective or self-aware people, the recognition that a belief results from indoctrination will destroy our attachment to the belief. Suppose you realize that your only reason for believing that earth is flat is that you were indoctrinated by members of the Flat Earth Society. Your realization that this is the only account of why you believe earth is flat will be enough to loosen the grip that the belief has on you. Similarly, if I have only prudential reasons for believing in God and, consequently, my belief can only be acquired by indoctrination, then my belief will not be stable—it will be undermined by my own knowledge of why I have the belief. If Pascal's wager is to succeed, then, it will not be enough to submit to indoctrination; to make our indoctrination stick we *also* need to conceal from ourselves that we have been indoctrinated. At a minimum, we need to find ways to insulate our belief in God from any serious scrutiny, even scrutiny by ourselves. To maintain a belief arrived at in this way, we have to prevent ourselves from engaging in any serious self-reflection and to forgo any self-knowledge that such reflection might bring.

A fourth and more famous reason for declining Pascal's wager needs more than a brief mention. In the next section we'll let physicist and mathematician **William K. Clifford** (1845–1879) present the objection that it is immoral to believe anything on faith, and we will then consider the fideist's reply to Clifford as it was formulated by William James.

William K. Clifford: A prominent physicist and mathematician who defends an *ethics of belief* and argues that it is immoral to believe anything without sufficient justifying reasons.

ETHICS AND BELIEF

Pascal's wager is intended to demonstrate that it is pragmatically rational—that is, prudent—to adopt the belief that there is a God, even if there is nothing in the wager that makes it plausible to think God exists. But if the evidence for the proposition that God exists is not the source of our assent to it, then that assent must have another source. Pascal, like other fideists, allows that we can bring ourselves to assent by self-indoctrination. This might be more common than we think—sometimes people allow themselves to slide imperceptibly from *wishing or hoping* that something is true to *believing* it is true. If the incentives for believing are great enough, it might take great strength of will to prevent ourselves from going down that slide.

Clifford illustrates how easily one might make the transition from wanting something to be true to sincerely believing it, and argues that it is *immoral* to make the transition. If he is right, then a fourth objection to Pascal's wager is that *it is immoral to believe in God without good justifying reasons*. We will let Clifford explain the objection in his own words.

"The Ethics of Belief" (W. K. Clifford, 1877)[8]

A shipowner was about to send to sea an emigrant-ship. He knew that she was old, and not over-well built at the first; that she had seen many seas and climes, and often had needed repairs. Doubts had been suggested to him that possibly she was not seaworthy. These doubts preyed upon his mind, and made him unhappy; he thought that perhaps he ought to have her thoroughly overhauled and refitted, even though this should put him to great expense. Before the ship sailed, however, he succeeded in overcoming

[8] "The Ethics of Belief", in W. K. Clifford, Lectures and Essays, Vol. II, ed. by Leslie Stephen and Frederick Pollock (MacMillan and Co., London, 1879). Used by permission.

these melancholy reflections. He said to himself that she had gone safely through so many voyages and weathered so many storms that it was idle to suppose she would not come safely home from this trip also. He would put his trust in Providence, which could hardly fail to protect all these unhappy families that were leaving their fatherland to seek for better times elsewhere. He would dismiss from his mind all ungenerous suspicions about the honesty of builders and contractors. In such ways he acquired a sincere and comfortable conviction that his vessel was thoroughly safe and seaworthy; he watched her departure with a light heart, and benevolent wishes for the success of the exiles in their strange new home that was to be; and he got his insurance-money when she went down in mid-ocean and told no tales.

What shall we say of him? Surely this, that he was verily guilty of the death of those men. It is admitted that he did sincerely believe in the soundness of his ship; but the sincerity of his conviction can in no wise help him, because *he had no right to believe on such evidence as was before him*. He had acquired his belief not by honestly earning it in patient investigation, but by stifling his doubts. And although in the end he may have felt so sure about it that he could not think otherwise, yet inasmuch as he had knowingly and willingly worked himself into that frame of mind, he must be held responsible for it. . . .

. . . For it is not possible so to sever the belief from the action it suggests as to condemn the one without condemning the other. . . .

. . . Nor is it that truly a belief at all which has not some influence upon the actions of him who holds it. . . . If a belief is not realized immediately in open deeds, it is stored up for the guidance of the future. . . . No real belief, however trifling and fragmentary it may seem, is ever truly insignificant; it prepares us to receive more of its like, confirms those which resembled it before, and weakens others; and so gradually it lays a stealthy train in our inmost thoughts, which may some day explode into overt action, and leave its stamp upon our character for ever.

And no one man's belief is in any case a private matter which concerns himself alone. Our lives our guided by that general conception of the course of things which has been created by society for social purposes. Our words, our phrases, our forms and processes and modes of thought, are common property, fashioned and perfected from age to age; an heirloom which every succeeding generation inherits as a precious deposit and a sacred trust to be handled on to the next one, not unchanged but enlarged and purified, with some clear marks of its proper handiwork. Into this, for good or ill, is woven every belief of every man who has speech of his fellows. An awful privilege, and an awful responsibility, that we should help to create the world in which posterity will live.

. . . [I]t has been judged wrong to believe on insufficient evidence, or to nourish belief by suppressing doubts and avoiding investigation. The reason of this judgment is not far to seek: it is that . . . the belief held by one man was of great importance to other men. But forasmuch as no belief held by one man, however seemingly trivial the belief, and however obscure the believer, is ever actually insignificant or without its effect on the fate of mankind, we have no choice but to extend our judgment to all cases of belief whatever. Belief, that sacred faculty which prompts the decisions of our will, and knits into harmonious working all the compacted energies of our being, is ours not for ourselves but for humanity. . . . Whoso would deserve well of his fellows in this matter will guard the purity of his beliefs with a very fanaticism of jealous care, lest at any time it should rest on an unworthy object, and catch a stain which can never be wiped away.

It is not only the leader of men, statesmen, philosopher, or poet, that owes this bounden duty to mankind. Every rustic who delivers in the village alehouse his slow, infrequent sentences, may help to kill or keep alive the fatal superstitions which clog his race. Every hard-worked wife of an artisan may transmit to her children beliefs which shall knit society together, or rend it in pieces. No simplicity of mind, no obscurity of station, can escape the universal duty of questioning all that we believe.

It is true that this duty is a hard one, and the doubt which comes out of it is often a very bitter thing. It leaves us bare and powerless where we thought that we were safe and strong. To know all about anything is to know how to deal with it under all circumstances. We feel much happier and more secure when we think we know precisely what to do, no matter what happens, than when we have lost our way and do not know where to turn. . . . It is the sense of power attached to a sense of knowledge that makes men desirous of believing, and afraid of doubting.

. . . But if the belief has been accepted on insufficient evidence, the pleasure is a stolen one. Not only does it deceive ourselves by giving us a sense of power which we do not really possess, but it is sinful, because it is stolen in defiance of our duty to mankind. That duty is to guard ourselves from such beliefs as from pestilence, which may shortly master our own body and then spread to the rest of the town. What would be thought of one who, for the sake of a sweet fruit, should deliberately run the risk of delivering a plague upon his family and his neighbours?

. . . Every time we let ourselves believe for unworthy reasons, we weaken our powers of self-control, of doubting, of judicially and fairly weighing evidence. . . . But a greater and wider evil arises when the credulous character is maintained and supported, when a habit of believing for unworthy reasons is fostered and made permanent. . . . In like manner, if I let myself believe anything on insufficient evidence, there may be no great harm done by the mere belief; it may be true after all, or I may never have occasion to exhibit it in outward acts. But I cannot help doing this great wrong towards Man, that I make myself credulous. The danger to society is not merely that it should believe wrong things, though that is great enough; but that it should become credulous, and lose the habit of testing things and inquiring into them; for then it must sink back into savagery.

. . . Habitual want of care about what I believe leads to habitual want of care in others about the truth of what is told to me. Men speak the truth of one another when each reveres the truth in his own mind and in the other's mind; but how shall my friend revere the truth in my mind when I myself am careless about it, when I believe thing because I want to believe them, and because they are comforting and pleasant? Will he not learn to cry, 'Peace,' to me, when there is no peace? By such a course I shall surround myself with a thick atmosphere of falsehood and fraud, and in that I must live. It may matter little to me, in my cloud-castle of sweet illusions and darling lies; but it matters much to Man that I have made my neighbours ready to deceive. . . .

To sum up: it is wrong always, everywhere, and for anyone, to believe anything upon insufficient evidence.

If a man, holding a belief which he was taught in childhood or persuaded of afterwards, keeps down and pushes away any doubts which arise about it in his mind, purposely avoids the reading of books and the company of men that call in question or discuss it, and regards as impious those questions which cannot easily be asked without disturbing it—the life of that man is one long sin against mankind.

One of the objections to accepting Pascal's wager is that we cannot succeed in voluntary belief or self-indoctrination unless we also successfully conceal from ourselves the sources of our belief. But this very move, in which we nourish belief by suppressing doubts and avoiding investigation, is, Clifford thinks, deeply immoral. The immorality is visible when we combine two of Clifford's ideas: First, our beliefs determine how we act: A belief is not "truly a belief at all which has not some influence upon the actions of him who holds it." Second, our actions affect and involve other people, so "no man's belief is in any case a private matter which concerns himself alone." If our actions are properly the concern of other people, and our beliefs determine our actions, then our beliefs are properly the concern of other people. Thus, Clifford argues, there are ethical issues involved in acquiring and holding beliefs.

On Clifford's view, we have a moral obligation to believe only what the evidence supports. The shipowner in his example had only prudential reasons to believe his ship was seaworthy. But his belief did not fit with the evidence, so his sincerity was no defense of his belief or actions. To believe something we have no right to believe on the basis of the evidence is always morally wrong.

Do We Owe Others Reasons?

Perhaps we can take Clifford's idea one step further. I don't feel any need to justify my behaviour to the flies that I swat or banish from my house by putting up screens. This shows how I regard flies. Similarly, if my actions affect you and your well-being, but I feel that I need not offer you justifications for my actions, then I treat you as less than fully human. This suggests to some philosophers that a minimum requirement for regarding other persons as *fully human* is to regard them as *beings to whom we owe reasons* for our treatment of them. To be fully human is, from a moral perspective, to deserve reasons. Now, as long as my actions arise from beliefs that I hold only because *I want to hold them*—because *I have willed myself to believe*—then the only accounting I can give for my actions is "I have willed it." When this is all I have to offer you, I treat you as not deserving of reasons for my treatment of you, and so as less than fully human. On this view all voluntary belief risks being immoral.

In short, Clifford claims that we must struggle to believe whatever the evidence tells us, and that this not a mere fetish for the truth, but a moral obligation. To believe something only because it is prudent to do so is to fail in both our intellectual *and moral* obligations, to others and to ourselves. If Clifford is right, it will follow that those who take Pascal's wager will be acting immorally.

These are strong charges, so we should give defenders of prudential reasoning and voluntary belief an opportunity to respond. William James directly challenges Clifford's claim that we have a moral obligation to believe on the basis of evidence. In the following sections, we will explore what James says about matters of faith.

"The Will to Believe" (William James, 1896)[9]

> Does it not seem preposterous on the very face of it to talk of our opinions being modifiable at will? Can our will either help or hinder our intellect in its perceptions of truth? . . . Can we, by any effort of our will, or by any strength of wish that it were true, believe ourselves well and about when we are roaring with rheumatism in bed, or

[9] From James, W. (1896). *The Will to Believe and Other Essays in Popular Philosophy*. Retrieved on August 10, 2014, from http://www.gutenberg.org/cache/epub/26659/pg26659.txt

feel certain that the sum of the two one-dollar bills in our pocket must be a hundred dollars? . . .

The talk of believing by our volition seems, then, from one point of view, simply silly. From another point of view it is worse than silly, it is vile. . . .

. . . Yet if any one should thereupon assume that intellectual insight is what remains after wish and will and sentimental preference have taken wing, or that pure reason is what then settles our opinions, he would fly quite as directly in the teeth of the facts.

. . . As a matter of fact we find ourselves believing, we hardly know how or why. . . . Here in this room, we all of us believe in molecules and the conservation of energy, in democracy and necessary progress . . . all for no reasons worthy of the name. . . . Our reason is quite satisfied, in nine hundred and ninety-nine cases out of every thousand of us, if it can find a few arguments that will do to recite in case our credulity is criticised by some one else. . . .

Evidently, then, our non-intellectual nature does influence our convictions. . . . pure insight and logic, whatever they might do ideally, are not the only things that really do produce our creeds.

. . . The thesis I defend is, briefly stated, this: *Our passional nature not only lawfully may, but must, decide an option between propositions, whenever it is a genuine option that cannot by its nature be decided on intellectual grounds; for to say, under such circumstances, "Do not decide, but leave the question open," is itself a passional decision,—just like deciding yes or no,—and is attended with the same risk of losing the truth.* . . .

. . . [N]ot only as a matter of fact do we find our passional nature influencing us in our opinions, but that there are some options between opinions in which this influence must be regarded both as an inevitable and as a lawful determinant of our choice. . . .

. . . Wherever the option between losing truth and gaining it is not momentous, we can throw the chance of *gaining truth* away, and at any rate save ourselves from any chance of *believing falsehood*, by not making up our minds at all till objective evidence has come. In scientific questions, this is almost always the case; and even in human affairs in general, the need of acting is seldom so urgent that a false belief to act on is better than no belief at all. . . . But in our dealings with objective nature we obviously are recorders, not makers, of the truth; and decisions for the mere sake of deciding promptly and getting on to the next business would be wholly out of place. . . .

The Sentiment of Rationality

. . . Faith means belief in something concerning which doubt is still theoretically possible; and as the test of belief is willingness to act, one may say that faith is the readiness to act in a cause the prosperous issue of which is not certified to us in advance. . . .

. . . We cannot live or think at all without some degree of faith. Faith is synonymous with working hypothesis. The only difference is that while some hypotheses can be refuted in five minutes, others may defy ages. . . .

. . . [B]elief (as measured by action) not only does and must continually outstrip scientific evidence, but there is a certain class of truths of whose reality belief is a factor as well as a confessor; and that as regards this class of truths faith is not only licit and pertinent, but essential and indispensable. The truths cannot become true till our faith has made them so.

Suppose, for example, that I am climbing in the Alps, and have had the ill-luck to work myself into a position from which the only escape is by a terrible leap. Being without similar experience, I have no evidence of my ability to perform it successfully;

> but hope and confidence in myself make me sure I shall not miss my aim, and nerve my feet to execute what without those subjective conditions would perhaps have been impossible. . . . In this case (and it is one of an immense class) the part of wisdom clearly is to believe what one desires; for the belief is one of the indispensable preliminary conditions for the realization of its object. *There are then cases where faith creates its own verification.* . . .
>
> . . . The thought becomes literally the father to the fact, as the wish was father to the thought.

James's challenge to Clifford begins with the observation that, as a matter of fact, we all believe a great many things without sufficient evidence for those beliefs. So justifying reasons are not what make up our minds most of the time. This might seem to miss Clifford's point, for he does not say that *we do in fact* make up our minds only on the basis of evidence and reasons—only that *we have an obligation to do so*. But James takes the next step and claims that our doing so is both necessary and legitimate.

James locates and defends a much broader role for faith—and not merely for religious faith. Nevertheless, he finds only limited occasions for the use of faith. In certain very special cases,

i. We cannot leave undecided what to believe (i.e., we cannot be agnostic); and
ii. The truth or falsity of a belief cannot be decided on the basis of the evidence.

In just those special, perhaps even rare, cases where both conditions apply, James tells us that "the part of wisdom is clearly to believe what one desires," and also that our desires "not only lawfully may, but must" settle what we should believe.[10] Faith only contributes additional beliefs where the evidence does not already favour a conclusion. So James is a transrationalist fideist—on his view, there is room for faith, but it cannot legitimately supply beliefs on matters that are already decidable on the basis of evidence, and it cannot conflict with or overrule the evidence. We can and should believe what we want to be true only when a belief is required, and the evidence leaves open the matter of which belief is best.

As illustrated by James's case of the climber in the Alps, he thinks there are at least some cases where our *wanting* something to be true, and our believing what we want, can *make our belief true*. Furthermore, James is a *direct voluntarist* about belief: He thinks the mountain climber can simply "will himself to believe" that he can make the jump. James's story only seems plausible in a limited range of cases. For example, sometimes doubts about our own abilities may prevent us from trying, or, when our doubts become disabling, prevent us from succeeding if we do try. In such cases only confidence that we will succeed can get us to so much as try. But our confidence that we can do something may also conflict with overwhelming contrary evidence, and no amount of confidence will result in success if our doubts are well justified. What makes it possible for the mountain climber to "will" himself to believe is, in part, that there is no opposing evidence to overcome (as there would be if he knew his legs were broken).

There are severe limitations on the idea that we can make something true by willing it to be true. The only plausible cases are those in which a belief that we can do something is required for us to take action, and our taking the appropriate action then makes true our

[10] *Ibid.*

belief. There are common examples of this: My belief that I can find coffee is a requirement of looking for it; and my looking for coffee is a requirement of finding it. Here, my believing that I can find coffee contributes to my finding it, but the role of willing is very indirect—I can't just will myself to have coffee and expect it to appear. Notice that in this example I already have abundant evidence that I can find coffee—it's something I do regularly, so "faith" seems entirely unnecessary. Furthermore, my belief that I can jump to the moon fails to make it true that I can jump to the moon. However *sincere* my belief, faith will not *make it true*, and by acting on faith alone, I will fall flat on my face. In such cases—where the evidence is overwhelmingly against us—it is highly unlikely that we can directly will ourselves to believe; but, even if we can, it is highly unlikely that the belief we will ourselves to have will be true.

James's Definition of *Faith* Considered

James offers a definition of *faith* that many have found attractive: *Faith* is "the readiness to act in a cause the prosperous issue of which is not certified to us in advance."[11] The idea is that when we believe or act on occasions when there still remains some prospect that our belief is false or that our action will fail, we are believing or acting on faith. We do this all the time: Prosperous results are rarely "certified to us in advance." When I cross the street, there is no guarantee that I will successfully get to the other side, so James thinks it is appropriate to say I am acting on faith that I will. If he is right, then some form of *faith* is far more common that we usually recognize—without faith of this sort, we would cease to act altogether. If that is so, and some amount of faith is involved in all our actions, then Clifford must be wrong to think that it is morally and intellectually irresponsible to act and believe on faith.

James's definition doesn't capture what many theists have in mind by *faith*. For one thing, theists typically expect their faith to result in true belief. But faith of the sort James characterizes, while far more universal, can easily yield beliefs that are false. Suppose I buy a lottery ticket, with one chance in a million of winning. It is not certified in advance that I will win—indeed, although it is theoretically possible I will win, it is very close to certain that I will not. Nonetheless, by prudential reasoning of the right sort, plus a little manipulation of my will, I might be able to acquire considerable confidence that I will win. But none of this improves my odds of winning. However much I *want* it to be true that I will win, and however convinced I become that I really will win, it remains just as unlikely that I will. Of course, I can always *hope* I will win, but the slide from hope to belief is almost certain to result in a false belief. This seems to be a case of acting on what James calls "faith" but, if it is, having faith does not make an irrational belief any more likely to be true.

James's definition of *faith* displays a curious assumption: It assumes that if the evidence does not conclusively *determine* what we believe, leaving us no possibility of believing otherwise, then our belief must, at least in part, be determined by an act of will. That is, if the evidence does not *compel* a conclusion, but leaves some wiggle room, then our desire to believe one thing rather than another must make up the difference and contribute to our belief. Is this really so? The beliefs on which we act may be very strongly supported by reasons, even though those reasons are not conclusive and the conclusion is not compelled.

---

[11] *Ibid.*

My belief that I can cross the street safely is well grounded by many previous successful crossings, and my belief that I will not win the lottery is strongly justified by the numbers. But neither outcome, however probable, is certified in advance. So James thinks faith must contribute to my believing that I can safely cross the street or that my lottery ticket will lose. But although the evidence may not *compel* my belief, it does *justify* it, and that may be all that is needed to act on it. In those cases, it seems plausible to say that my belief or action is fully rational, and therefore that I have no need for faith as James understands it.

Believing What We Want

We have been examining cases of belief that are not based on argument or observation, but on the will. Why are these even a matter for philosophical discussion? *Why shouldn't we be allowed to believe whatever we want?* Three answers to these questions emerge from the preceding discussion.

First, the conception of faith offered by James has the consequence that beliefs held on faith will be, as often as not, false beliefs. Indeed, on occasions where we "will" ourselves to believe something *for no other reason than that we want it to be true*, then it is probably not true. Therefore, if we want our beliefs to be true, we have a reason not to believe whatever we want.

Second, faith is belief that is insulated from critical scrutiny. Clifford thinks this makes belief *morally irresponsible*. If our beliefs are merely expressions of our wills, then when we act on our beliefs, we are imposing our wills on those affected by our actions. In such cases, we cannot give others reasons for our treatment of them, since we have no reasons, but can only say that *it is our will* that others should be treated this way. Faith, when understood as a freely willed or freely chosen conviction, runs the risk of transforming the faithful into tyrants.

Third, at the end of the day, the fideist owes an explanation of the difference between believing on faith and believing because we have been indoctrinated or brainwashed. If faith is only willed belief, and weak voluntarism is the best account of how belief can be willed, then it is exceedingly difficult to see how there could be any difference.

Naturally, these charges against faith have arisen when we are still early in our philosophical reflections, and there may be further considerations that will put it in a better light. But the ball is now in the court of the faithful, and if they reply with arguments of their own, they will be playing the game of reason—the philosopher's game.

CONCLUSION

We explored the question of whether it might be legitimate to believe in God on faith. We discussed two models of what faith is—revelation or willed belief—and the problems each faces. Locke urged great caution in the use of revelation to ground beliefs since, although we can be certain that beliefs based on revelation are true, we can't be certain when a belief is based on revelation.

A second model of faith says that it is willed belief—that is, belief owed to a free choice or a free decision to believe. On this (Pascal's) view of faith, if there are strong prudential reasons for choosing to believe something, we needn't concern ourselves with whether there are any justifying reasons. Having this sort of faith requires believing what we want to believe, and that is no easy thing to do—we aren't usually able to believe whatever we want. Although there are indirect ways of getting ourselves to believe what we want, those are forms of indoctrination. Clifford argues that when we undertake to change our beliefs by submitting to indoctrination—even to self-indoctrination—important moral problems arise. Others are affected by the beliefs on which we act, and if those beliefs are willed, we cannot justify our treatment of others. In that event, our beliefs, and our methods of arriving at them, might have to be justified—and so be rational—in order to meet moral standards. Epistemology and ethics might not be very far apart.

Key Terms and Figures

revelation p. 316
compatibilism (of faith and reason) p. 316
transrational fideism p. 317
irrationalist fideism p. 317
enthusiasm p. 322
Søren Kierkegaard p. 325
willed belief p. 325
voluntarism p. 325
direct voluntarism p. 325
indirect voluntarism p. 326
justifying reasons p. 326
prudential reasons p. 326
Blaise Pascal p. 327
Pascal's wager p. 328
William K. Clifford p. 329

Additional readings about faith

Bishop, J. (2010). Faith, *The Stanford Encyclopedia of Philosophy*, Fall Edition. (Edward N. Zalta, Ed.). Available at http://plato.stanford.edu/archives/fall2010/entries/faith

Kierkegaard, S. (1985). Thought-Project. *Philosophical Fragments*. Princeton: Princeton University Press, 9–22.

Niebuhr, H. R. (1961). On the Nature of Faith. In S. Hook, Ed., *Religious Experience and Truth*. New York: New York University Press, 93–102.

Saka, P. (n.d.). Pascal's Wager about God. *Internet Encyclopedia of Philosophy*. (James Fieser, Ph.D., founder & general editor, Bradley Dowden, Ph.D., general editor). Available at http://www.iep.utm.edu/pasc-wag

APPENDIX A Evaluating Reasoning

I. LOGIC: THE VERY IDEA

Reasoning is something we do all the time, and it is something we do reasonably well. But there is much room for improvement. *Logic* is a set of tools that enables us to step back from our own reasoning, to reflect on it, to dissect it, and to critique it, all with an eye to improving it. In philosophy the primary use of logic is to help us *evaluate* reasoning—both our own and that of others. Until we can distinguish good reasoning from bad, we cannot know what is needed to do it better. Every philosopher needs some logic in her toolkit.

When we speak and think in the vocabulary of *arguments*, *premises*, and *conclusions*, we are employing concepts from logic to analyze, clarify, and restructure reasoning. With these simple concepts alone, we can dismantle a piece of reasoning and reassemble it in a form that allows us to inspect its inner workings—to see what the parts are and how they are connected. This is an essential preliminary to deciding if the reasoning is any good. Throughout the text, we frequently find *reconstructions* of a philosopher's reasoning that use these conventions: Premises are separated, numbered, and stacked above the conclusion. Studying the reconstructions in the text will train your eye to see the premises and conclusions as you read a passage of philosophy. At some point, you should attempt similar reconstructions on your own.

II. LOGIC BOXES

Twenty boxes containing brief logic lessons are located throughout the text in places where those lessons are relevant to the topics or arguments under discussion. In some cases it is possible (but not recommended) to skip the brief lesson in logic and proceed without it. It is always possible to detach the logic lesson from the context in which it appears and understand it on its own. Table A.1 shows one way to reorganize the Logic Boxes into three distinct clusters so that, along with an instructor's lecture, they might serve as the basis for a brief stand-alone introduction to informal logic.

Logic Boxes (A–D) in the first cluster explain the essential vocabulary and concepts needed to discuss and evaluate arguments. Boxes in the second cluster (E–J) discuss and illustrate some common forms of argument and styles of reasoning—most of these are forms you will encounter frequently. The third cluster (K–T) introduces some common errors in reasoning—that is, *fallacies*. These fallacies are *common* precisely because they are *tempting* errors to make, but it becomes easier to resist them after we have exposed the source of their charms.

Logic Box C in Table A.1 provides a strategy that emphasizes the importance of distinguishing an evaluation of the *reasoning* in an argument, which can be valid or invalid, or strong or weak, from an evaluation of the *premises*, which can be true or false, or plausible or implausible. The ability to keep these tasks separate distinguishes those who merely *react* to reasoning with approval or disapproval and those who have begun to develop informed appraisals of arguments.

Table A.1 Logic Boxes

	A. Logical Basics		
A	The Components of Arguments	p. 23	*Introduction to basic vocabulary and some essential distinctions for discussing and appraising arguments.*
B	Valid vs. Sound	p. 26	
C	A Strategy for Evaluating Reasoning	p. 40	
D	Contradiction and Logical Impossibility	p. 298	
	B. Common Forms and Styles of Reasoning		
E	*Modus Ponens*	p. 254	*Some common forms of argument.*
F	*Modus Tollens*	p. 296	
G	Argument from Analogy	p. 285	
H	Inference to the Best Explanation	p. 245	
I	*Reductio Ad Absurdum* Argument	p. 60	
J	Inconsistent Triads	p. 125	
	C. Common Errors and Fallacies		
K	Illicit Appeal to Authority	p. 8	*Some tempting errors in reasoning.*
L	Argument from Popularity	p. 18	
M	*Ad Hominem* Arguments	p. 309	
N	*Non Sequitur*	p. 248	
O	Fallacy of Equivocation	p. 92	
P	Dilemma and False Dilemma	p. 92	
Q	Fallacy of Begging the Question	p. 219	
R	Circular Definitions	p. 113	
S	Fallacies of Composition and Division	p. 266	
T	Scope Fallacies	p. 169	

III. EVALUATING REASONING

For quite simple arguments, a clear head and a little reflection will enable you to determine whether they are valid or invalid. If you set aside concern with the truth or falsity of the statements in the argument and focus only on whether the conclusion *follows from* the premises, then when a simple argument smells rotten, it often is rotten. But our logical "intuitions" are generally unreliable for complicated arguments, and are sometimes unreliable for even very simple ones. Without some training in logic, you cannot be expected to distinguish valid from invalid arguments in every case. Nonetheless, your nose for an invalid argument will grow sharper and more reliable after you are exposed to more arguments, and as you think more carefully about them. Meanwhile, the following ideas will help to extend your logical reach.

First, it is important to keep track of the fact that the validity or invalidity of an argument does not depend on what the argument is about—that is, it does not depend on the subject matter or the content of the argument. Rather, *whether an argument is valid depends only on its logical form.* The idea of "logical form" can be roughly discerned from the following arguments, both of which have the *same* form:

1. All cats are mammals.
2. Zora is a cat.
3. So, Zora is a mammal.

1. All droobs are zeelogs.
2. Hammy is a droob.
3. So, Hammy is a zeelog.

You probably don't know what droobs or zeelogs are, but that doesn't matter. You can still *see* that the two arguments have the same form. The first premise of each argument tells us that *all* of one category of things (cats or droobs) is contained within a second category of things (mammals or zeelogs). The second premise of each tells us that some individual thing (Zora or Hammy) is contained within the first category. Each argument then concludes that this same individual is also contained in the second category. It's like saying, "If Dahlia and Samara are hiding in the car and the car is in the garage, then Dahlia and Samara are hiding in the garage."

If we set aside the content of each argument, we might express their common form as follows:

All Xs are Ys.
Z is an X.
So, Z is a Y.

It doesn't matter what we replace X, Y, or Z with, so long as we replace both Xs with the same thing, both Ys with the same thing, and both Zs with the same thing. *Countless* arguments can be created by replacing X, Y, and Z with different terms, but they will all have the same logical form.

The importance of the idea that arguments have a form is that whether or not an argument is valid depends on its logical form, not on its content. If some argument is valid, then any argument with the same logical form is also valid, and if an argument is invalid, then any argument with the same logical form is also invalid. *This way of establishing validity and invalidity is widely used in the text.* It turns out that our argument concerning cats and mammals is a valid argument—perhaps this is already obvious when you inspect it. And, since the argument about droobs and zeelogs has the same logical form as that argument, we must conclude that it is also valid. So you don't have to give any thought to whether the premises in the second argument are true or false (which is a good thing, since you probably don't have a clue whether all droobs really are zeelogs). The idea that arguments have a logical form on which their validity depends should help you understand why you don't need to know if the statements in an argument are true in order to decide whether it is valid.

IV. EVALUATING PREMISES

Even a valid argument cannot promise to deliver a true conclusion unless its premises are all true. In philosophy, where we often find ourselves in a deep fog, we cannot be confident of agreement about the truth or falsity of premises. So we settle for the next best thing and look for premises that are *plausible* or *acceptable*. We are then assured, if we reason validly, of conclusions that are plausible or acceptable.

If the truth of a premise cannot be directly demonstrated, the following sorts of considerations count in favour of classifying it as acceptable:

- There are readily available grounds that can be provided for believing the premise and no strong grounds for disbelieving it.
- The premise is common knowledge—it is something we can expect to be accepted by any audience of informed and reasonable people or by an audience with no stake in the outcome of the argument.
- The premise is already accepted by the persons to whom the argument is addressed.

These criteria are deliberately vague, but the idea behind them is simple: Each argument is addressed to an audience, and an acceptable premise must be one that is acceptable *to that audience*. There is no better evidence that a premise is *acceptable* to an audience than the fact that they already accept it. The final consideration on this list makes this point explicit. In philosophy it is often the case that an argument is directed to those who already believe a particular doctrine or set of doctrines, so the argument is designed to persuade or dissuade a particular group of people. For example, a theist may wish to persuade an atheist that God exists, or someone who thinks we have free will may wish to dissuade a determinist from her views. In such cases, a premise is acceptable if it is one we can reasonably expect the argument's audience to already accept or be prepared to accept with a little reflection. A premise is unacceptable if it is one we can expect those same people to reject.

APPENDIX B Writing Philosophy Essays

I. THE STUDENT PHILOSOPHY ESSAY

In broad outline, philosophy essays do not differ from other kinds of essay—they share the familiar three-part structure of *introduction*, *body*, and *conclusion*. Your *introduction* lets your reader know what topic you intend to address, what you intend to say about that topic, and perhaps even *why that topic* is worth writing about. The *body* of the essay then addresses your topic in the ways you have promised in your introduction to do. Your *conclusion* tells your reader how you have dealt with the topic and how the body of your essay has successfully fulfilled the promises made in the introduction. There is a simple way to fit all three parts together properly: Write the body of the essay first, look carefully at what you have accomplished, and then write an introduction stating your intention to accomplish exactly that. Then write your conclusion, pointing out how the body of the essay manages to do just what you said it would—no more and no less.

Any details beyond this standard three-part format will vary from one instructor to another, but as a student of philosophy you will be expected to produce two kinds of writing: expository and critical writing. A standard philosophy essay combines both.

II. EXPOSITORY WRITING

In expository writing, we seek to illuminate, clarify, or explain someone else's ideas. Usually this needs to be done because the original author was writing for a very different audience—for readers with different background knowledge or different vocabulary, for example. The purpose of expository writing is therefore *to make someone else's ideas accessible* to a new or different audience. In a student essay, however, your primary aim is to *demonstrate your comprehension* of an author's ideas by explaining and clarifying them for others.

In order of importance, the characteristics of good expository writing are *clarity*, *accuracy*, and *originality*. These are your goals. To reach them, you must solve the problem of *finding an appropriate distance* from the text you are explaining. That is, you should never stray too far from the original text, and you should never stay too close to it.

On the one hand, *don't stray too far* from the text you are explaining. You must maintain sufficient contact with the text so that it is clear you are giving an accurate account of the original author's ideas and not just presenting your own thoughts. You can do this by providing plausible paraphrases and by making use of occasional but relevant quotations from the original text. But don't let an author's way of presenting her ideas limit you too much—remember that your objective is to find *another way* of explaining the *same* ideas.

On the other hand, you should *not stay too close* to the author's way of expressing an idea or limit yourself to using the author's own examples or illustrations. In order to demonstrate that you understand what you are writing about, you should try to be original even when you are explaining someone else's ideas. To do this, look for your own ways to express the author's main points, and illustrate those points with your own examples. Only by doing these things can you illuminate, clarify, or explain a text, rather than merely repeat what it says. Being faithful to another person's ideas is in tension with giving an original presentation, so expository writing is always a delicate balancing act.

III. CRITICAL WRITING

In critical writing, you subject ideas to close scrutiny; you examine and evaluate them. In its most ambitious form, you take a position on an issue or propose a solution to a problem, and then defend your position or your solution. You might also argue against alternative positions. There are less ambitious forms of critical writing, such as attempts to rebut someone else's position or to rebut one particular line of reasoning—without committing to any side on the issue. In all these cases, critical writing aims *to make a case* for some idea, even if only for the modest idea that someone else's reasoning is unpersuasive.

One goal of critical writing is to make a contribution to a discussion or debate by helping shape which ideas your reader finds plausible or implausible. But critical writing has another goal that, for the philosophy student, is more important: It enables you to develop and clarify your own ideas, to locate their strengths and weaknesses, and to discover which of your ideas might need to be repaired or even abandoned.

The characteristics of good critical writing are *persuasiveness*, *fair and respectful treatment* of the views you oppose, and *demonstrated insight* into the complexities of the issues discussed. Critical writing challenges us to practice and demonstrate impartiality by giving fair treatment to the views we oppose as well as to the views we hold dear. You should try to write as an impartial judge of ideas even if you are aligned with one side on an issue. The best way to accomplish this is to:

1. Ensure that any presentation and criticism of the views you oppose represents them fairly and accurately. This was also required for good expository writing, but here it serves another purpose: Whenever you fail to give a fair representation of the ideas you oppose, you *weaken the case against them* and thereby make the case for your own position appear suspect.
2. Ensure that any defense of your own views is designed to persuade those who do not already agree with you; a defense that only seems persuasive to those who agree with you is a poor one.
3. Whenever possible, show an appreciation of any weaknesses of your own views and of the objections others might have to them. Again, your position is weakened by a failure to appreciate why others are not persuaded by what you have to say. There is no better way to strengthen your view than by incorporating into your essay the strongest objections you can find to it, and then disarming those objections by showing why they are unpersuasive. When you cannot successfully disarm the objections to your own views, it is time to ask whether you might be on the wrong side of an issue.

Although a standard philosophy essay combines expository and critical writing, it is a useful exercise to separate the two: Try writing a short expository essay that abstains from taking any critical stance on the issues and arguments. In the process of pushing yourself towards a better understanding of other people's views, you will discover that points of agreement and disagreement begin to emerge naturally. Our own views are often first awakened by encounters with the ideas of others, and our ideas take on their distinctive shapes through ongoing interactions with the thoughts of others. Even if you are alone at your desk, writing philosophy is not a solitary exercise.

References

Aquinas, St. Thomas. (1981). *Summa Theologica*. (Fathers of the English Dominican Province, Trans.). Retrieved August 8, 2014, from http://www.gutenberg.org/cache/epub/17611/pg17611.txt

Aristotle. (1928). *The Categories*. (E. M. Edghill, Trans.). Retrieved June 29, 2014, from http://www.gutenberg.org/cache/epub/2412/pg2412.txt

Augustine, Saint. (1913). *The City of God*. (M. Dods, G. Wilson, & J. J. Smith, Trans.).

Augustine, Saint. (1921). *The Confessions of Saint Augustine*. (E. B. Pusey, Trans.) Retrieved August 1, 2014, from http://www.gutenberg.org/cache/epub/3296/pg3296.txt

Ayer, A. J. (1965). Freedom and Necessity. *Philosophical Essays*. London: MacMillan: 271–284. Originally published in *Polemic* No. 5, 1946.

Baehr, P. (Ed.) (2000). *The Portable Hannah Arendt*. New York: Penguin Books.

Baier, A. C. (1985). *Postures of the Mind: Essays on Mind and Morals*. Minneapolis: University of Minnesota Press.

Baier, A. C. (1995). A Naturalist View of Persons. *Moral Prejudice: Essays on Ethics*. Cambridge, Mass.: Harvard University Press: 313–26.

Baier, A. C. (1997). *The Commons of the Mind: The Paul Carus Lectures*. Chicago: Open Court Publishing Co.:

Broad, C. D. (1939). Arguments for the Existence of God. In *Religion, Philosophy and Psychical Research*. Routledge & Keagan Paul, 1953: 156–67. Originally published in *Journal of Theological Studies* 40: 16–30.

Burnet, J. (1908). *Early Greek Philosophy*. London: Adam and Charles Black.

Chan, Wing-Tsit; (trans. and ed., 1963). *A Source Book in Chinese Philosophy*. Princeton, NJ: Princeton University Press.

Clarke, S. (1704). *A Discourse Concerning the Being and Attributes of God*. Retrieved on August 8, 2014, from http://demorrieaux.files.wordpress.com/2013/09/a-discourse-concerning-the-being-and-attributes-of-god.pdf

Clifford, W. K.(1879). The Ethics of Belief in *W.K. Clifford, Lectures and Essays*. Vol. II. (Leslie Stephen and Frederick Pollock, Ed.). London: Macmillan and Co. Press:177–211.

d'Holbach. (1770). *The System of Nature*. Retrieved August 1, 2014, from http://www.gutenberg.org/cache/epub/8909/pg8909.txt

de Sade, Marquis. (1990). *Justine, Philosophy in the Bedroom and Other Writings*. (R. Seaver & A. Wainhouse, Ed.). New York, NY, 1965: Grove Press.

Descartes, R. (1901). *Discourse on the Method of Rightly Conducting the Reason*. (John Veitch, Trans.). Retrieved from www.gutenberg.org/cache/ epub/59/pg59.txt

Descartes, R. (1911). *Meditations on First Philosophy*, in *The Philosophical Works of Descartes*. (Elizabeth S. Haldane, Trans.). London: Cambridge University Press.

Descartes, R. (1971). Correspondence with Princess Elisabeth. *Philosophical Writings*. (E. Anscombe & P. T. Geach, Trans.) Indianapolis: Bobs-Merrill.

Descartes, R. (1984) *The Philosophical Writings of Descartes*, John Cottingham, Robert Stoothoff, and Dugal Murdoch, edited and trans. Volume I. London: Cambridge: Cambridge University Press.

Dewey, J. (1922). *Human Nature and Conduct: An Introduction to Social Psychology*. New York: Henry Holt and Company. Retrieved July 19, 2014, from http://www.gutenberg.org/cache/epub/41386/pg41386.txt

di Lampedusa, G. T. (1958). *The Leopard*. (A. Colquhoun, Trans.) London: The Harvill Press.

Dostoyevsky, F. (1912). *The Brothers Karamazov*. (Constance Garnett, Trans.). Retrieved on August 10, 2014, from http://www.gutenberg.org/files/28054/28054-0.txt

Eddington, A. S. (1928). *The Nature of the Physical World*. Retrieved on August 4, 2014, from http://www.gutenberg.ca/ebooks/eddingtona-physicalworld/eddingtona-physicalworld-01-h-dir/eddingtona-physicalworld-01-h.html

Epicurus. (n.d.). *Letter to Menoeceus*. (Peter Saint-Andre, Trans.). Retrieved July 20, 2014, from http://www.monadnock.net/epicurus/letter.html

Freud, S. (1961). *The Future of an Illusion*. (James Strachey, Trans.) New York: W.W. Norton & Co. Inc.

Glazer, N. (Ed.). (1972). *Franz Kafka: The Complete Stories*. New York: Shocken Books.

Gunnerman, J. P. (1979). *The Moral Meaning of Revolution*. New Haven: Yale University Press.

Hume, D. (1739). *A Treatise of Human Nature*. Retrieved August 3, 2014, from http://www.gutenberg.org/cache/epub/4705/pg4705.txt

Hume, D. (1758). Of the Immortality of the Soul. *Essays, Moral, Political, and Literary*. Retrieved July 20, 2014, from http://www.econlib.org/library/LFBooks/Hume/hmMPL49.html

Hume, D. (1748). *An Enquiry Concerning Human Understanding*. Retrieved August 9, 2014, from http://www.gutenberg.org/cache/epub/9662/pg9662.txt

Hume, D. (1779). *Dialogues Concerning Natural Religion*. Retrieved on August 9, 2014, from http://www.gutenberg.org/cache/epub/4583/pg4583.txt

James, W. (1896). *The Will to Believe and Other Essays in Popular Philosophy*. Retrieved on August 10, 2014, from http://www.gutenberg.org/cache/epub/26659/pg26659.txt

James, W. (1907). *Pragmatism; A New Name for Some Old Ways of Thinking*. Retrieved August 3, 2014, from http://www.gutenberg.org/cache/epub/5116/pg5116.txt

Kant, I. (1999). *An answer to the question: What is Enlightenment?*. In Mary J. Gregory (Trans. & Ed.). *Practical Philosophy*. Cambridge: Cambridge University Press.

Kant, I. (1986). *Lectures on Philosophical Theology*. (Allen Wood & Gertrude M. Clark, Trans.). Ithaca, NY: Cornell University Press.

Laertius, D. (1925). *Lives of Eminent Philosophers*. R. D. Hicks (Ed.). Retrieved June 29, 2014, from http://www.perseus.tufts.edu/hopper/text?doc=D.%20L.%206&lang=original

Laplace, P. S. (1902). *A Philosophical Essay on Probabilities*. (F. W. Truscott & F. L. Emory, Trans.). Retrieved August 1, 2014, from http://archive.org/stream/philosophicaless00lapliala/philosophicaless00lapliala_djvu.txt

Larkin, P. (1977). *Collected Poems*. (Anthony Thwaite, Ed.). Farrar, Straus, and Giroux. London: The Marvel Press and Faber & Faber Ltd.

Leibniz, G. (1985). *Theodicy*. Retrieved on August 10, 2014, from http://www.gutenberg.org/cache/epub/17147/pg17147.txt

Leibniz, G. F. W. (1898). *Mondalogy*. (Robert Latta, Trans.). London: The Claredon Press.

Lichtenberg, G. C. (2000). *The Wastebooks*. (R. J. Hollingdale, Trans.) New York: *New York Review Books*.

Locke, J. (1690). *An Essay Concerning Human Understanding*. Vols. I and II. Retrieved July 11, 2014, from http://www.gutenberg.org/cache/epub/10615/pg10615.txt

Longino, H. E. Feminist Epistemology. In John Greco and Ernest Sosa, Eds. (1999), *The Blackwell Companion to Epistemology*. Oxford: Blackwell Publishers: 327–53.

Lucretius. (1916). *On the Nature of Things*. (William Ellery Leonard, Trans.). Retrieved July 20, 2014, from http://www.gutenberg.org/cache/epub/785/pg785.txt

Mackenzie, C., & Stoljar, N., Eds. (2000). Introduction: Autonomy Refigured. *Relational Autonomy*. Oxford: Oxford University Press: 3–31.

Paley, W. (1802). *Natural Theology*. Retrieved on August 9, 2014, from http://archive.org/stream/naturaltheologyo1802pale#page/n5/mode/2up

Parfit, D. (1971). Personal Identity. *Philosophical Review*, *80*: 3–27.

Pascal, B. (1958). *Pensées*. (W. F. Trotter, Trans.) Retrieved August 10, 2014, from http://www.gutenberg.org/files/18269/18269-0.txt

Peirce, C. (1868). Some Consequences of Four Incapacities. *Journal of Speculative Philosophy 2*: 140–157.

Peirce, C. (1905). What Pragmatism Is. *The Monist*, *15*:2: 161–181.

Peirce, C. S. (1998). The First Rule of Logic. In *The Essential Peirce: Selected Philosophical Writings, Volume 2 (1893–1913)*. Peirce Edition Project (Ed.). Bloomington: Indiana Press: 42–56.

Plantinga, A. (2007). The Dawkins Confusion; Naturalism ad absurdum. *Christianity Today*, March/April. Retrieved on August 9, 2014, from http://www.philvaz.com/apologetics/DawkinsGodDelusionPlantingaReview.pdf

Plato. (1892). *Republic*. (Benjamin Jowett, Trans.). Retrieved June 29, 2014, from http://www.gutenberg.org/cache/epub/150/pg150.txt

Plato. (1892). *Phaedo: The Last Hours of Socrates*. (Benjamin Jowett, Trans.). Retrieved July 20, 2014, from http://www.gutenberg.org/cache/epub/1658/pg1658.txt

Plato. (1892). *Symposium*. (Benjamin Jowett, Trans.) Retrieved July 11, 2014, from http://www.gutenberg.org/cache/epub/1600/pg1600.txt

Plato. (1892). *Euthyphro*. (Benjamin Jowett, Trans.) Retrieved June 29, 2014, from http://www.gutenberg.org/cache/epub/1642/pg1642.txt

Proust, M. (1949). *Within a Budding Grove*. London :Chatto & Windus.

Reid, T. (1969). *Essays on the Intellectual Powers of Man*. Cambridge, Mass.: MIT Press.

Rushdie, S. (2002). India's Fiftieth Anniversary. *Step Across This Line: Collected Nonfiction 1992–2002*. Toronto: Alfred A. Knopf Canada.

Russell, B. (1912). *The Problems of Philosophy*. Retrieved August 4, 2014, from http://www.gutenberg.org/cache/epub/5827/pg5827.txt

Russell, B. (1948). *Human Knowledge: Its Scope and Limits*. New York: Simon and Schuster.

Ryle, G. (1949). *The Concept of Mind*. London: Penguin Classics,.

Searle, J. (1980). Minds, Brains, and Programs. *Behavioral and Brain Sciences*, *3*: 417–457.

Shoemaker, S. (1963). *Self-Knowledge and Self-Identity*. Ithica, NY: Cornell University Press.

Swift, M. I. (1905). *Human Submission*. Part Second. Philadelphia: Liberty Press.

Taylor, R. (1992). *Metaphysics*, 4th edition. New Jersey: Prentice Hall, Inc.

Tennyson, A. (1865). *Enoch Arden*. Retrieved July 20, 2014, from http://www.gutenberg.org/cache/epub/1358/pg1358.html

Teresa of Avila. *The Life of Teresa of Jesus*, (E. A. Peters, Trans., 1960). Retrieved August 9, 2014, from http://catholicfirst.com/thefaith/catholicclassics/stteresa/life/teresaofavila07.html#CHAPTER%20XXVII

Turing, A. M. (1950). Computing Machinery and Intelligence. *Mind*. Vol. LIX no. 236: 433–460.

Wiggins, D. (1967). *Identity and Spatio-Temporal Continuity*. Oxford: Blackwell Publishers.

William, B. (2002). *Truth and Truthfulness*. Princeton, NJ: Princeton University Press.

Williams, B. (1956–57). Personal Identity and Individuation. *Proceedings of the Aristotelian Society, LVII*: 229–253; also (1960–61). *Analysis, 21*: 43–48.

Williams, B. (1973). The Makropulos Case: Reflections on the Tedium of Immortality. *Problems of the Self*. Cambridge: Cambridge University Press: 82–100.

Wittgenstein, L. (1953). *Philosophical Investigations*. (G. E. M. Anscombe, Trans.) New York: The MacMillan Company.

Yee, S. (Ed.). (2009). Philosophical Fragments. In *The Portable Kiekegaard*. (D. F. Swenson, Trans.) Vancouver, British Columbia: Emerald Knight Publishing:.

Index

D

E

F

G

H

I

J

K

L

M

N

O

P

Q

R

U

V

W

Z